Comparing Health-Related Policies & Practices in Sports:

The NFL and Other Professional Leagues

Christopher R. Deubert

I. Glenn Cohen

Holly Fernandez Lynch

Petrie-Flom Center for Health Law Policy, Biotechnology, and Bioethics

Harvard Law School

May 2017

TABLE OF CONTENTS

ABOUT THE AUTHORS

Christopher R. Deubert is the Senior Law and Ethics Associate for the Law and Ethics Initiative of the Football Players Health Study at Harvard University. Previously, Deubert practiced commercial litigation, sports law, securities litigation, and labor/employment litigation at Peter R. Ginsberg Law, LLC f/k/a Ginsberg & Burgos, PLLC in New York City. His sports practice focused primarily on representing National Football League (NFL) players in League matters, including appeals for Commissioner Discipline, under the NFL's Policy and Program on Substances of Abuse and under the NFL's Policy on Anabolic Steroids and Related Substances (now known as the Policy on Performance-Enhancing Substances), and related litigation. Deubert also previously worked for Sportstars, Inc., one of the largest NFL-player representation firms, performing contract, statistical, and legal analysis, and he performed similar work during an internship with the New York Jets. Deubert graduated with a joint JD/MBA degree from Fordham University School of Law and Graduate School of Business in 2010, and a BS in Sport Management from the University of Massachusetts in 2006.

I. Glenn Cohen is a professor at Harvard Law School; Faculty Director of the Petrie-Flom Center for Health Law Policy, Biotechnology, and Bioethics; and, Co-Lead of the Law and Ethics Initiative of the Football Players Health Study. His award-winning work at the intersection of law, medicine, and ethics—in particular, medical tourism and assisted reproduction—has been published in leading journals, such as the *Harvard Law Review*, *Stanford Law Review*, *New England Journal of Medicine*, *Journal of the American Medical Association*, *American Journal of Bioethics*, and *American Journal of Public Health*. He was previously a fellow at the Radcliffe Institute for Advanced Study and a faculty scholar in bioethics with the Greenwall Foundation. He is the author, editor, and/or co-editor of several books from Oxford, Columbia, John Hopkins, and MIT University Presses. Prior to joining the Harvard faculty, Cohen served as a clerk to Chief Judge Michael Boudin, United States Court of Appeals for the First Circuit, and as an appellate lawyer in the Civil Division of the Department of Justice. He graduated from the University of Toronto with a BA (with distinction) in Bioethics (Philosophy) and Psychology and earned his JD from Harvard Law School.

Holly Fernandez Lynch is Executive Director of the Petrie-Flom Center for Health Law Policy, Biotechnology, and Bioethics; Faculty at the Harvard Medical School Center for Bioethics; and, Co-Lead of the Law and Ethics Initiative of the Football Players Health Study. Her scholarly work focuses on the regulation and ethics of human subjects research and issues at the heart of the doctor-patient relationship. Her book, *Conflicts of Conscience in Health Care: An Institutional Compromise*, was published by MIT Press in 2008; she is also co-editor with I. Glenn Cohen of *Human Subjects Research Regulation: Perspectives on the Future* (MIT Press 2014), *FDA in the 21st Century: The Challenges of Regulating Drugs and New Technologies* (Columbia University Press 2015), and *Nudging Health: Health Law and Behavioral Economics* (Johns Hopkins University Press 2016). Lynch practiced pharmaceuticals law at Hogan & Hartson, LLP (now Hogan Lovells), in Washington, DC, and worked as a bioethicist in the Human Subjects Protection Branch at the National Institutes of Health's Division of AIDS. She also served as senior policy and research analyst for President Obama's Commission for the Study of Bioethical Issues. Lynch is currently a member of the Secretary's Advisory Committee on Human Research Protections at the US Department of Health and Human Services. She graduated Order of the Coif from the University of Pennsylvania Law School, where she was a Levy Scholar in Law and Bioethics. She earned her master's degree in bioethics from the University of Pennsylvania's School of Medicine, and her BA with a concentration in bioethics, also from the University of Pennsylvania.

ACKNOWLEDGMENTS

First, the authors would like to thank the staff and research assistants who assisted in the creation of this Report: Daniel Ain; Tom Blackmon; Jay Cohen; Louis Fisher; Nicholas Hidalgo; Scott Sherman; Jamie Smith-George; and, Samuel Stuckey. These individuals assisted with a variety of administrative and research tasks. Relatedly, the authors would like to thank Professor Peter Carfagna for helping to coordinate research assistance by his students. Particular thanks are due to Justin Leahey, Project Coordinator for the Law & Ethics Initiative of the Football Players Health Study, who provided important administrative and research assistance throughout the creation of the Report.

Second, the authors would like to thank the members of the Law & Ethics Advisory Panel for their comments and guidance during the creation of this Report: Nita Farahany; Joseph Fins; Ashley Foxworth; Walter Jones; Isaiah Kacyvenski; Bernard Lo; Chris Ogbonnaya; and, Dick Vermeil.

Third, the authors would like to thank the expert reviewers of this Report who provided valuable comments during the editing process: Marc Edelman, Zicklin School of Business, Baruch College, City University of New York; and, Michael McCann, University of New Hampshire School of Law.

Fourth, the authors would like to thank the professors and academic professionals who reviewed and provided comments for parts of this Report: Neil Longley; Stephanie Morain; and, Karen Roos. Relatedly, the authors would like to thank The Hastings Center, who initially proposed the idea of this Report.

Fifth, the authors would like to thank the professionals who helped finalize this Report and its release: Lori Shridhare and Angela Rakauskas from the Football Players Health Study at Harvard University; Cristine Hutchison-Jones, who provided proofreading and editing services; and, Fassino/Design, Inc., which designed and formatted the Report.

Finally, the authors would like to thank the leagues and players unions that agreed to provide relevant information and/or review this Report prior to its publication. In the Introduction, we provide more detail as to those leagues and unions that provided relevant information and/or reviewed this Report prior to its publication. The cooperation of the leagues and players unions was essential to the accuracy, fairness, and comprehensiveness of this Report.

ENSURING INDEPENDENCE & DISCLOSURE OF CONFLICTS

The 2011 Collective Bargaining Agreement between the National Football League Players Association ("NFLPA") and the National Football League ("NFL") set aside funds for medical research. The NFLPA directed a portion of those funds to create the Football Players Health Study at Harvard University, of which this Report is a part. Our analysis has been independent of any controlling interest by the NFLPA, the NFL, or any other party; this independence was contractually protected in Harvard's funding agreement with the NFLPA. Per that contract, the NFLPA was only entitled to prior review of this Report to ensure that no confidential information was disclosed.[a] Additional information about how this Report came to be is provided in the Preface.

The present Report is part of the Law and Ethics Initiative of the Football Players Health Study at Harvard University. Additional background information about the Football Players Health Study is provided in the Preface. We provide more specific information about the Law and Ethics Initiative here.

The Statement of Work agreed to between the NFLPA and Harvard included as one of the Law and Ethics Initiative's projects to "Conduct Comparative Sports League Analysis." More specifically, Harvard described the work to be done as follows:

> We will analyze governance and stakeholder obligations in other professional sports leagues in order to identify best practices and situate the ethics framework developed for professional football. This project will examine, for example, how medical practices in other leagues may result in the encouragement and tolerance of behavior that is risky to health. The project will examine influences among health behaviors of players and team policies regarding player health.

This project description was intended to be preliminary. The actual scope of this Report developed over time, as expected, as the result of considerable research, internal discussion, and conversations with experts. Beyond agreeing to the Statement of Work, the NFLPA did not direct the scope or content of this Report.

As is typical with sponsored research, we provided periodic updates to the sponsor in several formats: Pursuant to the terms of Harvard-NFLPA agreement, the NFLPA does receive an annual report on the progress of the Football Players Health Study as well as one Quad Chart progress report each year. Additionally, on two occasions (August 22, 2014, and January 23, 2015), we presented a summary of the expected scope and content of the Report to the Football Players Health Study Executive Committee, comprised of both Harvard and NFLPA personnel. Those meetings did not alter our approach in constructing this Report, the conclusions reached, or the recommendations made. Moreover, none of the comments made during those meetings altered the content of the Report.

In the Introduction, Section E(2): Describe, we discuss our research process for this Report. Additional information about our communications with the NFLPA and NFL is also relevant here. During the course of our research, we had multiple telephone and email communications with both NFLPA and NFL representatives to gain factual information. These communications were not about the progress, scope, or structure of our Report.

We also concluded that it was essential to provide the applicable stakeholders the opportunity to substantively review the Report. These stakeholders are the leagues discussed in this Report: the National Football League ("NFL"); Major League Baseball ("MLB"); the National Basketball Association ("NBA"); the National Hockey League ("NHL"); the Canadian Football League ("CFL"); and, Major League Soccer ("MLS"). This was necessary to try to fully account for the realities at hand, avoid factual errors, and fairly

---

a   The applicable contract language provides that the NFLPA is permitted to review publications 30 days in advance "for the sole purpose of identifying any unauthorized use of Confidential Information."

consider all sides. Accordingly, we provided each league the opportunity to review the Report before publication. Additional information about the leagues' and their corresponding labor unions' cooperation with and review of this Report or failure to do so is included in the Introduction.

The leagues had the opportunity to identify any errors, provide additional information, comment on what action we expected from them going forward, and raise further suggestions or objections. Sometimes these comments led to valuable changes in the Report. We found other comments unpersuasive and they did not result in any changes. It is critical to recognize that no external party, including the NFLPA and NFL, had the ability to direct or alter our analysis or conclusions.

In addition, we subjected the draft Report to peer review by outside experts. We engaged two independent experts in sports law to review the Report for accuracy, fairness, comprehensibility, and its ability to positively impact the health of NFL players. These experts were Marc Edelman, Zicklin School of Business, Baruch College, City University of New York, and, Michael McCann, University of New Hampshire School of Law.

Finally, the content of this Report is solely the responsibility of the authors and does not represent the official views of the NFLPA or Harvard University.

DISCLOSURES:

- The Law and Ethics Initiative's allocated budget is a total of $1,257,045 over three years, which funds not only the present Report, but also several other projects.[b]

- Deubert's salary is fully supported by the Football Players Health Study at Harvard University. From August 2010 to May 2014, Deubert was an associate at the law firm of Peter R. Ginsberg Law, LLC f/k/a Ginsberg & Burgos, PLLC. During the course of his practice at that firm, Deubert was involved in several legal matters in which the NFL was an opposing party. Of relevance to this Report, Deubert represented players disciplined pursuant to the NFL's Policy and Program on Substances of Abuse and the Policy on Anabolic Steroids and Related Substances (now known as the Policy on Performance-Enhancing Substances). Also, since 2007, Deubert has provided research assistance to the Sports Lawyers Association, whose Board of Directors includes many individuals with interests related to this work.

Lastly, in March 2017, as this Report's content was finalized except for incorporating some changes related to new collective bargaining agreements in MLB and the NBA, and with the Law & Ethics Initiative of the Football Players Health Study ending in May 2017 as the funding period came to a close, Deubert communicated with organizations with interests relevant to this work about potential job opportunities, including law firms that represent sports leagues, unions, and players. Following finalization of the Report, Deubert also communicated with some of the sports unions themselves about potential job opportunities. All changes to the Report, including those that occurred during or after March 2017, were reviewed and approved by Cohen and Lynch.

- 20% of Cohen's salary is supported by the Football Players Health Study at Harvard University. Cohen has no other conflicting interests to report.

- 30% of Lynch's salary is supported by the Football Players Health Study at Harvard University. Lynch has no other conflicting interests to report.

---

b   Other Law and Ethics projects include: (1) our Report, *Protecting and Promoting the Health of NFL Players: Legal and Ethical Analysis and Recommendations* (2016); (2) our Report, *NFL Player Health: The Role of Club Doctors*, 46 Hastings Center Rep. 2 (2016); (3) our law review article, *Evaluating NFL Player Health and Performance: Legal and Ethical Issues*, 165 Univ. Penn. L. Rev. 227 (2017); and, (4) a qualitative interview study ("listening tour") with players and their families to better understand their legal and ethical concerns related to health and well-being.

EXECUTIVE SUMMARY

1) INTRODUCTION

What can the NFL and NFLPA learn from the policies and practices of other elite professional sports leagues about protecting and promoting player health? This is the fundamental question motivating this Report, authored by members of the Law & Ethics Initiative of the Football Players Health Study at Harvard University.[a]

This Report, *Comparing Health-Related Policies and Practices in Sports: The NFL and Other Professional Leagues,* seeks to answer that question. The leagues share considerable similarities—at their core, they are organizations that coordinate elite-level athletic competitions for mass audiences. In this respect, the leagues are competitors within the professional sports industry, with each of them competing for fans' dollars and attention. The policies by which the leagues operate, and their practices, are thus often very similar. However, as in any industry, there are also differences between the leagues. This Report seeks to identify and understand those different policies and practices that have the possibility to affect player health such that the leagues may be able to learn from one another.

While leagues and their games are different in many important respects, making it impractical and unfair to opine as a definitive matter on which of the leagues' policies and practices in their totality best protect player health, the Report generally concludes that the NFL's policies concerning player health appear superior to the other leagues. Nevertheless, through the nine recommendations contained in this Report, we hope to elucidate several ways in which the NFL can learn from other leagues and further improve player health.

This Report has four functions. First, to **identify** the various policies that do or could influence the health of players in the various leagues. Second, to **describe** the policies and their relation to protecting and promoting player health. Third, to **evaluate** the capacity of these policies to protect and promote player health, in particular, by comparing policies on similar issues. And fourth, to **recommend** changes to policies that affect NFL players grounded in our evaluation of certain approaches taken by other leagues that appear to be more favorable. Where possible, we perform the same analysis concerning the leagues' practices related to player health.

In this Executive Summary, we provide only summaries of the key issues discussed in the Report, while the Report covers more issues and provides more complexity, nuance, and all relevant citations. Appendix A of the Report is a compilation of the Report's recommendations with explanatory text and Appendix B is a compilation of tables summarizing and comparing the leagues' policies and practices.

In the remainder of this summary Introduction, we identify the leagues and player unions relevant to our analysis and summarize the areas of potential improvement we found when comparing the policies and practices of the NFL to the other leagues. Then, we provide a summary of each of the issues analyzed in the Report: (1) Club Medical Personnel; (2) Injury Rates and Policies; (3) Health-Related Benefits; (4) Drug and Performance-Enhancing Substance Policies; (5) Compensation; and, (6) Eligibility Rules.

a   This Report is part of Law and Ethics Initiative of the Football Players Health Study at Harvard University. The 2011 Collective Bargaining Agreement (CBA) between the NFL and NFLPA allocated funds for research, and in 2014, the NFLPA and Harvard University entered into an agreement to create and support The Football Players Health Study using a portion of these funds. The contract governing this project protects our academic integrity as researchers; no external party has any editorial control over our work. A version of this Report was shared with the NFLPA prior to publication. We also invited the NFL and the other leagues and unions discussed in this Report to review the Report prior to its publication and to provide comments. As detailed in the Report, some of the leagues and unions accepted our invitation while others did not. The NFLPA was treated the same as other stakeholders, with the exception of a contractually guaranteed 30-day review to ensure that we did not use any confidential information. We considered all feedback provided to us from all stakeholders but retained final editorial control. The content is solely the responsibility of the authors and does not necessarily represent the official views of the NFLPA or Harvard University.

A) The Leagues

This Report analyzes the policies and practices of the following professional sports leagues:

- **The National Football League ("NFL"):** The world's premier professional football league, consisting of 32 member clubs. The NFL's 2017 revenues are estimated to reach $14 billion.

- **Major League Baseball ("MLB"):** The world's premier professional baseball organization, consisting of 30 member clubs. MLB's 2016 revenues were an estimated $10 billion.

- **National Basketball Association ("NBA"):** The world's premier professional basketball league, consisting of 30 member clubs. The NBA's 2016–17 revenues are projected to be approximately $8 billion.

- **National Hockey League ("NHL"):** The world's premier professional hockey league, consisting of 30 member clubs. The NHL's 2015–16 revenues were an estimated $4.1 billion.

- **Canadian Football League ("CFL"):** A professional football league consisting of 9 member clubs, all of which are located in Canada. The CFL's revenues are an estimated $200 million annually.

- **Major League Soccer ("MLS"):** A professional soccer league consisting of 20 clubs. As is explained in further detail in the Report, MLS is uniquely organized—rather than having each club owned and controlled by a different person or entity (like in the other sports leagues), all of the clubs in the MLS are owned and controlled by Major League Soccer, LLC. MLS' 2016 revenues were an estimated $600 million.

We chose these leagues because of their similarity to the NFL, both structurally and legally. The NFL, MLB, NBA, and NHL are particularly similar. Each of these leagues has been operating for nearly a century (or more in the case of MLB) and is an entrenched part of the American sports and cultural landscape. Their revenue streams also dwarf those of any other professional sports leagues, including the CFL and MLS. For these reasons, the NFL, MLB, NBA, and NHL are commonly referred to collectively as the "Big Four" sports leagues. We nevertheless acknowledge that other sports and sports leagues can provide lessons for the NFL and the other sports leagues concerning player health. The CFL was included in our analysis because it is the only other long-standing and continuous professional football league. Finally, the MLS was included because it is a major North American professional sports league.

B) The Unions

Each of the leagues discussed in this Report has an important counterpart. The leagues are the constructs of the individual clubs (or operator-investors in MLS) and thus are principally interested in protecting and advancing the rights of the clubs. To protect and advance their rights and interests, the players in each of the leagues have formed a players association, a labor union empowered with certain rights and responsibilities under federal labor laws. The players associations are:

- **National Football League Players Association ("NFLPA")**

- **Major League Baseball Players Association ("MLBPA")**

- **National Basketball Players Association ("NBPA")**

- **National Hockey League Players Association ("NHLPA")**

- **Canadian Football League Players Association ("CFLPA")**

- **Major League Soccer Players Union ("MLSPU")**

C) Areas for Improvement

As stated earlier, the NFL's player health provisions are generally the most protective of player health among the relevant comparators. Nevertheless, we also identified many areas in which the policies and practices of the NFL concerning player health could potentially be improved by comparison to the other leagues:

1 The CFL CBA, unlike the NFL CBA, requires that pre-season physicals "to determine the status of any pre-existing condition" be performed by a neutral physician.

2 The standard of care articulated in the NHL and MLS CBAs, unlike the NFL CBA, seemingly requires club doctors to subjugate their duties to the club to their duties to the player *at all times*.

3 MLB, unlike the NFL, has a concussion-specific short-term injury list.

4 The MLB, NHL, and CFL injury reporting policies, unlike the NFL, do not require the disclosure of the location on the body of a player's injury.

5 MLB, the NBA, and the NHL, unlike the NFL, generally offer health insurance to players for life.

6 Among the Big Four leagues, the retirement plan payments offered by the NFL are the lowest.

7 MLB and NHL players, unlike in those in the NFL, are vested in their pension plans on the first day they play in the league.

8 The NBA and CFL, unlike the NFL, offer treatment to players who have violated their performance-enhancing substance policies.

9 The amount of player compensation that is guaranteed in the NFL is substantially lower than in the other Big Four leagues.

10 The NFL has the most prohibitive eligibility rule of the leagues (except the CFL).

In the full Report, for each of these possible improvements we discuss whether the NFL's policies might be justifiably different than the other leagues'.

Learning from Other Leagues

Major League Baseball
- Concussion-specific injury list
- No disclosure of player injury location
- Length and amount of health insurance for former players
- Earlier pension accrual date
- More guaranteed compensation
- Eligibility age and education

National Hockey League
- No disclosure of player injury location
- Length and amount of health insurance for former players
- Earlier pension accrual date
- More guaranteed compensation
- Eligibility age and education

National Basketball Association
- Length and amount of health insurance for former players
- Treatment for performance-enhancing substance usage
- More guaranteed compensation
- Eligibility age and education

Canadian Football League
- Neutral doctor pre-season physical
- No disclosure of player injury location
- Treatment for performance-enhancing substance usage

Major League Soccer
- More guaranteed compensation
- Eligibility age and education

CHAPTER 1: Club Medical Personnel

This Chapter discusses the role of club medical staff, including both doctors and athletic trainers, in each of the sports leagues as set forth in the leagues' various controlling policies, most principally, their CBAs. In particular, we focus on: (1) the types of medical personnel required, if any; (2) the medical personnel's obligations; (3) the obligations of the players concerning club medical personnel; (4) the relationship between the medical personnel and the clubs; and, (5) the existence of sponsorship arrangements between medical personnel and the clubs, if any.

Our focus here is on the structural issues that are generally governed by the CBA or other policies rather than how each individual club hires and supervises its medical personnel and how individual medical personnel interact with individual players, matters that are not the subject of extensive reporting or publicly available research. By understanding what is required or permitted pursuant to the CBA or other policies we can understand the scope of possible practices, including those that might be concerning as they relate to player health.

Our analysis suggests that the NFL's policies concerning club medical personnel are overall, by comparison to the other leagues, the most protective of player health in almost all cases by providing players with superior control and information about their healthcare. Nevertheless, there are four areas in which the NFL might appear deficient as compared to one or more of the other leagues. Two of these apparent deficiencies (access to medical records and prescription medication monitoring) are not a problem in practice. We believe that a third deficiency—the inherent conflict of interest in the structure of club medical staffs and related standard of care provisions—are not adequately addressed by any of the leagues. This issue and our proposed recommendation is discussed at length in our report *Protecting and Promoting the Health of NFL Players: Legal and Ethical Analysis and Recommendations.* Thus, here, we focus on the lone issue resulting in a recommendation for the NFL.

While the CFL Standard Player Contract requires players to submit to a pre-season physical by the club's doctors, the CFL CBA also requires that pre-season physicals "to determine the status of any pre-existing condition" be performed by a neutral physician. The stated purpose of this requirement is to help determine "in the future" whether there was "an aggravation of . . . [a] pre-existing condition." In contrast, NFL club doctors perform all pre-season physicals and would be the ones to opine about a player's prior injury history. We believe the CFL's approach is preferred, and thus recommend that the NFL consider adopting such an approach:

- **Recommendation 1-A:** Pre-season physicals for the purpose of evaluating a player's prior injuries should be performed by neutral doctors.

CHAPTER 2: Injury Rates and Policies

An important measurement of player health is the incidence and type of injuries players may sustain in the course of their work. Additionally, given the importance of player injuries, the manner in which player injuries are handled administratively and reported can indicate a league's approach to player health issues more generally. In this Chapter, we examine the leagues': (1) injury tracking systems; (2) injury rates; (3) injury-related lists; and, (4) policies concerning public reporting of injuries. In summarizing our analysis, it is important to note that there are important limitations in analyzing and comparing the leagues' injury data, described at length in the full Report, including but not limited to the underreporting of injuries (concussions in particular), and differences between the leagues, including scheduling, electronic medical record systems, and injury definitions.

Statistic	NFL	MLB	NBA	NHL	CFL[b]	UEFA[c]
Mean Injuries Per Game	5.90	0.45	0.16	0.59	N/A	0.53
Concussions Per Game	0.625	0.007	0.007	0.067	0.704	0.010
Rate of Concussion Per Player-Game[d]	0.00679	0.00026	0.00035	0.00180	0.00800	0.00072

This Table provides some of the key injury statistics in comparing the leagues, though we provide many more statistics and caveats in the Report itself. The NFL's injury rates are much higher than those of the other leagues. The mean number of injuries suffered per game in the NFL is approximately 3.4 times higher than the combined rates of MLB, the NBA, NHL, and UEFA combined. Similarly, the NFL's concussion per game rate is approximately 6.9 times higher than the combined rates of those same leagues. We excluded the CFL from this comparison because it is also a football league, but we note that the CFL's concussion per game rate is actually higher than the NFL's.

At the same time, the NFL's rate of concussions per player-season is 0.073, lower than the NHL's of 0.108. Thus, if one compared one NFL player and one NHL player, the NHL player would be *more likely* to suffer a concussion in his next regular season than the NFL player during his next season. However, this difference is due to the fact that the NHL plays substantially more regular season games than the NFL (82 versus 16). When comparing concussion statistics on a per game basis, an NFL player is approximately 3.8 times more likely to suffer a concussion in a regular season game as compared to an NHL player (0.00679/0.00180).

One other caveat is worth emphasizing. Due to data availability these statistics and those in the Report are limited to the leagues' regular season games, which underestimates injury rates. As we emphasize in the full Report, there are a significant number of injuries and concussions sustained during NFL practices and during the pre-season (90 concussions in 2015 practices and pre-season games).

Injury Tracking Systems

Each of the Big Four leagues and the MLS has an injury tracking system of some kind. Discussions with experts on this issue indicated that the injury tracking systems are generally comparable; each of them is a sophisticated and modern system that should enable accurate reporting and provide interesting and useful data. The differences may come in how the leagues use the data that is available to them.

The NFL and NBA employ Quintiles, a health information technology firm, to perform sophisticated data analysis concerning player injuries. While other leagues have occasionally made injury data available for analysis, our research has not revealed whether the other leagues perform an ongoing annual analysis like Quintiles does for the NFL and NBA.

Injury-Related Lists

The NFL, NBA, and NHL all permit their clubs to declare players inactive one game at a time, which is generally advantageous to players. We use the NFL as an example. In the NFL, clubs have a 53-man Active/Inactive List, only 46 of whom can be active for the game each week. The remaining seven players are placed on the Inactive List for the game, *i.e.,* benched, either for injury or skill purposes, but are available to play in the next week's game. This arrangement permits players the opportunity to remain on the roster but to rest and treat an injury without immediately rushing back to play. At the same time, because clubs are constantly struggling with having the best players available as well as likely having multiple injured players, players will still likely feel pressure to return as soon as possible so that the club can deactivate other injured players and avoid seeking a replacement.

b   As discussed in the full Report, there was no publicly available data on CFL injuries.
c   As discussed in the full Report, there is no recent data concerning player injuries in MLS. However, there is injury data from the Union of European Football Associations ("UEFA"), a European soccer organization whose members generally include the best soccer clubs in the world. While UEFA and MLS are different soccer organizations, we nonetheless believe that data from UEFA, an elite soccer organization like the MLS, can be instructive of the injury rates in MLS. Indeed unless and until MLS makes its own data public, we think the UEFA data provides the best proxy estimate of the underlying injury rate in that league.
d   We emphasize that this statistic is a mean of all player positions. As discussed in the full Report, we know that rates vary depending on a player's position. Unfortunately, we do not have sufficient data to do position-by-position analysis. Nevertheless, even in the absence of that data we think the comparison of means is useful.

The Active/Inactive List is also interrelated with the Injured Reserve list, designated for players with longer-term injuries. Generally, once a player is on Injured Reserve, he is no longer eligible to play that season. However, by placing the player on Injured Reserve, the club can replace the player on the 53-man Active/Inactive List. Thus, there are important implications in determining whether the player's injury is short-term and the club only has to declare him inactive for a game or two, or whether the player's injury is more severe and requires the player to be placed on Injured Reserve (which also allows the club to obtain a replacement player to join the 53-man roster).

The interplay between the short-term Inactive List and the longer term Injured Reserve list is particularly important concerning concussions. As discussed in the full Report, concussions present uncertain recovery times, are challenging to diagnose and treat, and present particularly acute long-term concerns. MLB is the only sport with a concussion-specific injured list. Because of these concussion-specific concerns, we recommend that the NFL also adopt a concussion-specific injured list.

Injury Reporting Policies

There are three variations in the leagues' injury reporting policies.

First, the NFL, NBA, NHL, and MLS require clubs to disclose publicly players' injury statuses.

Second, the NFL, NBA, and MLS require clubs to disclose publicly the nature of player injuries. While the NHL requires clubs to disclose whether a player will miss a game or not return to a game due to injury, the NFL and NBA (in practice) that the club identify the player's body part that is injured. Below, we make a recommendation concerning this issue.

Third, in MLB, the NBA, the NHL, and MLS, the CBAs specifically describe what type of information the clubs are permitted to disclose publicly. The NFL CBA is silent on this issue. Instead, NFL clubs seemingly rely on players' to execute waivers providing the clubs with permission to disclose publicly player health information.

In the full Report, we discuss in detail three concerns related to the NFL's Injury Reporting Policy: (1) a general concern about an individual's medical information being made publicly available; (2) the possibility that players will target other players' injuries that have been publicly disclosed; and, (3) the Injury Reporting Policy's role in preventing gamblers from receiving inside information about player health issues. Ultimately, we believe that it is debatable whether the NFL's gambling-related concerns are sufficiently substantial today to justify overriding a player's right to have his health information treated confidentially. We lack the relevant expertise, insight, and information, however, to recommend that the NFL no longer obligate clubs to report information on the status of players. Instead, we recommend the NFL consider the issue more closely, in addition to other injury-related issues:

- **Recommendation 2-A:** The NFL, and to the extent possible, the NFLPA, should: (a) continue to improve its robust collection of aggregate injury data; (b) continue to have the injury data analyzed by qualified professionals; and, (c) make the data publicly available for re-analysis.

- **Recommendation 2-B:** Players diagnosed with a concussion should be placed on a short-term injured reserve list whereby the player does not count against the Active/Inactive 53 man roster until he is cleared to play by the NFL's Protocols Regarding Diagnosis and Management of Concussions.

- **Recommendation 2-C:** The NFL should consider removing the requirement that clubs disclose the location on the body of a player's injury from the Injury Reporting Policy.

CHAPTER 3: Health-Related Benefits

In this Chapter, we summarize the various health-related benefits available to the players in each of the leagues. Specifically, for each league, we examine: (1) retirement benefits; (2) insurance benefits; (3) disability benefits; (4) workers' compensation benefits; (5) education-related benefits; and, (6) the existence of health-specific committees jointly run by the league and players association. Each of these domains is relevant to protecting players should they experience negative health effects during and after their playing years, and also to promoting their ability to maintain their health and well-being over the longer term. Given that a decision to play or continue to play professional sports, like many other decisions, is a matter of weighing risks and benefits, those decisions must be made against a backdrop of available benefits. It is for this reason that we spend considerable space describing and evaluating the available benefits in each league.

According to the NFLPA, NFL players have "the very best benefits package in professional sports." This claim seems substantially true. First, the NFL offers every benefit that is provided by any of the other leagues. Second, the NFL offers several benefits that are not provided by any of the other leagues, including severance pay, long term care insurance, the Former Player Life Improvement Plan, and neurocognitive disability benefits for former players. Third, there are several benefits that only the NFL and a limited number of the other leagues provide: (a) only the NFL, MLB, NBA, and NHL provide health insurance (beyond COBRA) for former players; (b) only the NFL, MLB, and NBA provide players with mental health and substance abuse treatment; (c) only the NFL and NBA offer a health reimbursement account; (d) only the NFL and MLB offer disability benefits to former players; (e) only the NFL and NBA offer education-related benefits for all players; and, (f) only the NFL, NBA, NHL, and MLS guarantee workers' compensation benefits to all of their players.[e]

While overall the NFL thus appears to be the best league for benefits, there are, however, three areas in which the NFL might appear deficient as compared to one or more of the other leagues.

First, the NFL's health insurance options for former players appear to be less favorable than those offered by MLB, the NBA and the NHL. Currently, for players who have vested under the Retirement Plan (which requires at least three years of Credited Service for players after 1992), the NFL provides the same health insurance as available to current players for five additional years or the former player can also obtain health insurance via COBRA. However, COBRA is designed to be a temporary solution and is generally regarded as expensive relative to other health insurance plans. In contrast, MLB's Benefit Plan provides former players the option to continue (or obtain) the same health insurance benefits as current players *for life*. While former MLB players have to pay more for their health insurance than current MLB players, presumably the plans offered are cheaper than COBRA coverage or players would select that option. Similarly, the NBA's Retiree Medical Plan is available to former players for life (at varying rates) and the NHL allows former players who played at least 160 games to continue with the NHL's insurance plan for life.

The NFL does offer a variety of health benefits that might partially fill the gap for former players, including health reimbursement accounts, long term care insurance, benefits for uninsured former players, and disability benefits. Nevertheless, players often have to go through a difficult process to obtain some of these benefits after they have already had to pay for the care, or care is delayed until they can obtain the benefits. We suggest that there may be advantages to allowing former players to continue to obtain some form of the health insurance that they were able to receive while playing.

Second, as shown in the full Report (Tables 3-J and 3-K) the monthly payments to former NFL players under the Retirement Plan are seemingly the smallest in the Big Four leagues. Nevertheless, when all of the benefits available to former players are packaged together, it is likely that the NFL's benefits are the most valuable due to the number of benefits that are available. Consequently, lower Retirement Plan payments might simply reflect the NFLPA's preferred allocation of total benefits, *i.e.*, a shifting of the value of benefits away from the Retirement Plan and to other benefits instead. As with health insurance benefits, the NFL's Retirement Plan payments require players to undertake relatively little administrative work to receive benefits and they are a more secure and stable income source and benefit than some of the other benefits made available by the NFL. Nevertheless, some might believe it is a better use of player benefit money to fund benefits and programs for former players who are disabled or impaired in some way as opposed to providing larger Retirement Plan payments to all eligible former players. All of the benefits available to NFL players must be viewed collectively. For these reasons, we recommend the NFL and NFLPA consider whether the current allocation of player benefits is the preferred, most just, and most effective allocation.

Third, MLB and NHL players are vested in their pension plans on the first day they play in those leagues. By comparison, the NFL requires players to accrue three years of experience (or more depending on when they played), before they are eligible for retirement benefits (as well as many other benefits). The mean career of NFL and MLB players are both around five years long. Yet, the NFL's Retirement Plan likely excludes and has excluded thousands of former players who did not earn three Credited Seasons. It is unclear why the NFL and NFLPA require three years of service (the NBA does as well). The minimum service time clearly reduces costs for the Retirement Plan, but might also reflect a policy decision as to when an NFL player has sufficiently contributed to the NFL to deserve pay under the Retirement Plan. Below, we make a recommendation concerning the vesting requirement for the NFL's Retirement Plan:

- **Recommendation 3-A:** The NFL and NFLPA should consider whether change is necessary concerning player benefit plans.

  - The NFL and NFLPA should consider providing former players with health insurance options that meet the needs of the former player population for life.

---

e   While NFL clubs do provide workers' compensation benefits, as discussed in the full Report, the NFL and its clubs have sponsored legislation in several states to restrict players' workers' compensation benefits.

– The NFL and NFLPA should consider increasing the amounts available to former players under the Retirement Plan.

– The NFL and NFLPA should consider reducing the vesting requirement for the Retirement Plan.

CHAPTER 4: Drug and Performance-Enhancing Substance Policies

This Chapter summarizes the policies of each of the leagues concerning performance-enhancing substances ("PES") and drugs of abuse. As explained below, the leagues differ at times in their categorizations and treatments of different drugs and substances. Where appropriate, we will separate our analysis of the leagues' policies by PES and drugs of abuse (collectively "drug policies.") The leagues' definitions are discussed at length in the full Report.

With the possible exception of how marijuana is regulated, the Big Four's drug policies do not vary substantially. Leagues and unions balance multiple factors in creating drug policies, including but not limited to deterrence, treatment, privacy, and integrity of the game, and rely on difficult value judgments. The three features of the policies we view as most important to player health and those which we analyze are: (1) the availability of Therapeutic Use Exemptions ("TUEs"); (2) the availability of treatment; and, (3) the opportunity to receive treatment without being subject to initial discipline. With these issues in mind, we turn to our analysis of how the NFL compares to the other leagues.

Concerning TUEs, the NFL, MLB and the NBA all offer TUEs for both their PES and drugs of abuse policies. In contrast, the CFL offers TUEs for its PES policy but does not have a drugs of abuse policy. We also found no evidence that the NHL offers a TUE for its Substance Abuse Program or that the MLS offers any TUEs. Thus, the NFL's use of TUEs is at least as good as the other leagues.

All of the leagues, including the NFL, have robust treatment programs for drugs of abuse. However, the NBA, CFL, and potentially MLS are the only leagues that offer treatment for a player who has violated a PES Policy. On this issue, the NFL might appear deficient compared to the NBA and CFL. However, there are other relevant considerations concerning the treatment programs offered to players, discussed next.

The NFL, NBA, NHL, MLS and maybe MLB provide a safe-harbor for players who voluntarily refer themselves for treatment for drugs of abuse. These provisions importantly allow players to seek help they might recognize they need without the fear of immediate adverse employment action.

In contrast, no Big Four league offers a safe-harbor for players who have used PES. It is possible that these leagues view PES users as players intentionally looking to cheat the game and their competitors, whereas those using drugs of abuse are in need of medical care. However, there is robust scientific evidence supporting the need to provide treatment to PES users, as well. PES usage has shown to be addictive, and has been associated with the use of drugs of abuse (opioids in particular), body dysmorphic disorder, depression, antisocial traits, mood and personality disorders, other psychological disorders, and cognitive deficits in impulsivity, risk-taking, and decision-making. As a result, PES users may experience withdrawal symptoms, and may be at an increased risk of suicide. Consequently, many experts recommend and provide treatment and counseling for PES users. We adopt that recommendation for purposes of this Report:

• **Recommendation 4-A:** The NFL should consider amending the PES Policy to provide treatment to any NFL player found to have violated the PES Policy.

CHAPTER 5: Compensation

This Chapter examines the form and nature of player compensation in the leagues. In reviewing this Chapter, it is important to understand that the structures, operations and finances of the "Big Four" are considerably different from those of the CFL and MLS due to, among other things, their long histories and the amount of their revenues (billions versus millions).

Compensation is an important component of player health. First, the different compensation structures and systems in the leagues can influence players' decisions about their physical and mental health, for example when to play through injury and when to retire. In their efforts to maximize their earnings (and sometimes, eligibility for various benefits), some players might sacrifice their short- and/or long-term physical and mental health. The compensation structures dictate when or if a player faces such a trade-off.

Compensation may also be related to health in a second way. Without adequate savings and benefits during and after NFL play, players may find themselves insufficiently prepared to meet their physical and mental health needs, especially in the event of crisis. In addition, as we discussed in greater detail in Chapter 3, crises in physical and mental health are closely tied to bankruptcy, home foreclosure, and other serious financial setbacks. NFL players suffer these outcomes as well, despite their relatively high (but short-lived) compensation.

We are most concerned with how compensation and compensation structures affect player behavior and decision-making concerning their health, *i.e.*, what are the consequences of the current compensation regimes on players' short- and long-term health. Unfortunately, these are questions that we cannot fully answer at the present.

To effectively and rigorously compare how the different leagues' compensation structures affect player health decisions would require the ability to control for a range of variables, including but not limited to free agency rules, salary and contract limitations, salary cap structure, the level of guaranteed compensation, career length, career earnings, and injury outcomes. This is a challenging analysis that requires more data than is currently available and thus we cannot fairly assess which leagues' overall compensation structures among the Big Four are best for players.

Some have suggested that NFL player health could be improved through guaranteeing more of their compensation, which would potentially mitigate pressure to play through injuries in order to protect a player's status on the club. On this and related issues, many would argue that MLB's system is the most player-friendly, because compensation is almost entirely guaranteed, there is no hard Salary Cap, there is no maximum salary, and, there is no maximum contract length. It is thus not surprising that, as of February 2017, the 23 largest contracts among these sports leagues are all for MLB players. However, MLB players are not guaranteed a share of the revenue like in other leagues and must wait six years before becoming an Unrestricted Free Agent, the longest wait of the Big Four; thus, it is not clear that their compensation arrangement is preferable.

The NFL and NFLPA are frequently criticized—by players, the media and academics, among others—for what is perceived as the lack of guaranteed contracts as compared to the other leagues. However, the issue is complicated, as discussed in detail in the Report, including the effect of guaranteed compensation on opportunities for less proven players, and the possibility of reduced compensation and roster sizes. As a preliminary matter, when discussing the compensation paid to players, one must also consider the other benefits the players receive. As is discussed in Chapter 3 of this Report, the NFL provides a benefits package superior to those offered in all of the other leagues. We nonetheless make the following recommendation:

- **Recommendation 5-A:** The NFL and NFLPA should research the consequences and feasibility of guaranteeing more of players' compensation as a way to protect player health.

CHAPTER 6: Eligibility Rules

Each of the leagues has rules governing when individuals become eligible to play in their leagues. While we fully acknowledge the unique nature and needs of the leagues and their athletes, we believe the leagues can learn from the other leagues' policies.

Leagues' eligibility rules affect player health in two somewhat opposite directions: (1) by potentially forcing some players who might be ready to begin a career playing for the leagues to instead continue playing in amateur or lesser professional leagues with less (or no) compensation and at the risk of being injured; and, (2) by protecting other players from entering the leagues before they might be physically, intellectually, or emotionally ready. As discussed in the full Report and recommendation, the NCAA's Bylaws are an important factor in considering the eligibility rules and their effects on player health.

The leagues' eligibility policies vary. MLS has the most liberal eligibility policy, with no minimum age requirement, while, by requiring several years of college, the NFL and CFL are the most restrictive.

All of the eligibility rules seemingly are at least partially concerned with when a player is "ready" to enter a professional league. Readiness is an important concept, but difficult to define. In our view, a player is ready when he is able to enter the league safely, in terms of protecting his health, and maximize his success across various domains, including physically, mentally, and emotionally. Each of the leagues, often through negotiations with the unions, has made a judgment as to when they think the typical player is ready, or at least ready enough. In so doing, the leagues have helped protect clubs from drafting and investing in players who are not ready, and also potentially helped to protect players who need more time to prepare for a successful and healthy career. However, without more empirical analysis, we cannot say for certain when players—individually or collectively—are ready and thus whether the eligibility rule is fair or successful. No such data currently exists and would be challenging to gather.

The comparison of the leagues' policies highlights two clear issues with the NFL's eligibility rule, but, generally, neither is of the NFL's making.

First, the NFL's requirement that players effectively play at least three years of college football might ensure that only sufficiently physically mature players enter professional football, but it also requires players to risk their physical health longer without getting paid—and in a sport with higher injuries rates than that of the other leagues, as discussed in Chapter 2: Injury Rates and Policies. While the NCAA's Exceptional Student-Athlete Disability Insurance program tries to alleviate some of these issues, players have legitimate concerns that they will suffer a career-altering or ending injury before they are able to reach the professional level and earn any money from their athletic skills. This is at least in part a result of the NCAA's prohibition on student-athletes being compensated. Whether the NCAA's rules are fair is beyond the scope of this Report, but it is clear that the rules create a problem for players who have the potential to reach the NFL but who are required — or might prefer — to continue playing college football.

Second, in light of the fact that players are not paid for playing in college, it is understandable that many want to enter the NFL as soon as possible. Specifically, players will want to enter the NFL after their junior year of college, the first time they are permitted under the NFL's eligibility rule. However, whether the player is ready to leave college for the NFL is a difficult question to answer and may not be resolved until many years later — if ever. If the player is undrafted, NCAA rules effectively prohibit the player from returning to college football, and the player's football future is in serious doubt. Once again, although this problem intersects with the NFL's eligibility rule, it is the primary result of the NCAA's rules, not the NFL's.

It is challenging to assess the reasonableness of the NFL's current eligibility rule. The rule seemingly prevents players from joining the NFL before they are ready, which both protects those players from injury in the NFL and protects the clubs from investing in players who are not yet ready to play at a professional level. While there are likely to occasionally be players who are ready to join the NFL before the end of their junior season, there are going to be outliers to any rule and, without data suggesting otherwise, we cannot say the NFL's eligibility rule is unreasonable or not sufficiently considerate of player health. For this reason our main recommendation is for the NFL to continue to gather data to permit a better evidence-based evaluation of its current policy, as well to consider the interplay of its rules with the NCAA's:

- **Recommendation 6-A:** The NFL should consider performing or funding research analyzing when a player might be "ready" for the NFL.

- **Recommendation 6-B:** The NFL should reconsider the interplay of its eligibility rules with the NCAA's rules as they concern player health and take appropriate action if necessary.

CONCLUSION

This Report begins by explaining the pressing need for research into the overall health of NFL players; the need to address player health from all angles, both clinical and structural; and the challenges presented in conducting such research and analysis. The issues and parties involved are numerous, complex, and interconnected. To address these issues — and ultimately, to protect and improve the health of NFL players — requires a diligent and comprehensive approach to create well-informed and meaningful recommendations for change.

We believe part of that comprehensive approach is for the NFL and NFLPA to learn from other professional sports leagues when possible. In many respects, the leagues and their games are very different and thus it can be challenging to draw comparisons. Nevertheless, the leagues face a series of common issues, such as labor negotiations, stadiums and arenas, fan interest, multimedia platforms, and many others. But perhaps the most important issue is player health. In recent years, each of the leagues has had to make a fresh and comprehensive examination of its player health policies and practices. We anticipate the leagues will continue to engage in this examination for many years to come.

As demonstrated by our Report's analysis and recommendations, the leagues have the opportunity to learn a great deal from one another in light of their shared interest in player health. Additionally, our Recommendations are only as useful as their implementation. For these reasons, we make the following final Recommendations.

- **Final Recommendation 1:** The leagues and unions should continue to coordinate on player health issues and to consider each other's policies and practices.

- **Final Recommendation 2:** The media, academics, the leagues, and the unions should continue to police the advancement of player health.

* * *

NFL football has a storied history and holds an important place in this country. The men who play it deserve to be protected and have their health needs met and it is our fervent hope that they will be met. We hope this Report furthers that cause.

Summary Table of Recommendations

1   Pre-season physicals for the purpose of evaluating a player's prior injuries should be performed by neutral doctors. (Recommendation 1-A).

2   The NFL, and to the extent possible, the NFLPA, should: (a) continue to improve its robust collection of aggregate injury data; (b) continue to have the injury data analyzed by qualified professionals; and, (c) make the data publicly available for re-analysis. (Recommendation 2-A).

3   Players diagnosed with a concussion should be placed on a short-term injured reserve list whereby the player does not count against the Active/Inactive 53 man roster until he is cleared to play by the NFL's Protocols Regarding Diagnosis and Management of Concussions. (Recommendation 2-B).

4   The NFL should consider removing the requirement that clubs disclose the location on the body of a player's injury from the Injury Reporting Policy. (Recommendation 2-C).

5   The NFL and NFLPA should consider whether change is necessary concerning player benefit plans. (Recommendation 3-A).

6   The NFL should consider amending the Performance-Enhancing Substance Policy ("PES Policy") to provide treatment to any NFL player found to have violated the PES Policy. (Recommendation 4-A).

7   The NFL and NFLPA should research the consequences and feasibility of guaranteeing more of players' compensation as a way to protect player health. (Recommendation 5-A).

8   The NFL should consider performing or funding research analyzing when a player might be "ready" for the NFL. (Recommendation 6-A).

9   The NFL should reconsider the interplay of its eligibility rules with the NCAA's rules as they concern player health and take appropriate action if necessary. (Recommendation 6-B).

PREFACE

THE FOOTBALL PLAYERS HEALTH STUDY AT HARVARD UNIVERSITY

In response to ongoing concerns about NFL player health, the 2011 Collective Bargaining Agreement ("CBA") between the NFL and the National Football League Players Association ("NFLPA") added a number of new health, safety, and welfare provisions. One of these provisions sets aside $11 million per year through 2021 to be dedicated to medical research.[1] Thus, in the summer of 2012, the NFLPA issued a request for proposals to conduct original research and scientific exploration to be supported by these funds, focusing on "new and innovative ways to protect, treat, and improve the health of NFL players." The NFLPA's request for proposals specified a number of areas of particular interest, including sports medicine, repetitive brain trauma, wellness, aging, and cardiovascular disease. At the top of the list, however, was not a particular medical problem, but instead "Medical Ethics (*e.g.*, examination of health care contexts to obtain a better understanding of internal morality of these practices, accountability, new interventions that avoid harms currently incurred, appropriate informed consent in the context of professional athletics, and consideration of medical care in the labor-management context of professional football.)."[2]

To meet the challenge of protecting and improving player health, it is necessary to move beyond clinical issues to simultaneously address structural and organizational issues as well. This is true for healthcare more generally, where it is essential to invest not only in scientific research and development to create new clinical interventions, but also to invest in systems to efficiently administer those interventions to patients in need, as well as public health approaches that can help minimize the need for intervention in the first place. Likewise, to make headway in protecting and improving the health of NFL players, we must go beyond a single-minded focus on their clinical care and instead implement a more comprehensive strategy capable of addressing the myriad of stakeholders and contextual factors (past, present, League-wide, and individual) that play a role in their health. These include not only players' physical issues and risk factors, but also their relationships with clinicians, professional motivations, financial pressures, and family responsibilities, as well as the centrality of their health to their careers, the competitive nature of the business, constraints on alternative opportunities for many players, and the like. The relevant stakeholders are similarly varied and extensive.

Thus, when submitting its proposal to the NFLPA, our Harvard team included a variety of critical clinical projects alongside an equally robust set of law and ethics proposals. We agreed from the outset that a focus on diagnosing and treating player health issues—while essential—would be insufficient on its own to comprehensively resolve those issues. Instead, our approach has been to also address precisely those structural and organizational factors that are so important to player health but would be neglected by a purely clinical approach.

The NFLPA ultimately agreed, selecting Harvard to receive the funding after a multi-round competitive process involving several universities. In February 2014, Harvard Medical School entered into an agreement with the NFLPA to create the **"Football Players Health Study at Harvard University."** Drawing on expertise from across Harvard University, the Football Players Health Study is dedicated to understanding the causes of conditions NFL players face, with the goal of improving their health and wellbeing.

The "Law and Ethics Initiative," led by the **Petrie-Flom Center for Health Law Policy, Biotechnology, and Bioethics** at Harvard Law School, encompasses a variety of distinct projects with the primary goal of understanding the legal and ethical issues that may promote or impede player health, and developing recommendations to promote player health through structural change.[a]

The existence of the Law and Ethics component differentiates the Football Players Health Study from other studies concerning NFL player health. While there have been many important studies concerning the medical components of

---

a   Other Law and Ethics projects include: (1) our Report, *Protecting and Promoting the Health of NFL Players: Legal and Ethical Analysis and Recommendations* (2016); (2) our Report, *NFL Player Health: The Role of Club Doctors*, 46 Hastings Center Rep. 2 (2016); (3) our law review article, *Evaluating NFL Player Health and Performance: Legal and Ethical Issues*, 165 Univ. Penn. L. Rev. 227 (2017); and, (4) a qualitative interview study ("listening tour") with players and their families to better understand their legal and ethical concerns related to health and well-being.

player health, we are not aware of any that have conducted a comprehensive analysis of the relevant legal and ethical environment.

Additionally, in the Section: Ensuring Independence and Disclosure of Conflicts, we discuss the ways in which the Law and Ethics Initiative interacted with, but was independent of, both the NFLPA and NFL in creating this Report.

In the Introduction that follows, we will describe the scope of this Report, its goals, process, and limitations. First, however, it is essential to explain the guiding principles of the Football Players Health Study as a whole.

Most importantly, the Football Players Health Study is interested in health issues beyond concussions and neurological trauma. Although we recognize that concussions and their possible long-term sequelae are on the minds of many, and are among the most critical health issues facing players today, we simultaneously recognize that player health is larger than concussions alone. Players also have concerns about cardiac health, arthritis and other joint damage, pain management, and a wide variety of other issues. Moreover, their primary concerns are likely to change over time from their playing days to retirement to old age. Thus, we have adopted the following mantra for our work: "The Whole Player, The Whole Life." Rather than a myopic approach, we are taking a wide and long view in order to make players as healthy as they possibly can be over every conceivable dimension of their entire lives.

We approached this project as scholars and social scientists whose goal is to improve NFL player health. We are independent academic researchers first and foremost, regardless of the source of our funding. We have no "client" in this endeavor, other than players themselves, and we have no agenda other than to improve the lives of former, current, and future players. Indeed, the Football Players Health Study is funded pursuant to money set aside under the 2011 CBA for research designed to help players. Because of the way the clubs and players split revenues from NFL games and other operations, the funds used for the Football Players Health Study can reduce the amount of money available to current players in the form of salary.[b] Thus, the players have chosen to pay for the Football Players Health Study. In addition, although our contractual relationship is with the NFLPA, that very same contract protects our academic integrity without exception; no external party has any control whatsoever over our conclusions.

One of our primary concerns is that too little is known about player health. Specifically, too little is known from a rigorous scientific perspective about the risks and benefits of playing professional football because available data are insufficient in a variety of respects. For example, "[w]e do not know what factors exacerbate or mitigate an individual's risk, including genetics, nutrition, lifestyle, as well as length of time and position played, and injuries sustained during playing years."[3] Professional football players are an elite and unique group of men who must be studied directly and often in large numbers before we can really understand how football has affected them. Only then can we fully address any health problems they may have. We come to this work with no pre-existing agenda—we have neither any interest in ending professional football nor any interest in looking the other way if confronted with compelling data of its downsides. Again, we are interested only in helping players lead the healthiest and most productive lives they possibly can. We are committed to going where the science takes us.

Finally, we are forward-looking. Our role is not to evaluate fault or assign blame for player health problems, and the Football Players Health Study is uninvolved in any litigation related to these issues. Instead, we are working with a single-minded focus to develop a clear path for addressing and remediating existing player health problems, and for preventing such problems from continuing or occurring in the future—from both clinical and organizational perspectives. Although this process does include assignment of shared responsibility for protecting and promoting players' health to a wide variety of parties, the past is relevant only to the extent that it demonstrates ways to successfully improve going forward.

These are the guiding principles motivating every aspect of the Football Players Health Study at Harvard University.

---

b   The players' share of NFL revenues is referred to as the Player Cost Amount. 2011 CBA, Art. 12, § 6(c)(i). The Football Players Health Study is funded from a pool of money known as the Joint Contribution Amount. *See* 2011 CBA, Art. 12, § 5. If the NFL generates new revenue streams, the players are entitled to 50% of the net revenues from those new ventures less 47.5% of the Joint Contribution Amount. 2011 CBA, Art. 12, § 6(c)(ii). Thus, if the NFL generates new revenue streams, the amount that is passed on to the players is reduced by 47.5% of the Joint Contribution Amount, which includes the Football Players Health Study.

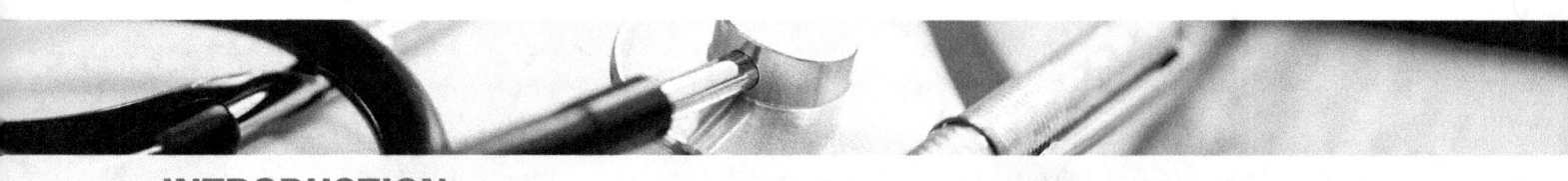

INTRODUCTION

This Report seeks to improve the health of NFL players (former, current, and future) by comparing policies, and, where information is available, practices, in the NFL to other elite professional sports leagues. The leagues share considerable similarities—at their core, they are organizations that coordinate elite-level athletic competitions for mass audiences. In this respect, the leagues are competitors within the professional sports industry, with each of them competing for fans' dollars and attention. The practices and policies by which the leagues operate are thus often very similar. However, there are also differences between the leagues. This Report seeks to identify and understand those different policies and practices that have the possibility to affect player health. Organizations operating within the same industry often can learn better practices and policies from one another. While leagues and their games are different in many important respects, making it impractical and unfair to opine as a definitive matter on which of the leagues' policies and practices in their totality best protect player health the Report generally concludes that the NFL's policies concerning player health appear superior to the other leagues. Nevertheless, through the nine recommendations contained in this Report, we hope to elucidate several ways in which the NFL can learn from other leagues and further protect player health.

With the purpose of this Report in mind, the remainder of this Introduction provides additional background information on the subject matter of the Report and then further introduces the Report by describing its audience, articulating the process we used to develop our ultimate recommendations, and clarifying important points about scope.

A) The Leagues

This Report analyzes the policies and practices of the following professional sports leagues:

- **The National Football League ("NFL"):** The world's premier professional football league, consisting of 32 member clubs. The NFL began play in 1920, has its headquarters in New York City, and is led by Commissioner . The NFL's 2017 revenues are estimated to reach $14 billion.[4]

- **Major League Baseball ("MLB"):** The world's premier professional baseball organization, consisting of 30 member clubs. MLB began play in 1903,[a] has its headquarters in New York City, and is led by Commissioner Rob Manfred. MLB's 2016 revenues were an estimated $10 billion.[5]

- **National Basketball Association ("NBA"):** The world's premier professional basketball league, consisting of 30 member clubs. The NBA began play in 1946, has its headquarters in New York City, and is led by Commissioner Adam Silver. The NBA's 2016–17 revenues are projected to be approximately $8 billion.[6]

- **National Hockey League ("NHL"):** The world's premier professional hockey league, consisting of 30 member clubs. The NHL began play in 1917, has its headquarters in New York City, and is led by Commissioner Gary Bettman. The NHL's 2015–16 revenues were an estimated $4.1 billion.[7]

- **Canadian Football League ("CFL"):** A professional football league consisting of 9 member clubs, all of which are located in Canada. The CFL began play in 1958, has its headquarters in Toronto, and is currently looking for a new Commissioner. The CFL's revenues are an estimated $200 million annually.[8]

Although both are professional football leagues, the NFL and CFL playing rules vary in several important ways. Some of the key distinctions include: (1) in the NFL, a team has four downs to advance the ball ten yards, while in the CFL a team only has three downs; (2) an NFL field is 120 yards long (including two ten-yard end zones) and 160 feet wide, while an CFL field is 130 yards long (including two twenty-yard end zones) and 65 yards wide; (3) in the NFL, goalposts are at the back of the end zone while in the CFL they are on the goal line; and, (4) in the NFL, players in the backfield are not allowed to be moving forward when the ball is snapped, while in the CFL, all offensive backfield players (except the quarterback) can be moving forward at the snap.

---

a   MLB consists of the National League and American League. The National League began play in 1876 and the American League in 1901. The leagues merged to create Major League Baseball in 1903. *See History of baseball in the United States*, Baseball-Reference.com, http://www.baseball-reference.com/bullpen/History_of_baseball_in_the_United_States (last visited Mar. 10, 2016), *archived at* https://perma.cc/DSK5-6VRN.

The NFL's skill level is considered by most outside observers as superior to the CFL. Many CFL players aspire to make the NFL while many players who were unable to make it in the NFL turn to the CFL.

- **Major League Soccer ("MLS"):** A professional soccer league consisting of 20 clubs. As is explained in further detail in Chapter 5, Section F: Compensation in MLS, MLS is uniquely organized—rather than having each club owned and controlled by a different person or entity (like in the other sports leagues), all of the clubs in MLS are owned and controlled by Major League Soccer, LLC, a Delaware limited liability company.[9] The reasoning for this structure is discussed in Chapter 5. MLS began play in 1996, has its headquarters in New York City, and is led by Commissioner Don Garber. MLS' 2016 revenues were an estimated $600 million.[10]

Soccer, as a global game, has dozens of professional leagues around the world. Although MLS has made strides and is an internationally respected league, it is not the world's premier soccer league. The European leagues, such as the English Premier League, Bundesliga in Germany, and La Liga in Spain are generally considered the best in the world. Nevertheless, we chose to focus our review on MLS for a few reasons: (1) the European leagues are organized and regulated in materially different ways than MLS and American sports leagues; (2) the European leagues generally are not governed by CBAs or a labor-management dynamic like in MLS and North American sports leagues; and, (3) European laws on a variety of relevant issues are materially different from American (and Canadian) laws. For these reasons, MLS was the best soccer league from which to draw useful comparisons to the NFL.

We chose these leagues because of their similarity to the NFL, both structurally and legally. The NFL, MLB, NBA, and NHL are particularly similar. Each of these leagues has been operating for nearly a century (or more in the case of MLB) and is an entrenched part of the American sports and cultural landscape. They share similar structures and operational practices, at least in part because they have shared many executives, lawyers, stadiums, and fans over the years. Their revenue streams also dwarf those of any other professional sports leagues, including the CFL and MLS. For these reasons, the NFL, MLB, NBA, and NHL are commonly referred to collectively as the "Big Four" sports leagues.[11] Where appropriate, we also adopt this moniker.

We nevertheless acknowledge that other sports and sports leagues can provide lessons for the NFL and the other sports leagues concerning player health.[b] Sports of all kinds present health risks and rewards to their athletes and thus how those sports manage those risks and rewards is relevant. We have not undertaken this analysis here, focusing instead on the sports and leagues most similar to the NFL.

B) The Unions

Each of the leagues discussed in this Report has an important counterpart. The leagues are the constructs of the individual clubs (or operator-investors in MLS) and thus are principally interested in protecting and advancing the rights of the clubs. To protect and advance their rights and interests, the players in each of the leagues have formed a players association, a labor union empowered with certain rights and responsibilities under federal labor laws.[c] The players associations are:

- National Football League Players Association ("NFLPA"): The NFLPA was formed in 1956,[12] has its headquarters in Washington, DC, and is led by Executive Director DeMaurice Smith.

- Major League Baseball Players Association ("MLBPA"): The MLBPA was formed in 1953,[13] has its headquarters in New York City, and is led by Executive Director Tony Clark, a 15-year MLB veteran.

- National Basketball Players Association ("NBPA"): The NBPA was formed in 1954,[14] has its headquarters in New York City, and is led by Executive Director Michelle Roberts.

- National Hockey League Players Association ("NHLPA"): The NHLPA was formed in 1957,[15] has its headquarters in Toronto, and is led by Executive Director Don Fehr, who served as Executive Director of the MLBPA from 1985–2009.

- Canadian Football League Players Association ("CFLPA"): The CFLPA was formed in 1965,[16] has its headquarters in Stoney Creek, Ontario, and is led by President Scott Flory, a 15-year CFL veteran.

- Major League Soccer Players Union ("MLSPU"): The MLSPU was formed in 2003,[17] has its headquarters in Bethesda, Maryland, and is led by Executive Director Bob Foose.

---

b   Boxing, in which fighters are subjected to repeated hits to the head, draws obvious comparisons to playing in the NFL. Of note, the Muhammad Ali Boxing Reform Act provides for certain safety standards for professional boxing matches. 15 U.S.C. § 6304.

c   To avail themselves of federal labor laws, the unions must be certified by the National Labor Relations Board ("NLRB"). Here, we provide the dates the players associations were formed and began working on behalf of the players, which were generally several years before they gained official recognition from the NLRB.

The principal right and purpose of the unions is to negotiate with the leagues concerning many of the policies examined in this Report, as is discussed in the next Section.

C) Collective Bargaining Agreements

Nearly all of the policies and practices that we discuss in this Report are contained in and governed by collective bargaining agreements ("CBA") agreed to by the league and its respective players association. In this Section, we provide a brief explanation of CBAs to provide context for and assist in the comprehension of the Report.

Pursuant to the National Labor Relations Act ("NLRA"), the unions are "the exclusive representative[] of all the employees in [the bargaining] unit[d] for the purposes of collective bargaining in respect to rates of pay, wages, hours of employment, or other conditions of employment."[e] Also pursuant to the NLRA, each league's clubs, acting collectively as the league, are obligated to bargain collectively with the unions concerning the "wages, hours, and other terms and conditions of employment" for the players.

We acknowledge that many commentators believe that MLBPA has historically been the strongest union, and that the NFLPA has been regarded as having been less effective by comparison.[18][f] However, complexity and nuance belie any easy comparisons. For context, the NFLPA's union membership is roughly the same size of all of the other major unions combined and NFL players generally have shorter careers than other athletes, creating challenges for building and maintaining solidarity among the players. Ultimately, the CBAs speak for themselves as the result of the negotiations between the leagues and the unions. Rather than speculate on the leagues' and unions' approaches to player health, we can objectively analyze the collectively bargained provisions and policies. Nevertheless, the ability to effectuate change, including the areas in need of change highlighted in this Report, is a function of each union's strength.

Since the 1960s, the Big Four leagues and their respective players associations have each negotiated approximately ten to 15 CBAs.[g] The CBAs are hundreds of pages long and govern nearly every aspect of the sports. Collective bargaining is inherently a give-and-take dynamic where the negotiating power and leverage of each side plays an important role in the outcome. Both league and union leadership and the dynamics between the leagues and unions have changed over time, resulting in varied CBA negotiations and results. Nevertheless, generally speaking, most important changes in leagues' policies and practices are the result of the CBA process. Consequently, CBAs are of paramount importance to understanding how the leagues function and making recommendations for improvement.

The CBA represents the key covenant between players and club owners, on all matters pertaining to player health (alongside many other important issues that matter to these parties). The most straightforward way to implement many of the changes we recommend to protect and promote player health would be to include them in the next CBA. That said, whenever change is possible outside of the CBA negotiating process, it should not wait. Moreover, although the CBA will often be the most appropriate mechanism for implementing our recommendations, we do not want to be understood as suggesting that player health should be treated like just another issue for collective bargaining subject to usual labor-management dynamics. As an ethical matter, players should not be expected to make concessions in other domains in order to achieve gains in the health domain. To the contrary: player health should be a joint priority, and should not be up for negotiation.

Finally, it is important to clarify our writing process concerning the MLB-MLBPA CBA. MLB reviewed a draft of this Report in the fall of 2016 and provided comments in September 2016. We made edits based on those comments and asked MLB for additional information in October 2016. On November 30, 2016, MLB and the MLBPA agreed to the terms of a new CBA.[19] On December 2, the league and union issued a joint press release providing the terms of the new CBA,[20] and on December 14, the MLB owners and the MLBPA Executive Board (consisting of player representatives) ratified the new CBA.[21] Nevertheless, as of the date that our Report went to press on March 18, 2017, the full length CBA had not yet been publicly released. Thus, while we were able to update the Report based on the information contained in the joint press

---

d   A "bargaining unit" is the group of employees sufficiently similar to be represented by the union. *See* 29 U.S.C. § 159(b) (describing the factors for determining whether a bargaining unit is appropriate for collective bargaining).

e   29 U.S.C. § 159(a). Similarly, Canada's Labour Code declares that unions certified by the Canada Industrial Relations Board "has exclusive authority to bargain collectively on behalf of the employees in the bargaining unit[.]" Canada Labour Code, § 36(1)(a).

f   Indeed, DeMaurice Smith, Executive Director of the NFLPA, has effectively admitted as much. At a public event in 2017, Smith stated that he "aspire[s] for our union to be as strong as the baseball union." *See* University of Houston, Health Law & Policy Institute, Medical and Legal Ethics in the NFL and Sports (Jan. 31, 2017), http://www.uh.edu/infotech/services/streaming-media/events/hlpi/ (last visited Feb. 1, 2017), *archived at* https://perma.cc/K7JK-DKG5.

g   Throughout this Report, we will refer to the CBAs by years, such as the 1968 CBA, 1993 CBA, or 2011 CBA. The years reference the dates the CBAs became effective, which is usually, but not always, the year in which the CBA was agreed to, *i.e.*, some CBAs had retroactive application.

release, additional details, nuance or context may be contained in the full length CBA when it is publicly released. On February 27, 2017, we provided MLB with the sections of this Report relevant to MLB, including those which were edited based on the press release about the new CBA. In March 2017, MLB provided additional comments on the revised sections of the Report before it went to press.

D) Audience

This Report has several key audiences. There are those that we see as the major change agents: current players; club owners; the NFL; the NFLPA; club medical staff; and, various player advisors (*e.g.*, contract advisors, financial advisors, and family members). If change is to occur, these are the key individuals and entities that will need to effectuate it. But we live in an era where discussions about protecting and promoting player health extend far beyond these change agents. Fans, the media, the NFL's business partners, and others all have a stake in—and more importantly, some power to shape—how the policies and practices of NFL football will evolve to best protect and promote player health. Finally, while our focus is on promoting the health of NFL players, much of what we have learned and discuss here is likely useful to the other leagues as well.

Writing for such divergent audiences is a significant challenge. Ultimately, we decided to err in favor of providing a more comprehensive analysis, with all the complexity and length that entails.

E) Goals and Process

This Report has four functions. First, to identify the various policies that do or could influence the health of players in the various leagues. Second, to describe the policies and their relation to protecting and promoting player health. Third, to evaluate the capacity of these policies to protect and promote player health, in particular, by comparing policies on similar issues. And fourth, to recommend changes to policies that affect NFL players grounded in our evaluation of certain approaches taken by other leagues that appear to be more favorable.

It is worth describing those functions in greater depth.

1) IDENTIFY

To arrive at the policy domains analyzed herein, we considered for potential analysis any policy or practice that can, does, or should affect player health. Our prior Report, *Protecting and Promoting the Health of NFL Players: Legal and Ethical Analysis and Recommendations,* offers a comprehensive analysis of stakeholders and issues affecting NFL player health. That Report mapped a wide variety of issues, and this Report more closely examines how the NFL and other leagues have handled some of them. This Report includes six Chapters analyzing different policies concerning player health: (1) Club Medical Personnel; (2) Injury Rates and Policies; (3) Health-Related Benefits; (4) Drug and Performance-Enhancing Substance Policies; (5) Compensation; and, (6) Eligibility Rules.

One important limitation to the domains we include in this Report deserves explicit discussion. This Report focuses primarily on *written* policies and rules. We have intentionally avoided analysis about *unwritten* practices within the leagues, which is a practical limitation to our work. The policies we have analyzed are generally codified in the CBAs and other documents and can easily be reviewed. To accurately understand unwritten practices would require gathering substantial data from individuals working in the leagues. For example, understanding the relationship among clubs, club medical personnel, and players—and the ways in which these relationships might vary among the leagues—is interesting and important. However, without collecting data from representative portions of both players and club medical personnel in all of the leagues, we cannot fairly compare club medical personnel practices across the leagues. Gathering such data is beyond the scope of the current project. Therefore, we focus on the written policies that govern club medical personnel.

We similarly researched the role and practices of clubs, coaches, agents, and financial advisors concerning player health across the different leagues. However, again, reliable data about the practices of these groups across each of the leagues—as opposed to their policies—generally does not exist and is challenging to gather. Such information would clearly be useful, and thus we encourage others to conduct such research if sufficient funding and access to the relevant populations can be obtained. However, for practical purposes, this Report focuses primarily on the relevant policies in each of the leagues. By understanding these policies, we can understand the range of relationships and actions expressly permitted and analyze whether existing policies could allow for or give rise to potentially problematic situations could arise.

Figure Introduction-A: The Report's Goals and Process

1	Identify	the various policies that do or could influence the health of players in the various leagues.
2	Describe	the policies and their relation to protecting and promoting player health.
3	Evaluate	the capacity of these policies to protect and promote player health.
4	Recommend	changes to policies that affect NFL players grounded in our evaluation of certain approaches taken by other leagues that appear to be more favorable.

2) DESCRIBE

As discussed above, our analysis of the leagues' policies stemmed largely from reviewing the CBAs and other publicly available policies and documents, such as court filings, medical studies, law review articles, and news articles. To supplement our review, in some cases we requested that the leagues and/or unions provide us with information and documents that were not otherwise available. The leagues and unions provided varying degrees of cooperation:

- The NFL provided documents and information relevant to our prior report, *Protecting and Promoting the Health of NFL Players: Legal and Ethical Analysis and Recommendations,* as well as this Report. However, the NFL declined our invitation to review this Report.

- The NFLPA provided documents and information relevant to our prior report, *Protecting and Promoting the Health of NFL Players: Legal and Ethical Analysis and Recommendations,* as well as this Report. The NFLPA was also provided with a draft of this Report to review but did not provide comments.

- MLB provided documents and information that we requested, reviewed the Report, and provided comments.

- The MLBPA declined our invitation to review the Report.

- The NBA provided documents and information that we requested, reviewed the Report, and provided comments.

- The NBPA was provided with a draft of this Report to review but did not provide comments.

- The NHL reviewed the Report but declined to provide specific comments. The NHL stated "[w]ith respect to NHL-related information contained in the draft report, there are numerous factual and data-related inaccuracies. By way of example, the report references and relies upon certain outdated/superceded (sic) NHL/NHLPA policies and procedures. In addition, certain of the cited analytical data appears to be inaccurate. As a result, analysis of and conclusions drawn from such policies, procedures and data are flawed."[22] In response to this statement, on multiple occasions we requested additional information or specification about those items the NHL believed were inaccurate. The NHL did not respond.

In addition, the NHL declined to provide copies of the following requested documents: (1) the NHL/NHLPA Authorization Form for Health Care Providers to Release Health Information; (2) the NHL/NHLPA Concussion Program Authorization Form; (3) the Authorization for Management and Release of Neuropsychological Test Results; (4) the Substance Abuse and Behavioral Health Program; (5) the Prohibited Substances List for the Performance Enhancing Substances Program; and, (6) the NHL Concussion Protocol.

- The NHLPA reviewed the Report and provided comments and relevant documents. The NHLPA requested that the following statement appear in the Report to explain its involvement:

  – The NHLPA is pleased to have been able to respond to the authors' request for comments regarding a late draft of the study, and to provide certain of the information requested. The information and comments were provided to the authors of the study on the strict understanding that they were not to be attributed to the NHLPA in the text of the study, either directly or by implication. Nothing in the study, including the study's decision not to address a question or issue, is to be construed as reflective of the position of the NHLPA.

- MLS declined our invitation to review the Report and declined to provide relevant documents, including a Medical Policies and Procedures Manual and MLS' injury reporting policy.

- The MLSPU provided documents and information that we requested, reviewed the Report, and provided comments.

- The CFL provided some degree of cooperation by providing some information during a telephone call. However, after that call, the CFL declined to provide additional information or documents and declined our invitation to review the Report.[h]

- The CFLPA provided documents and information that we requested, and was provided a draft of the Report to review but did not provide comments.

As a result of the varying degrees of cooperation from the leagues and unions, we were not able to explore certain issues as deeply as we would have liked, in particular the relationships among clubs, club medical staff, and players. We again highlight this and other practices as areas calling for further research, provided the leagues provide the necessary access and information.

Importantly, while the leagues and unions had the opportunity to comment, and their comments in many instances did inform the content of this Report, we retained control over the final content of the Report. We carefully considered the comments from the leagues and unions and made changes we determined were appropriate but no reviewer had the authority to demand that any change be included. Thus,

review should not be considered an individual endorsement of any part of the final Report.

3) EVALUATE

Once we understood the leagues' varying policies, we could compare and contrast them. In cases where other leagues had policies that differed from the NFL we asked, "If the NFL adopted this policy, would it improve player health?" In doing so, we were careful to take into account the leagues' different circumstances and motivations. Nevertheless, in certain situations, we were able to identify gaps and opportunities for better protecting and promoting the health of NFL players. On the other hand, in some instances, we discovered that the NFL has more protective policies in place than other leagues, indicating that the learning from this Report can be multi-directional.

4) RECOMMEND

The primary goal of this Report is to make recommendations that improve the overall health of NFL players. Our analysis is thus principally focused on understanding other leagues' policies and practices and comparing them to the NFL's. As will be shown in this Report, it would be reasonable to conclude that *overall* the NFL's policies and practices concerning player health are the most protective of player health among the leagues. However, there are still some areas in which the NFL might learn lessons as compared to one or more comparator leagues and we have made corresponding recommendations. Additionally, even though our analysis likely reveals many areas in which other leagues can and should improve concerning the health of their players, as described above, it is beyond the scope of this Report to make those recommendations—we focus only on advancements for NFL players.

For every recommendation we describe both the *reason* for the change and, where applicable, potential *mechanisms* by which it may be implemented. However, we avoided being overly specific or prescriptive when multiple options for implementation may exist, and/or when we lacked sufficient information to determine which mechanism might be best.

While we consider and discuss a wide range changes that could improve player health, we purposefully chose to focus on *actionable recommendations* that could be realistically achieved between the publication of this Report and execution of the next NFL-NFLPA CBA.[i] This pragmatic approach does not mean that we are giving relevant

---

h   During the course of our research, both the NHL and CFL were defending themselves in lawsuits brought by former players alleging that the leagues had acted negligently concerning player concussions. Nevertheless, we do not believe our requests concerned issues relevant to those cases nor did either league indicate the ongoing litigation was the reason for their decisions not to cooperate. Additionally, the NFL was and is the subject of more litigation than either the NHL or CFL, but it substantially cooperated with our requests related to this Report.

---

i   The 2011 NFL CBA expires in March 2021.

Figure Introduction-B: Summary of League and Union Involvement

League/Union	Provided Documents/ Information	Accepted Invitation to Review Draft Report	Provided Comments
NFL	✓	✗	✗
NFLPA	✓	✓	✗
MLB	✓	✓	✓
MLBPA	None requested	✗	✗
NBA	✓	✓	✓
NBPA	None requested	✓	✗
NHL	✗	✓	Yes, but no details
NHLPA	✓	✓	✓
CFL	✓	✗	✗
CFLPA	✓	✓	✗
MLS	✗	✗	✗
MLSPU	✓	✓	✓

stakeholders a pass to simply accept the many current barriers to change that may exist, but it does recognize that change may be difficult in this complex web of relationships and in a culture that has developed over the course of many decades and is deeply entrenched. Furthermore, certain changes might require further information, research, or discussion than we were able to achieve in this Report. When we concluded that was the case, we so indicated by recommending only that a change be "considered" or that additional information be sought. Our recommendations may not be easy to achieve, but we have taken into account various realities in making them.

Finally, it is important to recognize that we do not view our recommendations as the exclusive changes that the various stakeholders should consider. We do, however, view these as minimum next steps forward—a floor, not a ceiling.

Appendix A is a compendium of all of the recommendations made in this Report. As discussed above, the NFL's policies concerning player health on the whole appear superior to the other leagues. Consequently, we include only nine recommendations in this Report. This is not to say there are not other areas in which the NFL can improve player health. Indeed, in our Report *Promoting the Health of NFL Players: Legal and Ethical Analysis and*

Recommendations, we included 76 recommendations for improving player health directed at a variety of stakeholders, including the NFL and NFLPA. This Report is focused only on those Recommendations that are derived from an understanding of other leagues' policies.

F) Scope

As already alluded to, the scope of this project is to generate legal and ethical recommendations that will improve the overall health of NFL players, current, future, and former. To fully grasp what is to come, it is essential to clarify these parameters.

As described at length in the Introduction to our Report *Promoting the Health of NFL Players: Legal and Ethical Analysis and Recommendations*, we adopt a broad definition of health that extends beyond the sort of clinical measurements that might immediately be evoked by the phrase. We maintain the importance of considering the full range of non-medical inputs that can influence health, also known as the "social determinants of health." These social determinants extend beyond the sorts of things for which one would seek out a doctor's care, and include broadly "the conditions in which people are born, grow, live, work, and age," as affected by the "distribution of money, power, and resources at global, national and local levels."[23] Indeed, the NFL's Player Engagement Department itself includes "physical strength," "emotional strength," "personal strength," and "financial strength" within its concept of "total wellness."[24]

Ultimately, for the purposes of all of our work, we define health for purposes of this Report as "a state of overall wellbeing in fundamental aspects of a person's life, including physical, mental, emotional, social, familial, and financial components."

In making recommendations regarding NFL player health, we have taken as our threshold the moment that a player has exhausted or foregone his remaining college eligibility and has taken steps to pursue an NFL career—from that point on, what needs to happen to maximize his health, even after he leaves the NFL? The reason we have selected this frame is not because the health of amateur players— those in college, high school, and youth leagues—is secure or unimportant. Instead, the reason is largely pragmatic: there is only so much any one report can cover. We recognize that what happens at the professional level can have a trickle-down effect on the culture of football across the board, and also that some amateur players may be taking health risks in hopes of eventually reaching the NFL, even when that may be highly unlikely. Nonetheless, our goal with this Report, prompted by the limited scope of the request for proposals for this project and in part by the fact that further analysis will be possible by others, is only to address the already complicated set of factors influencing the health of NFL players, current, future, and former.

That said, many of our recommendations will be most relevant to current and future players, simply because former players may not continue to be engaged with or affected by many of the stakeholders that we are analyzing, or may be past the point at which implementation of particular recommendations could help them. For example, no matter what improvements we recommend related to club doctors, these simply could not affect players who are no longer affiliated with any club.

Endnotes

1 CBA, Art. 12, § 5.

2 Nat'l Football League Players Ass'n, *Request for Proposals Advancing the Frontiers of Research in Professional Football* (2012), § 1(a).

3 Alvaro Pascual-Leone and Lee M. Nadler, *Let's not kill football yet,* Pitt. Post. Gazette, May 10, 2015, http://www.post-gazette.com/opinion/Op-Ed/2015/05/10/Let-s-not-kill-football-yet-Yes-players-get-injured-but-the-scope-of-the-problem-is-far-from-clear/stories/201505100034, *archived at* http://perma.cc/V3DN-Z2F3.

4 Mike Florio, *NFL will reach $14 billion in 2017 revenue*, ProFootballTalk (Mar. 6, 2017, 11:29 AM), http://profootballtalk.nbcsports.com/2017/03/06/nfl-will-reach-14-billion-in-2017-revenue/, *archived at* https://perma.cc/X57A-VRXU. Mark Leibovich, *Roger Goodell's Unstoppable Football Machine,* N.Y. Times, Feb. 3, 2016, http://www.nytimes.com/2016/02/07/magazine/roger-goodells-unstoppable-football-machine.html?_r=0, *archived at* https://perma.cc/Y7L5-A99L.

5 Maury Brown, *MLB Sees Record Revenues Approaching $10 Billion for 2016,* Forbes (Dec. 5, 2016, 3:22 PM), http://www.forbes.com/sites/maurybrown/2016/12/05/mlb-sees-record-revenues-approaching-10-billion-for-2016/#7704e2e21845, *archived at* https://perma.cc/775E-WE9A.

6 Dan Feldman, *Report: NBA Revenue Projected to Reach $8 Billion Next Season*, Pro Basketball Talk (Sep. 16, 2016, 10:05 AM), http://nba.nbcsports.com/2016/09/16/report-nba-revenue-projected-to-reach-8-billion-next-season/, *archived at* https://perma.cc/73NP-QRJN.

7 *See The Business of Hockey*, Forbes (Nov. 30, 2016), http://www.forbes.com/nhl-valuations/list/, *archived at* https://perma.cc/545K-NQBV (listing NHL clubs' estimated revenues).

8 Andrew Bucholtz, *What percentage of league-wide revenues did CFL players get in 2013 under the old CBA?*, Yahoo! Sports Can. (June 9, 2014, 6:49 PM), https://ca.sports.yahoo.com/blogs/cfl-55-yard-line/percentage-league-wide-revenues-did-cfl-players-2013-224954281.html, *archived at* http://perma.cc/F5NU-FWE3.

9 *See* Fraser v. Major League Soccer, L.L.C., 284 F.3d 47, 53-55 (1st Cir. 2002) (discussing MLS' structure and operations).

10 *See* Chris Smith, *Major League Soccer's Most Valuable Teams 2016,* Forbes (Sep. 7, 2016, 10:32 AM), http://www.forbes.com/sites/chrissmith/2016/09/07/major-league-soccers-most-valuable-teams-2016-new-york-orlando-thrive-in-first-seasons/, *archived at* https://perma.cc/K7B6-DJ86.

11 *See* Michael A. McCann, *The NBA and the Single Entity Defense: A Better Case?* 1 Harv. J. Sports & Ent. L. 39, 40 (2010) (referring to the NFL, MLB, NBA and NHL as the "Big Four"); Marc Edelman, *How to Curb Professional Sports Bargaining Power Vis-à-Vis the American City*, 2 Va. Sports & Ent. L.J. 280, 291 (2003).

12 *History,* Nat'l Football League Players Ass'n, https://www.nflpa.com/about/history (last visited Aug. 7, 2015), *archived at* https://perma.cc/3D2R-8EQG?type=pdf [hereinafter "NFLPA History"].

13 *See* Glenn M. Wong, *Essentials of Sports Law*, § 11.3 (4th ed. 2010) (providing history of the unions in the Big Four sports leagues).

14 *Id.*

15 *Id.*

16 *Id.*

17 *Id.*

18 *See, e.g.,* A. Jason Huebinger, 16 Sports Law. J. 279, 281-82 (2009); Matthew Levine, *Despite His Antics, T.O. Has a Valid Point: Why NFL Players Deserve a Bigger Piece of the Pie*, 13 Vill. Sports & Ent. L.J. 425, 435-36 (2006); Mark Bradley, *NFL players may hate Roger Goodell, but he's their biggest ally,* Atl. J.-Const., Jun. 4, 2012, *available at* 2012 WLNR 28612021; Larry Brooks, *Head-Less Iceman Lead to the Slaughter,* N.Y. Post, Aug. 15, 2010, *available at* 2010 WLNR 16396767 Jon Saraceno, *Mawae's labor of love: Fighting for players*, USA Today, Oct. 21, 2010, *available at* 2010 WLNR 21102155.

19 Bill Baer, *Report: Owners, Union Agree on New Collective Bargaining Agreement*, Hardball Talk (Nov. 30, 2016, 8:51 PM EDT), http://mlb.nbcsports.com/2016/11/30/report-owners-union-agree-on-new-collective-bargaining-agreement/, *archived at* https://perma.cc/3JRF-PTYF.

20 *MLBPA, MLB Announce Details of New Labor Agreement*, MLBPA (Dec. 2, 2016), http://www.mlbplayers.com/ViewArticle.dbml?DB_OEM_ID=34000&ATCLID=211336390, *archived at* https://perma.cc/4XUA-2DAW.

21 Craig Calcaterra, *Owners, Players Ratify New Collective Bargaining Agreement*, Hardball Talk (Dec. 14, 2016, 5:16 AM EDT), http://mlb.nbcsports.com/2016/12/14/owners-ratify-new-collective-bargaining-agreement-29-1/, *archived at* https://perma.cc/YYK2-GLSR.

22 Email from Julie Grand, NHL, Deputy General Counsel, to authors (Nov. 1, 2016).

23 *Social Determinants of Health,* World Health Org., http://www.who.int/social_determinants/sdh_definition/en/ (last visited Aug. 2, 2016), *archived at* http://perma.cc/USS7-8C9J; *see also* Michael Marmot & Richard G. Wilkinson, Social Determinants of Health (2d ed. 2005); For discussions of the relationship between these social determinants and ethics and political philosophy, *see, e.g.,* Sridhar Venkatapuram, Health Justice: An Argument from the Capabilities Approach (2011); Norman Daniels, Just Health: Meeting Health Needs Fairly (2007); Madison Powers & Ruth Faden, Social Justice: The Moral Foundations of Public Health and Health Policy (2006).

24 *See NFL Total Wellness*, NFL Player Engagement.com, https://www.nflplayerengagement.com/total-wellness/ (last visited Aug. 7, 2015), *archived at* https://perma.cc/Z368-BBV4.

Chapter 1

Club Medical Personnel

This Chapter discusses the role of club medical staff, including both doctors and athletic trainers, in each of the sports leagues as set forth in the leagues' various controlling policies, most principally, the CBAs. In particular, we focus on: (1) the types of medical personnel required, if any; (2) the medical personnel's obligations; (3) the obligations of the players concerning club medical personnel; (4) the relationship between the medical personnel and the clubs; and, (5) the existence of sponsorship arrangements between medical personnel and the clubs, if any.

Our focus here is on the structural issues that are generally governed by the CBA or other policies rather than how each individual club hires and supervises its medical personnel and how individual medical personnel interact with individual players, matters that are not the subject of extensive reporting or publicly available research. By understanding what is required or permitted pursuant to the CBA or other policies we can understand the scope of possible practices, including those that might be concerning as they relate to player health.

To provide context for the policies we examine in this Chapter, it is important to provide background on the subjects most relevant to player health. We discuss those below, and then provide background on two additional issues relevant to club medical personnel and this Chapter, before reviewing the policies of each league.

1) SUBJECTS RELEVANT TO PLAYER HEALTH

There are a wide variety of laws, statutes, regulations, and ethical codes that govern the actions of sports medical professionals. For example, the American Medical Association ("AMA")'s Code of Medical Ethics ("AMA Code")[1] governs the conduct of nearly all doctors, and contains multiple provisions applicable to the duties and obligations of club doctors. Similarly, the leading sports medicine organization, Fédération Internationale de Médecine du Sport ("FIMS"), publishes a Code of Ethics.[2] And, for athletic trainers, the National Athletic Trainers Association ("NATA") has a fairly robust Code of Ethics.[3]

The full panoply of laws, statutes, regulations, and ethical codes and their application to professional sports is complex and discussed at length in our prior Report: *Protecting and Promoting the Health of NFL Players: Legal and Ethical Analysis and Recommendations.* Here, we identify some of the principles discussed in that Report most relevant to understanding the different leagues' efficacy in protecting and promoting player health: (a) quality of medical care; (b) disclosure and player autonomy; (c) confidentiality; and, (d) conflicts of interest. While we do not organize the Chapter by these issues, they served as the framework for our analysis and we thus elaborate on them here.

a) Quality of Medical Care

Playing professional sports comes with a risk of injury that likely exceeds most traditional employment situations. Moreover, a player's health is essential to his performance and career longevity. Consequently, it is important that players have access to high quality healthcare and healthcare that is suited to meet their sport-specific needs. In this respect, we are interested in whether the leagues have policies that require certain types of medical professionals and certain certifications that are likely to be most responsive to a professional athlete's healthcare needs. Additionally, we are interested in whether the leagues clarify the standard of care to be provided to players.

b) Disclosure and Player Autonomy

There is broad support in law and ethics for a patient's right to autonomy—the right to make his or her own choices concerning healthcare.[4] A key correlate of a patient's right to make his or her own decisions is the obligation of the healthcare provider to disclose relevant medical information. Players are patients too and deserve the same protections we all seek in our medical decision-making.[a] As it concerns professional sports leagues, we are interested in what types of information or records the clubs are required to provide to players, what type of healthcare options are available to players outside of the club, and what level of control the club retains over the player's healthcare choices.

c) Confidentiality

One of the fundamental principles of the doctor-patient relationship is that a patient's medical information must be treated confidentially.[5] However, this principle is put under pressure in situations where an employee's health is relevant to the employee's ability to perform his job, and his healthcare is provided in the employment context, both of which are the case in professional sports. While we recognize club interests and rights in accessing certain player health information, appropriate safeguards are needed in dictating the degree to which player medical information can be disclosed and disseminated. We look carefully to see which leagues have put such safeguards in place and to what extent. We also examine confidentiality protections when a player obtains care from a healthcare professional outside of the club, including whether the club has any rights to view that information.

d) Conflicts of Interest

Club medical staff—such as doctors and athletic trainers—are clearly fundamental to protecting and promoting player health. However, they face an inherent structural conflict of interest. This is not a moral judgment about them as competent professionals or devoted individuals, but rather a simple fact of the current organizational structure of their positions, in which they simultaneously perform at least two roles that are not necessarily compatible. On the one hand, they are hired by clubs to provide and supervise player medical care. As a result, they have a legal and ethical responsibility to protect and promote the health of their player-patients, in line with players' interests as defined by the players themselves. This means providing care and medical advice aligned with player goals, and also working with players to help them make decisions about their own

---

a   Indeed, as part of our prior Report, *Protecting and Promoting the Health of NFL Players: Legal and Ethical Analysis and Recommendations,* we included a Patient Bill of Rights for NFL Players, modeled on the Patient's Bill of Rights common in hospitals and other healthcare settings.

self-protection, including when they should play, rest, and potentially retire.

On the other hand, clubs engage medical staff because medical information about and assessment of players is necessary to clubs' business decisions related to a player's ability to perform at a sufficiently high level in the short- and long-term. Additionally, clubs engage medical staff to advance the clubs' interest in keeping their players healthy and helping them recover as fully and quickly as possible when they are injured. These dual roles for club medical staff may sometimes conflict because players and clubs often have conflicting interests, but club medical staff are called to serve both parties. We examine what the leagues are doing (or are not doing) to protect players from these conflicts.

Similarly, many healthcare organizations are interested in being associated with professional sports clubs to enhance their reputation and exposure. Consequently, these organizations seek to enter into a variety of commercial arrangements with clubs, including some whereby a healthcare organization pays the club for the right to provide medical care to the players. Such arrangements may raise concerns about how medical professionals treating players are being selected (*e.g.*, skill or payment) and whether these relationships have the potential to undermine the care provided to players or trust in the healthcare professionals providing that care.

2) ADDITIONAL INTRODUCTORY ISSUES

a) Independent Contractors Versus Employees

Where possible, we have provided information concerning whether club doctors in a particular league are independent contractors or employees of the club. The distinction has important ramifications from a potential liability perspective vis-à-vis workers' compensation laws.

Workers' compensation statutes provide compensation for workers injured at work and thus generally preclude lawsuits against co-workers based on the co-workers' negligence.[6] Thus, in cases where the club doctor is an employee of the club—as opposed to an independent contractor as is the case for most club doctors—a player's lawsuit against the doctor is likely to be barred by the relevant state's workers' compensation statute. This has been the result in multiple cases brought by athletes against clubs and club doctors,[7] as well as in cases brought by athletes against athletic trainers,[8] who are almost always employees of the club. Where the club doctors are independent contractors instead of employees, the players can pursue medical malpractice cases against the doctor,[9] but the club is not likely to be held legally responsible for any negligence by the doctor.[10]

b) Healthcare in Canada

The second issue worth mentioning now concerns Canadian clubs. MLB (one club), the NBA (one), NHL (seven), CFL (all nine), and MLS (three) have Canadian clubs. As Canadian and United States laws differ concerning healthcare, an understanding of the Canadian healthcare system is necessary for any discussion of the relationship between Canadian clubs and medical personnel.

The Canadian healthcare system is a social, welfare-based system, wherein "access to health care is viewed as a right" and is financed through government funding.[11] The ten Canadian provinces and three territories separately administer healthcare plans modeled off of the federal Canada Health Act of 1984.[12] The federal government ensures provincial compliance with the federal template through the threat of loss of federal funding.[13] Compliant plans must cover "insured services"—a defined term in the Canada Health Act that includes medically necessary hospital services, hospital facilities, drugs used in hospitals, medically necessary services rendered by medical practitioners, and medically required surgical/dental services performed in a hospital. In addition, plans must also meet the five principles of the Canada Health Act: public administration; provincial portability; universality; comprehensiveness; and, accessibility.[14] Given the gaps in coverage (for example, drugs outside of hospitals and vision/dental services performed outside of hospitals are generally not covered), private spending still makes up 29% of Canadian healthcare expenditures.[15]

"As far as delivery of services is concerned, most physicians are independent contractors operating on a fee-for-service basis."[16] These physicians receive fees that are fixed through negotiations between medical associations and provincial governments, and there is no additional billing.[17] To collect payment, physicians directly bill the provincial medical services association.[18] Physicians providing non-covered services, however, directly bill patients, who pay through private insurance or out-of-pocket.[19] Of course, this is different from the United States. Outside of some specific populations, including but not limited to those covered by Medicare, Medicaid, or the Veterans Affairs healthcare system, most Americans have private health insurance either through their own insurance plan or one sponsored by their employer.

* * *

With these introductory issues in mind to provide context, we turn now to analyzing club medical personnel policies in each of the leagues. For each league, we analyze: (1) Types of Medical Personnel; (2) Medical Personnel's Obligations; (3) Players' Obligations; (4) Relationship between Medical Personnel and Clubs; and, (5) Sponsorship Arrangements.

A) Club Medical Personnel in the NFL

1) TYPES OF MEDICAL PERSONNEL

a) Doctors

The CBA obligates NFL clubs to retain certain kinds of doctors:

- **Club Physicians:** Clubs must retain[20] a board-certified orthopedic surgeon and at least one physician board-certified in internal medicine, family medicine, or emergency medicine. All physicians must also have a Certificate of Added Qualification in Sports Medicine. In addition, clubs are required to retain consultants in the neurological, cardiovascular, nutritional, and neuropsychological fields.[21]

- **Physicians at Games:** "All home teams shall retain at least one [Rapid Sequence Intubation] RSI physician who is board certified in emergency medicine, anesthesia, pulmonary medicine, or thoracic surgery, and who has documented competence in RSI intubations in the past twelve months. This physician shall be the neutral physician dedicated to game-day medical intervention for on-field or locker room catastrophic emergencies."[22]

Of note, these two provisions do not require clubs to retain and have available neurological doctors at the games. The absence of this requirement is offset by the Concussion Protocol's[b] requirement that for every game each club be assigned an Unaffiliated Neurotrauma Consultant to assist in the diagnosis of concussions.

Most (if not all) of the doctors retained by NFL clubs are members of the National Football League Physicians Society ("NFLPS"). The stated mission of the NFLPS, founded in 1966, "is to provide excellence in the medical and surgical care of the athletes in the National Football League and to provide direction and support for the athletic trainers in

charge of the care for these athletes."[23] Approximately 175 doctors work with NFL clubs,[24] an average of 5.5 per club. The NFLPS holds annual meetings at the NFL Combine to discuss medical and scientific issues pertinent to its membership.[25]

According to the NFLPS, 22 of the 32 clubs' head orthopedists and 14 of the 32 clubs' head "medicine" doctors are board-certified in sports medicine.[26] In addition, although the 2011 CBA requires club doctors to have a Certificate of Added Qualification in Sports Medicine, currently only 11 out of the 32 head club doctors have such a Certificate. The remaining club doctors were with clubs before the 2011 CBA and were grandfathered in under the new policy.

Notably, the NFLPS does not have a code of ethics for its members.[c]

b) Athletic Trainers

The CBA dictates the required presence, education, and certification of athletic trainers:

> All athletic trainers employed or retained by Clubs to provide services to players, including any part time athletic trainers, must be certified by the National Athletic Trainers Association and must have a degree from an accredited four-year college or university. Each Club must have at least two full-time athletic trainers. All part-time athletic trainers must work under the direct supervision of a certified athletic trainer.[d]

Each NFL club employs approximately four athletic trainers, including a head athletic trainer and three assistants. Head athletic trainers have an average of 21.9 years of experience in the NFL, while assistants average approximately 8.4 years of experience in the NFL.[27] In the 2014 season, 26 athletic trainers had at least 20 years of experience and eight had more than 30 years of experience.[28] Athletic trainers—unlike most club doctors—are full-time employees of the club and not independent contractors.

The Professional Football Athletic Trainers Society ("PFATS") is an organization that represents the athletic trainers of NFL clubs.[29] "[M]embership in PFATS is limited to those professionally certified in accordance with the most

---

b   The Concussion Protocol refers to the NFL Head, Neck and Spine Committee's Protocols Regarding Diagnosis and Management of Concussion.

c   This information was provided by the NFLPS. In Recommendation 2:1-B of our Report *Protecting and Promoting the Health of NFL Players: Legal and Ethical Analysis and Recommendations*, we recommend the NFLPS adopt a code of ethics.

d   2011 NFL CBA, Art. 39, § 2. The CBA's requirement that athletic trainers be certified by NATA is actually in error and a requirement with which athletic trainers cannot comply. NATA is a voluntary professional association but does not *certify* athletic trainers. Athletic trainers are certified by the Board of Certification for the Athletic Trainer ("BOC"). Nevertheless, all NFL athletic trainers are certified by the BOC.

current NFL Collective Bargaining Agreement and who are employed full-time as head or assistant athletic trainers by any of the 32 NFL franchises."[30] PFATS' mission statement is as follows:

> The Professional Football Athletic Trainers Society (PFATS) is a Professional Association representing the athletic trainers of the National Football League. We serve the players of the NFL, the member Clubs, and other members of the community. Our purpose is to ensure the highest quality of health care is provided to the National Football League. We are dedicated to the welfare of our members and committed to the promotion and advancement of athletic training through education and research. The Society is founded on the professional integrity and the ethical standards of our members and the fellowship that exists among us.[31]

PFATS does have a Code of Ethics for its members. However, as discussed in greater depth in our Report, *Protecting and Promoting the Health of NFL Players: Legal and Ethical Analysis and Recommendations*, the Code of Ethics is seriously flawed and requires substantial changes to be protective of player health.[32]

2) MEDICAL PERSONNEL'S OBLIGATIONS

The CBA requires each NFL club to "use its best efforts to ensure that its players are provided with medical care consistent with professional standards for the industry."[33] The CBA expounds on this provision by articulating its conception of the club doctor's standard of care:

> [E]ach Club physician's primary duty *in providing medical care* shall be not to the Club but instead to the player-patient. This duty shall include traditional physician/patient confidentiality requirements. In addition, all Club physicians and medical personnel shall comply with all federal, state, and local requirements, including all ethical rules and standards established by any applicable government and/or other authority that regulates or governs the medical profession in the Club's city.[34] (Emphasis added.)

This CBA provision is susceptible to multiple interpretations. On a generous reading (*i.e.*, one that does not give the italicized language any special emphasis), club doctors' primary duty is to the player at all times. On a less generous reading, the CBA provision demands a primary duty to the player-patient *only* in situations where the club doctor

is "providing medical care," and thus is inapplicable when the club doctor is rendering services to the club. Importantly, however, the way club doctors are currently situated within the club precludes the two roles from being truly separated, and thereby precludes club doctors from having their exclusive duty be to the players. This is because at the same time that the club doctor is providing care to the player, he is simultaneously performing duties for the club by judging the player's ability to play and help the club win.

Thus, the club doctor is required by the CBA to provide medical care that puts the player-patient's interests above the club's (in the event these interests conflict), which is as it should be. However, in most instances—and as seemingly recognized by the CBA—it is impossible under the current structure for the club doctor to *always* have a primary duty to the player-patient over the club, because sometimes the club doctor is not providing care, but rather is advising the club on business decisions, *i.e.*, fitness-for-play determinations. In other words, the club doctor cannot always hold the player's interests as paramount and at the same time abide by his or her obligations to the club. Indeed, a club doctor could provide impeccable player-driven medical care (treating the player-patient as primary in accord with the CBA), while simultaneously hurting a player's interests by informing a club that the player's injury and treatment course will negatively impact his ability to play. Thus, under any reading of the CBA provision, players lack a doctor who is concerned with their best interests at all times— an unacceptable situation.

Relatedly, the CBA provision also seems to require that the care relationship between players and club doctors be afforded "traditional" confidentiality protections. However, clubs request or require players to execute collectively-bargained waivers effectively waiving this requirement— and no player refuses to sign the waiver.[e] Questions might be raised as to whether the players are providing meaningful and voluntary informed consent in their execution. Players are being compelled to waive certain legal rights concerning their health without meaningful options. There is no doubt that players execute the waivers because they fear that if they do not, they will lose their job. Indeed, the waivers (which are collectively bargained with the NFLPA)[35] permit the athletic trainer and club doctors to disclose the player's medical information to club employees, such as coaches and the general manager. Thus, it is unclear what work this CBA language is doing. Of course, given this communication, it is inevitable that players will be less

---

e   For more on this issue, see our Report, *Protecting and Promoting the Health of NFL Players: Legal and Ethical Analysis and Recommendations*. A copy of the waiver at issue is included as Appendix L to that Report.

than forthcoming about their medical needs, lest it negatively affect their career prospects.

In reviewing a draft of our Report, *Protecting and Promoting the Health of NFL Players: Legal and Ethical Analysis and Recommendations,* the NFL rejected our claim that the CBA provision "requires the traditional patient-physician confidentiality requirements of a private system,"[36] even though the provision in question specifically says club doctors have a duty to provide "traditional physician/patient confidentiality requirements." The CBA provision does not qualify the club doctor's duty in the context of the employer-employee relationship. The NFL should abide by its obligations under the CBA.

The CBA also imposes disclosure requirements on club doctors:

> All Club physicians are required to disclose to a player any and all information about the player's physical condition that the physician may from time to time provide to a coach or other Club representative, whether or not such information affects the player's performance or health. If a Club physician advises a coach or other Club representative of a player's serious injury or career threatening physical condition which significantly affects the player's performance or health, the physician will also advise the player in writing. The player, after being advised of such serious injury or career-threatening physical condition, may request a copy of the Club physician's record from the examination in which such physical condition was diagnosed and/or a written explanation from the Club physician of the physical condition.[37]

Additionally, club doctors are obligated to permit a player to examine his medical records once during the pre-season and once after the regular season. Club doctors are also obligated to provide a copy of a player's medical records to the player upon request in the off-season.[38] Nevertheless, in reality, the NFL now has an electronic medical record system that permits players to obtain access to their medical records at any time.

Finally, there are no CBA provisions that address an athletic trainer's obligations.

3) PLAYERS' OBLIGATIONS

The CBA and Standard NFL Player Contract impose certain obligations on players concerning their relationship with club medical personnel.

First, players are required to "undergo the standardized minimum pre-season physical examination and tests" that are agreed to as part of the CBA.[39]

Second, players are obligated to "undergo a complete physical examination by the club physician upon club request, during which physical examination Player agrees to make full and complete disclosure of any physical or mental condition known to him which might impair his performance . . . and to respond fully and in good faith when questioned by the Club physician about such condition."[40]

Third, players seemingly have an ongoing obligation to report injuries to the club. The CBA permits clubs to fine players up to $1,770 if the player does not "promptly report" an injury to the club doctor or athletic trainer.[41] We are not aware of any guidance on what constitutes "promptly report[ing]."

Fourth, whenever a player seeks a second medical opinion or exercises his right to have the surgeon of his choice perform an operation, the player must first consult with the club doctor if he wishes to have the club pay for the second medical opinion or surgery.[42] Additionally, if the player sees a second opinion doctor and wants the club to pay for it, "the Club physician must be furnished promptly with a report concerning the diagnosis, examination and course of treatment recommended by the other physician."[43]

4) RELATIONSHIP BETWEEN MEDICAL PERSONNEL AND CLUBS

As a preliminary matter, each member of an NFL club's medical staff is typically chosen by the club's front office executives, *e.g.,* the club president or general manager.[44]

a) Doctors

Club doctors are affiliated with a wide variety of private practice groups, hospitals, academic institutions, and other professional sports leagues. Some of these institutions have long-standing relationships with clubs which often help lead to the doctor being retained by the club. The NFLPA plays no role in the selection of club doctors other than ensuring they have the qualifications required by the CBA and are properly licensed in the relevant state(s), via Synernet, a third-party vendor jointly selected by the NFL and NFLPA.[45] Additionally, of the NFL's 32 head club doctors, two are employees and 30 are independent contractors.[46]

Also, while it is our understanding that club doctors' contracts are generally reviewed and renewed on an annual basis, there is very little turnover among club doctors.

Actual statistics and practices of club doctor compensation are difficult to ascertain. In the course of our research, we were informed by some familiar with the industry that club doctors are generally paid in relatively nominal amounts compared to what one might expect ($20,000–$30,000).[f] In reviewing a draft of our Report, *Protecting and Promoting the Health of NFL Players: Legal and Ethical Analysis and Recommendations,* the NFL stated that this estimate "grossly underestimates compensation to Head Team Physicians, Head Team Orthopedists and Head Team Internists."[47] Nevertheless, the NFL did not provide alternative compensation statistics.

In addition, despite the relatively high scrutiny club doctors face, it is our understanding that their contracts with the clubs do not include any type of indemnification whereby the club would pay for the defense, settlement, or verdict of a medical malpractice claim.

Despite the various challenges, club doctors have a variety of reasons for being interested in the position. Many of them are sports fans and thus the opportunity to work up close and personal with some of the best athletes in the world is exciting. From a business perspective, a doctor's association with an NFL club could be powerful in terms of professional respect and name recognition, resulting in more patients.

b) Athletic Trainers

Athletic trainers—unlike most club doctors—are full-time employees of the club and not independent contractors.

Athletic trainers are generally an NFL player's first and primary source of medical care.[48] Club doctors are only with the club sporadically during the week of practice and then attend the games, whereas the athletic trainers are with the club at all times. Players will first meet with the athletic trainer concerning a medical issue and the athletic trainer then typically determines whether the player should meet with the club doctor. The athletic trainers and club doctors are in regular communication about players' conditions and treatment. The club doctors are responsible for directing and supervising the care of the players by the athletic trainers.

Players execute waivers permitting the athletic trainer and club doctors to disclose the player's medical information to club employees, such as coaches and the general manager.[g] Athletic trainers—in consultation with the club doctors—thus keep coaches and general managers apprised of players' injury statuses during regular meetings so the general manager can make a decision about whether or not to sign another player in the event a player is unable to play.[49] These waivers effectively undermine the confidentiality protections outlined in the CBA.

5) SPONSORSHIP ARRANGEMENTS

The NFL first instituted a Medical Sponsorship Policy in 2004.[h] At its core, the Policy, most recently amended in 2014, permits clubs to enter into a Sponsorship Agreement[i] with a medical services provider ("MSP")[j], but prohibits such agreements that also include the provision of medical services. Stated another way, "[n]o Club may enter into a contract for the provision of medical services to its players that is interdependent with, or in any way tied to a Sponsorship Agreement with a [MSP]." The Medical Sponsorship Policy does not define "interdependent" and instead the NFL reviews the arrangements to ensure there is no interdependence.[50]

The Policy also explicitly declares that clubs are permitted to enter into agreements with MSPs whereby the MSP obtains the right to advertise itself as an "official" or "proud" "sponsor," "partner," or "provider."[51] A review of club websites and media guides shows that at least 25 clubs currently have some type of "official" healthcare sponsor or partner.

Additionally, the Medical Sponsorship Policy does not prohibit MSPs from paying for the right to provide medical services to players, although, according to the NFLPS, no MSP currently pays for the right to provide medical services to players. The Policy also does not limit an MSP's ability to bargain for the right to provide healthcare to a club by offering discounted or free services.

f   In 2001, the Minnesota Vikings paid their three club doctors $4,000, $19,600, and $47,500 per year, respectively. The amounts varied based on the extent of the doctors' obligations. *See* Memorandum and Order, Stringer v. Minn. Vikings Football Club, No. 02-415, 20–23 (Minn. Dist. Ct. Apr. 25, 2003).

g   These waivers are included as Appendices L and M in our Report, *Protecting and Promoting the Health of NFL Players: Legal and Ethical Analysis and Recommendations.*

h   For a complete history of the NFL's Medical Sponsorship Policy, *see* Christopher R. Deubert, I. Glenn Cohen, Holly Fernandez Lynch, *Protecting and Promoting the Health of NFL Players: Legal and Ethical Analysis and Recommendations,* § 2(A) (2016).

i   The 2014 Medical Sponsorship Policy defines "Sponsorship Agreements" as "agreements with MSPs involving the sale or license by the club of commercial assets such as naming rights, stadium signage, advertising inventory within club-controlled media, promotional inventory (e.g., day-of-game promotions), hospitality, and rights to use club trademarks for marketing and promotional purposes."

j   According to the Policy, MSPs include "hospitals, universities, medical practice groups, rehabilitation facilities, laboratories, imaging centers and other entities that provide medical care and related services." Although doctors are not specifically included in the definition of MSPs, the NFL includes doctors as MSPs for purposes of the Policy. Email with Larry Ferazani, Vice President, Labor Litigation & Policy, Nat'l Football League (Apr. 15, 2015) (on file with author).

Table 1-A:
Arrangements *Prohibited* by Medical Sponsorship Policy

Description	Explanation
Agreement with MSP to provide medical services to club on an exclusive basis.	Policy prohibits agreements with MSPs for the exclusive provision of medical services, thus enabling clubs and players to seek necessary medical care elsewhere.
Agreement allowing institutional MSP to select the doctors mandated by the CBA to provide care to the club's players.	Policy prohibits agreements that permit MSP to select CBA-mandated doctors; these doctors must be selected by the club.
Agreement with MSP to provide medical services to club on a non-exclusive basis alongside the right to post advertisements in the club's stadium using club trademarks.	Each of these agreements would be permitted on its own, but not jointly; Policy prohibits medical services agreements that are interdependent with Sponsorship Agreements with MSPs.
Agreement with MSP to provide medical services to club on a non-exclusive basis alongside naming rights to the club's practice facility.	Each of these agreements would be permitted on its own, but not jointly; Policy prohibits medical services agreements that are interdependent with Sponsorship Agreements with MSPs.
Agreement with doctor to provide medical services to club on a non-exclusive basis alongside agreement for his or her institutional MSP to post advertisements in the club's stadium using club trademarks.	Each of these agreements would be permitted on its own, but not jointly; Policy prohibits medical services agreements that are interdependent with Sponsorship Agreements with MSPs.
Agreement with doctor to provide medical services to club on a non-exclusive basis but doctor reports to institutional MSP concerning care provided to players.	Policy requires doctors to report directly to the club.

Importantly, even in situations where an MSP enters into an agreement to provide medical services to a club but has not entered into a sponsorship agreement of any kind, the MSP can benefit from the association. The MSP could still identify itself as a healthcare provider for the club on its website and in advertisements, within the bounds of relevant intellectual property, professional advertising, and consumer protection laws and regulations. In other words, the MSP likely could not use the club's logo without permission or try to make it appear that the club was actively endorsing the MSP's services. In 2004, the marketing director of Methodist Hospital explained the value of the hospital's association with the Houston Texans:

> We track phone calls coming in from new patients . . . . The No. 1 driver of our calls is the association with our local teams. People say they heard that Methodist is where the players go, so it must be the best. It's not a coincidence that we are the best, but there isn't a better way to convince them. That's a win-win situation.[52]

Finally, it is worth noting that institutional MSPs can be a party to the doctor's contract with the club to the extent that such an arrangement is necessary for medical malpractice insurance or for practice privileges.

When asked for its position on medical sponsorship in the NFL, the NFLPA stated only that it "insisted upon changes that minimized conflicts of interest resulting in changes to the NFL's Medical Sponsorship Policy in 2014/15." The NFLPA declined to provide further detail on the negotiations or what specific changes it insisted upon, indicating that the discussions were confidential and that the Medical Sponsorship Policy is unilaterally promulgated by the NFL. The NFLPA indicated that its "sole objective" regarding the Medical Sponsorship Policy "is to reduce conflicts of interest and to ensure the best care possible for its members." Nevertheless, the NFLPA did not indicate that it is opposed to medical sponsorship agreements. In addition, we recognize the medical sponsorship agreements provide clubs — and thus the players — with a lucrative source of revenue.

Above and below are examples of relationships between MSPs, including doctors, and clubs with a discussion of whether these relationships would be prohibited or permitted by the 2014 Medical Sponsorship Policy. However, it is important to keep in mind that the 2014 Medical

Table 1-B:

Arrangements *Permitted* by Medical Sponsorship Policy

Description	Explanation	Potential Concerns with Practices Still Permitted
Agreement with MSP to pay the club to provide medical services to club on a non-exclusive basis.	Policy does not prohibit MSPs from paying for the right to provide medical services.	Club might choose MSP that is willing to pay the most rather than the best MSP.
Agreement with MSP to provide medical services to club on a non-exclusive basis, whereby MSP has agreed to no compensation or compensation at rates below the MSP's standard rate and market rates.	Policy does not prohibit MSPs from discounting the costs of their services for the right to provide medical services.	Club might choose MSP willing to charge lowest rates rather than the best MSP.
Agreement with MSP to provide medical services to club on a non-exclusive basis and MSP has the right to call itself the "official" doctor or healthcare provider of the club.	Policy expressly permits agreements that permit MSPs to call themselves the "official" doctor or healthcare provider.	MSP will attach monetary value to "official designation," and alter payment structure as a result, leading to clubs choosing MSPs based on reduced rates rather than skills.
Agreement with MSP to provide medical services to club on a non-exclusive basis and a separate agreement to post advertisements in the club's stadium using club trademarks.	Policy permits MSPs and clubs to enter into medical services and Sponsorship Agreements so long as they are not "interdependent."	Whether the two agreements are "interdependent" is difficult to enforce. Implied agreements and long-standing practices could result in clubs choosing MSPs based on Sponsorship Agreements rather than skills.
Agreement with MSP to pay the club for the right to call itself the "official" healthcare provider of the club and to post advertisements in the club's stadium using club trademarks but does not actually provide any medical services to the club.	Policy expressly permits Sponsorship Agreements with MSPs "so long as these agreements do not involve the provision of medical service to players."	Does not directly affect player health but raises concerns about whether the general public will falsely rely on the MSP's declaration that it is the "official" healthcare provider.

Sponsorship Policy is complex and, at times, unclear. Additionally, the document is not collectively bargained and there is no generally available guidance. Thus, what follows is our best interpretation of the Policy. A more detailed discussion of the Medical Sponsorship Policy can be found in our Report, *Protecting and Promoting the Health of NFL Players: Legal and Ethical Analysis and Recommendations.*[53]

In reviewing a draft of our Report, *Protecting and Promoting the Health of NFL Players: Legal and Ethical Analysis and Recommendations*, the NFL stated that it "disagree[d] entirely with the conclusions reached in Table [1]-B,"[54] without explaining why it reads the plain text of the Policy so differently than we do. The fact that two sets of trained attorneys (those who authored this Report and those at the NFL) interpret the Policy differently demonstrates that it should be clarified. Ideally, the NFL will make the Policy public to allow for further discussion and review.[k]

---

k   In a written response to our Report, the NFL again disagreed with us, stating: "Despite the clear language in the policy prohibiting the exchange of medical services for sponsorship, the initial draft of the Report asserted, '[a]dditionally the Medical Sponsorship Policy does not prohibit medical service providers from paying for the right to provide medical services to players.' The NFL identified this inaccurate statement, and advised the authors that, '[t]he Policy on Medical Services Agreements and Sponsorships does [prohibit a physician from paying for the right to provide medical care to NFL Players].' Incredibly, the Report rejected the NFL's interpretation of the language in its own policy, which we enforce, by asserting the interpretation of the language was unclear to the authors, and as result refused to remove this reference from the Report. The Report cites no example where the policy has not been followed." For the reasons stated above, we continue to disagree with the NFL's interpretation and recommend that it be clarified.

As these charts demonstrate, while the NFL has made progress in regulating the payment to and from club doctors for sponsorship, on a plain reading of the Policy, there are still a number of ethically fraught arrangements the current Policy appears to leave in place.[I]

With this understanding of the NFL policies, we are now ready to begin the comparison to the other leagues.

B Club Medical Personnel in MLB

As explained in the Introduction, Section C: Collective Bargaining Agreements, in the fall of 2016, MLB and the MLBPA agreed to and ratified the terms of a new CBA. However, as of the date this Report went to press, the parties had not yet published the new CBA. Thus, this Section summarizes the information contained in the 2012 CBA, with relevant changes revealed in a joint press release issued by the parties summarizing the changes agreed to in 2016. Additional details, nuance or context may be contained in the full length CBA when it is publicly released.

1) TYPES OF MEDICAL PERSONNEL

a) Doctors

MLB policy requires "[t]he home Club [to] have a Club physician (medical or surgical) present for every game."[55] The home club doctor is also "expected to provide medical coverage for the visiting Club."[56] In addition, MLB policy requires each club to appoint a head doctor to be "responsible for all medical decisions of the Club, and [to] serve as the primary liaison between the Club and the Office of the Commissioner's Medical Director on all medical issues."[57]

A club's head doctor must be "licensed to practice medicine in the club's home state and be Board Certified in his or her specialty."[58] In addition, club doctors providing medical coverage at games must be "able to handle all common injuries and illnesses that would be expected during a professional baseball game, including the evaluation and management of concussions."[59]

MLB's policies concerning club doctors differ from the NFL's in four important respects. First, while there are several provisions referencing club doctors in the CBA,[60] there is no CBA provision that explicitly requires clubs to retain doctors. Second, of the policies that do exist, none are in the CBA, which permits MLB to change them without MLBPA input or approval. Third, neither MLB policy nor the CBA requires clubs to retain certain kinds of doctors, whereas the NFL CBA requires clubs to retain a board-certified orthopedic surgeon at least one physician board-certified in internal medicine, family medicine, or emergency medicine, and consultants in the neurological, cardiovascular, nutritional, and neuropsychological fields.[61] Fourth, unlike the NFL, MLB does not require that all club doctors have a Certificate of Added Qualification in Sports Medicine.

The professional organization for MLB club doctors is the MLB Team Physicians Association ("MLBTPA"). MLBTPA's "mission is to maintain the earned trust of the athletes and teams of Major and Minor League Baseball, as well as the public, by providing the highest quality medical care and services aimed at securing and enhancing their safety, health and well-being."[62] The MLBTPA website lists 117 members, an average of 3.9 per MLB club. Research did not reveal an MLBTPA code of ethics specific to its members.

The 2012 CBA did not require clubs to retain doctors and the publicly released details of the 2016 CBA do not indicate that anything has changed in that regard. However, the 2016 CBA did make two relevant additions: (1) clubs are now required to provide access to a sports psychologist;[63] and, (2) MLB and the MLBPA agreed to jointly retain a dietician to provide recommendations to players and clubs on nutrition and supplements.[64]

b) Athletic Trainers

Like the NFL CBA, the MLB CBA requires the employment of certified athletic trainers:

> Each Club shall employ two Certified Athletic Trainers on a full-time basis. Both trainers will travel with the Club on the road; provided, that one trainer may remain in the Club's home city if necessary for the Club to fulfill its obligations to disabled players who do not travel with the Club.

> Individuals newly appointed as trainers shall be certified by the National Athletic Trainers Association (NATA) or the Canadian Athletic Therapists

Association (CATA), or shall be physical therapists licensed by an appropriate state authority.[65,m]

The professional organization for MLB club athletic trainers is the Professional Baseball Athletic Trainer Society ("PBATS"). "PBATS mission is to serve as an educational resource for the Major League and Minor League Baseball athletic trainers. PBATS serves its members by providing for the continued education of the athletic trainer as it relates to the profession, helping to improve his understanding of sports medicine so as to better promote the health of his constituency—professional baseball players."[66] Research did not reveal a PBATS code of ethics specific to its members.

In reviewing a draft of this Report, MLB stated as follows:

> The insinuation in the report that MLB team physicians and certified athletic trainers do not have a code of ethics is patently untrue. All MLB physicians are board certified in their respective specialties and are obligated to practice medicine under general ethical codes that govern all licensed physicians, as well as the more specific codes of ethics of the appropriate licensing bodies and other professional organizations by which they are a member (e.g., AAOS, AMSSM, etc.). Since all MLB athletic trainers are members of the National Athletic Trainers Association and are also licensed by their respective state authorities, these codes of ethics apply to and govern this group of medical professionals. MLB takes the position that the duties and obligations of Club medical representatives are **not** negotiable subjects of bargaining, and are not an appropriate part of our CBA.

We understand MLB's point and revised the report to clarify that there are not codes of ethics *specific* to members of the MLBTPA and PBATS. Nevertheless, we disagree with MLB that medical personnel working with professional sports clubs do not need their own codes of ethics. Club medical personnel face a variety of complex situations that are not adequately contemplated or addressed by existing codes of ethics, most notably balancing their obligations to provide care to the player while also advising the club about players' health. Codes of ethics adopted by professional organizations for club medical personnel would

supplement existing codes of ethics by providing guidance and tenets for the unique and competitive environment in which they must operate.[n]

2) MEDICAL PERSONNEL'S OBLIGATIONS
a) Doctors

The CBA contains the following provisions concerning the club doctor's duties or obligations.[o]

First, club doctors are "prohibited from making any public disclosure of a Player's medical information absent a separate, specific written authorization from the Player authorizing such public disclosure."[67] The NFL CBA does not contain a specific prohibition such as this, but the AMA's Code of Ethics does.[68]

Second, "[i]f a player on a visiting Club receives medical treatment from the home Club's physician, certified athletic trainer or other medical professional for a work-related injury, a copy of any written medical evaluation prepared by the home Club's medical professional shall be provided to the Player and his Club's physician."[69]

Third, if a player is a free agent and requests a copy of his medical records from his prior club, the "Club shall provide such records within 10 days of such request."[70]

Fourth, the CBA requires club doctors to use a standardized medical history questionnaire when conducting initial physical examinations of players.[71]

Fifth, the CBA requires that for a player to be placed on the Disabled List, a standard form of diagnosis, including an estimated time period for recovery, must be submitted by the club doctor, a copy of which must be provided to the player.[72]

Sixth, the CBA sets forth MLB's policy concerning the assessment and management of concussions.[73] Club doctors are involved in determining whether a player has suffered a

---

m   The MLB CBA's requirement that athletic trainers be certified by NATA or CATA is actually in error and a requirement with which athletic trainers cannot comply. NATA and CATA are voluntary professional associations but do not *certify* athletic trainers. Athletic trainers are certified by the Board of Certification for the Athletic Trainer ("BOC"). The NFL CBA also erroneously requires athletic trainers to be certified by NATA.

n   In reviewing a draft of this Report a second time, MLB stated that "MLB maintains our position regarding a code of ethics, and do not find it appropriate to ask physicians to comply with a code of ethics that differs from the Hippocratic Oath or other professional/ethical oaths they took as a physician." To be clear, we do not recommend the addition of codes of ethics that differ from or conflict with existing codes. Instead, we believe it is appropriate that additional codes of ethics tailored for the specific circumstances of professional sports supplement existing codes. For more discussion on the challenges of the sports healthcare environment, see our Special Report, *NFL Player Health: The Role of Club Doctors*, 46 Hastings Center Rep. 2 (2016).

o   In addition to those obligations listed here, club doctors are also involved in determining whether a player's injury will prevent him from playing in the All-Star Game. 2012 MLB CBA, Art. XV, § O.

concussion, whether the player should be placed on the Disabled List, and clearing the player to return to play.[74]

We turn now to the standard of care for MLB club doctors. When asked specifically about this issue, MLB directed us to its minimum game day standards and the MLBTPA mission statement, both of which were discussed above. However, neither the game day standards nor the mission statement sets forth a standard of care for club doctors specific to MLB club doctors or that goes beyond what is already required by codes of ethics and relevant law applicable to all doctors. By comparison, the NFL, NHL and MLS CBAs all set forth standards of care for their club doctors which, in particular, attempt to address the conflict of interest inherent in having doctors that treat players while also providing services to the club.[p]

Also unlike the NFL, MLB policies do not: require club medical staff to inform players about communications between the medical staff and the club; entitle players to the surgeon of their choice (discussed further below); or, entitle players to their medical records as a general matter.

> Neither MLB game day standards nor the MLBTPA mission statement sets forth a standard of care for club doctors specific to MLB club doctors.

Concerning medical records, in reviewing a draft of this Report, MLB "dispute[d] . . . that players are not entitled to their medical records as a general matter. The medical records maintained in MLB's league-wide electronic medical records system is a player's legal medical file, and players are entitled to this information upon request." While it is useful that players can obtain their medical records upon request, players would likely view their records more if they were able to access their records without having to obtain the club's assistance, as NFL players can.

b) Athletic Trainers

The CBA is also sparse concerning athletic trainers' obligations. The only provision governing athletic trainers is their

involvement in MLB's protocol for assessing and managing concussions. MLB's concussion protocol requires that players "involved in an incident during a game that is associated with a high risk of concussion . . . will be evaluated on the field for a potential concussion by a Certified Athletic Trainer ('ATC') following the National Athletic Trainers' Association ('NATA') guidelines for management of sports-related concussions."[75] As stated above, the player cannot return to play until he has been cleared by the club doctor.[76]

Additionally, MLB regulations require that "[a]ll ATCs comply with the NATA definition of an athletic trainer, which states that 'athletic trainers work under the direction of physicians, as prescribed by state licensing statutes.'"[77]

3) PLAYERS' OBLIGATIONS

Players are subjected to the following requirements concerning their relationships with club medical personnel.

First, MLB's Uniform Player Contract requires players, "when requested by the Club, [to] submit to a complete physical examination at the expense of the Club, and if necessary to treatment by a physician, dentist, certified athletic trainer or other medical professional in good standing."[78] While the NFL CBA requires players to submit to physical examinations, it does not directly require players to submit to treatment. Nevertheless, in practice, if an NFL player failed to undergo treatment recommended by the club medical staff, the club could argue that the player failed to fulfill his obligations under the contract.

Second, "[p]rior to undergoing a 'second evaluation,' a Player shall inform the Club in writing of his decision to seek a second medical opinion, and the name of the physician who will be performing the diagnosis and medical evaluation."[79] In order for the club to pay for the cost of the second medical opinion, the doctor providing the opinion must be on a list of doctors created by MLB's Medical Advisory Committee and a medical professional designated by the MLBPA.[80] The NFL CBA similarly requires players to consult with the club before seeking a second medical opinion but does not limit a player's options to a pre-approved list.

Third, if a player seeks medical treatment from a doctor unaffiliated with the club for a baseball-related injury, the player must advise the club in advance and obtain the club's authorization for the treatment.[81] The player does not have to notify the club of consulting with another doctor if the player does not receive treatment for the injury, and is not invoking his right to have the club pay for a second medical opinion.[82] Additionally, a player does not have to advise

---

p   In our Report *Protecting and Promoting the Health of NFL Players: Legal and Ethical Analysis and Recommendations* we set forth a comprehensive recommendation to address this issue. We propose restructuring NFL club medical staff in such a way that the doctor treating the players has as his or her only concern the well-being of the player-patient and has no advisory role to the club.

the club about treatment for a non-baseball-related injury, provided the injury does not affect his ability to play.[83]

4) RELATIONSHIP BETWEEN MEDICAL PERSONNEL AND CLUBS

MLB does not have any policies concerning how clubs select or monitor medical personnel.[84] Club-doctor relationships, including compensation, duration of a contract, supervisory control, and hiring and termination, are decisions made by each individual club.[85] Perhaps partially as a result, club doctors' roles, employment situations, and compensation vary significantly around MLB.[86] In 2004, MLB attorneys reportedly suggested that clubs consider classifying their doctors as employees in order to reduce medical malpractice insurance premiums.[87] Despite this report, as in the NFL, most club doctors are independent contractors and "only a few" club doctors are employees.[88]

Clubs retain certain rights concerning a player's healthcare. Specifically, "the Club has the right to designate the doctors and hospitals when a Player is undergoing a surgery for an employment related injury," but are required to "take a Player's reasonable preferences into account when designating doctors to perform surgery[.]"[89] In contrast, NFL players have the right to a surgeon of their choice.

MLB and the MLBPA have collectively bargained a form that permits club medical personnel to disclose any of the player's health information to "the Owner, President, General Manager, Assistant General Manager, Field Manager, Physicians and such medical personnel as they may designate, Certified Athletic Trainer, Assistant Certified Athletic Trainer, Club Rehabilitation Coordinator, In-House Counsel, Risk Manager and Workers' Compensation Coordinator of the Club" "for any purpose relating to [the player's] employment as a player for the Club[.]"[90] The player has the right to revoke the authorization (assuming he signed it).[91] However, any revocation appears to be effectively meaningless because, as part of the Uniform Player Contract, the player agrees "that the Club's physician and any other physician or medical professional consulted by the Player . . . may furnish to the Club all relevant medical information relating to the Player."[92] The club also has the right to provide the player's medical information to clubs with which the player's club is in trade negotiations.[93] MLB's practices in this regard are comparable to the NFL, where players generally sign broad waivers permitting clubs to obtain, use, and disclose their medical information.

Turning to athletic trainers' practices specifically, like in the NFL, MLB athletic trainers are the primary caregivers for injuries suffered during the season.[94] Indeed, club doctors are not permitted by MLB regulations to sit in the dugout.[95] Club doctors reportedly do not travel to regular season away games, and, instead, the home club's doctors are responsible for overseeing the healthcare of both the home and visiting clubs, as well as all managers, coaches, and umpires.[96] MLB regulations also require that athletic trainers "comply with the [National Athletic Trainers Association] definition of an athletic trainer, which states that 'athletic trainers work under the direction of physicians, as prescribed by state licensing statutes.'"[97]

5) SPONSORSHIP ARRANGEMENTS

In 2004, MLB prohibited sponsorship arrangements between clubs and medical providers that included "the right of the [sponsor] to be the medical service provider for the club's players and employees."[98] Under MLB's policy, clubs must negotiate at arm's length for medical services, and the Commissioner must approve all sponsorship agreements with healthcare providers.[99] The Commissioner has approved such sponsorship arrangements with medical providers where "the Club has had a pre-existing relationship with the hospital or doctors prior to the sponsorship, and the terms of the health care agreement were unaffected by the sponsorship."[100] Additionally, MLB's medical sponsorship policy is the result of negotiations with the MLBPA.[101]

Nevertheless, MLB's policy does not prohibit clubs from "enter[ing] into traditional sponsorship arrangements with [medical service providers] involving, for example, advertising, hospitality or the use of trademark rights, provided that such agreements are otherwise consistent with Major League Baseball policy and applicable law."[102] Thus, it appears that MLB clubs are permitted to enter into sponsorship agreements with medical service providers so long as those agreements do not involve the provision of medical care to the players. Indeed, many MLB clubs have sponsorship relationships with regional healthcare providers.[103]

MLB's medical sponsorship policy is substantially similar to the NFL's. While there are gaps and room for interpretation, the general purpose of both policies is to prevent healthcare providers from paying for the right to provide medical care to the players. Additionally, MLB's medical sponsorship policy is slightly less concerning from a player perspective since it was negotiated with the MLBPA. In contrast, the NFL's Medical Sponsorship Policy is unilaterally imposed.

C) Club Medical Personnel in the NBA

1) TYPES OF MEDICAL PERSONNEL

a) Doctors

Like the NFL CBA, the NBA CBA requires clubs to retain doctors with certain qualifications:

> Each Team agrees to secure the services of at least two (2) physicians as team physicians. Beginning with the 2017–18 Season, each individual hired for the first time to perform services as a team physician must be a duly licensed physician who as of the hiring date: (i) is board certified and fellowship trained in his/her field of medical expertise; (ii) has at least five (5) years of post-fellowship clinical experience; and (iii) has successfully completed a fellowship in sports medicine, has a Certification of Added Qualification (CAQ) in sports medicine, or has other "sports medicine" qualifications as the parties may agree.[104]

In addition, the CBA provides that:

> Each Team has the sole and exclusive discretion to select any doctors, hospitals, clinics, health consultants, or other health care providers ("Health Care Providers") to examine and/or treat players pursuant to the terms of this Agreement and the Uniform Player Contract; provided, however, no Team will engage any such Health Care Provider based primarily on a sponsorship relationship (or lack thereof) with the Team, and without considering the Health Care Provider's qualifications (including, *e.g.*, medical experience and credentials) and the goal of providing high quality care to all of its players.[105]

This provision's application to potential sponsorships will be discussed below.

The professional organization for NBA club doctors is the NBA Physicians Association ("NBAPA").[q] A review of NBA club websites and media guides demonstrates that NBA clubs are typically affiliated with two to three doctors. Research did not reveal an NBAPA code of ethics specific to

its members. However, according to the NBA, the NBAPA By-Laws provide that the first purpose of the organization is "to achieve the best possible medical care for the professional basketball player." Finally, NBAPA representatives are permitted to participate in meetings of the NBAPA "for the purpose of discussing matters related to the medical care and treatment of players."[106]

b) Athletic Trainers

Like the NFL CBA, the NBA CBA dictates the required presence, education, and certification of athletic trainers:

> Each Team agrees to secure the services of at least one (1) athletic trainer to serve as the Head Athletic Trainer and one (1) athletic trainer to serve as an Assistant Athletic Trainer on a full-time basis. Beginning with the 2017–18 Regular Season: (i) each individual hired for the first time to perform services as an athletic trainer for a Team must as of the hiring date: (a) be certified by the National Athletic Trainers Association (NATA)[r] or the Canadian Athletic Therapists Association (CATA) (or a similar organization as the parties may agree), and (b) hold a current certification in Basic Cardiac Life Support or Basic Trauma Life Support; and (ii) each individual hired for the first time to perform services as a Head Athletic Trainer for a Team must, as of the hiring date, have at least three (3) years of experience as an athletic trainer since he/she first received the foregoing NATA/CATA certification.[107]

The professional organization for NBA club athletic trainers is the National Basketball Athletic Trainers Association ("NBATA"). The NBATA describes itself as "a professional organization of highly skilled certified athletic trainers who provide specialized health care and critical support services to the athletes and organizations of the National Basketball Association."[108] The NBATA further describes its purpose as to: "[l]ead the management and practice of exceptional health care; [p]rovide continuing education to our members; [p]rovide education and conduct basketball-related sports medicine research to benefit our athletes, the National Basketball Association, and the National Basketball Athletic Trainers Association, and our communities; [and,] [u]phold the athletic training profession's highest moral and ethical standards."[109] According to the NBATA,

---

q   The NBAPA's website is password-protected and thus additional information is not available.

r   The NBA CBA's requirement that athletic trainers be certified by NATA or CATA is actually in error and a requirement with which athletic trainers cannot comply. NATA and CATA are voluntary professional associations but do not *certify* athletic trainers. Athletic trainers are certified by the Board of Certification for the Athletic Trainer ("BOC"). The NFL CBA also erroneously requires athletic trainers to be certified by NATA.

there are 57 athletic trainers, approximately 1.9 per club. Research did not reveal an NBATA code of ethics specific to its members, beyond its statement of purpose.

The role of NBA athletic trainers is similar to that of athletic trainers in the other leagues. Athletic trainers are typically with the club at all times, are the player's first line of medical care and will liaise with doctors and other medical professionals as necessary.[110]

2) MEDICAL PERSONNEL'S OBLIGATIONS

The NBA CBA contains two notable provisions concerning club medical personnel's obligations.[s]

First, the CBA requires that "a player requiring the care and treatment of an orthopedic surgeon will, as far as practicable, be referred to and treated by one (1) orthopedic surgeon (rather than several.)"[111]

Second, the club must provide a player with his medical records within 48 business hours of the player's request.[112] In contrast, the NFL CBA only entitles players to their medical records once during the pre-season, once after the regular season, and upon request in the off-season.[113] However, in practice, the NFL's electronic medical records system provides players with 24/7 access to their medical records. Similarly, the NBA CBA says that one of the goals of its electronic medical records system is to "give players the ability to easily access their own health information" but it is unclear whether there is a portal through which players can access their medical records 24/7.

In addition to the above CBA provisions, according to the NBA, the NBA Operations Manual also regulates medical personnel's obligations including but not limited to their "timing of presence at games, handling of situations involving blood, gloves, washing skin surfaces, cleaning procedures for skin, and additional obligations under cardiac and concussion screenings, prescription drug policies, etc."

Notably, unlike the NFL, no NBA policy sets forth the standard of care for club doctors. Also unlike the NFL, NBA policies do not: require club medical staff to inform players about communications between the medical staff and the club; or, entitle players to the surgeon of their choice. The

NBA CBA—like the NFL's—does entitle players to their own medical records.

The 2017 NBA CBA did, however, introduce an interesting CBA provision that is worth discussing. In the event the NBA, a club or the NBPA

> has been advised by a physician that a player is medically unable and/or medically unfit to perform his duties as a professional basketball player as a result of a potentially life-threatening injury, illness or other health condition and/or that performing such duties would create a materially elevated risk of death for the player, then the NBA, a Team, or the Players Association may refer the player to a Fitness-to-Play Panel . . . . Once so referred, the player will not be permitted to play or practice in the NBA until he is cleared to do so by the Panel[.][114]

Beginning in 2017, the NBA and NBPA are creating Fitness-to-Play Panels with respect to: (i) cardiac illnesses and conditions; and, (ii) blood clots and other blood conditions and disorders, and will consider others as necessary.[115] The three-member Panels are to consist of expert doctors in these fields, with one doctor appointed by the NBA, one doctor appointed by the NBPA, and the third doctor appointed by the first two doctors.[116,t]

> The determination to be made by the Panel is whether, in the panel's reasonable medical judgment and experience, and having considered current medical knowledge and the best available objective evidence: (i) the player is medically able and medically fit to perform his duties as a professional basketball player; and (ii) performing such duties would not create a materially elevated risk of death for the player.[117]

If a player's condition is referred to a Fitness-to-Play Panel, prior to the Panel's review of his condition, he must "(on behalf of himself, his heirs and assigns) . . . sign a release and covenant not to sue agreement in the form agreed upon" by the NBA and NBPA.[118] Similarly, if the player is cleared to play, the player must sign an "informed consent and assumption of risk agreement" in a form agreed to by

s   In reviewing a draft of this Report, the NBA stated "[t]here are other terms governing obligations of medical personnel, including additional provisions regarding furnishing relevant information, not making public certain medical information, conducting certain health screenings, etc." Information concerning confidential player health information is discussed below. Otherwise, while other provisions of the CBA reference club doctors, they do not necessarily create obligations for them and thus we do not discuss them here.

t   The creation of a committee of medical experts with members selected by the league, the union, and the members of the committee matches the composition of the Medical Committee we proposed for the NFL in our report, *Protecting and Promoting the Health of NFL Players: Legal and Ethical Analysis and Recommendations*. We proposed a neutral Medical Committee be responsible for the hiring, compensation levels, review and possible termination of doctors treating NFL players as part of a process to remove the structural conflict of interest inherent in having doctors that both treat players and provide services to the club. Additional details and explanation can be found in our report.

the NBA and NBPA.[119] These forms are not publicly available, and thus we cannot opine on whether they comport with applicable law and codes of ethics.

Nevertheless, even if the Panel clears the player to play, the club is not required to let him play or practice.[120] Instead, if the club continues to believe that the player should not play, within 60 days the club must trade the player, release him from the club or amend his contract in such a way that might enable him to play.[121]

The "Fitness-to-Play" provision is, as far as we know, unprecedented in professional sports and seemingly arises out of a challenging situation in the NBA. In February 2015, Miami Heat star player Chris Bosh was diagnosed with a blood clot in his calf muscle, that later spread to his lungs.[122] As a result, Bosh missed a significant portion of the Heat's games in the 2014–15 and 2015–16 seasons.[123] Then, in September 2016, with the 2016–17 season approaching, Bosh failed his physical with the club when the Heat's doctor determined Bosh's need for blood thinners made playing professional basketball too risky.[124] Bosh's desire to continue playing may have prompted the creation of the Fitness-to-Play Panels though, as of February 2017, it is unclear whether Bosh intends to utilize the process.[125]

The new Fitness-to-Play Panels are interesting and innovative but new. Thus, we recommend that the NFL monitor their use and consider their potential application to the NFL. In its review of the Report, the NBA indicated its belief that the Fitness-to-Play Panels are an important new right for players. However, we note that NBA clubs retain considerable discretion in choosing whether to play players and thus it is unclear how much value the Panels provide to players. Lastly, we note that the Fitness-to-Play provision may implicate the Americans with Disabilities Act and/or the Genetic Information Nondiscrimination Act. For more on the intersection of these statutes and professional sports, see our law review article, *Evaluating NFL Player Health and Performance: Legal and Ethical Issues*, 165 U. Penn. L. Rev. 227 (2017).

---

3) PLAYERS' OBLIGATIONS

NBA players are entitled to a second medical opinion at the club's expense provided the player's injury or illness meets one of the following criteria:

> (i) has prevented the player from participating in a Regular Season or playoff game for two (2) weeks or more; (ii) in the opinion of a Team physician for the player's Team, is more likely than not to prevent the player from being able to participate

in an NBA game for two (2) weeks or more (or during the off-season, from participating in competitive basketball without restriction for two weeks or more); (iii) in the opinion of the Team physician will not be significantly aggravated by the player continuing to participate in NBA games (or during the offseason participating in basketball without restriction) when the player reasonably believes that continued participation will significantly aggravate his injury, illness or condition; (iv) results in direction from the Team physician that the player should undergo surgery; or (v) results in direction from the Team physician that the player should not undergo surgery when the player reasonably believes that surgery is necessary for the injury, illness or other health condition.

Additionally, the club will only cover the cost of the second medical opinion if: (1) the doctor providing the second medical opinion is from a list of doctors jointly maintained by the NBA and NBPA;[126] and, (2) prior to obtaining the second medical opinion, the player provides the club with the "name of the physician who will be performing the evaluation, and the date and location of the evaluation."[127]

The circumstances under which NBA players can obtain second opinions are limited as compared to players' options in the NFL. NBA players can only obtain second opinions in the above described scenarios whereas NFL players can obtain a second opinion whenever they would like, provided that if the club is to pay for the second opinion, the player first consults with the club doctor. Nevertheless, NBA players' rights to a second opinion was only added as part of the 2017 CBA. It thus remains to be seen how the provision operates in practice. For example, NBA players may be able to obtain second opinions as freely as NFL players.

Despite the player's right to obtain a second medical opinion, the club is only required to "*consider* the second opinion in connection with [the player's] diagnosis or treatment" (emphasis added).[128] In other words, the club doctor's opinion as to the proper course of treatment controls even if it conflicts with the second opinion doctor's opinion. If the player fails to comply with the club doctor's recommended course of treatment, it is possible the player could be found to be in violation of his obligations under his contract, including "to keep himself throughout each NBA Season in good physical condition."[129] While this provision potentially provides club doctors with the authority to determine the course of treatment against a player's wishes, we are not aware of any circumstance in which that has been the case. Nevertheless, this arrangement contrasts with the situation in the NFL, where the CBA does not grant club doctors the ultimate authority to determine the diagnosis and treatment for the player. In practice, players are generally free to follow the course of treatment recommended by the second opinion doctor, a clear positive for NFL players.

In addition to obligations in order to obtain a second medical opinion, the NBA Uniform Player Contract imposes several requirements on players concerning their cooperation with the club's medical personnel.

First, a player must "provide to the Team's coach, trainer, or physician prompt notice of any injury, illness, or medical condition suffered by him that is likely to affect adversely the Player's ability to render the services required under [his] Contract, including the time, place, cause, and nature of such injury, illness, or condition."[130] NFL players are similarly obligated to report their injuries.

Second, "[s]hould the Player suffer an injury, illness, or medical condition, he will submit himself to a medical examination, appropriate medical treatment by a physician designated by the Team, and such rehabilitation activities as such physician may specify."[131] NFL players are also obligated to submit to a medical examination but are not obligated to follow the treatment recommended by the club medical staff. Instead, NFL players are entitled to a second medical opinion and the surgeon of their choice.

Third, a player must "submit to a physical examination at the commencement and conclusion of each Contract year . . . and at such other times as reasonably determined by the Team to be medically necessary.[132] Relatedly, players are required to "submit to reasonable screening and baseline testing (e.g., pursuant to NBA cardiac and concussion protocols) and, in connection with such screening and testing, shall accurately and completely answer all reasonable health questions (including, upon request, providing accurate and complete medical histories)."[133] Again, NFL players are also obligated to submit to medical examinations and to provide an accurate medical history.

Fourth, a player must "at the commencement of [his] Contract, and upon the request of the Team . . . provide a complete prior medical history."[134] Similarly, the Standard NFL Player Contract and standardized minimum pre-season physical both require NFL players to provide a complete medical history.

Fifth, a player must "supply complete and truthful information in connection with any medical examinations or requests for medical information authorized by [his] Contract."[135] "A player who knows he has an injury, illness, or condition that renders, or he knows will likely render, him physically unable to perform the playing services required under a Player Contract may not validly enter into such Contract without prior written disclosure of such injury, illness, or condition to the Team."[136] If a player does not make the required disclosure, he risks having his contract voided. The Standard NFL Player Contract imposes similar disclosure obligations on NFL players.

Sixth, if a player "consults or is treated by a physician (including a psychiatrist) or a professional providing non-mental health related medical services (e.g., chiropractor, physical therapist) other than a physician or other professional designated by the Team [the player] shall give notice of such consultation or treatment to the Team and shall authorize and direct such other physician or professional to provide the Team with all information it may request concerning any condition that in the judgment of the Team's physician may affect the Player's ability to play skilled basketball."[137] The NBA CBA imposes this obligation on players regardless of whether the club is paying for the outside consultation or treatment. In contrast, the NFL CBA does not require NFL players to make their clubs aware of treatment sought outside of the club's medical staff unless the player wishes to have that care paid for by the club.

Seventh, "[a] Player who engages in five (5) or more training or workout sessions with a trainer, performance coach, strength and conditioning coach, or any other similar coach or trainer other than at the direction of the Team (each a "Third-Party Trainer"), shall give notice of such training or workout to the Team prior to the first such training or work out (sic) session, provided that if the player does not initially plan to continue working with any such Third-Party Trainer for five (5) or more sessions, such notice must be provided no later than prior to the fifth such session.[138,u] The NFL does not contain any requirement for players to give notice to their clubs of training with third-party trainers.

Eighth, a player is required to "execute such individual authorization(s) as may be requested by the Team . . . or as may be required by health care providers who examine or treat the Player."[139] Although the NFL CBA does not require players to execute authorizations permitting disclosure of their medical information, in practice all players execute such authorizations.

---

u   "This notice requirement [does] not apply to workouts or training that exclusively involve jogging, road bicycling, swimming, yoga, Pilates and/or dance." NBA Uniform Player Contract, § 7(h)(ii).

4) RELATIONSHIP BETWEEN MEDICAL PERSONNEL AND CLUBS

Our research was unable to determine how many NBA club doctors are employees versus independent contractors. We also were unable to find reliable information about the typical compensation of NBA club doctors. The NBA also did not provide non-public information concerning club doctors' employment relationships and structures.[140]

Clubs are permitted broad access to player medical information. Club doctors are permitted to "disclose all relevant medical information concerning a player to (i) the General Manager, coaches, and trainers of the Team by which such player is employed, (ii) any entity from which any such Team seeks to procure, or has procured, an insurance policy covering such player's life or any disability, injury or illness such player may suffer or sustain, and (iii) . . . the media or public on behalf of the Team."[141,v] Clubs considering acquiring a player via trade are also entitled to a player's medical records.[142] Additionally, according to the NBA, "[e]ach player in the NBA signs a health information authorization form each season that references disclosure to the media." These policies are similar to the practices of NFL clubs, whereby players execute waivers permitting broad disclosure and use of their medical information.

5) SPONSORSHIP ARRANGEMENTS

As discussed above, the NBA CBA prohibits clubs from retaining medical personnel or entering into agreements with healthcare providers to treat players if those agreements are "based primarily on a sponsorship relationship."[143] Thus, the NBA does not prohibit agreements whereby a healthcare provider pays for the right to be the club doctor and to be a sponsor of the club, provided the sponsorship is not the *primary* reason for the relationship. Consequently, it is not surprising that several clubs are engaged in sponsorship relationships with healthcare providers that include the provision of care to the players.[144] In this respect, the NBA policy falls short of the NFL and MLB's general prohibitions on healthcare providers paying for the right to provide care to players. However, in reviewing a draft of this Report, the NBA noted the possible difference between policy and practice: stating that "[t]he practical differences of the NBA and NFL/MLB policies may not be as pronounced as the statement in the report

implies." We acknowledge this distinction between policy and practice. Without additional information concerning medical sponsorship arrangements, which the leagues were generally unwilling to provide, we cannot fully evaluate the effects of the leagues' different medical sponsorship policies.

D Club Medical Personnel in the NHL

1) TYPES OF MEDICAL PERSONNEL

The NHL CBA, like the NFL CBA, contains robust requirements for club medical personnel.

a) Doctors

The CBA requires doctors to be present at all games:

> Each Club shall have a minimum of two (2) team physicians in attendance at all home games. At least one of the team physicians shall have successfully completed hockey-specific trauma management training or Advanced Trauma Life Support training during the previous three (3) years. Each Club shall have consultant specialists at each home game (the selection of whom shall be at the discretion of the head team physician) to complement the skill set of the two (2) team physicians. Each Club's team physicians in attendance at home games shall include, either as part of the two (2) main team physicians or as consultants, (i) an orthopedist, and (ii) an internal medicine, emergency medicine or primary care sports physician. At least one of the team physicians shall have familiarity with the NHL Modified SCAT2 or other comprehensive standardized acute concussion assessment tool as recommended by the NHL/NHLPA Concussion Working Group.[145]

Since the execution of the CBA, the above requirements have been amended. Clubs are now required to have three doctors in attendance at each home game, including: (1) an orthopedic surgeon; (2) an internal medicine or primary care physician; and, (3) a doctor certified and active in emergency medicine. In addition, now the club's two primary doctors, their athletic trainers, and any doctor that travels with the club to away games must be proficient with the X2 SCAT3 App used for evaluating possible concussions.

---

v A club is then permitted to "make public information relating to the players in its employ, provided that such information relates solely to the reasons why any such player has not been or is not rendering services as a player." 2017 NBA CBA, Art. XXII, § 4(d). In the NFL, players similarly sign waivers permitting the public disclosure of such information.

The CBA also dictates club doctors' required qualifications:

> Each medical doctor hired or otherwise retained by the Club after the Effective Date of [the CBA] to treat its Players as part of the Club's primary medical team shall, in the United States be board certified in his or her respective field(s) of medical expertise, and in Canada be board certified by either the Royal College of Physicians and Surgeons (for specialists) or the College of Family Practice of Canada (for family physicians). Each Club medical doctor who is part of the primary medical team hired or retained after the Effective Date of this Agreement, and any head team physician hired or promoted to such position after the Effective Date of this Agreement, shall have successfully completed a fellowship in Sports Medicine or have other "sports medicine" qualifications as the parties may agree.[w]

Nevertheless, our research did not reveal a code of ethics specific to NHL club doctors, which was confirmed to us by one NHL club athletic trainer that reached out to us concerning our work.[x]

b) Athletic Trainers

The NHL CBA also requires the full-time employment and presence of athletic trainers:

> Each Club shall employ at least two (2) ATs on a full-time basis. In the event both ATs do not travel with the Club on the road, and to the extent reasonably necessary in the Club's reasonable discretion to provide adequate services and treatment, the Club shall arrange for alternative means to provide athletic training services by providing at least one AT, and either an additional AT or other person of equal or greater medical training, or a massage therapist. All ATs employed or retained by a Club to provide services to Players must be certified by the National Athletic Trainers Association ("NATA") or the Canadian Athletic Therapists Association ("CATA"), or shall be physical therapists licensed by an appropriate state or provincial authority and/or certified as a specialist in physical therapy, and shall hold current certification in Basic Cardiac Life Support or Basic Trauma Life Support. At least one of the ATs shall have familiarity with the NHL Modified SCAT2 or other comprehensive standardized acute concussion assessment tool as recommended by the NHL/NHLPA Concussion Working Group.[y]

> An AT shall be available on the bench at all times during games and practices. If the AT must leave the bench for any reason, either (A) another AT must be available to immediately replace such AT on the bench, or (B) another person with equal or greater medical training must be available to immediately replace the AT on the bench.[146]

As with the CBA provision governing club doctors, the parties have also amended the policies governing athletic trainers. The new policy requires that, when on the road, each club shall arrange to have at least one athletic trainer and either an additional athletic trainer or a person of equal or greater medical training available to the players. The revised policy eliminates discretion clubs previously enjoyed as to whether to provide such services, and now makes this mandatory.

The professional organization for NHL club athletic trainers is the Professional Hockey Athletic Trainers Society ("PHATS"). PHATS' stated mission is to:

1. Encourage and promote the consistent application of the most advanced knowledge and techniques of the science of athletic training in the prevention, treatment, and rehabilitation of sports injuries to professional hockey players.

2. Function as a professional association for professional hockey athletic trainers to promote the welfare of its members, the profession of athletic training, and safe participation in the sport of hockey.

3. Provide for the exchange among its members of current ideas, techniques, and scientific data relating to the prevention and care of hockey injuries.

4. Support the continued advancement of the athletic training profession.[147]

---

w 20113 NHL CBA, § 34.2(a). Similarly, when the 2011 NFL CBA added a requirement that all club doctors have a Certificate of Added Qualification in Sports Medicine, the existing club doctors were not required to obtain the Certificate.

x For the reasons described in the Introduction, Section E: Goals and Process, we did not seek to survey NHL medical club personnel. Nevertheless, in response to our report, *Protecting and Promoting the Health of NFL Players: Legal and Ethical Analysis and Recommendations*, one NHL club athletic trainer reached out to us and provided us information via email and telephone. At the athletic trainer's request, we do not identify him or the club for which he works. It is important to recognize that the opinions of the athletic trainer are only that of one individual and cannot be considered representative of the viewpoints of all NHL club athletic trainers or medical staff. Nevertheless, we believe the athletic trainer's personal experiences are informative and thus include them here.

y The NHL's concussion protocol does not require the use of an independent neurologist. In contrast, the NFL's concussion protocol requires that, during games, any player suspected of having suffered a concussion be examined by an unaffiliated neurotrauma consultant. The difference in policies might result at least in part for practical reasons. There are 256 regular season NFL games versus 1,312 regular season NHL games.

Nevertheless, research did not reveal a PHATS code of ethics specific to its members, which was confirmed to us by an anonymous NHL club athletic trainer.

The role of NHL athletic trainers is similar to that of athletic trainers in the other leagues. Athletic trainers are typically with the club at all times, are the player's first line of medical care, and will liaise with doctors and other medical professionals as necessary.[148]

2) MEDICAL PERSONNEL'S OBLIGATIONS

The NHL CBA directs that "[e]ach Club shall provide its Players with high quality health care appropriate to their needs as elite professional hockey players, including access to health care professionals[.]"[149] Seemingly in accordance with this obligation, the CBA also outlines the required relationship between the club medical personnel and the players:

> The primary professional duty of all individual health care professionals, such as team physicians, certified athletic trainers/therapists ("ATs"), physical therapists, chiropractors, dentists and neuropsychologists, shall be to the Player-patient regardless of the fact that he/she or his/her hospital, clinic, or medical group is retained by such Club to diagnose and treat Players. In addition, all team physicians who are examining and evaluating a Player pursuant to the Pre-Participation Medical Evaluation (either pre-season and/or in-season), the annual exit examination, or who are making a determination regarding a Player's fitness or unfitness to play during the season or otherwise, shall be obligated to perform complete and objective examinations and evaluations and shall do so on behalf of the Club, subject to all professional and legal obligations vis-a-vis the Player-patient.[150]

Above, we discussed problems with a similar standard of care outlined in the NFL CBA. The NFL's provision requires that "each Club physician's primary duty in providing medical care shall be not to the Club but instead to the player-patient." However, the NFL's standard of care fails to account for the club doctor's obligations to the club—namely to perform fitness-for-play evaluations. The NHL's provision seemingly resolves this concern in part, by requiring—without limitation to the circumstances of providing medical care—that the Club doctor be subject to

his or her obligations to the player "regardless of the fact that he/she . . . is retained by such Club[.]"[z]

The CBA imposes other health-related requirements on clubs and club medical personnel.

First, "If a Player on a visiting team receives medical and/or health diagnosis, treatment, or fitness to play determination(s)" from the home club medical personnel, the home club must send the visiting club a written medical report.[151] The NFL CBA has no such provision.

Second, "[e]ach Club shall identify one (1) individual who is responsible for monitoring on an ongoing basis, or auditing on a regular basis, prescription drugs that have been given to each Player on the Club, with a particular emphasis on monitoring controlled substances and sleeping pills, if any, that have been prescribed."[152] The NFL has no such provision, however, NFL clubs do not store controlled substances and any prescription drugs are obtained from a retail pharmacy.[153]

Third, the club is required to provide a doctor giving a second opinion all relevant medical information regarding the player, as long as the second opinion doctor is on a "list of medical specialists mutually agreed upon" by the Joint Health and Safety Committee,[154] a medical advisory committee consisting of five NHL members and five NHLPA members.[aa] The NFL does not explicitly require such cooperation but, in practice, the second opinion doctor receives all relevant medical information.[155]

Fourth, "[a]t the conclusion of each season, the Club shall provide each Player with a complete copy of his medical records at the time of his annual exit physical (to the extent the Club maintains physical possession of the Player's medical records; otherwise the Club's physician will provide the Player with a complete copy of his medical records upon the Player's direction to do so). The exit physical shall document all injuries that may require future medical or dental treatment either in the near future or post-career."[156]

---

z The NHL club athletic trainer who contacted us believes the club for which he works treats players "poorly." The athletic trainer believes there is an "inherent conflict of interest" where club doctors treat players while also reporting to the club. As a result, the athletic trainer believes club doctors often place the interests of the club ahead of those of the player. Although the athletic trainer believes there is "widespread" agreement in the NHL medical community about these problems, we remind the reader that the opinions of this particular athletic trainer should not be considered representative of all NHL club athletic trainers.

aa The athletic trainer who contacted us expressed his belief that this process does not adequately protect player health. As an initial matter, the athletic trainer believes club doctors often try to dissuade players from receiving a second medical opinion, including by telling players that the club doctor has already consulted with other club doctors. Second, the athletic trainer expressed his belief that many of the second opinion consultations are with doctors from other clubs, who are unlikely to render an opinion that disagrees with the initial club doctor's opinion.

This provision is outdated, as the NHL's electronic medical record system now provides players with access to their medical records. NFL players are also able to access their electronic medical records at any time.[157]

3) PLAYERS' OBLIGATIONS

Like the NFL CBA, the NHL CBA provides players the right to a second medical opinion concerning diagnoses or courses of treatment[ab] and the surgeon of their choice, but imposes obligations on players related to that care.

When seeking a second medical opinion, the player must "advise the Club in writing of his decision to seek a Second Medical Opinion and the name of the Second Medical Opinion Physician."[158] The club is only obligated to pay for the second medical opinion if the player consults with a doctor from the Joint Health and Safety Committee's list or otherwise obtains the approval of the club.[159] If the player uses a doctor from the approved list or approved by the club, the player (or the second opinion doctor) must provide the club doctor "with a report concerning the diagnosis, examination, and course of treatment recommended by the Second Medical Opinion Physician[.]"[160] Players do not have to provide the club with information from a second opinion doctor if the second opinion is obtained outside of the process outlined in the CBA and if the player arranges and pays for the consultation himself.

If the club doctor and second opinion doctor disagree, the two doctors can agree to have the player examined by a third doctor.[161] Nevertheless, in the NHL, the club doctor is ultimately entitled to "determine the diagnosis and/or course of treatment,"[162] including whether "a surgical procedure is the appropriate course of treatment for the Player."[163] If the player fails to comply with the recommended course of treatment, it is possible the player could be found to be in violation of his obligations under his contract, including "to keep himself in good physical condition[.]"[164ac] Nevertheless, we are not aware of any circumstances in which surgery was performed or recommended against the player's wishes. In contrast, the NFL CBA does not set forth how to resolve a dispute between the club doctor and second opinion doctor. More importantly, the NFL CBA does not grant club doctors the ultimate authority to determine the diagnosis and treatment for the player. In practice, players are generally free to follow the course of treatment recommended by the second opinion doctor, a clear positive for NFL players.

An NHL player is entitled to the surgeon of his choice, but the club will only cover the cost of the surgery if the doctor is on the Joint Health and Safety Committee's list or is otherwise approved by the club.[165] After any such surgery, the player (or his doctor) must provide the club doctor "with all relevant records from the surgeon regarding the surgery[.]"[166] The NFL CBA imposes similar requirements.

Finally, if a player wishes to rehabilitate an injury during the off-season in a city of his choice, the player must obtain permission from the club and send periodic status reports to the club.[167] If the club is not satisfied with the player's progress, the club can require the player to continue his rehabilitation in the club's city.[168] The NFL CBA does not address player's off-season training locations.

4) RELATIONSHIP BETWEEN MEDICAL PERSONNEL AND CLUBS

The NHL declined to provide any information concerning the employment or financial relationships between NHL clubs and their doctors, and our independent research did not uncover more information.[169] The only information we received on this issue was from the anonymous athletic trainer discussed above, who explained that the club medical staff is typically hired by the club's general manager.

Most of our information about the relationship between NHL clubs and their medical staff is based on the CBA itself. The CBA permits clubs to disclose player medical information in a variety of situations. The CBA requires players to execute three different health-related authorizations: (1) the NHL/NHLPA Authorization Form for Health Care Providers to Release Health Information; (2) the NHL/NHLPA Concussion Program Authorization; and, (3) the Authorization for Management and Release of Neuropsychological Test Results.[170] The content of the authorization forms is unknown, but the CBA does explicitly allow disclosure of player medical information "as reasonably required for professional sports operations, between and among a Club's Club Personnel[ad] for purposes related to the Player's employment as an NHL hockey Player."[171]

---

ab NHL players are also entitled a second medical opinion where a club doctor has determined the player is physically unable to perform his duties as a hockey player. 2013 NHL CBA, § 17.7. The player is responsible for the costs of this consultation. If no consensus is reached between the club doctor and the player's second opinion doctor in the fitness for play context, a third physician chosen by them decides the matter. *Id.* The club and player share the costs for the third physician's opinion. *Id.*

ac If there is a question as to whether the player is disabled or unable to perform his duties, the Standard Player Contract sets forth a process by which that determination is made by an independent doctor. *See* Standard Player Contract, § 5, included as Exhibit 1 to the 2013 NHL CBA. If the player is found to be physically able to play and refuses to do so, he can be immediately suspended without pay. *Id.* at § 5(j).

ad "'Club Personnel' means a Club's coaching staff, owners, presidents, executives, hockey operations staff, general managers, assistant general managers, human resources personnel, and Club Health Professionals." 2013 NHL CBA, Art. 1.

Additionally, club personnel, the NHL and the NHLPA may disclose a player's medical information: (1) as required by the player's Standard Player Contract or the CBA, *e.g.,* determining a player's fitness to play; (2) when the information is relevant to a grievance; (3) when the information is relevant to an investigation of whether the player or club violated the CBA or Standard Player Contract; (4) as permitted by the authorization forms discussed above; (5) for purposes of the club seeking advice regarding its rights and obligations; (6) for purposes of injury surveillance and as authorized by the electronic medical record system; (7) to a club considering acquiring the player via trade; (8) to the player's agent; (9) as part of the player obtaining a second opinion; (10) to treat the player in an emergency; (11) to doctors and individuals involved in managing the Performance Enhancing Substances Program or the Substance Abuse and Behavioral Health Program; and, (12) to vendors and administrators as necessary.[172] These disclosure policies are similar to the practices of NFL clubs.

5) SPONSORSHIP ARRANGEMENTS

Our research has not revealed whether the NHL has a medical sponsorship policy and the NHL declined to provide any information on the matter. In 2012, the Canadian newspaper *The Globe and Mail* reported that at least ten US-based NHL teams had an "official medical provider."[173] According to the report, these clubs had a variety of relationships with their healthcare providers, with some clubs paying their club doctors a salary, others exchanging perks for pro bono services, and a minority of clubs accepting payment from medical groups.[174] Additionally, some clubs entered into a sponsorship agreement with a medical service provider but independently retained club doctors from outside of that service provider's network.[175]

The anonymous athletic trainer who contacted us confirmed that in his experience these sponsorship arrangements exist. The athletic trainer expressed his belief that many NHL clubs enter into long-term agreements whereby medical service providers such as local hospitals pay the club millions of dollars per year for the right to provide medical services to the club's players, including the right to select the club's doctors. Moreover, the athletic trainer indicated to us that under these agreements, medical specialists needed by the players, such as neurologists and ophthalmologists, are chosen by the hospital. In sum, the athletic trainer expressed his belief that players are "forced" to see doctors from a specific hospital, rather than the best doctors for the players' needs. The NHL did not respond to an email asking if the athletic trainer's assertions are accurate.

In contrast, as discussed above, the NFL has indicated that its medical sponsorship policy prohibits the type of arrangement that might occur in the NHL, *i.e.,* where medical service providers pay for the right to provide care to players. Nevertheless, also as discussed above, the boundaries of the NFL's medical sponsorship policy are not clear. Additionally, the NFL's medical sponsorship policy prohibits agreements whereby medical service providers provide exclusive care to players, which might be a problem in the NHL.

E Club Medical Personnel in the CFL

1) TYPES OF MEDICAL PERSONNEL

Unlike the NFL CBA, the CFL CBA does not require clubs to retain doctors. However, like the NFL CBA, the CFL CBA does require clubs to retain certified athletic trainers, known in Canada as "Athletic Therapists":

> Member Clubs shall employ or retain a minimum of one trainer who is certified by the Canadian Physiotherapists Association and/or the Canadian Athletic Therapists Association (CATA) or equivalent qualifications. All head therapists in the C.F.L. must be certified athletic therapists in good standing with CATA. The head therapists from each Member Club will be required to submit their CATA certification indicating that they are in good standing with CATA to the C.F.L. Office on an annual basis.[176]

Nevertheless, a review of CFL club websites reveals that CFL clubs are typically affiliated with five to ten medical professionals.[177] These professionals typically include orthopedists, emergency physicians, sports medicine physicians, chiropractors, and optometrists.[178] The clubs also generally employ 3–4 athletic trainers.[179]

2) MEDICAL PERSONNEL'S OBLIGATIONS

The CFL CBA's only requirement of medical personnel is that they provide players with their medical records upon request.[180]

Unlike the NFL, the CFL lacks policies concerning: (1) the standard of care for club medical personnel; (2) communications between medical personnel and the club; (3) a player's right to a second opinion; and, (4) a player's right to a surgeon of his choice. The CFL CBA — like the NFL's — does entitle players to their own medical records.

3) PLAYERS' OBLIGATIONS

The CFL's Standard Player Contract imposes only one medical personnel-related obligation on players:

> Prior to the start of each football season, the Player shall attend before the Club's Medical Committee for a complete physical and medical examination, and, shall answer completely and truthfully all questions asked of him with respect to his physical and medical condition[.][181]

The NFL CBA similarly requires players to submit to a pre-season physical and "to make full and complete disclosure of any physical or mental condition known to him which might impair his performance . . . and to respond fully and in good faith when questioned by the Club physician about such condition."[182]

4) RELATIONSHIP BETWEEN MEDICAL PERSONNEL AND CLUBS

According to the CFL, all CFL club doctors are independent contractors.[183] The CFL's characterization of its relationship with club doctors accords with Canadian physicians' general status as independent contractors within its government-sponsored healthcare system; however, two 1980s Canadian cases that considered whether NHL Canadian club doctors were independent contractors or employees for liability purposes both looked beyond the parties' understanding of their relationship.[184] Based on the differing factual scenarios, the British Columbia Supreme Court — which heard both cases — concluded that club doctors were employees in one case and independent contractors in another. In both cases, the perceived level of control proved to be dispositive. Thus, a court considering the status of CFL club doctors for vicarious liability purposes may look beyond the manner in which the club doctors receive compensation or the title that the league ascribes to clubs' relationships with doctors. In doing so, the court will likely examine the degree of control clubs have over the doctors.

Concerning the duties of CFL club doctors, the CBA provides that a club has "the right to conduct a medical examination at any time[.]"[185] However, the CBA also dictates that a pre-season physical "to determine the status of any pre-existing condition" is to be performed by a neutral physician.[186]

Although there is limited information available on CFL club doctors, in 2007, the Saskatchewan Roughriders' club doctor, Dr. Robert McDougall, acknowledged the complications in being a club doctor:

> You have a responsibility to the organization for which you work . . . but in addition you have a responsibility to the athlete and you can't function independently from that athlete. Because you administer care to the athlete, he/she needs to be fully informed of the events. . . . So I feel like there is a triad of duties: the organization you work with, the athlete, and in the end, yourself as a physician. Above all, you have a responsibility as a physician to make the right medical decision.[187]

These concerns were echoed by CFL Hall of Fame player Chris Walby, who explained that there are many situations "where the physician definitely supports the team before the player."[188] According to Walby, the club doctor's "job is to get you back on the field in as short a time frame as possible."[189]

5) SPONSORSHIP ARRANGEMENTS

According to the CFL's former President and Chief Operating Officer, Michael Copeland, no CFL clubs engage in sponsorship arrangements whereby a healthcare provider pays the club for the right to provide healthcare to the club's players.[190] The practice of leagues and their member clubs accepting payment from medical groups is reportedly "frowned upon" in Canada.[191]

F) Club Medical Personnel in MLS

MLS' most recent CBA was agreed to in March 2015. In addition, MLS' Medical Policies & Procedures Manual ("MLS Medical Manual"), which is not collectively bargained, provides guidance on these issues.[192] The MLS Medical Manual is a league-imposed manual with which MLS clubs and their doctors and athletic trainers are required to comply.[193]

1) TYPES OF MEDICAL PERSONNEL

The MLS CBA declares that after its execution, MLS and the MLSPU would "meet to agree on a side letter/provision to include in the CBA regarding the required number of medical/training personnel each Team shall retain (e.g., Team physician, athletic trainers, therapists, and appropriate minimum certification requirements for such personnel)."[194] As of the date of publication, it is unclear whether the side letter has been executed. Nevertheless, the MLS Medical Manual suggests that MLS clubs "establish a network" of the following medical professionals:

- Head club physician/ chief medical officer;
- Orthopedic sub-specialists (special attention given to foot and ankle specialists);
- Primary care sports medicine;
- Internal medicine;
- Head athletic trainer;
- Assistant athletic trainer;
- Strength and conditioning coach;
- Cardiologist;
- Neuropsychologist;
- Neurosurgeon;
- Dentist;
- Oral and maxillofacial surgeon;
- Massage therapist;
- Physical therapist;
- Chiropractor;
- Nutritionist;
- Podiatrist;
- Dermatologist;
- Ophthalmologist; and,
- Imaging center.[195]

The professional organization for MLS club doctors is the MLS Team Physicians Society ("MLSTPS"). MLSTPS' stated mission is "[t]o be a global leader and collaborator in the science of soccer medicine focused on research, education and athlete care."[196] Research did not reveal an MLSTPS code of ethics specific to its members.

The corresponding organization for MLS club athletic trainers is the Professional Soccer Athletic Trainers' Society ("PSATS"). According to PSATS, the organization "serves to enhance the personal and professional development of its membership. PSATS strives to provide educational opportunities for its members so they may better serve Major League Soccer, their organization, and the professional soccer players under their care."[197] Our research did not reveal a PSATS code of ethics specific to its members.

According to the MLS Medical Manual, MLS athletic trainers are required to be certified by the National Athletic Trainers Association ("NATA").[198] However, this is an error and a requirement with which athletic trainers cannot comply. NATA is a voluntary professional association but does not *certify* athletic trainers. Athletic trainers are certified by the BOC.[199] The BOC used to be part of NATA, but split from the voluntary association in 1989.[200]

As in all of the leagues, MLS athletic trainers are the players' first line of medical care.[201] The athletic trainers are with the club on a constant basis, preparing them for practices and games, treating conditions as needed, and updating the club on players' health statuses.[202] In addition, the athletic trainers liaise with club doctors when the players need more extensive care.[203]

2) MEDICAL PERSONNEL'S OBLIGATIONS

The CBA directs that "[e]ach Team shall provide its Players with high quality health care that is reasonably appropriate to their needs as elite professional soccer players, including access to health care professionals[.]"[204] Seemingly in accordance with this obligation, the CBA also outlines the required relationship between the club medical personnel and the players:

> The primary professional duty of all individual health care professionals (such as Team physicians, athletic trainers, physical therapists chiropractors, dentists and neuropsychologists) providing health care to a Player, shall be to the Player-patient regardless of the fact that the health care professional or his/her hospital, clinic, or medical group is retained by such Team to diagnose and treat Players. In addition, all individual health care professionals, such as Team physicians who are examining and evaluating a Player shall be obligated to perform complete and objective examinations and evaluations and shall do so on behalf of the Team and League, subject to all professional and legal obligations vis-a-vis the Player-patient.[205]

These provisions are almost verbatim replicas of the NHL CBA provisions. Above, we discussed problems with a similar standard of care outlined in the NFL CBA as compared to the NHL CBA. The same analysis applies here. The NFL's provision requires that "each Club physician's primary duty in providing medical care shall be not to the Club but instead to the player-patient." However, the NFL's standard of care fails to account for the club doctor's obligations to the club—namely to perform fitness-for-play evaluations. The NHL's and MLS' provision seemingly resolves this concern in part, by requiring—without limitation to the circumstances of providing medical care—that the club doctor be subject to his or her obligations to the player "regardless of the fact that he/she . . . is retained by such Club[.]" Nevertheless, we still do not believe the NHL's and MLS' provisions sufficiently protect player health as discussed in the Analysis Section.

In addition to the CBA provision, the MLS Medical Manual directs in multiple provisions some form of the following: "Club physicians and Athletic Trainers are always expected to comply with the highest standards of medical care and to use their best professional judgment."[206]

Finally, the MLS CBA also requires clubs to "cooperate with all requests by a Player or former player and/or his representative(s) for copies of the Player's or former player's medical recording, including athletic trainers' notes, and shall provide such records and notes within fourteen (14) days of any request by a Player or former player."[207]

3) PLAYERS' OBLIGATIONS

The CBA imposes numerous health-related obligations on players.

First, as part of the Standard Player Agreement, the player represents that "he knows of no physical or mental conditions that could impair his ability to play skilled professional soccer during the Term of th[e] Agreement and he has not knowingly concealed any such conditions[.]"[208] The standard NFL Player Contract also requires players to represent that they are in "excellent physical condition."[209]

Second, the Standard Player Agreement also obligates a player to "maintain a high level of physical and mental conditioning and competitive skills, not engage in alcohol abuse, not use drugs or any other substances in contravention of the MLS Player Substance Abuse and Behavioral Health Program and Policy, and generally develop and maintain a physical and mental readiness necessary to play for the Team."[210] The NFL Player Contract also requires players to "maintain" themselves in "excellent physical condition."[211]

Third, a player must "immediately . . . notify the Team's coach, trainer or physician of any illness or injury contracted or suffered by him which may impair or otherwise affect, either immediately or over time, his ability to play skilled professional soccer."[212] The CBA does not describe the punishment in the event a player fails to disclose an injury. NFL players are similarly required to report their injuries.

Fourth, "[p]rior to the start (including, during the season, when a Player first joins his Team) and at the conclusion of each League season, Players shall submit to complete medical examinations by a physician designated by MLS, at times designated by MLS and at MLS's expense. Such medical examinations may include, without limitation, blood tests . . . . The Player shall answer completely and truthfully all questions asked of him concerning his physical and mental condition."[213] The NFL CBA imposes similar requirements on its players.

Fifth, "[i]n addition to the Pre-season and end of League Season medical and physical examinations, Players may also be required to submit, on reasonable dates and times at the expense of MLS, to such reasonable additional medical examinations (including blood tests . . .) as may be requested by his Team or MLS."[214] NFL players are also required to submit to medical examinations.

Sixth, a "Player is required to execute any authorizations required to release all of his medical records to MLS and/or Team physicians, relevant officials, and to the workers' compensation insurance carrier of MLS . . . . It is understood that medical information relating solely to the reasons why such Player has not been, is not or may not be rendering services as a Player may be released to the public by MLS or a Team. A medical information release . . . shall be executed by each Player during Pre-Season each year or upon joining MLS during the League Season."[215] Although the NFL CBA does not require players to execute authorizations permitting disclosure of their medical information, in practice, all players execute such authorizations.

Seventh, if a player seeks a second medical opinion and the second opinion doctor disagrees with the club doctor, "[t]he physician for the player shall evidence his determination by completing [a form], which shall be provided to the Player's Team no later than forty-eight (48) hours after completion of the examination."[216] If the second opinion doctor and club doctor are unable to resolve the disagreement, the "relevant medical issue(s)" are determined by a neutral doctor agreed upon by the club's doctor and the second opinion doctor.[217] The player is obligated to "promptly submit to treatment recommended by" the club doctor or the neutral doctor, as applicable.[218] If the player refuses to submit to the treatment recommended by the club doctor, the player is considered in breach of his contract and thus subject to suspension or termination.[219]

In contrast, the NFL CBA does not set forth how to resolve a dispute between the club doctor and second opinion doctor. More importantly, the NFL CBA does not grant club doctors the ultimate authority to determine the diagnosis and treatment for the player, or require players to submit to any treatment. In practice, players are generally free to follow the course of treatment recommended by the second opinion doctor. However, it is important to remember that NFL players have an obligation to maintain themselves in excellent physical condition.[220] If the player does not take certain steps to recover from an injury—including perhaps the treatment recommended by one or more doctors—it is possible that the player could be found to have breached his contract and thus subject to suspension or termination.

4) RELATIONSHIP WITH CLUBS

The MLS Medical Manual dictates that clubs are responsible for negotiating agreements with doctors and athletic trainers for the treatment of players.[221] In addition, while the MLS Medical Manual requires that athletic trainers be "year-round employees,"[222] there is no direction on whether club doctors should be employees or independent contractors. Otherwise, we were unable to discover information about the financial relationships between MLS clubs and their doctors. MLS declined to provide any information related to these issues. Additionally, according to the MLSPU, there are no "collectively bargained provisions regarding the relationships between team medical personnel and the clubs."[223]

Some information about the relationships between MLS clubs and their doctors can be gleaned from a 2012 lawsuit filed by former D.C. United player Bryan Namoff against the club, the club's coach, Tom Soehn, the club doctor, Christopher Annunziata, and the club athletic trainer, Brian Goodstein.[224] Namoff alleged that the D.C. United medical staff had failed to properly treat his concussion, resulting in a variety of physical and mental conditions.[225]

In a May 8, 2014, order, a District of Columbia court determined that Namoff's claims against D.C. United, Soehn, and Goodstein were barred by workers' compensation laws.[226] The court noted that Goodstein was employed by D.C. United as an athletic trainer,[227] and found that MLS and D.C. United were "concurrent employers" of Namoff.[228] Consequently, the workers' compensation laws barred Namoff's lawsuit against his co-employee Goodstein.

In an August 12, 2014, order, the court found that Annunziata was an independent contractor.[229] The court based its decision largely on Annunziata's ethical requirements as a doctor to "make clinical decisions and exercise his independent professional medical judgment when managing, caring for, and treating patients."[230] Additionally, the court found that the MLS Medical Policies and Procedures Manual "directs team physicians to provide care based on their own 'best professional judgment' and recognizes that they are ultimately responsible' for treating players."[231] Thus, because D.C. United could not direct his work, Annunziata was not an employee of the club.

The court's order also revealed some interesting details about the relationship between Annunziata and D.C. United. There was no written contract between the parties and Annunziata was not paid for his work.[232] Instead, D.C. United provided Annunziata "tickets to games, permissions to use his association with D.C. United in his promotional and marketing materials, and paid travel expenses."[233]

The arrangement revealed by the Namoff lawsuit comports with the typical arrangements in the NFL, where the club doctor is generally an independent contractor and the athletic trainer is an employee.

As mentioned above, MLS players are required to sign an authorization permitting disclosure of their medical information. The authorization form is broad.[ae] The authorization form permits "all physicians, hospitals, laboratories, pharmacies, clinics, and other health care providers (including, but not limited to, all athletic trainers/therapists) (collectively, 'Health Providers')" to release the player's medical information to:

> (a) the Health Providers, coaches, soccer operations staff, player operations staff, legal staff, human resources staff, owners, executives, general managers, assistant general managers, and other officials (collectively "Soccer Personnel") of Major League Soccer, L.L.C., MLS Canada LP, and the Major League Soccer ("MLS") Team or Teams (and such MLS Team Operators) for which [the player] ha[s] agreed (or may agree) to play while this authorization is in effect, (and, in the event of any contemplated assignment of my playing services to another MLS Team or Teams, the Soccer Personnel of such other MLS Team or Teams (and such MLS Team Operators); (b) at the direction of

ae The authorization's breadth stands in contrast to the MLS Medical Manual's multiple provisions requiring that "[c]onfidentiality regarding a Player's medical condition will be maintained at all times." MLS Medical Policies & Procedures Manual § I (2015). *See also id.* § IV.4; *id.* § IX.A.1.

MLS and consistent with the collective bargaining agreement, to the Soccer Personnel of the United States Soccer Federation, the Canadian Soccer Association, and any other National Federation (and their respective Teams) for which [the player] ha[s] agreed (or may agree) agree *[sic]* to play while this authorization is in effect; and (c) at the direction of MLS, any individual or entity from which MLS or an MLS Team may receive services in furtherance of uses and disclosure of [the player's] Health Information permitted by this authorization, such as electronic medical records vendors and worker's *[sic]* compensation insurance carriers, provided that such individual or entity shall be required to maintain the confidentiality of my Health Information.[234]

These disclosure policies are similar to the practices of NFL clubs.

5) SPONSORSHIP ARRANGEMENTS

Research has not revealed an MLS medical sponsorship policy. However, some MLS clubs have entered into sponsorship arrangements with healthcare providers and hospitals while at the same time retaining a doctor from that healthcare provider as the club doctor. For example, the Hospital for Special Surgery in New York is the "Official Hospital of the New York Red Bulls,"[235] and a doctor affiliated with the Hospital for Special Surgery is listed as one of the Red Bulls' two club doctors.[236] Similarly, Orlando Health is both the jersey sponsor and "official medical team" of the Orlando City Soccer Club,[237] and a doctor from Orlando Health serves as Orlando City's club doctor.[238]

In addition, the MLS Medical Manual tangentially admits that medical sponsorship is permitted. In outlining policies concerning whether certain healthcare costs are the responsibility of the league or the club, the MLS Medical Manual states that clubs are responsible for healthcare costs where "[c]lubs have created either written or verbal marketing agreements in which clubs funnel billable therapy to a particular club sponsor group."[239] This provision thus strongly suggests that MLS permits sponsorship arrangements whereby healthcare providers pay for the right to provide care. In contrast, the NFL does not permit such arrangements.

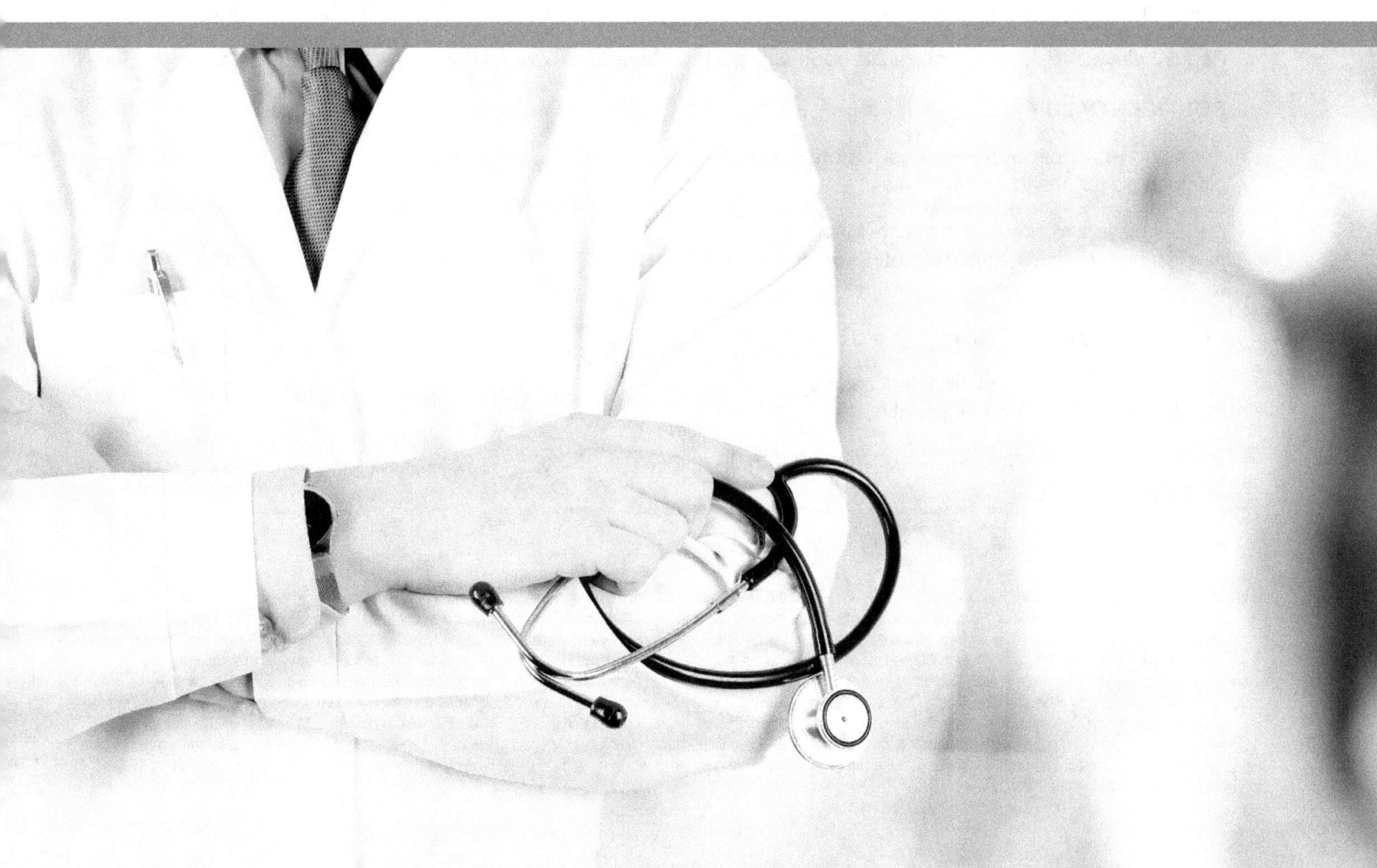

G Analysis

Table 1-C below summarizes the leagues' handling of certain issues concerning the different principles identified at the beginning of this Chapter.

Table 1-C:

Summary of Club Medical Personnel Policies and Practices

Do the Leagues' policies:	NFL	MLB	NBA	NHL	CFL	MLS
QUALITY OF MEDICAL CARE						
Require retention of doctors?	Yes	Yes	Yes	Yes	No	No
Require retention of athletic trainers?	Yes	Yes	Yes	Yes	Yes	No
Require sports-specific certification for doctors?	Yes	No	Yes	Yes	No	No
Set forth a standard of care?	Yes	No[af]	No	Yes	No	Yes
DISCLOSURE AND PLAYER AUTONOMY						
Require medical staff to disclose communications with club to player?	Yes	No	No	No	No	No
Require club to pay for second opinion?	Yes	Yes	Yes	Yes	No	Yes
Provide club doctor right to determine a player's course of treatment?	No	No	Yes	Yes	No	Yes
Entitle players to surgeon of their choice?	Yes	No[ag]	No	Yes	No	No
Entitle players to medical records?	Yes	Yes	Yes	Yes	Yes	Yes
Require players to submit to physicals upon request?	Yes	Yes	Yes	No	Yes	Yes
CONFIDENTIALITY						
Permit non-medical club personnel to obtain and disclose player health information?	No	Yes	Yes	Yes	No	Yes
Require players to inform club of care by other medical professionals, regardless of payment source?	No	If baseball-related	Yes	No	No	No
CONFLICTS OF INTEREST						
Insulate club medical staff from influence by coaches and other club personnel?	No	No	No	No	No	No
Prohibit healthcare providers from paying for right to provide care?	Yes	Yes	Partially	Unknown	No	No

---

af As discussed above, when asked specifically about this issue, MLB directed us to its minimum game day standards and the MLBTPA mission statement, both of which were discussed above. However, neither the game day standards nor the mission statement sets forth a standard of care for club doctors specific to MLB club doctors or that goes beyond what is already required by codes of ethics and relevant law applicable to all doctors. By comparison, the NFL, NHL and MLS CBAs all set forth standards of care for their club doctors which, in particular, attempt to address the conflict of interest inherent in having doctors that treat players while also providing services to the club.

ag In reviewing a draft of this Report, MLB stated that our indication that MLB players do not have the right to the surgeon of their choice was "inaccurate." We disagree. As discussed above, while MLB clubs are directed to "take a Player's reasonable preferences into account when designating doctors to perform surgery," "the Club has the right to designate the doctors and hospitals when a Player is undergoing a surgery for an employment related injury[.]" 2012 MLB CBA, Attachment 35. In addition, "in no event should they force a Player to have a surgery performed by the Club physician but should instead, in any case in which a Player has objected to the surgery being performed by the Club physician, designate another physician to perform the surgery." *Id.* Thus, the decision of which surgeon to use ultimately rests with the club, subject to player's ability to object to the club doctor performing the surgery.

Before analyzing the results of the above Table, it is important to note that some of the leagues' practices concerning these issues might be positive towards player health but are not codified in the CBA or other policy document. Therefore we cannot capture them in our analysis, especially since some leagues were unwilling to provide us information we requested. With that caveat in mind, we turn to our analysis of the leagues' policies concerning medical personnel. In particular, our focus is on how the NFL compares to the other leagues.

The above Table suggests that the NFL's policies concerning club medical personnel are the most protective of player health in almost all cases by providing players with superior control and information about their healthcare. The NHL's policies are similarly protective of player health, with one worrisome provision that permits club doctors to "determine the diagnosis and/or course of treatment,"[240] including whether "a surgical procedure is the appropriate course of treatment for the Player."[241] The NHL's policy would seemingly permit players to be compelled to undergo a surgery even if they (or their own doctor) believe it inappropriate, at risk of having their contract voided should they refuse. That the NFL and NHL lead on these issues is perhaps not surprising considering they are generally the two leagues with the highest rates of serious injuries (See Chapter 2: Injury Rates and Policies) and the most controversies concerning player health. The CFL is a football league too of course, but it does not compare in size to the NFL or NHL and thus does not engage in the same level of collective bargaining, policy making, or litigation.

While overall the NFL appears to offer the medical personnel policies most protective of player health, there are, however, four areas in which the NFL might learn lessons as compared to one or more of the other leagues. We explain these areas below, including those resulting in recommendations for the NFL.

First, it appears the NFL might learn lessons when it comes to players' access to medical records. The NBA requires club medical personnel to provide players with medical records within 48 hours of a player's request. In contrast, the NFL CBA only entitles players to their medical records once during the pre-season, once after the regular season, and upon request in the off-season.[242] However, in practice, the NFL's recently implemented electronic medical records system provides players with 24/7 access to their medical records. Consequently, the NFL's deviation on this issue is no longer relevant.

Similarly, the NHL CBA requires club medical personnel to provide players with a complete copy of their medical

records during their end-of-season physical. In contrast, while NFL players have 24/7 access to electronic versions of their records, there is no NFL CBA provision that obligates clubs to provide players with their medical records as a matter of course. It is not clear whether providing players with paper copies of their medical records versus electronic access is preferable. It is possible that one approach—or the two approaches combined—could increase the possibility that a player will review his records and seek appropriate or necessary care. However, without additional information, it is speculative to say the NHL's policy is superior.

Second, the NHL CBA requires clubs to identify an individual responsible for monitoring the club's prescription drug use. The NFL CBA has no such requirement. Nevertheless, the absence of any such provision is mitigated by the NFL's policies concerning medications. NFL clubs do not store controlled substances at their facilities and any prescription medications are filled through a local pharmacy.

Third, while the CFL Standard Player Contract requires players to submit to a pre-season physical by the club's doctors, the CFL CBA also requires that pre-season physicals "to determine the status of any pre-existing condition" be performed by a neutral physician.[243] The stated purpose of this requirement is to help determine "in the future" whether there was "an aggravation of . . . [a] pre-existing condition."[244] Furthermore, the provision is housed within the Injury Grievance article of the CBA,[ah] and thus it appears that the provision is designed to ensure that there is an accurate record of a player's injury history. In contrast, NFL club doctors perform all pre-season physicals and would be the ones to opine about a player's prior injury history. We believe the CFL's approach is preferred, for reasons explained below.

Fourth, the NHL's and MLS' required standards of care appear preferable to that of the NFL, in that they seemingly require club doctors to subjugate their duties to the club to their duties to the player at all times. In contrast, the NFL CBA only explicitly requires that the doctor's first priority be the player when the doctor is "providing medical care." Club doctors have important roles for the club beyond providing medical care, specifically performing fitness-for-play evaluations, the outcomes of which might not be in the player's interests. Consequently, by its specific terms,

---

ah Under the CFL Standard Player Contract, clubs are obligated to pay an injured player's medical expenses and salary (provided the player is a veteran) for so long as the player is physically unable to play. CFL Standard Player Contract ¶¶ 20–21. An Injury Grievance would be filed if the player and club disputed the extent of the player's injuries, and thus the club's obligations to pay the player's salary and medical expenses.

the NFL CBA only requires club doctors to consider players as their principal responsibility some of the time. But while the NHL's and MLS' provisions are preferable in their specificity and demands, they still fail to sufficiently protect player health.[ai]

Despite the possible protections provided by the NHL's and MLS' standards of care, they do not—nor do any of the other leagues—address perhaps the most fundamental structural issue concerning player health: the conflicts of interest faced by club medical personnel. In each of the leagues, the club's medical staff treats the players, but is selected by, reports to the club, including providing advice on the players' short-term and long-term usefulness to the club. While the Canadian healthcare system seemingly insulates the Canadian club doctors from payment as a source of conflict, American clubs have financial or other arrangements with their club doctors that can influence doctors' decision-making and care (consciously or unconsciously). While the various player health provisions discussed herein can improve a player's options and empower him to receive better care, there will be concerns about the quality and primacy of player health, and trust in club medical personnel, so long as it is principally clubs that control the medical staff.

For these reasons, in our report *Protecting and Promoting the Health of NFL Players: Legal and Ethical Analysis and Recommendations*, we recommended that club doctors and medical staff be redefined as "Players' Doctors" and "Players' Medical Staff," to reflect their exclusive responsibility to advance the health of players.[245] Moreover, we recommended that these medical professionals should be chosen and subject to review and termination by a Committee of medical experts selected equally by the NFL and the NFLPA and that their only interaction with clubs should be via the head Players' Doctor's written reports on the status of players currently receiving medical treatment. Finally, we recommend that a Players' Doctor's determination of a player's playing status should be controlling. The rationale for this proposed structure is discussed at length in our report but, generally, this arrangement removes the structural conflicts of interest that can and do impede player health. The NHL's standard of care supports our proposed approach, but does not go far enough. To ensure the best possible and most independent care, a standard of care is insufficient—structural changes are needed.

---

ai   In our report *Protecting and Promoting the Health of NFL Players: Legal and Ethical Analysis and Recommendations,* Chapter 3: Club Doctors, we describe in depth doctors legal and ethical obligations in the two different situations: providing medical care; and, performing fitness-for-play evaluations.

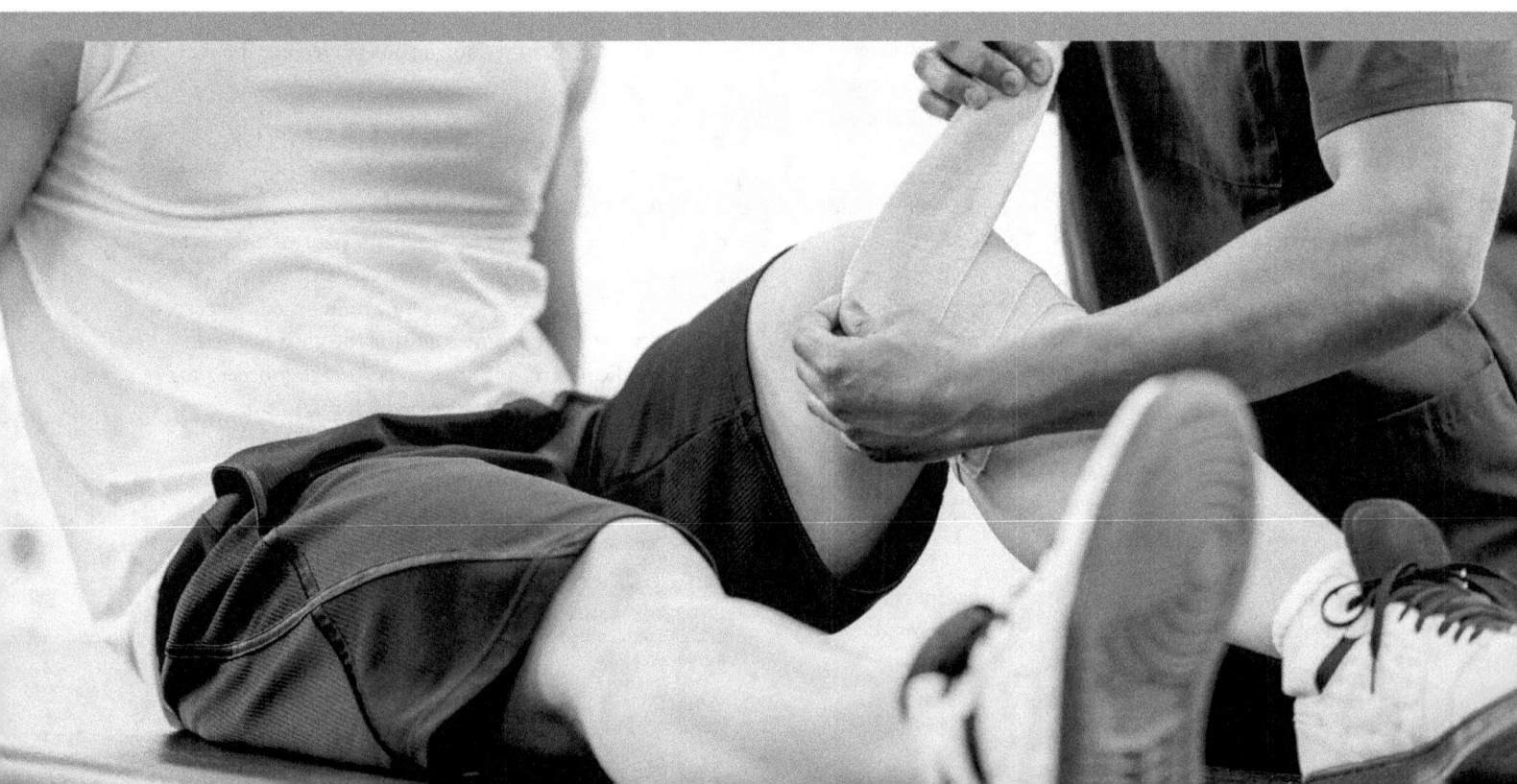

H Recommendation

Given the general superiority of NFL policies compared to other leagues, and uncertainty about possible areas where the NFL can learn by comparison, we have only one recommendation related to medical care, generated by comparison to the CFL.

Recommendation 1-A: Pre-season physicals for the purpose of evaluating a player's prior injuries should be performed by neutral doctors.

The CFL requires pre-season physicals for the purpose of evaluating a player's prior injuries to be performed by a neutral doctor. The NFL should adopt the same rule. The use of neutral doctors ensures that players' medical history is being recorded in an accurate manner, *i.e.*, in a manner that correctly details a player's injury history and the ways in which those prior injuries are manifesting themselves today. Clubs—and thus club doctors—have an incentive to minimize players' injuries and declare them fit to play in order to avoid further financial liability. For example, if an NFL player is injured during one season, and fails the pre-season physical the next season, the player is entitled to an Injury Protection benefit, an amount equal to 50% of his Paragraph 5 Salary (*i.e.,* base) for the season following the season of injury, up to a maximum payment of $1,150,000 (in 2016).[246] If the player is still injured during the next pre-season, he can obtain Extended Injury Protection, a benefit that permits a player to earn 50% of his salary up to $500,000 for the *second* season after suffering an injury that prevented the player from continuing to play. Additionally, similar to the CFL, if the club doctor finds that a player is healthy enough to play, a player's potential Injury Grievance[aj] is undermined. In these situations, the club doctor, acting in the interests of the club, might be motivated to find that the player is healthy enough to play during the pre-season physical, preventing the player from receiving benefits and compensation to which he is entitled. While we do not know if such practices are common or widespread, in our Report *Protecting and Promoting the Health of NFL Players: Legal and Ethical Analysis and Recommendations*, we provided examples from players attesting that such situations do occur.[247] Whatever the frequency, a structural conflict still exists and needs to be addressed. A neutral doctor avoids the potential for bias, and ensures players are receiving their just compensation and care.

As discussed in the Introduction, the NFL declined to review this Report. However, MLB did provide comments on the Report which may provide insight into the viewpoints of the other professional leagues. In reviewing a draft of this Report, MLB expressed its disagreement with this recommendation, stating:

> The recommendation (1-A) that preseason physical examinations be performed by a neutral doctor misses the point of the PPE [preparticipation physical evaluation]. Continuity of care is an important aspect of player health care and it is the view of our medical experts that having a separate physician for the preseason exam would result in worse care during the season. The recent Consensus Monograph on PPE, which was prepared by several national physician groups and is viewed as the governing document on these types of exams, does **not** include a recommendation for independent physicians.

While we generally agree with MLB that continuity of care is important, we disagree with MLB's comment for several reasons.

First, it is important to understand we believe there is a structural conflict of interest whereby NFL club doctors provide care to players while also providing services for the club.[ak] As a result, players have business reasons to be concerned about the outcome of the pre-season physical. As explained above, club doctors may not accurately record a player's condition, which can negatively affect his contract status and benefits to which he is entitled.

---

aj An Injury Grievance is "a claim or complaint that, at the time a player's NFL Player Contract or Practice Squad Player Contract was terminated by a Club, the player was physically unable to perform the services required of him by that contract because of an injury incurred in the performance of his services under that contract." 2011 NFL CBA, Art. 45, § 1.

ak In our Report *Protecting and Promoting the Health of NFL Players: Legal and Ethical Analysis and Recommendations* we set forth a comprehensive recommendation to address this issue. We propose restructuring NFL club medical staff in such a way that the doctor treating the players has as his or her only concern the well-being of the player-patient and has no advisory role to the club.

Recommendation Concerning Club Medical Personnel – continued

Second, our recommendation would not affect continuity of care as MLB's comment seems to suggest. Assuming doctors working for the club continue to treat players (which is not what we recommend as explained in footnote ak), the club doctor would have full access to the results of the pre-season physical and is also permitted to re-examine the player at any time, including during the pre-season. However, a physical performed by a neutral doctor should be used to establish the player's pre-existing conditions in order to better protect the player's business interests.

Third, MLB's reference to the consensus monograph[al] is misplaced. The monograph specifically states that it "is intended to provide a state-of-the-art, practical, and effective screening tool for physicians who perform PPEs for athletes in *middle school, high school, and college*."[248] Thus, the monograph does not apply to *professional sports*, and does not speak to the issues raised above.

---

al   *See* Am. Acad. Pediatrics, Preparticipation Physical Evaluation (4th ed. 2010). This monograph was created through the coordination of the American Academy of Family Physicians, American Academy of Pediatrics, American College of Sports Medicine, American Medical Society for Sports Medicine, American Orthopaedic Society for Sports Medicine, and the American Osteopathic Academy of Sports Medicine.

Endnotes

1   The AMA's Code of Medical Ethics can be found on its website at http://www.ama-assn.org/ama/pub/physician-resources/medical-ethics/code-medical-ethics.page (last visited Aug. 22, 2016), *archived at* http://perma.cc/8JJ4-MYJX.

2   FIMS' Code of Ethics is available from its website at http://www.fims.org/en/general/code-of-ethics. FIMS also published a Team Physician Manual which is one of the preeminent manuals for sports injuries and also covers the same ethical considerations espoused in its Code of Ethics.

3   *See NATA Code of Ethics,* Nat'l Athletic Trainers Ass'n, Sept. 28, 2005, http://www.nata.org/codeofethics, *archived at* http://perma.cc/7ZXQ-KP5U.

4   *See, e.g.,* John Lantos, Ann Marie Matlock, David Wendler, *Clinician Integrity and Limits to Patient Autonomy,* 305 J. Am. Med. Ass'n 495–9 (Feb. 2, 2011) ("Respect for patient autonomy plays a central role in modern clinical ethics"); Simon N. Whitney, Amy L. McGuire, Laurence B. McCullough, *A Typology of Shared Decision Making, Informed Consent, and Simple Consent,* 140 Ann. Intern. Med 54–59 (2003) ("Enhancing patient choice is a central theme of medical ethics and law."); Cathy Charles, Amiram Gafni, Tim Whelan, *Decision-making in the physician-patient encounter: revisiting the shared treatment decision-making model,* 49 Social Science & Medicine 651–61 (1999) (emphasizing the need to respect differences in patient preferences). *See also* Stedman's Medical Dictionary (28th ed. 2006) (defining "autonomy" as "[t]he condition or state of being autonomous, able to make decisions unaided by others."); Black's Law Dictionary (9th ed. 2009) (defining "autonomy" as: "the right of self-government"; "an individual's capacity for self-determination.")

5   *See* Mark A. Hall, et al., Health Care Law and Ethics 168–69 (2003) (collecting cases and statutes discussing doctors' obligations to keep patient information confidential); AMA Code, Fourth Principle ("A physician shall respect the rights of patients, colleagues, and other health professionals, and shall safeguard patient confidences and privacy within the constraints of the law.")

6   *See* Alexander Cornwell, *Trapped: Missouri Legislature Seeks to Close Workers' Compensation Loophole with Some Co-Employees Still Inside,* 77 Mo. L. Rev. 235, 235 (2012); David J. Krco, *Case Note: Torts — Narrowing the Window: Refining the Personal Duty Requirement for Coemployee Liability Under Minnesota's Workers' Compensation System — Stringer v. Minnesota Vikings Football Club, LLC,* 33 Wm. Mitchell L. Rev. 739, 739 (2007); John T. Burnett, *The Enigma of Workers' Compensation Immunity: A Call to the Legislature for a Statutorily Defined Intentional Tort Exception,* 28 Fla. St. U. L. Rev. 491, 497 (2001).

7   *See Lotysz v. Montgomery,* 309 A.D.2d 628 (N.Y.App. 2003) (NFL player's medical malpractice claim against club doctor barred by state workers' compensation statute); *Daniels v. Seattle Seahawks,* 92 Wash.App. 576 (Wash.App. 1998) (same); *Hendy v. Losse,* 54 Cal.3d 723 (Cal. 1991) (same); *Rivers v. New York Jets,* 460 F.Supp. 1233 (E.D.Mo. 1978) (NFL player's claim that club wrongfully concealed the true nature of player's condition barred by workers' compensation statute); *Brinkman v. Buffalo Bills Football Club Division of Highwood Service, Inc.,* 433 F.Supp. 699 (W.D.N.Y. 1977) (NFL player's claim that club failed to provide adequate medical care barred by workers' compensation law). *See also Bryant v. Fox,* 162 Ill.App.3d 46 (Ill.App. 1987) (NFL player's medical malpractice claim against club doctor not barred by workers' compensation statute where evidence established that doctor was an independent contractor); Pam Louwagie and Kevin Seifert, *Stringer claims against Vikings dismissed,* Newspaper of the Twin Cities (Minneapolis, MN), Apr. 26, 2003, *available at* 2003 WLNR 14250471 (medical malpractice claims against club doctors barred by workers' compensation statute). *Martin v. Casagrande,* 159 A.D.2d 26 (N.Y.App. 1990) (NHL player's claim that club doctor and general manager conspired to withhold information about player's medical condition barred by workers' compensation statute);

Bayless v. Philadelphia National League Club, 472 F.Supp. 625 (E.D.Pa. 1979) (former MLB player's claim that club negligently administered pain-killing drugs barred by workers' compensation statute).

8   *See Stringer v. Minnesota Vikings Football Club, LLC,* 705 N.W.2d 746 (Minn. 2005) (estate of former NFL player against athletic trainers barred by workers' compensation statute); *McLeod v. Blase,* 290 Ga.App. 337 (Ga.App. 2008) (former NBA player's claim against athletic trainer for alleged negligent treated barred by workers' compensation statute).

9   *See* Memorandum and Order, *Stringer v. Minnesota Vikings Football Club, LLC,* No. 02-415, at 11-14 (Minn.Dist.Ct. Apr. 25, 2003) (denying club doctor's motion to dismiss certain claims on ground that doctor was independent contractor); *Bryant v. Fox,* 162 Ill.App.3d 46 (Ill.App. 1987) (NFL player's medical malpractice claim against club doctor not barred by workers' compensation statute where evidence established that doctor was an independent contractor).

10 Lawsuits against clubs are difficult to pursue. The CBAs present the biggest obstacle against any such claim. Common law claims such as negligence are generally preempted by the Labor Management Relations Act ("LMRA"). 29 U.S.C. § 185. The LMRA bars or "preempts" state law claims where the claim is "substantially dependent upon analysis of the terms" of a CBA, *i.e.,* where the claim is "inextricably intertwined with consideration of the terms of the" CBA. *Allis-Chambers Corp. v. Lueck,* 471 U.S. 202, 213, 220 (1985). In order to assess a club's health-related duties to a player — an essential element of a negligence claim — a Court would likely have to refer to and analyze the terms of the CBA, resulting in the claim's preemption. *See, e.g., Givens v. Tennessee Football, Inc.,* 684 F.Supp.2d 985 (M.D.Tenn. 2010) (player's tort claims against club arising out of medical treatment preempted); *Williams v. Nat'l Football League,* 582 F.3d 863 (8th Cir. 2009) (players' tort claims arising out of drug test preempted).

11 Jon R. Johnson, *Session 8: Canada and U.S. Approaches to Health Care: How the Canadian and U.S. Political, Regulatory, and Legal Systems Impact Health Care,* 31 Can.-U.S. L.J. 251, 254 (2005).

12 *Id.* at 257.

13 *Id.* Under the 1966 Medicare Act, the federal government covered one half of the cost of eligible provincial plans covering physician services, but the government has since shifted to a "block-funding system" where it pays the provinces a lump sum for healthcare that covers about 15–20% of the cost of the plans. *Id.* at 257, 262–63.

14 *Id.* at 258–59.

15 *Id.* at 255, 260.

16 *Id.* at 264. *See also* Roy Romanow, *Directions in Canadian Health Care After the Romanow Report,* 67 Sask. L. Rev. 1, 3 (2004) ("And most doctors [in Canada] are effectively independent contractors paid according to fee schedules."); Colleen M. Flood & Bryan Thomas, *Canadian Medical Malpractice Law in 2011: Missing the Mark on Patient Safety,* 86 Chi. Kent L. Rev. 1053, 1056–57 (2011) ("In general, the provinces supply publicly funded health services by contracting with physicians — who are private, for-profit contractors — through provincial medical associations. The dominant method of payment for these private physicians has been a fee-for-service system, although this is slowly changing."); Daniel W. Srsic, *Collective Bargaining by Physicians in the United States and Canada,* 15 Comp. Lab. L.J. 89, 9192 (1993) ("In Canada, doctors continue to work almost exclusively in private practice, while in the United States an increasing number of doctors are working as employees of hospitals and HMOs."). Most hospitals, meanwhile, are non-profit and publicly funded, although they are not government owned. Johnson, *supra* note 11 at 263. Also, for-profit clinics may contract with a province to provide "insured services" to patients without violating the Canada Health Act, so long as patients do not have to pay for those services. *Id.* at 264 n.62.

17 *Id.* at 264.

18 *See, e.g.*, Lonny Balbi, *The Liability of Professional Team Sports Physicians*, 22 Alberta L. Rev. 247, 249 (1984); *Wilson v. Vancouver Hockey Club*, (1983) 5 D.L.R. 4th 282, para. 7 (Can. B.C.S.C.) ("He explained that the reference to 'bill 0113' was a general practitioner billing code number that would have to be sent to the Medical Services Plan in order that Dr. Peers would be paid."); *Robitaille*, 19 B.C.L.R. at para. 57 ("The doctors rendered accounts to the medical services association for the account of the player for office consultations and other 'non-dressing room' services.").

19 *See* Roy Romanow, *Directions in Canadian Health Care After the Romanow Report*, 67 Saskatchewan L. Rev. 1, 3–4 (2004). Physicians providing these services include, for example, dentists, dental surgeons, ophthalmologists, psychologists, chiropractors, physiotherapists, osteopaths, and naturopaths. *Id.*

20 The CBA does not define "retain" or otherwise dictate the requisite scope of involvement by the various doctors.

21 NFL CBA, Art. 39, § 1.

22 NFL CBA, Art. 39, § 1(e).

23 *NFL Physicians Society Mission Statement*, Nat'l Football League Physicians Soc'y, http://nflps.org/about/ (last visited Aug. 7, 2015), *archived at* http://perma.cc/928Z-LVZ4.

24 *See* Dave Siebert, *What Is Medical Care Like on an NFL Sideline?*, Bleacher Report (Nov. 15, 2013), http://bleacherreport.com/articles /1850732-what-is-medical-care-like-on-an-nfl-sideline, *archived at* http://perma.cc/7JR4-HR3G (quoting then-NFLPS President Matthew Matava describing the "about 177 NFL team physicians"); *Team Physicians*, Nat'l Football League Physicians Society, http://nflps.org/team -physicians/ (last visited Feb. 24, 2016), *archived at* https://perma.cc/ HK8A-QJ9L (listing 153 club doctors as members of the NFLPS).

25 *See Frequently Asked Questions — How Often Do All NFLPS Members Meet?*, Nat'l Football League Physician's Soc'y, http://nflps.org/faqs/how -often-do-all-nflps-members-meet/ (last visited Aug. 7, 2015), *archived at* http://perma.cc/76P5-DRQX; *Frequently Asked Questions — What Are Typical Topics at Members Meetings?*, Nat'l Football League Physician's Soc'y, http://nflps.org/faqs/what-are-typical-topics-at-members -meetings/ (last visited Aug. 7, 2015), *archived at* http://perma.cc/LR79 -9AN3 ("The topics at these meetings vary and address any or all of the potential injuries that an NFL player may experience. This can include orthopaedic injuries such as ACL tears, meniscus tears, cartilage injuries to the knee, multiligamentous injuries to the knee, high ankle sprains, fractures, dislocations, foot injuries, surgical techniques, rehabilitation, hip injuries, arthroscopy of the hip, sports hernia challenges, shoulder injuries such as dislocations or labral tears, rotator cuff problems, elbow dislocation, biceps or triceps injuries, wrist injuries, and hand and finger injuries or dislocations. From a medical standpoint, there has been a recent emphasis on heat-related illnesses, cardiac conditions, MRSA infections, sickle cell traits, concussions and the management of acute blunt trauma to the chest or abdomen.").

26 This information was provided by NFLPS.

27 This information was provided by PFATS.

28 These figures were determined by compiling the data available on the Professional Football Athletic Trainers Society website. *See Member Directory*, Prof. Football Athletic Trainers Soc'y, http://www.pfats.com/ directory/ (last visited Aug. 7, 2015), *archived at* http://perma.cc/PG2S -C2KH.

29 *Mission*, Prof. Football Athletic Trainers Soc'y, http://www.pfats.com/ about/mission (last visited May 31, 2016), https://perma.cc/SV92-L2FC.

30 *History*, Prof. Football Athletic Trainers Soc'y, http://www.pfats.com/ about/history (last visited Aug. 7, 2015), *archived at* http://perma.cc /6P8N-PZTV.

31 *Mission*, Prof. Football Athletic Trainers Soc'y, *supra* note 29.

32 *See* Christopher R. Deubert, I. Glenn Cohen, Holly Fernandez Lynch, *Protecting and Promoting the Health of NFL Players: Legal and Ethical Analysis and Recommendations*, Ch. 3 (2016).

33 NFL CBA, Art. 39, § 3(e).

34 NFL CBA, Art. 39, § 1(c).

35 This information was provided by the NFLPA.

36 NFL Comments and Corrections (June 24, 2016).

37 NFL CBA, Art. 39, § 1(c).

38 NFL CBA, Art. 40, § 2(a).

39 NFL CBA, Art. 39, § 6.

40 NFL CBA, App. A, § 8.

41 NFL CBA, Art. 42, § 1(a)(iii).

42 NFL CBA, Art. 39, §§ 4–5.

43 NFL CBA, Art. 39, § 4.

44 *How does a physician become an NFL team physician?* NFL Physicians Soc'y, http://nflps.org/faqs/how-does-a-physician-become-an-nfl-team -physician/ (last visited Aug. 25, 2015), *archived at* http://perma.cc /72XA-N2KW.

45 *see Synernet Staff Visits NFL Headquarters*, Synernet (Feb. 11, 2015), http://www.synernet.net/news/news.aspx, *archived at* https://perma.cc /E4UC-WNWP.

46 Telephone Interview with Larry Ferazani, NFL, Vice President, Labor Litigation & Policy (Oct. 6, 2014).

47 NFL Comments and Corrections (June 24, 2016).

48 *See* Christopher R. Deubert, I. Glenn Cohen, Holly Fernandez Lynch, *Protecting and Promoting the Health of NFL Players: Legal and Ethical Analysis and Recommendations*, § 3(D) (2016).

49 Telephone Interview with Larry Ferazani, NFL, Vice President, Labor Litigation & Policy (Oct. 6, 2014).

50 *Id.*

51 *Id.*

52 Bill Pennington, *Sports Turnaround: The Team Doctors Now Pay the Team*, The New York Times, May 18, 2004, http://www.nytimes .com/2004/05/18/sports/sports-medicine-sports-turnaround-the -team-doctors-now-pay-the-team.html?pagewanted=1, *archived at* https://perma.cc/BDU2-ETSM.

53 *See* Christopher R. Deubert, I. Glenn Cohen, Holly Fernandez Lynch, *Protecting and Promoting the Health of NFL Players: Legal and Ethical Analysis and Recommendations*, § 2(A) (2016).

54 NFL Comments and Corrections (June 24, 2016).

55 Memorandum from Dan Halem to All Major League Clubs (Dec. 1, 2015).

56 *Id.*

57 Memorandum from Dan Halem to MLB General Managers and Medical Personnel (Nov. 7, 2012).

58 *Id.*

59 Memorandum from Dan Halem to All Major League Clubs (Dec. 1, 2015).

60 *See* 2012 MLB CBA, Art. XIII, Attachments 5, 6, 18, 35 and 36, and Schedule A.

61 NFL CBA, Art. 39, § 1.

62 *Home*, Major League Baseball Team Physicians Ass'n, http://mlbtpa.org/ (last visited Aug. 25, 2015), *archived at* http://perma.cc/2JTM-XMJ5.

63 *MLBPA, MLB Announce Details of New Labor Agreement*, MLBPA (Dec. 2, 2016), http://www.mlbplayers.com/ViewArticle.dbml?DB_OEM _ID=34000&ATCLID=211336390, *archived at* https://perma.cc/4XUA -2DAW (announcing replacement of 15-day DL with 10-day DL).

64 *Id.*

65 MLB CBA, Art. XIII, § E.

66 *About*, Professional Baseball Athletic Trainers Soc'y, http://pbats.com /about/ (last visited Aug. 25, 2015), *archived at* http://perma.cc/G9FP -42CS.

67 MLB CBA, Art. XIII, § G.

68 *See* AMA Code Opinion 3.1.5 — Professionalism in Relationships with Media: To safeguard patient interests when working with representatives of the media, all physicians should: (a) Obtain consent from the patient or the patient's authorized representative before releasing information; (b) Release only information specifically authorized by the

patient or patient's representative or that is part of the public record; (c) Ensure that no statement regarding diagnosis or prognosis is made except by or on behalf of the attending physician; and, (d) Refer any questions regarding criminal activities or other police matters to the proper authorities. *Opinion 3.1.5—Professionalism in Relationships with Media*, Am. Med. Ass'n, *available at* http://www.ama-assn.org/ama/pub/physician-resources/medical-ethics/code-medical-ethics.page (last visited Aug. 1, 2016), *archived at* https://perma.cc/ZR8K-FC93.

69 MLB CBA, Art. XIII, § G(6).

70 MLB CBA, Art. XIII, § G(7)(a).

71 MLB CBA, Art. XIII, § I.

72 MLB CBA, Art. XIII, § C.

73 MLB CBA, Attachment 36.

74 *Id.*

75 *Id.*

76 *Id.* at Concussion Return to Play Form.

77 Memorandum from Dan Halem to MLB General Managers and Medical Personnel (Nov. 7, 2012).

78 MLB Uniform Player Contract, at REGULATIONS ¶ 2.

79 MLB CBA, Art. XIII, § D.

80 MLB CBA, Art. XIII, § D.

81 MLB CBA, Art. XIII, § G.

82 *Id.*

83 *Id.*

84 Email from Jon Coyles, MLB Labor Counsel, to Chris Deubert (Oct. 6, 2014, 15:13 EST) (on file with author).

85 *Id.* MLB is not aware of any field managers that have the authority to hire or terminate medical personnel. *Id.*

86 *Id.*

87 Bill King, *Team Doctors Rattled by Threat of Malpractice Suits*, SportsBusinessDaily.com (June 21, 2004), http://www.sportsbusinessdaily.com/Journal/Issues/2004/06/20040621/SBJ-In-Depth/Team-Doctors-Rattled-By-Threat-Of-Malpractice-Suits.aspx, *archived at* http://perma.cc/5E7V-QMXX; *See generally* Dennis Durao, *An Endangered Species: Professional Sports Team Physicians*, 15 Quinnipiac Health L.J. 33 (2011) (detailing increases in insurance premiums for physicians treating professional athletes).

88 Email from Jon Coyles, *supra* note 84.

89 MLB CBA, Attachment 35.

90 MLB CBA, Attachment 18 at ¶¶ 2–3.

91 *Id.* at ¶ 8.

92 MLB Uniform Player Contract, ¶ 6(b)(1), included as Schedule A to the 2012 MLB CBA.

93 *Id.* at ¶ 6(b)(2). The receiving club must return all of the records within 30 days. *Id.*

94 Tom Haudricourt, *Milwaukee Journal Sentinel Tom Haudricourt column*, Milwaukee J. Sentinel, Apr. 6, 2008, *available at* 2008 WLNR 6507711; Alyson Footer, *Clearing up the term 'athletic trainer'*, MLB News, Mar. 25, 2008, http://m.mlb.com/news/article/2444052/, archived at http://perma.cc/S2CD-RXDE; *see also* Alison Gardiner-Shires, Scott C.Marley, John C. Barnes, Mark E. Shires, *Professional baseball athletic trainers' perceptions of preparation for job-specific duties*, 47 J. of Athletic Training 704 (2012).

95 Tim Johnson and Dr. Eric Berkson, *Life As a Red Sox Team Physician*, Mass. Gen. Hospital (Apr. 13, 2010), http://www.massgeneral.org/about/newsarticle.aspx?id=2165, *archived at* http://perma.cc/DAG9-X9AZ.

96 *Id.*

97 Memorandum from Dan Halem to MLB General Managers and Medical Personnel (Nov. 7, 2012).

98 Memorandum from MLB Commissioner Selig to All Major League Owners, President and General Managers re: Medical Service Provider Sponsorships (Nov. 17, 2004) (on file with author). Before this policy, some sponsorship arrangements involved payments from the sponsoring provider to the club, coupled with agreements to provide free healthcare to players and their families in exchange for advertising space in the club's stadium. *Healthy: Rangers Ink Deal With Medical Center of Arlington*, SportsBusinessDaily.com (Feb. 25, 2004), http://www.sportsbusinessdaily.com/Daily/Issues/2004/02/Issue-108/Sponsorships-Advertising-Marketing/Healthy-Rangers-Ink-Deal-With-Medical-Center-Of-Arlington.aspx, *archived at* http://perma.cc/3MQK-4DKP.

99 Memorandum from Daniel R. Halem to All Major League Club Presidents, General Managers, Assistant General Managers, Club Counsel, Team Physicians and Certified Athletic Trainers re: Medical Service Provider Sponsorships (Feb. 18, 2014) (on file with author).

100 Email from Jon Coyles, MLB Labor Counsel, to Chris Deubert (Oct. 6, 2014, 15:13 EST) (on file with author).

101 *Id.*

102 Memorandum from Daniel R. Halem to All Major League Club Presidents, General Managers, Assistant General Managers, Club Counsel, Team Physicians, and Certified Athletic Trainers re: Medical Service Provider Sponsorships (Feb. 18, 2014) (on file with author).

103 *See, e.g.,* Oliver Millerchip, *Kaiser Permanente Backs MLB's Nationals*, SportsProMedia.com (May 7, 2014), http://www.sportspromedia.com/news/kaiser_permanente_backs_mlbs_nationals, *archived at* http://perma.cc/XMQ3-TG2X (noting a managed care consortium's sponsorship of the Washington Nationals); *Pirates Announce Affiliation Renewals With Team Partners*, MLB.com (May 6, 2013, 9:23 am), http://m.mlb.com/news/article/46753608/pirates-announce-affiliation-renewals-with-team-partners, *archived at* https://perma.cc/U358-X9KR (noting a multiyear agreement for Highmark to be the "Official Healthcare Provider of the Pittsburgh Pirates").

104 NBA CBA, Art. XXII, § 1(a).

105 NBA CBA, Art. XXII, § 6.

106 NBA CBA, Art. XXII, § 3.

107 NBA CBA, Art. XXII, § 1(b).

108 *About*, Nat'l Basketball Athletic Trainers Ass'n, http://nbata.com/about-us/ (last visited Aug. 25, 2015), *archived at* https://perma.cc/AT3Z-N7TT.

109 *Id.*

110 *See* Travis Tate, *A Day in the Life of—Athletic Trainer*, NBA.com, http://www.nba.com/jazz/news/day_in_the_life_athletic_trainer.html (last visited Aug. 25, 2015), *archived at* http://perma.cc/V7CV-SFVW (describing duties of Utah Jazz athletic trainer); Jaimie Siegle, *Behind the Scenes at Philips Arena with NBA Head AT Wally Blase*, Nat'l Athletic Trainers Ass'n (May 22, 2014), http://www.nata.org/nata-news-blog/behind-scenes-philips-arena-nba-head-wally-blase, *archived at* http://perma.cc/BBF2-TE4G (describing duties of Atlanta Hawks athletic trainer); Fred Kerber, *Train of Thought—Walsh Keeps Nets in Working Order*, N.Y. Post, Nov. 15, 2008, *available at* 2008 WLNR 21933024 (describing duties of New Jersey Nets athletic trainer).

111 NBA CBA, Art. XXII, § 2.

112 NBA CBA, Art. XXII, § 4(f).

113 NFL CBA, Art. 40, § 2(a).

114 NBA CBA, Art. XXII, § 11(c).

115 NBA CBA, Art. XXII, § 11(b).

116 NBA CBA, Art. XXII, § 11(a).

117 NBA CBA, Art. XXII, § 11(d)(2).

118 NBA CBA, Art. XXII, § 11(d)(3).

119 NBA CBA, Art. XXII, § 11(d)(3).

120 NBA CBA, Art. XXII, § 11(g).

121 *Id.* The contract amendment possibility existed in CBAs prior to 2017 and thus is not limited to the Fitness-to-Play determinations. When a club doctor believes a player is not sufficiently fit to play (which would include general fitness as well as medical determinations), a player's contract can be amended to provide that the club can suspend the player for successive one-week periods until the club believes the player can play. *See id.*; 2017 NBA CBA, Art. II, § 3(l); NBA Uniform

Player Contract, Ex. 7. After each one-week suspension, the player has the right to be examined by a doctor selected by the President or a Vice President of the American Society of Orthopedic Surgeons (the "Reviewing Physician"). NBA Uniform Player Contract, Ex. 7. The Reviewing Physician's determination "concerning the physical condition of the Player to play skilled basketball" is binding on the club and the player. *Id.* If the Reviewing Physician determines that the player "is in physical condition sufficient to play skilled basketball," then the club can no longer suspend the player. *Id.* At this point, as a practical matter, the player would be allowed to suit up and presumably practice, but the club would still have the discretion not to play the player. Nevertheless, if the club is unwilling to play the player, the player is of no value to the club. Consequently, the club would likely play the player, trade him to another club, or release him. According to the NBA, this provision generally concerns players' physical fitness at the beginning of each season. Nevertheless, it has the potential to be applied to the Fitness-to-Play determinations as well.

122 *Chris Bosh fails Heat physical with blood clotting, no timetable for return*, Sports Illustrated (Sep. 23, 2016), http://www.si.com/nba/2016/09/23/chris-bosh-miami-heat-blood-clotting, *archived at* https://perma.cc/25X4-UYU3.

123 *Id.*

124 Howard Beck, *Stuck in Standoff Over Chris Bosh's Future, NBA to Create New Medical Panels*, Bleacher Rep. (Dec. 21, 2016), http://bleacherreport.com/articles/2683133-stuck-in-standoff-over-chris-bosh-future-nba-to-create-new-medical-panels?utm_source=facebook.com&utm_medium=share&utm_campaign=web-des-art-top-188, *archived at* https://perma.cc/GB52-PBHY.

125 *Id.*

126 NBA CBA, Art. XXII, § 10(b).

127 NBA CBA, Art. XXII, § 10(c).

128 NBA CBA, Art. XXII, § 10(g).

129 NBA Uniform Player Contract, § 7(a).

130 NBA Uniform Player Contract, § 7(d).

131 NBA Uniform Player Contract, § 7(e).

132 NBA Uniform Player Contract, § 7(f).

133 NBA CBA, Art. XXII, § 7.

134 NBA Uniform Player Contract, § 7(f).

135 NBA Uniform Player Contract, § 7(g).

136 NBA CBA, Art. II, § 13(i).

137 NBA Uniform Player Contract, § 7(h)(i).

138 NBA Uniform Player Contract, § 7(h)(ii).

139 NBA Uniform Player Contract, § 7(i).

140 Email from David Weiss, Associate Vice President and Assistant General Counsel, NBA, to author (Sept. 30, 2014).

141 NBA CBA, Art. XXII, § 4(a). However, a "player or his immediate family (where appropriate) shall have the right to approve the terms and timing of any public release of medical information relating to any injuries or illnesses suffered by that player that are potentially life- or career-threatening, or that do not arise from the player's participation in NBA games or practices." 2017 NBA CBA, Art. XXII, § 4(e).

142 NBA CBA, Art. XXII, § 4(b).

143 NBA CBA, Art. XXII, § 6.

144 *See, e.g., Sacramento Kings Announce Kaiser Permanente as Team's New Medical Provider*, Nat'l Basketball Ass'n, Oct. 3, 2013, http://www.nba.com/kings/news/sacramento-kings-announce-kaiser-permanente-teams-new-medical-provider, *archived at* http://perma.cc/FB55-RK6F; *DMC Sports Medicine — New Home*, Detroit Med. Center, http://www.dmc.org/detroit-medical-center-sports-medicine-new-home.html (last visited Aug. 25, 2015), archived at http://perma.cc/DEU3-G74H.

145 NHL CBA, § 34.2(a).

146 NHL CBA, § 34.2(b)(i).

147 *Mission Statement*, Prof. Hockey Athletic Trainers Soc'y, http://www.phats-sphem.com/mission (last visited Aug. 26, 2015), *archived at* http://perma.cc/74ZD-J2Z7.

148 *See* FrankD, *An interview with Tampa Bay Lightning Head Athletic Trainer Tommy Mulligan*, SB Nation (Feb. 9, 2010, 6:00 AM), http://fromtherink.sbnprivate.com/2010/2/9/1299657/an-interview-with-tampa-bay *archived at* http://perma.cc/BRC2-6A86 (discussing duties of Tampa Bay Lightning athletic trainer).

149 NHL CBA, § 34.1(a).

150 NHL CBA, § 34.1(b).

151 NHL CBA, § 34.3(b)(ii).

152 NHL CBA, § 34.8.

153 Christopher R. Deubert, I. Glenn Cohen, Holly Fernandez Lynch, *Protecting and Promoting the Health of NFL Players: Legal and Ethical Analysis and Recommendations*, § 2(l) (2016).

154 NHL CBA, § 34.4(a).

155 Christopher R. Deubert, I. Glenn Cohen, Holly Fernandez Lynch, *Protecting and Promoting the Health of NFL Players: Legal and Ethical Analysis and Recommendations*, § 4(D) (2016).

156 NHL CBA, § 23.10.

157 Christopher R. Deubert, I. Glenn Cohen, Holly Fernandez Lynch, *Protecting and Promoting the Health of NFL Players: Legal and Ethical Analysis and Recommendations*, § 3(A) (2016).

158 NHL CBA, § 34.4(c)(i).

159 NHL CBA, § 34.4(c)(ii).

160 NHL CBA, § 34.4(c)(iii).

161 NHL CBA, § 34.4(d).

162 NHL CBA, § 34.4(e).

163 NHL CBA, § 34.5(a).

164 Standard Player Contract, § 2, included as Exhibit 1 to the 2013 NHL CBA.

165 NHL CBA, § 34.5(a).

166 NHL CBA, § 34.5(b).

167 NHL CBA, § 34.6.

168 NHL CBA, § 34.6(d).

169 In a pair of cases from the early 1980s, Canadian courts were split about whether club doctors are employees or independent contractors. *See Robitaille v. Vancouver Hockey Club, Ltd.*, (1981) 124 D.L.R. 3d 228 (Can. B.C.C.A.), *available at* https://www.canlii.org/en/bc/bcca/doc/1981/1981canlii532/1981canlii532.html, *archived at* https://perma.cc/Q4N9-HGP4 (finding that the three club doctors were employees of the defendant club and holding the club vicariously liable); *Wilson v. Vancouver Hockey Club*, (1983) 5 D.L.R. 4th 282 (Can. B.C.S.C.), *available at* https://www.canlii.org/en/bc/bcsc/doc/1983/1983canlii340/1983canlii340.html, *archived at* https://perma.cc/JNG5-X593 (finding that the club doctor was an independent contractor and the defendant club was not vicariously liable for his negligence). *See also Martin v. Casagrande*, 559 N.Y.S.2d 68, 69 (N.Y.App.Div. 1990) (NHL player's recovery under workers' compensation laws barred player's lawsuit against club and club doctor); Frank Fitzpatrick, *Jury Starts Deliberations in Babych's Lawsuit*, Philly.com (Oct. 31, 2002), http://articles.philly.com/2002-10-31/sports/25352880_1_dave-babych-flyers-physician-deliberations, *archived at* http://perma.cc/5TE5-7TUU; *Dave Babych Wins Injury Lawsuit*, CBCSports (Nov. 1, 2002, 1:31 a.m.), http://www.cbc.ca/sports/hockey/dave-babych-wins-injury-lawsuit-1.304723, *archived at* http://perma.cc/C29K-ZK5T (former player awarded $1.37 million in damages against club doctor for alleged improper treatment of broken foot after court determined that club doctor was an independent contractor).

170 NHL CBA, § 34.3(a).

171 NHL CBA, 34.3(c)(x).

172 NHL CBA, § 34.3(c).

173 Sean Gordon & David Shoalts, *Diagnosing Sports Injuries Never an Exact Science*, Globe & Mail, Feb. 7, 2012, http://www.theglobeandmail.com

/sports/hockey/diagnosing-sports-injuries-never-an-exact-science/article544490/, *archived at* http://perma.cc/N26D-Q7WL. NHL spokespersons have been cagey about the number of teams with such deals in the past. *See* Tom Farrey, *A Snapshot of Sports' Medical Dilemma*, ESPN, Sept. 12, 2002, http://espn.go.com/gen/s/2002/0912/1430969.html, *archived at* http://perma.cc/N26D-Q7WL ("Spokespersons for the NHL and Major League Baseball say they don't know how many of their teams have such deals.").

174 Gordon & Shoalts, *supra* note 173. Accepting payment from medical groups is "frowned upon" in Canada. *Id.*

175 *See* Bill King, *Team Doctors Rattled by Threat of Malpractice Suits*, SportsBusinessDaily.com (June 21, 2004), http://www.sportsbusinessdaily.com/Journal/Issues/2004/06/20040621/SBJ-In-Depth/Team-Doctors-Rattled-By-Threat-Of-Malpractice-Suits.aspx, *archived at* http://perma.cc/5E7V-QMXX.

176 CFL CBA, § 34.18.

177 *See* Administration, Edmonton Eskimos, http://www.esks.com/page/administration (last visited Aug. 26, 2016), *archived at* https://perma.cc/6JNY-Y6U8 (listing nine doctors affiliated with Edmonton); *Football Op*, Montreal Alouettes, http://en.montrealalouettes.com/football-operations/ (last visited Aug. 26, 2016), *archived at* https://perma.cc/DC3G-LMAJ (listing nine doctors affiliated with Montreal Alouettes); *Front Office & Football Operations*, Toronto Argonauts, http://www.argonauts.ca/coaching-staff-football-operations/ (last visited Aug. 22, 2016), *archived at* https://perma.cc/P3C8-HDT7 (listing seven doctors affiliated with Toronto Argonauts).

178 *Id.*

179 *Id.*

180 CFL CBA, § 34.03.

181 CFL Standard Player Contract, ¶ 6.

182 NFL CBA, App. A, § 8.

183 Telephone interview by Chris Deubert with Michael Copeland, President and Chief Operating Officer, CFL (July 24, 2014).

184 *See Robitaille v. Vancouver Hockey Club, Ltd.*, (1981) 124 D.L.R. 3d 228 (Can. B.C.C.A.), *available at* https://www.canlii.org/en/bc/bcca/doc/1981/1981canlii532/1981canlii532.html, *archived at* https://perma.cc/Q4N9-HGP4 (finding that the three club doctors were employees of the defendant club and holding the club vicariously liable); *Wilson v. Vancouver Hockey Club*, (1983) 5 D.L.R. 4th 282 (Can. B.C.S.C.), *available at* https://www.canlii.org/en/bc/bcsc/doc/1983/1983canlii340/1983canlii340.html, *archived at* https://perma.cc/JNG5-X593 (finding that the club doctor was an independent contractor and the defendant club was not vicariously liable for his negligence).

185 CFL CBA, § 24.09.

186 CFL CBA, § 24.08.

187 *Dr. Robert McDougall and the Saskatchewan Roughriders*, 17 J. Can. Rheumatology Ass'n (2007), http://www.stacommunications.com/customcomm/Back-issue_pages/CRAJ/crajPDFs/2007/fall2007/english/04.pdf, *archived at* http://perma.cc/VAP5-8P59.

188 *An Athlete's Perspective: An Interview with CFL All-star Chris Walby*, 17 J. Can. Rheumatology Ass'n (2007), http://www.stacommunications.com/customcomm/Back-issue_pages/CRAJ/crajPDFs/2007/fall2007/english/04.pdf, *archived at* http://perma.cc/VAP5-8P59.

189 *Id.*

190 Telephone interview by Chris Deubert with Michael Copeland, President and Chief Operating Officer, Can. Football League (July 24, 2014).

191 Sean Gordon and David Shoalts, *Diagnosing Sports Injuries Never an Exact Science*, Globe & Mail, Feb. 7, 2012, http://www.theglobeandmail.com/sports/hockey/diagnosing-sports-injuries-never-an-exact-science/article544490/, *archived at* http://perma.cc/N26D-Q7WL.

192 The MLS Medical Manual states that "Club Physicians and Athletic Trainers are required to comply with the policies and procedures set forth in this manual." MLS Medical Policies & Procedures Manual § I (2015).

193 MLS Medical Policies & Procedures Manual § III.5 (2015).

194 MLS CBA, § 9.8.

195 MLS Medical Policies & Procedures Manual Introduction (2015).

196 *Home*, MLS Team Physician Soc'y, http://www.mlsteamdocs.com/ (last visited Aug. 26, 2015), *archived at* http://perma.cc/QJ7E-82SN.

197 *About*, Prof. Soccer Athletic Trainers' Soc'y, http://www.psats.net/#!psats-members-/cigi (last visited Aug. 26, 2015), *archived at* http://perma.cc/D22U-5SP7.

198 MLS Medical Policies & Procedures Manual § V.2 (2015).

199 Interview with MaryBeth Horodyski, Vice President, NATA, and Jim Thornton, President, NATA (Aug. 20, 2014).

200 *See BOC Vision & Mission*, Board of Cert. for Athletic Trainers, http://bocatc.org/about-us/boc-vision-mission (last visited Aug. 7, 2015), *archived at* http://perma.cc/3J98-WU2T.

201 *See An In Depth Look with an Athletic Trainer in Major League Soccer*, Board of Cert. for the Athletic Trainer, http://www.bocatc.org/blog/uncategorized/an-in-depth-look-with-an-athletic-trainer-in-major-league-soccer/ (last visited Aug. 26, 2015), *archived at* http://perma.cc/W86J-FAHW (interview with Houston Dynamo athletic trainer describing his duties); Luke Lohr, *Plight of the MLS Athletic Trainer*, The MLS Reserves, Apr. 4, 2012, www.mlsreserves.com/2012/04/plight-of-mls-athletic-trainer.html, *archived at* http://perma.cc/PZ6S-Z89R (interview with FC Dallas athletic trainer describing his duties).

202 *Id.*

203 *Id.*

204 MLS CBA, § 9.7.

205 *Id.*

206 MLS Medical Policies & Procedures Manual § I (2015). *See also id.* § IV.5 ("Club Physicians will always provide medical services based on their best medical judgment."); *id.* § X.A ("Club Physicians and Athletic Trainers will at all times comply with the highest standard of care when treating any injury or other medical problem.")

207 MLS CBA, § 9.1(v).

208 MLS Standard Player Agreement, ¶ 7(g).

209 NFL CBA, App. A, ¶ 8.

210 MLS Standard Player Agreement, ¶ 4(b).

211 NFL CBA, App. A, ¶ 8.

212 MLS CBA, § 9.5.

213 MLS CBA, § 9.1(i).

214 MLS CBA, § 9.1(iii).

215 MLS CBA, § 9.1(iv).

216 MLS CBA, § 9.3(i)(a).

217 MLS CBA, § 9.3(i).

218 MLS CBA, § 9.4.

219 *Id.*

220 NFL Player Contract, § 8, included as Appendix A to the 2011 NFL CBA.

221 MLS Medical Policies & Procedures Manual § III.1, § V.2 (2015).

222 MLS Medical Policies & Procedures Manual § V.3 (2015).

223 Email from Bob Foose, Executive Director, MLS Players Union, to author (Aug. 29, 2014).

224 *See Docket*, *D.C. Soccer LLC, et al. v. Commonwealth Orthopaedics & Rehabilitation, P.C., et al.*, 2012-CA-007050 (D.C. Sup. Ct.), available by searching the District of Columbia courts website at https://www.dccourts.gov/cco/maincase.jsf.

225 *See* Complaint, *Namoff v. D.C. Soccer LLC* (D.C. Sup. Ct. Aug. 29, 2012).

226 Order, *Namoff v. D.C. Soccer LLC*, No. 2012-CA-7050 (D.C. Sup. Ct. May 8, 2014); Steven Goff, *Namoff's lawsuit was dismissed*, Wash. Post, Jan 14, 2015, https://www.washingtonpost.com/news/soccer-insider/wp/2015/01/14/namoffs-lawsuit-was-dismissed//, *archived at* https://perma.cc/5JEK-EZCE.

227 Order, *Namoff v. D.C. Soccer LLC*, No. 2012-CA-7050, *2 (D.C. Sup. Ct. May 8, 2014).

228 *Id.* at 8.

229 *See* Order, *Namoff v. Annunziata,* No. 2012-CA-008981 (D.C. Sup. Ct. Aug. 12, 2014).

230 *Id.* at 7.

231 *Id.* at 9.

232 *Id.* at 6.

233 *Id.*

234 MLS CBA, Ex. 2.

235 *New York Red Bulls and Hospital for Special Surgery Announce Partnership,* Hospital for Special Surgery (Mar. 21, 2007), http://www.hss.edu /newsroom_hss-partnership-new-york-red-bulls-soccer-team-sports -medicine.asp, *archived at* http://perma.cc/UR8C-JAFC.

236 *See Technical Staff,* N.Y. Red Bulls, http://www.newyorkredbulls.com/ technicalstaff (last visited Aug. 26, 2015), *archived at* http://perma.cc /88X2-LF4A.

237 *Orlando City SC and Orlando Health Unveil Inaugural MLS Home Jersey,* Orlando City Soccer Club (Nov. 5, 2014), *available at* http://www .orlandocitysc.com/post/2014/11/05/orlando-city-sc-and-orlando-health -unveil-inaugural-mls-home-jersey, *archived at* http://perma.cc/RL3N -6VJY.

238 *See Daryl Christopher Oshbar,* Orlando Health, http://www.orlandohealth .com/physician-finder/daryl-christopher-osbahr-md?hcmacid =a0bi000000HyCQ3AAN (last visited Aug. 22, 2016), *archived at* https://perma.cc/66C5-6U7X.

239 MLS Medical Policies & Procedures Manual § X.B.2.d (2015).

240 NHL CBA, § 34.5(a).

241 NHL CBA, § 34.4(f).

242 NFL CBA, Art. 40, § 2(a).

243 CFL CBA, § 24.08.

244 *Id.*

245 *See* Christopher R. Deubert, I. Glenn Cohen, Holly Fernandez Lynch, *Protecting and Promoting the Health of NFL Players: Legal and Ethical Analysis and Recommendations,* § 2(H) (2016).

246 NFL CBA, Art. 45, § 2.

247 *See* Christopher R. Deubert, I. Glenn Cohen, Holly Fernandez Lynch, *Protecting and Promoting the Health of NFL Players: Legal and Ethical Analysis and Recommendations,* Recommendation 1:1-F (2016).

248 Am. Acad. Pediatrics, Preparticipation Physical Evaluation 3 (4th ed. 2010).

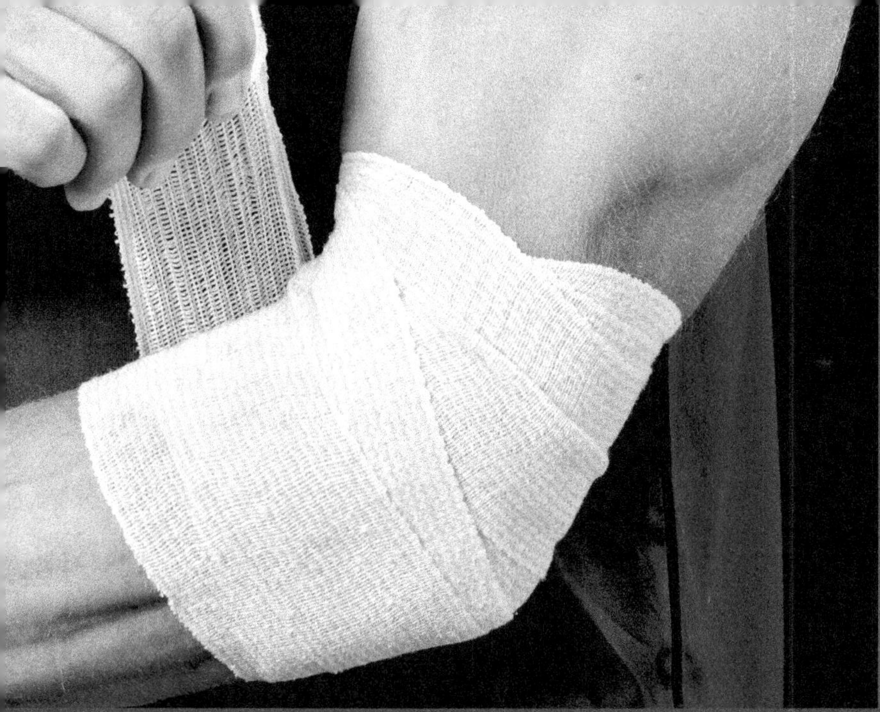

Injury Rates and Policies[a]

An important measurement of player health is the incidence and type of injuries players may sustain in the course of their work. Additionally, given the importance of player injuries, the manner in which player injuries are handled administratively and reported can indicate a league's approach to player health issues more generally. In this Chapter, we examine the leagues': (1) injury tracking systems; (2) injury rates; (3) injury-related lists; and, (4) policies concerning public reporting of injuries. At the conclusion of this Chapter, Table 3-E will summarize some of the key statistics and policies concerning injuries.

Before beginning our analysis, we provide some background information and qualifications on some of the topics we will discuss.

a   We are immensely grateful for the assistance of Karen G. Roos, PhD, MSPT, ATC, from California State University, Long Beach in preparing this Chapter.

1) INJURY TRACKING SYSTEMS AND RATES

As will be discussed below, all of the leagues (except the CFL) have an electronic medical record ("EMR") system into which the club's medical staff enters player injuries and through which the club and league are then able to track player injuries and conduct a variety of statistical analyses, all on a de-identified basis.[b] While these data are valuable, they are not routinely made available to the public. Consequently, obtaining data on injury incidence, specifically in the form of injury incidence rates, requires release of the data either by the leagues themselves or through academic studies (many of which have requested the data from the leagues).

There are additional limitations with the injury tracking systems.

As a general matter, injuries in sports are underreported.[1] Players routinely hide their medical conditions from the club. Players principally do this to protect their status on the club and due to fear of being viewed as less tough by the coaches.[2] Players know that their careers are tenuous and also know that if the club starts perceiving a player to be injury-prone, it is often not long before the club no longer employs that player.[3]

Similarly, club medical staff might not enter player injuries into the system or might discourage players from seeking help for a medical condition so that it appears players are healthier than they actually are. Medical staff also might not input injuries in order to: (1) make it appear they are doing their job well and keeping players healthy; or, (2) to help the club in a potential dispute with the player. For example, if an NFL club terminates a player's contract while he is injured, the club is responsible for the player's salary for so long as the player is injured. A club's medical staff might not include the full extent of a player's injuries in the system in order to support the club's potential argument that the player was not injured when the club terminated the player's contract. While we do not mean to imply such actions are common, and we have no way of estimating the incidence, in our report *Protecting and Promoting the Health of NFL Players: Legal and Ethical Analysis and Recommendations*, we discuss evidence from interviews with players who attest that such actions do occur in the NFL.[4] It is not known whether there is any prescribed punishment in any of the leagues if a club's medical staff fails to fully and accurately report player injuries. Beyond non-reporting by club medical staff, some injuries might not be documented because the athlete does not report the injury to the medical staff.

In particular, as other scholars have noted, concussions are underreported.[5] Diagnosing concussions requires review of various criteria, such as whether the player has balance problems, a blank or vacant look, disorientation, or cognitive issues.[6] Additionally, a concussion diagnosis often requires a player to self-report symptoms, such as headaches, dizziness, vision problems, and/or sensitivity to light or sound.[7] As a result of the varied diagnostic criteria and the ability of players to hide symptoms, concussion rates are likely higher than the reported statistics.

In light of the above, we emphasize that the injury statistics we provide in this Chapter reflect only those that are reported and that actual injury rates are likely higher. Aside from underreporting, our analysis is also limited by differences between the leagues, including scheduling, EMR systems, and injury definitions.

Injury severity is a potentially interesting statistic to calculate and compare. Indeed, several of the studies discussed below attempt to quantify injury severity by the amount of time players lost, *i.e.*, the number of practices or games a player missed. However, because the leagues' practice and game schedules vary considerably, a cross-league comparison of the severity data would not be useful. For example, NFL clubs play a 16-game regular season and practice four to five times per week. In contrast, MLB clubs play a 162-game regular season and have almost no practices during the season. An injury that might cause an MLB player to miss four or five games might not cause an NFL player to miss any games. Consequently, determining the severity of injuries by the number of games or practices missed does not provide for an accurate comparison across the leagues.[8]

Finally, in this Chapter, unless otherwise indicated, we are only comparing data from *regular season games*, not pre-season or post-season games or practices. We generally limit our analysis in this way because in many cases only regular season injury data are available. Additionally, several other domains we discuss such as the number of games, players, and plays, have more readily available and consistent data in the regular season, permitting better comparisons. Lastly, the number of practices per season in each of the sports varies considerably, making comparisons that include practices problematic. While this method results in reporting lower aggregate injury incidence, we believe statistics focused on injuries per regular season game, and

---

b   Nonetheless, we are uncertain what types of internal statistical analyses the leagues may be performing.

injuries per player-season[c] provide the best understanding of the incidence of injury in each sport.

2) INJURY STUDIES

In this Chapter, we utilize data from several studies concerning injury rates in the respective leagues. Several of these studies retrieved data from the leagues' injury tracking system. Consequently, those studies (and our use of that data) are limited in the same way that the injury tracking systems are limited, as discussed above. In addition, we identify other limitations of the studies that are relevant to our analysis. Despite these limitations, the studies we have used are the best publicly-available sources for injury data in the leagues and, we believe, provide useful data. Nevertheless, in light of these limitations and the limited number of studies, we caution the reader about interpreting our findings too strongly. Indeed, one important recommendation we make is that more research is needed on injury rates in the NFL, as well as more sharing of league data on injuries. Similarly, while our focus is on the NFL, it is likely desirable for the other leagues to engage in the same type of research.

3) CONCUSSIONS

Given the above concerns about underreporting of injuries, specifically concussions, it is also important to know what we mean by "concussion." The leading definition of a concussion comes from the 4th International Conference on Concussion in Sport held in Zurich, Switzerland, in November 2012, and published in the *British Journal of Sports Medicine*. The publication (identified by lead author Paul McCrory of the Florey Institute of Neuroscience and Mental Health in Australia) is a consensus statement from 28 of the leading sports medicine and sports concussion professionals, including many with ties to the leagues and unions.[9] The consensus statement (which improves on definitions from prior conferences) defines a concussion "as a complex pathophysiological process affecting the brain, induced by biomechanical forces."[10,d] In addition, the consensus statement lists symptoms and conditions associated with concussions, including headaches, cognitive impairment, behavioral and emotional changes, loss

of consciousness, amnesia, and sleep disturbance.[11] The NFL, MLB, NBA, NHL, and MLS concussion protocols specifically cite the consensus statement's criteria for a concussion.[12]

> The NFL, MLB, NBA, NHL, and MLS concussion protocols specifically cite the consensus statement's criteria for a concussion.

Given the nature of this Report, some may wonder why we are not providing analysis of each of the leagues' concussion protocols, that is, the policies that dictate how the clubs treat players who have suffered or are suspected of having suffered a concussion. We have chosen not to discuss these policies in depth because they are substantially similar. The consensus statement sets forth the leading medical opinion as to the appropriate process for evaluating a possible concussion, including the diagnostic tests to be performed (both pre-season and post-concussion), and a recommended return-to-play process, consisting of a graduated increase in activity, provided the player remains free of concussion-symptoms.[13] In reviewing the leagues' concussion protocols (or reports describing the protocols where the protocols themselves were not available), it is clear that all of the leagues' protocols are in line with the procedures recommended by the consensus statement.[14,e]

We acknowledge that at times questions have been raised as to whether certain leagues or clubs are sufficiently following the protocols.[15] While these are important questions, we were unable to find any objective data from which to

---

c   In this Chapter, we utilize the terminology commonly used by experts in sports injury data analysis. As such, the term "player-game" represents one player playing in one game. Similarly, the term "player-season" represents one player playing in one season regardless of how many games that player played in that season.

d   We also acknowledge that there are concerns about subconcussive impacts, Steven P. Broglio, et al., *Cognitive Decline and Aging: The role of Concussive and Subconcussive Impacts*, 40 Exerc. Sport Sci. Rev. 138 (2012), but are unaware of any data on this issue from the leagues discussed in this Report.

e   MLS' Concussion Evaluation and Management Protocol does contain two provisions that appear unique and potentially concerning. First, "[th]e Team Physician has the ultimate and absolute authority to decide when a player should be removed for evaluation[.]" In contrast, the NFL empowers both officials and independent athletic trainers to require a player to be removed from a game for evaluation. Second, while the MLS Protocol does require a player who has suffered a concussion to consult with the club's neuropsychologist, "[t]he team neuropsychologist should NOT communicate to the player whether he or she thinks that the player should/should not return to play." Instead, "[th]e Team Physician has the ultimate and absolute authority to decide . . . whether that player is fit to return to play." In the event of a conflict between the Team neuropsychologist and Team Physician, Dr. Ruben Echemendia, chair of MLS' concussion program, is to be consulted. Nevertheless, the player is being deprived of potentially important medical information concerning his health.

analyze the leagues' compliance. This is an issue that the leagues and unions must investigate and enforce.[f]

4) INJURY-RELATED LISTS

In this Chapter, we also discuss injury-related lists—a type of roster on which injured players are placed for a certain number of days or games. All of the leagues have such lists. The lists vary in their meaning and duration, potentially alleviating or creating pressure on the player to play through, or return from, an injury. We will discuss each league's approach to injury lists and analyze their effects in the Analysis Section.

* * *

With this background in hand we now turn to an analysis of each of the leagues on the relevant issues relating to player injuries.

A) Injuries in the NFL

1) INJURY TRACKING SYSTEM

In 1980, the NFL created the NFL Injury Surveillance System ("NFLISS") to document, track, and analyze NFL injuries and provide data for medical research.[16] When an injury occurs, each club's athletic trainer is responsible for opening an NFLISS injury form and recording the medical diagnosis (including location, severity, and mechanism of injury) and details about the circumstances (*e.g.*, date, game or practice, field surface) in which it occurred.[17] Prior to 2015, a reportable injury was defined as only those injuries, football-related or not, associated with any time lost from practice or games or specific conditions regardless of time lost, including but not limited to concussions, fractures, dental injuries requiring treatment, health-related illness

requiring IV fluid administration, and injuries or illness requiring special equipment (*e.g.*, a knee brace). Beginning with the 2015 season, all injuries, regardless of whether or not they result in time lost from practice or games, are included in the NFLISS.[18] The athletic trainer is required to update the injury form with details about all medical treatments and procedures the player receives, including surgery.[19] Since 2011, the NFLISS has been managed by the international biopharmaceutical services firm Quintiles.[20] Quintiles analyzes injury data and provides reports to the NFL and NFLPA throughout the year.[21]

The NFLISS provides the best available data concerning player injuries and we thus use it here. Although the NFL's past injury reporting and data analysis have been publicly criticized as incomplete, biased, or otherwise problematic, those criticisms have been in response to studies separate from the NFLISS[22] and we are not aware of any criticism of the NFLISS.[g] The next Section is a compilation of NFLISS data on player injuries, which was reviewed and updated (where necessary) by the NFL. However, in considering this data, it is important to recognize that the NFL's injury reporting systems have undergone substantial change in recent years. An electronic version of the NFLISS was launched as a pilot with five clubs in 2011;[23] the electronic NFLISS expanded to all 32 clubs in 2012;[24] then, in 2013, the NFL launched an electronic medical record ("EMR") system on a pilot basis with eight NFL clubs, which was expanded to all clubs in 2014.[25] The EMR system integrates with the NFLISS and provides the most accurate injury reporting data in NFL history. Consequently, the different reporting structures over time almost certainly contributed to fluctuations in the injury rates identified below. Therefore, it is not possible to be certain whether injury *rates* have increased in recent years, or if, instead, the apparent increases are due to improved injury *reporting,* or some combination of the two. Similarly, increased attention to player injuries in recent years, concussions in particular, might also lead to higher *reported* injury totals.

f   Indeed, the NFL in 2015 and the NHL in 2016 adopted policies whereby they discipline clubs for failing to comply with the concussion protocols. *See* James O'Brien, *NHL Plans on Fining Teams Who Violate New Concussion Protocol,* Pro Hockey Talk (Oct. 11, 2016, 6:30 PM), http://nhl.nbcsports.com/2016/10/11/nhl-plans-on-fining -teams-who-violate-new-concussion-protocol/, *archived at* https://perma.cc/34YL -VF85; Darin Gantt, *NFL to fine, suspend teams who don't follow injury protocols,* ProFootballTalk (Dec. 17, 2015, 6:00 AM), http://profootballtalk.nbcsports.com/2015 /12/17/nfl-to-fine-suspend-teams-who-dont-follow-injury-protocols/, *archived at* https://perma.cc/8CH3-77F9.

g   Other studies of NFL injury rates have been conducted using the clubs' publicly released injury reports. *See, e.g.,* David W. Lawrence, Paul Comper, and Michael G. Hutchison, *Influence of Extrinsic Risk Factors on National Football League Injury Rates,* Orthopaedic J. Sports Med. (2016); David W. Lawrence, Paul Comper, and Michael G. Hutchison, *Descriptive Epidemiology of Musculoskeletal Injuries and Concussions in the National Football League, 2012–2014,* Orthopaedic J. Sports Med. (2015). While these studies provide interesting analyses, NFL injury reports are not the best data source, for reasons discussed in Chapter 17: The Media of our Report, *Protecting and Promoting the Health of NFL Players: Legal and Ethical Analysis and Recommendations.*

2) INJURY STATISTICS

The tables below summarize key injury statistics of NFL players.

Table 2-A:
Number of Practice, Game, and Total Injuries in NFL Pre-season (2009–2015)[26]

Year	Number of Practice Injuries	Number of Game Injuries	Total Injuries
2009	551	360	911
2010	560	410	970
2011	641	399	1,040
2012	675	431	1,106
2013	688	416	1,104
2014	823	503	1,326
2015	780	498	1,278
Totals	**3,138**	**2,016**	**7,735**

Table 2-B:
Mean Number of Practice, Game, and Total Injuries in NFL Pre-season per Year, over 6 Seasons (2009–2015)[h]

Mean Number of Practice Injuries	Mean Number of Game Injuries	Mean Number of Total Injuries
623.0	403.2	1026.8

Table 2-C:
Number of Practice, Game, and Total Injuries, and Mean Number of Injuries Per Game in NFL Regular Season (2009–2015)[i]

Year	Number of Practice Injuries	Number of Game Injuries	Total Regular Season Injuries	Injuries per Regular Season Game
2009	165	1,372	1,537	5.36
2010	176	1,346	1,522	5.25
2011	295	1,426	1,721	5.57
2012	262	1,380	1,642	5.39
2013	264	1,500	1,764	5.86
2014	401	1,823	2,224	7.12
2015	336	1,730	2,066	6.76
Totals	**1,899**	**10,577**	**12,476**	**N/A**

h   As a reminder, the injury reporting systems have changed in recent years. Consequently, the figures cannot be strictly compared across the seasons and the mean is not definitively accurate.

i   Each year, there are 256 regular season NFL games. Thus, this figure is derived by dividing the number of injuries in the "Games" column by 256.

Table 2-D:
Mean Number of Practice, Game, and Total Injuries per Year, and Mean Number of Injuries per Game in NFL Regular season, over 6 seasons (2009–15)

Mean Number of Practice Injuries	Mean Number of Game Injuries	Mean Number of Total Regular Season Injuries	Mean Number of Injuries per Regular Season Game[j]
271.3	1,511.0	1,782.3	5.90

Table 2-E:
Number of Practice, Game, and Total Concussions, and Mean Number of Concussions per Game in NFL Regular Season (2009–16)[27]

Year	Number of Practice Concussions (Pre- And Regular Season)	Number of Preseason Game Concussions	Number of Regular Season Game Concussions	Total Concussions	Mean Number of Concussions per Regular Season Game
2009	25	40	159	224	.62
2010	45	50	168	263	.66
2011	37	48	167	252	.65
2012	45	43	173	261	.68
2013	43	38	148	229	.58
2014	50	41	115	206	.45
2015	38	54	183	272	.71
2016	32	45	167	244	.65
Totals	**315**	**359**	**1,280**	**1,951**	**N/A**

Table 2-F:
Mean Number of Practice, Game, and Total Concussions, and Mean Number of Concussions per Game in NFL Regular Season, over 8 Seasons (2009–16)[28]

Mean Number of Practice Concussions (Pre- And Regular Season)	Mean Number of Pre-season Game Concussions	Mean Number of Regular Season Game Concussions	Mean Number of Total Concussions	Mean Number of Concussions per Regular Season Game
39.4	44.9	160.0	243.9	.625

j   Each year, there are 256 regular season NFL games. Thus, this figure is derived by dividing the number of injuries in the "Games" column by 256.

Table 2-G:
Number of Regular Season Game Concussions per Player, and Mean Number of Regular Season Game Concussions per Player per Season (2009–2016)[k]

Year	Number of Regular Season Game Concussions	Number of Regular Season Players	Rate of Concussions per Player-Season
2009	159	2,123	0.075
2010	168	2,187	0.077
2011	167	2,144	0.078
2012	173	2,183	0.079
2013	148	2,188	0.067
2014	115	2,202	0.052
2015	183	2,251	0.081
2016	167	2,274	0.073
Totals/Rate	**1,112**	**15,278**	**0.073**

In considering the mean number of concussions per player-season, it is important to point out that the number of players who played in a regular season NFL game includes both players who played all 16 games in a season and those who played only 1 game in a season. Thus, while there is a mean of 0.073 concussions per player per regular season, the mean is likely different for different subsets of players, *i.e.*, depending on how many games a player played in that season.

Table 2-H:
Concussion Incidence by Player Position in the Regular Season (2013)

Position	2013
Offensive Line	19
Running Back	15
Tight End	16
Quarterback	6
Wide Receiver	17
Offense Total	**73 (49.3%)**
Defensive Secondary	25
Defensive Line	12
Linebacker	11
Defense Total	**48 (32.4%)**
Special Teams Total	**27 (18.2%)**

Table 2-I:
Mean Number of Injuries Per Play, NFL Regular Season Games (2013)

Total Number of Injuries	Total Number of Plays[l]	Mean Number of Injuries per Play[m]
1,500	43,090	0.035 injuries/play

k   The number of regular season players' statistics were obtained from official NFL and NFLPA playtime figures. To be clear, these statistics only include players who played in a regular season game and thus do not include players who only played in the pre-season.
l   This statistic was obtained from calculations derived from official NFL and NFLPA playtime figures.
m   This Report does not include per-play injury data for the other leagues as that data is generally not available and the definition of a "play" in other leagues can vary.

As shown in Table 2-I, the mean number of injuries per play in 2013 was 0.035, indicating that there was an injury on 3.5% of all plays. Additionally, from the available information regarding the total number of injuries, total number of players per game, games per year, and years of data, we can calculate the overall rate of injury as 0.064 per player-game.[n] In other words for every particular game there is a mean of 5.90 injuries (0.064 injuries per player-game x 92 players per game). That equates to one injury for every 15.6 players in that game.

We can also determine the mean rate of how often concussions occur in a game. Between 2009 and 2016 there were a total of 1,280 regular season concussions. Using the available information regarding the total number of concussions, total number of players per game, games per year, and years of data, we can calculate the overall rate of concussion per player-game as 0.0068 concussions per player-game.[o]

We can also determine the rate of injuries per player-season. During the 2009–15 seasons, there were a total of 15,278 player-seasons played.[p] During this same time period there were a total of 10,577 game injuries. This equates to an overall rate of 0.69 injuries per player-season (10,577/15,278). Some readers—particularly players—may be surprised that this statistic is not higher. It is important to remember that this statistic is the mean of *all* players who played in the NFL during these seasons, including players who might have only played in one game. Additionally, the statistic does not include injuries that occurred during pre-season practices or games or regular season practices. Thus, while helpful, this statistic is an incomplete picture of the injuries suffered by NFL players during the course of a season.

Readers might be interested in the mean number of games a player plays before suffering an injury. We calculated above that the rate of injuries per player-game was 0.064. Thus, we can calculate that players play a mean of 15.6 games before suffering one injury (1/0.064). We can also calculate the mean number of games a player plays before suffering a concussion. We calculated above that the rate of concussion per player-game was 0.0068. Thus, we can calculate

that players play a mean of 147.10 games before suffering one concussion (1/0.0068). With 16 regular season games, players theoretically play a mean of 9.2 seasons before suffering a concussion. For context, although there is a debate about career lengths generally, the mean career length for a *drafted* player is about 5 years.[q] Nevertheless, it is important to remember that these are *mean* statistics and thus include players who play very little in the game or players who play positions less likely to suffer injuries or concussions. Players with more game time and players at certain positions are likely to suffer injuries and/or concussions at rates higher than those provided here.

Finally, we can calculate what percentage of player injuries are concussions. Between 2009 and 2015, there were a total of 10,577 regular season injuries (Table 2-C). During this same time period, there were 1,113 regular season concussions (Table 2-E). Thus, concussions represented 10.5 percent of all regular season injuries (1,113/10,577).

Figure 2-A: NFL Regular Season Mean Number of Concussions as Compared to All Other Injuries

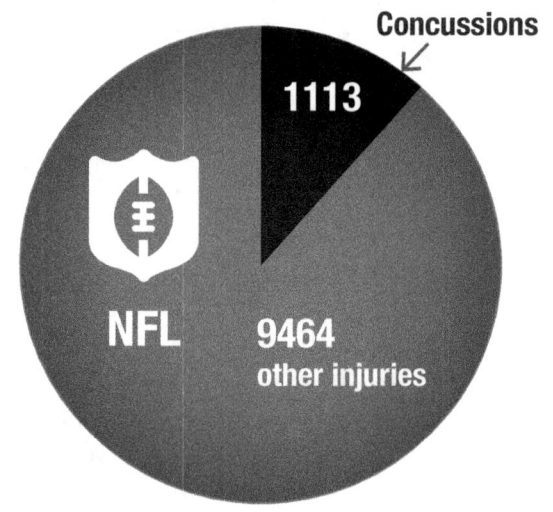

Concussions
1113

NFL
9464
other injuries

---

n   This statistic is calculated by dividing the total number of regular season game injuries from 2009–15 (10,577) by the total number of game exposures over the same time period (164,864). The 164,864 statistic is calculated by multiplying 7 seasons by 256 regular season games per season by 92 players per game. Clubs are limited to 46 active players during a game, 2011 NFL CBA, Art. 25, § 1, thus, 92 players have the opportunity to play each week.

o   This statistic is calculated by dividing the total number of regular season game concussions from 2009–16 (1,280) by the total number of game exposures over the same time period (188,416). The 188,416 statistic is calculated by multiplying 7 seasons by 256 regular season games per season by 92 players per game.

p   In other words, a mean of 2,182.6 players played in a regular season NFL game each season. The number of player-seasons was obtained from official NFL and NFLPA playtime figures.

q   The NFL and NFLPA disagree on the mean career length of NFL players. The NFLPA has long stated that the mean career is about 3.2 years. The NFL insists players' mean career length is about 6 years. The difference arises from which population of players is being examined. The NFLPA seems to include in their calculation every player who ever signed a contract with an NFL club, regardless of whether they ever make the club or play in an NFL regular season game, while also including players who are still active (and whose careers will thus exceed their current length). On the other hand, the NFL's calculation comes from players who made the opening day roster and that played between 1993–2002, a slightly different era from today's NFL. The website sharpfootballanalysis.com ultimately found that players who were drafted between 2002 and 2007 have a mean career length of 5.0 years. *Average NFL Career Length*, Sharp Football Analysis (Apr. 30, 2014), http://www .sharpfootballanalysis.com/blog/?p=2133, *archived at* http://perma.cc/KR58-R8DA.

Finally, below is some additional information from the NFLISS:[r]

- The most common types of injuries during regular season practices in 2013 were hamstring strains (46), groin adductor strains (10), high ankle sprains (6), and shoulder sprains (6).

- The five most common types of injuries during regular season games in 2013 were concussions (147), hamstring strains (approximately 128[s]), medical collateral ligament (MCL) sprains (approximately 76), high ankle sprains (approximately 58), and groin adductor strains (approximately 47).

- The most common mechanisms of concussions during regular season games in 2013 were contact with other helmets (49.0%), contact with the playing surface (16.3%), contact with another player's knee (10.2%), and contact with another player's shoulder (7.5%).

3) INJURY-RELATED LISTS

Injured NFL players are placed on different lists depending on the expected duration of the injury and the timing of the injury.

If a player fails the pre-season physical, i.e., the club doctor determines the player is not physically ready to play football, and is unable to participate in training camp but is expected to be able to play later in the season, the player can be placed on the Physically Unable to Perform ("PUP") List. A player on the PUP List cannot practice or play until after the sixth game of the regular season and does not count towards the club's 53-man Active/Inactive List during that time.[29]

Players who are injured during the pre-season or regular season and are unable to return that season are placed on Injured Reserve, which typically precludes them from practicing or playing further that season. Players on Injured Reserve do not count towards the club's 53-man Active/Inactive List. In 2012, the NFL and NFLPA amended the rules to permit clubs to allow one player in any season to return from Injured Reserve after a minimum of six weeks.[30]

Finally, players who suffer short-term injuries are only given a different status on the day of the game. NFL clubs have a 53-man Active/Inactive List.[31] This is the roster of players clubs have to choose from each week. On the day of the game, the number of players who are permitted to play, i.e., the Active List, is reduced to 46 players.[32] Thus, seven players are declared Inactive and cannot play on each game day. Generally, at least some of the seven players declared Inactive have been so declared due to injury (the rest would be for skill reasons). A player is Inactive for that particular game, but can be Active for the next game. In this way, the Inactive List serves as a short-term, non-durational injured list.

4) INJURY REPORTING POLICIES

The NFL's "Personnel (Injury) Report Policy" ("Injury Reporting Policy") requires each club to report information on injured players to both the NFL and the media each game week ("Injury Report").[33] The stated purpose of this reporting is "to provide a full and complete rendering of player availability" to all parties involved, including the opposing team, the media, and the general public.[34] According to the NFL, the policy is of "paramount importance in maintaining the integrity of the game,"[35] i.e., preventing gambling on inside information concerning player injuries.[36]

The Injury Report is a list of injured players, each injured player's type or location of injury, and the injured player's status for the upcoming game. Each injury must be described "with a reasonable degree of specificity," e.g., ankle, ribs, hand. For a quarterback's arm injury or a kicker's or punter's leg injury, the description must designate left or right. No other injuries require the side of the injury to be disclosed. Historically, the player's status for the upcoming game was classified into four categories: "Out (definitely will not play)"; "Doubtful (at least 75 percent chance will not play)"; "Questionable (50-50 chance will not play)"; and, "Probable (virtual certainty player will be available for normal duty)".[37] In 2016, the NFL changed the classifications for player injuries by: (1) eliminating the "probable" designation; (2) changing the definition of "questionable" to "uncertain as to whether the player will play in the game"; (3) changing the definition of "doubtful" to "unlikely the player will participate"; and, (4) only using the "out" designation two days before a game.[38] The Injury Report also indicates whether a player had full, limited, or no participation in practice, whether due to injury or any other cause (e.g., team discipline, family matter, etc.).

For a typical Sunday game, clubs must issue an Injury Report after practice each Wednesday, Thursday, and Friday of game week. If there are any additional injuries after the Friday deadline, the club must report these injuries to

---

r   This information is from the year-end NFLISS reports prepared by Quintiles for the year 2014, and the reports presented at the NFL's annual Health & Safety Press Conference during the week of the Super Bowl.

s   Statistics for injuries other than concussions are only available in bar graph form. Consequently, we estimate the injury figure based on the graph available.

the NFL, the club's opponent, the televising network, and the local media on Saturday and Sunday.

The Injury Reporting Policy dictates that all injury reports be "credible, accurate, and specific within the guidelines of the policy." In "unusual situations," clubs are requested to contact the League's public relations office and, when in doubt, clubs should include a player in the Injury Report. Clubs and coaches that violate the policy are subject to disciplinary action. If a question arises as to why a player did not participate in a game, the club can be required to provide a written explanation to the NFL within 48 hours.

Despite the enforcement system and disciplinary action for abuse (typically fines of $5,000 to $25,000[39]), many in the media along with coaches and players have questioned the Injury Report's accuracy and value. A 2007 *USA Today* analysis of two-and-a-half seasons of Injury Reports found a high variance in the number of injuries reported by teams, with 527 reported by the Indianapolis Colts versus just 103 by the Dallas Cowboys.[40] Interviews with coaches in that article as well as others suggested that the different philosophies of coaches to report even minor injuries versus only major injuries accounted for this variance.[41] In the same article, former Pittsburgh Steelers coach Bill Cowher was quoted as saying that he deliberately changed the location of injuries (*e.g.,* reporting hip instead of knee) to protect his players from having their injuries targeted by opponents.[42] Baltimore Ravens head coach Jim Harbaugh, after being fined for not listing an injured player in 2012, told the media that "[t]here's no credence on the injury report now . . . . It doesn't mean anything. It has no value."[43] In March 2014, two former players on the New England Patriots stated that head coach Bill Belichick filed inaccurate and false injury reports.[44] Many in the media have referred to the Injury Report as a "game" or "joke."[45] Nevertheless, some believed that the 2016 changes to the injury reporting policy allowed for even more gamesmanship.[46]

Many clubs have policies prohibiting players from speaking to the media about injuries.[47]

Finally, to facilitate the Injury Reporting Policy, clubs, request or require players to execute waivers permitting broad disclosure and use of their medical information.[48]

With this understanding of the NFL's policies, we can now begin our comparison to the other leagues.

B) Injuries in MLB

1) INJURY TRACKING SYSTEM

In 2010, MLB—with agreement and assistance from the MLBPA—launched a web-based electronic medical record ("EMR") system "designed to allow trainers to have more and better information at their fingertips."[49] The EMR system is linked to MLB's electronic Baseball Information System ("eBIS"),[50] that clubs use to complete the Standard Form of Diagnosis for Disabled List applications,[51] which will be discussed in more detail below. With the EMR system, clubs' athletic trainers enter data on "all injuries, illnesses, and preventative events"[52]—whether baseball-related or not.[53] In addition, the EMR system provides MLB with robust data, which—once de-identified and centralized in MLB's Health and Injury Tracking System ("HITS")—MLB can use to monitor, study, and analyze injuries in baseball.[54] "HITS includes any injury or physical complaint sustained by a player that affects or limits participation in any aspect of baseball-related activity (e.g., playing in a game, practice, warm up, conditioning, weight training)."[55]

2) INJURY STATISTICS

MLB's efforts to study injury data should serve as a model for other leagues. Since the creation of MLB's EMR and HITS systems, MLB has undertaken, in partnership with the Johns Hopkins University Bloomberg School of Public Health, to conduct and publish comprehensive studies of injuries by major and minor league baseball players for the purpose of amending policies and practices to better protect player health.[56] As of the fall of 2016, doctors affiliated with MLB and their research partners have published studies on overall injury trends,[57] hamstring injuries,[58] knee injuries,[59] hip and groin injuries,[60] and traumatic brain injuries,[61] in major and minor league players. Moreover, additional studies are forthcoming.[62]

In 2016, the researchers discussed above published a study describing the implementation of the EMR and HITS systems, which included aggregate MLB injury data, shown below in Table 2-J.[63] Importantly, "[f]or research studies, injuries are operationally defined as those that are work-related, did not occur in the off-season (i.e., occurred only [in] spring training, the regular season, or the postseason), were a primary diagnosis, and resulted in at least 1 day out of play."[64] In the Analysis Section at the end of this Chapter, we explain how this definition varies slightly from injury data we provide from other leagues.

Table 2-J:

Number of Injuries during Spring Training, the Regular Season, or Postseason over Five Seasons (2010–14)

Year	2010	2011	2012	2013	2014	Total
Injuries	2,076	1,641	1,347	1,270	1,249	**7,583**

Importantly, the number of injuries recorded in HITS is considerably more than the number of players placed on the Disabled List ("DL"), as shown in Table 2-K.

The DL is a roster designation for players "unable to render services because of a specific injury or ailment."[65] During the time players are on the DL, clubs are permitted to replace the player on the club's active roster. However, not all injured players are placed on the DL. DL designations only include injuries that result in time loss.[t] Thus, DL data underrepresents the actual total number of injuries and for that reason we do not use it here.

Between 2010 and 2014, there were 4,614 spring training games,[66] 12,150 regular season games,[67] and 32 postseason games,[68] for a total of 16,941 games. We can thus estimate that there are 0.45 injuries per game (7,583/16,941). It is important to note that injuries that would occur during practice are included in the total number of injuries and thus the actual mean number of injuries per game is probably lower. However, we think the number of injuries that occur during practice are minimal—players play 162 games in 183 days[69] and there are very limited practices during the season.[70]

Table 2-K:

Number of Disabled List Designations over Five Seasons (2010–14)[71]

Year	2010	2011	2012	2013	2014	Total
Designations	459	515	504	519	488	**2,485**

We can also calculate a rate of injuries per player-game. A 2015 study conducted by MLB's Medical Director Dr. Gary Green ("Green Study")[72,u] revealed that during the 2011 and 2012 seasons, players played a total of 138,085 regular season games.[73] During this same time period, there were 2,988 injuries.[74] However, these statistics include spring training and postseason injuries. From the data above, we know that 71.7% of all MLB games between 2010 and 2014 were regular season games (12,150/16,941). If we assume that the rate of injuries is constant among spring training, regular season, and postseason games,[v] we can estimate that between 2011 and 2012, there were 2,142 injuries in regular season games (2,988 x 71.7%). We can thus estimate that the rate of injuries per player-game during this time period is 0.016 (2,142/138,085) assuming players only suffer one injury per game.

Finally, we can calculate the rate of injuries per player-season. Approximately 1,337 players played in an MLB regular season game in 2014.[75] During 2014, there were 1,249 injuries. Thus, the rate of injuries per player during

the 2014 regular season was 0.93 per player-season (1,249/1,337). There are two important points concerning this statistic: (1) this statistic represents a per player per season statistic, regardless of whether they played one game or all 162 games; and, (2) there is likely variation in injury rates among the different positions on the field.

Between 2011 and 2014, the five most commonly injured body parts were upper leg (thigh) (724 injuries), shoulder/clavicle (672), hand/finger/thumb (501), elbow (430), and knee (410).[76]

We turn now to the incidence of concussions in MLB. The Green Study focused on exactly this issue.

The Green Study reported that there were 41 concussions in MLB during the 2011 and 2012 seasons, but only 36 occurred during games.[77] It is important to note that the Green Study acknowledged that the possible underreporting of concussions was a limitation of its study.[78] Nevertheless, the Green Study offers the most reliable data on MLB concussions and we thus use it here.

---

t   Between 1998 and 2015, the average duration of a player's time on the DL was 55.1 days. Stan Conte, Christopher L. Camp and Joshua S. Dines, *Injury Trends in Major League Baseball Over 18 Seasons: 1998–2015*, 45 Am. J. Orthopedics 116, 118 (2016).

u   According to MLB, the study was conducted pursuant to its partnership with Johns Hopkins and MLB did not provide any funding or financial support.

v   This is likely not the case, as more injuries may be suffered as the season goes on due to cumulative strain. *See* Randall Dick et al., *Descriptive Epidemiology of Collegiate Men's Baseball Injuries: National Collegiate Athletic Association Injury Surveillance System, 1988–89 through 2003–04*, 42 J. Athletic Training 183 (2007). Nevertheless, any variance in the injury rates is challenging to determine and thus proceed based on this assumption. While imperfect, we still believe the data and these calculations are sufficiently reliable and useful.

With 4,860 regular season MLB games occurring during these two seasons,[79] there is a mean of 0.007 concussions per game (36/4,860). From the available information regarding the total number of concussions, total number of players per game, games per year, and years of data, we can calculate the overall rate of concussion as 0.00026 per player-game.[w]

Finally, we can estimate the rate of concussions per player-season. As stated above, in 2014, 1,337 players played in an MLB regular season game. In the same year, players were placed on the DL due to a concussion or concussion-like symptoms 21 times.[x] Thus, in 2014, the rate of concussion per player-season was 0.016 (21/1,337).

The Green Study also examined the number of concussions by "athlete exposures," or "AE." The Green Study based the number of AEs on the actual number of games played by players.[80] This methodology resulted in 138,085 AEs over the two seasons. With 36 concussions occurring in the two seasons, that is the equivalent of 0.26 concussions per every 1,000 AEs, or, put another way, players experienced 0.26 concussions for every 1,000 games played. The Green Study also found that catchers experience more concussions than fielders,[81] and "struck by batted ball" is the most likely mechanism by which a player sustains a concussion.[82]

Readers might be interested in the mean number of games a player plays before suffering an injury. We calculated above that the rate of injuries per player-game was 0.016. Thus, we can calculate that players play a mean of 62.5 games before suffering one injury (1/0.016). We can also calculate the mean number of games a player plays before suffering a concussion. We calculated above that the rate of concussion per player-game was 0.00026. Thus, we can calculate that players play a mean of 3,846.15 games before suffering one concussion (1/0.00026). With 162 regular season games, players theoretically play a mean of 23.74 seasons before suffering a concussion. For context, the mean career length for a drafted player is about 5.6 years.[83] Nevertheless, it is important to remember that these are *mean* statistics and thus includes players who play very little in the game or players who play positions less likely to suffer injuries or concussions. Players with a lot of play time and players at

certain positions are likely to suffer injuries and/or concussions at rates higher than those provided here.

Finally, we can calculate what percentage of player injuries are concussions. In 2014, there were 1,249 injuries and 22 instances in which players were placed on the DL due to a concussion or concussion-like symptoms. Concussions thus represented 1.8% of all injuries (22/1,249).

Figure 2-B: MLB Regular Season Mean Number of Concussions as Compared to All Other Injuries

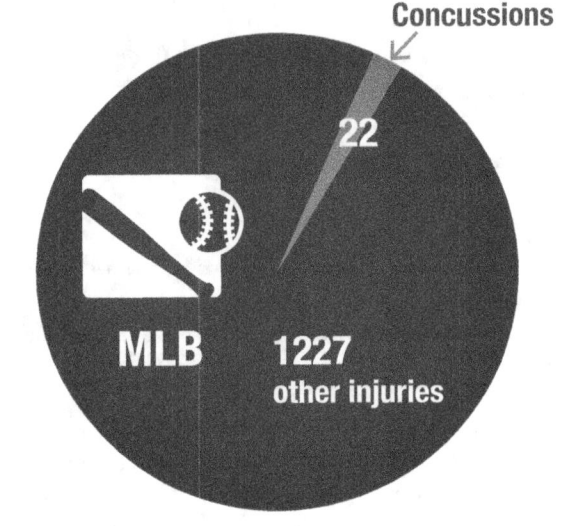

3) INJURY-RELATED LISTS

MLB has three DLs: a 7-day DL, which is exclusively for players who have suffered "acute" concussions;[84] a 10-day DL; and, a 60-day DL.[85] To place a player on one of the DLs, a club must submit an application to MLB that includes the Standard Form of Diagnosis (appended to the MLB CBA) and a separate document indicating the estimated time period of recovery.[86] The club doctor-prepared Standard Form of Diagnosis provides MLB with information about the nature of the player's injury (including "Body Side," "Part of Body Injured," and "Body Part Detail"), the date of the injury, and the club doctor's diagnosis.[87] MLB may request "that a Club provide additional information in support of a Disabled List placement before the application is approved[.]"[88] Once MLB has accepted a DL application, the player covered by the application must remain inactive for at least the number of days enumerated in the title of the DL to which he has been assigned.[89]

---

w   This statistic is calculated by dividing the total number of regular season game concussions from 2011–12 (41) by the total number of game exposures over the same time period (138,024). The 138,024 statistic is calculated by multiplying 2 seasons by 2,430 regular season games per season by 28.4 players per game. The Green Study provided that there were 69,043 games played per season. With 2,430 regular season games per season, we can thus calculate that a mean of 28.4 players play in each MLB game.

x   MLB has a 7-day DL "solely for the placement of players who suffer a concussion." 2012 MLB CBA, Att. 36, ¶ 2. Given the specific nature of this DL, there are likely very few (if any) instances in which a player suffered a concussion and was not placed on the DL.

4) INJURY REPORTING POLICIES

Unlike the NFL, MLB does not obligate clubs to report player injuries publicly. However, the CBA permits clubs to disclose the following "about *employment-related* injuries: (a) the nature of a Player's injury, (b) the prognosis and the anticipated length of recovery from the injury, and (c) the treatment and surgical procedures undertaken or anticipated in regard to the injury."[90] Despite this permission, club doctors are "prohibited from making any public disclosure of a Player's medical information absent a separate, specific written authorization from the Player authorizing such public disclosure."[91] Thus, club officials, such as coaches or the general manager (and not the doctor), are most likely the ones to update the media on player injuries.

As a matter of course, clubs effectively report injuries through roster transactions. An MLB club's active roster is limited to 25 players (except during September).[92] If a player is injured and placed on the DL, his spot on the active roster will be filled by another player. Clubs publicly update their active rosters and DL as needed. Thus, when a player is moved from the active roster to the DL, the club is indicating that the player is injured.

C) Injuries in the NBA

1) INJURY TRACKING SYSTEM

Since 2012, the NBA has employed an EMR system, called HealtheAthlete. Cerner Corporation, the creator of HealtheAthlete, describes the "secure electronic platform" as "enhanc[ing] the standard of medical record keeping for all NBA athletes."[93] The system allows each player to have an integrated record of their care, gives medical personnel easy access to these records, and improves the NBA's ability to track trends in player health and healthcare.[94] The EMR system also "allow[s] for authorized academic researchers to access the data (on a de-identified basis) and conduct studies designed to improve player health and broaden medical knowledge" (with the NBPA's approval, which cannot be unreasonably withheld).[95] The CBA specifically permits disclosures of player health information to be made via "secure systems" with EMRs to the extent that medical disclosures are otherwise allowed by the CBA.[96]

Prior to the EMR system, the National Basketball Athletic Trainers Association ("NBATA"), comprised of all athletic trainers working for an NBA club, maintained a record of "all injuries and illnesses sustained by NBA players."[97] An injury or illness was considered reportable if it: (1) required physician referral, prescription medication, or both; (2) resulted in a missed game or practice; or, (3) necessitated emergency care.[98] Entries into the NBATA system were "completed by the team's athletic trainer and cosigned by the team physician."[99] The reported data included pathology, time and place of injury or onset of illness, activity, and the mechanism of injury.[100] The HealtheAthlete system collects the same data formerly recorded by the athletic trainers.[101] In reviewing a draft of this Report, the NBA stated that the HealtheAthlete system also provides additional unspecified information. Additionally, since 2014, the NBA has worked with the international biopharmaceutical services firm Quintiles to analyze injury data and provide reports to the NBA and NBPA.[102]

2) INJURY STATISTICS

The most recent comprehensive study on NBA injury rates was led by Dr. Mark C. Drakos and published in *Sports Health* in 2010.[103] The study looked at injury data from the NBATA injury database for 17 seasons (1988–89 through 2004–05).[104] The Drakos study stated that it did not examine injury rates "for practices and pre-season games" due to "unreliable reporting methods and lack of a standardized protocol."[105] Given the source of the data, "injuries" as defined in the study included those: (1) requiring physician referral, prescription medication, or both; (2) resulting in missed games or practices; and, (3) those requiring emergency care.[106] Additionally, the study only included injury data for injuries that occurred during the NBA regular season.[107]

The Drakos study acknowledged that it was limited by the fact that the injury data may be underreported for a variety of reasons.[108] Additionally, the length of study complicates the analysis, as it seems likely that over the 17 seasons knowledge about injuries and attitudes towards reporting injuries changed, resulting in changes in the data over time. Nevertheless, the Drakos study provides the most reliable publicly-available data on NBA player injuries and we thus use it here.

Like the Green Study discussed above in MLB, the Drakos study examined injury rates through AEs, defined as "1 athlete appearing in 1 game."[109] During the time period studied, there were 6,287 injuries in regular season games.[110] The study determined there was an injury rate of 19.1 per 1,000 AEs.[111]

Using the data from the Drakos study, we can also calculate several other statistics. Over the 17 seasons, there was a mean of 369.8 injuries per season (6,287/17). Also, during the time period studied, there were 38,268 regular season NBA games.[y] Thus, there were 0.16 injures per regular season NBA game (6,287/38,268).

To determine additional statistics, we used data from basketball-reference.com for the 17 seasons covered by the Drakos study. During these seasons, players made a total of 387,673 game appearances. Thus, the injury rate per player-game was 0.016 (6,287/387,673). Additionally, during the seasons of the study, there were a total of 7,115 player-seasons.[z] Using the Drakos study's calculation of 6,287 injuries, we can calculate that the injury rate per player-season was 0.88 (6,287/7,115). Again, there are two important limitations to this statistic: (1) this statistic represents a per player-season statistic, regardless of whether he played one game or all 82 games; and, (2) there is likely variation in injury rates among the different positions on the court.

According to data in the Drakos study, the most commonly injured body parts during regular season games were ankles (66.1 injuries per season), knee (29.5), femur (28.4), lumbar spine (28.3), and tibia (25.4).[112] Ankle sprains (distinct from *all* ankle injuries) were the most common injury (62.7 per season).[113]

Concussions were among the least-reported injuries in the study. During the 17-year period, there were only 53 reported concussions that occurred during games, which accounted for only 0.8% of total injuries reported during games and contributed to only 0.4% of games missed.[114] With 38,268 games played during the period, a diagnosed concussion occurred only once every 722.0 games, or a mean of 0.0014 per game. Over the length of the Drakos study, the rate of concussion was 0.00014 per player-game (53/387,673). During the 2013–14 season, there were only nine reported concussions,[115] a mean of one every 136.7 games, or 0.007 per game. Players made 25,618 game appearances during the 2013–14 season,[116] and therefore suffered a per player-game concussion rate of 0.00035 (9/25,618). Additionally, during the 2013–14 season, 483 players played in the NBA. Thus, there were 0.019 concussions reported per player-season (9/483).

Readers might be interested in the mean number of games a player plays before suffering an injury. We calculated above that the rate of injuries per player-game was 0.016. Thus, we can calculate that players play a mean of 62.50 games before suffering one injury (1/0.016). We can also calculate the mean number of games a player plays before suffering a concussion. We calculated above that the rate of concussion per player-game was 0.00035. Thus, we can calculate that players play a mean of 2,857.14 games before suffering one concussion (1/0.00035). With 82 regular season games, players theoretically play a mean of 34.8 seasons before suffering a concussion. For context, the mean career length for a player is about 4.8 years.[117] Nevertheless, it is important to remember that this is a *mean* statistic and thus includes players who play very little in the game. Players with more game time are likely to suffer concussions at rates higher than those provided here.

Finally, as stated above, during the time period of the Drakos Study (1988–2005), concussions represented only 0.8% of game injuries. Based on increased attention to concussions since 2005, it seems likely that this proportion has increased. However, we do not have more recent injury data against which to compare recent concussion data.[aa] For this reason, we also do not provide a Figure showing concussions as a percentage of injuries, as we do for the NFL, MLB, and NHL.

3) INJURY-RELATED LISTS

NBA rosters are generally limited to 15 players, divided between an Active List and an Inactive List.[118] A club typically has 12 or 13 players on its Active List, who are eligible to play in games, and then has 2 to 3 players on the Inactive List who cannot play.[119] While NBA clubs generally place their injured players on the Inactive List, healthy players can also be on the Inactive List.[120] Thus, the NBA has no list specific to injured players. Moreover, players are not required to be on the Inactive List for any specific period of time. Consequently, like in the NFL, NBA clubs can declare players inactive for as little as one game at a time.

4) INJURY REPORTING POLICIES

Like the NFL, the NBA obligates clubs to report player injuries publicly, including the nature of the player's injury.[121] The CBA authorizes each club to make public

---

y   NBA clubs play 82 games a season, except in the 1998–99 season they only played 50 due to a lockout. Additionally, the NBA added clubs prior to the 1989–90, 1995–96 and 2004–05 seasons.

z   This statistic was calculated by adding together the number of players who played in at least one NBA game in each of the 17 seasons covered by the Drakos study. During the seasons in question, a range of 353 to 464 players would make an appearance in an NBA game during any given season.

aa   If we assume that the total number of player injuries in a season has remained constant at the mean of 369.8 observed during the period studied in the Drakos Study, we can calculate that the 9 concussions that occurred during the 2013–14 season represented 2.4% of all player injuries (369.8/9). Nevertheless, because the data is not from the same year, this calculation method is of questionable validity.

injury information relating to its players, so long as the information relates solely to the reasons that a player is not rendering his services as a player.[122] Further, a player or his immediate family (where appropriate) "shall have the right to approve the terms and timing of any public release of medical information relating to any injuries or illnesses suffered by that player that are potentially life- or career-threatening, or that do not arise from the player's participation in NBA games or practices."[123]

In practice, NBA clubs release injury reports prior to every game, describing a player's status (out, doubtful, questionable, probable) and the nature of the player's injury, including the injured body part.

D) Injuries in the NHL

1) INJURY TRACKING SYSTEM

The NHL's injury tracking system is part of the Athlete Health Management System ("AHMS"). The AHMS is the NHL's "electronic health records system focusing on the diagnosis, treatment and rehabilitation of injuries suffered by athletes in the course of athletic competition and training."[124] The AHMS "has an injury surveillance component," which requires "NHL Athletic Team Trainers/Therapists and Team Physicians [to] document[] all injuries using a standardised 'injury/illness event' (IIE) form for each event causing a player to miss one or more games."[125] "Medical staff [are] also instructed to create an IIE for each event needing medical assessment and treatment, regardless of time loss."[126]

2) INJURY STATISTICS

The most comprehensive study on NHL injury rates was led by Carly McKay and published in the *British Journal of Sports Medicine* in 2014.[127] The study looked at injury data from the AHMS for six seasons (2006–07 through 2011–12).[128]

The McKay study acknowledged that it was limited by the potential underreporting of injuries,[129] as is a common and complex occurrence in injury surveillance. Additionally, it acknowledged the possibility that athletic trainers' practices in reporting injuries vary among the clubs.[130] Nevertheless, the McKay study provides the best available data on NHL player injuries and we thus use it here.

Like the MLB and NBA studies discussed above, the McKay study examined injury rates through AEs. This study defined 1 AE as 1 player participating in 1 game.[131] During the time period studied, there were 4,368 injuries during regular season games.[132] Thus, using this methodology, there was an injury rate of 15.58 injuries per 1,000 AEs.

However, the study also presented injury rates per hours of ice time, where exposure was measured in terms of the number of hours on the ice. Using this methodology, the study determined that there were 49.4 injuries per 1,000 hours on the ice.[133] The study explained that the approximately threefold increase in injury rate is due to the fact that no player (other than the goaltender) plays the entire 60-minute game.[134]

Using the data from the McKay study, we can also calculate several other statistics. During the time period studied, there were 7,380 NHL regular season games.[135] Thus, there were 0.59 injuries per game (4,368/7,380).

From the available information regarding the total number of injuries, total number of players per game, games per year, and years of data, we can calculate the overall rate of injury per player-game as 0.015.[ab] Additionally, during the seasons of the study, there were a total of 5,145 player-seasons.[136] With 4,386 injuries during this span, there was thus a mean of 0.85 injuries per player-season (4,386/5,145). Again, there are two important limitations to this statistic: (1) this statistic represents a per player-season rate, regardless of whether they played one game or all 82 games; and, (2) there is likely variation in injury rates among the different positions on the ice.

The study found that the most common injuries were to the head (16.8%), thigh (14.0%), and knee (13.0%).[137] Additionally, body checks were the most frequent cause of injury at 28.6%.[138]

ab This statistic is calculated by dividing the total number of regular season game injuries from 2006–12 (4,368) by the total number of game exposures over the same time period (299,136). The 299,136 statistic is calculated by multiplying 6 seasons by 1,312 regular season games per season by 38 players per game. Although NHL clubs are permitted to have 20 players active for each game, *see* Jay Levin, *The Business of the Game: Roster Limits*, Nashville Predators, July 11, 2008, http://predators.nhl.com/club/news.htm?id=439739, *archived at* http://perma.cc/W9FB-MUW8 (describing a 20-player 'dressed list' for games); *Bounty of riches for Carbonneau; Wounded return*, Montreal Gazette, Oct. 17, 2008, *available at* 2008 WLNR 28430795 (Montreal Canadians coach discussing challenge of choosing which 20 players will dress for the game), the backup goalie normally does not play, making 19 players per game per club a more accurate statistic. *See* Brian Benson et al., *A Prospective Study of Concussions Among National Hockey League Players During Regular Season Games: The NHL-NHLPA Concussion Program*, 183 Canadian Med. Ass'n J. 905, App. 2 (2011) (basing athlete-exposure calculations on only "one goalie playing per team, per game").

Turning to concussions in the NHL, there are two principal studies.[ac] In an independent study led by Dr. Richard A. Wennberg and published in the *Canadian Journal of Neurological Sciences* in 2008 examined concussion as reported in the media for ten NHL seasons (1997–98 through 2007–08).[139] While media reported concussion data is not the ideal data set, the NHL and NHLPA declined our requests for data on the number of concussions suffered over the last ten years. The Wennberg study concluded that the concussion incident rate during these seasons was 1.45 per 1,000 AEs, with an AE defined as one player playing in one NHL game.[140] The Wennberg study reported that there was a total of 688 concussions over the ten years studied,[141] which we can calculate equals a mean of 68.8 reported concussions per season, or .058 per regular season game.[ad] From data provided by the Wennberg study, we can calculate that player exposures (*i.e.*, games played) was a total of 477,240 games during the seasons studied.[142] Thus, the rate of concussions per player-game is 0.0014 (0.688/477,240).

In 2011, the doctors in charge of the NHL/NHLPA Concussion Program[143] published their own study concerning NHL concussion rates.[144] The NHL/NHLPA study examined concussions reported by club doctors on standardized injury reporting forms for the seasons of 1997–98 through 2003–04.[145] The NHL/NHLPA study reported a total of 559 concussions during the time period studied,[146] equaling a mean of 79.9 concussions per season, or 0.068 per regular season game.[ae] If we estimate that 38 players play per game,[af] we can estimate that during the seasons analyzed by the NHL/NHLPA study, players played a total of 313,158 games.[ag] Thus, according to the data from the NHL/NHLPA study, the rate of concussions per player-game is

0.0018 (559/313,158). The NHL/NHLPA study also calculated those statistics as the equivalent of 1.8 concussions per 1,000 player-hours on the ice.[147]

As awareness of concussions has grown, and reporting of concussions has likely improved, more recent data concerning concussions are more useful. The NHL does not make its concussion data publicly available like the NFL, but, nevertheless, it was reported that there were 78 concussions during the 2012–13 regular season and 53 concussions during the 2013–14 regular season.[148] However, because of a work stoppage, there were only 48 games during the 2012–13 regular season, rather than the normal 82. We can extrapolate that 78 concussions during 48 regular season games is the equivalent of 133 concussions during a normal 82 game regular season.[ah] 53 concussions reportedly suffered during a full-length 2013–14 regular season is considerably less (60.2%) than the 133 concussions during a hypothetical full-length 2012–13 regular season, which necessarily calls the data into question. Nevertheless, as stated earlier, the NHL and NHLPA declined to provide more recent or reliable data on concussions and thus we rely on the best available data.

There were a total of 1,950 regular season games in the 2012–13 and 2013–14 regular seasons.[ai] With 131 concussions having occurred during these season, we can calculate that a concussion occurred once every 14.9 regular season games,[aj] equivalent to a rate of 0.067 per regular season game.[ak] Again, estimating that 38 players play per game, we can estimate that players played a total of 74,100 games during the 2012–13 and 2013–14 seasons.[al] We can thus calculate that the rate of concussions per player-game during those seasons was 0.0018 (131/93,480). This rate is slightly more than that from the Wennberg study and matches the rate calculated using data from the NHL/NHLPA study.

---

ac An additional study on concussions in the NHL worth considering is Michael G. Hutchison et al., *A systematic video analysis of National Hockey League (NHL) concussions, part 1: who, when, where and what?* Br. J. Sports Med. 1 (2013). This study analyzed the situational factors associated with concussions in the NHL, such as contact with an opponent and position. The study analyzed concussions that occurred during the 2006–07, 2007–08, 2008–09, and 2009–10 seasons. However, the analysis did not include all concussions that occurred during the 2009–10 season. Instead, the authors stopped their data collection as of December 31, 2009. Consequently, the data from this study is not the best data for determining the number of concussions that occur during an NHL regular season.

ad This statistic was calculated by dividing 688 concussions by 11,931 regular season games. There are 82 regular season games in the NHL each season. The number of games per season, however, depends on the number of clubs. There were 26 clubs in 1997–98, 27 in 1998–99, 28 in 1999–00, and 30 from 2000–01 and beyond. Thus, the total number of games played by clubs during this time equals 23,862 [(26 clubs x 82 games x 1 season) + (27 clubs x 82 games x 1 season) + (28 clubs x 82 games x 1 season) + (30 clubs x 82 games x 7 seasons)]. Because each game involves two clubs, you then divide the total number of games (23,862) by 2 to reach the number of unique games.

ae This statistic was calculated by dividing 559 concussions by 8,241 regular season games. The 8,241 regular season game statistic was calculated using the same methodology as described in footnote ad.

af *See* footnote ab for an explanation of this assumption.

ag This statistic was calculated by multiplying 8,241 regular season games (*see* footnote ad for methodology) by 38 players per game.

ah This statistic is calculated by dividing 82 by regular season games by 48 regular season games and multiplying it by 78 concussions that occurred during the shortened 2012–13 regular season.

ai The number of games in the 2012–13 season is calculated by multiplying 30 clubs x 48 regular season games and then dividing by 2 clubs per game, to reach 720 games. The number of games in the 2013–14 season is calculated by multiplying 30 clubs x 82 regular season games and then dividing by 2 clubs per game, to reach 1,230 games. 720 + 1,230 = 1,950.

aj This statistic was calculated by dividing 1,950 regular season games over the two seasons by 131 concussions.

ak This statistic was calculated by dividing 131 concussions by 1,950 regular season games.

al This statistic is calculated by multiplying 1,950 regular season games over the two seasons by 38 players.

We can also try to calculate the number of concussions per player-season. Using the extrapolated concussion data for the 2012–13 season, we can estimate a hypothetical total of 186 concussions during the 2012–13 and 2013–14 seasons. Using data from the McKay study, we can calculate that there during the time period studied (2006–12), a mean of 857.3 players played each season.[149] If we assume that the mean number of players played for the 2012–13 and 2013–14 seasons was the same as during the time period of the McKay study, we can estimate that there are 0.108 concussions per player-season (186/1,714.6).[am]

Readers might be interested in the mean number of games a player plays before suffering an injury. We calculated above that the rate of injuries per player-game was 0.016. Thus, we can calculate that players play a mean of 62.5 games before suffering one injury (1/0.016). We can also calculate the mean number of games a player plays before suffering a concussion. We calculated above that the rate of concussion per player-game was 0.0018. Thus, we can calculate that players play a mean of 555.56 games before suffering one concussion (1/0.0018). With 82 regular season games, players theoretically play a mean of 6.8 seasons before suffering a concussion. For context, the mean career length for a player is about 5.6 years.[150] Nevertheless, it is important to remember that this is a *mean* statistic and thus includes players who play very little in the game. Players with more game time are likely to suffer concussions at rates higher than those provided here.

Finally, by combining data from the different studies, we can estimate what percentage of player injuries are concussions. The McKay study found that there was a mean of 728 injuries per season during the 2006–07 through 2011–12 regular seasons. Again in an effort to use the most recent data, there was an estimated mean of 93.0 concussions per season during the 2012–13 and 2013–14 regular seasons, assuming the 2012–13 season was normal length (186/2). Based on these statistics, we can estimate that 12.8% of regular season injuries are concussions (93/728).[an]

Figure 2-C: NHL Regular Season Mean Number of Concussions As Compared to All Other Injuries

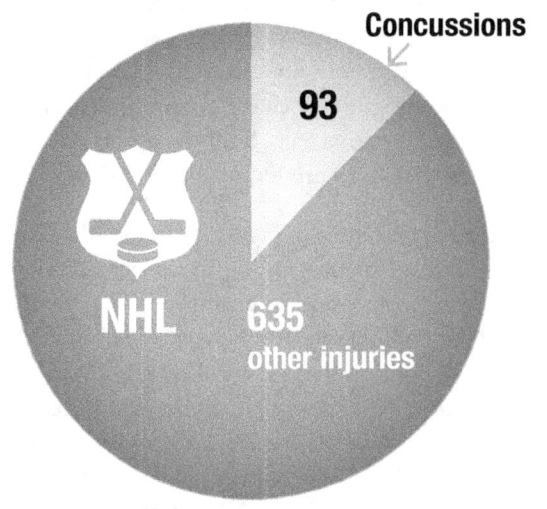

3) INJURY-RELATED LISTS

Like the NFL, injured NHL players are placed on different lists depending on the expected duration of the injury and the timing of the injury.

First, the Injured Reserve List ("IR") is for a player "reasonably expected to be injured, ill or disabled and unable to perform his duties as a hockey Player for a minimum of seven (7) days from the onset of such injury, illness or disability."[151] NHL club rosters are limited to 23 players.[152] During the time a player is on IR, the club can replace him on the roster.[153]

Second, players who fail the pre-season physical are placed on the Injured Non-Roster list.[154] A player on the Injured Non-Roster list does not count against the club's 23-man roster.[155] NHL clubs are permitted to have up to 50 players under contract,[156] thus, the purpose of the Injured Non-Roster list is unclear.

Third, like the NFL, players injured for only a short period of time are only temporarily declared inactive. NHL clubs have 23-man rosters. But clubs are only permitted to have 20 players play in each game. Thus, clubs declare three players inactive for each game. As in the NFL, the players declared inactive are frequently players with an injury that is expected to keep them out of only for a game or two.

---

am Readers should be cautioned that this calculation applies statistics from the time period of the McKay study to other years. In normal statistical methods, this is not preferred as it makes assumptions that various considerations do not change over time. We are unaware of any policy or practice changes that would have caused a meaningful change in the number of players per regular season between the years of the McKay study (2006–12) and the years of the most recent concussion data (2012–14). However, we again caution that we are extrapolating data from the 2012–13 season as if it were a full 82 game regular season.

an As explained in the preceding footnote, this estimate is limited by the fact that we are comparing data from two different time periods.

4) INJURY REPORTING POLICIES

Like the NFL, the NHL requires clubs to report publicly information about player injuries. Specifically, clubs are "required to disclose that a player is expected to miss a game due to injury, or will not return to a game following an injury."[157] Additionally, "Clubs are prohibited from providing untruthful information about the nature of a player injury or otherwise misrepresenting a player's condition."[158]

The CBA authorizes clubs to publicly disclose the nature of a player's injury, the prognosis and anticipated recovery time, and the treatment and surgical procedures that have been or will be undertaken.[159],[ao] Nevertheless, unlike in the NFL, clubs are not required "to disclose the specific nature of player injuries."[160] Accordingly, individual clubs may disclose information as they see fit, and designations such as "upper-body injury" and "lower-body injury" are both common and acceptable.[161] The NHL may fine clubs for failing to abide by the policy, but the NHL does not publicly disclose those fines.[162]

E) Injuries in the CFL

1) INJURY TRACKING SYSTEM

Research has not revealed any injury tracking system in use by the CFL.

2) INJURY STATISTICS

There has not been a comprehensive study of general injury rates in the CFL, perhaps because CFL clubs are not required to publicly report injuries, as will be discussed below.[163]

In 2010, the CFL implemented a concussion protocol, requiring the standardization of concussion reporting and allowing the League to more accurately track concussions.[164] In the first year of the new protocol, there were 50 reported concussions in 85 CFL games for a mean of 0.59 per game.[165] It is unclear whether this data includes pre-season or postseason games.[166]

The CFL does not publicize its concussion data in the same manner as the NFL. Thus, it is challenging to find more recent statistics concerning the number of concussions in the CFL. However, in a 2015 news article, Dr. Dhiren Naidu, the club doctor for the CFL's Edmonton club, stated that in 2014, there was a mean of slightly more than eight concussions per club.[167] With nine CFL clubs, that means there were slightly more than 72 concussions in the CFL in 2014. In the same article, it was reported that concussions in the CFL "dropped by 25 percent in 2015."[168] Thus, if we assume that the number of concussions in 2014 was 76 (which is closer to eight per club than nine per club), a 25% reduction would mean that there were 57 concussions in 2015. Thus, in 2015, there was an estimated mean of 0.704 concussions per game.[ap]

Using this estimated number of concussions in 2015, total number of players per game, and games per year, we can calculate a rate of 0.0080 concussions per player-game.[aq] With this statistic we can also calculate that the mean number of games a player plays before suffering one concussion is 125.0 (1/0.0080). With 18 regular season games, players theoretically play a mean of 6.9 seasons before suffering a concussion. Nevertheless, it is important to remember that this is a *mean* statistic and thus includes players who play very little in the game or players who play positions less likely to suffer concussions. Players who play a lot and players at certain positions are likely to suffer concussions at rates higher than those provided here.

3) INJURY-RELATED LISTS

CFL clubs maintain a 44-player active roster, a two-player reserve list,[169] and a 10-player practice-squad roster.[170] In the event that a player is injured, his club may place him on either a six-game or one-game Injured List, depending on the severity of the injury.[171] Players on either Injured List do not count toward the club's roster limits.[172]

---

ao Despite the authorizations contained in the CBA, *in re: Nat'l Hockey League Players' Concussion Injury Litigation,* 120 F. Supp.3d (D. Minn. 2015), the Court expressed that the NHL's disclosure of player medical information might violate the Americans with Disabilities Act ("ADA") confidentiality provisions. *See id.* at 951.

ap This statistic is calculated by dividing the estimated number of concussions (57) by the total number of games in a regular season (81). We can calculate that there are 81 regular season games by multiplying the number of CFL clubs (9) by the number of regular season games each club plays (18), and dividing by two to factor in that in each game there are two clubs playing.

aq This statistic is calculated by dividing the estimated number of concussions (57) by the total number of game exposures over the same time period (7,128). The 7,128 statistic is calculated by multiplying 81 regular season games per season by 88 players per game. CFL clubs maintain a 44-player active roster. *Rosters Glossary,* CFLDB, https://cfldb.ca/glossary/rosters/ (last visited Sept. 22, 2015), *archived at* http://perma.cc/77LF-2E4Y.

4) INJURY REPORTING POLICIES

The CFL does not require public disclosure of injuries, but clubs report injuries to the CFL through the process of placing a player on the Injured List, and clubs must report concussions to the League.[173]

F) Injuries in MLS

1) INJURY TRACKING SYSTEM

Like the NBA, MLS uses the "HealtheAthlete" EMR system for recording player medical information and tracking injuries.[174] Cerner Corporation, the creator of HealtheAthlete, describes the "secure electronic platform" as providing the ability to "improve the standard of medical record keeping for injured athletes, as well as ease communication between the athlete's key care providers."[175] Additionally, according to Cerner, the platform "allows MLS athletic trainers to increase the accuracy of injury documentation by accessing the platform from any location and integrating care-related media, like notes, X-rays, and MRIs, directly into the athlete's injury report."[176] Athletic trainers are required to "document soccer related Player complaints, injuries, treatments, [and] medications, including over-the-counter medications[.]"[177]

2) INJURY STATISTICS

The only study ever done of MLS injury rates was performed by San Jose Earthquakes athletic trainer Bruce E. Morgan following MLS' inaugural 1996 season.[178] The study determined that MLS players suffered injuries at a rate of 35.3 per 1,000 hours of game play.[179]

Data from the MLS' HealtheAthlete system are not publicly available and thus it is difficult to provide current MLS injury data. More helpful data can be derived from studies or reports concerning injury rates in the Union of European Football Associations ("UEFA"), a European soccer organization whose members generally include the best soccer clubs in the world and who play in some of the best soccer leagues in the world (such as the English Premier League and Spain's La Liga). While UEFA and MLS are different soccer organizations, we nonetheless believe that data from UEFA, an elite soccer organization like MLS, can be instructive of the injury rates in MLS. Indeed unless and

until MLS makes its own data public, we think the UEFA data provides the best proxy estimate of the underlying injury rate in that league.

In 2014, UEFA released a report on injuries suffered by players playing for a selection of 29 (out of 54) UEFA member clubs ("UEFA Report").[180] The UEFA Report does not provide a definition for a reportable injury. Nevertheless, the UEFA Report stated that the mean match injury incidence for all clubs was 23.2 injuries per 1,000 hours of match play during the 2013–14 season.[181] Additionally, a study done of UEFA injuries from 2001 to 2008 determined that players suffered injuries at a rate of 27.5 per 1,000 hours of game play.[182]

The UEFA Report acknowledges two relevant limitations. First, it acknowledged that the Report only includes injuries from one season.[183] Second, the UEFA Report acknowledged that there is variation among the clubs in injury incidence,[184] which might be explained by different practices in the reporting of injuries. For example, the UEFA Report does not discuss a standardized injury reporting system or process among the clubs. Nevertheless, the UEFA Report provides the most reliable data on UEFA player injuries and we thus use it here.

The UEFA Report determined that the body parts most commonly injured during games are thigh (27.0%), knee (17.5%), ankle (14.6%), hip/groin (13.8%), and lower leg/Achilles tendon (7.6%).[185]

Using the data from the UEFA Report, we can also calculate several other statistics. The UEFA Report included data from 29 clubs.[186] Additionally, the UEFA Report found there to be a total of 739 injuries from games,[187] for a mean of 25.5 injuries per club for the 2013–14 season (739/29).

The UEFA report also reported that the clubs participating in the study played a mean of 59 games,[188] for a total of 1,711 games played by the clubs (59 x 29). To provide an accurate analysis of the injuries per game, we can only count games in which the clubs played against one another as one game, i.e., we only count the unique games. We thus reviewed the 2013–14 seasons of the 29 clubs (which participate in 12 different leagues) and determined that the clubs played 327 games against one another. Thus, the clubs played in a total of 1,384 unique games (1,711 less 327). With this number of games, we can calculate that there were 0.53 injuries per UEFA game (739/1,384).

We can also calculate injury rates per player. Data on player participation during the 2013–14 season was not readily available. Thus, we make our best estimates. There are generally 11 players per club in a soccer game at a time.

FIFA's[189] rules limit clubs to three substitutions in official games.[190] Thus, we can estimate that 14 players play in each game per club, assuming clubs use all of their substitutions. As a result, we can estimate that were 19,376 player appearances during 2013–14 games (14 x 1,384). We can then estimate a rate of 0.038 injuries per player-game (739/19,376). We again remind the reader there is likely variation among the different positions on the field.

The UEFA Report found that the most common injuries were to the thigh (27.1%), knee (18.5%), and hip/groin (14.5%).[191]

The UEFA Report reported 14 concussions during games.[192] Using the above statistic of 1,384 unique games, we can calculate a mean of 0.010 concussions per game (14/1,384). With an estimated 19,376 player appearances, we can thus also estimate that the rate of concussion per player-game was 0.00072 (14/19,376).

Readers might be interested in the mean number of games a player plays before suffering an injury. We calculated above that the rate of injuries per player-game was 0.038. Thus, we can calculate that players play a mean of 26.32 games before suffering one injury (1/0.038). We can also calculate the mean number of games a player plays before suffering a concussion. We calculated above that the rate of concussion per player-game was 0.00072. Thus, we can calculate that players play a mean of 1,388.89 games before suffering one concussion (1/0.00072). Nevertheless, it is important to remember that this is a *mean* statistic and thus includes players who play very little in the game. Players who play a lot are likely to suffer concussions at rates higher than those provided here.

Finally, we can calculate what percentage of injuries were concussions. The UEFA report found that 14 of 739 injuries were concussions, equal to 1.9%.

MLS, without explanation, has refused to publicly release data on the number of concussions suffered by its players.[193]

3) INJURY-RELATED LISTS

MLS club rosters are limited to 28 players.[194] Injured players can be placed on two different lists, depending on the severity of the injury.

First, players with "short-term" injuries are placed on the Disabled List ("DL") and replaced on the roster with another player.[195] The player must remain on the DL for a minimum of six matches.[196]

Second, players who have suffered season-ending injuries are placed on the Season Ending Injury List.[197] These players are then replaced on the club's roster.[198]

4) INJURY REPORTING POLICIES

Like NFL clubs, MLS clubs are required to submit injury reports about players' statuses.[199] MLS requires clubs to include in their "Match Notes" information about player injuries.[200] Match Notes are programs of pre-game information including rosters, statistics, and other information about the game that are publicly available. In the Match Notes, the clubs must designate a player either as "out" or "questionable," indicate the affected part of the body, and provide an injury diagnosis.[201] According to the MLS Medical Manual, the "injury reports should be as accurate as possible."[202]

Policies concerning the public reporting of injuries can seem somewhat contradictory. The CBA dictates that public reporting of player injuries be limited to medical information relating to why the player "ha[s] not been, [is] not, or may not be rendering playing services as an MLS player."[203] However, the MLS Medical Manual directs that "[i]n circumstances where a player injury or illness requires a complex medical examination (e.g., to review a surgical procedure)," the club doctor or athletic trainer can publicly describe "the nature of the injury or illness, the prescribed treatment or rehabilitation, and the excepted timing of the player's return to action."[204] While the MLS Manual does say the club doctor or athletic trainer should first consult with the player,[205] there is no indication the player can prevent the club doctor or athletic trainer from discussing his medical condition.

G) Analysis

Tables 2-L and 2-M on the next page summarize some of the key injury-related statistics and policies. Nevertheless, it is important to understand the limitations of the injury statistics. At the beginning of this Chapter, we identified various limitations with analyzing injury statistics, including that injuries in sports are likely underreported and that there are important differences between the leagues including practice and game scheduling, EMR systems, and injury definitions. Moreover, for each of the leagues, we described various limitations or statistical assumptions we made to calculate the statistics discussed in these tables. Additionally, for the reasons discussed above, the injury statistics for MLS include MLS-specific data as well as the data provided by the UEFA Report.

Table 2-L:
Comparison of Leagues' Regular Season Injury Statistics[ar]

	NFL	MLB	NBA	NHL	CFL[as]	UEFA	MLS[at]
Electronic Tracking System	Yes	Yes	Yes	Yes	No	N/A[au]	Yes
Mean Injuries Per Season[av]	1,511.0	1,516.6	369.8	728.0	N/A	N/A	N/A
Rate of Injuries Per Player-Season	0.69	0.93	0.88	0.85	N/A	N/A[aw]	N/A
Mean Concussions Per Season[ax]	160.0	18.0	9.0	93.0	57.0[ay]	N/A[az]	N/A[ba]
Rate of Concussions Per Player-Season	0.073	0.016	0.019	0.108	N/A[bb]	N/A[bc]	N/A
Concussions As Percentage of Injuries[bd]	10.5%	1.8%	2.4%	12.8%	N/A	1.9%	N/A
Mean Injuries Per Game	5.90	0.45	0.16	0.59	N/A	0.53	N/A
Rate of Injury Per Player-Game	0.064	0.016	0.016	0.016	N/A	0.038	N/A
Regular Season Games Per Player-Injury	15.60	62.50	62.50	62.50	N/A	N/A	N/A
Most Common Injury/ Injured Body Part[be]	Concussion	Upper leg (thigh)	Ankle Sprain	Head	N/A	Thigh	N/A
Concussions Per Game	0.625	0.007	0.007	0.067	0.704	0.010	N/A
Rate of Concussion Per Player-Game[bf]	0.00679	0.00026	0.00035	0.00180	0.00800	0.00072	N/A
Games Per Concussion Per Player	147.10	3,846.15	2,857.14	555.56	125.00	1,388.89	N/A

ar We remind the reader that we use the data that we consider the most reliable—and generally the most recent—in order to provide the most accurate assessment of injury rates in sports today. We also remind the reader that our data is limited to regular season data.

as As mentioned above, there was no publicly available data on CFL injuries.

at There is no recent data concerning player injuries in MLS.

au As mentioned above, UEFA is not a league but instead an organization of member clubs who participate in many different leagues. Consequently, our review of UEFA here is constrained to injury data and does not include an analysis of the policy issues covered in this Chart.

av This statistic includes injuries that occurred during regular season games, not practices, except for MLB. Data for MLB only includes as injuries those injuries that caused a player to be placed on the Disabled List, regardless of the reason the player was placed on the Disabled List. Nevertheless, we remind the reader that practices are infrequent during the MLB regular season.

aw The UEFA Report did not provide data on how many players played in the games for which injury data was compiled and, due to the variations in season types and lengths among the different UEFA clubs, this figure is difficult to calculate.

ax This statistic only includes concussions that occurred during regular season games.

ay It is unclear whether the CFL data concerning concussions includes pre-season or postseason games.

az The UEFA Report only provided data from a select number of clubs.

ba MLS refuses to provide data on the number of concussions suffered by its players.

bb Although some concussion data are available concerning the CFL, reliable data on the number of players per season are not.

bc The UEFA Report did not provide data on how many players played in the games for which injury data was compiled and, due to the variations in season types and lengths among the different UEFA clubs, this figure is difficult to calculate.

bd It is important to remember that this statistic is a relative statistic—it does not reflect the actual number of concussions in the leagues.

be Here, we use the terminology from the studies relevant to each of the leagues—some identify the most common injury while others identify the most commonly injured body part.

bf We emphasize that this statistic is a mean of all player positions. As discussed in the full Report, we know that rates vary depending on a player's position. Unfortunately, we do not have sufficient data to do position-by-position analysis. Nevertheless, even in the absence of that data we think the comparison of means is useful.

Table 2-M:

Comparison of Leagues' Injury Policies

	NFL	MLB	NBA	NHL	CFL	UEFA	MLS
Authorized to Disclose Injuries (Existence and Nature)	By waiver	Yes	Yes	Yes	No	N/A	Yes
Required to Disclose Existence of Injuries	Yes	No	Yes	Yes	No	N/A	Yes
Required to Disclose Nature of Injuries	Yes	No	Yes[bg]	No	No	N/A	Yes

Before proceeding with our analysis, there are some important limitations to our comparison of injury statistics across the leagues that should be noted.

First, in describing the leagues' injury statistics, we are limited by the injury definitions used by the leagues and studies. These definitions vary slightly among the leagues. Generally speaking, the NFL, NBA, and NHL report all player injuries that result in treatment, regardless of whether the injury causes the player to miss a practice or game. In contrast, MLB's publicly available injury data (through the research studies conducted by its partners and affiliates), only includes injuries that cause a player to miss "at least 1 day . . . of play." Thus, MLB's injury data is low as compared to the other leagues.

Second, the data comes from different time periods. Generally speaking, the injury data for the NFL is from 2009–16, for MLB from 2010–14, for the NBA from 1988–2005, and the NHL from 2006–12. It is possible that injury rates and injury reporting practices have changed over time. Nevertheless, we believe that this is still sufficiently reliable and transferrable to the present and thus provides useful information for examining the injury rates across the different sports leagues.

With these limitations in mind, we turn now to an analysis of the data.

The NFL's injury rates appear to be much higher than those of the other leagues. Indeed, if one combines the estimated mean number of injuries suffered per game in MLB, the NBA, and the NHL, the estimated mean number of injuries suffered per game in the NFL is approximately 4.9 times higher than the sum of those other leagues. Additionally,

if one combines the per-game concussion rates of all of the non-football leagues (including UEFA), the NFL's concussion rate is approximately 6.9 times higher than the sum of those other leagues.

Nevertheless, it is important to point out one area in which the NFL may not be more injurious. The NFL's rate of concussions per player-season is 0.073; the NHL's is 0.108. Thus, if one were to imagine a comparison of one NFL player and one NHL player, the NHL player would be *more likely* to suffer a concussion in his next regular season than the NFL player during his next season. However, this discrepancy is due to the fact that the NHL plays substantially more regular season games than the NFL (82 versus 16). When comparing concussion statistics on a per game basis, an NFL player is approximately 3.8 times more likely to suffer a concussion in a regular season game as compared to an NHL player (0.00679/0.00180).

In addition, limiting our analysis to the leagues' regular season games (a function of available data) underestimates injury rates. As shown in Section II.A on NFL injury rates, there are a significant number of injuries and concussions sustained during NFL practices and during the pre-season (90 concussions in 2015 practices and pre-season games). In particular, pre-season NFL training camps can often be extremely physical as players fight to prove themselves and make the club.[bh] With that increased level of intensity and physicality comes injuries and concussions. The reader should bear this limitation in mind.

It is beyond our expertise to recommend specific on-the-field rule changes for professional football, but we acknowledge that the rules of play can have an important impact on minimizing player injury. Rule changes have historically

---

bg   However, a player or his immediate family (where appropriate) "shall have the right to approve the terms and timing of any public release of medical information relating to any injuries or illnesses suffered by that player that are potentially life- or career-threatening, or that do not arise from the player's participation in NBA games or practices." 2017 NBA CBA, Art. XXII, § 4(e).

bh   While the other leagues also have pre-season training camps and practices, it is generally believed that the physical intensity and competitiveness of an NFL training camp surpasses the training camp environment in the other leagues.

been implemented to increase the safety of the game, and that trend continues today.[206] However, the effects of these changes are not always clear at the outset: some injury-reducing rule changes may inadvertently induce other types of risk-taking behavior, or reduce certain injuries while exacerbating others. As in any contact sport, a certain number of injuries in football are unavoidable. Which on-the-field changes would be desirable depends on a multi-factorial analysis of the benefits and drawbacks of the current version of the game (in regards to health and otherwise), the benefits and drawbacks of moving to a radically different game, and a method of weighing those benefits and drawbacks against the welfare consequences of injuries to players and players' own desires and goals as they define them. Thus, while we welcome recommendations for rule changes to improve player safety made by appropriate experts, evaluated in light of what players themselves want, we are not in a position to make these determinations as a definitive matter. Ultimately, we conclude that we are likely to be far more effective in protecting and promoting player health via off-the-field intervention than by suggesting that the game itself fundamentally change.

In our efforts to improve and promote player health, we instead focus our analysis on three of the issues discussed above: (1) injury tracking systems; (2) injury-related lists; and, (3) policies concerning public reporting of injuries.

1) INJURY TRACKING SYSTEMS

Each of the Big Four leagues and MLS has an injury tracking system of some kind. Discussions with experts on this issue indicated that the injury tracking systems are generally comparable; each of them is a sophisticated and modern system that should enable accurate reporting and provide interesting and useful data. The differences may come in how the leagues use the data that is available to them.

The NFL and NBA employ Quintiles, a health information technology firm, to perform sophisticated data analysis concerning player injuries. While the studies discussed above demonstrate that the other leagues have occasionally made injury data available for analysis, our research has not revealed whether the other leagues perform an ongoing annual analysis like Quintiles does for the NFL and NBA. The academic studies discussed above demonstrate that such analyses are possible. We will discuss this issue and others in the Recommendations Section below.

2) INJURY-RELATED LISTS

The NFL, NBA, and NHL all permit their clubs to declare players inactive one game at a time,[207] which is generally advantageous to players. We use the NFL as an example. In the NFL, clubs have a 53-man Active/Inactive List, only 46 of whom can be active for the game each week. The remaining seven players are placed on the Inactive List for the game, *i.e.*, benched, either for injury or skill purposes, but are available to play in the next week's game. This arrangement permits players the opportunity to remain on the roster but to rest and treat an injury without immediately rushing back to play. At the same time, because clubs are constantly struggling with having the best players available as well as likely having multiple injured players, players will still likely feel pressure to return as soon as possible so that the club can deactivate other injured players and avoid seeking a replacement.

The Active/Inactive List is also interrelated with the Injured Reserve list, designated for players with longer-term injuries. Generally, once a player is on Injured Reserve, he is no longer eligible to play that season. However, by placing the player on Injured Reserve, the club can replace the player on the 53-man Active/Inactive List. Thus, there are important implications in determining whether the player's injury is short-term and the club only has to declare him inactive for a game or two, or whether the player's injury is more severe and requires the player to be placed on Injured Reserve (which also allows the club to obtain a replacement player to join the 53-man roster).

The interplay between the short-term Inactive List and the longer term Injured Reserve list is particularly important concerning concussions. As discussed in the full Report, concussions present uncertain recovery times, are challenging to diagnose and treat, and present particularly acute long-term concerns. MLB is the only sport with a concussion-specific injured list. We discuss this in more detail in the Recommendations Section.

3) INJURY REPORTING POLICIES

There are three variations in the leagues' injury reporting policies.

First, the NFL, NBA, NHL, and MLS require clubs to disclose publicly players' injury statuses.

Second, the NFL, NBA and MLS require clubs to disclose publicly the nature of player injuries. While the NHL requires clubs to disclose whether a player will miss a game or not return to a game due to injury, the NFL and NBA (in practice) require that the club identify the player's body part that is injured. Below, we make a recommendation concerning this issue.

Third, in MLB, the NBA, the NHL, and MLS, the CBAs specifically describe what type of information the clubs are permitted to disclose publicly. The NFL CBA is silent on this issue. Instead, NFL clubs seemingly rely on players' individually executed waivers to obtain permission to disclose publicly player health information.

In considering whether the NFL should make changes to its Injury Reporting Policy, it is important to understand what the concerns might be with the current Policy. We discuss two possibilities.

First, there is a general concern about an individual's medical information being made publicly available. Codes of ethics[208] and laws[209] relevant to the medical profession generally prohibit the disclosure of an individual's medical information to a third party without permission. These codes and laws are grounded in the historical notion that an individual's health information is "sacred."[210] However, the relevant codes of ethics and laws also permit an individual's medical information to be disclosed to a third party without permission in certain contexts, including where the employer is providing healthcare to an employee,[211] as is the case in the NFL. These laws recognize that in certain situations employers have a legitimate interest in an employee's medical information, such as where the employee's medical information pertains to the employee's ability to perform the job or for workers' compensation purposes.[212]

Nevertheless, disclosure to employers is different from disclosure to the general public. The question is then whether the public or the NFL has sufficient interest in a player's medical information to override a player's right to keep his medical information confidential. The reasons the NFL favors disclosure are also relevant to our second concern with the NFL's Injury Reporting Policy.

The second concern with publicly disclosing player health information relates to the potential for targeting injuries. The NFL's Injury Reporting Policy requires clubs to disclose the location of a player's injury. This disclosure creates the possibility that opposing players will target the location of a player's injury in an attempt to knock the player out of the game. For example, prior to the 2015 Super Bowl, New England Patriots cornerback Brandon Browner said he would encourage his teammates to target and try to hit the injured shoulder of Seattle Seahawks safety Earl Thomas and the injured elbow of Seahawks cornerback Richard Sherman.[213] Similarly, in the 2012 NFC Championship game, New York Giants special teams players Jacquian Williams and Devin Thomas discussed targeting San Francisco 49ers kick returner Kyle Williams due to his history of concussions.[214] We discuss this concern further in the Recommendation Section.

The purpose for the NFL's Injury Reporting Policy, including the requirement that the nature of a player's injury be disclosed, largely relates to gambling. The NFL's Injury Reporting Policy was created specifically for the purpose of preventing gamblers from having inside information about player injuries.[215] More specifically, the NFL is concerned with how the importance of inside information might affect the integrity of its games. Gamblers will seek inside information, including player injury information, and there is no better source for player injury information than the players themselves. Inside information about player injuries can lead to closer relationships between gamblers and players, leading to concern that gamblers might cause players (through pay or intimidation) to alter their play, diminish their effort, or intentionally try to lose to benefit the gamblers.[216] If that is the case, the legitimacy of the games is undermined and, if exposed, public confidence and interest in the games would likely erode.[217] Consequently, the NFL prohibits players from having any association with gamblers or gambling institutions.[218]

The NFL's stance on gambling was established in the 1960s when gambling was closely associated with organized crime.[219] And the NFL's concerns were well-founded. Among other incidents, in 1963, two of the leagues' best players, Alex Karras of the Detroit Lions and Paul Hornung of the Green Bay Packers were suspended one year for betting on NFL games and associating with known criminals.[220]

All that said, it is debatable whether the NFL's gambling-related concerns are sufficiently substantial today to justify overriding a player's right to have his health information treated confidentially. These questions are beyond the scope of this report. In particular, it would be important to consider federal law enforcement's opinions on the state of organized crime and the role of gambling within organized crime's activities. Without this information, we cannot recommend that the NFL no longer obligate clubs to report information on the status of players.[221]

An additional purpose of the NFL's Injury Reporting Policy also concerns the integrity of the game. Certain types of injuries on certain players are more important than other types of injuries. For example, an injury to the starting quarterback's throwing shoulder has the potential to impact the game more than a leg injury. Similarly, an injury to a defensive back's ankle is generally more important than whether he has a hand injury. Nevertheless, disclosure of the nature of a player's injury presupposes that it is somehow unfair if the other club does not know the nature of the opposing club's player injuries. That is not necessarily the case. If neither club knows the nature of the other club's injuries, both clubs have an equal (and fair) level of uncertainty.

Having identified areas of concern, we now turn to Recommendations for change.

H) Recommendations

Recommendation 2-A: The NFL, and to the extent possible, the NFLPA, should: (a) continue to improve its robust collection of aggregate injury data; (b) continue to have the injury data analyzed by qualified professionals; and, (c) make the data publicly available for re-analysis.

As explained above, each of the Big Four leagues and MLS seems to have a quality injury tracking system, allowing for the accumulation of current information about the nature, duration, and cause of player injuries. As stated above, we rely on this data in this Report because it provides the best available data concerning player injuries, although we cannot independently verify the data's accuracy. Nevertheless, if accurately collected, this data has the potential to improve player health through analysis by qualified experts so long as it is made available to them. In particular, analysis potentially could be performed to determine, among other things, the effects of rule changes, practice habits, scheduling, new equipment, and certain treatments, while also identifying promising or discouraging trends and injury types in need of additional focus.[222] Notably, the NFL already conducts this type of analysis through Quintiles.

However, the NFL does not publicly release its aggregate injury data (nor does any other league).[223] The NFL does release some data at its annual Health & Safety Press Conference at the Super Bowl. However, the data released at the Press Conference is minimal compared to the data available and the analyses performed by Quintiles. For the data to have the potential meaningful applications mentioned above, it must be made available in a form as close to its entirety as possible. Such disclosure would permit academics, journalists, fans, and others to analyze the data in any number of ways, likely elucidating statistical events, trends, and statistics that have the opportunity to improve player health. To be clear we are recommending the release of more *aggregate* data, not data that could lead to identification of the injuries of any particular player or cause problems concerning gambling.

Publicly releasing injury data, nevertheless, comes with complications that we must acknowledge. While more transparency in injury reporting is necessary, the nuances of such data can easily be lost on those without proper training. Sports injury prevention priorities in public health can be swayed by public opinion and heavily influenced by those with the most media coverage. Making injury data publicly available may allow those with the media access to dictate the agenda regardless of the actual implications of the data. As a result, it may be harder for injury trends that may be more hazardous, but less visible in the media, to get the attention they need, even when the data clearly shows the importance of these issues. Thoughtful, balanced, peer-reviewed results may have difficulty competing against those statistics which garner the most media attention. For this and other reasons, in our report *Protecting and Promoting the Health of NFL Players: Legal and Ethical Analysis and Recommendations*, we recommended that "[t]he media . . . engage appropriate experts, including doctors, scientists, and lawyers, to ensure that its reporting on player health matters is accurate, balanced, and comprehensive."[224] The medical, scientific, and legal issues concerning player health are extremely complicated, which demands that the media take care to avoid making assertions that are not supported or that do not account for the intricacies and nuance of medicine, science, and the law.

In light of these concerns, one possible intermediate solution is to create a committee of experts that can review requests for data and determine whether or not the usage of the data is appropriate and will advance player health. Indeed, the Datalys Center for Sports Injury Research and Prevention performs this role concerning access to NCAA student-athlete injury data.[225] Moreover, such committees have also been formed in the clinical research setting.[226]

Recommendations Concerning Injury Rates and Policies – continued

Recommendation 2-B: Players diagnosed with a concussion should be placed on a short-term injured reserve list whereby the player does not count against the Active/Inactive 53 man roster until he is cleared to play by the NFL's Protocols Regarding Diagnosis and Management of Concussions.[bi]

According to the leading experts, 80–90% of concussions are resolved within seven to ten days.[227] Thus, concussion symptoms persist for longer than ten days for approximately 10–20% of athletes. In addition, there are a variety of factors that can modify the concussion recovery period, such as the loss of consciousness, past concussion history, medications, and the player's style of play.[228] Consequently, a player's recovery time from a concussion can easily range from no games to several games. The uncertain recovery times create pressure on the player, club, and club doctor. Each roster spot is valuable and clubs constantly add and drop players to ensure they have the roster that gives them the greatest chance to win each game day. As a result of the uncertain recovery times for a concussion, clubs might debate whether they need to replace the player for that week or longer. The club doctor and player might also then feel pressure for the player to return to play as soon as possible. By exempting a concussed player from the 53 man roster, the club has the opportunity to sign a short-term replacement player in the event the concussed player is unable to play. At the same time, the player and club doctor would have some of the return-to-play pressure removed.

In fact, MLB already has such a policy. MLB has a seven-day Disabled List (as compared to its normal 10- and 60-day Disabled Lists) "solely for the placement of players who suffer a concussion."[229]

Why treat concussions differently than other injuries in this respect? This is a fair question to which there are a few plausible responses. First, in terms of the perception of the game by fans, concussions have clearly received more attention than any of the other injuries NFL players might experience and thus the future of the game depends more critically on adequately protecting players who suffer from them. Second, concussions are much harder to diagnose than other injuries, such that there may be a period of uncertainty in which it would be appropriate to err on the side of caution.[230] Third, both players and medical professionals have more difficulty anticipating the long-term effects of concussions as compared to other injuries, given current scientific uncertainties concerning brain injury.[231] Fourth, and perhaps most importantly, it is much harder to determine the appropriate recovery times for concussions as compared to other injuries.[232] These reasons all support a recommendation to exclude concussed players from a club's Active/Inactive roster, but we recognize that the key feature of players potentially feeling or facing pressure to return before full recovery may be shared across any injury a player may experience. Thus, it may also be reasonable to consider extending this recommendation to injuries beyond concussions.[bj]

In reviewing a draft of our Report, *Protecting and Promoting the Health of NFL Players: Legal and Ethical Analysis and Recommendations,* the NFL argued that "[t]he current NFL roster rules actually provide greater flexibility" than is recommended here.[233] The NFL explained that because "[t]here is no limitation on how long a player may be carried on the 53-man roster throughout the season without being 'activated,' . . . a player who is concussed routinely is carried on his club's 53-man roster without being activated until he is cleared."[234] However, for the reasons explained above, we believe concussions should be treated differently. All 53 spots on the roster are precious to both the club and the players. The uncertainty surrounding recovery from a concussion presents unique pressures that can be lessened with the approach recommended here.

---

bi   This recommendation also appears as Recommendation 7:1-E in our Report *Protecting and Promoting the Health of NFL Players: Legal and Ethical Analysis and Recommendations.* Due to the fact that the recommendation was inspired by MLB's concussion-specific DL list, we include it here as well.

bj   We recognize that this new injured reserve list is subject to gaming by clubs, whereby a club might designate a player as concussed in order to add another player and effectively expand the roster. We do not view this this concern to be sufficient to outweigh the health benefits of the proposal. Moreover, all injury lists are subject to some risk of being gamed in this manner, and thus the issue is not unique to what we propose.

Recommendations Concerning Injury Rates and Policies – continued

Indeed, the NFL's practice has been to treat concussions differently from other injuries. As part of its Concussion Protocol, players suspected of having suffered a concussion during a game are examined by doctors unaffiliated with the club, and to be cleared to play in the next game they must be cleared by doctors unaffiliated with the club. For all other injuries, club doctors are the only ones to examine and clear players to play. Additionally, in 2016, the NFL sent a memo to all clubs directing them not to comment on a player's progress in returning from a concussion.[235] Instead, the NFL directed clubs to state only "that the player is in the concussion protocol under the supervision of the medical team, and the club will monitor his status."[236] This is in contrast to the clubs' open discussion of players' other injuries.

The Washington football club essentially proposed our recommendation at the 2016 owners' meetings. Washington proposed amending the NFL bylaws to provide that a player who has suffered a concussion, and who has not been cleared to play, be placed on the club's Exempt List, and be replaced by a player on the club's Practice Squad on a game-by-game basis until the player is cleared to play. Unfortunately, the proposal was not adopted.

Recommendation 2-C: The NFL should consider removing the requirement that clubs disclose the location on the body of a player's injury from the Injury Reporting Policy.

In our Report *Protecting and Promoting the Health of NFL Players: Legal and Ethical Analysis and Recommendations*, we recommend the NFL consider fining and/or suspending players if they discuss or encourage targeting another player's injury.[237] However, the need for this Recommendation would be reduced if the NFL's Injury Reporting Policy did not openly disclose the location on the body of players' injuries, a requirement imposed only by the NFL, NBA and MLS.

The gambling-related interests of full disclosure likely do not outweigh the risks of targeting by other players created by the Injury Reporting Policy.[238] While additional data—including from federal law enforcement authorities—could inform this analysis—it seems unlikely that the risks of injury information being sold on a black market are so high to justify a known risk of players intentionally aiming to hit a player in an area known to be injured because of the Injury Reporting Policy. Similarly, we see no inequity in clubs not knowing the full extent of an opposing club's player injuries. Consequently, we recommend that the NFL consider removing the requirement that clubs disclose the location of a player's injury from the Injury Reporting Policy.

Endnotes

1 Gary A. Green et al., *Mild Traumatic Brain Injury in Major and Minor League Baseball Players*, 43 Am. J. Sports Medicine 5, 1124 (2015) (discussing historic underreporting of concussions in sports); Carly D. McKay et al., *The Epidemiology of Professional Ice Hockey Injuries: A Prospective Report of Six NHL Seasons*, 48 Brit. J. Sports Med. 57, 61 (2014) (discussing possibility that injuries in the NHL are underreported); Kristen L. Kucera et al., *Validity of Soccer Injury Data from the National Collegiate Athletic Association's Injury Surveillance System*, 46(5) J. Athletic Training 489 (2011).

2 *See* Christopher R. Deubert, I. Glenn Cohen, Holly Fernandez Lynch, *Protecting and Promoting the Health of NFL Players: Legal and Ethical Analysis and Recommendations*, § 1(C) (2016); Christine M. Baugh et al., *Perceived Coach Support and Concussion Symptom-Reporting: Differences between Freshmen and Non-Freshmen College Football Players*, 42 J. L. Med., & Ethics 314 (2014) (analyzing possible explanations for under-reporting of concussions by college football players); Zachary Y. Kerr et al., *Disclosure and non-disclosure of concussion and concussion symptoms in athletes: Review and application of the socio-ecological framework*, 28 Brain Inj. 1009 (2014) (analyzing factors influencing athletes' disclosure of sports-related concussions and concussion symptoms).

3 *See* Christopher R. Deubert, I. Glenn Cohen, Holly Fernandez Lynch, *Protecting and Promoting the Health of NFL Players: Legal and Ethical Analysis and Recommendations*, § 1(C) (2016).

4 *See* Christopher R. Deubert, I. Glenn Cohen, Holly Fernandez Lynch, *Protecting and Promoting the Health of NFL Players: Legal and Ethical Analysis and Recommendations* Recommendation 1:1-F (2016).

5 Gary A. Green et al., *Mild Traumatic Brain Injury in Major and Minor League Baseball Players*, 43 Am. J. Sports Med. 5, 1124 (2015) (discussing historic underreporting of concussions in sports), *available at* http://ajs.sagepub.com/content/early/ 2015/02/06/0363546514568089.full.pdf+html; E. Kroshus, L. D. Kubzansky, R. E. Goldman, and S. B. Austin, Norms, *Athletic Identity, and Concussion Under-Reporting among Male Collegiate Ice Hockey Players: A Prospective Cohort Study*, Annals of Behav. Med. (forthcoming, 2014); Christine M. Baugh et al., *Frequency of head-impact-related outcomes by position in NCAA division I collegiate football players*, 32 J. Neurotrauma 5 (2015); Brad Partridge, *Dazed and confused: sports medicine, conflicts of interest, and concussion management*, 11 J. Bioethical Inquiries 1, 67 (2014).

6 *See NFL Head, Neck and Spine Committee's Protocols Regarding Diagnosis and Management of Concussions*, Nat'l Football League, http://images.nflplayers.com/mediaResources/lyris/pdfs/NFL_Diagnosis_Mgmt_Concussion.pdf (last visited Sep. 18, 2015), *archived at* http://perma.cc/H2M7-U2KL (listing "potential concussion signs (observable)" and "potential concussions symptoms").

7 *Id.*

8 For discussion on the appropriate methodology for measuring player injuries, *see* John Orchard and Wayne Hoskins, *For Debate: Consensus Injury Definitions in Team Sports Should Focus on Missed Playing Time*, 17 Clin. J. Sport Med. 192 (2007); Lisa Hodgson et al. *For Debate: Consensus Injury Definitions in Team Sports Should Focus on Encompassing All Injuries* 17 Clin. J. Sport Med. 188 (2007).

9 Paul McCrory, *Consensus statement on concussion in sport: the 4th International Conference on Concussion in Sport, Zurich, November 2012*, 48 J. Athletic Trainers 4 (2013) ("Consensus Statement").

10 *Id.* at 1.

11 *Id.*

12 *See* 2011 MLB CBA, Att. 36 (MLB Concussion Protocol); *NFL Head, Neck and Spine Committee's Protocols Regarding Diagnosis and Management of Concussions*, Nat'l Football League, http://images.nflplayers.com/mediaResources/lyris/pdfs/NFL_Diagnosis_Mgmt_Concussion.pdf (last visited Sep. 18, 2015), *archived at* http://perma.cc/H2M7-U2KL (NFL Concussion Protocol); NHL Concussion Evaluation and Management Protocol 2015/16 (on file with authors); *Concussion Evaluation and Management Protocol*, MLS (2015) (on file with authors). Information about the NBA's concussion protocol was provided by the NBA—we did not review the protocol directly.

13 *See* Consensus Statement at 1-4.

14 *Compare Consensus Statement with* NFL Concussion Protocol, *supra* note 12; MLB Concussion Protocol, *supra* note 12; *NBA.com: Official—Concussion Policy Summary*, Nat'l Basketball Ass'n, http://www.nba.com/official/concussion_policy_summary.html (last visited Sep. 18, 2015), *archived at* http://perma.cc/D84E-JHLM; NHL Concussion Protocol, *supra* note 12; CFL Concussion Guidelines 2014 (on file with author); *MLS discusses concussion protocol*, ESPN, Jan. 7, 2012, http://espn.go.com/sports/soccer/news/_/id/7436065/mls-medical-staffers-target-concussion-protocol, *archived at* http://perma.cc/78EF-6DWZ (describing MLS Concussion Protocol); *Concussion Evaluation and Management Protocol*, MLS (2015) (on file with authors).

15 *See, e.g.,* Dan Feldman, *Clippers Violate NBA's Concussion Policy, Play Austin Rivers With Concussion*, Pro Basketball Talk (Dec. 13, 2016, 11:54 AM), http://nba.nbcsports.com/2016/12/13/clippers-violate-nbas-concussion-policy-play-austin-rivers-with-concussion/, *archived at* https://perma.cc/JE73-D9ZV.

16 *Injury Surveillance in the NFL: an Update from Quintiles Outcome,* Applied Clinical Trials, Aug. 30, 2012, http://www.appliedclinicaltrialsonline.com/injury-surveillance-nfl-update-quintiles-outcome (last visited Jan. 21, 2016), *archived at* https://perma.cc/5ZUF-9NF7.

17 *Id.*

18 *Transcript—2016 Injury Data Results Conference Call*, NFL Communications, Jan. 29, 2016, https://nflcommunications.com/Pages/Transcript---2016-Injury-Data-Results-Conference-Call.aspx, *archived at* https://perma.cc/RKC6-352G.

19 *Id.*

20 *Id.*

21 This information was provided by the NFLPA.

22 Alan Schwarz, Walt Bogdanich, Jacqueline Williams, *N.F.L.'s Flawed Concussion Research and Ties to Tobacco Industry*, N.Y. Times, Mar. 26, 2016, http://www.nytimes.com/2016/03/25/sports/football/nfl-concussion-research-tobacco.html, *archived at* https://perma.cc/NM4N-SW4Q. *See also NFL response to New York Times' concussion research story*, NFL.com (Mar. 24, 2016, 4:11 PM), http://www.nfl.com/news/story/0ap3000000647389/article/nfl-response-to-new-york-times-concussion-research-story, *archived at* https://perma.cc/Z3XE-8FQ6.

23 *Injury Surveillance in the NFL: an Update from Quintiles Outcome,* Applied Clinical Trials, Aug. 30, 2012, http://www.appliedclinicaltrialsonline.com/injury-surveillance-nfl-update-quintiles-outcome (last visited Sep. 18, 2014), *archived at* http://perma.cc/FH93-5259.

24 *Id.*

25 This information was provided by the NFLPA.

26 These tables were created by examining the year-end NFLISS reports prepared by Quintiles for the year 2014, and the reports presented at the NFL's annual Health & Safety Press Conference during the week of the Super Bowl.

27 The reports do not provide postseason data.

28 The reports do not provide postseason data.

29 *See* 2012 NFL Constitution and Bylaws, § 12.3(E).

30 Socalisteph, *NFL PUP list, Injured Reserve, NFI List rules and the 2014 San Francisco 49ers*, Superbowl Nation Blog—Niners Nation (Jul. 18, 2014, 5:30 AM), http://www.ninersnation.com/2014/7/18/5914295/nfl-pup-list-rules-injured-reserve-nfi-list-rules-49ers-2014, *archived at* https://perma.cc/D5YZ-87HX.

31 NFL CBA, Art. 25, § 4.

32 NFL CBA, Art. 25, § 1.

33 NFL Personnel (Injury) Report Policy, *available at* http://operations.nfl.com/media/2235/06-07-16-2016-injury-report-policy.pdf, *archived at* https://perma.cc/D822-PXDN.

34 *Id.*

35 *Id.*

36 For additional information on gambling's role in the NFL, *see* Christopher R. Deubert, I. Glenn Cohen, Holly Fernandez Lynch, *Protecting and Promoting the Health of NFL Players: Legal and Ethical Analysis and Recommendations*, § 18(A) (2016).

37 NFL Personnel (Injury) Report Policy, *supra* n. 33.

38 Tom Pelissero, *Major change to NFL's injury report will take some getting used to*, USA Today (Aug. 21, 2016, 4:33 PM), http://www.usatoday.com/story/sports/nfl/2016/08/21/injury-report-probable-bill-belichick-patriots/89080582/, *archived at* https://perma.cc/QT4C-MAA6.

39 *See* Scott Boeck, Skip Wood, *Analysis: Injury report is game within the game*, USA Today, Nov. 22, 2007, http://usatoday30.usatoday.com/sports/football/nfl/2007-11-22-injury-report-cover_N.htm, *archived at* http://perma.cc/SRU4-ZWY4. Midway through the 2012 season, 4 NFL teams had been fined $20,000 each for injury report violations. Mike Florio, *Rams rack up an injury-reporting fine, too*, ProFootballTalk (Nov. 2, 2012, 10:44 PM), http://profootballtalk.nbcsports.com/2012/11/02/rams-rack-up-an-injury-reporting-fine-too/, *available at* http://perma.cc/S8TF-G78N. In 2009, the Jets were fined a total $125,000 for former quarterback Brett Favre's injury for the last 5 games of the season ($75,000 for the team and $25,000 each for G.M. Mike Tannenbaum and former head coach Eric Mangini), the highest injury-reporting violation fine publicly announced. *See* Greg Bishop, *Jets Still Paying Price for Favre and Mangini*, N.Y. Times, Sept. 16, 2009, http://www.nytimes.com/2009/09/17/sports/football/17favre.html, *archived at* http://perma.cc/XV4N-GMTB.

40 Scott Boeck, Skip Wood, *Analysis: Injury report is game within the game*, USA Today, Nov. 22, 2007, http://usatoday30.usatoday.com/sports/football/nfl/2007-11-22-injury-report-cover_N.htm.

41 *See id.*; Gregg Rosenthal, *Redskins play the "questionable" game, again*, ProFootballTalk.com (Sept. 25, 2010, 10:07 AM), http://profootballtalk.nbcsports.com/2010/09/25/redskins-play-the-questionable-game-again/, *archived at* https://perma.cc/7MBX-ZXL4. Players reporting that coaches report the wrong injuries: Michael David Smith, *Spikes, Talib say Patriots file false injury reports* (Mar. 19, 2014, 7:01 AM), http://profootballtalk.nbcsports.com/2014/03/19/spikes-talib-say-patriots-file-false-injury-reports/, *archived at* https://perma.cc/X6YP-H33S.

42 *See* Scott Boeck and Skip Wood, *Analysis: Injury report is game within the game*, USA Today, Nov. 22, 2007, http://usatoday30.usatoday.com/sports/football/nfl/2007-11-22-injury-report-cover_N.htm, *archived at* http://perma.cc/SRU4-ZWY4.

43 Jeff Zrebiec, *John Harbaugh: 'The injury report has no value'*, Balt. Sun, Nov. 2, 2012, http://www.baltimoresun.com/sports/ravens/ravens-insider/bal-harbaugh-criticizes-nfl-over-injury-report-20121102-story.html, *archived at* https://perma.cc/E9TQ-3JPY.

44 Michael David Smith, *Spikes, Talib say Patriots file false injury reports*, ProFootballTalk (Mar. 19, 2014, 7:01 AM) http://profootballtalk.nbcsports.com/2014/03/19/spikes-talib-say-patriots-file-false-injury-reports/, *archived at* http://perma.cc/3GKS-GL5T.

45 See Gregg Rosenthal, *Redskins play the "questionable" game, again*, ProFootballTalk (Sept. 25, 2010, 10:07 AM), http://profootballtalk.nbcsports.com/2010/09/25/redskins-play-the-questionable-game-again/, *archived at* http://perma.cc/N6S6-SULJ; John Niyo, *NFL injury reports a weekly joke*, Detroit News, Nov. 10, 2012, http://www.detroitnews.com/article/20121110/OPINION03/211100317, *archived at* http://perma.cc/K8PQ-GST6; Scott Boeck, Skip Wood, *Analysis: Injury report is game within the game*, USA Today, Nov. 22, 2007, http://usatoday30.usatoday.com/sports/football/nfl/2007-11-22-injury-report-cover_N.htm, *archived at* http://perma.cc/SRU4-ZWY4. The Pittsburgh Tribune-Review found "the NFL's 1999 [Injury Reports]

data was so suspect, the Trib didn't use it" (from Carl Prine, *Bloody Sundays*, Pittsburgh Trib.-Rev., Jan. 9, 2005, http://triblive.com/x/pittsburghtrib/sports/steelers/s_291033.html#axzz3OdCi5UC7, *archived at* http://perma.cc/4A89-N7AB.

46 Mike Florio, *New Injury report creates plenty of questions, concerns*, ProFootballTalk (Aug. 21, 2016, 8:20 PM), http://profootballtalk.nbcsports.com/2016/08/21/new-injury-report-creates-plenty-of-questions-concerns/, *archived at* https://perma.cc/ZMX9-XQT2.

47 *See* Darin Gantt, *Julian Edelman won't say whether he had concussion tests*, ProFootballTalk (Feb. 1, 2015, 11:30 PM), http://profootballtalk.nbcsports.com/2015/02/01/julian-edelman-wont-say-whether-he-had-concussion-tests/, *archived at* http://perma.cc/BS7C-2AUQ (discussing Patriots policy of prohibiting players from speaking about injuries).

48 Copies of these waivers are included as Appendices L and M in our other report, *Protecting and Promoting the Health of NFL Players: Legal and Ethical Analysis and Recommendations* (2016).

49 John Schlegel, *MLB Instituting New Medical Records System*, Major League Baseball, Mar. 1, 2010, http://m.mlb.com/news/article/8632528/, *archived at* http://perma.cc/EH3X-B6CP.

50 Keshia M. Pollack, *"Of Course They Are an Occupational Group!" Preventing Injuries Among Professional Baseball Players*, Johns Hopkins Center for Injury Res. & Policy, Mar. 4, 2014, http://www.ucdenver.edu/academics/colleges/PublicHealth/research/ResearchProjects/piper/resources/Documents/Injury%20seminar%20Co%20March%204%202014_revised.pdf, *archived at* http://perma.cc/7YJ2-429E.

51 *See* MLB CBA, Attachment 5 (Standard Form of Diagnosis); MLB CBA, Attachment 36, Ex. B (Concussion Diagnostic Form for 7-Day Disabled List Placement).

52 It is unclear what is meant by a "preventative event." Preventative events typically include specific strength or balance training and exercise programs for the purpose of injury prevention and are common in sports. The programs are coordinated by athletic trainers or strength and conditioning coaches to improve specific strength or coordination in order to preemptively avoid injuries. However, it is unclear what the authors meant by preventative events in this case.

53 Pollack, *supra* note 50. Players must provide consent for their records to be included in the system. *Id. See also* Christopher S. Ahmad et al., *Major and Minor League Baseball Hamstring Injuries: Epidemiologic Findings From the Major League Baseball Injury Surveillance System*, 42 Am. J. Sports Med. 1464, 1466 (2014) ("In the MLB EMR, athletic trainers record all injuries, illnesses, and preventative visits for both baseball-related and non-baseball related events for all players on their respective team as their medical-legal record.")

54 *See, e.g.*, Gary A. Green et al., *Mild Traumatic Brain Injury in Major and Minor League Baseball Players*, 43 Am. J. Sports Med. 5, 1118–26 (2015).

55 Keshia M. Pollack et al., *Developing and Implementing Major League Baseball's Health and Injury Tracking System*, 183 Am. J. Epidemiology 1, 3 (2016).

56 *See id.*

57 Stan Conte, Christopher L. Camp, Joshua S. Dines, *Injury Trends in Major League Baseball Over 18 Seasons: 1998–2015*, 45 Am. J. Orthopedics 116 (2016).

58 Christopher S. Ahmad et al., *Major and Minor League Baseball Hamstring Injuries: Epidemiologic Findings From the Major League Baseball Injury Surveillance System*, 42 Am. J. Sports Med. 1464 (2014).

59 Diane L. Dahm et al., *Epidemiology and Impact of Knee Injuries in Major and Minor League Baseball Players*, 45 Am. J. Orthopedics E54 (2016).

60 Struan H. Coleman et al., *The Epidemiology of Hip and Groin Injuries in Professional Baseball Players*, 45 Am. J. Orthopedics 168 (2016).

61 Gary A. Green et al., *Mild Traumatic Brain Injury in Major and Minor League Baseball Players*, 43 Am. J. Sports Med. 5 (2015).

62 Keshia M. Pollack et al., *Developing and Implementing Major League Baseball's Health and Injury Tracking System*, 183 Am. J. Epidemiology 1, 5 (2016).

63 *Id.* at 4.

64 *Id.* at 3.

65 Stan Conte, Christopher L. Camp and Joshua S. Dines, *Injury Trends in Major League Baseball Over 18 Seasons: 1998–2015*, 45 Am. J. Orthopedics 116, 118 (2016).

66 Major League Rule 2(g).

67 MLB's website provides spring training standings from which to calculate the number of spring training games. *See Standings*, Major League Baseball, http://mlb.mlb.com/mlb/standings/exhibition.jsp?ymd =20161002 (last visited Oct. 14, 2016), *archived at* https://perma.cc/ W6KQ-ZBBZ.

68 Each of the 30 clubs plays 162 regular season games against another club, resulting in 2,430 games per season (162 x 15). 2,430 games x 5 seasons = 12,150 games.

69 *See World Series Winners, Records, and Results and Postseason Series*, Baseball-Reference.com, http://www.baseball-reference.com/ postseason/ (last visited Oct. 14, 2016), *archived at* https://perma.cc/ KP2W-NRXR.

70 MLB CBA, Art V.

71 *See* Gary A. Green et al., *Mild Traumatic Brain Injury in Major and Minor League Baseball Players*, 43 Am. J. Sports Med. 5, 1118, 1125 (2015) (describing "the few practices in professional baseball").

72 *See Dr. Gary Green named Medical Director of Major League Baseball*, Major League Baseball, April 14, 2010, http://mlb.mlb.com/news/press _releases/press_release.jsp?ymd=20100414&content_id=9290282 &vkey=pr_mlb&fext=.jsp, *archived at* http://perma.cc/5EW8-7XRP.

73 *See* Gary A. Green et al., *Mild Traumatic Brain Injury in Major and Minor League Baseball Players*, 43 Am. J. Sports Med. 5, 1118, 1121 (2015).

74 *See Disabled List Data*, Baseball Heat Maps, http://www .baseballheatmaps.com/disabled-list-data/, (last visited Jan. 21, 2016), *archived at* http://perma.cc/2VNP-GD9P (providing spreadsheets of all players placed on the DL for the 2010–15 seasons by gathering data from MLB.com).

75 This figure was gathered from MLB.com's "Sortable Player" statistics page by adding together all players who had a plate appearance and all pitchers, and then removing those pitchers that also had a plate appearance.

76 Keshia M. Pollack et al., *Developing and Implementing Major League Baseball's Health and Injury Tracking System*, 183 Am. J. Epidemiology 1, 5 (2016).

77 Gary A. Green et al., *Mild Traumatic Brain Injury in Major and Minor League Baseball Players*, 43 Am. J. Sports Med. 5, 1118, 1118–21 (2015). By comparison, a 2014 study examining DL data from 2001 to 2010 found only 33 concussions over that 10-season period. Leslie E. Schwindel et al., *Epidemiology and Outcomes of Concussions in Major League Baseball*, 2 Annals of Orthopedics & Rheumatology 3, 1022, 1022 (2014). The smaller figures were likely the result of lesser awareness and failure to diagnose concussions in the earlier seasons. Indeed, the study found that 0 concussions were reported in 2001, while 10 were reported in 2010. *Id.*

78 Gary A. Green et al., *Mild Traumatic Brain Injury in Major and Minor League Baseball Players*, 43 Am. J. Sports Med. 5, 1118, 1125 (2015).

79 Each of the 30 clubs plays 162 games, resulting in a total of 2,430 games per season (because each game involves two clubs, we multiplied 162 x 15). Thus, in two seasons, there are 4,860 games (2,430 x 2).

80 Gary A. Green et al., *Mild Traumatic Brain Injury in Major and Minor League Baseball Players*, 43 Am. J. Sports Med. 5, 1118, 1120 (2015) ("To estimate exposure, we based the average number of players per team per game on analysis of regular-season game participation via box scores that are publicly available. This average number over a season, multiplied by the number of team games . . . was used as an estimate of game exposures[.]")

81 Green, *supra* note 77 at 1122 (finding catchers accounted for 40% of concussions); *see also* Schwindel, *supra* note 77, at 1022–23 (finding that 30.3% of concussions were suffered by catchers).

82 Green, *supra* note 77 at 1122; *see also* Schwindel, *supra* note 77 at 1022–23.

83 William D. Witnauer, Richard G. Rogers & Jarron M. Saint Onge, *Major league baseball career length in the 20th century*, 26 Population Res. & Pol'y Rev. 4, 371–386 (2007).

84 MLB CBA, Attachment 36 § 2(A). "Acute" is not defined in the CBA.

85 Major League Rule 2(g)(1); *MLBPA, MLB Announce Details of New Labor Agreement*, MLBPA (Dec. 2, 2016), http://www.mlbplayers.com/ ViewArticle.dbml?DB_OEM_ID=34000&ATCLID=211336390, *archived at* https://perma.cc/4XUA-2DAW (announcing replacement of 15-day DL with 10-day DL).

86 MLB CBA, Attachment 5 (Standard Form of Diagnosis). There is a different form for clubs attempting to place a player who has suffered a concussion on the 7-day DL. MLB CBA, Attachment 36, Ex. B (Concussion Diagnostic Form for 7-Day Disabled List Placement). The Concussion Diagnostic Form for 7-Day Disabled List requires clubs to provide such information as the date of injury, diagnosis description, event that cause the injury, whether the player was removed from the game, and the basis of the concussion diagnosis (including the SCAT2 Assessment Form). The form also requests video information if available. *Id.*

87 MLB CBA, Attachment 5 (Standard Form of Diagnosis).

88 MLB CBA, Art. XIII(C).

89 *See* Major League Rule 2(g)(1). For example, a player placed on the 15-day DL is not eligible to play in an MLB game until at least 15 days have passed, though he may remain out of play longer if his rehabilitation is not complete after 15 days

90 MLB CBA, Art. XIII(G)(4) (emphasis added).

91 *Id.*

92 Major League Rule 2(a).

93 *Center to Standardize Health Care for NBA Players with Easy-to-Use and Automated System "HealthAthlete"*, Globe Newswire, Nov. 14, 2012, http://globenewswire.com/news-release/2012/11/14/505082 /10012449/en/Cerner-to-Standardize-Health-Care-for-NBA-Players-With -Easy-to-Use-and-Automated-System-HealtheAthlete.html, *archived at* http://perma.cc/8TEG-9LKQ.

94 *See id.*

95 NBA CBA, Art. XXII, § 8.

96 NBA CBA, Art. XXII, §§ 3, 7.

97 Mark C. Drakos, Benjamin Domb, Chad Starkey, Lisa Callahan, Answorth A. Allen, *Injury in the National Basketball Association: A 17-Year Overview*, 2 Sports Health 284, 285 (2010).

98 *Id.*

99 *Id.*

100 *Id.*

101 *See Athletic Health Management*, Cerner Corp., https://www.cerner.com /solutions/individuals_and_families/athletic_health_management/ (last visited Sept. 22, 2015), *archived at* http://perma.cc/4BGH-HNB5.

102 Baxter Holmes and Tom Haberstroh, *The Cutting Edge: Injury Prediction and Prevention*, ESPN (Jun. 7, 2016), http://www.espn.com/nba/story /_/id/16009403/cutting-edge-injury-prediction-prevention, *archived at* https://perma.cc/PF6G-GDTZ.

103 Mark C. Drakos, Benjamin Domb, Chad Starkey, Lisa Callahan, Answorth A. Allen, *Injury in the National Basketball Association: A 17-Year Overview*, 2 Sports Health 284 (2010).

104 *Id.* at 285.

105 *Id.*

106 *Id.*

107 *Id.*

108 *Id.* at 289–90.

109 *Id.* at 285.

110 *Id.* at 286.

111 *Id.* at 286.

112 Mark C. Drakos, Benjamin Domb, Chad Starkey, Lisa Callahan, Answorth A. Allen, *Injury in the National Basketball Association: A 17-Year Overview*, 2 Sports Health 284, 287 (2010). The Drakos Study provided the total number of game-related injuries by body part. To obtain the figures in this Report, we divided these totals by the 17 seasons of the study.

113 *Id.* at 288. There were 1,066 ankle sprains during the 17 years of the study, equaling 62.7 per year (1,066/17).

114 *Id.*

115 Jeff Stotts, *Only 9 NBA Players Got Concussion This Year*, FiveThirtyEight (May 21, 2014, 1:43 pm), http://fivethirtyeight.com/datalab/only-9-nba-players-got-concussions-this-year/, *archived at* http://perma.cc/KY4L-B32Y.

116 This data was gathered from basketball-reference.com.

117 Susan Konig, *Financial Planning for the Pros,* 34 Registered Representative (Apr. 2010), *available at* 2010 WLNR 26366417.

118 *See* Larry Coon, *NBA Salary Cap FAQ*, CBA FAQ, July 8, 2015, http://www.cbafaq.com/salarycap.htm#Q79, *archived at* http://perma.cc/X3CS-F58N; NBA CBA, Art. XXIX § 2.

119 Coon, *supra* n. 118.

120 *Id.*

121 This information was provided by the NBA—we did not review the policy directly.

122 NBA CBA, Art. XXII, § 4(d).

123 NBA CBA, Art. XXII, § 4(e).

124 *Athlete Health Management System*, Athlete RMS, http://athleterms.com/Solutions/AHMSPro.aspx (last visited Sept. 22, 2015), *archived at* http://perma.cc/7L67-4AZT.

125 Carly D. McKay et al., *The Epidemiology of Professional Ice Hockey Injuries: A Prospective Report of Six NHL Seasons*, 48 Brit. J. Sports Med. 57, 57 (2014).

126 *Id.*

127 *Id.*

128 *Id.*

129 *Id.* at 61.

130 *Id.*

131 *Id.* at 58. The study calculated total AEs by multiplying 82 games per season per club by 30 NHL clubs by 19 players per game, equaling 46,740 per season. The 19 players per game figure is the equivalent of a club's entire roster each night, less a backup goaltender. We find this calculation to be reliable. Unlike in other sports, every player on an NHL club's roster will play every game, except for the backup goaltender.

132 *See id.* at 59.

133 *Id.*

134 *Id.* at 60.

135 There are 82 games per season and 30 NHL clubs. Thus, this statistic was determined by multiplying 82 by 15 (30 NHL clubs divided by 2 clubs per game) by the 6 seasons in the study.

136 The study provides the following number of players for each season: 840 in 2006–07; 843 in 2007–08; 837 in 2008–09; 838 in 2009–10; 891 in 2010–11; and, 895 in 2011–12. *See* McKay at 58.

137 *Id.* at 59.

138 *Id.* at 60.

139 Richard A. Wennberg & Charles H. Tator, *Concussion Incidence and Time Lost from Play in the NHL During the Past Ten Years*, 35 Can. J. Neurological Sci. 647, 649 (2008).

140 *See id.* at 649.

141 *Id.*

142 *Id.* at Table 2.

143 The NHL/NHLPA Concussion Program, launched in 1997, was the first professional sports working group program that addressed concussions. *See Frequently Asked Questions About Concussions*, Nat'l Hockey League, Feb. 7, 2011, http://www.nhl.com/ice/news.htm?id=551900,

archived at http://perma.cc/63YK-8C8H. Through input from the NHLPA, physicians, and athletic trainers, the Concussion Program has sought to better understand concussions. *See id.* The Program has resulted in the implementation of mandatory neurophysiological baseline testing for all players, as well as changes to rules, equipment, and the playing environment. *Id.*

144 Brian Benson et al., *A Prospective Study of Concussions Among National Hockey League Players During Regular Season Games: The NHL-NHLPA Concussion Program*, 183 Can. Med. Ass'n J. 905 (2011).

145 *See id.*

146 *Id.* at 907.

147 *See id.*

148 James Wisniewski, *NHL still grappling with concussions*, ESPN, June 8, 2014, http://espn.go.com/nhl/playoffs/2014/story/_/id/11051889/nhl-says-concussions-decreased-protocol-remains-imperfect, *archived at* http://perma.cc/YD2R-CPUE ("According to data from STATS provided to The Associated Press, there were 53 concussions during the regular season, a sharp decline from the 78 reported during the league's last full season two years ago.")

149 The study provides the following number of players for each season: 840 in 2006–07; 843 in 2007–08; 837 in 2008–09; 838 in 2009–10; 891 in 2010–11; and, 895 in 2011–12. *See* McKay at 58.

150 *Average Length of an NHL Player Career,* QuantHockey.com, http://www.quanthockey.com/Distributions/CareerLengthGP.php (last visited Aug. 28, 2015), *archived at* http://perma.cc/95QB-X9P9.

151 NHL CBA, § 16.11(a).

152 NHL CBA, § 16.4(a).

153 NHL CBA, § 16.11(d).

154 NHL CBA, § 16.11(a).

155 *Id.* Although clubs have a 23-man Active Roster, only 20 players (18 skaters and 2 goaltenders) are permitted to dress for each game. NHL Official Rules, Rule 5.1 (2014–15).

156 *See* 2013 NHL CBA, Art. 1 (defining "Reserve List" as, among other things, "all Players signed to a[] [Standard Player Contract]," and limiting the Reserve List to "[n]o more than 50 Players signed to a[] [Standard Player Contract]").

157 Stu Hackel, *The Morning Skate: N.H.L.'s New Injury-Disclosure Policy Draws Heavy Criticism*, Slapshot Blog, N.Y. Times (Nov. 10, 2008, 3:26 p.m.), http://slapshot.blogs.nytimes.com/2008/11/10/the-morning-skate-nhls-new-injury-disclosure-policy-draws-heavy-criticism/, *archived at* http://perma.cc/X5FS-JD9Q (quoting the policy).

158 *Id.*

159 CBA, Art. 34, § 3(c)(iii).

160 Stu Hackel, *The Morning Skate: N.H.L.'s New Injury-Disclosure Policy Draws Heavy Criticism*, Slapshot Blog, N.Y. Times (Nov. 10, 2008, 3:26 p.m.), http://slapshot.blogs.nytimes.com/2008/11/10/the-morning-skate-nhls-new-injury-disclosure-policy-draws-heavy-criticism/, *archived at* http://perma.cc/X5FS-JD9Q.

161 *See* Curtis Rush, *The "Upper-Body" Injury—from Pat Quinn's Brain to NHL Lexicon*, Toronto Star, Mar. 18, 2014, http://www.thestar.com/sports/leafs/2014/03/18/the_upperbody_injury_from_pat_quinns_brain_to_nhl_lexicon.html, *archived at* http://perma.cc/7KDB-B6Q6; *see also NHL Injuries*, ESPN, http://espn.go.com/nhl/injuries (last visited Oct. 28, 2015).

162 A.J. Perez, *NHL Unlikely to Get Closer to Ending Little Disclosure on Injuries*, CBS Sports, Mar. 24, 2011, http://www.cbssports.com/nhl/story/14850387/nhl-unlikely-to-get-closer-to-ending-little-disclosure-on-injuries, *archived at* http://perma.cc/5YED-UDL7.

163 *See* Chris Zelkovich, *CFL Concussions Not Always Revealed to Fans*, Toronto Star, Apr. 7, 2011, http://www.thestar.com/sports/football/argos/2011/04/07/cfl_concussions_not_always_revealed_to_fans.html, *archived at* http://perma.cc/T3Q8-2AZW.

164 Mark Masters, *'Awareness Is Half The Battle' for CFL and Concussions*, Nat'l Post, Apr. 7, 2011, http://sports.nationalpost.com/2011/04/07

/awareness-is-half-the-battle-for-cfl-and-concussions/, *archived at* http://perma.cc/T3Q8-2AZW ("There were 50 concussions recorded in 85 CFL games last year").

165 *Id.* The only other study our research revealed concerning CFL injuries concerned concussions suffered by CFL players during the 1997 season. J. Scott Delaney et al., *Concussions During the 1997 Canadian Football League Season*, 10 Clin. J. Sport Med. 9 (2000). The data was self-reported in the form of a voluntary questionnaire and the understanding of concussions has changed significantly since 1997. For these reasons, the data in the study cannot be considered useful today. Nevertheless, of the 289 players who responded to the questionnaire, 8.4% reported that they had suffered a concussion, but 44.8% reported one or more concussion symptoms. Based on these responses, the researchers concluded that concussions are likely substantially underreported. *Id.*

166 The nine CFL clubs each play 18 regular season games, for a total of 81 games. In addition, there are five playoff games, for a total of 86 regular season and postseason games. It is thus unclear what games may or may not have been included to reach a figure of 85 games.

167 Marika Washchynshyn, *Is the Canadian Football League Safer than the NFL?*, Complex (Nov. 25, 2015), http://www.complex.com/sports/2015/11/cfl-concussions, *archived at* https://perma.cc/G47Y-RTT5.

168 *Id.*

169 The reserve list consists of two players who do not dress for a club's game. *Rosters Glossary*, CFLdb, https://cfldb.ca/glossary/rosters/ (last visited Sept. 22, 2015), *archived at* http://perma.cc/77LF-2E4Y. Players on the injured list do not count toward the reserve list. *Id.*

170 *The Game*, Can. Football League, http://www.cfl.ca/page/game_rule_ratio (last visited Sept. 22, 2015), *archived at* http://perma.cc/5RRT-RSGZ.

171 *See Rosters Glossary*, CFLdb, https://cfldb.ca/glossary/rosters/ (last visited Sept. 22, 2015), *archived at* http://perma.cc/77LF-2E4Y; CFL CBA, § 14.02(F).

172 *See Id.*

173 *See* Zelkovich, *supra* note 163; CFL CBA, Art. 29 § 2.

174 *Cerner Collaborates With Major League Soccer to Improve Medical Care for Professional Athletes*, Cerner Corp., August 9, 2011, http://phx.corporate-ir.net/phoenix.zhtml?c=118401&p=irol-newsArticle&ID=1594607, *archived at* http://perma.cc/R74X-993X.

175 *Id.*

176 *Id.*

177 MLS Medical Policies and Procedures Manual § V.11 (2015).

178 Bruce E. Morgan and Michael A. Oberlander, *An Examination of Injuries in Major League Soccer*, 29 Am. J. Sports Med. 426 (2001).

179 *Id.* at 427.

180 */14 Season Report—UEFA Elite Club Injury Study*, UEFA (2014), http://www.uefa.org/MultimediaFiles/Download/uefaorg/Medical/02/19/04/32/2190432_DOWNLOAD.pdf, *archived at* http://perma.cc/Q6GL-RTAA.

181 *Id.* at § 5.2.1.

182 Jan Ekstrand, Martin Haägglund, and Markus Waldén, *Injury Incidence and Injury Patterns in Professional Football: The UEFA Injury Study*, 45 Brit. J. Sports Med. 553, 553 (2011).

183 *Id.* at 3.

184 *Id.*

185 */14 Season Report—UEFA Elite Club Injury Study*, § 5, Table 1, UEFA (2014), http://www.uefa.org/MultimediaFiles/Download/uefaorg/Medical/02/19/04/32/2190432_DOWNLOAD.pdf, *archived at* http://perma.cc/Q6GL-RTAA.

186 *Id.* at § 1, § 4.

187 *Id.* at § 5.

188 *Id.* at § 4.

189 The Federation International de Football Association ("FIFA") is the international governing body for the sport of soccer. *See Who We Are,*

190 *Law of the Game 2013–2014*, FIFA (2013), http://www.fifa.com/mm/document/footballdevelopment/refereeing/81/42/36/log2013en_neutral.pdf, *archived at* http://perma.cc/VJJ8-6G7V, at p. 17.

191 */14 Season Report—UEFA Elite Club Injury Study*, § 5, Table 1, UEFA (2014), http://www.uefa.org/MultimediaFiles/Download/uefaorg/Medical/02/19/04/32/2190432_DOWNLOAD.pdf, *archived at* http://perma.cc/Q6GL-RTAA.

192 *Id.* at Table 2.

193 *See Concussion policies by league*, USA Today, Oct. 11, 2012, http://www.usatoday.com/story/sports/2012/10/11/concussions-nascar-nfl-mlb-nhl-nba/1628129/, *archived at* http://perma.cc/WV7S-5PG3.

194 *Roster Rules and Regulations*, Major League Soccer, http://pressbox.mlssoccer.com/content/roster-rules-and-regulations (last visited Sept. 22, 2015), *archived at* http://perma.cc/9BLN-R7QD.

195 *Id.*

196 *Id.*

197 *Id.*

198 *Id.*

199 *Major League Soccer Fines LA Galaxy for Violating Injury Report Policy*, Major League Soccer, June 24, 2011, http://pressbox.mlssoccer.com/content/major-league-soccer-fines-la-galaxy-violating-injury-report-policy, *archived at* http://perma.cc/EC3H-HY5C.

200 MLS Medical Policies & Procedures Manual, § IX.B (2015).

201 *Id.*

202 *Id.*

203 MLS CBA, Ex. 2.

204 MLS Medical Policies & Procedures Manual, § IX.B.11 (2015).

205 *Id.*

206 *See* Christopher R. Deubert, I. Glenn Cohen, Holly Fernandez Lynch, *Protecting and Promoting the Health of NFL Players: Legal and Ethical Analysis and Recommendations*, App. I (2016) (discussing and providing history of health-related rule changes in the NFL). *See also* Joseph S. Torg et al., *The National Football Head and Neck Injury Registry, 14-Year Report on Cervical Quadriplegia, 1971- Through 1984*, 254 J. Am. Med. Ass'n 3439 (1985) (discussing NCAA rule changes in response to player health data).

207 Short-term inactive lists are not practical in MLB. MLB rosters are limited to 25 players, including the five-man starting pitching staff, each of whom only pitches every fifth game. Players on the club's Disabled List do not count towards a club's 25-man roster. Thus, if MLB's Disabled List did not include time requirements and clubs could place players on the Disabled List one game at a time, the club could place the starting pitchers on the Disabled List and only take them off the list when they were going to pitch. If, on any given day, four of the five starting pitchers are on the Disabled List, the club could then have four other players on the roster in their place, effectively creating a 29-man roster since the starting pitchers would return to action without having missed any games in which they were scheduled to pitch.

208 *See, e.g.,* AMA Code Opinion 3.1.5—Professionalism in Relationships with Media, Am. Med. Ass'n, *available at* http://www.ama-assn.org/ama/pub/physician-resources/medical-ethics/code-medical-ethics.page (last visited Aug. 1, 2016), *archived at* https://perma.cc/ZR8K-FC93 ("To safeguard patient interests when working with representatives of the media, all physicians should: (a) Obtain consent from the patient or the patient's authorized representative before releasing information; (b) Release only information specifically authorized by the patient or patient's representative or that is part of the public record"); Fédération Internationale de Médecine [du Sport, Code of Ethics, ¶ 11 ("[n]o information about an athlete may be given to a third party without the consent of the athlete.")

209 *See, e.g.,* Mark A. Hall, et al., Health Care Law and Ethics 168–69 (2003) (collecting cases and statutes for the proposition that doctors have

both common law and statutory obligations to keep patient information confidential); Health Insurance Portability and Accountability Act ("HIPAA"), 45 C.F.R. § 164.502 (prohibiting use or disclosure of health information except in certain situations, including where patient has provided consent).

210 *See, e.g.,* Charles A. Welch, *Sacred Secrets—The Privacy of Medical Records*, 435 N. Eng. J. Med. 371 (2001); Mark A. Rothstein, *Improve Privacy in Research By Eliminating Informed Consent? IOM Report Misses the Mark*, 37 J.L. Med. & Ethics 507, 510 (2009) (describing the confidentiality of medical information as a "sacred trust" with healthcare providers). *See also U.S. v. Westinghouse Elec. Corp.*, 638 F.2d 570, 577 ("Information about one's body and state of health is matter which the individual is ordinarily entitled to retain within the private enclave where he may lead a private life.") (Internal quotations and citations omitted).

211 *See* Christopher R. Deubert, I. Glenn Cohen, Holly Fernandez Lynch, *Protecting and Promoting the Health of NFL Players: Legal and Ethical Analysis and Recommendations*, § 2(C) (2016) (discussing NFL club doctors' legal and ethical obligations to keep player health information confidential, including when such information can be provided to the clubs).

212 *See id.*

213 Josh Alper, *Brandon Browner on Earl Thomas, Richard Sherman: Hit that shoulder, hit that elbow*, ProFootballTalk (Jan. 26, 2015, 3:15 PM), http://profootballtalk.nbcsports.com/2015/01/26/brandon-browner -on-earl-thomas-richard-sherman-hit-that-shoulder-hit-that-elbow/, *archived at* http://perma.cc/B5YF-NT3C.

214 Mike Florio, *Concussions take on a strategic component*, ProFootball-Talk (Jan. 23, 2012, 10:09 PM), http://profootballtalk.nbcsports.com /2012/01/23/concussions-take-on-a-strategic-component/, *archived at* http://perma.cc/5D6N-AMVT.

215 Mike Florio, *Disclosure of injury information continues to put NFL players in a delicate spot*, ProFootballTalk (July 10, 2015, 12:34 PM), http://profootballtalk.nbcsports.com/2015/07/10/disclosure-of-injury -information-continues-to-put-nfl-players-in-a-delicate-spot/, *archived at* http://perma.cc/PYL4-KMRY ("When it comes to disclosing injury information, the NFL has struggled at times to strike the right balance. To create a sense of transparency (and in turn to discourage gamblers from pursuing inside information by cozying up to players, coaches, and other team employees), the NFL has developed an injury-reporting system far more complex than, for example, hockey's upper-body/lower-body shell game.")

216 *Id.*

217 *See* NFL League Policies for Players, 52 (2013) ("The NFL opposes all forms of illegal gambling, as well as legal betting on NFL games or other professional, college or Olympic sports. Such activity negatively affects the interests, welfare and integrity of the NFL, its games, clubs, players and coaches, and diminishes public confidence in legitimate sport. Equally important, even social gambling among co-workers can lead to discord, violence and a loss of team cohesion.")

218 *See* NFL League Policies for Players, 52–58 (2013) ("League policy strictly prohibits NFL Personnel [including players] from participating in or facilitating any form of illegal gambling," "League policy prohibits advertising or promotional activities by NFL Personnel [including players] that reasonably can be perceived as constituting affiliation with or endorsement of gambling or gambling-related activities").

219 *See* Christopher R. Deubert, I. Glenn Cohen, Holly Fernandez Lynch, *Protecting and Promoting the Health of NFL Players: Legal and Ethical Analysis and Recommendations*, § 18(A) (2016).

220 *See* Michael B. Engle, *The No-Fantasy League: Why the National Football League Should Ban Its Players from Managing Personal Fantasy Football Teams*, 11 DePaul J. Sports L. & Contemp. Probs. 59, 85 (2015) (discussing Karras and Hornung cases).

221 Additionally, gambling on football represents approximately 45% of all legal gambling. *See* David Purdum, *Wagers, Bettor Losses Set Record*, ESPN (Jan. 30, 2015), http://espn.go.com/chalk/story/_/id/12253876 /nevada-sports-bettors-wagered-lost-more-ever-2014, *archived at* http://perma.cc/RKR8-WPD7. Thus, there is substantially less gambling in the other sports, which might explain their less robust injury reporting policies.

222 For examples of such studies in high school and college sports, *see* Barry P. Boden et al., *Catastrophic Injuries in Pole Vaulters, A Prospective 9-Year Follow-up Study*, 40 Am. J. Sports Med. 1488 (2012); Frederick O. Mueller and Robert C. Cantu, *Catastrophic injuries and fatalities in high school and college sports, fall 1982–spring 1988*, 22 Med. & Sci. in Sports & Exercise 737 (1990).

223 Some of the studies discussed in this Report were the result of the leagues' willingness to provide some injury data upon request. While it is commendable that the leagues occasionally provide the data when requested, this does not entirely address the concerns outlined in Recommendation 1.

224 Christopher R. Deubert, I. Glenn Cohen, Holly Fernandez Lynch, *Protecting and Promoting the Health of NFL Players: Legal and Ethical Analysis and Recommendations*, Recommendation 17:1-B (2016).

225 *See The Datalys Center for Sports Injury Research and Prevention*, NCAA, http://www.ncaa.org/health-and-safety/medical-conditions /datalys-center-sports-injury-research-and-prevention (last visited Aug. 3, 2016), *archived at* https://perma.cc/2M75-B24L.

226 *See, e.g., Data transparency*, GlaxoSmithKline, http://www.gsk.com/ en-gb/behind-the-science/innovation/data-transparency (last visited June 20, 2016), *archived at* https://perma.cc/M5HN-NLHN; *Frequently Asked Questions*, the YODA Project, http://yoda.yale.edu/frequently -asked-questions-faqs#Data (last visited June 20, 2016), *archived at* https://perma.cc/2Z98-R7HC.

227 *See* Paul McCrory et al., *Consensus statement on concussion in sport: the 4th Int'l Conference on Concussion in Sport held in Zurich, November 2012*, 47 Br. J. Sports Med. 250, 251 (2013).

228 *Id.* at 253.

229 MLB CBA, Att. 36, ¶ 2.

230 *See* Paul McCrory et al., *Consensus statement on concussion in sport: the 4th Int'l Conference on Concussion in Sport held in Zurich, November 2012*, 47 Br. J. Sports Med. 250, 250–58 (2013) (discussing the challenges of and best practices for diagnosing concussions).

231 *See id.*

232 *See id.* at 252–58 (discussing generally the challenges of determining when an athlete has recovered from a concussion).

233 Letter from Larry Ferazani, NFL, to authors (July 18, 2016).

234 *Id.*

235 Mike Florio, *NFL tells teams to stop commenting about concussed players*, ProFootballTalk (Nov. 11, 2016, 7:50 PM), http://profootballtalk .nbcsports.com/2016/11/11/nfl-tells-teams-to-stop-commenting-about -concussed-players/, *archived at* https://perma.cc/Z7ML-ZP7W.

236 *Id.*

237 Christopher R. Deubert, I. Glenn Cohen, Holly Fernandez Lynch, *Protecting and Promoting the Health of NFL Players: Legal and Ethical Analysis and Recommendations* Recommendation 7:4-B (2016).

238 Mike Florio, *Disclosure of injury information continues to put NFL players in a delicate spot*, ProFootballTalk (July 10, 2015, 12:34 PM), http://profootballtalk.nbcsports.com/2015/07/10/disclosure-of-injury -information-continues-to-put-nfl-players-in-a-delicate-spot/, *archived at* http://perma.cc/PYL4-KMRY ("many players would like to keep [injury information] secret, in order to keep an opponent from hitting, poking, and/or kicking the injured region.")

Chapter 3

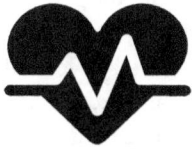

Health-Related Benefits

In this Chapter, we summarize the various health-related benefits available to the players in each of the leagues. Specifically, for each league, we examine: (1) retirement benefits; (2) insurance benefits; (3) disability benefits; (4) workers' compensation benefits; (5) education-related benefits;[a] and, (6) the existence of health-specific committees jointly run by the league and players association. Each of these domains is relevant to protecting players should they experience negative health effects during and after their playing years, and also to promoting their ability to maintain their health and well-being over the longer term. Given that a decision to play or continue to play professional sports, like many other decisions, is a matter of weighing risks and benefits, those decisions must be made against a backdrop of available benefits. It is for this reason that we spend considerable space describing and evaluating the available benefits in each league.

---

a   By "education-related benefits," we mean programs that assist players to obtain or complete their college degree, or to obtain training for a second career.

Before we begin our analysis of the leagues' health-related benefits, there are a few prefatory notes that should frame our analysis.

1) FINANCIAL HEALTH

Our goal is to examine all the inputs that may influence players' health, including the so-called "social determinants of health." Financial health is a major contributor to physical and mental health, and also, in turn, affected by physical and mental health.[b] Indeed, many studies have shown a correlation between financial debt and poor physical health.[1] While the actual career earnings of NFL players are difficult to ascertain,[c] there have been multiple studies about NFL player financial health with a variety of results.

According to a 2009 *Sports Illustrated* article, by the time NFL players have been retired for two years, 78% of them are bankrupt or in financial distress.[2] But other studies have somewhat different findings. According to a 2009 NFL-funded study of former NFL players by the University of Michigan, the median income of a former player between the ages of 30 and 49 is $85,000, compared to $55,000 for the general population. The study also found that 8.4% of former players between 30 and 49 were below the poverty level, as compared to 9.5% of the general population.[3] A 2015 academic study also found different results than those arrive at in the *Sports Illustrated* article, finding that within

two years of the end of their career, only 1.9% of players were bankrupt—while also finding that one in six players was bankrupt within 12 years of leaving the NFL.[4] Moreover, in 2012, ESPN released the documentary *Broke* detailing the financial problems of professional athletes, and exploring how they had gotten there.[5] And in a 2014–15 survey of 763 former players by *Newsday*, 50.59% of former players interviewed said they had struggled financially since their playing career ended.[6]

There are, however, important limitations to the above-mentioned studies.

First, to support its claims *Sports Illustrated* cited "reports from . . . athletes, players' associations, agents and financial advisers"[7] but no additional details and no information that can be independently verified.

Second, there are two potential limitations to the Michigan Study. First, the study population only included players who had vested rights under the NFL's Retirement Plan; meaning, the players generally had been on an NFL roster for at least three games in at least three seasons. However, there is likely a significant but unknown percentage of NFL players that never become vested under the Retirement Plan. Second, responders to the survey were 36.8% African-American and 61.4% White—almost a complete reversal of the NFL's population of current players. While the racial demographics of former players is likely closer to the population of the Michigan Study, *i.e.*, there were formerly more white players than in the current NFL, the Michigan Study did not provide such data on the former player population and did not adjust or account for the racial demographics of the former player population. We discussed the Michigan Study in a telephone call with Dr. David Weir, the Study's lead author. Dr. Weir explained that: (1) due to limited resources, the population of players to be studied and contacted was limited to the data and contact information available to and provided by the NFL; and, (2) the NFL did not provide racial demographics of former players and thus the study could not adjust for that factor. Weir also believes that the racial demographics of former players is substantially similar to the racial demographics of the Michigan Study's participants. Finally, Weir explained that, during the internal review process with the NFL, the study was leaked to the media, preventing the study from being amended and submitted to a peer-reviewed publication.

Finally, there are also limitations to the *Newsday* survey: (1) the survey was sent via email and text message by the NFLPA to more than 7,000 former NFL players, thus eliminating former players who were less technologically savvy

---

b   Many experts have recognized that "financial insecurity can cause people to 'cut corners in ways that may affect their health and well-being,' like spending less on food, clothing, or prescriptions." Nadia N. Sawicki, *Modernizing Informed Consent: Expanding the Boundaries of Materiality,* Univ. Ill. L. Rev. (2016), *citing* Kevin R. Riggs and Peter A. Ubel, *Overcoming Barriers to Discussing Out-of-Pocket Costs With Patients,* 174 Jama Int. Med. 849 (2014); Peter A. Ubel, Amy P. Abernethy, and S. Yousuf Zafar, *Full Disclosure — Out-of-Pocket Costs as Side Effects,* 369 New Eng. J. Med. 1484 (2013). Indeed, to many, "financial well-being is certainly within the boundaries of most peoples' concept of health." *Id.,* quoting Michael S. Wilkes and David L. Schriger, *Caution: The Meter is Running: Informing Patients About Health Care Costs,* 165 Western J. Med 74, 78 (1996) (noting that "discussions about the cost of care are an important part of the physician-patient relationship").

c   Based on an average career length of approximately three years, the NFLPA has estimated that the average career earnings of an NFL player are $4 million after taxes. *See* Adam Molon, *Why So Many Ex-NFL Players Struggle With Money,* CNBC (Jan. 31, 2014, 12:29 PM), www.cnbc.com/id/101377457#, *archived at* http://perma.cc/F5YN-FJE2. Using an average salary of $1.9 million and an average career length of 3.5 years, others have estimated NFL players earn about $6.7 million in their careers, a figure largely on par with that of the NFLPA's. *See* Nick Schwartz, *The Average Career Earnings Of Athletes Across America's Major Sports Will Shock You,* USA Today, Oct. 24, 2013, http://ftw.usatoday.com/2013/10/average-career-earnings-nfl-nba-mlb-nhl-mls, *archived at* http://perma.cc/9DFP-WPQ2. However, the NFL has disputed the 3.5 years figure generally provided by the NFLPA, stating instead that players who actually make an NFL club have, on average, careers of about 6 years. *See What is average NFL player's career length? Longer than you might think, Commissioner Goodell says,* NFL (Apr. 18, 2011), http://nflcommunications.com/2011/04/18/what-is-average-nfl-player%E2%80%99s-career-length-longer-than-you-might-think-commissioner-goodell-says/, *archived at* http://perma.cc/PX5U-9SFK. Finally, it is important to point out that the average in this case does not reflect the median career earnings of NFL players, *i.e.,* the career earnings of your typical NFL player—the calculation of which would depend on how you define the typical player.

and also possibly skewing the sample towards those former players closer to the NFLPA; (2) the response rate for the survey was low (approximately 11%); and, (3) the study does not discuss the demographics of respondents, making it difficult to ascertain whether those who responded are a representative sample of all former players.

Despite these limitations, we provide the reader with the best existing data. Moreover, while there are limitations to the data collected to date as well as differences in the figures presented, it is clear that there are serious concerns about former players' financial difficulties.[8]

The relationship between physical and financial health goes in both directions. Without adequate savings and benefits during and after NFL play, players may find themselves insufficiently prepared to meet their physical and mental health needs, especially in the event of crisis. Furthermore, crises in physical and mental health are closely tied to bankruptcy, home foreclosure, and other serious financial setbacks.[9] At its worst, these circumstances can lead to a vicious cycle—poor health outcomes lead to financial losses, which worsen the ability to combat physical and mental health impairments, which in turn further deplete financial resources.

Financial health is also in and of itself an important component of a person's health. Financial difficulties can cause stress that contributes to or exacerbates psychological and physical ailments.

For all of the above reasons, it is thus critical that we examine the financial benefits available to players, including but not limited to retirement and investment plans.

2) WORKERS' COMPENSATION

Most of the benefits discussed herein are fairly straightforward, but it is helpful to explain workers' compensation benefits more fully. "Workers' compensation laws provide protections and benefits for employees who are injured in the course of their employment. In the typical case, the workers' compensation regime grants tort immunity to employers in exchange for the regime's protections and benefits to the employee,"[10] without the employee having to prove the employer was at fault, as they would have to in a typical tort lawsuit. While workers' compensation laws, systems and benefits vary widely among the states, workers' compensation generally provides two important benefits to workers: (1) monetary compensation; and, (2) coverage for medical care. We discuss each of these benefits in turn.

Workers' compensation payments typically depend on the employee's level of injury or disability and the extent to which the injury or disability affects the employee's ability to continue working. Generally, workers receive "around one-half to two-thirds of the employee's average weekly wage."[11] In addition, the amount of benefits is subject to maximums which are usually tied to the state's average weekly wage,[12] and are generally between $500 and $1,000.[13] The benefits continue so long as the employee is disabled or unable to work. Additionally, the amount a player receives in workers' compensation often reduces the amount a club is obligated to pay the player for certain other CBA-provided benefits.[14] Again, it is important to bear in mind that these benefits and schemes can vary widely among the states.

Medical care coverage is an important benefit available to players through workers' compensation. Often, if a player is injured during the season, he is entitled to medical care from the club during the season of injury only.[15] Consequently, if a player suffers an injury that causes him to have ongoing or recurring healthcare needs (such as surgeries) well beyond the season of injury (and for perhaps the rest of his life), the club will have no obligation to pay for such care. Workers' compensation fills that gap. Workers' compensation statutes generally require the employer (in practice, usually the employer's insurance carrier) to pay for reasonable and necessary medical expenses that are the result of an injury suffered in the workplace in perpetuity. More importantly, the worker does not have to pay for any part of the care.

3) AVAILABILITY OF PLAN DOCUMENTS

Although we analyze the leagues' various benefit programs, many of the actual plan documents—to the extent they exist—are not publicly available.[16] Typical plan documents for these kinds of benefits are dozens or hundreds of pages long, detailing a variety of intricacies and nuances in the plans. Without the ability to review those plans in detail, we rely on the summaries provided in the CBAs (which vary in detail) and other publicly available information. Consequently, readers should not consider these summaries as definitive statements concerning the leagues' various benefit programs, but instead as informed general explanations.

4) COMPARING THE PLANS

In Tables 3-J and 3-K below, we provide our best estimates of the Big Four Leagues' retirement/pension plans. While we do our best to summarize the amounts potentially available to players under all of the various plans, we stress caution in extrapolating data from our analyses and summaries. The benefit plans contain intricate legal, financial, and actuarial components that determine a player's ultimate entitlement. For example, many of the plans contain offsets concerning other benefits, such that if a player is receiving payments under a retirement plan, any amounts he could receive for disability benefits are likely to be decreased. The eligibility criteria for the various benefits also vary within and across the leagues. Consequently, it is difficult to determine in generalities the amounts to which a former player might be entitled.

5) OTHER BENEFITS

In considering the scope of health-related benefits available to players, it is important also know that the degree to which players are able to collect the full balance of their contracts varies depending on the league and the player's individual contract. In Chapter 5: Compensation, we examine the degree to which player compensation is guaranteed. For our purposes here, we are focused on those benefits available to protect and promote player health other than the compensation available as part of a player's contract.

In addition, while this Chapter focuses on those benefits that are agreed to as part of the CBA, many if not all of the leagues—and the corresponding unions—have other programs and benefits available to players that are not a part of the CBA. For example, the NFL's Player Engagement Department operates many programs designed to help future, current, and former NFL players, with particular focus on transitioning to a life after football.[17] Similarly, the NFLPA offers a variety of internships and educational programs for players.[18,d] Other leagues and unions likely have similar programs, but they are not well-publicized and publicly-available details can be sparse. Consequently, while we focus on the benefits for which more information is available, readers should understand that the leagues likely offer additional benefits to the players.

* * *

With those prefatory and explanatory notes in mind, we turn to our analysis of the leagues' various benefit plans.

A) NFL Health-Related Benefits

As a preliminary matter, NFL player eligibility for many of the collectively-bargained benefits discussed below depends on the number of "Credited Seasons" a player has earned. Generally, a player earns a Credited Season when he is entitled to be paid for at least three regular season games.[19]

Additionally, it is important to understand the relationship between player benefits and player salaries. In the NFL, the players' share of revenues is referred to as the Player Cost Amount.[20] The Player Cost Amount is one of two essential components for calculating the Salary Cap, which is the "absolute maximum amount of Salary that each club may pay or be obligated to pay or provide to players . . . at any time during a particular League Year."[21] The other essential component of the Salary Cap calculation is Player Benefit Costs. Player Benefit Costs are the total amounts the NFL and its clubs spend on all the programs and benefits described herein, in addition to the costs of providing medical care to NFL players.[22] The Salary Cap is determined by subtracting Player Benefit Costs from the Player Cost Amount and dividing by the number of clubs in the NFL.[23] In other words, the Salary Cap equals Player Cost Amount minus Player Benefit Costs divided by 32. *Thus, the more that is paid to NFL players—including retired players—in the form of benefits and medical care, i.e., Player Benefits Cost, the less they are able to receive in the form of salary.* Indeed, in 2015, when the Salary Cap was $143,280,000 per club, each club was charged $37,550,000 in Player Benefit Costs. Thus, out of a possible $180,830,000 that could have been spent on player salaries by each club, 26.2% was allocated to player benefits.

It is important to clarify these numbers. As Figure 3-A shows on the next page, about 50% of a club's revenue is allocated toward the players. The club keeps the other 50%. Of the 50% allocated for the players (the Player Cost Amount), in 2015, 26.2% of that was used on player benefits. Thus, in 2015, we can estimate that each club had approximately $361,660,000 in revenue, $180,830,000 of which would be available for players. $37,550,000 was spent on player benefits. The $37,550,000 is 26.2% of the Player Cost Amount and 10.4% of the club's revenue.

---

d   These programs are discussed in Appendices D and E of our Report, *Protecting and Promoting the Health of NFL Players: Legal and Ethical Analysis and Recommendations.*

Figure 3-A: Division of All Revenue

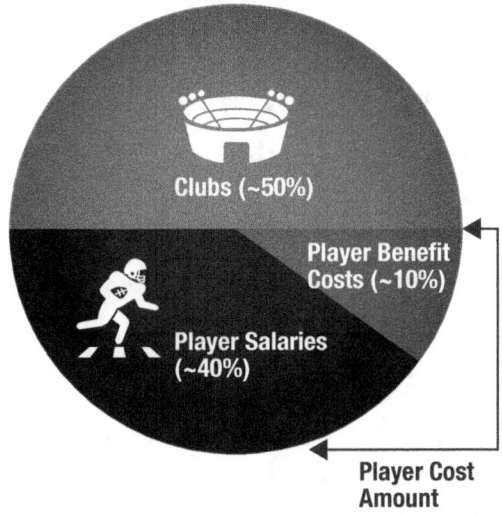

Table 3-A:
Severance Pay Benefits[e]

Seasons	Amount for Each Credited Season
1989–92	$5,000
1993–99	$10,000
2000–08	$12,500
2009	$15,000
2010	0
2011	$15,000
2012–13	$17,500
2014–16	$20,000
2017–20	$22,500

1) RETIREMENT BENEFITS

The NFL provides four retirement-focused benefits: (a) the Severance Pay Plan; (b) the Bert Bell/Pete Rozelle NFL Player Retirement Plan ("Retirement Plan"); (c) the Player Annuity Plan; and, (d) the Second Career Savings Plan.

a) Severance Pay Plan[24]

The Severance Pay Plan, first created in 1982, entitles eligible players to severance pay for each Credited Season. To be eligible, a player must have at least two Credited Seasons, at least one of which was in 1993 or later. A player becomes eligible for the lump sum severance payment 12 months after his last contract expired or was terminated. Table 3-A below summarizes the amount of benefits available to players under the Severance Pay Plan.

For example, a player who played from 1998 through 2009 would be entitled to a severance payment of $147,500: $10,000 for each of his two seasons between 1998 and 1999 ($20,000); $12,500 for each of his nine seasons between 2000 and 2008 ($112,500); and, $15,000 for 2009.

b) Retirement Plan[25]

The NFL's Retirement Plan, first created in 1968, provides eligible players with retirement benefits, and offers survivor benefits for players' wives and family. Generally, only "Vested Players" are eligible for retirement benefits. A Vested Player is a player who fits one of the following criteria: (1) has three or more Credited Seasons, including at least one Credited Season after 1992; (2) has four or more Credited Seasons, including at least one Credited Season after 1973; or, (3) has five or more Credited Seasons.

Vested Players can receive monthly retirement benefits for life beginning at age 55. Players with a Credited Season before 1993 can receive reduced monthly benefits as early as age 45. A player can elect to receive retirement benefits until his death or defer some of the benefits to his family upon death. In order to begin receiving his retirement benefits at age 55, a player must file for them. If a player has not filed for them, he will automatically begin receiving the benefits at age 65. Table 3-B on the next page shows the monthly benefits per credit season of the Retirement Plan. These benefits are additive, meaning the player's monthly benefits are the sum of the monthly benefits to which he is entitled for each Credited Season.

---

e   Pursuant to the terms of the 2006 CBA, the NFL was not required to fund several benefit plans, including the Severance Pay Plan in 2010 if the 2010 season was not played with a Salary Cap — a situation which would only exist if the NFL and NFLPA were unable to agree to an extension of the CBA, which is what actually transpired. See 2006 CBA, Art. L; Art. LVI.

Table 3-B:

NFL Retirement Plan Benefits (If Taken after Age 55):

Credited Season	Monthly Benefit Credit per Credited Season
Before 1982	$250
1982 through 1992	$255
1993 through 1994	$265
1995 through 1996	$315
1997	$365
1998 through 2011	$470
2012 through 2014	$560
2015 through 2017	$660
2018 through 2020	$760

In addition, the Retirement Plan includes $620 million in Legacy Benefits created as part of the 2011 CBA for players who played before 1993. The Legacy Benefits listed in Table 3-C below are in addition to the Retirement Benefits listed above.

Table 3-C:

NFL Retirement Plan Legacy Benefits

Credited Season	Monthly Benefit Credit per Credited Season
Before 1975	$124
1975 through 1992	$108

According to the NFL, as of 2015, 3,641 former players receive an average monthly retirement benefit of $1,656,[26] for a total of approximately $72,353,952 annually. In addition, about 90% of those former players also received Legacy Benefit payments, with an average monthly payment of $723.85,[27] for a total of approximately $28,464,677 in Legacy Benefit payments. Thus, in 2015, the NFL Retirement Plan paid a little over $100 million to former NFL players.

The Retirement Plan—which until 2011 also covered disability benefits—historically has been viewed negatively by former players. The filing process has been considered complex and lengthy,[28] resulting in many former players suing the Retirement Plan concerning their benefits.[29] During a 2007 hearing before the United States Senate Committee on Commerce, Science, and Transportation, it was revealed that only 317 former players were receiving disability benefits, out of the thousands that were eligible.[30]

Of additional concern, in recent years the NFLPA has been warning players that the Retirement Plan is underfunded.[31] Currently, the Plan only takes in enough money to cover about 54.5% of what it pays out,[32] jeopardizing its ability to pay retirement benefits in the future.

Tables 3-J and 3-K at the conclusion of this Chapter put these numbers in context, comparing monthly payments under the leagues' various retirement/pension plans.

c) Player Annuity Plan[33]

The Player Annuity Plan, first created in 1998, provides deferred compensation to players.[34] Players automatically contribute to the Annuity Plan through payroll deductions, which are then invested. The Annuity Plan is divided between a Qualified Account and a Nonqualified Account. The Qualified Account includes the maximum amount of compensation that can be deferred on a pre-tax basis pursuant to IRS rules. The maximum amount that could be deferred on a pre-tax basis in 2016 was $53,000.[35] The amount contributed to the Annuity Plan above this amount is the Nonqualified Account portion and must be taxed before being invested as part of the Annuity Plan.

To be eligible for the Annuity Plan, a current or former player must have at least one Credited Season. So long as the player is active, compensation will be deducted from his pay to fund his Annuity Plan account. A player does not vest[f] in his Qualified Account until he has earned at least three Credited Seasons, but a player is always vested in his Nonqualified Account.

A player can elect to receive a distribution at any time after he is done playing, provided the player is at least 45, or is at least 35 and five years have elapsed since the player last earned a Credited Season. Distributions must begin no later than the first day of the month after the player turns 65. Players can also elect different forms of distribution for each of their accounts and different dates for payments to begin. Payment forms include: (1) annual installments until the player reaches 45; (2) an annuity for life; (3) a reduced annuity for life, with a survivor annuity beginning after the player's death; (4) a lump sum, if the former player is at least 45 when the lump sum is to be paid; and, (5) a partial lump sum, if the player is at least 45 when the partial lump sum is paid, with the remainder paid in one of the other payment forms. Table 3-D on the next page provides details on this program.

---

f   "Vest" means "[t]o give (a person) an immediate, fixed right of present or future enjoyment." Black's Law Dictionary (9th ed. 2009). In essence, "vesting" in a benefit or retirement plan generally means the individual has earned the right to the benefit or retirement plan, typically by meeting a minimum number of years of employment.

Table 3-D:
NFL Player Annuity Plan Deferred Compensation Amounts (2016 Season)

Credited Seasons	Total Amount Allocated to Annuity Plan for That Season
1	$0
2	$5,000
3	$5,000
4	$70,000
5 or more	$80,000

The reason for the large increase in allocation from the third to fourth Credited Season is likely due to the vesting requirements. As stated earlier, a player is not vested in his Qualified Account—which represents the bulk of the Annuity Plan contribution—until after his third Credited Season. If he does not vest in the Qualified Account, it is forfeited. Thus, by minimizing the amounts allocated before players vest in the Annuity Plan, the Annuity Plan minimizes the amount of deferred compensation that might be forfeited.

d) Second Career Savings Plan[36]

The Second Career Savings Plan, first created in 1993, is a 401(k)[37] plan that helps players save for retirement in a tax-favored manner. All NFL players are eligible for the Plan, regardless of the number of Credited Seasons.

To fund the Plan, the player's club is required to contribute a minimum of: $1,000 if the player has exactly one Credited Season; $7,200 if the player has exactly two Credited Seasons; and, $3,600 if the player has three or more Credited Seasons. In addition, the club will contribute $2 for every $1 contributed by a player during a year in which the player earned a Credited Season, provided the player already has at least one Credited Season, up to a maximum of $26,000 between 2015 and 2018, and $28,000 between 2019 and 2020. Players are automatically enrolled in the plan, with 10% of their pre-tax salary going towards the plan. Players can change the amount of their contributions or opt out of the plan at any time.

A player can receive benefits after he is 45 provided the player is not employed by a club,[38] or after the player is 59½. The player can receive the benefits in a variety of forms: (1) a single lump sum payment; (2) installments over ten years; (3) an annuity for the player's life; or, (4) an annuity for the player's life and surviving spouse's life.

According to the NFLPA, 99% of NFL players are enrolled in the Second Career Savings Plan.[39]

2) INSURANCE BENEFITS

The NFL provides four insurance-related benefits: (a) the Player Insurance Plan; (b) the Health Reimbursement Account Plan; (c) the Long Term Care Insurance Plan; and, (d) the Former Player Life Improvement Plan.

a) Player Insurance Plan[40]

The NFL Player Insurance Plan, first created in 1968, provides players and their immediate family with life insurance, accidental death and dismemberment insurance, medical coverage, dental coverage, and wellness benefits. The wellness benefits include access to clinicians for mental health, alcoholism, and substance abuse, child and parenting support services, elder care support services, pet care services, legal services, and identity theft services.

Any player in the NFL, including a practice squad player, is eligible for the Player Insurance Plan. Players who are vested under the Retirement Plan continue to receive coverage for five years after their career ends. Players who are not vested are only covered through the end of the plan year in which they play their last game.

After their career has ended, players have the option of continuing coverage pursuant to the Consolidated Omnibus Budget Reconciliation Act ("COBRA")[41] for a period of 18, 29, or 36 months. Players are required to pay the full cost of coverage plus 2% for administrative costs.

It is important to note that COBRA is an extension of healthcare coverage that employers are required to provide as a matter of law. Thus, NFL clubs are not unique in providing COBRA coverage, and all of the American clubs in the leagues discussed herein are also be obligated to provide COBRA coverage to their former players. In contrast, former players who are residents of Canada can generally obtain healthcare through government-funded plans at any time during or after their playing career.

b) Health Reimbursement Account ("HRA") Plan[42]

The HRA Plan, first created in 2006, helps to pay out-of-pocket healthcare expenses after players are no longer employed by an NFL club and after the period of extended medical coverage under the Player Insurance Plan that is paid by the NFL has ended.[43] To be eligible, players whose last Credited Season was in 2004 or 2005 must have at least eight Credited Seasons, or, players whose last Credited Season was in 2006 or later must have at least three Credited Seasons.

A player is eligible to withdraw amounts from his HRA Plan account for medical expenses incurred provided he files for reimbursement within 24 months of receiving the medical bill to be reimbursed.

To fund the players' HRA Plan accounts, clubs contribute the amounts to each player's Health Account. Players do not contribute their own money to their Health Account. Details on the HRA plan contribution scheme can be found in Table 3-E.

Table 3-E:
NFL HRA Plan Account Contributions

Credited Seasons	Health Account Contribution per Credited Season
2009 and prior	$25,000
2010	$0
2011 through 2015	$25,000
2016 through 2020	$30,000

c) Long Term Care Insurance Plan

The Long Term Care Insurance Plan, first created in 2011, provides medical insurance to cover the costs of long-term care for NFL players (but not their family members). Players are eligible for the Long Term Care Insurance Plan if they are: (1) vested players under the Retirement Plan; (2) between the ages of 50 and 76; and, (3) have been certified by a licensed healthcare provider as requiring critical supervision, or requiring the presence of another person within arm's reach due to inability to perform a required number of defined activities of daily living. The Plan provides benefits of $150 a day for a maximum of four years.[g]

Players are not required to contribute to the funding of the Plan. In addition, the Plan provides benefits to all former players who are eligible.

d) Former Player Life Improvement Plan[44]

The Former Player Life Improvement Plan, first created in 2007, permits qualifying former players (and in some cases their dependents) not otherwise covered by health insurance to receive reimbursement for medical costs for "joint replacements, prescription drugs, assisted living, Medicare supplemental insurance, spinal treatment, and neurological treatment." Former NFL players who are vested under the

---

g   For comparison, according to the U.S. Department of Health and Human Services, the average cost of long-term care in a semi-private room in a nursing home is $205 per day, and $229 per day for a private room. *Costs of Care*, U.S. Dep't of Health and Human Services (last visited Aug. 25, 2016), http://longtermcare.gov /costs-how-to-pay/costs-of-care, *archived at* https://perma.cc/RZ4N-BFHB.

Retirement Plan are eligible for the plan. However there are many benefits under this plan, some of which have additional eligibility requirements, so not every player is eligible for every benefit.

---

3) DISABILITY BENEFITS

The NFL provides two disability-related benefits: (a) the Disability & Neurocognitive Benefit Plan; and, (b) the 88 Plan.

a) Disability & Neurocognitive Benefit Plan[45]

The Disability & Neurocognitive Benefit Plan provides eligible players with disability benefits, including benefits based on neurocognitive disability. The Plan provides four types of benefits: (1) Total and Permanent Disability Benefits; (2) Line-of-Duty Disability Benefits; (3) Mild Neurocognitive Disability Benefits; and, (4) Moderate Neurocognitive Disability Benefits.

A player is eligible for "Total and Permanent Disability Benefits" if the Initial Claims Committee[46] or Disability Board[47] determines "(1) that he has become totally disabled to the extent that he is substantially prevented from or substantially unable to engage in any occupation or employment for remuneration or profit . . . , and (2) that such condition is permanent."

A player is awarded Total and Permanent Disability Benefits pursuant to one of four categories: (1) Active Football: the player is an active player and the disability results from NFL activities;[48] (2) Active Nonfootball: the player is an active player but the disability does not result from NFL activities; (3) Inactive A: the player is a former player who filed for disability benefits within 15 years of his last Credited Season; or, (4) Inactive B: the player is a former player who filed for disability benefits more than 15 years after his last Credited Season. Inactive A and Inactive B disability benefits do not have an eligibility requirement that the disability resulted from NFL activities.

A player is eligible for Line-of-Duty Disability Benefits if the Initial Claims Committee or Disability Board determines that the player "incurred a substantial disablement . . . arising out of [NFL] football activities." Line-of-Duty Disability Benefits address those injuries or disabilities that are not considered permanent.

A player is eligible for Neurocognitive Disability Benefits if: (1) the player is vested under the Retirement Plan; (2) the player is under age 55; (3) the player had at least one Credited Season after 1994; (4) the player does not receive retirement benefits; (5) the player does not receive total and permanent disability benefits; (6) the player executes a release releasing the NFL and clubs from any liability for head or brain injuries; and, (7) the player is determined to have mild or moderate neurocognitive impairment.

A player has "mild neurocognitive impairment if he has problems with one or more domains of cognitive functioning which reflect acquired brain dysfunction but are not severe enough to cause marked interference in day-to-day activities."

A player has "moderate neurocognitive impairment if he has problems with one or more domains of cognitive functioning which reflect acquired brain dysfunction resulting in marked interference with everyday life activities, but not severe enough to prevent the Player from working."

A player must submit to a medical examination by a doctor of the Disability Board's choosing to determine if the player has neurocognitive impairment.

Details on the disability and neurocognitive benefits can be found in Table 3-F.

Table 3-F:
NFL Disability and Neurocognitive Benefits

Type of Disability	Monthly Benefit
Total & Permanent: Active Football	$22,084
Total & Permanent: Active Nonfootball	$13,750
Total & Permanent: Inactive A	$11,250
Total & Permanent: Inactive B	$5,000
Line-of-Duty	$3,000
Mild Neurocognitive	$2,250

A player can only receive one of the above benefits at any one time.

According to a 2010 analysis of the NFLPA's disability claims database, disability benefit applications had never exceeded 200 applications in a year until 2008 and 2009, when there were more than 400 claims in both years.[49] As of 2010, NFL disability benefit claims were approved approximately 38% of the time.[50] Importantly, the benefits criteria changed after the 2011 CBA, so current data would not be comparable. Moreover, according to the same analysis, of the players who filed for disability benefits, the mean age at which they retired from the NFL was 30.2 years.[51] Additionally, the mean age at which the player filed for disability benefits was 38.1 years.[52]

Finally, through the year 2009, there had been a total of 2,670 disability benefit claims, with 2,423 (90.7%) for orthopedic conditions, 52 (1.9%) for neurological conditions, 18 (0.7%) for psychological conditions, 18 (0.7%) for cardiovascular conditions, and 159 for other unspecified conditions (6.0%).[53]

b) The 88 Plan[54]

The 88 Plan, first created in 2006, provides former players suffering from dementia, ALS, or Parkinson's disease with benefits. The 88 Plan is named for John Mackey, a Hall of Fame tight end for the Baltimore Colts and San Diego Chargers from 1963–72, who wore number 88 during his career. Mackey suffered from dementia later in life and died in 2011 at the age of 69.

Vested Players under the Retirement Plan and players who have received Total and Permanent Disability Benefits under the Disability & Neurocognitive Benefit Plan who have been diagnosed with dementia, ALS, or Parkinson's disease are eligible. The 88 Committee, consisting of an NFL designee and an NFLPA designee, determines whether the player qualifies for the benefit.

The 88 Plan will reimburse or pay the following costs for medical care that are related to a player's Dementia, ALS, or Parkinson's disease: (1) institutional care; (2) home custodial care provided by an unrelated third party; physician services; (3) durable medical equipment; and, (4) prescription medication. The maximum benefits are $130,000 per year so long as the player continues to suffer from Dementia, ALS or Parkinson's disease. Finally, there is no requirement that the player prove that his condition is related to his NFL career.

4) WORKERS' COMPENSATION BENEFITS

The NFL CBA requires clubs to provide workers' compensation coverage or comparable benefits, including clubs that are "in any state where workers' compensation coverage is not compulsory or . . . [are] excluded from a state's workers' compensation coverage[.]"[55] The second part of the preceding sentence is important. Florida, for example, does not require employers to provide workers' compensation coverage.[56] Consequently, players with the Miami Dolphins, Tampa Bay Buccaneers, and Jacksonville Jaguars would not have workers' compensation coverage without this provision. Nevertheless, workers' compensation benefits and statutes have been contentious issues in the NFL. In recent years, the NFL and its clubs have reportedly sponsored legislation in several states, including California, Illinois and Louisiana, to restrict players' workers' compensation benefits.[57]

5) EDUCATION-RELATED BENEFITS

The NFL's Tuition Assistance Plan, first created in 2002, reimburses players for tuition, fees, and book costs associated with attending an eligible educational institution. All current NFL players with at least one Credited Season are eligible for the plan. In addition, former players with at least five Credited Seasons are also eligible, provided that the costs are incurred within four years of the player's last season.

For any course in which players seek to use this benefit for reimbursement, the player must have received a "C" or better in the course and submit his claim for reimbursement within six months of when the final grade is issued. The maximum reimbursement is $20,000 per year.[h] A former player with at least five Credited Seasons is eligible for up to $60,000 in reimbursements total.

In recent years, the NFL and its clubs have reportedly sponsored legislation in several states, including California, Illinois and Louisiana, to restrict players' workers' compensation benefits.

6) JOINT HEALTH-SPECIFIC COMMITTEES

There are two health-related committees provided for in the NFL CBA: (a) the Joint Committee on Player Safety and Welfare ("Joint Committee"); and, (b) the Accountability and Care Committee ("ACC").

a) Joint Committee on Player Safety and Welfare

The Joint Committee, first established in 1977, consists of three representatives chosen by the NFL and three chosen by the NFLPA.[58] The Joint Committee's purpose is to "discuss[] the player safety and welfare aspects of playing equipment, playing surfaces, stadium facilities, playing rules, player-coach relationships, drug abuse prevention programs and other relevant subjects."[59] In addition, the NFLPA has "the right to commence an investigation before the Joint Committee if the NFLPA believes that the medical care of a team is inadequate.[60]

While a complaint to the Joint Committee results in a review by neutral physicians, the definition of the scope of that review process' authority is vague. The Joint Committee is obligated to act upon the recommendations of the neutral physicians, but it is unclear what it means for the Joint Committee to act and there is nothing obligating the NFL or any club to abide by the neutral physicians' or Joint Committee's recommendations. Moreover, there is no indication that the neutral physicians or Joint Committee could award damages to an injured player.[61]

In 2012, the NFLPA commenced the first and only Joint Committee investigation.[62] The nature and results of that investigation are confidential per an agreement between the NFL and NFLPA.[63]

b) Accountability and Care Committee

The ACC, created in 2011, consists of the NFL Commissioner or his designee; the NFLPA Executive Director or his designee; and six additional members "experienced in fields relevant to healthcare for professional athletes," three appointed by the Commissioner and three by the NFLPA Executive Director.[64] The CBA dictates that the ACC is to: (1) encourage and support programs for outstanding professional training by club medical staffs; (2) develop a standardized pre-season and postseason physical examination and education protocol to inform players of the risks associated with playing football; (3) conduct research into prevention and treatment of illness and injury commonly experienced by professional athletes; (4) conduct a confidential player survey at least once every two years to solicit the players' input and opinion regarding the adequacy of medical care; (5) assist in the development and maintenance of injury surveillance and medical record systems; and, (6) undertake such other duties as the Commissioner and Executive Director may assign.[65] Additionally, players can make complaints about their medical care to the ACC—but the ACC then refers those complaints to the NFL and club involved.[66]

* * *

With an understanding of the NFL's health-related benefits, we now turn to our analysis of the other leagues' health-related benefits.

---

h   According to the College Board, the average tuition at a public four-year university for an in-state student is $9,410; the average tuition at a public four-year university for an out-of-state student is $23,893; and, the average tuition at a private four-year university is $32,405. See Average Published Undergraduate Charges by Sector, 2015-16, CollegeBoard, http://trends.collegeboard.org/college-pricing/figures-tables /average-published-undergraduate-charges-sector-2015-16 (last visited Mar. 17, 2016), archived at https://perma.cc/HNW6-FBKG.

B) MLB Health-Related Benefits

As explained in the Introduction, Section C: Collective Bargaining Agreements, in the fall of 2016, MLB and the MLBPA agreed to and ratified the terms of a new CBA. However, as of the date this Report went to press, the parties had not yet published the new CBA. Thus, this Section principally relies on information contained in the 2012 CBA and other documents that existed prior to the new CBA. Specifically, most of MLB's health-related benefits are contained in the Major League Baseball Players Benefit Plan ("Benefit Plan")[67] includes many of the benefits in which we are interested.[i] In addition to these documents, we rely on a joint press release issued by the parties summarizing the changes agreed to in 2016. Nevertheless, the press release does not provide specifics of the changes to the Benefit Plan and other benefits, *i.e.*, it generally does not provide the amounts by which certain benefits increased. In discussing certain benefits below, we will indicate those that we understand to have been changed as part of the 2016 CBA negotiations, but caution the reader that important additional details, nuance or context are likely to be contained in the full length CBA and a revised Benefit Plan when they are complete.

1) RETIREMENT BENEFITS

The Benefit Plan includes a Pension Plan and an Investment Plan.

a) Pension Plan

The Pension Plan provides monthly payments to eligible former players based on the time period during which the player played, the player's retirement age, years of service, and annual compensation.[68] In 2016, MLB and the MLBPA agreed that pension benefits for certain but unspecified classes of retired players would be increased.[69] However, as discussed above, the specific amounts by which the benefits increased is not yet publicly known. Thus, what follows is a summary of the Pension Plan prior to the 2016 CBA negotiations.

Fixed monthly payments range from a low of $85.10 to a high of $13,666, with higher payments for players in more recent eras, players who retire at an older age, players with more years of service, and—where applicable—players with higher average annual salaries.[70] Players also receive variable monthly pension payments determined by a base monthly rate (calculated using the same factors as a player's fixed monthly payment) weighted by the investment performance of a fund for the variable benefits relative to a baseline interest rate.[71] Variable monthly payments range from a low of $82 to a high of $3,000.[72]

Players who played in 1980 or later are eligible for the Pension Plan on the first day they are on an MLB club's roster.[73] Players who played prior to 1980 are eligible for the Pension Plan in three ways: (1) they have four years of service;[74] (2) if they played prior to 1970, they reached the age of 65 prior to April 1, 1980;[75] and, (3) if they played in 1970 or later, they reached the age of 62 prior to April 1, 1980.[76] Players with fractional years of credited service receive an adjusted benefit amount.[77]

Table 3-G on the next page provides an abbreviated review of the Pension Plan benefits available to MLB players who played after 1991 and earned a mean of at least $68,212 during the three years of their career during which their salary was the highest. At the end of this Chapter, Tables 3-J and 3-K compare the monthly payments of the Big Four leagues' retirement/pension plans.

In reviewing the Tables below, it is important to understand that the "Retirement Age" is not the age at which a player retired from MLB. Instead, it is a term used in the Pension Plan to indicate the age at which a player begins to receive Pension Plan benefits. A player may "retire" for Benefit Plan purposes at any time between his 45th and 70½th birthday.[78] It is unclear whether a player will receive any Pension Plan benefits if they do not file for them. Finally, it is also important to note that the maximum annual pension amounts for players who played after 1991 are generally adjusted annually to equal the limitations on such plans set by the Internal Revenue Service.[79] In 2016, the limitation on the annual contributions to pension plans was $210,000.[80]

---

i   Although there is one Canadian MLB club (Toronto Blue Jays), the Benefit Plan does not include any special provisions for providing benefits under Canadian law.

Table 3-G:
MLB Player Combined Fixed and Variable Monthly Pension Payments for Players after 1991 (Abbreviated)

Retirement Age	Years of Credited Service						
	1	2	3		8	9	10+
45	$525	$1,050	$1,575		$4,200	$4,725	$5,250
46	$557	$1,115	$1,673	***	$4,462	$5,020	$5,578
47	$593	$1,186	$1,779		$4,744	$5,337	$5,930
***							
60	$1,427	$2,855	$4,283		$11,422	$12,850	$14,278
61	$1,541	$3,082	$4,624		$12,330	$13,872	$15,413
62	$1,666	$3,333	$5,000		$13,333	$15,000	$16,666

b) Investment Plan

The Investment Plan is a 401(k) plan. Under the Investment Plan, players have the option of having a portion of their compensation for any given year placed into the Investment Plan before taxes are withheld. The player can determine the amount to be placed into the Plan, subject to maximums set by the Internal Revenue Service.[81] Generally speaking, if the player does not elect to place any money into the Plan, an amount equal to the Internal Revenue Service maximum ($18,000 in 2016) will automatically be placed into the Plan for the player.[82] Although the clubs are not obligated to contribute anything to the Plan,[83] according to MLB, the clubs contribute millions of dollars each year to the players' accounts.[84] Additionally, all players are fully vested in their accounts at all times.[85] The NFL also offers a 401(k) plan.

2) INSURANCE BENEFITS

In 2016, MLB and the MLBPA agreed that players' medical and dental benefits for players would be "improved in a variety of areas."[86] However, as discussed above, the specific ways in which the benefits improvement is not yet publicly known. Thus, what follows is a summary of disability benefits prior to the 2016 CBA negotiations.

Like the NFL's Player Insurance Plan, MLB's Benefit Plan provides players and their families with life insurance, accidental death and dismemberment insurance, medical coverage, and dental coverage. A player and his dependents become eligible for health insurance as soon as the player is listed on a club's 40-man roster.[87] Disabled players and their dependents are also eligible for health insurance.[88] Additionally, former players may continue coverage through COBRA or by enrolling in the inactive health benefits program.[89] In 2016, according to MLB, "MLB spent over

$13 million to subsidize health care for retired (inactive) MLB players."[90] MLB expects this amount "to grow in the coming years."[91] Both the active and inactive player health care programs cover hospitalizations, visits to physicians, standard preventative care, and prescription drug costs through the use of preferred provider organizations.[92]

MLB's Benefit Plan also provides some wellness benefits, including access to clinicians for mental health and treatment for alcohol or drug abuse. However, the plan does not include other benefits included in the NFL Player Insurance Plan, including child and parenting support services, elder care support services, pet care services, legal services, and identity theft services.

3) DISABILITY BENEFITS

Before a player is old enough to begin receiving a pension, he may be eligible for disability benefits under the Pension Plan. In 2016, MLB and the MLBPA agreed that disability benefits for players would be "improved."[93] However, as discussed above, the specific amounts by which the benefits increased is not yet publicly known. Thus, what follows is a summary of disability benefits prior to the 2016 CBA negotiations.

Former players with at least four years of service who become totally and permanently disabled and all active players who become totally and permanently disabled are eligible for disability benefits.[94] Disability payments range from $2,500 to $5,000 a month for the player and $300 to $600 for dependents, depending on whether the player is active or inactive when he is disabled, the player's salary the year before his disability, and whether the player, if inactive, can show by clear and convincing evidence that he became disabled as a result of his baseball career.[95] Players

urchases annuities for players to provide a source of post-employment income.[113] To fund the Plan, the NBA con-ibutes 1% of Basketball Related Income,[114,k] and players ave the option of contributing up to 10% of their post-tax ncome into the plan.[115] Annuities under the Plan are pay-ble to a player a year after his retirement from the NBA or x months after his 30th birthday, whichever is later.[116] The enefit is paid in the form of installment payments until the layer reaches 50 years old or a joint life annuity paid over he player's life and his surviving spouse's life.[117] This is imilar to the NFL, which also offers an annuity plan.

) INSURANCE BENEFITS

he NBA offers three different health insurance or benefit rograms through a Voluntary Employees' Beneficiary association ("VEBA"): (a) a standard health insurance rogram; (b) a health reimbursement account ("HRA Benefit"); and, (c) a Retiree Medical Plan. VEBAs, created ursuant to Section 501(c)(9) of the Internal Revenue Code, raditionally provide "life, sick, accident, or similar benefits for] members or their dependents, or designated beneficia-ies."[118] The VEBA is described in the CBA as providing for at least some of the benefits discussed in this Section, but its ull scope is unclear. By comparison, the NFL does not have a VEBA.

In addition, the 2017 CBA provides that the NBA and National Basketball Players Association ("NBPA") are to "meet and confer to discuss the establishment of a long-term care insurance benefit."[119] In contrast, the NFL already offers a long-term care insurance plan.

a) Health Insurance

The NBA provides players and their families with life insurance, accidental death and dismemberment insur-ance, medical coverage, vision coverage, dental coverage, and prescription drug insurance benefits.[120] The 2017 CBA also states that the parties will "establish a mental wellness program for current players."[121] The extent of the NBA's intended mental wellness program is unclear, but, by com-parison, the NFL does offer a variety of wellness benefits, including: access to clinicians for mental health, alcoholism, and substance abuse; child and parenting support services; elder care support services; pet care services; legal services; and, identity theft services.

b) HRA Benefit

The HRA Benefit (formerly known as the Supplemental Medical Benefits Program) covers healthcare costs not oth-erwise covered by players' primary insurers, such as costs incurred in connection with the payment of premiums for health insurance.[122] The benefit is available during players' careers or after.

HRA plans can help to pay out-of-pocket healthcare expenses after players' careers have ended. The 2017 CBA provides for an HRA Benefit to be created for each player in the amount equal to "the lesser of: (A) $30,000 and (B) the difference between $150,000 and the sum of all contributions previously made to fund an HRA Benefit for such player in respect of prior Salary Cap Years . . . or, if such difference is $0 or a negative number, then $0."[123] However, the plan is only available to players who played in the NBA during and/or after the 2000–01 season, and also appears limited to current players.[124] By comparison, the NFL offers a health reimbursement account and Former Player Life Improvement Plan to help former players with medical costs not covered by insurance.

Players who play for the Toronto Raptors are not eligible for the HRA Benefit for the period of time during which the player is a resident of Canada (instead, they receive an alternative benefit).[125]

c) Retiree Medical Plan

The 2017 CBA established medical benefits for former play-ers for the first time.[126] According to the NBPA, under the new program:

- Retired players with between three and six years of NBA ser-vice time but who are not yet eligible for Medicare would be offered a plan that includes medical, hospital, and prescription drug coverage with modest out-of-pocket costs for deduct-ibles and co-pays.

- Those with between seven and nine years of service who are not eligible for Medicare would be offered the same coverage as the three-to-six-year players with lower out-of-pocket costs.

- Retired players with at least 10 years of service who are not eligible for Medicare would be offered the same coverage as the seven-to-nine-year players, as well as coverage for their families.

- Retired players who are eligible for Medicare who have three to nine years of service would be offered a $0 deductible and $0 co-pay plan along with a low-cost prescription drug plan; those with 10+ years of service would receive this coverage for themselves and their spouse.[127]

k   Basketball Related Income, generally speaking, "means the aggregate operating revenues" of the NBA and NBA clubs. 2017 NBA CBA, Art. VII, § 1(a)(1).

may receive a stabilizing disability supplement if, once they begin receiving their pension, their pension is less than their disability payment.[96]

MLB's disability benefits are significantly less than those provided by the NFL. NFL benefits for total and permanent disability range from $5,000 to $22,084 per month depending on the cause of the disability. In addition, the NFL offers benefits for disabilities which are less than total and permanent disabilities, and also offers neurocognitive disability benefits. MLB does not offer either of these benefits, although there is likely much less of a need for neurocognitive disability benefits in MLB than in the NFL.

4) WORKERS' COMPENSATION BENEFITS

Although not explicitly provided for in the CBA, MLB clubs, like NFL clubs, pay workers' compensation benefits to their players.[97] However, unlike the NFL, there is no provision in the MLB CBA that requires clubs to provide comparable benefits in states where workers' compensation coverage is not required. Consequently, it appears that players in states that do not require coverage, like those for the Tampa Bay Rays and Miami Marlins in Florida, are not automatically covered.[98] Nevertheless research suggests that the clubs generally do choose to provide coverage.

5) EDUCATION-RELATED BENEFITS

MLB offers a "College Scholarship Plan" to its players.[99] As part of the 2016 CBA negotiations, the parties agreed to "[i]mprovements to the College Scholarship Plan, particularly for players living outside of the U.S."[100] In October 2016, we asked MLB for more information about the College Scholarship Plan, including the criteria for receiving benefits under the Plan and the actual benefits received under the Plan. MLB responded only by directing us to the description of the College Scholarship Plan in the 2012 CBA, which does not clearly set forth the information we requested.

6) JOINT HEALTH-SPECIFIC COMMITTEES

MLB has a Safety and Health Advisory Committee ("SHAC"), comprised of representatives of both the clubs and the MLBPA, to "deal with emergency safety and health problems" and to review player working conditions.[101] The SHAC has advisory authority only,[102] but the parties have agreed to make "every reasonable effort" to utilize the SHAC before pursuing safety- and health-related grievances through the CBA's arbitration procedures.[103]

C) NBA Health-Related Bene

As a preliminary matter, it is important to po the NBA, like the NFL, the amounts paid to rent and former) in the form of benefits in m decreases the amounts available to current pl salary.[104]

1) RETIREMENT BENEFITS

The NBA offers three retirement programs: (a Pension Plan; (b) the 401(k) Savings Plan; and Career Income Plan.[j]

a) Players' Pension Plan

The NBA Players' Pension Plan allows for full after three years of service in the league,[105] the requirement as the NFL's Retirement Plan for played after 1991. Players can begin drawing t at age 45.[106] Under the 2017 CBA, beginning a Pension Plan pays players $572.13 per month of credited NBA service,[107] with the possibility increases to that figure based on actuarial calcu According to the NBA, the pension benefits pe service are the same for all players that played regardless of when they played. The NBA also that players automatically receive Pension Plan they do not file for them. Lastly, the Pension Pla by the clubs.[109]

b) 401(k) Savings Plan

Under the 401(k) Savings Plan, players can cont portion of their salary, subject to the maximum permitted by the Internal Revenue Service ($18, 2016[110]), into a 401(k) plan.[111] Clubs match 14C players' allowed contributions.[112] This is similar NFL, which also offers a 401(k) plan. However, contribute 200% of a player's contribution. NBA contributions are automatic, unless the player af opts out.

c) Post-Career Income Plan

The Post-Career Income Plan (formerly called the Employment Annuity Benefit Plan) is a retirement

---

j   The NBA CBA also provides that players employed by the Toronto Rap required to receive comparable benefits as those described in this Se permitted under Canadian Law.

According to the NBA, eligible former players are not required to pay any premiums for coverage for themselves. The players can add their family to the insurance by paying premiums at varying amounts depending on the player's years of credited service.[128]

3) DISABILITY BENEFITS

NBA players are entitled to disability insurance benefits.[129] The CBA does not specify the benefit amounts available to the players.

4) WORKERS' COMPENSATION BENEFITS

The 2017 NBA CBA provides that players are entitled to workers' compensation benefits "in accordance with applicable statutes."[130] In reviewing this Report, the NBA explained that the CBA provision is meant to indicate the clubs' compliance with workers' compensation statutes. In practice, the NBA operates a league-wide workers' compensation program in which all clubs are required to participate with two exceptions. The Cleveland Cavaliers and Toronto Raptors play in what are known as "monopolistic" jurisdictions, Ohio and Ontario respectively, where employers are required to obtain workers' compensation insurance from a state fund or qualify as a self-insurer. According to the NBA, the NBA's workers' compensation program is long-standing but not negotiated with the NBPA. Thus, while unlikely, the NBA could unilaterally decide to dissolve the program and clubs that play in states where workers' compensation is not required, such as Florida and Texas, would no longer be required to provide workers' compensation benefits to its players. Nevertheless, in current practice, all NBA players can receive workers' compensation benefits.

5) EDUCATION-RELATED BENEFITS

Beginning with the 2017 CBA, the VEBA provides for "reimbursement of eligible tuition and career transition expenses."[131] Players are entitled to a maximum reimbursement of $33,654 per year, and $101,000 over their lifetime.[132] These benefits are available to players while playing and when their playing career is over.

Similarly, the NFL's Tuition Assistance Plan reimburses players for tuition, up to a maximum reimbursement of $20,000 per year.

6) JOINT HEALTH-SPECIFIC COMMITTEES

The NBA and NBPA have a Labor-Management Cooperation and Education Trust ("Education Trust"). While the Education Trust's role is unclear, it seems that could address player health issues.

According to the CBA, the Education Trust is designed to provide "(i) health education programs and (ii) education and career counseling programs designed to assist the NBA, NBA Teams and NBA players in solving problems of mutual concern not susceptible to resolution within the collective bargaining process and to enhance the involvement of NBA players in making decisions that affect their working lives."[133] The 2017 CBA states that the parties will "meet and confer to discuss the Education Trust establishing a modified financial education program."[134]

In addition to the Education Trust, there are other committees that have some health-related duties.

First, there is a Committee of Team Physicians with which NBPA representatives meet in order to discuss "matters related to the medical care and treatment of players,"[135] but this group is not a joint committee in and of itself and has limited authority of any kind under the CBA. The Committee of Team Physicians is responsible for periodically reviewing the NBA's Concussion Policy "in order to keep it current and consistent with the evolving science of concussion management,"[136] and must consult with NBPA representatives before making any changes to the Concussion Policy.[137,I]

Second, there is a Prohibited Substances Committee that consists of one NBA representative, one NBPA representative, and three jointly selected representatives who are "experts in the field of testing and treatment for drugs of abuse and performance-enhancing substances."[138] The Prohibited Substances Committee advises the NBA and NBPA on its anti-drug policy.[139]

In contrast, the NFL's Joint Committee and Accountability and Care Committee are principally focused on player health and safety issues.

[I]   In reviewing a draft of this Report, the NBA also highlighted that it and the NBPA have a Wearables Committee for the purpose of reviewing and approving wearable devices for use by players. 2017 NBA CBA, Art. XXII, § 13. We know from our research that the NFL and NFLPA have also collaborated on this issue. It is possible other leagues too have also considered this issue. However, because it is a rapidly evolving issue with questionable ties to player health, we have not endeavored to cover this issue across the leagues and thus do not include additional information here. For more information on potential legal concerns with wearable technologies, see our law review article, Jessica L. Roberts, et al., *Evaluating NFL Player Health and Performance: Legal and Ethical Issues*, 165 U. Penn. L. Rev. 227 (2017).

D) NHL Health-Related Benefits

As a preliminary matter, it is important to point out that in the NHL, like the NFL and NBA, the amounts paid to players (current and former) in the form of benefits decreases the amounts available to current players in salary.[140]

1) RETIREMENT BENEFITS

The NHL has two retirement plans available to its players: (1) the Retirement Plan, which is a defined benefit plan; and, (2) a 401(k) plan.

The NHL's Retirement Plan provides pension payments to players beginning on their 62nd birthday, except the player may receive actuarially equivalent[141] pension benefits as early as one month after his 45th birthday.[142] A player becomes eligible for participation in the Retirement Plan as of the date of his first NHL regular season game,[143] and he accrues fractional credited service[144] for each regular season game during which he is on a club's roster.[145] The NHL contributes $38 million each year to fund the Retirement Plan.[146] The application of the NHL's Retirement Plan to players who played prior to the 2013 CBA is unclear.

To determine the pension payment amounts, the NHL uses a player with ten years of credited service as its baseline. A player with ten or more years of credited service is eligible to receive the maximum pension payment permitted under the Internal Revenue Code, which was $210,000 in 2016[147] ($17,500/month). A player with less than ten years of credited service will receive a proportional share of the maximum payment permitted.[148] Thus, if a player played only seven years, he would be eligible to receive pension payments up to 70% of $210,000 ($147,000).

It is unclear whether players automatically receive Retirement Plan payments or if they must file for them.

In addition to the Retirement Plan, as part of the 2005 CBA, the NHL and NHLPA established the Fund for Senior Retired Players.[149] The Fund provides money to approximately 350 former players over the age of 65 or their widows depending on how many seasons the player played.[150] Both the NHL and NHLPA contribute $3 million annually toward the Fund.[151]

We turn now to the NHL's 401(k) plan. The 401(k) plan was created as part of the 2012 CBA, replacing a prior pension plan. A 401(k) plan is a retirement plan created pursuant to section 401(k) of the United States Internal Revenue Code. There are, however, seven Canadian clubs in the NHL for whom the United States Internal Revenue Code would not apply. Nevertheless, Canadian tax law does provide for a retirement plan substantially similar to an American 401(k). Consequently, the NHL has two separate 401(k)-type plans—one for players on American clubs, and one for players on Canadian clubs. To avoid confusion, for our purposes here, we refer to both of these plans as the NHL's 401(k) plan.

The 401(k) plan allows players to contribute pre-tax and post-tax portions of their pay into an investment account up to the limits set by the IRS. In 2016, the maximum pre-tax contribution was $18,000 and the maximum post-tax contribution was $53,000.[152] While clubs formerly contributed to the old pension plan, the new 401(k) plan is funded entirely by the players. Additionally, players must voluntarily enroll in the plan. In contrast, under the NFL's 401(k) plan, clubs contribute $2 for every $1 contributed by a player and players are automatically enrolled in the plan.

2) INSURANCE BENEFITS

The NHL provides insurance benefits for players that include medical coverage, dental coverage, life insurance, and accidental death insurance.[153] While not a part of its insurance coverage, the NHL, through its Substance Abuse and Behavioral Health Program, offers players substance abuse and mental health treatment free of charge. This program is discussed further in Chapter 4: Drug and Performance-Enhancing Drug Policies. However, there is no indication that the NHL offers other wellness benefits provided by the NFL, including: child and parenting support services, elder care support services, pet care services, legal services, and, identity theft services.

Former players who played at least 160 games in the NHL can continue to receive the above benefits for life provided they apply for coverage within 120 days of the date the player was last covered under the plan.[154] The former players have to contribute to the costs of their health insurance in amounts that had not yet been agreed upon in the 2013 CBA.[155] In contrast, former NFL players are only entitled to health insurance for five years after they are done playing. Finally, for Canadian residents, the health insurance plan provides coverage for treatment that is not covered by the player's provincial Canadian health plan.[156]

3) DISABILITY BENEFITS

The NHL offers a variety of disability benefits.

First, under the Retirement Plan, a player who has at least five years of credited service and becomes totally and permanently disabled is entitled "to receive disability pension benefits from the Retirement Plan equal to the value of his accrued pension benefits, actuarially reduced to the age of commencement."[157]

Second, the NHL provides a "career ending disability policy" providing for a one-time benefit, subject to the player signing a release, ranging in amount from $200,000 to $1,000,000.[158] To obtain the payment, the player must release "the Club, the League, the NHLPA, all other Clubs, the insurance carrier, and the servants, employees, officers and agents of each of the above from any and every additional obligation, liability, claim or demand[.]"[159] The NFL's Neurocognitive Disability Benefit also requires players to execute a release of liability. The NFL's disability benefits differ in that they are paid monthly, rather than in a lump sum.

Third, the NHL offers a "serious disability policy" that provides a one-time benefit for the player in the event he suffers a serious disability, contingent on execution of the above-described release.[160] Table 3-H below lists the potential serious disabilities and the related benefit amounts:

There is an important difference between the disability benefits offered by the NFL and the NHL. NHL disability benefits are only available to players currently on a club's roster.[161] In contrast, NFL players can and generally do apply for disability benefits after their career has ended. In particular, the NFL offers several neurocognitive disability benefits to former players, while the NHL only provides disability payments for loss of brain function if the player is currently playing.

4) WORKERS' COMPENSATION BENEFITS

NHL players are entitled to workers' compensation benefits.[162] In addition, like the NFL CBA, the NHL CBA requires clubs located in states where workers' compensation coverage is not required for professional athletes to provide equivalent benefits to the players.[163] Thus, players for the Tampa Bay Lightning and Florida Panthers are able to receive workers' compensation benefits despite the fact that Florida does not require employers to obtain workers' compensation coverage.

5) EDUCATION-RELATED BENEFITS

The CBA contemplates the creation or expansion of education-related benefits. Although there is no formal program, the 2011 CBA states that "[t]he League and the NHLPA shall work together on developing and improving career counseling and continuing education programs[.]"[164] Indeed, in 2015, the NHL and NHLPA announced plans to

Table 3-H:
NHL Serious Disability Benefits

Disability	Benefit Amount
Loss of Brain Function	$5,000,000
Paralysis	$5,000,000
Organ Failure	$3,000,000
Diagnosis of Terminal Illness	$3,000,000
Loss of a Limb*	$2,500,000
Loss of Two (2) Limbs*	$4,000,000
Loss of Sight in Both Eyes	$4,000,000
Loss of Sight in One (1) Eye	$2,000,000
Loss of Hearing or Speech	$750,000
Loss of Hearing and Speech	$1,000,000
Loss of One Hand or One Foot*	$750,000
Loss of Both Hands or Both Feet or One Hand and One Foot[a]	$1,000,000

* Loss includes loss of use.

launch a program that would pay for players' tuition at colleges and trade schools.[165] The NHL and NHLPA each have committed approximately $1.5 million to the program, which will begin with current players and hopes to expand to former players.[166]

6) JOINT HEALTH-SPECIFIC COMMITTEES

The NHL and NHLPA have formed the Joint Health and Safety Committee, which consists of five members from each side.[167] The Committee is responsible for "mak[ing] recommendations to the NHL and the NHLPA for consideration and approval regarding all issues related to Player health and regarding the safety of the playing environment."[168] To do so, the Committee is empowered to create working groups and subcommittees as necessary.[169] The Committee is also responsible for resolving issues concerning whether club doctors have violated their obligations to the players,[170] monitoring the electronic medical record system,[171] and creating a list of second opinion doctors.[172]

E) CFL Health-Related Benefits

1) RETIREMENT BENEFITS

The CFL provides a pension plan for players. The CFL pension plan is a defined contribution plan, with clubs and players paying matching amounts.[173] In 2016, for example, each parties contributed $3,900 (CAD).[174] However, clubs will only contribute the amounts for players who are on the club's roster for nine or more games in that season.[175] As a defined benefit plan, the players seemingly are vested in the pension plan as soon as any money is contributed to their account.

2) INSURANCE BENEFITS

The CFL medical plan provides medical coverage,[m] life insurance, and accidental death and dismemberment insurance coverage.[176] Dental benefits are not included in the medical plan but a "Benefit Plan Advisory Committee may agree to change the benefits, including the addition of

dental coverage and disability" if there is sufficient surplus from the amounts paid by the clubs.[177]

In contrast, the NFL provides dental benefits as well as a variety of wellness benefits, including access to clinicians for mental health, alcoholism, and substance abuse; child and parenting support services; elder care support services; pet care services; legal services; and, identity theft services.

Also unlike the NFL, the CFL offers no health insurance benefits for former players. However, as long as the players are residents of Canada, they can obtain healthcare through government-sponsored plans.

3) DISABILITY BENEFITS

As explained above, disability benefits are not guaranteed under the CFL CBA, but are possible if funding exists. In contrast, the NFL provides many different types of disability benefits for current and former players.

4) WORKERS' COMPENSATION BENEFITS

Some provincial statutes prohibit professional athletes, such as CFL players, from receiving workers' compensation benefits.[178] However, in 2016, the CFLPA submitted an application for players to be eligible for workers' compensation benefits in the province of Alberta,[179] where two CFL clubs play. If successful, the CFLPA reportedly plans to try and expand coverage for workers' compensation benefits to other provinces.[180] By contrast, although workers' compensation payments have been a controversial issue, all NFL players are currently entitled to such benefits.

5) EDUCATION-RELATED BENEFITS

The CFL does not offer any education-related benefits, unlike the NFL's Tuition Assistance Plan.

6) JOINT HEALTH-SPECIFIC COMMITTEES

The CFL and CFLPA have a Joint Committee on Players' Safety and Welfare.[181] The Committee's purpose is to discuss player safety and welfare aspects of playing equipment, playing surfaces, stadium facilities, playing rules, player-coach relationships, drug abuse prevention programs, and any other relevant subjects.[182] Any proposed change in a playing rule must be referred to the Committee for consideration and a recommendation.[183] However, the Committee has no authority to bind either the CFL or CFLPA on any issue.[184]

m   The relationship between the CFL's medical plan and the Canadian healthcare system, under which the government pays for the majority of healthcare expenses, is unclear. The Canadian healthcare system is described in more detail in Chapter 1: Club Medical Personnel.

F) MLS Health-Related Benefits

1) RETIREMENT BENEFITS

MLS offers a 401(k) plan to its players.[185] Regardless of whether a player contributes, MLS makes employer contributions equivalent to 3.75% of a player's base salary.[186] Contributions vest immediately.[187]

2) INSURANCE BENEFITS

MLS provides players and their family members with medical insurance, dental insurance, and life insurance.[188]

In contrast, the NFL provides a variety of wellness benefits, including access to clinicians for mental health, alcoholism, and substance abuse; child and parenting support services; elder care support services; pet care services; legal services; and, identity theft services.

Also unlike the NFL, MLS offers no health insurance benefits for former players.

3) DISABILITY BENEFITS

MLS does provide long-term disability insurance for its players equivalent to 60% of a player's salary, with a monthly maximum benefit of $10,000.[189] The monthly maximum benefit is the same in the 2015 CBA as it was in the 2004 CBA.[190]

4) WORKERS' COMPENSATION BENEFITS

MLS players are entitled to workers' compensation benefits.[191] Additionally, like the NFL and NHL, MLS clubs that are in states that are not required to provide workers' compensation benefits are required to provide equivalent benefits.[192] Thus, players on Orlando City FC are able to obtain the equivalent of workers' compensation benefits when they otherwise would have been denied coverage because Florida does not require employers to provide workers' compensation benefits. Alternatively, MLS and the MLSPU have agreed that players can file for benefits in New York state, regardless of where they play.[193] In other words, MLS will not challenge the jurisdiction of the claim.[194]

5) EDUCATION-RELATED BENEFITS

MLS does not offer any league-wide education-related benefits. However, for players who participate in the Generation adidas program, an initiative designed to grow domestic talent, players can leave college early and money is placed in escrow for them to complete their college education at a later date.[195] Nevertheless, this benefit is available only to a select group of the most highly-skilled young players—it is not a league-wide benefit to all players like the NFL's Tuition Assistance Plan.

6) JOINT HEALTH-SPECIFIC COMMITTEES

MLS has a Health and Safety Committee, which includes one MLSPU representative, that is responsible for making "recommendations to the Commissioner concerning health and safety procedures and protocols."[196]

G) Analysis

While we provide an analysis that compares the leagues on the benefits they provide players, it is worth emphasizing at least two reasons why this is not a full apples-to-apples comparison. First, the mean number of seasons of play varies across the leagues,[n] such that in some leagues fewer individuals will make the milestones necessary for vesting or activation of some benefits. Second, while we lack complete data on the health risks of playing each of the sports, from what we do know the risks associated with each sport are heterogeneous in at least some respects, such that the need for health insurance and disability benefits varies from league to league.

With that caveat, Table 3-I provides a comparison of the leagues' benefits while Tables 3-J and 3-K provide a comparison of monthly payments under the Big Four leagues' retirement/pension plans in two different scenarios.

Table 3-I:
Comparison of Leagues' Benefits

Benefit	NFL	MLB	NBA	NHL	CFL	MLS
Pension Plan	Yes	Yes	Yes	Yes	Yes	No
Pension Plan Vesting Requirement	3 years (post 1992)	1 day	3 years	1 day	9 games	N/A
Severance Plan	Yes	No	No	No	No	No
401k Plan	Yes	Yes	Yes	Yes	No	Yes
Other Deferred Compensation Plan	Yes	No	Yes	No	No	No
Health Insurance (Current Players)	Yes	Yes	Yes	Yes	Yes	Yes
Health Insurance (Former Players, other than COBRA)	5 years	For life potentially	For life potentially	For life potentially	No	No
Life Insurance	Yes	Yes	Yes	Yes	Yes	Yes
Dental Insurance	Yes	Yes	Yes	Yes	Maybe	Yes
Health Reimbursement Account	Yes	No	Yes	No	No	No
Long Term Care Insurance	Yes	No	Potentially	No	No	No
Wellness Benefits	Many	Some	Some	None	None	None
Disability Benefits (Current Players)	Yes	Yes	Yes	Yes	Maybe	Yes
Disability Benefits (Former Players)	Yes	Yes	No	No	No	No
Neurocognitive Disability Benefits	Yes	No	No	Only for current players	No	No
Workers' Compensation	Yes	Partial	Yes	Yes	Prohibited by law	Yes
Education-Related Benefits	Yes	No	Yes	Yes	No	For some players
Joint Health-Specific Committee(s)	Yes	Yes	Yes	Yes	Yes	Yes

---

n   In Chapter 5: Compensation, Table 5-I, we use the following mean career lengths: NFL – 5.0 years; MLB – 5.6 years; NBA – 4.8 years; NHL – 5.6 years; CFL – 3.2 years; and, MLS – 3.2 years.

In examining the projected monthly payouts under the Big Four Leagues' retirement/pension plans, we caution that the plans are complicated and involve many different variables to determine what a former player's monthly payment will be, including but not limited to the player's current income and cost of living adjustments. In Tables 3-J and 3-K below, we try to provide a picture of the type of retirement benefits available to players in each of the leagues. For this analysis, we chose the age of 62 for the age at which the retired player would begin to receive benefits because in the NHL this is the earliest age at which a player can receive retirement benefits. Then, we chose to analyze players who last played in 2000 and 2015 to provide a spectrum of how the benefits change depending on when the player last played.

Table 3-J:
Projected Monthly Payments under the Big Four Leagues' Retirement Plans (Last Played in 2000 and Will Take Retirement Benefits at Age 62)

League	Experience			
	1 Year	3 Years	5 Years	10 Years
NFL	$470	$1,410	$2,090	$3,661
MLB	$1,666	$5,000	$8,333	$16,666
NBA[197]	$1,792	$5,375	$8,958	$17,917
NHL	Uncertain°			

Table 3-K:
Projected Monthly Payments under the Big Four Leagues' Retirement Plans (Last Played in 2015 and Will Take Retirement Benefits at Age 62)

League	Experience			
	1 Year	3 Years	5 Years	10 Years
NFL	$470	$1,720	$2,810	$5,160
MLB	$1,666	$5,000	$8,333	$16,666
NBA	$1,792	$5,375	$8,958	$17,917
NHL	$1,750	$5,250	$8,750	$17,500

According to the NFLPA, NFL players have "the very best benefits package in professional sports."[198] This claim seems substantially true. First, the NFL offers every benefit that is provided by any of the other leagues. Second, the NFL offers several benefits that are not provided by any of the other leagues, including severance pay, long term care insurance, the Former Player Life Improvement Plan, and neurocognitive disability benefits for former players. Third, there are several benefits that only the NFL and a limited number of the other leagues provide: (a) only the NFL, MLB, NBA, and NHL provide health insurance (beyond COBRA) for former players; (b) only the NFL, MLB, and NBA provide players with mental health and substance abuse treatment; (c) only the NFL and NBA offer a health reimbursement account; (d) only the NFL and MLB offer disability benefits to former players; (e) only the NFL and NBA offer education-related benefits for all players; and, (f) only the NFL, NBA, NHL, and MLS guarantee workers' compensation benefits to all of their players.

While overall the NFL thus appears to be the best league for benefits, comparing the leagues' benefit offerings is challenging and not without judgment calls. For example, considering the NFL's higher injury rates (see Chapter 2: Injury

---

o   Prior to 2012, when a new CBA established a new Retirement Plan and 401(k) plan, clubs contributed amounts into investment accounts on behalf of the players on an annual basis. For example, in 2012, if a player had played less than 160 games in his career, the club contributed $23,820 in Canadian dollars into the player's account that season. If the player had played 160 or more career games, the club contributed $50,000 into the player's account. The amounts a player would receive under this plan after their career depends on investment results and when the player starts to draw benefits from the account.

Rates and Policies), it seems appropriate that NFL players would be entitled to more benefits, such as the NFL's Long Term Care Insurance Plan and Former Player Life Improvement Plan. In particular, given the disparities in concussion rates, neurocognitive disability benefits are likely appropriate in the NFL but may not be needed in some of the other leagues. Moreover, we have identified three areas in which the NFL might learn lessons for improvement from one or more of the other leagues.

First, the NFL's health insurance options for former players appear to be less favorable than those offered by MLB, the NBA and the NHL. Currently, for players who have vested under the Retirement Plan (which requires at least three years of Credited Service for players after 1992), the NFL provides the same health insurance as available to current players for five additional years or the former player can also obtain health insurance via COBRA. However, COBRA is designed to be a temporary solution and is generally regarded as expensive relative to other health insurance plans.[199] In contrast, MLB's Benefit Plan provides former players the option to continue (or obtain) the same health insurance benefits as current players for life. While former MLB players have to pay more for their health insurance than current MLB players, presumably the plans offered are cheaper than COBRA coverage or else the players would have opted for COBRA coverage. Similarly, the NBA's Retiree Medical Plan is available to former players for life free of charge and the NHL allows former players who played at least 160 games to continue with the NHL's insurance plan for life.[200]

The NFL does offer a variety of health benefits that might partially fill the gap for former players, including health reimbursement accounts, long term care insurance, benefits for uninsured former players, and disability benefits. Nevertheless, players often have to go through a difficult process to obtain some of these benefits after they have already had to pay for the care, or care is delayed until they can obtain the benefits. We believe there may be advantages to allowing former players to continue to obtain some form of the same health insurance that they were able to receive while playing—ensuring, among other things, that they can remain in the same network of doctors.

Second, as shown in Tables 3-J and 3-K, the monthly payments to former NFL players under the Retirement Plan are seemingly the smallest payments of the Big Four leagues. Nevertheless, when all of the benefits available to former players are packaged together, it is likely that the NFL's benefits are the most valuable due to the number of benefits that are available. Consequently, lower Retirement Plan payments might simply reflect the NFLPA's preferred

allocation of total benefits, *i.e.*, a shifting of the value of benefits away from the Retirement Plan and to other benefits instead. As with health insurance benefits, the NFL's Retirement Plan payments require players to undertake relatively little administrative work to receive and they are a more secure and stable income source and benefit than some of the other benefits made available by the NFL. Nevertheless, some might believe it is a better use of player benefit money to fund benefits and programs for former players who are disabled or impaired in some way as opposed to providing larger Retirement Plan payments to all eligible former players. All the benefits available to NFL players must be viewed collectively. For these reasons, as discussed in the Recommendation, we recommend the NFL consider whether the current allocation of player benefits is the preferred, most just, and most effective allocation.

Third, MLB and NHL players are vested in their pension plans on the first day they play in those leagues. By comparison, the NFL requires players to accrue three years of experience (or more depending on when they played), before they are eligible for retirement benefits (as well as many other benefits). The mean career of NFL and MLB players are both around five years long.[201] Yet, the NFL's Retirement Plan likely excludes and has excluded thousands of former players who did not earn three Credited Seasons. It is unclear why the NFL requires three years of service (the NBA does as well). The minimum service time clearly reduces costs of the Retirement Plan, but might also reflect a policy decision as to when an NFL player has sufficiently contributed to the NFL to deserve pay under the Retirement Plan. Below, we make a recommendation concerning the vesting requirement for the NFL's Retirement Plan.

In addition to the above-described potential deficiencies, there is another issue worthy of comment. To obtain Neurocognitive Disability Benefits after their career is over, the NFL requires players to execute a release releasing the NFL and clubs from any liability for head or brain injuries when they apply for the benefits. Similarly, the NHL requires players to release the NHL, clubs, and a variety of other parties for players to obtain career-ending disability insurance benefits. It could be argued that these releases unfairly condition benefits to which players are entitled on the relinquishment of their legal rights. On the other hand, the releases could be seen to ensure players do not seek more benefits than those to which they are entitled and to prevent litigation. As there are persuasive points for and against the releases, we do not make a recommendation concerning them. Instead, we merely highlight the issue for potential future consideration by the leagues, unions, and others.

H) Recommendation

Recommendation 3-A: The NFL and NFLPA should consider whether change is necessary concerning player benefit plans.

As discussed above, we identified three potential areas of concern regarding the benefit plans offered by the NFL. Also as discussed above, the benefits available to NFL players must be viewed in the context of one another: increasing one benefit might mean a decrease in another benefit. Below, we identify and discuss possible changes to the benefit plans, the implementation of which must be weighed collectively.

- The NFL and NFLPA should consider providing former players with health insurance options that meet the needs of the former player population for life: While the NFL provides significant benefits to former players, players likely do not take full advantage of those benefits due to the associated administrative burdens.[202] Additionally, a consistent and reliable health insurance plan seems preferable to ad hoc and uncertain benefits. The NFL and NFLPA should consider whether it would be more appropriate to shift some of the value of benefits away from the unplanned benefits (*e.g.,* disability benefits and the health reimbursement account) to more stable health insurance options.[p] Where players have only played one or two seasons (and perhaps games), there might be questions as to whether it is appropriate to provide lifetime health insurance to someone who was employed for such a short period of time. On the other hand, only a few games or seasons can have life-lasting effects on a player. One option worth considering is tiering health insurance benefits and allowing those with less Credited Seasons to qualify for some but not full benefits.

- The NFL and NFLPA should consider increasing the amounts available to former players under the Retirement Plan: The monthly retirement benefits represent a more stable benefit than the other valuable but still uncertain benefits. Consequently, the NFL and NFLPA should consider whether it would be more beneficial to shift some of the value of benefits away from the unplanned benefits to the more stable Retirement Plan monthly payments.

- The NFL and NFLPA should consider reducing the vesting requirement for the Retirement Plan: The purpose of the NFL's three-year vesting requirement is unclear. The vesting requirement results in a considerable portion of former players being unable to collect any retirement benefits. We acknowledge that there may be appropriate policy reasons for such a limitation, such as a determination as to when a player has sufficiently contributed to the NFL. Indeed, many employers require a certain number of years of service before accruing certain benefits.[q] If the vesting requirement is instead principally motivated by cost, then the distribution of benefits among former players should be reconsidered to determine what is maximally beneficial for player health. In other words, is the current distribution of benefits among former players, which largely excludes players with less than three years of experience, preferred by the NFL, NFLPA, and players, or would it be preferable to reduce the benefits to players with more than three years of experience to provide some benefits to those with less than three years of experience? While these considerations are not easy and require a delicate balance, the exclusion of a significant portion of former players from the Retirement Plan requires an examination of the vesting requirement. As with health insurance benefits, one option worth considering is tiering Retirement Plan benefits and allowing those who have played less than three Credited Seasons to qualify for some if not full benefits.

---

p   According to columnist Mike Freeman, the NFLPA did analyze the potential costs of providing NFL players with health insurance for life and found the cost to be approximately $2 billion. Mike Freeman, *Two Minute Warning: How Concussions, Crime, and Controversy Could Kill the NFL (and What the League Can Do to Survive),* xxv (2015).

q   The principal distinction would be that employers require a certain number of years of service to, in part, encourage employees to continue working for them rather than obtaining employment elsewhere. This incentive structure is not needed in the NFL—where the vast majority of players play in the NFL for as long as they are able.

Endnotes

1   *See* Thomas Richardson et al., *The relationship between personal unsecured debt and mental and physical health: A systematic review and meta-analysis*, 33 Clinical Psychol. Rev. 8, 1148-62 (2013).

2   Pablo S. Torre, *How (and Why) Athletes Go Broke*, Sports Illustrated, Mar. 23, 2009, http://www.si.com/vault/2009/03/23/105789480/how-and-why-athletes-go-broke, *archived at* http://perma.cc/7KVD-QA72.

3   David R. Weir, et al., *National Football League Player Care Foundation Study of Retired NFL Players* 37, Inst. for Social Res. at Univ. of Mich. (2009), http://ns.umich.edu/Releases/2009/Sep09/FinalReport.pdf, *archived at* http://perma.cc/WY8A-HZ8Z.

4   Kyle Carlson, et al., *Bankruptcy Rates Among NFL Players with Short-Lived Income Spikes* 8, Nat'l Bureau of Economic Res. (April 2015), http://www.nber.org/papers/w21085.pdf, *archived at* http://perma.cc/Y8A5-NJLZ. The study found that the rate of bankruptcy among the general population in the 25–34 year age group was very similar to the bankruptcy rate of NFL players. However, the general population's average income is almost certainly substantially less than that of the average NFL player.

5   Linda Holmes, *ESPN's 'Broke' Looks At The Many Ways Athletes Lose Their Money*, NPR (Oct. 2, 2012, 1:35 PM), http://www.npr.org/blogs/monkeysee/2012/10/02/162162226/espns-broke-looks-at-the-many-ways-athletes-lose-their-money, *archived at* https://perma.cc/VPK7-QLBX.

6   *See* Jim Baumbach, *Life After Football*, Newsday, Jan. 22, 2015, http://data.newsday.com/projects/sports/football/life-football/, *archived at* http://perma.cc/77DP-LUUE.

7   Pablo S. Torre, *How (and Why) Athletes Go Broke*, Sports Illustrated, Mar. 23, 2009, http://www.si.com/vault/2009/03/23/105789480/how-and-why-athletes-go-broke, *archived at* http://perma.cc/7KVD-QA72.

8   *See* Ken Belson, *When Settlement Buys Time*, N.Y. Times, Jul. 19, 2014, http://www.nytimes.com/2014/07/19/sports/football/former-nfl-players-make-difficult-choice-in-opposing-concussion-settlement.html, *archived at* http://perma.cc/5P3D-94A8; Sally Jenkins and Rick Maese, *Do No Harm: Who Should Bear The Costs Of Retired NFL Players' Medical Bills?* Wash. Post, May 9, 2013, http://www.washingtonpost.com/sports/redskins/do-no-harm-who-should-bear-the-costs-of-retired-nfl-players-medical-bills/2013/05/09/2dae88ba-b70e-11e2-b568-6917f6ac6d9d_story.html, *archived at* http://perma.cc/VER2-EM24.

9   *See, e.g.*, Melissa B. Jacoby, Teresa A. Sullivan, Elizabeth Warren, *Rethinking the Debates over Health Care Financing: Evidence from the Bankruptcy Courts*, 76 N.Y.U. L. Rev. 375 (2001) (empirical data demonstrating how many American families declare bankruptcy in the aftermath of illness or other healthcare crisis); Christopher Tarver Robertson, Richard Egelhof, Michael Hoke, *Get Sick, Get Out: The Medical Causes of Home Mortgage Foreclosures*, 18 Health Matrix 65 (2008) (empirically demonstrating and discussing the role that health crises have in home foreclosures).

10 Gabe Feldman, *Closing the Floodgates: The Battle Over Workers' Compensation Rights in California*, 8 FIU L. Rev. 107, 109 (2012).

11 Lex Larson, Workers' Compensation Law, § 1.01 (Matthew Bender 2014).

12 Lex Larson, Workers' Compensation Law, § 1.03 (Matthew Bender 2014).

13 Howard Berkes, *Injured Workers Suffer As 'Reforms' Limit Workers' Compensation Benefits*, Nat'l Pub. Radio, Mar. 4, 2015, http://www.npr.org/2015/03/04/390441655/injured-workers-suffer-as-reforms-limit-workers-compensation-benefits, *archived at* https://perma.cc/6MB8-56Y4 (discussing states' reductions in maximum workers' compensation benefits).

14 *See, e.g.* 2011 NFL CBA, Art. 41, § 4.

15 *See, e g.*, 2011 CBA, App. A, ¶ 9.

16 With the assistance of the NFLPA, we were able to gain access to lengthy summaries of NFL plan documents.

17 These programs can be found at the NFL's Player Engagement Department website at https://www.nflplayerengagement.com.

18 *See NFLPA Externship Program Enters Second Year*, Nat'l Football League Players Ass'n, Feb. 23, 2015, https://nflpa.com/news/all-news/nflpa-externship-program-enters-second-year, *archived at* https://perma.cc/AZX7-G8AY; *Active Players — Grow Experience*, Nat'l Football League Players Ass'n, https://nflpa.com/active-players/playerdevelopment/experience (last visited Apr. 7, 2015), *archived at* https://perma.cc/AZX7-G8AY; *A Winning Team: Kelley School of Business and the NFLPA*, Kelley Sch. of Bus., https://nflpawebqa.blob.core.windows.net/media/Default/PDFs/Player%20Development/NFLPA-Kelley_%20Program.pdf (last visited Apr. 7, 2015), *archived at* https://perma.cc/E4UJ-N6CT.

19 *See* Bert Bell/Pete Rozelle NFL Player Retirement Plan (Apr. 1, 2012) § 1.11 (defining "Credited Season"); 2011 CBA, Art. 26, § 2 (same).

20 CBA, Art. 12, § 6(c)(i).

21 CBA, Art. 1.

22 CBA, Art. 12, § 2.

23 CBA, Art. 12, § 6(c)(v).

24 The summary provided in this Section comes from reviewing a Summary Plan Description for the Severance Pay Plan prepared for NFL players by the NFL Management Council, the administrators of the Severance Pay Plan.

25 The summary provided in this Section comes from reviewing a Summary Plan Description for the Bert Bell/Pete Rozelle NFL Player Retirement Plan ("Retirement Plan") prepared for NFL players by the Retirement Board, the administrators of the Retirement Plan.

26 Aaron Gordon, *Battle for Benefits, Part 3: "Don't Make Proud Men Beg"*, Vice Sports (Sept. 18, 2015), https://sports.vice.com/en_us/article/battle-for-benefits-part-3-dont-make-proud-men-beg, *archived at* https://perma.cc/YP4J-8AGY.

27 *Id.*

28 *See* Mark Fainaru & Steve Fainaru, *League of Denial: The NFL, Concussions, and the Battle for Truth* 86–87 (2013).

29 Pursuant to the Employee Retirement Income Security Act ("ERISA"), individuals claiming entitlement to benefits under a retirement plan are entitled to bring a civil action to enforce or clarify their rights under the plan. 29 U.S.C. § 1132(a). Former players routinely sue the Retirement Plan alleging they were wrongfully denied benefits, with mixed success. *See, e.g.*, Atkins v. Bert Bell/Pete Rozelle NFL Player Retirement Plan, 694 F.3d 557 (5th Cir. 2012) (plan administrator's determination that player was not entitled to additional benefits was not an abuse of discretion); Giles v. Bert Bell/Pete Rozelle NFL Player Retirement Plan, 925 F. Supp. 2d 700 (D.Md. 2012) (Retirement Board's classification of participant's disability as "Inactive" rather than "Football Degenerative" was not reasonable decision supported by substantial evidence in the record); Moore v. Bert Bell/Pete Rozelle NFL Player Retirement Plan, 282 Fed.Appx. 599 (9th Cir. 2008) (Retirement Board's decision to terminate player's benefits was not based on reasonable interpretation of plan's terms); Johnson v. Bert Bell/Pete Rozelle NFL Player Retirement Plan, 468 F.3d 1082 (8th Cir. 2006) (plan administrator did not abuse its discretion in setting date of disability as time of disability determination by physician to whom plan had referred former player); Boyd v. Bert Bell/Pete Rozelle NFL Players Retirement Plan, 410 F.3d 1173 (9th Cir. 2005) (administrator did not abuse its discretion in rejecting retiree's claim, given ambiguity as to cause of neurologic disability at issue); Courson v. Bert Bell NFL Player Retirement Plan, 75 F. Supp. 2d 424 (W.D.Pa. 1999) *aff'd* 214 F.3d 136 (3d Cir. 2000) (plan administrator's determination that former player was not disabled was not arbitrary or

capricious); Brumm v. Bert Bell NFL Retirement Plan, 995 F.2d 1433 (8th Cir. 1993) (trustees' interpretation of ERISA plan to allow higher level of disability benefits only in cases involving single, identifiable football injury, and excluding cases of disability resulting from football career's overall impact on body, was unreasonable in light of plan's goals).

30 *Oversight of the Nat'l Football League (NFL) Retirement System: Hearing Before the Comm. On Commerce, Sci. & Transp.*, 110th Cong. 1177 (2007), *available at* http://www.gpo.gov/fdsys/pkg/CHRG-110shrg76327 /html/CHRG-110shrg76327.htm, *archived at* https://perma.cc/RK38 -GBYQ?type=pdf.

31 Aaron Gordon, *Battle for Benefits, Part 3: "Don't Make Proud Men Beg"*, Vice Sports (Sept. 18, 2015), https://sports.vice.com/en_us/article /battle-for-benefits-part-3-dont-make-proud-men-beg, *archived at* https://perma.cc/YP4J-8AGY.

32 *Id.*

33 The summary provided in this Section comes from reviewing a Summary Plan Description for the Player Annuity Plan prepared for NFL players by the Annuity Board, the administrators of the Player Annuity Plan.

34 An annuity plan is one in which a person contributes money to an investment account and then, at a later date (typically in retirement), the account makes regular payments to the person. *Definition of Annuity*, Investopedia, http://www.investopedia.com/terms/a/annuity.asp (last visited Sep. 18, 2015), *archived at* http://perma.cc/CV69-CQC7.

35 *See IRS Announces 2016 Pension Plan Limitations; 401(k) Contribution Limit Remains Unchanged at $18,000 for 2016*, Internal Revenue Service, Oct. 21, 2015, https://www.irs.gov/uac/Newsroom/IRS-Announces -2016-Pension-Plan-Limitations%3B-401(k)-Contribution-Limit -Remains-Unchanged-at-$18,000-for-2016, *archived at* https://perma .cc/G28S-9K6R.

36 The summary provided in this Section comes from reviewing a Summary Plan Description for the Second Career Savings Plan prepared for NFL players by the Savings Board, the administrators of the Second Career Savings Plan.

37 A 401(k) is a retirement plan provided for in Section 401(k) of the Internal Revenue Code 26 U.S.C. § 401(k). Under a 401(k), employees contribute a certain percentage of their salary to an investment account before taxes are withheld from the salary. Taxes on the income are deferred until the employee withdraws money from the 401(k) account, which is generally not permitted until the employee reaches age 59½. An additional benefit of 401(k) plans is that often times employers contribute to the accounts and these contributions are also tax-deferred. *See 401k Plans*, Internal Revenue Service, http://www.irs.gov /Retirement-Plans/401k-Plans (last visited Sep. 18, 2015), *archived at* http://perma.cc/DN7N-WVKS.

38 The Summary Plan Description for the Second Career Savings Plan does not specify whether a player who is employed by a club as a coach or in some other capacity is not eligible for the benefits at 45.

39 *Quotes from NFLPA Press Conference*, Nat'l Football League Players Ass'n (Feb. 4, 2016), https://www.nflpa.com/news/all-news/quotes -from-nflpa-sb50-press-conference, *archived at* https://perma.cc/2GZH -FQ37.

40 The summary provided in this Section comes from reviewing a Summary Plan Description for the Player Insurance Plan prepared for NFL players by Aon Hewitt, the administrators of the Player Insurance Plan.

41 COBRA, 29 U.S.C. §§ 1161–69, requires continuation coverage to be offered to covered employees, their spouses, former spouses, and dependent children when group health coverage would otherwise be lost due to certain specific events, including, as would be relevant in the NFL, "the termination (other than by reason of such employee's gross misconduct), or reduction of hours, of the covered employee's employment." 29 U.S.C. § 1163(2).

42 The summary provided in this Section comes from reviewing a Summary Plan Description for Health Reimbursement Account Plan prepared for NFL players by the HRA Board, the administrators of the Health Reimbursement Account Plan.

43 Upon the player's death, the player's spouse and dependents can continue to utilize the HRA Plan until the account is exhausted or they die.

44 The summary provided in this Section comes from reviewing a Summary Plan Description for the Former Player Life Improvement Plan prepared for NFL players by Aon Hewitt, the administrators of the Former Player Life Improvement Plan.

45 The summary provided in this Section comes from reviewing the NFL Player Disability & Neurocognitive Benefit Plan.

46 The Initial Claims Committee consists of three members: one appointed by the NFL; one appointed by the NFLPA; and, a medical professional jointly chosen by the parties.

47 The Disability Board consists of three members selected by the NFL and three members selected by the NFLPA.

48 League football activities include any NFL "pre-season, regular-season, or post-season game, or any combination thereof, our out of League football activity supervised by a[] [Club], including all required or directed activities."

49 Edgeworth Economics, *DRAFT Dangers of the Game: Injuries in the NFL—Analysis for the NFLPA* (Sept. 6, 2010), http://esq.h-cdn.co/assets /cm/15/07/54dae83730ce3_-_Dangers-of-the-Game-Draft-Esquire.pdf, *archived at* http://perma.cc/T3MH-YTVU.

50 *Id.*

51 *Id.*

52 *Id.*

53 *Id.*

54 The summary provided in this Section comes from reviewing a Summary Plan Description for the 88 Plan prepared for NFL players by the 88 Board, the administrators of the 88 Plan.

55 CBA, Art. 41, § 1.

56 *See* 2011 CBA, Art. 41, § 3 (identifying Florida as a state that does not require workers' compensation coverage).

57 For more on the role of workers' compensation in the NFL, *see* Christopher R. Deubert, I. Glenn Cohen, Holly Fernandez Lynch, *Protecting and Promoting the Health of NFL Players: Legal and Ethical Analysis and Recommendations,* § 8(B) (2016).

58 CBA, Art. 50, § 1(a).

59 CBA, Art. XI.

60 CBA, Art. 50, § 1(d). "Within 60 days of the initiation of an investigation, two or more neutral physicians will be selected to investigate and report to the Joint Committee on the situation. The neutral physicians shall issue a written report within 60 days of their selection, and their recommendations as to what steps shall be taken to address and correct any issues shall be acted upon by the Joint Committee." *Id.*

61 In *Stringer v. Nat'l Football League*, the Court also expressed concerns about the effectiveness of the Joint Committee: "While the NFL is required to give 'serious and thorough consideration' to recommendations of the Joint Committee, the CBA imposes no independent duty on the NFL to consider health risks arising from adverse playing conditions, or to make recommendations for rules, regulations or guidelines for the Clubs to follow." 474 F. Supp.2d 894, 906 (S.D. Ohio 2007).

62 This information was provided by the NFLPA.

63 *Id.*

64 CBA, Art. 39, § 3(a).

65 *Id.*

66 The three NFL-appointed members of the ACC are: Dr. Matthew Matava, club doctor for the St. Louis Rams and former President of the NFL Physicians Society ("NFLPS"); Rick Burkholder, athletic trainer for the Kansas City Chiefs and President of the Professional Football Athletic Trainers ("PFATS"); and, Dr. Elliott Hershman, Chairman of NFL Injury and Safety Panel, Department of Orthopaedic Surgery, Lenox Hill Hospital, and Team Orthopedist, New York Jets. The three NFLPA-appointed members of the ACC are: Dr. Anthony Alessi, neurologist and Associate Clinical Professor of Neurology, University of Connecticut; Dr. Ross McKinney, Director, Trent Center for Bioethics, Humanities & History

of Medicine, Duke University & School of Medicine; and, Dr. Johnny Benjamin, orthopedist and Director, Pro Spine Center.

67 The Benefit Plan can be found as an exhibit in a lawsuit brought by the widow of former MLB pitcher Jose Lima. *See* Lima-Leclerc v. Major League Baseball Players Benefit Plan, 13-cv-271 (S.D.N.Y.), ECF No. 11-5.

68 *Id.* § 7.2.

69 *MLBPA, MLB Announce Details of New Labor Agreement*, MLBPA (Dec. 2, 2016), http://www.mlbplayers.com/ViewArticle.dbml?DB_OEM _ID=34000&ATCLID=211336390, *archived at* https://perma.cc/4XUA -2DAW.

70 *See* Benefit Plan at Tables 1–9.

71 *Id.* § 7.12–13. *See also id.* at Tables 1–9. U.S. Department of Treasury Regulations cap maximum annual player benefits at $200,000. *Id.* § 9.1.

72 *See id.*

73 *Id.* § 27.62.

74 *Id.*

75 *See id.* (defining a "Vested Member"); *id.* § 27.37 (defining "Normal Retirement Date").

76 *Id.*

77 *See* Benefit Plan at Tables 1–9 ("For fractional years of credited service, benefits shall be determined by interpolation.")

78 Benefit Plan § 6.1.

79 *Id.* § 7.6(b).

80 *IRS Announces 2016 Pension Plan Limitations*, Internal Revenue Service, Oct. 21, 2015, https://www.irs.gov/uac/newsroom/irs-announces-2016 -pension-plan-limitations-401-k-contribution-limit-remains-unchanged -at-18-000-for-2016, *archived at* https://perma.cc/8AQV-YZN8.

81 Benefit Plan § 8.1. In 2016, the maximum amount an employee could contribute to a 401(k) plan was $18,000. *IRS Announces 2015 Pension Plan Limitations*, Internal Revenue Service, Oct. 23, 2014, http://www.irs .gov/uac/Newsroom/IRS-Announces-2015-Pension-Plan-Limitations-1, *archived at* http://perma.cc/4DFY-BQAL.

82 Benefit Plan § 8(g).

83 *See id.* § 8.1(b)(i) (permitting clubs to make contributions "in their discretion").

84 MLB Comments and Corrections (Sept. 30, 2016).

85 Benefit Plan § 8.5.

86 *MLBPA, MLB Announce Details of New Labor Agreement*, MLBPA (Dec. 2, 2016), http://www.mlbplayers.com/ViewArticle.dbml?DB_OEM _ID=34000&ATCLID=211336390, *archived at* https://perma.cc/4XUA -2DAW.

87 Benefit Plan § 13.2(a)(i)–(iv).

88 *Id.* § 13.2(a)(iv).

89 *Id.* §§ 13.3, 13.4(a). Players are entitled to extend their healthcare coverage under the inactive health benefits program until they are eligible for Medicare at age 65. *Id.* § 13.4(d).

90 MLB Comments and Corrections (Mar. 15, 2017).

91 *Id.*

92 Benefit Plan §§ 14.3–14.8.

93 *MLBPA, MLB Announce Details of New Labor Agreement*, MLBPA (Dec. 2, 2016), http://www.mlbplayers.com/ViewArticle.dbml?DB_OEM _ID=34000&ATCLID=211336390, *archived at* https://perma.cc/4XUA -2DAW.

94 Benefit Plan § 10.1.

95 *Id.* § 10.2(a). If the player was not injured as an active member or within five years of becoming inactive—or if the player cannot prove by clear and convincing evidence that his disability is the result of his active services—he may still receive disability benefits equal to one-twelfth of his total income from employment or self-employment during the year preceding his disability (capped at a high of $5,000 and a low of $2,500) if he is otherwise eligible. *Id.*

96 *Id.* § 10.3(b).

97 *See* 2012 MLB CBA, Art. IX, § E (entitling player to receive unpaid balance of salary if contract was terminated after injury "less all workers' compensation payments received by the Player"); Art. XXIII, § D(1) (g) (including medical "costs reimbursed or paid for through workers' compensation" as part of the definition for Player Benefit Costs).

98 As discussed in the Introduction to this Section, the normal trade-off for workers' compensation benefits is that the injured employee cannot sue the employer for injuries suffered in the course of employment. Even though Florida players do not receive workers' compensation benefits, they likely still cannot sue the club. The CBA also presents a potential obstacle against any such claim. Common law claims such as negligence are generally preempted by the Labor Management Relations Act ("LMRA"). 29 U.S.C. § 185. The LMRA bars or "preempts" state common law claims where the claim is "substantially dependent upon analysis of the terms" of a CBA, *i.e.*, where the claim is "inextricably intertwined with consideration of the terms of the" CBA." Allis-Chambers Corp. v. Lueck, 471 U.S. 202, 213 (1985). In order to assess a club's duty to a player—an essential element of a negligence claim—the Court may have to refer to and analyze the terms of the CBA, resulting in the claim's preemption. So long as the player's claim is "inextricably intertwined" with the CBA, it will be preempted. Instead, such claims are intended to be brought pursuant to the arbitration provisions in the CBA.

99 MLB CBA, Art. XV, § D.

100 *MLBPA, MLB Announce Details of New Labor Agreement*, MLBPA (Dec. 2, 2016), http://www.mlbplayers.com/ViewArticle.dbml?DB_OEM _ID=34000&ATCLID=211336390, *archived at* https://perma.cc/4XUA -2DAW.

101 MLB CBA, Art. XIII, § A(1).

102 MLB CBA, Art. XIII, § A(3).

103 MLB CBA, Art. XIII, § A(4). Nevertheless, the SHAC does not appear to have completed any serious investigations, other than looking into a rise in broken bats in 2008. *Major League Baseball, MLB, MLBPA Adopt Recommendations of Safety and Health Advisory Committee*, Major League Baseball (Dec. 9, 2008), *available at* http://mlb.mlb.com/pa/pdf /health_advisory_120908.pdf, *archived at* https://perma.cc/QN49-XDBJ.

104 *See* 2017 NBA CBA, Art. VII, § 2(a) (explaining that the Salary Cap, *i.e.*, the amounts available to players in the form of salary, is reduced by the amount spent on player benefits).

105 *See* Sonya Stinson, *Go Long: Retirement Plans for Pro Athletes*, Fox Bus., http://www.foxbusiness.com/personal-finance/2012/09/25/go -long-retirement-plans-for-pro-athletes/, Sep. 25, 2012, *archived at* http://perma.cc/TR69-SG8Z; Ron Kroichick, *Pensions in Pro Sports: NBA All-Star break brought big boost to Ezersky*, S.F. Chron., Mar. 18, 2007, http://www.sfgate.com/sports/kroichick/article/PENSIONS-IN-PRO -SPORTS-NBA-All-Star-break-2609494.php, *archived at* https://perma .cc/9JTS-W7S6. "'Years of Service' means the number of years of NBA service credited to a player in accordance with the following: a player will be credited with one (1) year of NBA service for each year that he is on an NBA Active List or Inactive List for one (1) or more days during the Regular Season." 2017 NBA CBA, Art. I, § 1(iiii).

106 *See* Scott Soshnick, *NBA Players Forced to Save Toward Retirement for First Time*, Bloomberg Bus., Jul. 12, 2012, http://www.bloomberg .com/news/articles/2012-07-12/nba-players-forced-to-save-toward -retirement-for-first-time, *archived at* http://perma.cc/EV83-V42Z (mentioning that NBA players can begin receiving their pension at 45).

107 NBA, CBA Art. IV, § 1(a)(1).

108 NBA, CBA Art. IV, § 1(a)(2).

109 NBA CBA, Art. IV, § 1(c).

110 *IRS Announces 2015 Pension Plan Limitations*, Internal Revenue Service, Oct. 23, 2014, http://www.irs.gov/uac/Newsroom/IRS-Announces-2015 -Pension-Plan-Limitations-1, *archived at* http://perma.cc/4DFY-BQAL.

111 NBA, CBA, Art. IV, § 2.

112 *See* Jay MacDonald, *Professional Athletes' Big-League Tax Bills*, Fox Bus., Mar. 15, 2012, http://www.foxbusiness.com/personal-finance /2012/03/15/professional-athletes-big-league-tax-bills/, *archived*

at http://perma.cc/2WDF-RULG; Mark Riddix, *Top Pro Athlete Pension Plans*, Investopedia, July 16, 2010, http://www.investopedia.com /financial-edge/0710/top-pro-athlete-pension-plans.aspx, *archived at* http://perma.cc/SR8A-HV72. *See also Top 15 Sports Organizations with the Best 401k Plans*, BrightScope, Jun. 25, 2013, http://blog.brightscope .com/2013/06/25/top-15-sports-organizations-with-the-best-401k -plans/, *archived at* http://perma.cc/XKT4-NNDZ (rating the plan as the best in professional sports, in part because of generous contributions of NBA clubs).

113 NBA CBA, Art. IV § 4(a).

114 NBA CBA, Art. IV, § 4(d)(1).

115 This information was provided by the NBA.

116 *See* 2011 NBA CBA, Art. IV, § 4(b)(3).

117 *Id.*

118 *Voluntary Employee Beneficiary Association — 501(c)(9)*, Internal Revenue Service, Jan. 13, 2015, http://www.irs.gov/Charities-&-Non-Profits /Other-Non-Profits/Voluntary-Employee-Beneficiary-Association-501 %28c%29%289%29, *archived at* http://perma.cc/XGW2-WXEK. The VEBA is funded through 1% of Basketball Related Income. 2011 NBA CBA Art. IV § 4(c).

119 NBA CBA, Art. IV, § 3(a)(9).

120 NBA CBA, Art. IV, § 3(a).

121 NBA CBA, Art. IV, § 3(a)(9).

122 *NBPA-NBA Supplemental Benefit Plan*, CitizenAudit, July 2014, http://pdfs.citizenaudit.org/2014_07_EO/20-1260597_9900_201306 .pdf, *archived at* http://perma.cc/EG2S-XXCL.

123 *Id.*

124 *See* 2011 NBA CBA, Art. IV, § 3(b).

125 The CBA does not define what it means to be a "resident" of Canada.

126 NBA CBA, Art. IV, § 3(a)(6)(i).

127 *Current NBA Players Break New Ground by Choosing to Fund Health Insurance for Retired NBA Players*, Nat'l Basketball Players Ass'n (July 27, 2016), *available at* http://nbpa.com/current-nba-players-break-new -ground-by-choosing-to-fund-health-insurance-for-retired-nba-players/, *archived at* https://perma.cc/4UKC-6KUU.

128 This information was provided by the NBA.

129 NBA CBA, Art. IV § 3(a)(2)(ii).

130 NBA CBA, Art. IV, § 6(a).

131 NBA CBA, Art. IV, § 3(a)(7).

132 *Id.*

133 NBA CBA, Art. IV, § 5(b).

134 *Id.*

135 NBA CBA, Art. XXII § 2.

136 NBA CBA, Art. XXII § 8.

137 NBA CBA, Art. XXII, § 9(b).

138 NBA CBA, Art. XXXIII, § 2 (d)(i).

139 NBA CBA, Art. XXXIII, § 2 (d)(ii).

140 *See* 2013 NHL CBA, § 50.4(a)-(b) (explaining that "Players' Share" of league revenues is equal to the clubs' aggregate salaries plus player benefits).

141 "Actuarial equivalence" is a "[g]eneral term used for applying some measurement to two benefit plans to see if resulting values are sufficiently close for the specified purpose." John M. Bertko and Cori E. Uccello, *Comparing Health Benefit Plans: Demystifying "Actuarial Equivalence,"* Am. Acad. of Actuaries, Jun. 11, 2008, http://www.actuary .org/briefings/pdf/equivalence2_july08.pdf, *archived at* http://perma.cc /23VS-LBLP.

142 NHL CBA, § 21.15.

143 NHL CBA, § 21.13.

144 A player earned "credited service" for each regular season game he is on the club's roster. 2013 NHL CBA, § 21.14.

145 *Id.* Additionally, a player who has five years of credited service is eligible,

upon becoming totally and permanently disabled, to receive pension benefits under the Retirement Plan equal to "the value of his accrued pension benefits, actuarially reduced to the age of commencement." 2013 NHL CBA, Art. 21, § 18.

146 NHL CBA, § 21.11(a)(i).

147 *See IRS Announces 2016 Pension Plan Limitations; 401(k) Contribution Limit Remains Unchanged at $18,000 for 2016*, Internal Revenue Service, Oct. 21, 2015, https://www.irs.gov/uac/Newsroom/IRS-Announces -2016-Pension-Plan-Limitations%3B-401(k)-Contribution-Limit -Remains-Unchanged-at-$18,000-for-2016, *archived at* https://perma .cc/G28S-9K6R.

148 NHL CBA, § 21.16.

149 *Senior Retired Players Fund Increased,* Nat'l Hockey League Player Ass'n, Jul. 31, 2013, www.nhlpa.com/news/senior-retired-players-fund -increased, *archived at* http://perma.cc/YYD8-KZCQ.

150 *Id.*

151 *Id.*

152 *See IRS Announces 2016 Pension Plan Limitations; 401(k) Contribution Limit Remains Unchanged at $18,000 for 2016*, Internal Revenue Service, Oct. 21, 2015, https://www.irs.gov/uac/Newsroom/IRS-Announces -2016-Pension-Plan-Limitations%3B-401(k)-Contribution-Limit -Remains-Unchanged-at-$18,000-for-2016, *archived at* https://perma .cc/G28S-9K6R.

153 NHL CBA, § 23.2.

154 NHL CBA, § 23.6(a).

155 *See* 2013 NHL CBA, § 23.6(d).

156 NHL CBA, § 23.7(b).

157 NHL CBA, § 21.18.

158 NHL CBA, § 23.3(a).

159 NHL CBA, § 23.3(d).

160 NHL CBA, § 23.3(b).

161 *See* 2013 NHL CBA, § 23.3(a) (limiting career ending disability benefits to "a Player who is on a Club's Insured Roster"); § 23.3(b) (limiting serious disability benefits to "a Player who is on a Club's Insured Roster").

162 NHL CBA, § 31.5.

163 NHL CBA, § 31(5).

164 NHL CBA, Art. 29.

165 Rick Westhead, *NHLPA readies $3M 'back to school' program,* TSN, Jun. 9, 2015, www.tsn.ca/nhlpa-readies-3m-back-to-school-program-1 .303734, *archived at* http://perma.cc/G6BQ-WGSL.

166 *Id.*

167 NHL CBA, § 34.9(b).

168 NHL CBA, § 34.9(a).

169 NHL CBA, § 34.9(e).

170 NHL CBA, § 34.1(c).

171 NHL CBA, § 34.3(b)(i).

172 NHL CBA, § 34.4(a).

173 CFL CBA, § 13.02.

174 *Id.*

175 *Id.*

176 CFL CBA, Art. 16.

177 *Id.*

178 *See* Rick Westhead, *CFL, union need to step up and protect the players,* Toronto Star, Nov. 27, 2007, *available at* 2007 WLNR 23396716; *Wealthy athletes go after compensation,* Edmonton J. (Canada), Aug. 16, 1996, *available at* 1996 WLNR 3805939.

179 Farhan Lalji, *CFLPA submits application for WCB coverage,* TSN (Aug. 23, 2016), http://www.tsn.ca/cflpa-submits-application-for-wcb-coverage-1 .553968, *archived at* https://perma.cc/ZKB8-VCVP.

180 *Id.*

181 CFL CBA, § 31.01.

182 *Id.*

183 CFL CBA, §31.06.

184 CFL CBA, § 31.03.

185 MLS CBA, § 10.8.

186 *Id.*

187 *Id.*

188 MLS CBA, § 22.

189 MLS CBA, § 22.4.

190 *Compare* 2015 MLS CBA, § 22.4 and 2004 MLS CBA, § 22.4.

191 MLS CBA, § 22.5.

192 *Id.*

193 This information was provided by the MLSPU.

194 *Id.*

195 *See* L. E. Eisenmenger, *McCabe Explains Generation adidas,* USSoccer-Players.com, Jan. 8, 2010, http://www.ussoccerplayers.com/2010/01/mccabe-explains-generation-adidas.html, *archived at* https://perma.cc/RWK5-4R64.

196 MLS CBA, § 24.1.

197 The retirement benefit amounts for NBA players were provided by the NBA.

198 *Benefits and Services,* Nat'l Football League Players Ass'n, https://www.nflpa.com/active-players/benefits-and-services (last visited Sep. 18, 2015), *archived at* https://perma.cc/45QW-DPZC.

199 *See FAQs about COBRA Continuation Health Coverage,* U.S. Dept. of Labor, http://www.dol.gov/ebsa/faqs/faq-consumer-cobra.html (last visited Sep. 18, 2015), *archived at* http://perma.cc/79A8-EKUQ *(*discussing COBRA's temporary nature); Anna Rapa, *Individual Health Insurance, Sometimes a Bane, Sometimes a Benefit, and Increasingly the Only Option,* 88 Mich. B. J. 16, 17 (2009) ("Maintaining insurance coverage under COBRA rather than having a separate individual policy between jobs may provide the best coverage, even if COBRA premiums are notoriously expensive."); Tiffany M. Alexander, *Are You Covered? Your Health Insurance Options,* 32 Sum Fam. Advoc. 20 (2009) ("COBRA disadvantages are (1) it tends to be much more expensive than a private policy because it often offers better coverage, and (2) it is only a temporary solution.")

200 While speculative, some similarity in the plans offered by MLB and the NHL may be due to overlapping leadership at the MLBPA and NHLPA. Don Fehr was Executive Director of the MLBPA from 1983 until 2009, during which time Fehr helped established the MLBPA's reputation as one of the strongest unions in the country. After leaving the MLBPA in 2009, Fehr became the NHLPA's Executive Director in 2010. In addition, Steve Fehr, Don's brother, serves as outside counsel to both the MLBPA and NHLPA.

201 *See Average NFL Career Length,* Sharp Football Analysis, Apr. 30, 2014, http://www.sharpfootballanalysis.com/blog/?p=2133, *archived at* http://perma.cc/X8QV-77A3 (discussing disagreement between NFLPA and NFL and determining that the average drafted player plays about 5 years); William D. Witnauer, Richard G. Rogers, Jarron M. Saint Onge, *Major league baseball career length in the twentieth century,* 26 Population Res. & Policy Rev. 4, 371-386, Jun. 14, 2007, http://link.springer.com/article/10.1007%2Fs11113-007-9038-5 (finding average MLB career to be 5.6 years).

202 For more on this issue, *see* Christopher R. Deubert, I. Glenn Cohen, Holly Fernandez Lynch, *Protecting and Promoting the Health of NFL Players: Legal and Ethical Analysis and Recommendations,* Recommendation 7:3-B (2016).

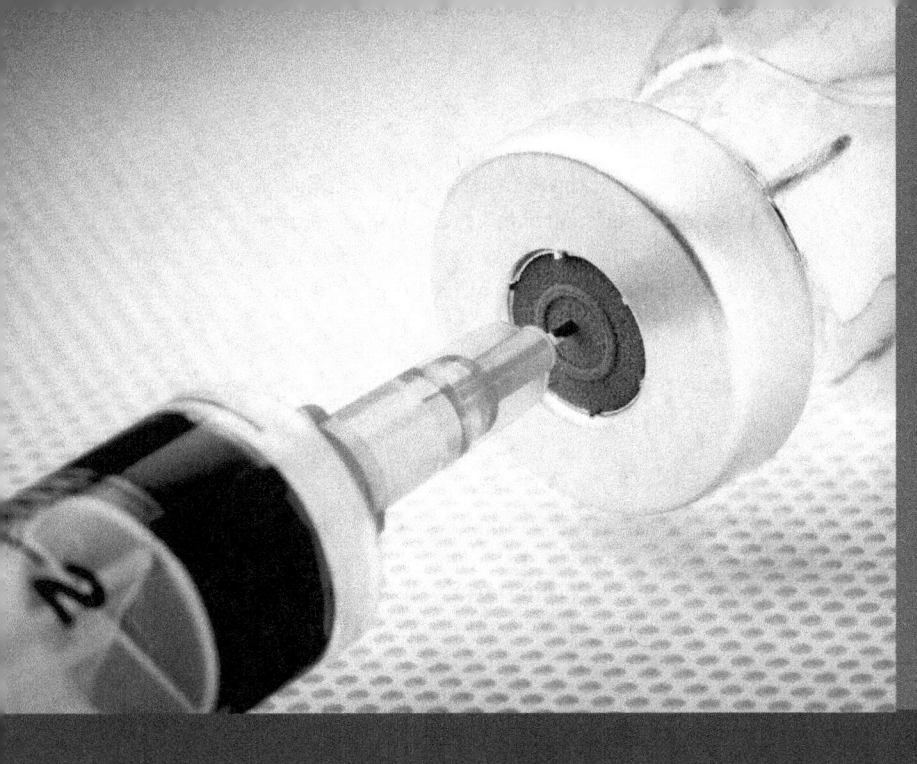

Chapter 4

Drug and Performance-Enhancing Substance Policies

This Chapter summarizes the policies of each of the leagues concerning performance-enhancing substances ("PES") and drugs of abuse. As explained below, the leagues differ at times in their categorizations and treatments of different drugs and substances. Where appropriate, we will separate our analysis of the leagues' policies by PES and drugs of abuse, but will collectively refer to the policies as the leagues' "drug policies."

Before analyzing the leagues' drug policies, there are a few concepts and issues that need to be discussed, including what is meant by a "PES" and a "drug of abuse"; the unique case of marijuana; the purpose for the drug policies; therapeutic use exemptions; and, the role of unions in drug policies.

1) MEANINGS OF PES AND DRUGS OF ABUSE

The leagues generally do not provide an overarching definition for PES but instead ban a long list of substances that have the potential to enhance a player's performance in ways that the league, sports community, and/or medical community has determined to be unfair, unnatural, and/or unsafe.[1] As will be shown below, PES are also sometimes referred to as "performance-enhancing drugs" ("PEDs"). This term is slightly outdated as the term PES now better captures a wider variety of substances that athletes might try to use to enhance their performance.

Drugs of abuse is a term generally used by the leagues in reference to illegal substances that do not have the potential to enhance a player's performance and which present serious health concerns. For example, MLB defines "drugs of abuse" to include marijuana, synthetic marijuana, cocaine, LSD, opiates, MDMA, GHB, and PCP.[2] Similarly, the NFL defines "substances of abuse" as all illegal drugs, including but not limited to, marijuana, cocaine, opiates, MDMA, and PCP.[3] Legal substances, including alcohol and prescription medications, can also fall within the purview of the leagues' drugs of abuse policies if abused, as will be discussed below.

Finally, we use the terms "substance" and "drug" interchangeably. While they are not exactly analogous terms, the terms are often used interchangeably in the context of professional sports and thus serve our purposes here.

2) MARIJUANA

Before we get into the details of the various policies it is worthwhile to discuss the special case of marijuana, which we also generally include in the category of drugs of abuse. Marijuana is banned under federal law and is listed as a Schedule I controlled substance under the Controlled Substances Act, thus classifying it as a substance which, according to the Act, "has a high potential for abuse" and "has no currently accepted medical use[.]"[4] Nevertheless, as of February 2017, 29 states have approved marijuana for medical use, and seven states (Alaska, Colorado, Massachusetts, Maine, Nevada, Oregon, and Washington) and the District of Columbia have approved it for recreational use in certain

amounts.[5,a] Moreover, there is a robust debate about what, if any, are the health and social consequences of marijuana use.[6] Thus, the argument exists that marijuana should be treated differently from other "drugs of abuse."

Some of the leagues have explicitly recognized the uniqueness of marijuana. As will be shown below, the NFL and NBA treat marijuana differently, and the NBA *does not* classify marijuana as a drug of abuse. Moreover, some believe marijuana use is common among NFL players to help manage pain.[7] Amidst at least some evidence that marijuana can be an effective pain management tool,[8] in 2016, the NFLPA announced that it would study the issue.[9] Nevertheless, the NFL has insisted that the legalization of marijuana in certain states (including those that are home to NFL clubs), does not change the NFL's position—a policy banning marijuana.[10] However, the NFL has stated that it is willing to consider medically appropriate uses of marijuana, such as for pain management and treatment of concussions, if recommended by medical experts.[11]

3) PURPOSE OF DRUG POLICIES

The case of marijuana raises the question about why certain drugs are banned, under either a PES or drugs of abuse policy. A list of reasons why specific drugs might be banned includes: (1) the drugs are associated with negative health consequences; (2) the drugs are illegal; and/or, (3) the drugs provide the player with an unfair competitive advantage.[b]

Many drugs meet one or more of these criteria. The criteria most closely related with the particular drug generally determine whether the drug is banned under a PES policy

---

a   Nineteen sports clubs play in these states and the District of Columbia: Denver Broncos (NFL); Colorado Rockies (MLB); Denver Nuggets (NBA); Colorado Avalanche (NHL); Colorado Rapids (MLS); New England Patriots (NFL); Boston Red Sox (MLB); Boston Celtics (NBA); Boston Bruins (NHL); New England Revolution (MLS); Portland Trail Blazers (NBA); Portland Timbers (MLS); Seattle Seahawks (NFL); Seattle Mariners (MLB); Seattle Sounders FC (MLS); Washington Nationals (MLB); Washington Wizards (NBA); Washington Capitals (NHL); and, D.C. United (MLS). The Washington football club is of course associated with Washington, D.C. but practices in Virginia and plays in Maryland.

b   In addition the reasons why certain drugs are banned, many would also likely add that the leagues regulate drugs to: (1) protect clubs' investments in the players; and, (2) to avoid negative publicity that results when players suffer adverse health or legal consequences associated with drug use. *See, e.g.,* Lee A. Linderman, *A Congressional Carve Out: The Necessity for Uniform Application of Professional Sports Leagues' Performance-Enhancing Drug Policies,* 84 S. Cal. L. Rev. 751, 772 (2011) ("Sports leagues have an obvious interest in preventing their athletes from severely damaging their own bodies through PED use. Leagues do not want their players—stars or otherwise—destroying their own bodies because such actions would bring negative publicity to the sport and force teams to deal with losing players to unnatural injuries."); Mark M. Rabuano, *An Examination of Drug-Testing as a Mandatory Subject of Collective Bargaining in Major League Baseball,* 4 U. Pa. J. Lab. & Emp. L. 439, 458 (2002) ("Within the League, the management-employer has a legitimate interest in controlling drug use to protect its investment and the job performance of its employees. Because the profitability of MLB is tied to the success of players and fan support, the preservation of League integrity through drug-testing is an issue that should thus be reserved for managerial prerogative.")

or a drugs of abuse policy. Drugs that provide an unfair competitive advantage would generally be those classified as a PES while illegal drugs would generally be considered drugs of abuse. Nevertheless, many PES are also illegal (or obtainable only with a prescription) and some illegal drugs of abuse can provide a competitive advantage (such as stimulants). Our analysis is focused on the health consequences of drug use rather than competitive advantage issues.

Finally, the health consequences of many of the drugs are a constant subject of debate and ongoing scientific assessment. Whether the positive purposes and effects of certain drugs sufficiently outweigh the negative consequences is a medical determination and beyond the scope of this Report, but this question does relate to the purpose of therapeutic use exemptions, an issue to which we now turn.

4) THERAPEUTIC USE EXEMPTIONS

Some prohibited substances might be appropriate or necessary for the treatment of specific medical conditions. Consequently, sports leagues generally permit what are known as therapeutic use exemptions ("TUEs"), that permit the player to use a banned substance without violating a drug policy. A good example of a TUE is the case of American Olympic sailor Kevin Hall. As a result of cancer, Hall needed testosterone injections to maintain normal levels of the hormone.[12] Hall received a TUE to take testosterone (normally a banned substance) so that he could participate in the 2004 Olympics.[13,c]

The availability of TUEs also raises the prospect of players seeking them more for performance-enhancing purposes as opposed to medical. In 2006, MLB began to test for stimulants, a banned substance but one nonetheless long considered to be commonly used in MLB.[14] In 2006, 28 players obtained a TUE for stimulants used to treat attention-deficit disorder ("ADD"), such as Adderall or Ritalin.[15] The next year, 103 players obtained TUEs for ADD drugs, raising concerns that the TUE process was being abused.[16] Nevertheless, the prevalence of TUEs for ADD drugs has remained fairly consistent: 119 in 2013; 112 in 2014;[17] 111

in 2015,[18] and 105 in 2016.[19] Approximately 1,375 players played in a MLB regular season game in 2016.[20] Thus, an estimated 7.6% of them had a TUE for ADD drugs.[d]

5) ROLE OF UNIONS

Each of the leagues' drug policies is the result of collective bargaining with the leagues' respective players unions. Indeed, drug testing is generally considered a mandatory subject of bargaining between employers and a union pursuant to the National Labor Relations Act.[21] The union will look to protect the players' rights and interests in all respects when negotiating the drug policy, but what that means is not always clear.

Players have heterogeneous views concerning the most desirable drug policy. When it comes to drugs of abuse, some players likely do not want any testing out of concerns for their privacy or so that they can engage in drug-related behavior off of the field. Other players might be concerned with the adverse health and legal consequences associated with drugs of abuse and instead want robust testing. Similarly, some players intentionally take PES to try to improve their performance and thus would like to see minimal testing and discipline for their use. Conversely, some players believe that PES undermine the integrity and fairness of the game and should be subject to frequent testing and harsh punishment.

Regardless of the players' and unions' balancing of these views, the unions always work to protect a player's legal and procedural rights. A drug test can be an invasive and personal process. Drug tests are conducted via the collection of either urine or blood. Urine specimen collection requires a player to be naked from his knees up and then urinate into a cup with the specimen collector standing directly in front of him.[22] Blood tests require blood to be withdrawn. Consequently, players and their unions generally seek to minimize the number of times players have to go through these uncomfortable experiences.

Additionally, the unions want to ensure that the drug tests are reliable in that testing procedures accurately determine whether a player has failed a drug test. In the 2011 CBA, the NFL and NFLPA agreed that the NFL would begin

---

c   It is important to understand that if a player does not obtain a TUE before beginning use of the banned substance he is likely to be disciplined, regardless of whether the drug has been prescribed. NFL player Robert Mathis was suspended for the first four games of the 2014 season after testing positive for a banned substance that was in a fertility drug Mathis had been prescribed to help Mathis and his wife conceive a child. Darin Gantt, *Robert Mathis balancing professional guilt and personal joy*, ProFootballTalk (Jul. 31, 2014), http://profootballtalk.nbcsports.com/2014/07/31/robert -mathis-balancing-professional-guilt-and-personal-joy/, *archived at* http://perma .cc/C8DS-7VCA. Mathis failed to obtain a TUE for the drug and was thus subject to discipline. Mike Florio, *NFL responds to agent's statement regarding Robert Mathis*, ProFootballTalk (May 17, 2014, 12:57 AM), http://profootballtalk.nbcsports.com /2014/05/17/nfl-responds-to-agents-statement-regarding-robert-mathis/, *archived at* http://perma.cc/7JUH-ZS9H.

d   It is hard to know how this usage compares to the general population. Our research did not reveal usage rates for a comparable control population. However, according to a national survey on drug use by the University of Michigan, in 2015, approximately 1.6% of people aged 19-30 reported using Ritalin, an ADD medication. Additionally, approximately 6.9% of people aged 19-30 reported using Adderall, also an ADD medication. However, the relationship between usage and prescriptions was not provided. *See* Lloyd D. Johnston et al., *Monitoring the Future national survey results on drug use, 1975– 2015: Volume 2, College students and adults ages 19–55* 111 (2015), available at http://monitoringthefuture.org/pubs.html#monographs.

to test for human growth hormone ("hGH"), with the specifics to be worked out at a later date. Nevertheless, it took nearly three years for the NFL and NFLPA to agree on the procedures of hGH testing due, in part, to concerns about the scientific reliability of the blood tests available at the time.[23]

Another procedural concern of the unions is "non-analytical positives," *i.e.*, those situations where the player has not tested positive for a banned substance but has violated a drug policy in some other way, such as by possessing the drug, engaging in illegal conduct, manipulating the test, or being accused of having used a banned substance through the testimony of others. Without clear proof that a player has taken a banned substance (such as through a failed drug test), the unions want to ensure that players are not unfairly punished for circumstantial evidence.

Finally, unions want to ensure that players receive a fair appeals process, typically understood to include the right to challenge the validity of the alleged drug policy violation before a neutral arbitrator. The appeals process and a player's legal rights thereunder are important issues for players. Nevertheless, they are legally complicated and more tangential to player health than is our focus in this Report. Consequently, we do not discuss them here.

* * *

With this background, we turn to our analysis of the leagues' drug policies. Specifically, for each of the leagues, we will describe: (1) the substances prohibited; (2) the types of tests and prohibited conduct; (3) the number of tests; (4) the administration of the policies; (5) therapeutic use; (6) discipline; (7) treatment; and, (8) confidentiality.

A drug test can be an invasive and personal process. Urine specimen collection requires a player to be naked from his knees up and then urinate into a cup with the specimen collector standing directly in front of him.

A) The NFL's Drug Policies

The NFL has two separate policies: (1) the Policy on Performance-Enhancing Substances ("PES Policy"); and, (2) the Policy and Program on Substances of Abuse ("Substance Abuse Policy"). Both policies were most recently amended in 2016. We will describe both policies for each issue of interest.

1) SUBSTANCES PROHIBITED

a) PES Policy

The PES Policy prohibits specifically listed substances in the following categories: (1) anabolic agents, including anabolic/androgenic steroids, hormones (including hGH), Beta-2-agonists, anti-estrogenic agents, and selective androgen receptor modulators ("SARMs"); (2) masking agents, including diuretics, epitestosterone, and probenecid; and (3) stimulants.[24] Doping methods, including enhancement of oxygen transfer, chemical and physical manipulation, and gene doping are also all strictly prohibited.[25] The NFL and NFLPA may mutually agree to modify the prohibited substances list included in the PES Policy.[26]

b) Substance Abuse Policy

The Substance Abuse Policy prohibits players "from the illegal use, possession, or distribution of drugs, including but not limited to cocaine; marijuana;[e] opiates and opioids; methylenedioxymethamphetamine (MDMA); and phencyclidine (PCP)," as well as the "abuse of prescription drugs, over-the-counter drugs, and alcohol."[27] Other substances not enumerated may be prohibited if included in a treatment plan required by the Substance Abuse Policy (explained further below).[28]

An important change concerning certain stimulants was made to the PES Policy and Substance Abuse Policy in 2014. Prior to 2014, several players tested positive for banned stimulants during the off-season.[29] Stimulants were banned under the PES Policy but provided the players no competitive advantage during the off-season. Instead, the players were using the stimulants as recreational drugs.[30] Under the revised PES Policy, if a player tests positive for a

---

e   Synthetic marijuana was banned in 2016. Mike Florio, *NFL, NFLPA agree on revised drug, PED policies*, ProFootballTalk (Oct. 9, 2016, 8:40 AM), http://profootballtalk .nbcsports.com/2016/10/09/nfl-nflpa-agree-on-revised-drug-ped-policies/, *archived at* https://perma.cc/4BVM-WYMT.

stimulant during the off-season, he is deemed to have violated the Substance Abuse Policy and not the PES Policy.[31] The change is dramatic in terms of the discipline to be imposed: four games for a first violation of the PES Policy versus no punishment under the Substance Abuse Policy, as will be explained below.

2) TYPES OF TESTS AND PROHIBITED CONDUCT

a) PES Policy

The PES Policy uses urine and blood tests.[32]

A test is "positive" under the PES Policy if the test result reveals the presence of a prohibited substance in the player's sample "at the level required by the testing protocols."[33] Players are also subject to punishment under the PES Policy for: (1) violations of law (demonstrated by convictions or player admissions) relating to the use, possession, acquisition, sale, or distribution of steroids, growth hormones, stimulants, or related substances, or conspiring to do so;[34] (2) using, possessing, or distributing PES as found through credible evidence;[35] (3) attempting to substitute, dilute, or adulterate a specimen;[36] and, (4) manipulating a test result.[37] While violations of law, non-analytical positives, attempts to substitute, dilute, or adulterate specimens, and test result manipulations are not expressly included in the definition of a "positive test," they are subject to discipline as will be explained below.

b) Substance Abuse Policy

The Substance Abuse Policy uses urine tests only.[38]

For the Substance Abuse Policy, "[t]ests . . . will be deemed positive if they are confirmed by laboratory analysis at the identified urine concentration levels."[39] A player who fails to cooperate fully in the testing process or who attempts to substitute or adulterate a specimen, alter a test result, or engage in doping methods will be treated as if he produced a positive test.[40] Players who fail to appear for testing are subject to discipline, but not on the same schedule as those whose specimens result in positive tests.[41]

A player also violates the Substance Abuse Policy if he commits a violation of law involving alcohol or drugs of abuse.[42] In addition to a conviction, a violation of law will also be found where the player enters into a diversionary program, deferred adjudication, disposition of supervision, or similar arrangement, including *nolo contendere* pleas.[43]

3) NUMBER OF TESTS

a) PES Policy

Under the PES Policy, free agent rookies and veterans are subject to pre-employment urine tests, including testing at the NFL Combine.[44] All players are also subject to at least one annual urine test for prohibited substances to occur at training camp or whenever a player reports as part of the player's pre-season physical.[45] Additionally, ten players per club are randomly selected for urine testing each week during the pre-season, regular season, and postseason.[46] During the off-season, players under contract who are not otherwise subject to reasonable cause testing (discussed below) may be tested at the discretion of the Independent Administrator (subject to a maximum of six combined urine and blood tests).[47]

The PES Policy also allows for blood testing under the following circumstances: (1) 20% of every club's roster will receive blood testing once annually; (2) each week during the pre-season, regular season, and postseason, five players from eight randomly selected clubs who are selected for urine testing will also receive blood testing;[f] (3) 10% of every club's roster will receive blood testing in the off-season; and, (4) pre-employment blood tests may be administered to free agent rookies and veterans, including 30 players randomly selected at the Combine who will undergo urine and blood testing.[48] The Independent Administrator randomly selects the players to be tested.

Finally, the PES Policy allows for reasonable cause testing for players who have previously tested positive for PES or for whom there is sufficient credible evidence[49] of prior PES involvement (up to two football seasons prior to the player's applicable college draft).[50] In no circumstance may a player undergo more than 24 combined urine and/or blood tests per year.[51]

b) Substance Abuse Policy

Under the Substance Abuse Policy, players are subject to testing on the following terms: (1) a rookie or veteran player not under contract may be subject to a pre-employment test if that player was not under contract to his last club on the date of its last game of the preceding season and the player has not had a test in the four-month period prior (excluding an NFL Combine test); (2) draft-eligible players are subject to pre-employment tests during the NFL Combine; (3) all players under contract are subject to one annual test during the off-season; (4) all players

---

f   In other words, for 8 of the NFL's 32 clubs, half of the ten players randomly selected for urine testing in any given week are also subject to blood testing.

in the Intervention Program[52] will be required to provide specimens when determined by the Medical Advisor (discussed below in Section 4: Administration); and, (5) a club and player may agree that the player will submit to unannounced testing during the term of his contract if the club has a reasonable basis for such testing.[53]

For players already in the NFL, it is fairly easy not to run afoul of the Substance Abuse Policy. Players are only tested for drugs of abuse during an off-season window that begins in April and ends in August.[54] So long as players do not use drugs of abuse during this time frame (or sufficiently in advance of this time frame), they will not test positive under the Substance Abuse Policy and can otherwise use drugs of abuse without detection or consequences under the Policy during the remainder of the year.[55] Moreover, the NFLPA issues a reminder about the drug testing dates to all players approximately a month before the drug testing window begins.[56] Because players should be able to avoid problems with the Substance Abuse Policy fairly easily, the off-season test is referred to even by NFL medical personnel as "an intelligence test."[57]

4) ADMINISTRATION

a) PES Policy

The Independent Administrator on Performance-Enhancing Substances, jointly selected by the NFL and the NFLPA, administers the PES Policy.[58] The current Independent Administrator is Dr. John Lombardo, an expert in PES.[59] Subject to limitations set in the PES Policy, the Independent Administrator is vested with the discretion to make determinations concerning, among other things, the method by which players will be subjected to testing each week, the selection of players to be tested each week, the number and frequency of reasonable cause and off-season tests to administer, the scheduling of medical evaluations associated with the use of prohibited substances, review and approval of therapeutic use exemptions, and finding and certifying violations for disciplinary action.[60]

The PES Policy also employs a chief forensic toxicologist jointly selected by the NFL and NFLPA. The toxicologist, among other things, audits the operation of testing laboratories, reviews and certifies lab results, and provides advice to the NFL and NFLPA on anti-doping. The PES Policy also includes a jointly selected collection vendor to implement a training and certification process for all persons involved in the collection of samples under the PES Policy.[61]

b) Substance Abuse Policy

The NFL and NFLPA jointly select a Medical Director, who is responsible for developing and implementing all aspects of the Substance Abuse Policy that relate to the treatment of players.[62] The NFL and NFLPA also jointly select a Medical Advisor, who has the responsibility of serving as medical review officer and overseeing selection and testing under the Substance Abuse Policy's treatment program, known as the Intervention Program and discussed in detail below.[63] Additional administrators for the Substance Abuse Policy include treating clinicians,[64] team substance abuse physicians,[65] a chief forensic toxicologist,[66] collection vendor(s),[67] and club physicians.[68]

5) THERAPEUTIC USE

Therapeutic use exceptions ("TUEs") are available for players under both the PES Policy and the Substance Abuse Policy by applying to the Independent Administrator of the PES Policy and the Medical Advisor for the Substance Abuse Policy.[69] "The TUE application should be filled out and submitted by the player's treating physician and should include all pertinent medical records documenting the diagnosis."[70] The NFL applies the following guidelines to all TUE requests:

1. The medication must be necessary and indicated for treatment of the specific medical problem for which it has been requested;

2. Acceptable alternative treatments with medications that are not prohibited were attempted but failed, or reasons for not prescribing these alternative treatments have been presented;

3. Appropriate evaluation has been completed and all medical records documenting the diagnosis have been submitted for review; and,

4. The applicant may not begin use of the prohibited substance until after the TUE is granted.[71]

6) TREATMENT

Some of the sports leagues' drug policies provide for the player to undergo treatment concerning his drug use in lieu of or in addition to punishment. We thus analyze that issue across the leagues, beginning here with the NFL.

a) PES Policy

The PES Policy does not provide for any treatment. Nevertheless, treatment might be available through the player's club-funded health insurance policy.

b) Substance Abuse Policy

According to the Substance Abuse Policy, "[t]he cornerstone of th[e] Policy is the Intervention Program."[72] "Under the Intervention Program, Players are tested, evaluated, treated, and monitored for substance abuse."[73] The Intervention Program consists of three possible stages of treatment. If the player complies with his treatment and does not fail any tests, he will be discharged from the Intervention Program. However, if the player does not comply or fails drug tests, he will be advanced into more aggressive stages of treatment and be subject to increasing discipline.

A player can enter the Intervention Program in three ways: (1) a positive test result; (2) "[b]ehavior (including but not limited to an arrest or conduct related to an alleged misuse of Substances of Abuse occurring up to two (2) football seasons prior to the Player's applicable scouting combine) which, in the judgment of the Medical Director, exhibits physical, behavioral, or psychological signs or symptoms of misuse of Substances of Abuse"; and, (3) "Self-Referral: Personal notification to the Medical Director by a Player of his desire voluntarily to enter Stage One of the Intervention Program prior to his being notified to provide a specimen leading to a Positive Test Result, and prior to behavior of the type described above becoming known to the Medical Director from a source other than the Player."[74]

Once in the Intervention Program, the players are referred to the appropriate clinical professionals to develop a treatment plan for the player.[75] The Medical Director must then approve the treatment plan.[76] Additionally, once in the Intervention Program, the player is subject to additional testing at the discretion of the Medical Director.[77]

If a player complies with his treatment plan, he can be discharged from the Intervention Program in as little as 90 days.[78] If the Medical Director believes the player needs additional treatment or if the player fails to comply with his treatment plan, such as by failing a test, the player will advance to Stage Two of the Intervention Program.[79] In Stage Two, a player can be subject to as many as ten unannounced drug tests per month.[80]

If a player complies with his treatment plan in Stage Two, he can be discharged from the Intervention Program in as little as 12 months.[81] However, again, if the Medical Director believes the player needs additional treatment or if the player fails to comply with his treatment plan, such as by failing a test, the player will advance to Stage Three of the Intervention Program and be subject to additional treatment and evaluation.[82]

A player's path through the Intervention Program is detailed further in Figure 4-A on page 143.

7) DISCIPLINE[g]

a) PES Policy

On the first violation, the PES Policy provides for different punishment based on the type of violation. All violations are treated similarly in the second and third instances, as illustrated in Table 4-A below.[83]

---

g   In all of the leagues, suspensions are without pay except in rare circumstances.

Table 4-A:
NFL PES Policy Discipline Schedule

Type of Violation	First Violation	Second Violation	Third Violation
Violation of Law or Sufficient Credible Evidence[84]	6 games	10 games	2 years
Positive Test (Diuretic or Masking Agent)	2 games	10 games	2 years
Positive Test (Stimulant or Anabolic Agent)	4 games	10 games	2 years
Positive Test (Prohibited Substance Plus Diuretic, Masking Agent, Attempt to Adulterate, or Attempt to Manipulate)	6 games	10 games	2 years

In 2016, approximately 19 NFL players were suspended for violating the PES Policy,[85] an increase from 13 players in 2015, and 16 players in 2014.[86]

In addition to the fines and suspensions described above, players potentially face contractual consequences for violating the PES Policy. When a player has violated the PES Policy, his club is entitled to proportional forfeiture of bonuses previously paid.[87] For example, if a player received a $10 million signing bonus for a five-year contract, and the player then fails a PES test after the second season, the player could be required to return $6 million of the signing bonus to the club.[88] Similarly, if a player is entitled to have his Paragraph 5 (*i.e.*, base) salary guaranteed in his second season, but fails a PES test between the first and second seasons, the contract might contain a clause permitting the club to void the guarantee in the second season.[89] Because

NFL compensation is generally not guaranteed, these financial punishments can be more harmful to a player than the suspensions listed above.

b) Substance Abuse Policy

Players are not disciplined for initial positive test results under the Substance Abuse Policy. Instead, players are entered into the Intervention Program, discussed above. Provided players comply with their treatment programs under the Intervention Program, they will not be disciplined.

However, players who fail to comply with the Intervention Program are subject to increasing levels of discipline. Figure 4-A on the next page demonstrates a player's potential path and discipline through the Intervention Program.

Figure 4-A: A Player's Path through the NFL's Intervention Program

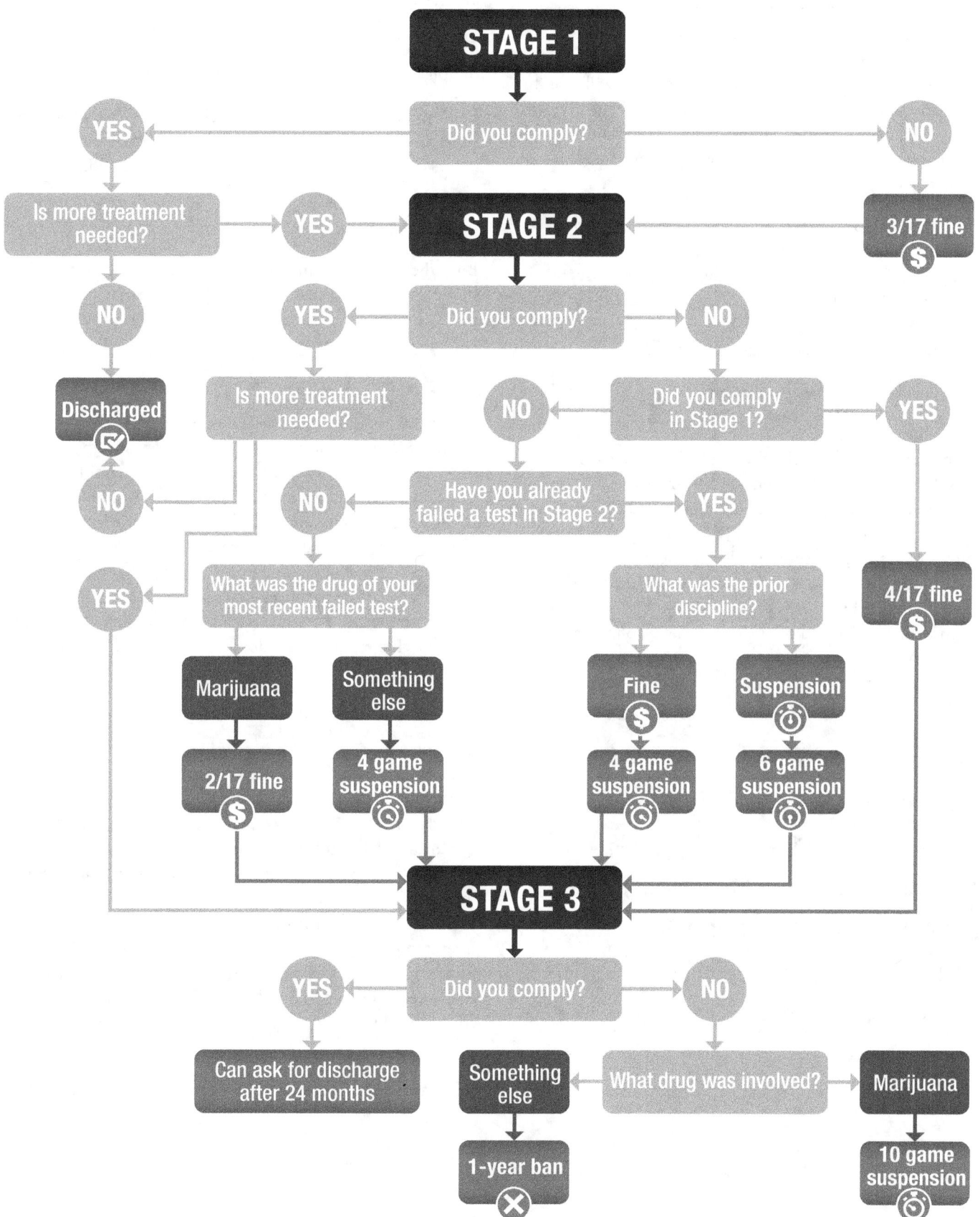

Additionally, a player who voluntarily enters the Intervention Program cannot be disciplined so long as he complies with his treatment plan.[90] In reality, this safe harbor provision is limited by the general tenuousness of NFL players' contracts and careers, which are often terminated for a variety of reasons. Because NFL players will look to avoid anything that sheds negative light on them—including voluntarily entering the Intervention Program—it is questionable how often players ever take advantage of the Substance Abuse Policy's safe harbor provision.

In 2016, approximately 26 players were suspended for violating the Substance Abuse Policy,[91] a decrease from 29 players in 2015, but more than the 23 players suspended in 2014.[92] Many more players were likely fined, but these statistics are not publicly available pursuant to the Policy's confidentiality provisions, discussed next.

Players are also subject to discipline for violations of law involving alcohol or drugs of abuse.

A player's first offense involving alcohol will generally result in a two-game suspension.[93] If there are "aggravating circumstances, including but not limited to felonious conduct, extreme intoxication (BAC of .15% or more), property damage or serious injury or death to the Player or a third party, and/or if the Player has had prior drug or alcohol-related misconduct, increased discipline may be imposed."[94] A second offense involving alcohol results in an eight-game suspension.[95]

A player's first offense involving drugs of abuse will generally result in a four-game suspension.[96] Discipline may be increased if there are aggravating circumstances similar to those discussed above.[97] A second offense involving drugs of abuse results in a six- to ten-game suspension.[98]

Finally, players who violate the Substance Abuse Policy are subject to the same potential contractual penalties as those discussed above arising out of violations of the PES Policy.

8) CONFIDENTIALITY

Both the PES Policy and Substance Abuse Policy mandate that players, clubs, the NFL, NFLPA, player agents, and all persons involved in administering the polices protect the confidentiality of matters covered by the policies.[99]

a) PES Policy

Under the PES Policy, "public disclosure, directly or indirectly, of information concerning positive tests, appeals or other violations of th[e] [PES] Policy is not permitted."[100] The PES Policy allows the NFL to publicly announce or acknowledge disciplinary action against a player when a suspension is upheld by an arbitrator and to publicly disclose information relating to the discipline of a player to correct inaccurate public claims made by the player or his representatives.[101] Finally, under the PES Policy, a player, club, or club employee is subject to a $500,000 fine for breaching the confidentiality provisions.[102]

b) Substance Abuse Policy

The Substance Abuse Policy requires confidentiality relating "to the history, diagnosis, treatment, prognosis, test results, or the fact of participation in the Intervention Program of any Player[.]"[103] The Substance Abuse Policy allows for disclosure under the same circumstances as the PES Policy and additionally allows for players to authorize or disclose information and allows the Medical Advisor or NFL to disclose to a club information about a player who the club is contemplating acquiring.[104] Finally, like the PES Policy, under the Substance Abuse Policy, a player, club, or club employee is subject to a $500,000 fine for breaching the confidentiality provisions.[105]

With this understanding of the NFL policies we are ready to compare them to what is in place for the other leagues.

> A player who voluntarily enters the Intervention Program cannot be disciplined so long as he complies with his treatment plan. In reality, this safe harbor provision is limited by the general tenuousness of NFL players' contracts and careers.

B) MLB's Drug Policies

MLB and the MLBPA have agreed to the Joint Drug Prevention and Treatment Program ("Joint Program"). The Joint Program, last amended in December 2016, covers both PES and drugs of abuse. Where it is helpful, we will discuss the Joint Program's treatment of the different drugs separately.

1) SUBSTANCES PROHIBITED

The Joint Program prohibits the use, possession, sale, or distribution of four categories of substances: drugs of abuse,[106] PES,[107] stimulants,[108] and Dehydroepiandrosterone ("DHEA").[109] During the term of the Joint Program, MLB and the MLBPA may jointly agree to ban any additional substances.[110] Additionally, if the federal government adds a substance to Schedule I, II, or III of the Code of Federal Regulations Schedule of Controlled Substances, then that substance is automatically added to the list of prohibited substances as a drug of abuse, PES, or stimulant.[111]

However, MLB does not test for stimulants during the off-season.[112]

2) TYPES OF TESTS AND PROHIBITED CONDUCT

Like the NFL, MLB uses urine tests for PES, stimulants, and DHEA,[113] and blood tests for hGH.[114]

> "[I]f any substance identified in the test results meets the levels set forth in the Collection Procedures and Testing Protocols of the Program," then that test shall be considered "positive."[115] Additionally if a player refuses or, without good cause, fails to take a test, or engages in activity to prevent the collection of a specimen, then the player will be deemed to have failed a test.[116] Likewise, a test will be considered positive if a player "attempts to substitute, dilute, mask or adulterate a specimen or in any other manner alter a test."[117] Players may also be subject to disciplinary action, under a just cause standard, for "any . . . violation of [the Joint Program's prohibitions], including, but not limited to, non-analytical positives."[118]

3) NUMBER OF TESTS

a) PES

Each player is tested for PES, stimulants, and DHEA upon reporting to spring training and receives at least one other unannounced test on a randomly selected date between the start of spring training and the final day of the post-season.[119] In total, 4,800 unannounced tests for PES and stimulants are administered to randomly selected players during the season[120] and 1,550 unannounced, random tests for only PES and DHEA are administered during the off-season, in order to ensure that all players are subject to at least one random off-season test.[121] Each player is also randomly tested for hGH once during spring training,[122] and 900 random, unannounced blood tests for hGH are performed throughout the year.[123] There is no limit on the number of times an individual player may be tested for hGH.[124]

During the 2016 season, MLB conducted 8,281 drug tests.[125] 6,634 of the tests were urine and 1,647 were blood.[126] There were 15 failed tests—12 for PES and three for stimulants.[127]

Players are also potentially subject to just cause testing or, in the case of players who violate the Joint Program, additional follow-up testing. If the Commissioner or the MLBPA notifies the other that it has "reasonable cause" to believe that a player has "engaged in the use, possession, sale or distribution of a [PES or stimulant]" in the past year," then the player may be subject to a test within 48 hours of notification.[128] Players who test positive for PES are subject to three unannounced tests in the year after the positive test, and players who test positive for stimulants are subject to six unannounced tests in the year after the positive test.[129]

b) Drugs of Abuse

Unlike in the NFL, MLB players are generally not required to undergo testing for drugs of abuse, unless the Commissioner or MLBPA presents the other with reasonable cause for testing.[130] If a player tests positive for a drug of abuse after undergoing reasonable cause testing, he is referred to the Treatment Board for an initial evaluation,[131] after which the Treatment Board may develop a treatment program consisting of some combination of counseling, in- or out-patient treatment, and follow-up testing.[132]

4) ADMINISTRATION

The Independent Program Administrator, jointly selected by the MLBPA and MLB, oversees the Joint Program.[133] The Independent Program Administrator administers and audits the Joint Program's testing regime and develops related educational programs.[134] Additionally, the Treatment Board—consisting of two representatives (a lawyer and a physician) appointed by the MLBPA, two representatives (a lawyer and a physician) appointed by MLB, and a fifth neutral labor arbitrator—supervises the treatment of players who have or are suspected to have used drugs of abuse.[135]

Of note, the Independent Program Administrator is responsible for publicly releasing a report by December 1, of each year that sets forth the number of tests conducted, the number of positive tests that resulted in discipline, the substances involved in the tests that resulted in discipline, the number of non-analytical positives that resulted in discipline, and the number of TUEs issued, broken down by the category of medication.[136]

MLB's PES report is a commendable exercise in transparency. By disclosing its drug testing efforts and results and subjecting them to public scrutiny, MLB is demonstrating its commitment to the integrity of the game. While we believe the NFL should seriously consider releasing a similar report, such a report has minimal (if any) direct impact on player health and thus it is outside the scope of our concern here.

5) THERAPEUTIC USE

As in the NFL, a player with a medical condition that requires treatment by a substance prohibited by the Joint Program can apply to the Independent Program Administrator for a TUE.[137] The Independent Program Administrator determines whether or not to grant the TUE after consultation with members of the Medical Advisory Panel or outside specialists.[138]

6) TREATMENT

a) PES

As with the NFL, the Joint Program does not provide for treatment in the case of PES use.

b) Drugs of Abuse

The Joint Program does provide for treatment in the case of drugs of abuse in a manner substantially similar to that of the NFL. Under the Joint Program, a player begins treatment for drugs of abuse if he has previously failed a drug test (as the result of reasonable cause testing), or "is otherwise found to have used or possessed" a drug of abuse.[139] The player's treatment program is determined by the medical professionals on the Treatment Board, who may consult with other treating doctors or experts in the field.[140] The treatment program "may include any or all of the following: counseling, impatient treatment, outpatient treatment and follow-up testing."[141] A player is subject to discipline for failing to cooperate with his treatment plan, as discussed below.

7) DISCIPLINE

Punishments for violations of the Joint Program depend on the category of prohibited substance involved, the nature of the offense, and the number of previous violations (if any). The rules are summarized in Table 4-B on the next page:

Table 4-B:
MLB Joint Program Discipline Schedule

Type of Violation	First Violation	Second Violation	Third Violation	Fourth Violation
PES Use[142]	80 games	162 games	Permanent suspension; can apply for reinstatement after 2 years	NA
PES Sale or Distribution[143]	80-100 games	162 games	Permanent suspension; can apply for reinstatement after 2 years	NA
Stimulant Use[144]	Follow-up testing	50 games	100 games	Permanent suspension
Stimulant-related Convictions[145]	25-50 games	50-100 games	Permanent suspension	NA
Stimulant Sale or Distribution[146]	60-90 games	2-year suspension	Permanent suspension	NA
DHEA Use[147]	Follow-up testing	25 games	80 games	Permanent suspension
DHEA-related Convictions[148]	25-50 games	50-100 games	Permanent suspension	NA
DHEA Sale or Distribution[149]	60-90 games	2-year suspension	Permanent suspension	NA
Failure to Comply with Treatment Program[150]	15-25 games	25-50 games	50-75 games	At least one year suspension[151]
Drugs of Abuse Sale or Distribution[152]	60-90 games	2-year suspension	Permanent suspension	NA
Drugs of Abuse-related Convictions[153]	25-50 games	50-100 games	Permanent suspension	NA

DHEA is treated differently than other PES. "DHEA is a hormone that is naturally made by the human body. . . . Athletes and other people use DHEA to increase muscle mass, strength, and energy."[154] DHEA is legal[155] and can be purchased over the counter as a dietary supplement,[156] which might explain its differential treatment. Despite its legality, MLB, the NFL, NBA, NHL, NCAA, and the World Anti-Doping Agency ("WADA")[h] have all banned the use of DHEA.[157]

It is unclear whether players who voluntarily refer themselves for treatment can be disciplined under the Joint Program. In reviewing a draft of this Report, MLB stated:

---

h   WADA, established in 1999, is an international agency funded by sports organizations and governments with its principal focus on eliminating the use of PES in sports. WADA publishes annually a "Prohibited List" that lists prohibited substances. The WADA Code and the Prohibited List are the governing anti-doping documents of all Olympic sports organizations and most sports organizations worldwide.

If a Player comes forward and discloses to the Joint Treatment Board that he has substance use problem, he will be evaluated and prescribed a treatment program. If he remains compliant with his treatment program and the Treatment Board's recommendations, he will not be subject to discipline under the Joint Drug Program. This process is described in Section 4 of the Joint Drug Program.

Nevertheless, based on our reading of the Joint Program, while Section 4 does describe the evaluation and treatment provided to players, it does not say anything about a player not being subjected to discipline for voluntarily referring himself for treatment.

8) CONFIDENTIALITY

Like in the NFL, information about an MLB player's test results, testing history, and treatment program are generally confidential.[158] However, there are many exceptions to this rule. First, MLB and the MLBPA may, upon request, provide a Congressional committee with an anonymized summary of tests conducted under the Joint Program.[159] Second, MLB may inform a club that the club's player has been placed in a treatment program.[160] Third, a club may disclose a player's treatment history to a potential trade partner;[161] MLB may publicly disclose that a player has been suspended for a specific number of days for violating the Joint Program or for refusing to take or tampering with a test.[162] Fourth, MLB, in announcing the suspension of a player, can reveal the specific substance which caused the violation of the Joint Program.[163] Finally, both MLB and the MLBPA may disclose details of a player's testing history to correct inaccurate or misleading claims made by that player.[164]

> Like in the NFL, information about an MLB player's test results, testing history, and treatment program are generally confidential. However, there are many exceptions to this rule.

C) The NBA's Drug Policies

The NBA and NBPA have agreed to the Anti-Drug Program. The Anti-Drug Program, last amended as part of the 2017 CBA, covers both PES and drugs of abuse. Where it is helpful, we will discuss the Anti-Drug Program's treatment of the different drugs separately.

1) SUBSTANCES PROHIBITED

Prohibited substances in the NBA fall into four categories: (1) drugs of abuse;[i] (2) marijuana and its by-products (including synthetic cannabinoids); (3) steroids, PES, and masking agents ("SPEDs");[j] and, (4) diuretics.[k] Additionally, any steroid or PES that is declared illegal[l] during the term of the CBA is automatically added to the list of prohibited substances, and either the NBA or NBPA can convene a meeting of the Prohibited Substances Committee to request that the Committee add a substance to the list of prohibited substances.[165]

2) TYPES OF TESTS AND PROHIBITED CONDUCT

The NBA's Anti-Drug program includes both urine and blood testing.[166] Any test under the Anti-Drug program will be considered "positive" for a prohibited substance if: (1) for a test for a drug of abuse or marijuana, the test confirms levels of the prohibited substance meeting or exceeding the levels set forth in the CBA;[167] (2) for a test for a SPED, the test confirms levels of the SPED meeting or exceeding the levels set forth in the CBA;[168] (3) for a test for a diuretic, the test confirms any detectable level of a diuretic;[169] (4) a player refuses to submit to a test or fully cooperate with the testing process;[170] (5) a player fails to submit to a scheduled test without reasonable explanation;[171] or, (6) a player attempts to substitute, dilute, or adulterate a specimen.[172]

Additionally, even if a player has not failed a test, the NBA's Anti-Drug Program prohibits the "use, possession, or distribution" of prohibited substances.[173]

---

i   Drugs of abuse include, among other substances, cocaine, LSD, methamphetamine, opiates, and PCP. 2017 NBA CBA, Ex. I-2.
j   Exhibit I-2 to the CBA specifically lists out over 150 banned SPEDs. hGH is included among banned SPEDs.
k   Exhibit I-2 to the CBA includes 24 banned diuretics.
l   The 2017 NBA CBA does not specify whether the illegality of the steroid or PES refers to federal and/or state law. However, according to the NBA, in practice, the league is concerned with federal law.

3) NUMBER OF TESTS

A player is required to undergo random urine testing for prohibited substances at any time, without prior notice, no more than four times during each season and no more than two times during the off-season.[174] Players can also be blood tested a maximum of two times during the season and once in the off-season.[175] The NBA can conduct a maximum of 1,525 total random tests during the season and a maximum of 600 total random tests during the off-season.[176]

Players are also subject to reasonable cause testing. If the NBA or NBPA has reasonable cause to believe that a player is engaged in the use, possession, or distribution of a prohibited substance, then that party may request a conference with the "Independent Expert," who will determine whether reasonable cause exists to test the player.[177] If reasonable cause exists, the player may be tested up to four times during the subsequent six-week period.[178]

4) ADMINISTRATION

A jointly selected NBA/NBPA Medical Director oversees the NBA's Anti-Drug Program concerning drugs of abuse and marijuana.[179] A separate Medical Director is responsible for overseeing the SPED portion of the Anti-Drug Program.[180] Additionally, a jointly selected Independent Expert issues authorizations for reasonable cause testing.[181] A five-member Prohibited Substance Committee, consisting of one NBA representative, one NBPA representative, and three jointly selected individuals, makes recommendations to the NBA and NBPA for changes to the list of Prohibited Substances, including laboratory analysis cutoff levels.[182] Finally, the NBA's Grievance Arbitrator (who handles a variety of potential grievances under the CBA) is responsible for resolving any and all disputes arising under the Anti-Drug program.[183]

5) THERAPEUTIC USE

Although it is not mentioned in the CBA, the NBA's Anti-Drug program does contain a TUE process.[184] A player can petition the Medical Director of the Anti-Drug program for permission to use a banned substance.[185] The Medical Director determines whether the player is entitled to the TUE based upon the player's diagnosis and relevant medical information submitted by the player, including but not limited to a validly issued prescription.[186]

6) TREATMENT

Like the NFL, the NBA's Anti-Drug Program includes a treatment component. The NBA's Anti-Drug Program has three different treatment programs depending on the substance involved: drugs of abuse (excluding marijuana); marijuana; and, PES. Discipline for the three programs differs and will be discussed in the next Section.

a) Drugs of Abuse Program

The Drugs of Abuse Program is a two-stage program that includes education, treatment, counseling, and additional testing as directed by the Medical Director.[187] Players enter the Drugs of Abuse Program in one of two ways: (1) by testing positive for a drug of abuse as a rookie;[188] or, (2) by voluntarily entering the Drugs of Abuse Program to seek treatment.[189]

b) Marijuana Program

The Marijuana Program also includes education, treatment, counseling, and additional testing as directed by the Medical Director.[190] Players enter the Marijuana Program by: (1) testing positive for marijuana;[191] (2) being found to have used or possessed marijuana by the Grievance Arbitrator;[192] (3) being convicted of the use or possession of marijuana;[193] or, (4) voluntarily entering the Marijuana Program to seek treatment.[194]

c) SPEDs Program

The SPEDs Program (for steroids, performance-enhancing substances, and masking agents), like the Drugs of Abuse Program and Marijuana Program, includes education, treatment, counseling, and additional testing as directed by the SPED Medical Director.[195] Players enter the SPEDs Program by: (1) testing positive for a SPED;[196] or, (2) being found to have used or possessed a SPED by the Grievance Arbitrator.[197] Under the 2011 CBA, players could voluntarily enter the SPEDs Program and avoid discipline,[198] but that option was eliminated in the 2017 CBA.[199]

7) DISCIPLINE

Discipline for a violation of the NBA's Anti-Drug Program depends on the type of prohibited substance triggering the violation and, for drugs of abuse only, whether a player is a rookie or a veteran.

a) Drugs of Abuse

Table 4-C on the next page outlines the types of discipline for drugs of abuse in the NBA.

Table 4-C:
NBA Drugs of Abuse Program Discipline Schedule

Player Status	First Violation	Second Violation
Rookie	Dismissed and disqualified for at least one year; contract voided subject to reinstatement by agreement of the NBA and NBPA; enters Drugs of Abuse Program.[200]	If in Stage 1, suspended until there is compliance and advanced to Stage 2.[201] If in Stage 2, dismissed and disqualified for at least two years, subject to reinstatement, and contract voided.[202]
Veteran	Dismissed and disqualified for at least two years' subject to reinstatement by agreement of the NBA and NBPA; contract voided.[203,m]	For players who entered the Drugs of Abuse Program voluntarily, if in Stage 1, suspended until there is compliance and advanced to Stage 2.[204] If in Stage 2, dismissed and disqualified for at least two years' subject to reinstatement by agreement of the NBA and NBPA and contract voided.[205]

Players who voluntarily enter the Drugs of Abuse Program will not be disciplined provided they comply with their treatment.[206]

In addition to the discipline outlined above, players who are convicted of crimes involving alcohol (including DUI or DWI) or controlled substances that are not prohibited substances are subject to discipline as determined by the Commissioner and will be evaluated by the Medical Director of the Anti-Drug Program, who can mandate counseling.[207]

b) Marijuana

Table 4-D below outlines the types of discipline for marijuana use in the NBA.

Table 4-D:
NBA Marijuana Program Discipline Schedule

Violation	Discipline
First	Required to enter Marijuana Program.[208]
Second	Fined $25,000 and required to enter Marijuana Program if not already.[209]
Third	Suspended for five games and required to enter Marijuana Program if not already in.[210]
Fourth or more	Suspended for five games longer than immediately preceding suspension and required to enter Marijuana Program if not already in.[211]

Players who voluntarily enter the Marijuana Program will not be disciplined provided they comply with their treatment. [212]

c) SPEDs

Table 4-E below explains the discipline meted out for PES use in the NBA.

Table 4-E:
NBA SPEDs Program Discipline Schedule

Violation	Discipline
First	Suspended for 25 games and required to enter SPEDs Program.[213]
Second	Suspended for 55 games and required to enter SPEDs Program if not already in.[214]
Third	Dismissed and disqualified for at least two years' subject to reinstatement by agreement of the NBA and NBPA, and required to enter SPEDs Program if not already in.[215]

Under the 2011 CBA, players who voluntarily entered the SPEDs Program were not disciplined provided they complied with their treatment.[216] However, the ability to come forward voluntarily without punishment was removed in the 2017 CBA.[217]

8) CONFIDENTIALITY

Except as "reasonably required" in connection with the suspension or dismissal of a player, the NBA, the clubs, the NBPA, and their affiliates and employees "are prohibited from publicly disclosing information about the diagnosis,

m   In reviewing a draft of this Report, the NBA confirmed that a veteran player that commits his first violation of the Anti-Drug Program in relation to a drug of abuse (excluding marijuana) is dismissed and disqualified from the NBA and is not entered into the Drugs of Abuse Program, i.e., the NBA does not provide or facilitate treatment for the player.

treatment, prognosis, test results, compliance, or the fact of participation of a player in the [Drug] Program."[218] If a player is suspended or disqualified for a violation involving a drug of abuse or marijuana, the NBA may not publicly disclose the prohibited substance involved, but, if the player is suspended for conduct involving a SPED, the particular SPED shall be disclosed.[219] The Medical Directors, drug program counselors, the Independent Expert, and Members of the Prohibited Substances Committee are also prohibited from public disclosure of information obtained in their roles.[220]

D) The NHL's Drug Policies

Like the NFL, the NHL has two separate policies concerning the use of drugs: (1) the Performance Enhancing Substances Program ("PES Program"); and, (2) Substance Abuse and Behavioral Health Program ("Substance Abuse Program"). The PES Program was most recently amended as part of the 2013 CBA. The Substance Abuse Program was put into place in 1996 and it has not been changed since then. We will describe both policies for each issue of interest.

1) SUBSTANCES PROHIBITED

a) PES Program

The Prohibited Substances List for the PES Program is based on the WADA Prohibited List, with specific prohibited substances selected jointly by the NHL and NHLPA for their relevance to professional hockey.[221] The Prohibited Substance List is not publicly available, but the parties agreed by letter agreement accompanying the 2013 CBA to include on the Prohibited Substances List "'illegal' stimulants and amphetamines . . . that are relevant to the sport of hockey."[222]

b) Substance Abuse Program

The Substance Abuse Program does not define "substances of abuse," but the Substance Abuse Program Collection and Laboratory Procedures for Samples includes threshold levels for marijuana, cocaine, opiates, PCP, amphetamines, and alcohol.[223]

2) TYPES OF TESTS AND PROHIBITED CONDUCT

a) PES Program

The PES Program does not detail the type of specimen that a player must submit, leaving the decision to the Program Committee (discussed below in Section 4: Administration). Recent news articles indicate that the PES Program uses urine samples rather than blood testing.[224]

Under the PES Program, a test is "positive," if: (1) the test indicates levels of the prohibited substance that exceed the established cutoff levels; (2) the player had an unexcused failure or refusal to take the test; or, (3) the player attempted to substitute, dilute, mask, or adulterate his test specimen.[225]

While the NHL, like the NFL, employs a "strict liability standard" (*i.e.*, the player will be disciplined regardless of whether he intended to take a banned substance),[226] a player has the right to offer an alternative medical explanation for an adverse analytical finding (*i.e.* a positive test) under the PES Program.[227] If, after considering relevant evidence, the Program doctors determine that a valid alternative medical explanation exists, then that alternative medical explanation renders the player's test result conclusively non-positive and the player is not subject to discipline.[228] If the Program doctors do not determine that a valid alternative medical explanation exists, then the doctors must promptly test the player's "B" sample,[229] which was gathered as part of the initial urine specimen collection process. If the "B" sample tests negative, then the player's test is conclusively non-positive and the player is not subject to discipline.[230]

b) Substance Abuse Program

The Substance Abuse Program uses urine samples.[231]

To establish a violation of the Substance Abuse Program, there are threshold levels for initial tests and confirmatory tests for the different substances of abuse.[232] However, as will be explained further below, it is important to note that only players who are currently enrolled in the Substance Abuse Program are tested in an identifiable manner. In other words, there is no identifiable random testing.

3) NUMBER OF TESTS

a) PES Program

Similar to the NFL, under the PES Program, each NHL club is subject to one team-wide, no-notice drug test during training camp and one team-wide, no-notice drug test randomly during the regular season.[233] In addition, "[i]ndividual Players will be randomly selected for no-notice testing during the Regular Season and Playoffs."[234] While the Program Committee may only test up to sixty players during the off-season, there is no regular season cap.[235] There is also no limit on the number of times the Program Committee may test an individual player.[236]

The Program Committee may also test players at any time for reasonable cause if it has "information that gives it reasonable cause to believe that a Player has, in the previous 12-month period, engaged in the use of a Prohibited Substance."[237] However, the player has 48 hours after receiving Reasonable Cause Notification to contest the information giving rise to the reasonable cause to an impartial arbitrator.[238]

b) Substance Abuse Program

Unlike the NFL, where all players under contract are subject to an identifiable drug test, the NHL's Substance Abuse Program does not subject NHL players to random identifiable testing for substances of abuse for disciplinary purposes. Tests conducted under the PES Program do report test results for drugs of abuse but on a de-identified basis.[239] Only "if a positive result shows a dangerously high level for a drug of abuse such that it causes concern for the health or safety of the Player or others," do the Program Doctors have the right to discover the identity of the player and refer the player for an evaluation under the Substance Abuse Program.[240] In response to concerns about cocaine use by NHL players, during the 2015 season it was announced that all tests conducted under the PES Program would include a test for the drug.[241] Previously, only one-third of PES Program drug tests tested for drugs of abuse.[242]

Players may also voluntarily enter the Substance Abuse Program.[243] In fact, voluntarily entering the program is the principal method by which players begin treatment. It is also possible that players can be required to undergo a test for a substance of abuse if the NHL or club has reasonable cause to believe the player has used a drug of abuse, similar to the provision contained in the PES Policy. The Substance Abuse Program doctors are authorized to require that players in the Substance Abuse Program "undergo periodic substance testing at a frequency and on a schedule to be determined by the doctors. Such testing may take place both in season and during the off-season."[244]

4) ADMINISTRATION

a) PES Program

The Program Committee, comprised of an equal number of NHL and NHLPA representatives and a consulting expert doctor from each side, administers the PES Program.[245] The Program Committee is responsible for, among other things, developing an educational program, overseeing the administration of PES testing, recommending to the NHL and NHLPA which PES from the WADA Prohibited List[n] they should include on the Prohibited Substances List, supervising player evaluation and treatment following positive tests, and administering the TUE process.[246]

b) Substance Abuse Program

"[Q]ualified doctors selected by the League and the NHLPA" administer the Substance Abuse and Program.[247] The Substance Abuse Program doctors' responsibilities include the development of an educational program, establishment of a multinational counseling network, development of standardized medical assessment tools for substance abuse problems, making decisions concerning treatment and follow-up care, and ensuring compliance with the program.[248]

5) THERAPEUTIC USE

a) PES Program

A player may apply to the PES Program Committee for a TUE with respect to a particular prohibited substance.[249] "[T]he Program Committee shall review, consider and act upon such Player's application expeditiously and approval of the application shall not be unreasonably withheld."[250]

b) Substance Abuse Program

There is no TUE provision in the Substance Abuse Program.

6) TREATMENT

a) PES Program

Players who violate the PES Program are referred to the Substance Abuse Program for evaluation and possible treatment. In contrast, the NFL's PES Policy does not refer violators to its Intervention Program for treatment.

---

n The NHL is the only of the four major American sports leagues to use the WADA Prohibited List in choosing its own prohibited substances.

b) Substance Abuse Program

Similar to the NFL's Intervention Program, the Substance Abuse Program is principally a "program of education, counseling, inpatient and outpatient treatment, follow-up care, and, where appropriate, sanctions."[251] Players who enter the Substance Abuse Program are given an initial evaluation and then a treatment plan as chosen by the Program Doctors.[252]

7) DISCIPLINE

a) PES Program

Table 4-F below explains the types of discipline for PES use by the NHL.

Table 4-F:
NHL PES Program Discipline Schedule

Violation	Discipline
First	Suspended for 20 games and referred to Substance Abuse Program.[253]
Second	Suspended for 60 games and referred to Substance Abuse Program.[254]
Third	Player permanently suspended, although player can apply for reinstatement after 2 years.[255]

From the time that the PES Policy was first instituted in 2005 through 2013, it was reported that only one player tested positive under the PES Policy, causing some to question the effectiveness of the Policy.[256] As of the date of publication, five players have been *disciplined* under the PES Policy—though that does not necessarily mean there have been five positive tests as players could be disciplined for other violations of the PES Policy. However, because hockey is an Olympic sport, NHL players wishing to play in the Olympics are also subject to testing by their country's respective Olympic drug-testing programs (such as the United States Anti-Doping Agency), and it is thus possible that PES are particularly uncommon in the NHL.[o]

b) Substance Abuse Program

Table 4-G below explains the types of discipline under the NHL's Substance Abuse Program. Again, we note that only

players in the Substance Abuse Program are tested in an identified manner, and thus only those players can be disciplined.

Table 4-G:
NHL Substance Abuse Program Discipline Schedule

Violation	Discipline
First	No discipline; enters Stage 1 of Substance Abuse Program.[257]
Second	Suspended during active treatment; enters Stage 2 of the Substance Abuse Program.[258]
Third	Suspended for a minimum of six months; enters Stage 3 of the Substance Abuse Program.[259]
Fourth	Suspended for a minimum of one year; enters Stage 4 of the Substance Abuse Program.[260]

In addition, a player who voluntarily enters the Substance Abuse Program cannot be disciplined provided he complies with his treatment.[261]

Outside the scope of the Substance Abuse Program, players might still be subject to discipline if they have violated the law concerning alcohol or a drug of abuse. Indeed, the Substance Abuse Program states that players may be subject to other discipline outside of the Substance Abuse Program.[262] The NHL CBA provides the Commissioner wide discretion to impose discipline for off-ice conduct, including fines, suspensions, and cancelling a player's contract.[263] Any discipline imposed is subject to appeal before a neutral arbitrator.[264]

8) CONFIDENTIALITY

a) PES Program

Test results under the PES Program are confidential except that: (1) once a positive test has been confirmed by the impartial arbitrator (or if no grievance has been filed), the player suspended will be identified and the fact of and length of his suspension under the Program will be announced; and, (2) if a player is subject to a transaction that results in a change to his status (*e.g.*, a trade) and that transaction was completed between the date on which the player tested positive and the date upon which he received his suspension, a club alleging that it was adversely affected by the player's nondisclosure of his positive test may file a grievance.[265]

---

o   Basketball and soccer are also Olympic sports and thus performance-enhancing drug usage in those sports might also be lowered as a result of the Olympic drug-testing programs.

b) Substance Abuse Program

The assessment of alcohol and drug problems under the Substance Abuse Program shall be conducted "with the assurance of confidentiality."[266] The Substance Abuse Program recognizes that "records which contain information pertaining to the diagnosis or treatment of psychiatric, alcohol- or drug-related disorders are subject to strict confidentiality" and therefore requires the player-patient's prior written authorization for disclosure.[267] The Substance Abuse program doctors are responsible for "[a]ppropriate maintenance of confidentiality of Player records."[268]

# E) The CFL's Drug Policies

The CFL-CFLPA Policy to Prevent the Use of Performance Enhancing Drugs ("PED Policy") was most recently amended in April 2016.

The CFL does not have a policy concerning drugs of abuse and the CFL CBA specifically declares that "there shall be no drug testing conducted in relation to any player in the C.F.L. except as provided for in the [PED Policy]."[269] However, the CFL CBA states that the CFLPA and the CFL Player Relations Committee ("CFLPRC") "shall continue with a Committee which shall have the mandate of studying and gathering information with respect to drug abuse related to both illegal and performance enhancing drugs."[270]

1) SUBSTANCES PROHIBITED

The PED Policy prohibits PES, stimulants, and masking agents.[271]

2) TYPES OF TESTS AND PROHIBITED CONDUCT

Like the NFL's PES Policy, the CFL's PED Policy authorizes the collection of blood and urine samples.[272]

According to the PED Policy, "[e]xcepting those drugs for which a quantitative reporting threshold is specifically identified in the Prohibited List, the detected presence of any quantity of a Performance Enhancing Drug, its Metabolites or Markers in a Player's sample shall result in an Adverse Analytical Finding."[273] In addition to adverse analytical findings, players are subject to discipline for refusing to comply with the testing provisions, tampering

or attempting to tamper with the sample collection process, administering or attempting to administer (or assisting with, encouraging, or covering up the administration of) a PES to any other player, and conviction in Canada of a criminal offense for possession or trafficking of a PES on the CFL Prohibited List.[274]

3) NUMBER OF TESTS

Beginning with the 2016 season, all players are tested under the PED Policy.[275] In addition, players are subject to targeted testing if: (1) "the laboratory has recommended follow-up testing based on their analytical investigation;" (2) "the Player is presently undergoing counseling and as a condition of their counseling, they are subject to further testing;" or, (3) "the Player has been granted a retroactive exemption" for previously refusing to submit to a drug test.[276] Finally, if a player has previously committed a violation of the PED Policy, then the player will be subject to mandatory testing for a two-year period following the violation, up to a maximum of eight drug tests.[277]

The CFL has the authority to reduce testing frequency, at any time and in its sole discretion.[278] All testing is done randomly, with no advance notice, and may occur at any time during the calendar year.[279]

4) ADMINISTRATION

The CFL and CFLPA are jointly responsible for administering the PED Policy, but the PED Policy does not elaborate on the specifics of that administration.[280]

5) THERAPEUTIC USE

The Designated Medical Authority,[281] a doctor jointly appointed by the CFL and CFLPA for the purpose of reviewing TUE applications, may grant a TUE to a player if: (2) the player could experience a significant health impairment if the substance "were to be withheld in the course of treating an acute or chronic medical condition"; (3) the use of the substance would "produce no additional achievement or performance other than that which might be anticipated by a return to a state of normal health"; and, (3) there is not a "reasonable therapeutic alternative" to using the prohibited substance.[282]

6) TREATMENT

The CFL's PED Policy makes treatment available to the players. "If a Player is suspended by the CFL pursuant to the terms of [the PED] Policy, such Player must participate in an assessment and clinical evaluation, to determine whether a counselling program would be recommended . . . . The program would be tailored to meet the specific needs of the Player and may include, but is not limited to, the following: (a) counselling from medical personnel or substance abuse experts; (b) remedial education that provides various information including alternatives to the use of performance enhancing substances; and (c) community service, including speaking to other Players or members of the public about the dangers of using Performance Enhancing Drugs in sport."[283] Nevertheless, "it is at the sole discretion of the player" whether he receives treatment.[284]

In contrast, the NFL makes treatment available as part of its Substance Abuse Policy but not its PES Policy.

7) DISCIPLINE

Table 4-H below explains the types of discipline for PES use by the CFL.

Table 4-H:
CFL PED Policy Discipline Schedule

Violation	Discipline
First	Suspended for two games, must complete educational course, undergo a clinical evaluation, and subject to additional drug testing for two years.[285]
Second	Suspended for nine games, must complete educational course, undergo a clinical evaluation, and subject to additional drug testing for two years.[286]
Third	Suspended for one year, must complete educational course, undergo a clinical evaluation, and subject to additional drug testing for two years.[287]
Fourth	Suspended for life.[288]

A player who voluntarily admits a problem using PES is not subject to discipline and will undergo a clinical evaluation.[289] In contrast, the NFL's PES Policy does not offer self-referrals a safe harbor from discipline.

> The CFL's PED Policy makes treatment available to the players. In contrast, the NFL makes treatment available as part of its Substance Abuse Policy but not its PES Policy.

8) CONFIDENTIALITY

The CFL, CFLPA, CFL Safety Committee, Sample Collection Authority, and the Substance Abuse Counseling Organization may not share a player's medical information.[290] However, the permitted disclosure of information about a player's failed drug test is much broader. As of 2016, the PED Policy dictates that "the CFL and CFLPA shall disclose the name of every Player who violates the [PED] Policy including disclosure of the summary details of the applicable violation (substance detected, sanction imposed, reasons for a sanction reduction, etc.) but only after all appeals available to the Player under the [PED] Policy have been exhausted."[291] Additionally, the PED Policy also authorizes "the CFL Commissioner and the President of the CFLPA, or their respective designees, . . . to speak publicly and disclose any information about a Player that has violated the [PED] Policy."[292]

F) MLS' Drug Policies

MLS' Substance Abuse and Behavioral Health Program and Policy ("Substance Abuse Policy") covers both PES and drugs of abuse. The Substance Abuse Policy was most recently amended as part of the 2015 CBA.

1) SUBSTANCES PROHIBITED

MLS' Substance Abuse Policy regulates four types of substances.

First, the Substance Abuse Policy "prohibits the use or possession of any controlled substance without a prescription issued by a physician licensed to practice medicine."[293] The Substance Abuse Policy also declares that "[p]rescription drugs, even if properly prescribed, may also be prohibited if such drug is not being used for an approved medical reason[.]"[294]

Second, the Substance Abuse Policy prohibits the use of "street drugs," including, "without limitation, (1) amphetamines, (2) barbiturates, (3) benzodiazepines, (4) cocaine, (5) marijuana, (6) methadone, (7) methaqualone, (8) opiates, (9) phencyclidine (PCP), (10) propoxyphene, (11) ecstasy, and (12) club drugs including GHB and their analogs[.]"[295]

Third, while MLS "recognizes that alcohol is a legal substance," the Substance Abuse Policy prohibits "the use of alcohol on work premises [unless as part of a Club or League function] or reporting to work under the influence of alcohol or otherwise being affected at work by the consumption of alcohol[.]"[296]

Fourth, the Substance Abuse Policy adopts the WADA Prohibited List for its list of prohibited PES.[297]

2) TYPES OF TESTS AND PROHIBITED CONDUCT

MLS' Substance Abuse Policy only provides for urine testing.[298]

A player violates the Substance Abuse Policy, in relevant part,[p] "(i) through receipt of a [failed test], (ii) use or possession of any controlled substance without a prescription, (iii) abuse of a prescription drug, (iv) use of alcohol on work premises or reporting to work under the influence of alcohol or otherwise being affected at work by the consumption of alcohol, (iv) use or possession of [street drugs], [or] (v) use or possession of [PES][.]"[299] "An adulterated or substituted drug test" is treated as a positive test.[300] Additionally, a refusal to submit to a drug test is also considered a positive test.[301]

3) NUMBER OF TESTS

The Substance Abuse Policy dictates that "[a]ll Players are subject to unannounced . . . testing" for all prohibited substances.[302] The Substance Abuse Policy does not set a limit on the number of times a player can be tested.[303]

4) ADMINISTRATION

The Substance Abuse Policy is "administered by qualified doctors, in associated with a certified substance abuse and behavioral health counselor ('Program Professionals')[.]"[304] The Program Professionals are "selected jointly by the [MLS] Commissioner or his designee and the MLS Players Union[.]"[305] The Program Professionals are responsible for:

1. Developing an educational program on substance abuse and behavioral health problems to be presented at least once each year to Players;

2. Overseeing Prohibited Substance and alcohol testing;

3. Establishing a comprehensive multi-national counseling network to include a 24-hour toll-free number and a network of designated counseling professionals in each MLS city;

4. Implementing a standardized medical and/or psychological assessment used to evaluate Players who have violated the [Substance Abuse] Policy or who self-refer to the [Substance Abuse] Program;

5. Making decisions concerning treatment and aftercare, and ensuring compliance with those treatment programs. The [Substance Abuse] Program Professionals shall determine all substance abuse and behavioral health treatments of Players; and,

6. Selecting and evaluating laboratory, treatment, and aftercare facilities.[306]

---

p   The Substance Abuse Policy also governs "violation[s] of criminal law," "domestic violence," and, "illegal or excessive gambling[.]" MLS Substance Abuse Policy, § 5(A). Such violations are subject to "discipline[] for just cause." *Id.* at § X(B)(2).

5) THERAPEUTIC USE

MLS' Substance Abuse Policy does not provide any exceptions for therapeutic use.

6) TREATMENT

MLS' Substance Abuse Policy provides the possibility of treatment for any violation of the Substance Abuse Policy, including PES.[307] A player is required to undergo an evaluation for possible treatment if the player: (1) refers himself for treatment; (2) has violated the Substance Abuse Policy; or, (3) is recommended to be evaluated by a league or club official who has "reasonable belief" that the player has violated the Substance Abuse Policy.[308] The Program Professionals will make a determination as to whether or not the player should enter treatment.[309]

Treatment can consist of counseling, outpatient treatment, in-residence treatment at a designated facility, and necessary aftercare.[310] Players must following the treatment determinations made by the Program Professionals.[311] Also, the costs of treatment are covered by MLS.[312]

7) DISCIPLINE

Like the NFL, MLS' Substance Abuse Policy contains a multi-stage treatment program in which the discipline is determined by the player's level of compliance with his treatment.[313] Importantly, this multi-stage treatment process applies only to drugs of abuse, not PES.[314] Figure 4-B on the next page shows an MLS player's path through the MLS Substance Abuse Policy Program. As compared to the NFL's Intervention Program, the level of discipline to be imposed by the MLS Substance Abuse Policy is far less clear. A player cannot be disciplined for voluntarily referring himself to the Program.[315] A player who fails a test for the first time is generally not disciplined for a first offense and is placed in Stage 1 of the Program.[316] However, upon the recommendation of the Program Professionals, a player can be placed in Stage 2 based on an initial failed test and players in Stage 2 are suspended without pay during treatment and are only reinstated at the Commissioner's discretion.[317] Generally, speaking, the MLS Substance Abuse Policy prescribes no specific punishments, leaving discipline to the discretion of the MLS Commissioner, with the consultation of the Program Professionals.[318] Moreover, the Substance Abuse Policy does not explicitly describe how players can exit the Program, which presumably occurs if they comply with treatment.

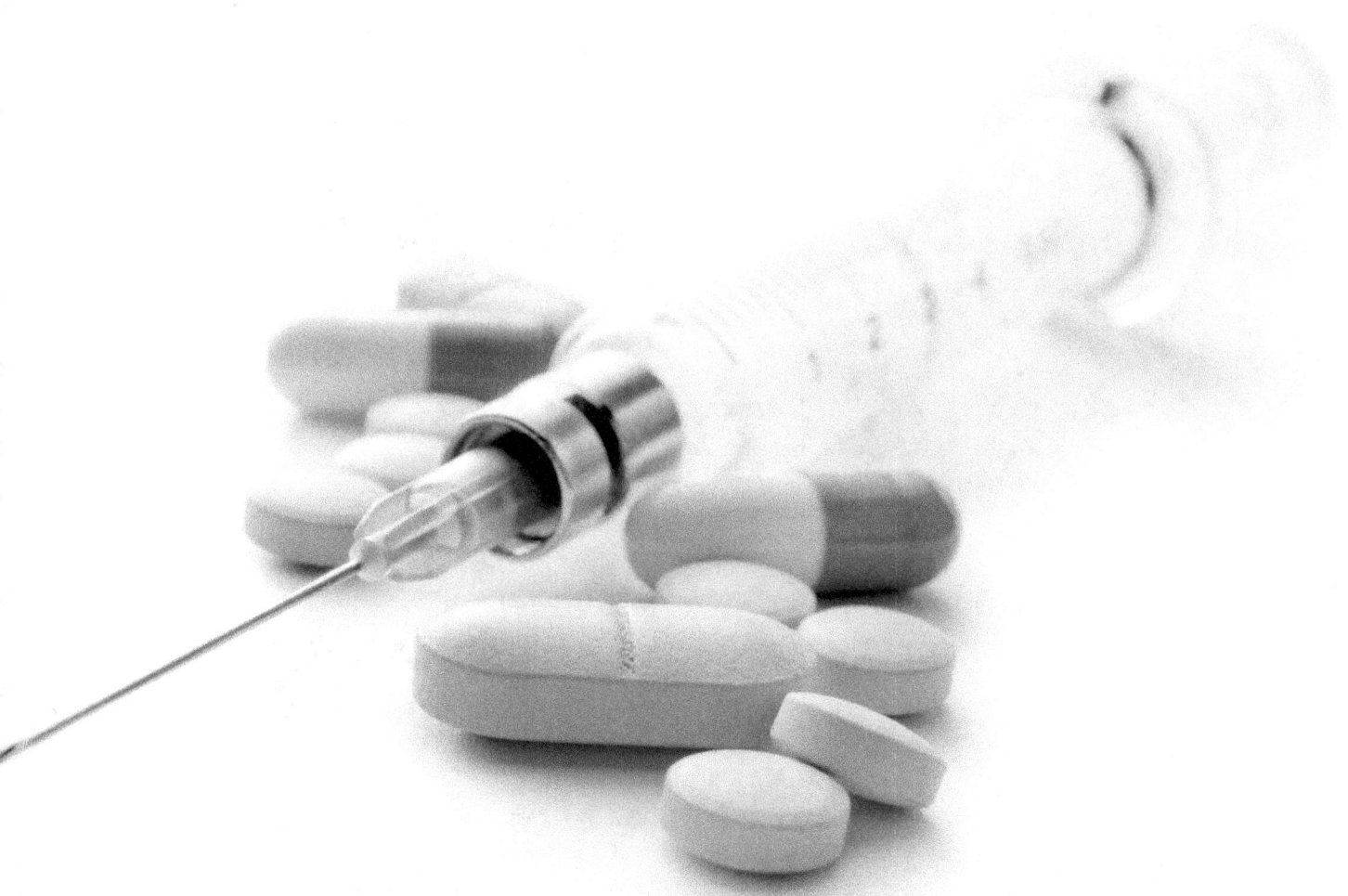

Figure 4-B: A Player's Path through MLS' Substance Abuse Policy Program

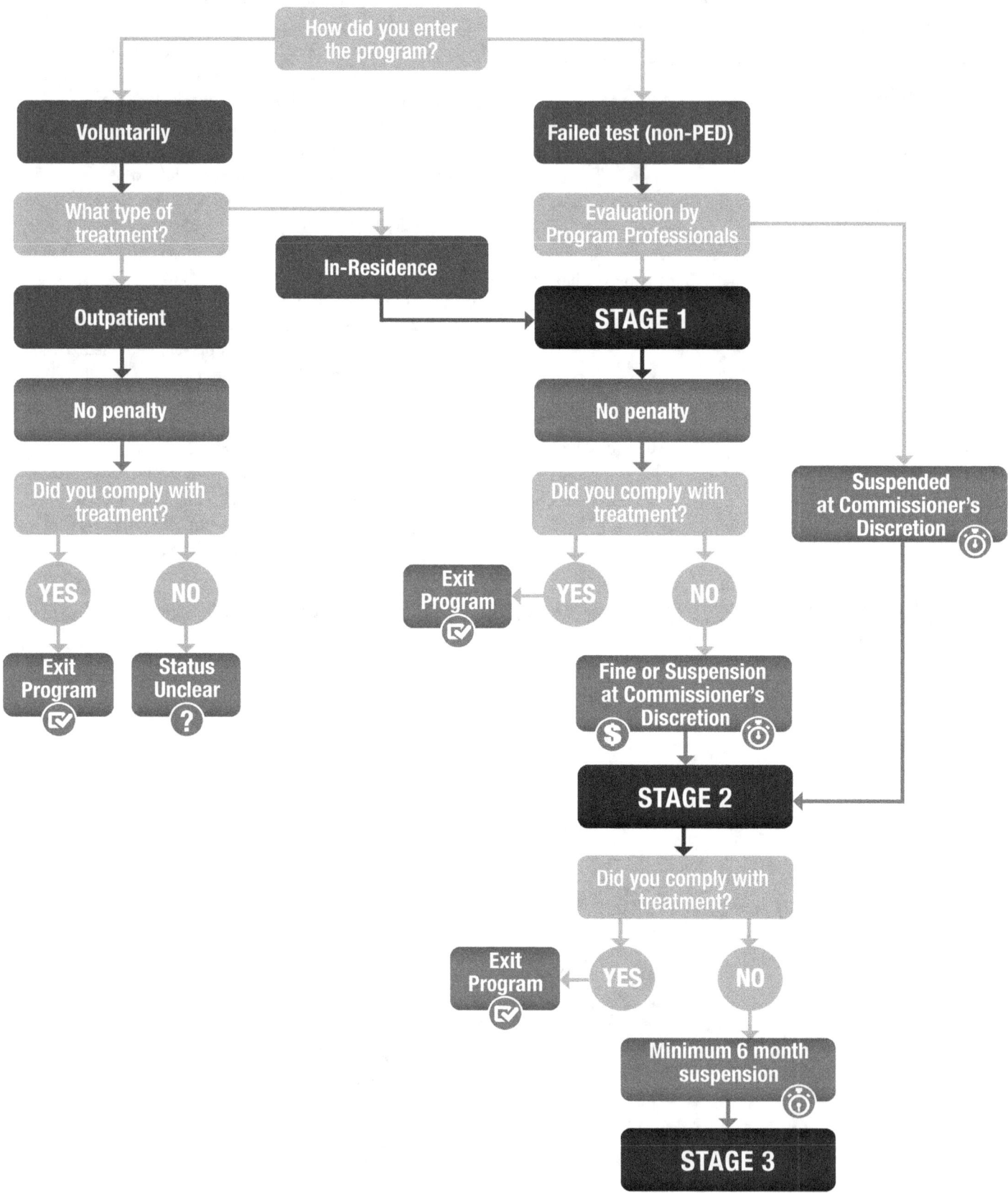

Finally, if a player violates the Substance Abuse Policy via the use or possession of PES, his discipline is determined in the "sole and absolute discretion" of the league, "including, without limitation, fines, suspension (with or without pay), and/or termination of the Player's [contract]."[319]

MLS is also the only league that does not provide its players with the possibility of challenging a violation of the Substance Abuse Policy through a neutral arbitration process. Instead, players can submit their challenge to a positive test in writing to the Program Professionals who then have the "absolute and sole" discretion to adjudicate the player's complaint.[320]

8) CONFIDENTIALITY

MLS' Substance Abuse Policy provides limited confidentiality protections for players. A player's participation in the treatment phase of the Program is only kept confidential if he is not yet in Stage 1 of the Program,[321] which can only occur through a self-referral. If a player is in treatment, MLS "may notify the Player's team of [the player's status and progress] as deemed reasonably necessary."[322] If a player has been suspended or terminated for a violation of the Substance Abuse Policy that did not involve PES, MLS may disclose "only that a Player has been suspended or terminated pursuant" to the Substance Abuse Policy.[323] "If a player is suspended or terminated for use or possession of a [PES], MLS may disclose such information as it deems necessary/appropriate."[324]

G) Analysis

The following tables summarize and compare the features of the leagues' drug policies.

Table 4-I:
Comparison of Leagues' PES Policies[q]

Feature	NFL	MLB	NBA	NHL	CFL	MLS
Independent administration	Yes	Yes	Yes	Yes	Yes	Yes
Urine tests permitted	Yes	Yes	Yes	Yes	Yes	Yes
Blood tests permitted	Yes	Yes	Yes	No	Yes	No
Maximum number of annual tests for player without prior violation	24	No maximum	Nine	No maximum	No maximum	No maximum
Therapeutic Use Exemptions available	Yes	Yes	Yes	Yes	Yes	No
Treatment available	No	No	Yes	No	Yes	Yes
Safe harbor for self-referrals	No	No	No	No	Yes	No
Discipline for first violation	Two–Six games	80 games	25 games	20 games	Two games	League discretion
Discipline for second violation	Ten games	162 games	55 games	60 games	Nine games	League discretion
Discipline for third violation	Two years	Life	Two years (subject to reinstatement)	Two years	One year	League discretion
Discipline for fourth violation	NA	NA	NA	NA	Life	League discretion
Confidential violations	Until discipline	Until discipline	Until discipline	Until discipline	Until discipline	Until discipline
Neutral appeal rights	In part	Yes	Yes	Yes	Yes	No

---

q For context, the NFL regular season is 16 games, the MLB regular season is 162 games, the NBA and NHL regular seasons are 82 games, the CFL regular season is 18 games, and the MLS regular season is 34 games.

Table 4-J:
Comparison of Leagues' Drugs of Abuse Policies

Feature	NFL	MLB	NBA	NHL	CFL	MLS
Independent administration	Yes	Yes	Yes	Yes	No Policy	Yes
Urine tests permitted	Yes	Yes	Yes	Yes	No Policy	Yes
Blood tests permitted	No	No	No	No	No Policy	No
Maximum number of annual tests for player without prior violation	One	No tests	Six	No tests	No Policy	No maximum
Therapeutic Use Exemptions available	Yes	Yes	Yes	No	No Policy	No
Treatment available	Yes	Yes	Yes	Yes	No Policy	Yes
Safe harbor for self-referrals	Yes	Maybe	Yes	Yes	No Policy	Yes
Discipline for first violation	None	None	No (Marijuana); One year for rookies only or two years (other drugs)	None	No Policy	Determined by Program Professionals evaluation
Discipline for second violation	Fine (Marijuana); Four games (other drugs)	15–25 games	$25,000 fine (Marijuana); 2 years for rookies or self-referrals (other drugs)	Suspended during treatment	No Policy	League discretion
Discipline for third violation	4–6 games	50–75 games	Five games (Marijuana)	Minimum of six months	No Policy	League discretion
Discipline for fourth violation	10 games (Marijuana); One year (other drugs)	At least One year	Ten games (Marijuana)	Minimum of one year	No Policy	League discretion
Confidential violations	Yes	Yes	Yes	Yes	No Policy	Until discipline
Neutral appeal rights	Yes	Yes	Yes	Yes	No Policy	No

With the possible exception of how marijuana is regulated, the Big Four's drug policies do not vary substantially. Before delving into specific issues of analysis, we note that the leagues and unions balance multiple factors in creating drug policies, including but not limited to deterrence, treatment, privacy, and integrity of the game. These policy considerations and value judgments are debatable in many spheres of the world, not just sports. To be sure, many aspects of these policies impact player health. The three features of the policies we view as most important and those which we focus on are: (1) the availability of TUEs; (2) the availability of treatment; and, (3) the opportunity to receive treatment without being subject to initial discipline. With these issues in mind, we turn to our analysis of how the NFL compares to the other leagues.

Concerning TUEs, the NFL, MLB and the NBA all offer TUEs for both their PES and drugs of abuse policies. In contrast, the CFL offers TUEs for its PES policy but does not have a drugs of abuse policy. We also found no evidence that the NHL offers a TUE for its Substance Abuse Program or that MLS offers any TUEs. Thus, the NFL's use of TUEs is at least as good as the other leagues.

All of the leagues, including the NFL, have robust treatment programs for drugs of abuse. However, the NBA, CFL, and potentially MLS are the only leagues that offer treatment for a player who has violated a PES Policy. On this issue, it might appear that the NFL can learn compared to the NBA and CFL. However, there are other relevant considerations concerning the treatment programs offered to players, discussed next.

The NFL, NBA, NHL, MLS and maybe MLB provide a safe-harbor for players who voluntarily refer themselves for treatment for drugs of abuse. These provisions importantly allow players to seek help they might recognize they need without the fear of immediate adverse employment action.

In contrast, no Big Four league offers a safe-harbor for players who have used PES. Under its prior CBA, NBA players did have a safe-harbor for PES use,[325] but that option was eliminated in the 2017 CBA.[326] The NBA does still, however, provide treatment for PES use.[327] The leagues that do not offer safe-harbor provisions for PES use may not offer such safe harbors because they believe that there are important differences between players who take PES and those who take drugs of abuse—we can only speculate because they have not publicly explained this policy difference. It is possible that these leagues view PES users as players intentionally looking to cheat the game and their competitors, whereas those using drugs of abuse need medical care.

However, there is robust scientific evidence supporting the need to provide treatment to PES users. PES usage has shown to be addictive,[328] and has been associated with the use of drugs of abuse[329] (opioids in particular),[330] body dysmorphic disorder,[331] depression,[332] antisocial traits,[333] mood and personality disorders,[334] other psychological disorders,[335] and cognitive deficits in impulsivity, risk-taking, and decision-making.[336] As a result, PES users may experience withdrawal symptoms,[337] and may be at an increased risk of suicide.[338] Consequently, many experts recommend and provide treatment and counseling for PES users.[339]

H) Recommendation

Recommendation 4-A: The NFL should consider amending the PES Policy to provide treatment to any NFL player found to have violated the PES Policy.

The NFL and the other leagues recognize that substance abuse is a serious medical issue and, as a result, provide players with robust counseling and treatment. As discussed above, PES usage has been shown to be associated with a variety of serious physical and mental ailments. However, only the NBA and CFL offer treatment for players who have used PES. In light of the potential negative health consequences associated with PES usage and the treatment provided by the NBA and CFL for PES usage, it seems prudent for the NFL to consider providing treatment to PES users similar to that provided for by the Substance Abuse Policy's Intervention Program.

There is an important clarification to this Recommendation. As stated earlier in this Chapter, we are not focused on the competitive advantage concerns associated with PES use or the discipline imposed by the leagues for drug or PES usage. We are focused on the health implications of drug and PES policies. Thus, our Recommendation should not be read to suggest that because players might need treatment for PES usage that they should not be disciplined — as is the case for first time offenders of the Substance Abuse Policy.

As discussed in the Introduction, the NFL declined to review this Report. However, MLB did provide comments on the Report which may provide insight into the viewpoints of the other professional leagues. MLB did not agree with this Recommendation, stating:

> There are no established treatment programs for PEDs, and since the recidivism rate for PEDs is fairly low, there is no support for the position that this class of prohibited substances warrants a response based on treatment. It is also an established practice of not just MLB, but all other professional leagues and international anti-doping organizations that the use of PEDs affects the integrity of play and should be responded with a disciplinary perspective as opposed to a clinical one. Our experts advise not including "PED treatment programs" as a recommendation in the report.

As a preliminary matter, we note that the NBA and CFL do provide treatment to PES users. Thus, there is a disagreement among the leagues (and potentially also the unions) on this issue, suggesting further research is needed.

We further reply to MLB with a clarification and with a disagreement. We understand sports organizations' need to discipline players who have violated PES policies. Our recommendation does not seek the elimination or reduction of discipline for PES violations in any way. Instead, we believe it is appropriate to consider providing players who have violated the PES Policy with counseling, regardless of any discipline imposed. This is where we and MLB disagree.

MLB rejects counseling for PES use on the grounds that "[t]here are no established treatment programs for PEDs." As discussed above, experts in the field recommend and do provide treatment for PES usage and its associated problems. Whether these programs are sufficiently "established," is beyond our expertise, but it nonetheless is an issue worth further consideration.

Endnotes

1   An exact definition for PES or PEDs is elusive. *See* Michael T. Lardon, *Performance-Enhancing Drugs: Where Should the Line be Drawn and by Whom?* 5 Psychiatry 58 (2008) (discussing the difficulty with determining what substances should be considered PEDs and thus banned). The United States Anti-Doping Agency describes PEDs as substances that "have the ability or potential to drastically alter the human body and biological functions, including the ability to considerably improve athletic performance in certain instances . . . [but that] can be extremely dangerous and, in certain situations, deadly." *Effects of PEDs*, U.S. Anti-Doping Agency, http://www.usada.org/substances/effects-of-performance-enhancing-drugs/, *archived at* http://perma.cc/CM2U-5SGK.

2   MLB JDA, § 2(A).

3   NFL Drug Policy, n.1. The NBA defines "drugs of abuse" as amphetamines, cocaine, LSD, opiates, and PCP.

4   U.S.C. § 812(b)(1)(B).

5   *State Marijuana Laws Map*, Governing, http://www.governing.com/gov-data/state-marijuana-laws-map-medical-recreational.html (last visited Feb. 21, 2017), *archived at* https://perma.cc/5U82-EAWN.

6   *See, e.g.,* Nora D. Volkow, Ruben D. Baler, Wilson M. Compton, Susan R.B. Weiss, *Adverse health effects of marijuana use*, 370 N. Engl. J. Med. 23 (2014); Editorial Board, *Repeal Prohibition, Again*, N.Y. Times, Jul. 27, 2014, http://www.nytimes.com/interactive/2014/07/27/opinion/sunday/high-time-marijuana-legalization.html?op-nav, *archived at* http://perma.cc/EH28-BZU6; Lawrence Downes, *The Great Colorado Weed Experiment*, N.Y. Times, Aug. 2, 2014, http://www.nytimes.com/2014/08/03/opinion/sunday/high-time-the-great-colorado-weed-experiment.html?op-nav, *archived at* http://perma.cc/H6W9-Y7ZE.

7   *See* Kevin Seifert, *Survey: Two-thirds of NFL players say legal pot equals fewer painkillers*, ESPN (Nov. 2, 2016), http://www.espn.com/nfl/story/_/id/17951858/nfl-players-legal-pot-equals-fewer-painkillers, *archived at* https://perma.cc/9JJV-WENY; Darin Gantt, *Former Broncos tight end says NFL should lift marijuana ban*, ProFootballTalk (Mar. 6, 2015, 6:37 AM), http://profootballtalk.nbcsports.com/2015/03/06/former-broncos-tight-end-says-nfl-should-lift-marijuana-ban/, *archived at* http://perma.cc/82MN-BCK7; Mike Freeman, *Banned, but Bountiful: Marijuana Coveted by NFL Players as Invaluable Painkiller*, Bleacher Rep., Jun. 30, 2015, http://bleacherreport.com/articles/2486218-banned-but-bountiful-marijuana-coveted-by-nfl-players-as-invaluable-painkiller, *archived at* http://perma.cc/L8QS-X2KD.

8   *See* Eric P. Baron, *Comprehensive Review of Medical Marijuana, Cannabinoids, and Therapeutic Implications in Medicine and Headache: What a Long Strange Trip It's Been . . .* , Headache 885 (2015) (collecting studies and concluding "[t]he literature suggests that the medicinal use of cannabis may have a therapeutic role for a multitude of diseases, particularly chronic pain disorders"); Arthur L. Caplan, Lee H. Igel, *It's Time to Normalize Medical Marijuana in Pro Sports*, Forbes (Dec. 7, 2016, 7:50 AM), http://www.forbes.com/sites/leeigel/2016/12/07/its-time-to-normalize-medical-marijuana-in-pro-sports/#7d1977dd2e3f, *archived at* https://perma.cc/H5SD-6ZYC (discussing marijuana as a pain management tool in professional sports and the US Food and Drug Administration's approval of two medications containing cannabinoids).

9   Zac Jackson, *NFLPA will study marijuana as a pain-management tool for players*, ProFootballTalk (Nov. 9, 2016, 7:19 PM), http://profootballtalk.nbcsports.com/2016/11/09/nflpa-will-study-marijuana-as-a-pain-management-tool-for-players/, *archived at* https://perma.cc/S2C5-EE67.

10 Gregg Rosenthal, *Marijuana legalization won't change NFL drug policy*, Nat'l Football League, Nov. 7, 2012, http://www.nfl.com/news/story/0ap1000000091645/article/marijuana-legalization-wont-change-nfl-drug-policy, *archived at* https://perma.cc/YV7M-G49B.

11 Mike Florio, *Goodell says league would consider marijuana as a concussion treatment*, ProFootballTalk (Jan. 23, 2014, 4:56 PM), http://profootballtalk.nbcsports.com/2014/01/23/goodell-says-league-would-consider-marijuana-as-a-concussion-treatment/, *archived at* http://perma.cc/7K93-FK93; Mike Florio, *NFL could indeed change its mind about marijuana, in time*, ProFootballTalk (Jan. 18, 2014, 1:47 PM), http://profootballtalk.nbcsports.com/2014/01/18/nfl-could-indeed-change-its-mind-about-marijuana-in-time/, *archived at* http://perma.cc/NTR2-NNW4.

12 Pete Thomas, *Hall's Olympic Dream Gets the Boost It Needs*, L.A. Times, Jul. 7, 2004, *available at* 2004 WLNR 19771636.

13 *Id.*

14 Amy Shipley, *Drug Exemptions Triple in MLB Majority Granted to Players to Treat Attention-Deficit Disorder*, Wash. Post, Jan. 16, 2008, *available at* 2008 WLNR 28017256.

15 *Id.*

16 *Id.*

17 Joy R. Absalon, *Orioles' Davis 'good to go' with new therapeutic-use exemption*, Fox Sports (Feb. 24, 2015, 9:12 PM), http://www.foxsports.com/mlb/story/baltimore-orioles-chris-davis-suspension-therapuetic-use-exemption-adderall-022415, *archived at* http://perma.cc/3VS5-MTBQ.

18 *Independent program administrator issues annual report*, Major League Baseball (Dec. 1, 2015), http://m.mlb.com/news/article/158704354, *archived at* http://perma.cc/BL74-JV9Q.

19 *Independent Program Administrator Annual Report*, Major League Baseball (Dec. 2, 2016), http://www.mlbplayers.com/ViewArticle.dbml?SPID=181313&ATCLID=211336296&DB_OEM_ID=34000, *archived at* https://perma.cc/RS3R-68H4.

20 This figure was gathered from MLB.com's "Sortable Player" statistics page by adding together all players who had a plate appearance and all pitchers, and then removing those pitchers that also had a plate appearance.

21 *See* Lid Elec., Inc. v. Int'l Broth. of Elec. Workers, Local 134, 362 F.3d 940, 944 (7th Cir. 2004); Bolden v. Southeastern Penn. Transp. Authority, 953 F.2d 807, 827-28 (3d Cir. 1991), *citing* National Labor Relations Board cases and memorandum.

22 The NFL's Specimen Collection Process is included in documents filed as part of lawsuit brought by then-Denver Broncos Linebacker D.J. Williams against the NFL. Specifically, the Specimen Collection Process states: "[t]he player must lower his pants and underwear below his knees"; [t]he player must not have any clothing above his knees (naked from 'Knees-to-Noggin')"; and, "[t]he collector . . . will monitor the furnishing of the specimen by direct frontal observation in order to assure the integrity of the specimen until the adequate volume of 100mL minimum is provided." *See* Exhibits in Support of Brief by Plaintiffs Ryan McBean and Genos "D.J." Williams, Williams, et al. v. Nat'l Football League, 12-cv-650 (D. Colo. Apr. 2, 2012), ECF No. 41-1.

23 Mike Florio, *League wants HGH testing, needs players to want it, too*, ProFootballTalk (May 4, 2013, 3:03 PM), http://profootballtalk.nbcsports.com/2013/05/04/league-wants-hgh-testing-needs-players-to-want-it-too/, *archived at* http://perma.cc/A8BD-ZRFW; Mike Florio, *NFLPA says NFL could have had HGH testing before MLB*, ProFootballTalk (Jan. 11, 2013, 2:23 PM), http://profootballtalk.nbcsports.com/2013/01/11/nflpa-says-nfl-could-have-had-hgh-testing-before-mlb/, *archived at* http://perma.cc/4LP5-879F.

24 NFL PES Policy, Appendix A.

25 *Id.*

26 NFL PES Policy, General Statement of Policy, n. 1.

27 NFL Substance Abuse Policy, General Policy, n. 1.

28 NFL Substance Abuse Policy, § 1.3.3.

29 Michael David Smith, *A new drug testing agreement could benefit Welker, Gordon*, ProFootballTalk (Sept. 4, 2014, 7:47 PM), http://profootballtalk.nbcsports.com/2014/09/04/a-new-drug-testing

-agreement-could-benefit-welker-gordon/, *archived at* http://perma.cc/X8UX-45KB; Darin Gantt, *Orlando Scandrick ready to rejoin Cowboys once new drug deal done,* ProFootballTalk (Sept. 13, 2014, 8:47 AM), http://profootballtalk.nbcsports.com/2014/09/13/orlando-scandrick-ready-to-rejoin-cowboys-once-new-drug-deal-done/, *archived at* http://perma.cc/6AJD-B9DK.

30 Smith, *supra* n. 29; Gantt, *supra* n. 29.

31 NFL PES Policy, § 6, n. 5.

32 NFL PES Policy, §§ 3.1, 7.

33 NFL PES Policy, § 11. If a player tests positive for a banned substance, he may either: "accept the result and the disciple, await the results of the scheduled 'B' sample analysis, or have an Observing Toxicologist witness the 'B' sample analysis." NFL PES Policy, § 4.2. If the "B" sample does not confirm a positive result, then the Independent Administrator never notifies the NFLMC or NFLPA of a positive test result. *Id.*

34 NFL PES Policy, § 5.

35 *Id.* Unlike other violations of the PED Policy, players who are convicted or otherwise admit to have used, possessed, or distributed PEDs are subject to discipline at the discretion of the Commissioner, including suspension up to six games for a first violation or, if appropriate, termination of a player's contract. *Id.* Other PED Policy violations follow the disciplinary schedule outlined in Section 6.

36 NFL PES Policy, §§ 3.3, 6, Appendix H. Players who fail to appear for testing for reasons other than attempting to deliberately evade or avoid testing are also subject to discipline—a fine of up to $25,000 and placement in the reasonable cause testing program for a first violation, a fine of two weeks' pay for a second violation, and a four-game suspension without pay for a third violation. NFL PES Policy, Appendix H.

37 NFL PES Policy, § 6.

38 *See, e.g.,* NFL Substance Abuse Policy, § 1.3.2.

39 NFL Substance Abuse Policy, § 1.3.3. If a player tests positive for a banned substance, he may either: "accept the result and the disciple, await the results of the scheduled 'B' sample analysis, or have an Observing Toxicologist witness the 'B' sample analysis." *Id.* If the "B" sample does not confirm a positive result, then the Independent Administrator never notifies the NFLMC or NFLPA of a positive test result. *Id.* The "B" sample need only show that the substance revealed in the "A" sample test is evidence to the "limits of detection." *Id.*

40 *Id.*

41 NFL Substance Abuse Policy, Appendix E. A player who fails to appear for testing, but who is adjudged not to have purposefully attempted to evade or avoid testing is subject to a $25,000 fine and placement in the Intervention Program for his first violation, a fine of 2/17ths of his Paragraph 5 NFL Player Contract salary for his second violation, and a four game suspension without pay for his third violation. *Id.*

42 NFL Substance Abuse Policy, § 2.

43 *Id.* A *nolo contendere* plea is one in which the accused does not contest or admit guilt. *See* Black's Law Dictionary (9th ed. 2009) (defining "nolo plea" as "[a] plea by which the defendant does not contest or admit guilt.").

44 NFL PES Policy, § 3.1.

45 *Id.*

46 *Id.*

47 *Id.*

48 NFL PES Policy, § 7.

49 "As used in this Policy, sufficient credible evidence includes but is not limited to: criminal convictions or plea arrangements; admissions, declarations, affidavits, authenticated witness statements, corroborated law enforcement reports or testimony in legal proceedings; authenticated banking, telephone, medical or pharmacy records; or credible information obtained from Players who provide assistance pursuant to Section 10 ["Appeals"] of the Policy." NFL PES Policy, § 3.1 n.4.

50 NFL PES Policy, §§ 3.1, 7.

51 *See, e.g.,* NFL PES Policy, § 7.

52 All NFL players are eligible for entrance into the Intervention Program. Players enter Stage One of the Intervention Program through a positive test result, behavior that exhibits symptoms of misuse of substances of abuse (e.g., an arrest for misuse of substance of abuse), or self-referral. NFL Substance Abuse Policy, § 1.4.1. A self-referred player always remains in Stage One of the Substance Abuse Policy. *Id.*

53 NFL Substance Abuse Policy, § 1.3.1.

54 Mike Florio, *Marijuana testing window opens today,* ProFootballTalk (Apr. 20, 2015, 8:12 AM), http://profootballtalk.nbcsports.com/2015/04/20/marijuana-testing-window-opens-today/, *archived at* http://perma.cc/DU9Z-RYGW.

55 *Id.*

56 Mike Florio, *NFLPA gives players 30-day marijuana warning,* ProFootballTalk (Mar. 19, 2015, 3:27 PM), http://profootballtalk.nbcsports.com/2015/03/19/nflpa-gives-players-30-day-marijuana-warning/, *archived at* http://perma.cc/Q4PC-NUEN.

57 *See* Ben Volin, *How did Aaron Hernandez not fail NFL drug tests?,* Bos. Globe, Apr. 4, 2015, http://www.bostonglobe.com/sports/2015/04/04/how-did-aaron-hernandez-not-fail-nfl-drug-tests/NXl7edYeTLKFhJlyfeOs1M/story.html, *archived at* http://perma.cc/DMU4-3GGX.

58 NFL PES Policy, § 2.1.

59 *See* John A. Lombardo, MD, Max Sports Medicine OhioHealth, http://maxsportscenter.com/Meet-Our-Team/John-A-Lombardo,-MD (last visited Aug. 31, 2015), *archived at* http://perma.cc/872S-R7C9.

60 NFL PES Policy, § 2.1.

61 NFL PES Policy, §§ 2.2, 2.3, 2.4.

62 NFL Substance Abuse Policy, § 1.1.1.

63 NFL Substance Abuse Policy, § 1.1.2.

64 Selected by the medical director, treating clinicians are responsible for administering the treatment plans for players assigned to them. NFL Substance Abuse Policy, § 1.1.3.

65 Each NFL club must designate one of its affiliated physicians as its team physician for substance abuse matters. NFL Substance Abuse Policy, § 1.1.4. The team substance abuse physician consults and coordinates club-level aspects of the player's treatment program, including the prescription or prohibition of certain medications necessary to facilitate compliance with the treatment program. *Id.*

66 The chief forensic toxicologist, jointly selected by the NFLMC and NFLPA, is responsible for laboratory evaluation of urine samples, providing scientific advice on toxicology matters, scientific interpretation of positive drug findings, and providing forensic testimony as needed. NFL Substance Abuse Policy, § 1.1.5.

67 "The NFL and NFLPA shall jointly agree upon one or more Collection Vendors to be responsible for specimen collection, storage and transportation to the designated laboratory." NFL Substance Abuse Policy, § 1.1.6.

68 Club physicians facilitate players' entrance into the Intervention Program on a self-referral basis. *See* NFL Substance Abuse Policy, § 1.4.1.

69 NFL PES Policy, Appendix I; NFL Substance Abuse Policy, Appendix F.

70 *Id.*

71 *Id.*

72 NFL Substance Abuse Policy at p. 1.

73 *Id.*

74 NFL Substance Abuse Policy, § 1.4.1.

75 NFL Substance Abuse Policy, § 1.5.1(a).

76 *Id.*

77 *Id.*

78 NFL Substance Abuse Policy, § 1.5.1(b).

79 *Id.*

80 NFL Substance Abuse Policy, § 1.5.2(a).

81 NFL Substance Abuse Policy, § 1.5.2(d).

82 *Id.*

83   NFL PES Policy, § 6.

84   "[S]ufficient credible evidence includes but is not limited to: criminal convictions or plea arrangements; admissions, declarations, affidavits, authenticated witness statements, corroborated law enforcement reports or testimony in legal proceedings; authenticated banking, telephone, medical or pharmacy records; or credible information obtained from Players who provide assistance[.]" NFL PES Policy, § 3.1, n. 4.

85   Spotrac.com provides a list of NFL suspensions. *NFL Fines & Suspensions 2016,* Spotrac, http://www.spotrac.com/nfl/fines-suspensions/ (last visited Jan. 23, 2017), *archived at* https://perma.cc/KAK9-63FG.

86   As stated above, Spotrac.com provides a list of NFL suspensions. *See NFL Fines & Suspensions 2015,* Spotrac, http://www.spotrac.com/ nfl/fines-suspensions/2015/ (last visited Mar. 10, 2016), *archived at* https://perma.cc/R3K4-FB74; *NFL Fines & Suspensions 2014,* Spotrac, http://www.spotrac.com/nfl/fines-suspensions/2014/ (last visited Mar. 10, 2016), *archived at* http://perma.cc/4VCB-PSCM. Additional research was then done on each player on the list to determine the reported cause of the suspension.

87   NFL PES Policy, § 14.

88   *See id., citing* 2011 NFL CBA, Art. 4, § 9. *See also* Chris Deubert, Glenn M. Wong, John Howe, *All Four Quarters: A Retrospective and Analysis of the 2011 Collective Bargaining Process and Agreement in the National Football League,* 19 UCLA Ent. L. Rev. 1, 48-51 (2012) discussing clubs' efforts to recoup portions of bonus money already paid to players); Chris Deubert, Glenn M. Wong, *Understanding the Evolution of Signing Bonuses and Guaranteed Money in the National Football League: Preparing for the 2011 Collective Bargaining Negotiations,* 16 UCLA Ent. L. Rev. 179, 202-26 (2009) (same).

89   *See* 2011 NFL CBA, At. 4, § 9(g) (discussing voiding of guarantees).

90   NFL PES Policy, § 1.4.1.

91   *See* Spotrac.com, *supra* note 86.

92   *Id.*

93   NFL Substance Abuse Policy, § 2.2.

94   *Id.*

95   *Id.*

96   *Id.* at § 2.3.

97   *Id.*

98   *Id.*

99   NFL PES Policy, § 12; NFL Substance Abuse Policy, § 1.2.

100 NFL PES Policy, § 12.1.

101 NFL PES Policy, § 12.

102 NFL PES Policy, § 12.2.

103 NFL Substance Abuse Policy, § 1.2.1.

104 *Id.*

105 NFL Substance Abuse Policy, § 1.2.3.

106 "Any and all drugs or substances included on Schedules I and II of the Code of Federal Regulations' Schedule of Controlled Substances . . . shall be considered Drugs of Abuse covered by the Program," in addition to synthetic and natural marijuana, cocaine, LSD, opiates, MDMA, GHB, and PCP (and their analogues). MLB Joint Program, § 2(A).

107 "Any and all anabolic androgenic steroids covered by Schedule III of the Code of Federal Regulations' Schedule of Controlled Substances . . . and [certain enumerated] categories of hormones and agents with antiestrogenic activity . . . shall be considered Performance Enhancing Substances covered by the Program. Anabolic androgenic steroids, hormones, and agents with antiestrogenic activity, that may not be lawfully obtained or used in the United States (including, for example, "designer steroids" and peptide hormones) also shall be considered Performance Enhancing Substances irrespective of whether they are covered by Schedule III." MLB Joint Program, § 2(B). Human Growth Hormone (hGH) is explicitly listed as a PED. *Id.*

108 Stimulants are defined in the Joint Program by an exhaustive list of 56 substances, including amphetamine, ephedrine, and methamphetamine. MLB Joint Program, § 2(C).

109 MLB Joint Program, § 2(D). "DHEA is a hormone that is naturally made by the human body. . . . Athletes and other people use DHEA to increase muscle mass, strength, and energy." *DHEA,* Medline Plus—U.S. Nat'l Library of Med., http://www.nlm.nih.gov/medlineplus/druginfo/ natural/331.html#Description (last visited Aug. 31, 2015), *archived at* http://perma.cc/R76C-YR75. As recently as 2009, MLB was the only of the big four American professional sports leagues to allow DHEA. *See* Jeff Passan, *Baseball still allows the steroid DHEA,* Yahoo! Sports, May 14, 2009, http://sports.yahoo.com/mlb/news?slug=jp-dhealegal051409, *archived at* http://perma.cc/5WJP-WSL8. MLB and the MLBPA often fought over inclusion of DHEA on the prohibited substance list, *see id.,* which may explain why DHEA was included in its own category when MLB finally added it to the list.

110 MLB Joint Program, § 2(E).

111 *Id.*

112 MLB Joint Program, § 3(A)(1).

113 *Id.*

114 MLB Joint Program, § 3(A)(3).

115 MLB Joint Program, § 3(F)(1). This situation is known as an "analytical positive."

116 MLB Joint Program, § 3(F)(2).

117 MLB Joint Program, § 3(F)(3).

118 MLB Joint Program, § 7(G)(2). Suspensions under this provision of the Joint Program do not follow a specified punishment schedule; they may, however, qualify as predicate offenses that increase the punishment for subsequent violations. *See* MLB Joint Program, § 7(A).

119 MLB Joint Program, § 3(A)(1).

120 *MLBPA, MLB Announce Details of New Labor Agreement,* MLBPA (Dec. 2, 2016), http://www.mlbplayers.com/ViewArticle.dbml?DB_OEM _ID=34000&ATCLID=211336390, *archived at* https://perma.cc/4XUA -2DAW.

121 *Id.;* MLB Joint Program, § 3(A)(2).

122 MLB Joint Program, § 3(A)(3)(a).

123 MLB Joint Program, § 3(A)(3). Of those 900 hGH tests, 500 are conducted during the season and 400 are performed during the off-season. MLB Joint Program, § 3(A)(3)(b)–(c); *MLBPA, MLB Announce Details of New Labor Agreement,* MLBPA (Dec. 2, 2016), http://www.mlbplayers.com/ ViewArticle.dbml?DB_OEM_ID=34000&ATCLID=211336390, *archived at* https://perma.cc/4XUA-2DAW.

124 *See* MLB Joint Program, § 3(A)(3).

125 *Independent Program Administrator Issues Annual Report,* Major League Baseball (Dec. 2, 2016), http://www.mlbplayers.com/ViewArticle.dbml ?SPID=181313&ATCLID=211336296&DB_OEM_ID=34000, *archived at* https://perma.cc/2PPQ-S397.

126 *Id.*

127 *Id.*

128 MLB Joint Program, § 3(C)(1). However, the party receiving the notification may dispute the reasonable cause basis, in which case the Arbitration Panel Chair will determine whether reasonable cause exists. MLB Joint Program, § 3(C)(1).

129 MLB Joint Program, §§ 3(D)(1)–(2). These follow-up tests do not count toward the 3,200 random urine tests or 400 random hGH tests otherwise permitted under the Joint Program. *Id.*

130 MLB Joint Program, §§ 3(B), 3(C)(2)(a).

131 MLB Joint Program, § 4(A).

132 MLB Joint Program, § 4(B)(1).

133 MLB Joint Program, § 1(A)(1).

134 MLB Joint Program, § 1(A)(2).

135 MLB Joint Program, §§ 1(B)(1)–(2). The Treatment Board made headlines in 2015 after deciding not to suspend former Los Angeles Angels (and current Texas Rangers) player Josh Hamilton. Hamilton, who had struggled with cocaine and alcohol addiction in the past, confessed to Major League Baseball in February that he had suffered a relapse

in his sobriety in an incident involving cocaine. Matt Schiavenza, *Josh Hamilton's Relapse Reveals Baseball's Double Standard on Drugs*, Atlantic, Apr. 4, 2015, http://www.theatlantic.com/entertainment/archive /2015/04/josh-hamiltons-relapse-reveals-baseballs-hypocrisy-on-drugs /389685/, *archived at* http://perma.cc/WXP8-M4JP. Because Hamilton self-reported the incident and had not failed a drug test since 2004, he appeared to technically qualify as a first-time offender under the Joint Program. *See* Jeff Todd, *Josh Hamilton Facing Discipline for Drug of Abuse*, MLB Trade Rumors (Feb. 25, 2015), http://www.mlbtraderumors .com/2015/02/josh-hamilton-meeting-with-mlb-regarding-disciplinary -matter.html, *archived at* https://perma.cc/SDB9-Y4K9; Cliff Corcoran, *Report: Josh Hamilton's Career Hits Roadblock as He Relapses on Drugs*, Sports Illustrated, Feb. 26, 2015, http://www.si.com/mlb/2015/02/25/ josh-hamilton-angels-relapse-drugs, *archived at* http://perma.cc/EWL4 -U5AT. However, MLB argued that Hamilton had violated his treatment program, which dated back as far as 2003 when Hamilton was in the minor leagues with the Tampa Bay Rays. Michael O'Keefe & Teri Thompson, *Arbitrator Rules for Josh Hamilton, Angels Outfielder Will Not Be Suspended by MLB for Substance Abuse Relapse*, N.Y. Daily News, Apr. 3, 2015, http://www.nydailynews.com/sports/baseball/arbitrator -rules-josh-hamilton-angel-dodges-suspension-article-1.2172441, *archived at* http://perma.cc/L7UN-MAX5. Hamilton and his camp, meanwhile, argued that he had faithfully followed his treatment program, which included counseling and drug testing, and he had a "one-night slip which he immediately self-reported." *Id.* Ultimately, an arbitrator ruled that Hamilton's conduct did not violate his treatment program and MLB thus could not suspend or impose any discipline on him. Ted Berg, *Josh Hamilton Will Not Be Suspended for Reported Offseason Drug Relapse*, USA Today, Apr. 3, 2015, http://ftw.usatoday.com/2015/04/josh -hamilton-los-angeles-angels-suspension-drug-relapse-mlb, *archived at* https://perma.cc/W8QC-GFM3 (quoting MLB's statement on the matter); *see also* MLB Joint Program, § 4(C)(3).

136   MLB Joint Program, § 1(A)(2)(g).

137   MLB Joint Program, § 3(I)(1).

138   MLB Joint Program, § 3(I)(3).

139   MLB Joint Program, § 4.

140   MLB Joint Program, § 4(B)(1).

141   *Id.*

142   MLB Joint Program, §§ 7(A)(1)–(3), 7(E)(1)–(3).

143   MLB Joint Program, § 7(F)(1)–(2).

144   MLB Joint Program, § 7(B)(1)–(4); *MLBPA, MLB Announce Details of New Labor Agreement*, MLBPA (Dec. 2, 2016), http://www.mlbplayers.com/ ViewArticle.dbml?DB_OEM_ID=34000&ATCLID=211336390, *archived at* https://perma.cc/4XUA-2DAW.

145   MLB Joint Program, § 7(B)(1)–(4).

146   MLB Joint Program, §§ 7(F)(1), (3).

147   MLB Joint Program, § 7(C)(1)–(4).

148   MLB Joint Program, § 7(E)(1)–(3).

149   MLB Joint Program, §§ 7(F)(1), (3).

150   MLB Joint Program, § 7(D)(1)–(5).

151   Additional failures to comply with the treatment program results in further discipline at the Commissioner's discretion. MLB Joint Program, § 7(C)(5).

152   MLB Joint Program, §§ 7(F)(1), (3).

153   MLB Joint Program, § 7(E)(1)–(3). However, absent a conviction, players are not subject to suspension for the use or possession of marijuana, hashish, or synthetic THC. MLB Joint Program, § 7(D)(5). Also, drug of abuse violations do not include alcohol or alcohol-related (e.g., DUI) violations.

154   *DHEA*, Medline Plus—U.S. Nat'l Library of Med., http://www.nlm.nih .gov/medlineplus/druginfo/natural/331.html#Description (last visited Aug. 31, 2015), *archived at* http://perma.cc/R76C-YR75.

155   DHEA is specifically exempt from the term "anabolic steroid" in the Controlled Substances Act. 21 U.S.C. § 802(41)(A).

156   *See, e.g., DHEA*, Walgreens, http://www.walgreens.com/store/c/dhea/ ID=361725-tier3 (last visited Aug. 31, 2015), *archived at* http://perma .cc/7E6P-PH4Y (listing DHEA for sale); *DHEA*, GNC, http://www.gnc .com/Vitamins/Specialty-Supplements/DHEA/family.jsp?categoryId =2166425&sr=1&origkw=dhea (last visited Aug. 31, 2015), *archived at* http://perma.cc/F79Z-K7WK (same).

157   *See* MLB Joint Program, § 2(D); NFL Steroid Policy, App. A—List of Prohibited Substances; 201 NBA CBA, Ex. I-2—Prohibited Substances; *The World Anti-Doping Code*, WADA (2015), https://wada-main-prod.s3 .amazonaws.com/resources/files/wada-2015-prohibited-list-en.pdf, *archived at* http://perma.cc/P2KM-KKKB. The NHL substantially uses the WADA Code.

158   MLB Joint Program, § 5(B)(1).

159   MLB Joint Program, § 5(B)(4).

160   MLB Joint Program, § 5(D)(1).

161   *Id.* Clubs must then keep that information confidential. *See* MLB Joint Program, § 5(B)(1).

162   MLB Joint Program, § 5(C).

163   MLB Joint Program, § 5(C)(1).

164   MLB Joint Program, § 5(E).

165   NBA CBA, Art. XXXIII § 16.

166   NBA CBA, Art. XXXIII, § 4(a).

167   NBA CBA, Art. XXXIII, § 4(d)(i).

168   NBA CBA, Art. XXXIII, § 4(d)(ii).

169   NBA CBA, Art. XXXIII, § 4(d)(vi).

170   NBA CBA, Art. XXXIII, § 4(d)(iii).

171   NBA CBA, Art. XXXIII, § 4(d)(iv).

172   NBA CBA, Art. XXXIII, § 4(d)(v).

173   NBA CBA, Art. XXXIII, § 5(a).

174   NBA CBA, Art. XXXIII, § 6(a). Off-season urine samples are only tested for SPEDs and diuretics. *Id.*

175   NBA CBA, Art. XXXIII, § 14(a).

176   NBA CBA, Art. XXXIII, § 6(a).

177   NBA CBA, Art. XXXIII, § 5(a). "In evaluating the information presented to him, the Independent Expert shall use his independent judgment based upon his experience in substance abuse detection and enforcement." 2017 NBA CBA, Art. XXXIII, § 5(b).

178   *Id.*; 2017 NBA CBA, Ex. I-1.

179   NBA CBA, Art. XXXIII, § 2(a). In addition to generally managing and overseeing the Program, the Medical Director is expressly responsible for selecting and supervising counselors (preferably, retired NBA players) and other personnel necessary for the effective implementation of the Program and evaluating and treating players subject to the Program. *Id.*

180   NBA CBA, Art. XXXIII, § 2(b).

181   NBA CBA, Art. XXXIII, § 2(c).

182   NBA CBA, Art. XXXIII, § 2(e).

183   NBA CBA, Art. XXXIII, § 2(g).

184   Email from David Weiss, Associate Vice President and Assistant General Counsel, NBA, to Christopher R. Deubert (Sep. 1, 2015).

185   *Id.*

186   *Id.*

187   NBA CBA, Art. XXXIII, § 1(f); Art. XXXIII, § 7.

188   NBA CBA, Art. XXXIII, § 6(b)(i).

189   NBA CBA, Art. XXXIII, 7(a).

190   NBA CBA, Art. XXXIII, § 1(k).

191   NBA CBA, Art. XXXIII, § 8(c).

192   *Id.*

193   *Id.*

194   NBA CBA, Art. XXXIII, § 8(a).

195   NBA CBA, Art. XXXIII, § 1(s).

196   NBA CBA, Art. XXXIII, § 9(b).

197   *Id.*

198   NBA CBA, Art. XXXIII, § 9(a).

199   *See* 2017 NBA CBA, Art. XXXIII, § 1(b) ("A player may not Come Forward Voluntarily for the use of a SPED").

200   NBA CBA, Art. XXXIII, § 6(b)(i).

201   NBA CBA, Art. XXXIII, § 10(a)(ii)(1).

202   NBA CBA, Art. XXXIII, § 10(a)(ii)(2).

203   *See* 2017 NBA CBA, Art. XXXIII, § 6(c); Art. XXXIII,§ 11(a).

204   NBA CBA, Art. XXXIII, § 10(a)(ii)(1).

205   NBA CBA, Art. XXXIII, § 10(a)(ii)(2).

206   NBA CBA, Art. XXXIII, § 7(a)(iv).

207   NBA CBA, Art. VI, § 14.

208   NBA CBA, Art. XXXIII, § 8(c)(A).

209   NBA CBA, Art. XXXIII, § 8(c)(B).

210   NBA CBA, Art. XXXIII, § 8(c)(C).

211   NBA CBA, Art. XXXIII, § 8(c)(D).

212   NBA CBA, Art. XXXIII § 8(a)(iii).

213   NBA CBA, Art. XXXIII, § 9(b)(A).

214   NBA CBA, Art. XXXIII, § 9(b)(B).

215   NBA CBA, Art. XXXIII, § 9(b)(C).

216   NBA CBA, Art. XXXIII § 9(a).

217   *See* 2017 NBA CBA, Art. XXXIII, § 1(b) ("A player may not Come Forward Voluntarily for the use of a SPED").

218   NBA CBA, Art. XXXIII § 3(a).

219   *Id.*

220   NBA CBA, Art. XXXIII § 3(b).

221   The list itself does not appear to be publicly available; however, the parties agreed by letter agreement accompanying the 2013 CBA to include on the Prohibited Substances List "'illegal' stimulants and amphetamines . . . that are relevant to the sport of hockey." NHL CBA, Issues Related to Article 47 of the CBA Letter Agreement.

222   NHL CBA, Letter Agreement, Don Zavelo, General Counsel, NHLPA, to William L. Daly, Deputy Commissioner, NHL re: Issues Related to Article 47 of the CBA (Feb. 15, 2013).

223   NHL/NHLPA, *Substance Abuse and Behavioral Program* Ex. A (Sep. 1996).

224   *See, e.g.*, Mark Craig, *Deer-Antler Spray Latest 'Thorny' Issue in Athlete Supplements*, Star Trib., Jul. 22, 2013, http://www.startribune.com /sports/vikings/216523471.html, *archived at* http://perma.cc/RUG5 -CCM9 ("The NHL and NBA don't test blood, although the NBA reportedly is getting closer to doing so."); Bill Simmons, *Daring to Ask the PED Question*, Grantland, Feb. 1, 2013, http://grantland.com/features/daring -ask-ped-question/, *archived at* https://perma.cc/Y3A6-52WZ ("We look the other way when the MLB, NFL, NBA and NHL players associations keep blocking blood testing in their respective sports (MLB finally started blood testing for the 2013 season)."). Additionally, while the NHL discussed implementing hGH testing over the summer of 2013, it had no policy in place as of April 2015. *See* Mark Zwolinski, *NHL Delays Testing for Human Growth Hormone Until 2014-15 Season at Earliest*, Toronto Star, Aug. 14, 2013, http://www.thestar.com/sports/hockey/2013/08 /14/nhl_delays_testing_for_human_growth_hormone_until_201415 _season_at_earliest.html#, *archived at* http://perma.cc/X89Z-RBYJ; Andrew Kehapril, *N.B.A. to Test Players for H.G.H. Starting Next Season*, N.Y. Times, Apr. 17, 2015, http://www.nytimes.com/2015/04/17/sports /basketball/nba-to-test-players-for-hgh-starting-next-season.html, *archived at* http://perma.cc/W7VM-85VS. Growth hormone is currently on WADA's 2015 Prohibited Substances List from which NHL chooses its prohibited substances, however. *See The World Anti-Doping Code*, WADA (2015), https://wada-main-prod.s3.amazonaws.com/resources /files/wada-2015-prohibited-list-en.pdf, *archived at* http://perma.cc/ P2KM-KKKB.

225   *See* 2013 NHL CBA, Art. 47 § 6(d). The determination of whether a player had an unexcused failure or refusal or whether a player attempted to substitute, dilute, mask, or adulterate a specimen rests with the Program Doctors, subject to appeal to the Impartial Grievance Arbitrator. *Id.*

226   NHL CBA, Art. 47.9(e).

227   NHL CBA, Art. 47, § 8(b).

228   *Id.*

229   NHL CBA, Art. 47, § 8(c).

230   *Id.*

231   NHL/NHLPA, *Substance Abuse and Behavioral Program* Ex. A (Sept. 1996).

232   NHL/NHLPA, *Substance Abuse and Behavioral Program* Ex. A (Sept. 1996). For example, the cutoff level for marijuana metabolites is 50 ng/ml for the initial test. If a specimen is identified as positive, then the program doctors should confirm the presence of marijuana metabolites using gas chromatography/mass spectrometry techniques at the cutoff value of 15 ng/ml. *Id.*

233   NHL CBA, Art. 47, § 6(a).

234   *Id.*

235   *See* 2013 NHL CBA, Art. 47, § 6.

236   *See id.*

237   NHL CBA, Art. 47, § 6(c).

238   *Id.*

239   NHL CBA, § 47.4(b).

240   *Id.*

241   Mike Halford, *Report: NHL to Implement Comprehensive Cocaine Testing By End of Season*, Pro Hockey Talk (Nov. 23, 2015, 2:31 PM), http://nhl .nbcsports.com/2015/11/23/report-nhl-to-implement-comprehensive -cocaine-testing-by-end-of-season/, *archived at* http://perma.cc/A66B -AL8Q.

242   *Id.*

243   NHL/NHLPA, *Substance Abuse and Behavioral Program* 4 (Sept. 1996).

244   NHL/NHLPA, *Substance Abuse and Behavioral Program* 4 (Sept. 1996). Players may voluntarily seek treatment through the SABH Program or Team Personnel (club physicians, trainers, coaches, and managers) may refer a player to the Program. *See id.* at 4.

245   NHL CBA, Art. 47 § 2.

246   *Id.*

247   NHL/NHLPA, *Substance Abuse and Behavioral Program* 2 (Sept. 1996). The SABH is available as Exhibit C to the Notice of Removal (ECF No. 1) in the case of Boogaard v. Nat'l Hockey League, No. 1:13-cv-04846 (N.D. Ill. July 3, 2013).

248   *Id.*

249   NHL CBA, Art. 47 § 10.

250   *Id.*

251   NHL/NHLPA, *Substance Abuse and Behavioral Program* 1 (Sept. 1996).

252   *Id.* at 3.

253   NHL CBA, Art. 47.7(a)(i).

254   NHL CBA, Art. 47.7(a)(ii).

255   NHL CBA, Art. 47.7(a)(iii).

256   Andrew DeWitt, *Are NHL players using PEDs? Jonathan Toews says naive to say no*, CBS Sports (Aug. 16, 2013, 10:49 AM), http://www .cbssports.com/nhl/eye-on-hockey/23177818/are-nhl-players-using -peds-jonathan-toews-says-naive-to-think-no, *archived at* http://perma .cc/4GMB-ENEH.

257   NHL/NHLPA, *Substance Abuse and Behavioral Program* 4 (Sept. 1996).

258   *Id.*

259   *Id.*

260   *Id.*

261   *Id.*

262   *Id.* at § 4(C).

263   NHL CBA, Art. 18-A.2.

264   *Id.* at Art. 18-A.4.

265   NHL CBA, Art. 47 § 11. If the grievance is upheld, the Arbitrator can fashion an appropriate remedy pursuant to traditional standards of contract law. *Id.*

266   NHL/NHLPA, *Substance Abuse and Behavioral Program* Ex. B (Sept. 1996).

267   *See id.* at Ex. C.

268   *Id.* at 2.

269   CFL CBA, § 32.02.

270   CFL CBA, § 32.01.

271   CFL PED Policy, Appendix D. HGH is included on the list. *Id.*

272   CFL PED Policy, § 2.01.3.

273   CFL PED Policy, § 7.02.

274   CFL PED Policy, §§ 6.01, 6.02.

275   *CFL, CFLPA Agree on New Drug Policy for the 2016 Season*, Can. Football League, http://www.cfl.ca/2016/04/21/cfl-cflpa-agree-new-drug-policy-2016-season/ (last visited Apr. 25, 2016), *archived at* https://perma.cc/4QY4-2SGL; 2016 CFL PED Policy, App. C.

276   CFL PED Policy, § 5.04.2.

277   CFL PED Policy, § 5.04.3.

278   CFL PED Policy, § 5.04.1.

279   *Id.*

280   CFL PED Policy, § 3.

281   The Designated Medical Authority is an individual jointly appointed by the CFL and CFLPA who has sole responsibility for reviewing Therapeutic Use Exemption applications. 2016 CFL PED Policy, § 5.03.1.

282   CFL PED Policy, § 5.03.4.

283   CFL PED Policy, § 9.01.1.

284   *Id.*

285   *CFL, CFLPA Agree on New Drug Policy for the 2016 Season*, Can. Football League, http://www.cfl.ca/2016/04/21/cfl-cflpa-agree-new-drug-policy-2016-season/ (last visited Apr. 25, 2016), *archived at* https://perma.cc/4QY4-2SGL; CFL PED Policy, § 7.03

286   *Id.*

287   *Id.*

288   *Id.*

289   CFL PED Policy, § 9.01.2.

290   CFL PED Policy, § 4.01.1.

291   CFL PED Policy, § 4.01.2.

292   *Id.*

293   MLS Substance Abuse Policy, § VI(A).

294   *Id.*

295   *Id.* at § VI(B).

296   *Id.* at § VI(C).

297   *Id.* at § VI(D).

298   *Id.* at § III(C) ("All specimen collection shall be done in accordance with the WADA Guidelines for Urine Sample Collection.")

299   *Id.* at § V(A).

300   *Id.* at § IX(A).

301   *Id.* at § VII(B).

302   *Id.* at § VII(A)(1).

303   *See id.*

304   *Id.* at § III(A).

305   *Id.*

306   *Id.*

307   *Id.* at § V.

308   *Id.* at § V(C).

309   *Id.*

310   *Id.* at § V(D).

311   *Id.*

312   This information was provided by the MLSPU.

313   MLS Substance Abuse Policy, § X(A).

314   *See id.* at § X(B) (providing different discipline scheme for players who have tested positive for PEDs).

315   *Id.* at § X(A).

316   *Id.*

317   *Id.* at § X(A)(3).

318   *See id.* at § X(A).

319   *Id.* at § X (B).

320   *See id.* at § VIII(D); § IX (B).

321   *See id.* at § XII(B)(1).

322   *Id.*

323   *Id.*

324   *Id.*

325   NBA CBA, Art. XXXIII, § 9(a).

326   *See* 2017 NBA CBA, Art. XXXIII, § 1(b) ("A player may not Come Forward Voluntarily for the use of a SPED").

327   *See* 2017 NBA CBA, Art. XXXIII, § 9.

328   *See* Alfhid Gronbladh, Erik Nylander, Mathias Halberg, *The neurobiology and addiction potential of anabolic androgenic steroids and the effects of growth hormone*, 126 Brain Res. Bulletin 127, 129–30 (2016) (discussing PES dependence); Harrison G. Pope et al., *Adverse Health Consequences of Performance-Enhancing Drugs: An Endocrine Society Specific Statement*, 35 Endocrine Reviews 341, 355 (2013) (discussing PES dependence); Gen Kanayama et al., *Treatment of anabolic-androgenic steroid dependence: Emerging evidence and its implications*, 109 Drug & Alcohol Dependence 6, 7 (2010) ("[PES usage] can cause a dependence syndrome where individuals may use these drugs almost continuously for years, often despite adverse effects"); Gen Kanayama et al., *Anabolic-androgenic steroid dependence: an emerging disorder*, 104 Addiction 12, 1966–78 (2009) (finding that About 30% of anabolic steroid users appear to develop a dependence syndrome, characterized by chronic steroid use despite adverse effects on physical, psychosocial, or occupational functioning).

329   *See* Anders Hakansson et al., *Anabolic androgenic steroids in the general population: user characteristics and associations with substance use*, 18 Eur. Addict Res. 2 (2012) ("[PED] use was most strongly associated with a lifetime history of illicit drug use and the misuse of prescription drugs."); Michael Bahrke et al., *Risk factors associated with anabolic-androgenic steroid use among adolescents*, 29 Sports Med. 6 (2000) ("studies have reported that the likelihood of using [PEDs] was associated with the use of several other drugs including marijuana, cocaine, stimulants, relaxants, heroin, caffeine, alcohol, cigarettes and smokeless tobacco.")

330   Alfhid Gronbladh, Erik Nylander, Mathias Halberg, *The neurobiology and addiction potential of anabolic androgenic steroids and the effects of growth hormone*, 126 Brain Res. Bulletin 127, 130 (2016) ("there is a strong association between [PES] dependence and opioid dependence"); Harrison G. Pope et al., *Adverse Health Consequences of Performance-Enhancing Drugs: An Endocrine Society Specific Statement*, 35 Endocrine Reviews 341, 348–49 (2013).

331   Gen Kanayama et al., *Treatment of anabolic-androgenic steroid dependence: Emerging evidence and its implications*, 109 Drug & Alcohol Dependence 6, 8–9 (2010).

332   *Id.* at 9.

333   Harrison G. Pope et al., *Adverse Health Consequences of Performance-Enhancing Drugs: An Endocrine Society Specific Statement*, 35 Endocrine Reviews 341, 348–49 (2013); Kanayama et al., *supra* n. 331 at 10.

334   Pope et al., *supra* n. 330 at 353; Kanayama et al., *supra* n. 331 at 10.

335   *See* Daria Paicentino et al., *Anabolic-androgenic Steroid Use and Psychopathology in Athletes. A Systematic Review*, 13 Current Neuropharmacology 101 (2015).

336 Pope et al., *supra* n. 33 at 348-49; Kanayama et al., *supra* n. 331 at 10.

337 Gronbladh, Nylander, Halberg, *supra* n. 330 at 130; Pope et al., *supra* n. 333 at 348-49.

338 Pope et al., *supra* n. 333 at 349; Kanayama et al., *supra* n. 333 at 349.

339 *See* Gronbladh, Nylander, Halberg, *supra* n. 330 at 133-34; Pope et al., *supra* n. 333 at 348-49; Kan ayama et al., *supra* n. 331 at 10; *Harrison G. Pope, MD, MPH*, McLean Hospital, http://www.mcleanhospital.org/biography/harrison-pope (last visited Dec. 15, 2016), *archived at* https://perma.cc/EK4G-7MWU ("Harrison G. Pope, MD, MPH, has conducted research in a wide range of areas in psychiatry and has authored more than 300 peer-reviewed papers. This work includes many publications on the diagnosis and treatment of psychotic disorders and major mood disorders, together with extensive research on eating disorders and related issues of body image in both women and men. More recently, Dr. Pope has also focused on substance abuse disorders, with emphasis on drugs such as cannabis, hallucinogens, ecstasy, and anabolic-androgenic steroids.").

Chapter 5

Compensation

This Chapter examines the form and nature of player compensation in the NFL, MLB, NBA, NHL, CFL, and MLS.[a] In reviewing this Chapter, it is important to understand that the structures, operations and finances of the NFL, MLB, NBA, and NHL — the "Big Four" — are considerably different from those of the CFL and MLS due to, among other things, their long-standing place in the United States and the amount of their revenues (billions versus millions).

---

a   In this Chapter, we are focused on the compensation structures of the players actually playing in the leagues, and not on practice squad, minor league, or development league players. The structure of play and compensation for players at these lower levels vary considerably across the leagues based on differing needs, and thus do not provide for a useful comparison.

Figure 5-A: The Leagues' Revenues

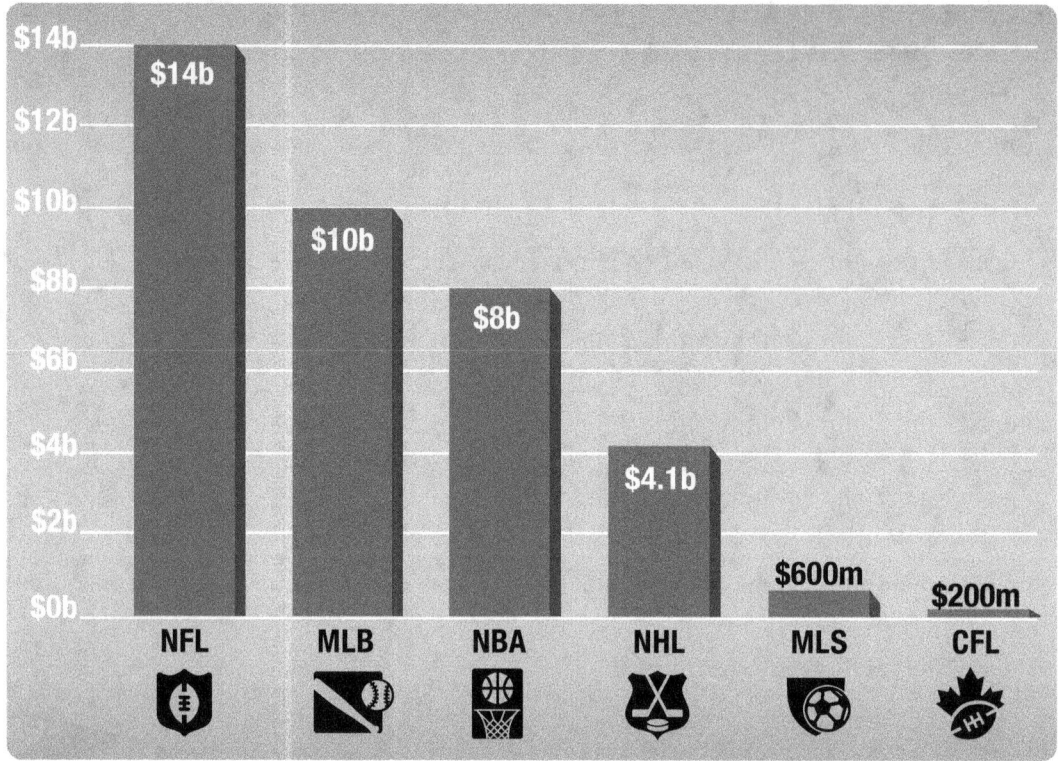

Compensation is an important component of player health. First, the different compensation structures and systems in the leagues can influence players' decisions about their physical and mental health, for example when to play through injury, when to retire, and the like. In their efforts to maximize their earnings (and sometimes, eligibility for various benefits), some players might sacrifice their short- and/or long-term physical and mental health.[1] The compensation structures dictate when or if a player faces such a trade-off.

Compensation may also be related to health in a second way. Without adequate savings and benefits during and after NFL play, players may find themselves insufficiently prepared to meet their physical and mental health needs, especially in the event of crisis.[2] In addition, as we discussed in greater detail in Chapter 3, crises in physical and mental health are closely tied to bankruptcy, home foreclosure, and other serious financial setbacks.[3] In the worst case scenario, these two outcomes can lead to a vicious cycle—poor health outcomes lead to financial losses, which worsen the ability to combat physical and mental health impairments, which in turn further deplete financial resources. Additionally, financial health is also in and of itself an important component of a person's health. Financial difficulties can cause stress that contributes to or exacerbates psychological and physical ailments. NFL players suffer these outcomes as well, despite their relatively high (but short-lived) compensation.

Before explaining the form and nature of compensation, it is important to discuss two concepts essential to the leagues' compensation structures: salary caps; and, free agency. After explaining these key terms, we then discuss, for each league: (1) its respective salary cap; (2) rookie compensation; (3) veteran compensation;[b] (4) minimum, maximum, and average (mean) salaries; and, (5) guaranteed compensation. At the conclusion of this Chapter, we provide a chart summarizing and comparing some of the key compensation figures and policies across the leagues.

1) THE SALARY CAP

Generally, a "Salary Cap" in sports is the maximum amount of money that a club can spend on its' players' salaries collectively in a season.[4] While some of the leagues use different terminology for their Salary Cap, and there are various nuances and differences among them, each of the leagues has some mechanism that restricts or reduces the

---

b   For purposes of this Chapter, we define a "rookie" as any player who has not yet played and a veteran as any player who has played.

amounts clubs can spend on player compensation. In each of the leagues, the Salary Cap is negotiated with a corresponding labor organization, or players association, that represents the players in negotiating the CBA. In the cases of the NFL, NBA, and NHL, the players associations have agreed to the Salary Caps in exchange for a minimum percentage of league revenues being spent on players. Moreover, in the cases of the NFL, NBA, NHL, and CFL, there is also a salary floor—a minimum amount that the clubs must spend on player salaries. How player contracts are calculated pursuant to these Salary Caps has a significant impact on the ways players are compensated in each sport.

2) FREE AGENCY

MLB is the oldest of the leagues, having begun play in 1903.[5] Beginning in the earliest days of professional baseball and MLB, every player contract contained what is known as a "reserve clause."[6] The reserve clause prohibited players from negotiating with other clubs and granted the clubs an option to renew the player's contract on the club's terms.[7] If players wanted to play professional baseball, they had almost no leverage in their contract negotiations.

The reserve clause raised concerns with the Sherman Antitrust Act. Section 1 of the Sherman Antitrust Act prohibits contracts, combinations, or conspiracies that unreasonably restrain trade.[8] The reserve clause was an agreement among the separate baseball clubs not to negotiate with each other's players and thus potentially unreasonably restrained the labor market for players' services. However, in 1922, in *Federal Baseball Club of Baltimore, Inc. v. National League of Professional Baseball Clubs* ("*Federal Baseball*"),[9] the Supreme Court of the United States held that MLB was not engaged in interstate commerce and was thus exempt from antitrust laws.[10]

As MLB grew into the large-scale, national business that it is today, the Supreme Court's holding in *Federal Baseball* seemed questionable, including to the Supreme Court itself. However, in 1953[11] and again in 1972,[12] the Supreme Court upheld MLB's antitrust exemption and the reserve clause on the grounds of *stare decisis*.[c] The Court reasoned that Congress had permitted MLB's antitrust exemption to stand for

50 years and that if anything were going to change, it had to be through legislation.[13,d]

The other leagues were not as fortunate. The reserve clause was used in all of the Big Four leagues, but the Supreme Court limited the antitrust exemption to baseball.[14] Consequently, as a result of antitrust litigation in the 1970s, the reserve clause was effectively eliminated in the NFL, NBA, and NHL.[15] In 1976, MLB players finally were able to extinguish further use of the reserve clause through the collectively bargained grievance process,[e] and subsequent collective bargaining efforts.

Without the reserve clause, club owners became concerned that open bidding for players' services would financially ruin the leagues. Consequently, the leagues each began to negotiate with their respective players unions. In 1976, MLB and the MLBPA, the NBA and NBPA, and the NHL and NHLPA all agreed to new CBAs.[16] In exchange for a variety of concessions, the players agreed to rules that reflected the reserve clause's intent: the clubs would be permitted to control a player's rights for a certain number of years, and then, after a player gained a certain level of experience, that player would become a "free agent," able to offer his services to any and all clubs at the highest price the market would bear. The club's ability to control the player for the first few years of his career is perhaps seen as fair consideration for the club's investment in the player's development, particularly at any minor league level.

While the NFL and NFLPA did not agree to free agency as it existed in the other leagues until 1993,[17] beginning in the 1970s free agency became and is an integral part of the modern sports landscape. Below, we generically define three terms common to the concept of free agency in professional sports that are key to understanding compensation in these leagues. While not all of the leagues use these exact terms, they all utilize the concepts:

---

d   Indeed, in 1998 Congress passed the Curt Flood Act, named for the plaintiff in the 1972 Supreme Court case, which substantially overruled *Federal Baseball* and its progeny by declaring that actions relating to the employment of Major League Baseball players are subject to antitrust law. However, the Act kept Major League Baseball's antitrust immunity concerning its handling of minor league baseball and franchise issues, such as relocation. *See* 15 U.S.C. § 26b; *City of San Jose v. Office of the Comm'r of Baseball*, 776 F.3d 686 (9th Cir. 2015).

e   After the 1974 season, Los Angeles Dodgers pitcher Andy Messersmith refused to sign the contract presented to him by the Dodgers. The club exercised its options under the reserve clause and Messersmith played the 1975 season without an executed contract. After the season, Messersmith claimed that he had played out the option year of the contract and was now a free agent, able to sign with any club he chose. An arbitrator ultimately sided with Messersmith. Joshua P. Jones, *A Congressional Swing and Miss: The Curt Flood Act, Player Control, and the National Pastime*, 33 Ga. L. Rev. 639, 659-60 (1999). The arbitrator's decision was affirmed in federal court. Kansas City Royals Baseball Corp. v. Major League Baseball Players Ass'n, 409 F. Supp. 233 (W.D. Mo. 1976) *aff'd*, 532 F.2d 615 (8th Cir. 1976).

---

c   *Stare decisis* is Latin for "to stand by things decided." It is "[t]he doctrine of precedent, under which a court must follow earlier judicial decisions when the same points arise again in litigation." Black's Law Dictionary (9th ed. 2009).

- **Exclusive Rights Player:** A player whose contract has expired and who, because he has minimal experience (defined differently by the various leagues), must sign a contract with his prior club, provided that club offers him a contract that meets the minimum requirements outlined in the CBA. Exclusive Rights Players have no leverage and thus generally must accept the contract offered by the club, which is typically for a salary at or near the league minimum.

- **Restricted Free Agent:** A player whose contract has expired and who can sign a contract with any club but, because the player has only a limited (but more than minimal) amount of experience (defined variously among the leagues), if the player signs with a new club his prior club is entitled to some form of compensation, typically draft picks. Further, the prior club has a right of first refusal on a contract offered by another club as long as it had already made the player an offer meeting certain minimum criteria outlined in the CBA ("Qualifying Offer"). Restricted Free Agents have minimal leverage as clubs generally prefer not to pay the required compensation to the player's prior club.

- **Unrestricted Free Agent:** A player whose contract has expired and, because he has reached a certain threshold of experience defined by the CBA, can sign a contract with any club without his prior club retaining any rights concerning the player. Unrestricted Free Agents have far more leverage and options as compared to Exclusive Rights Players or Restricted Free Agents. Becoming an Unrestricted Free Agent is an important opportunity for players to offer their services to any and all clubs at the highest price the market will bear (within the confines of the CBA).

With these important concepts and terms in mind, we turn to analyzing how they are effectuated in the leagues today and their effect on player health.

> The more that is paid to NFL players — including retired players — in the form of benefits and medical care, i.e., Player Benefits Cost, the less they are able to receive in the form of salary.

A) Compensation in the NFL

The most recent CBA agreed to by the NFL and the NFLPA was executed in 2011 and expires in 2021.

1) THE NFL'S SALARY CAP

NFL players, as a group, are entitled to different percentages of different revenue sources: (1) 55% of League Media, which consists of all NFL broadcasting revenues;[18] (2) 45% of NFL Ventures/Postseason revenue, which includes all revenues arising from the operation of postseason NFL games and all revenues arising from NFL-affiliated entities, including NFL Ventures,[19] NFL Network,[20] NFL Properties,[21] NFL Enterprises,[22] NFL Productions,[23] and NFL Digital;[24] and, (3) 40% of Local Revenues, which includes those revenues not included in League Media or NFL Ventures/Postseason, and specifically includes revenues from the sale of pre-season television broadcasts.[25] These revenues are collectively known as "All Revenue" or "AR."[26] AR in 2017 is estimated to reach $14 billion.[27] The players' share of AR cannot be less than 47% and cannot exceed 48.5%.[28]

The players' share of AR — the Player Cost Amount[29] — is one of two essential components for calculating the Salary Cap.[30] The other is Player Benefit Costs. Player Benefit Costs are the total amounts the NFL and its clubs spend on programs and benefits for players, including retired players, in addition to the costs of providing medical care to NFL players.[31] The Salary Cap is determined by subtracting Player Benefit Costs from the Player Cost Amount and dividing by the number of clubs in the NFL.[32] In other words, the Salary Cap equals Player Cost Amount minus Player Benefit Costs divided by 32. *Thus, the more that is paid to NFL players — including retired players — in the form of benefits and medical care, i.e., Player Benefits Cost, the less they are able to receive in the form of salary.* Indeed, in 2015, when the Salary Cap was $143,280,000 per club, each club was charged $37,550,000 in Player Benefit Costs. Thus, out of a possible $180,830,000 that could have been spent on player salaries for each club, 26.2% was allocated to player benefits.

It is important to clarify these figures. As Figure 5-B shows on the next page, about 50% of a club's revenue is allocated towards the players (the Player Cost Amount). The club keeps the other 50%. Of the 50% allocated for the players, in 2015, 26.2% of that was used on player benefits. Thus, in 2015, we can estimate that each club had approximately $361,660,000 in revenue, $180,830,000 of which would be available for players. $37,550,000 was spent on player benefits. The $37,550,000 is 26.2% of the Player Cost Amount and 10.4% of the club's revenue.

Figure 5-B: Division of All Revenue

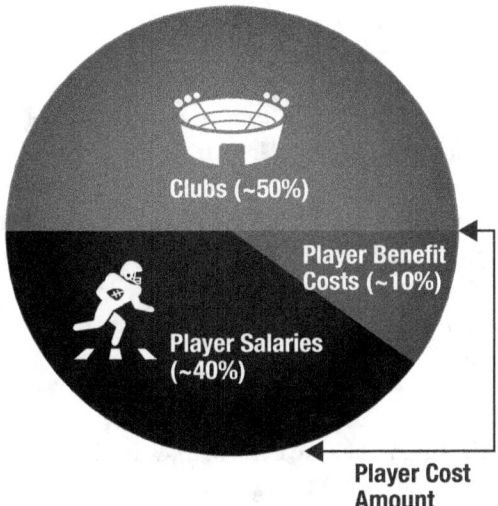

In 2016, the NFL Salary Cap was $155.27 million.[33] In 2017, the Salary Cap is $167 million.[34] Importantly, the NFL's Salary Cap is considered a "hard" Salary Cap in that, with some small exceptions or nuances, there is no way for a club to exceed the Salary Cap.[35] In exchange for the hard Salary Cap, clubs individually must spend at least 89% of their Salary Cap in cash over a four-year period,[36] and collectively must spend 95% of their Salary Caps in cash over a four-year period.[37] However, the Salary Cap in one season includes prorated portions of signing and option bonuses paid in previous years, even though no payment is actually made in the most recent season (*see* Section 4 below for additional explanation). Consequently, a club's Salary Cap figure does not represent the actual amount of money being paid to the players. The cash requirement measures the amount of compensation actually being paid and thus ensures that clubs are actually paying the players at least some threshold amount of money.

2) ROOKIE COMPENSATION

Rookie compensation was a major issue during the 2011 CBA negotiations. For example, the 2010 first overall Draft pick Sam Bradford agreed to a six-year, $78 million contract with the St. Louis Rams, including $50 million guaranteed before he ever played a game in the NFL.[38] By comparison, Tom Brady, at the time a three-time Super Bowl champion and two-time league MVP, received only a four-year, $72-million contract with $48.5 million guaranteed when he re-signed with the New England Patriots prior to the 2010 season.[39] With clubs—and, to some degree, players—unhappy with the amounts being paid to unproven rookies, the terms regarding rookie compensation were changed dramatically in the 2011 CBA.[40]

First, contracts for rookie players are now "fixed and unalterable."[41] First-round Draft picks are limited to four-year contracts, with the club retaining the option to extend the contract for a fifth year.[42] Rookies drafted in rounds two through seven are limited to four-year contracts, and undrafted rookies can only sign three-year contracts.[43]

Second, the amount of each rookie's compensation is largely determined by each club's Total Rookie Allocation, *i.e.*, how much a club can spend on its rookies (also known as the "Rookie Salary Cap"). Each club's Total Rookie Allocation is calculated based on the club's amount, round, and position of Draft picks.[44] Thus each drafted player has a value within each club's Total Rookie Allocation. Clubs and contract advisors (*i.e.*, agents) will not deviate much, if at all, from that assigned value in the total amount of compensation provided to the player in his rookie contract.[45] If one drafted player received more than was allotted for his salary under the Total Rookie Allocation, it means another drafted player would have to receive less than was allocated for his salary under the Total Rookie Allocation.

Third, a rookie's compensation generally consists of three items: (1) the base or "Paragraph 5" Salary, which is listed in Paragraph 5 of the Standard Player Contract; (2) a signing bonus, *i.e.*, a lump sum paid to the player shortly after signing the contract; and, (3) a Performance Incentive. The 2011 CBA prohibited several types of contract structures and bonuses that had previously been used to inflate rookies' contracts.[46] For most rookies, the signing bonus is the only portion of their compensation that is guaranteed, as Paragraph 5 salaries are typically only guaranteed (in whole or in part) for first round Draft picks.[47] The Performance Incentive is typically earned only if a player participates in a certain number of the club's plays and the club meets certain statistical performance criteria such as winning a certain number of games.[48]

In spite of these changes, rookie compensation still varies dramatically. 2016 first overall pick Jared Goff signed a four-year fully-guaranteed contract worth $27.9 million, including a $18.5 million signing bonus.[49] By contrast, the 253rd and final pick of the 2016 NFL Draft, Kalan Reed, signed a four-year deal worth $2.4 million, including a $58,540 signing bonus.[50] Only the signing bonus was guaranteed.[51]

3) VETERAN COMPENSATION

A veteran's compensation is typically determined by the new contract he signs when his existing contract has expired or is approaching expiration. Upon expiration of a player's contract, he meets one of three definitions of a veteran in the NFL. The three different types of veterans are determined by the number of Accrued Seasons a player has earned. Generally speaking, a player earns an Accrued Season for each season he is on the club's roster for six or more games.[52] Importantly, a player earns an Accrued Season for games missed as a result of a football-related injury.[53]

First, an Exclusive Rights Player is a player with less than three Accrued Seasons whose contract has expired.[54] An Exclusive Rights Player can only sign a contract with his prior club, provided the club offers him a contract for at least the minimum permissible salary.[55] Although drafted rookie contracts are required to be four years in length, players' contracts are often terminated before their expiration and the players then sign new contracts with other clubs. If the contract with the new club expires before the player has reached three Accrued Seasons, he will be an Exclusive Rights Player. There are dozens of exclusive rights players every year, most of whom are simply battling to remain on the roster.[f]

Chris Banjo, a safety for the Green Bay Packers is a recent example of an Exclusive Rights Player. Banjo was not selected in the 2012 NFL Draft, and was out of the NFL until signing with the Jacksonville Jaguars prior to the 2013 season. When the Jaguars cut Banjo during the 2013 pre-season, he signed a one-year deal with Green Bay for the league minimum. Banjo, as an Exclusive Rights Player, again signed one-year deals with Green Bay for the league minimum prior to the 2014 and 2015 seasons.[56]

Second, players with exactly three Accrued Seasons and an expired contract are Restricted Free Agents.[57] A Restricted Free Agents can negotiate with other clubs but his prior club, provided it makes an offer to the player, retains a right of first refusal and the right to receive Draft picks from the other club as compensation. The round of the Draft pick to which the prior club is entitled varies depending on the amount of money it offered the player.[58] There were 74 Restricted Free Agents in the 2015 off-season and 41 in the 2016 off-season.

Jermaine Kearse, a wide receiver for the Seattle Seahawks, is a recent example of a Restricted Free Agent. Kearse signed with Seattle as an undrafted free agent prior to the 2012 season. After being released by the club twice during the 2012 season, in October 2012 Kearse and the Seahawks agreed to a contract for the 2012, 2013, and 2014 seasons. When Kearse's contract expired after the 2014 season, Kearse became a Restricted Free Agent. In the 2015 off-season, the Seahawks offered Kearse a one-year contract worth $2,356,000, as they were required to do in order to retain their right of first refusal. Kearse signed the contract.[59]

Third, a player with four or more Accrued Seasons whose contract has expired is an Unrestricted Free Agent.[60] An Unrestricted Free Agent is "completely free to negotiate and sign a Player Contract with any Club, and any Club shall be completely free to negotiate and sign a Player Contract with such player without penalty or restriction[.]"[61] There are typically around 400 Unrestricted Free Agents each off-season.

A recent example of an Unrestricted Free Agent is Ndamukong Suh. Suh, a defensive lineman, was selected second overall in the 2010 NFL Draft by the Detroit Lions and signed a five-year contract. When Suh's contract expired after the 2014 season, he was an Unrestricted Free Agent and signed a six-year, $114 million contract with the Miami Dolphins.[62]

The nature of a player's compensation varies considerably depending on his status. Exclusive Rights Players typically have no leverage and thus generally must accept the contract offered by the club, which is typically at or near the league minimum Paragraph 5 Salary (non-guaranteed). Similarly, Restricted Free Agents typically have minimal leverage as clubs prefer not to pay the required compensation to the prior club. Consequently, Restricted Free Agents ordinarily sign the contracts the clubs are required to offer them to retain the right of first refusal. These contracts are non-guaranteed one-year contracts for between $1.2 and $2.6 million per year.[63]

Unrestricted Free Agents have far more leverage and options. While less skilled Unrestricted Free Agents might only sign contracts for the league minimum—if they are offered any contract at all—the best players are able to sign multi-year deals worth tens of millions of dollars, including tens of millions of dollars in guarantees.[64] An Unrestricted Free Agent contract includes Paragraph 5 salary as well as many different types of bonuses, such as a signing bonus; an option bonus (a lump sum paid in the event the club or player opts to extend or alter the contract in some way); a roster bonus (a lump sum paid in the event the player is still on the club's roster at a determined date); and, a workout

---

f   For context, 2,274 players played in at least one NFL game in 2016. This statistic is derived from official NFL-NFLPA playtime statistics.

Table 5-A:

NFL Minimum Paragraph 5 Salaries

Credited Seasons	2015	2016	2017	2018	2019	2020
0	$435,000	$450,000	$465,000	$480,000	$495,000	$510,000
1	$510,000	$525,000	$540,000	$555,000	$570,000	$585,000
2	$585,000	$600,000	$615,000	$630,000	$645,000	$660,000
3	$660,000	$675,000	$690,000	$705,000	$720,000	$735,000
4-6	$745,000	$760,000	$775,000	$790,000	$805,000	$820,000
7-9	$870,000	$885,000	$900,000	$915,000	$930,000	$945,000
10+	$970,000	$985,000	$1,000,000	$1,015,000	$1,030,000	$1,045,000

bonus (a lump sum paid in the event a player participates in a minimum number of the club's off-season workouts).[65] In addition, players' contracts might include incentive clauses, which provide players with bonuses based on the achievement of certain statistical accomplishments.[66]

Of course, players do not need to reach Unrestricted Free Agency to sign the types of contracts discussed above. The fact that a player's Unrestricted Free Agency is approaching often causes the player and his club to negotiate a contract extension that is generally commensurate with what the player would have received had he reached Unrestricted Free Agency.[g]

4) MINIMUM, MAXIMUM, AND AVERAGE (MEAN) SALARIES

NFL players' minimum salaries are dependent upon their number of Credited Seasons. Generally, a player earns a Credited Season (differentiated from an Accrued Season discussed above) when he is entitled to be paid for at least three regular season games.[67] Table 5-A above shows the minimum Paragraph 5 salaries for players based on their number of Credited Seasons and the League Year.[h]

The minimum salary is particularly important as nearly half of the players in the NFL only make the league minimum.[68]

The NFL does not prescribe a maximum salary. However, the Salary Cap and its complicated rules create barriers that effectively restrict player salaries. For example, when a player receives a signing bonus, even though the signing bonus is typically paid in one or two lump sums shortly after the contract is executed, only a portion of the signing bonus counts against the Salary Cap for the year in which the bonus was paid. For Salary Cap purposes, the signing bonus is prorated equally over the duration of the contract.[69] Thus, if a player receives an $8 million signing bonus as part of a four-year contract, the signing bonus will count against the Salary Cap for $2 million each year ($8 million divided by 4 years). However, a signing bonus can only be prorated over a maximum of five years.[70] Clubs thus generally prefer not to sign a player to a contract longer than five years to avoid losing the full benefit of proration.

The concept of an "average" salary in the NFL can be confusing. As discussed above, players often receive a significant portion of their compensation in upfront lump sum payments and then are paid less during the remainder of the contract. For example, when Unrestricted Free Agent Ndamukong Suh signed a six-year, $114 million contract with the Miami Dolphins in 2015, he received a $25.5 million signing bonus in the first year but his Paragraph 5 salaries for the remainder of the contract averaged $17.16 million.[71] Thus, it is unclear when the media is reporting "average" salary whether they are calculating that figure based on the compensation a player will receive in that particular season, or on the average amount owed to the player over the duration of the contract. Additionally, the details of NFL player contracts are typically not public, further calling into question the reliability of the data reported by the media.

g   For example, in 2014, two years before he would have been eligible for free agency, J.J. Watt signed a six-year contract extension with the Houston Texans for $100 million, $51.8 million of which was guaranteed. *Texans give J.J. Watt $100M deal,* ESPN, Sept. 2, 2014, http://espn.go.com/nfl/story/_/id/11451373/jj-watt-houston -texans-reach-agreement-6-year-100-million-deal, *archived at* http://perma.cc/ GUQ4-GP9J.

h   Credited Seasons are particularly important when it comes to NFL players' eligibility for health-related benefits, as discussed in Chapter 3: Health-Related Benefits.

In the NFL community, clubs and contract advisors (*i.e.,* agents) generally think of a player's salary in terms of the Average Per Year ("APY"). The APY is determined by dividing the contract's total compensation by its length. While there are nuances that might call into question whether to include certain years or forms of compensation in the calculation, the APY is generally a useful method for understanding the compensation provided to a player pursuant to a contract.

Based on our analysis, the website spotrac.com provides the most reliable publicly available data on player contracts. Using data from spotrac.com from the second week of the 2015 regular season, the average NFL player had a contract that was approximately 2.9 years in length and worth approximately $7.6 million total, or about $2.7 million per year. The median APY was approximately $710,000, and about 61% of the players had an APY of less than $1 million.

The value or duration of an NFL player contract is less meaningful when considering that NFL contracts are generally not guaranteed.

---

5) GUARANTEED COMPENSATION

Guaranteed compensation in the NFL is a complicated issue. Many people—particularly some players—feel that fully guaranteeing a player's contract is a fair trade for the health risks players undertake. More important for our purposes here, focused on protecting and promoting player health, if a player's contract were fully guaranteed, he would likely feel less pressure to play through injuries in an effort to continually prove himself to the club and avoid termination of his contract.[72] However, we have concerns about the possibility of unintended consequences as well as the feasibility of fully guaranteeing player compensation, which will be discussed in detail in the Analysis and Recommendation Sections below.

To understand these concerns, in this Section we provide an explanation of guaranteed compensation in the NFL. Generally, NFL clubs are permitted to terminate a player's contract without any further financial obligation to the player for five reasons:

1. the player "has failed to establish or maintain [his] excellent physical condition to the satisfaction of the Club physician";

2. the player has "failed to make a full and complete disclosure of [his] physical or mental condition during a physical examination";

3. "[i]n the judgment of the Club, [the player's] skill or performance has been unsatisfactory as compared with that of other players competing for positions on the Club's roster";

4. the player has "engaged in personal conduct which, in the reasonable judgment of the Club, adversely reflects on the Club"; and,

5. "[i]n the Club's opinion, [the player is] reasonably anticipated to make less of a contribution to the Club's ability to compete on the playing field than another player or players whom the Club intends to sign or attempts to sign, or already on the roster of the Club, and for whom the Club needs Room."[73]

Players and their contract advisors seek to curtail the clubs' termination rights as to individual players by negotiating for some of the player's compensation to be guaranteed in addendums to the Standard Player Contract. Guaranteed compensation takes a wide variety of forms (most notably in signing bonuses),[74] but generally players and their contract advisors seek to guarantee the player's contract even where he is terminated for "injury," "skill," or "Salary Cap." An "injury" guarantee will protect against the first reason listed above for which clubs can generally terminate a player's contract; a "skill" guarantee will protect against the third reason; and, a "Salary Cap" guarantee will protect against the fifth reason. A player might have all or just some seasons of his contract guaranteed for skill, injury, and/or Salary Cap. In addition, there are other mechanisms in the CBA which can effectively guarantee some or all of a player's salary, including Injury Protection[i] and Termination Pay.[j]

Generally, players and their contract advisors seek to obtain as much guaranteed money as possible in contract negotiations. Guaranteed compensation provides the player with a secure income that is otherwise typically threatened by injury. However, there are times when a player might not

---

i   Where a player is injured in one season, fails the pre-season physical the next season because of that injury, and is terminated by the club as a result, the player is entitled to 50% of his salary for that season up to a maximum of $1.1 million in the 2015 season. If the player is still physically unable to play two seasons after the injury, he is entitled to 30% of his salary up to a maximum for $525,000 in 2015. A player is only entitled to Injury Protection once in his career. *See* 2011 NFL CBA, Art. 45.

j   A player with at least four years of experience who has his contract terminated after the first game of the season is entitled to the remainder of his salary for that season once in his career. 2011 NFL CBA, Art. 30.

want to sign the contract that offers him the most money— guaranteed or unguaranteed. Younger players might eschew the last year or two of a contract and the money that comes with it in favor of a shorter contract. In doing so, the player is hoping or expecting that he will be able to complete the shorter contract, reenter the free agency market, and sign another contract. Such decisions are obviously risky— the player's career might end for skill or health reasons under the shorter contract and the player will never have another chance at another contract. However, if the player is healthy, securing a second free agent contract can be lucrative.

From a club's perspective, guaranteed compensation is something to be avoided. Guaranteeing all or a portion of a player's contract commits the club to a player financially, regardless of whether the player performs poorly or suffers a career threatening injury. Nevertheless, clubs regularly agree to guarantee compensation to players to persuade them to join or stay with the club.

Changes to the Salary Cap rules as part of the 2011 CBA potentially increased the use of guaranteed money. Technically, whether a player's compensation is guaranteed has no effect on the Salary Cap—a club is limited to a certain amount of player compensation costs regardless of whether that amount is guaranteed or unguaranteed. Importantly, the amount of player salary that is counted against a club's Salary Cap does not necessarily reflect the amount actually being paid to players. As a result of the Salary Cap's accounting rules, in any given year a significant portion of a club's Salary Cap allocation might be consumed by charges that do not actually reflect a payment being made from the club to players, such as prorated portions of a signing bonus paid in a prior year. However, the 2011 CBA addressed this discrepancy by adding a requirement that clubs spend a certain amount of the Salary Cap in cash, that is, actual payments to the players, regardless of the accounting rules. Probably the easiest way for a club to ensure that it spends a sufficient amount in cash is to pay lump sum signing bonuses. Signing bonuses are the most traditional form of guaranteed compensation.

Using the same data from spotrac.com discussed above, one finds that approximately 44% of all contracted compensation is guaranteed. The data also shows that approximately 70% of players had at least some guaranteed compensation in their contract and the average amount of guaranteed compensation in an NFL player contract was $3.4 million. Additionally, 251 players had a contract that included at least $10 million in guaranteed compensation and 740 players had a contract that included at least $1 million in guaranteed compensation.

> Approximately 44% of all contracted compensation is guaranteed and approximately 70% of players had at least some guaranteed compensation in their contract.

In recent years, the percentage of an NFL player's contract that is guaranteed appears to have risen. Although the scope of the guarantees is sometimes debated,[75] it is not uncommon for marquee players to sign contracts that guarantee 50% or more of their compensation.[76] Moreover, the 2011 CBA significantly curtailed rookie compensation, cutting the amount top Draft picks earned by more than 50%.[77] In exchange, however, many first round Draft picks' contracts are now fully guaranteed.[78]

There is also an important caveat to the guaranteed nature of the various bonuses players receive. The bonuses are almost always subject to proportional forfeiture or voiding if a player violates the contract in some way, such as by refusing to show up to training camp, failing a test under the NFL's Policy and Program on Substances of Abuse ("Substance Abuse Policy"), failing a test under the NFL's Policy on Performance-Enhancing Substances ("PES Policy"),[k] or otherwise engaging in conduct detrimental to the NFL or the club.[79] For example, if a player received a $10 million signing bonus for a five-year contract, and the player later refuses to report to the club for the fifth season in hopes of signing a more lucrative contract, the player could be required to return $2 million of the signing bonus to the club.[80] Similarly, if a player is entitled to have his Paragraph 5 salary guaranteed in his second season, but fails a drug test between the first and second seasons, the contract might contain a clause permitting the club to void the guarantee in the second season.[81]

With the structure of compensation in the NFL explained above, we are ready to compare it to the other leagues.

---

k   The Substance Abuse Policy and PES Policy are discussed at length in Chapter 4: Drug and Performance-Enhancing Substance Policies.

B) Compensation in MLB

The most recent CBA agreed to by MLB and the Major League Baseball Players Association ("MLBPA") was executed in 2016 and expires in 2021.

1) MLB'S TAX THRESHOLD

Unlike the NFL, MLB does not have a "Salary Cap" for its clubs, insofar as there is no maximum amount that clubs can spend on player salaries. Instead, MLB sets a Tax Threshold and applies a "Competitive Balance Tax" for compensation paid to players over that amount. For the 2016 season, the Tax Threshold was set at $189 million,[82] and will be $195 million in 2017.[83] This tax is also known as the "luxury tax" and is intended to encourage parity by forcing clubs not to exceed the Tax Threshold. The Competitive Balance Tax ranges from 20% to 50% depending upon how many times the club has previously exceeded the Tax Threshold.[84]

In 2016, MLB revenues were an estimated $10 billion.[85]

2) ROOKIE COMPENSATION

Rookies generally are paid the league minimum and have one-year contracts, as will be explained further below.[1]

3) VETERAN COMPENSATION

The 2012 MLB CBA and uniform player contract ("UPC") divide players into three categories based on the amount of time they have spent in the major leagues, and which category a player falls into has important consequences for his salary. A player's time in the major leagues is tracked by a metric known as Major League Service Time ("MLST"). A player accumulates one day of MLST for "each day of the . . . season [he] is on a Major League Club's Active List." One season of MLST is defined as 172 days.[86]

A player with less than three years of MLST is bound to his club by the terms of the UPC, which contains a reserve clause that effectively allows the club to unilaterally retain

his services so long as it pays him the minimum salary set in the CBA.[87] A player in this position is said to be "under reserve" to his club, and has essentially no leverage to influence his base salary—he can either accept his club's offer (almost certainly for a salary at or very near the minimum allowed by the CBA), attempt to hold out for higher pay, or find an occupation outside of MLB.[88] As a result, skilled players under reserve to their clubs are paid far less than they would be in an open market for their services.[89]

A player with more than three years but less than six years of MLST is said to be "arbitration eligible," and has the right under the CBA to submit the issue of his salary to an arbitration panel, with or without the consent of his club.[90] Certain players with more than two but less than three years of MLST are also arbitration eligible.[91] These players, known as "Super Two" players, must have accumulated 86 days of MLST in the immediately preceding season and rank in the top 22% in total MLST among all players eligible for Super Two consideration.[92]

If an arbitration-eligible player initiates arbitration, he and his club must exchange single-year salary figures with one another[93] and submit those figures to a salary arbitration panel consisting of three arbitrators jointly selected by the MLBPA and MLB.[94] Salary arbitration proceedings are summary and winner-take-all: each side has just 90 minutes to argue[95] for its proposed salary,[96] and the salary arbitration panel may award the player a single-year contract for either the proposed salary he submitted or the proposed salary the club submitted—it may not award any other figure.[97] This form of arbitration, also known as pendulum or final offer arbitration, forces the sides to submit reasonable figures in the hopes that the arbitrator believes their submission is closer to the player's value than the other side's submission.[98] As a result, approximately 90% of all salary arbitration cases settle before a hearing.[99] In effect, the salary arbitration mechanism permits players to receive their free market wages for one season without the ability to actually negotiate with other clubs.

A player with more than six years of MLST at the completion of the term of his contract becomes a free agent and is able to offer his services to any and all clubs at whatever price the market will bear.[100] In veteran free-agency contracts, there is often a trade-off between contract length and average annual compensation.[101] Due to risks of injury or performance drop-offs, a player might accept a lower average annual compensation in exchange for higher total compensation in a longer contract.[102]

MLB's three-tiered system is similar to the NFL's use of Exclusive Rights Players, Restricted Free Agents, and

---

I   Theoretically, a player could execute a long-term contract with the club before his rookie season that provides for greater pay in the rookie season, but such contracts are extremely rare. *See* Craig Calcaterra, *At Least One Major Leaguer is Not Pleased With the Jon Singleton Deal*, Hardball Talk (June 3, 2014, 8:55 AM), http://mlb.nbcsports.com/2014/06/03/at-least-one-major-leaguer-is-not-pleased-with-the-jon-singleton-deal/, *archived at* https://perma.cc/2BPJ-YCHU.

Unrestricted Free Agents. In both leagues, players gain more rights and compensation with experience.

Most MLB free agents obtain contracts that are short in duration. The share of one-year free agent contracts signed in each of the seasons from the 2007 season to the 2013 season, for example, has ranged from 51.43% to 76.52%, and the share of two-year free-agent contracts has ranged from 13.08% to 27.62%.[103] Between 2007 and 2014, only the 2013 free agency market had more than 20% of free agent contracts extend beyond three years.[104]

Though most free agents are only able to obtain short-term deals, superstars have been able to bargain for extremely lucrative long-term contracts. For example, in 2014, the Miami Marlins signed Giancarlo Stanton, a then-twenty-five-year-old right fielder, to a thirteen-year, $325 million contract,[105] breaking the previous record held by the Detroit Tigers infielder Miguel Cabrera's ten-year $292 million deal.[106]

MLB clubs are thought to have deployed two strategies to minimize players' opportunities to obtain large free-agent contracts.

First, clubs have kept star prospects in the minor leagues for a few weeks at the beginning of their rookie season before having the player join the major league roster. This plan prevents the young player from achieving the necessary number of days on the roster to accrue a full season of MLST, thus delaying the player's free agency by a year.[107] For example in 2015, the Chicago Cubs waited 11 days before calling up star rookie third baseman Kris Bryant.[108] By doing so, Bryant will not be a free agent until after the 2021 season.[109] Had Bryant started the season with the Cubs, he would be eligible for free agency after the 2020 season.[110]

Second, clubs have signed players to long-term contract extensions at reduced salaries years before the player reaches free agency or is salary arbitration eligible.[111] For example, in 2012, the Pittsburgh Pirates' star center fielder Andrew McCuthen had played two seasons and was a year away from being salary arbitration eligible—and thus likely earning a multi-million dollar salary commensurate with players of similar skill. Rather than go through salary arbitration in future years and have McCutchen potentially reach free agency, the Pirates signed McCutchen to a six-year contract worth $51.5 million, plus a seventh-year at the club's option for $14.75 million.[112] The contract means the Pirates control McCutchen's rights through his ninth season—three years after when he would have become a free agent if not for the long-term extension. For McCutchen, the long-term extension provides him long-term financial security when he otherwise would have been playing on year-to-year contracts

until he reached free agency. As for any player, there was no guarantee that McCutchen would have continued to be sufficiently healthy and productive to reach free agency and receive a long-term multi-million dollar contract.

4) MINIMUM, MAXIMUM, AND AVERAGE (MEAN) SALARIES

In 2016, the mean MLB salary was $4.4 million per year,[113] and the minimum salary was $507,500.[114] There is no maximum salary for MLB players.

Simple averages are not entirely revealing due to the fact that younger players are limited in their ability to obtain market wages by MLB's free agency and salary arbitration rules. Data on the distribution of average annual salaries in 2012 indicate that high salaries are concentrated among a relatively small number of the league's players according to the following distribution:[m]

- **Bottom 20%:** $481,593
  (The minimum 2012 salary was $480,000)
- **Second 20%:** $505,109
- **Third 20%:** $1,195,785
- **Fourth 20%:** $3,606,888
- **Top 20%:** $11,164,616
- **Top 5%:** $18,363,670
- **Top 1%:** $23,791,667[115]

5) GUARANTEED COMPENSATION

Unlike the NFL, MLB contracts are generally understood to be fully guaranteed.[116] According to Paragraph 7 of the UPC, clubs may terminate a player's contract if the player shall at any time:

1. fail, refuse, or neglect to conform his personal conduct to the standards of good citizenship and good sportsmanship or to keep himself in first-class physical condition or to obey the Club's training rules; or

2. fail, in the opinion of the Club's management, to exhibit sufficient skill or competitive ability to qualify or continue as a member of the Club's team; or

3. fail, refuse or neglect to render his services hereunder or in any other manner materially breach this contract.

m   For context, approximately 1,375 players played in an MLB regular season game in 2016.

However, in practice, Paragraph 7 is usually nullified in the contracts of any player other than those with minimal MLST or veterans with little to no leverage. Thus, MLB clubs generally cannot terminate a player's contract, *i.e.,* MLB player contracts are generally guaranteed.

C) Compensation in the NBA

The most recent CBA agreed to by the NBA and the National Basketball Players Association ("NBPA") was executed in 2017, takes effect on July 1, 2017, and expires in 2024. However, both parties have the option of terminating the CBA after the 2022–23 season by serving written notice of the exercise of such option by December 15, 2022.[117]

1) THE NBA'S SALARY CAP

NBA players are collectively entitled to approximately 50% of Basketball Related Income ("BRI").[118] BRI is "the aggregate operating revenues . . . received or to be received . . . " by the NBA, NBA Properties, Inc., NBA Media Ventures, LLC and any subsidiaries.[119] The NBA's Salary Cap is determined by multiplying BRI by 44.74%, subtracting player benefit costs, and dividing by the number of clubs.[120] The Salary Cap for the 2016–2017 season is $94.143 million,[121] and is expected to be $102 million in 2017–18.[122] The NBA's Salary Cap is in the process of considerable growth due to new multi-billion dollar television contracts for the NBA.[123] Each club is required to pay its players a total of at least 90% of the Salary Cap each year.[124] The NBA's 2016–17 revenues are projected to be an estimated $8 billion.[125] Unlike the NFL's "hard" Salary Cap, the NBA's Salary Cap is considered "soft," because there are multiple exceptions that permit clubs to exceed the Salary Cap. These exceptions will be discussed below in detail in Section 3: Veteran Compensation.

In addition to the Salary Cap, the NBA also has a Tax Level. The Tax Level is a threshold for a club's player salaries that is above the Salary Cap. While the 2016–17 Salary Cap was $94.143 million, the Tax Level was $113.287 million.[126] The Tax Level is expected to rise to $122 million in 2017–18.[127] If clubs exceed the Tax Level, they must pay the league a graduated tax based on how much they have exceeded the Tax Level.[128] The Tax Levels increase if the club has exceeded the Tax Level in three or more of the previous four seasons (*i.e.,* a "Repeater").[129] Up to 50% of the total tax payments may be distributed, at the NBA's

option, to non-taxpaying clubs, and amounts not distributed to non-taxpaying clubs can be used for other league purposes.[130] If a club's total salaries are higher than the Salary Cap but lower than the Tax Level, *e.g.,* $100 million in 2016–17, the club would not make a tax payment.

Table 5-B:
NBA Tax Levels (Non-Repeater)

Incremental Club Salary Above Tax Level	Tax Rate for Increment
$0–$4,999,999	$1.50 for $1
$5,000,000–$9,999,999	$1.75 for $1
$10,000,000–$14,999,999	$2.50 for $1
$15,000,000–$19,999,999	$3.25 for $1
$20,000,000 and over	Tax rates increase by $0.50 for each additional $5,000,000 increment above the Tax level (e.g., for Team Salary $20,000,000 to $24,999,999 above the Tax level, the Tax rate is $3.75-for-$1 for that increment).

Table 5-C:
NBA Tax Levels (Repeater)

Incremental Club Salary Above Tax Level	Tax Rate for Increment
$0–$4,999,999	$2.50 for $1
$5,000,000–$9,999,999	$2.75 for $1
$10,000,000–$14,999,999	$3.50 for $1
$15,000,000–$19,999,999	$4.25 for $1
$20,000,000 and over	Tax rates increase by $0.50 for each additional $5,000,000 increment above the Tax level (e.g., for Team Salary $20,000,000 to $24,999,999 above the Tax level, the Tax rate is $4.75-for-$1 for that increment).

In 2015–16, seven NBA clubs exceeded the Tax Level and were required to pay a tax, with the Cleveland Cavaliers paying the most at approximately $54 million.[131]

2) ROOKIE COMPENSATION

The NBA Draft has two rounds. The initial contract entered into by a first round NBA Draft pick and the club that drafts the player is called a Rookie Scale Contract.[132] Rookie Scale Contracts must cover two seasons, with a club option for the third and fourth seasons.[133] Clubs must exercise the option for the third season by October 31 following the player's first season and must exercise the option for the fourth season by the October 31 following the player's second season.[134] The values of these contracts can be negotiated between 80% to 120% of the Rookie Scale, agreed to by the NBA and NBPA. There is a different Rookie Scale for each year of the CBA, with values increasing or decreasing annually at the same rate as any increase or decrease in the Salary Cap. The first pick in the NBA Draft is given the greatest Rookie Scale amount, with each subsequent pick receiving a lesser Rookie Scale amount. For illustrative purposes, the Rookie Scale amounts for the first and last three first round NBA Draft positions for the 2017–2018 season are as follows[135]:

Table 5-D:
Sample of NBA Rookie Scale (2017–2018)

Pick	1st Year Salary	2nd Year Salary	3rd Year Salary	4th Year Option (Percentage Increase over 3rd Year Salary)
1	$5,855,200	$6,949,900	$8,121,000	26.1%
2	$5,238,800	$6,218,300	$7,266,100	26.2%
3	$4,704,500	$5,584,000	$6,525,000	26.4%
***				
28	$1,179,100	$1,399,600	$1,635,300	80.5%
29	$1,170,500	$1,389,300	$1,623,400	80.5%
30	$1,162,100	$1,379,300	$1,611,800	80.5%

Second round Draft picks do not operate under any scale. They may sign for any amount at or above the minimum salary.[136] Second round Draft picks, however, generally only command a minimum salary or an amount slightly above the minimum.[137] Initial contracts for second-round Draft picks are commonly one, two, or three years in length.[138]

Similar to the NBA, NFL rookie contracts operate on a scale based on the Total Rookie Allocation. However, the NFL rookies' salaries are not collectively bargained in the way the NBA's rookies' salaries are.

3) VETERAN COMPENSATION

As in the NFL, there are two types of free agency in the NBA: unrestricted and restricted.[139] Unrestricted Free Agents are able to sign with any club after their prior contract has terminated and there is nothing that the player's prior club can do to prevent him from signing with a new club.[140] Players become Restricted Free Agents only in limited circumstances: (1) following the fourth year of a player's Rookie Scale Contract; and, (2) for non-first round picks, when the player's contract has expired and he has been in the NBA for three or fewer seasons.[141,n] In order to make a player who meets these qualifications a Restricted Free Agent, the club for which the player last played must make the player a one-year Qualifying Offer.[142] The value of the Qualifying Offer is based on, among other things, the player's Draft position.[143]

The Restricted Free Agent may choose to accept the club's Qualifying Offer. In most cases, if he accepts the Qualifying Offer, the player would become an Unrestricted Free Agent after he completes the one-year Qualifying Offer contract. If he does not want to sign a contract with the club for which he last played, the player may sign an offer sheet (which includes principal terms such as base salary, number of years, and signing bonus) with another club.[144] The offer

---

n   In the case of first round draft picks, the player would only become a restricted free agent if the club did not exercise its option to extend his rookie contract for the next season.

sheet must be for more than two seasons.[145] The player's prior club then has a right of first refusal for a two-day period.[146] If the player's prior club exercises its right of first refusal, then the player will be under contract with his prior club under the principal terms of the offer sheet.[147] If the prior club does not match the terms of the offer sheet and the player joins a new club, the prior club does not receive any compensation for the loss of the player. In contrast, in the NFL, clubs that lose Restricted Free Agents are awarded compensatory draft picks depending on the amount of the player's new contract.

As mentioned above, there are exceptions to the Salary Cap. While there are ten different exceptions,[148] we list here the most important ones (as summarized by the NBA with minor clarifying edits):[149]

1. Qualifying Veteran Free Agent ("Bird") Exception:[o] A team may re-sign its own free agent to a first-year salary of up to the maximum player salary if he played for the team for some or all of each of the prior three consecutive seasons (or, if he changed teams, he did so by trade).

2. Early Qualifying Veteran Free Agent ("Early Bird") Exception: A team may re-sign its own free agent to a first-year salary of up to the greater of (a) 175% of the player's salary in the last season of his prior contract; or, (b) 105% of the average NBA player salary for the prior season, if he played for the team for some or all of each of the prior two consecutive seasons (or, if he changed teams, if he did so by trade or by assignment via the NBA's waiver procedures). A contract signed using the Early Bird Exception must be for at least two seasons.

3. Non-Taxpayer Mid-Level Salary Exception:

   a. A team may use the Non-Taxpayer Mid-Level Salary Exception to sign one or more players to contracts with first-year salaries that, in the aggregate, provide for a total up to $8.406 million in 2017–18 (the Exception amount grows annually by the same amount as the Salary Cap).

   b. Contracts signed under the Non-Taxpayer Mid-Level Salary Exception can cover up to four seasons.

   c. A team can use the Non-Taxpayer Mid-Level Salary Exception to re-sign its own free agent (as well as to sign another team's free agent), but cannot use this Exception to acquire a player by assignment.

4. Minimum Salary Exception: A team may sign a player to a one-year or two-year contract at the applicable minimum player salary (prorated as appropriate for a 10-Day or Rest-of-Season contract). This Exception may also be used to acquire by assignment a player who was signed to a one-year or two-year minimum contract.

The Bird and Early Bird Exceptions are the most significant. These exceptions permit clubs to resign their best players for maximum or close to maximum salaries without regard to the Salary Cap. If other clubs wanted to sign these players to maximum contracts, those contracts would count against the Salary Cap. These rules provide a clear advantage to a player's prior club in free agency negotiations.

In contrast, the NFL's Salary Cap has no meaningful exceptions.[150]

4) MINIMUM, MAXIMUM, AND AVERAGE (MEAN) SALARIES

The minimum salary in the NBA depends on the player's experience level and increases each season. The minimum salaries for the 2016–17 season (under the 2011 CBA)[151] and the 2017-18 season (under the 2017 CBA)[152] are as follows:

Table 5-E:
NBA Minimum Salaries

Years of Service	2016–17 (2011 CBA)	2017–18 (2017 CBA)
0	$543,471	$815,615
1	$874,636	$1,312,611
2	$980,431	$1,471,382
3	$1,015,696	$1,524,305
4	$1,050,961	$1,577,230
5	$1,139,123	$1,709,538
6	$1,227,286	$1,841,849
7	$1,315,448	$1,974,159
8	$1,403,611	$2,106,470
9	$1,410,598	$2,116,995
10+	$1,551,659	$2,328,652

o   The exception is named for Boston Celtics legend Larry Bird as the rule is believed to have been created to help the Celtics resign Larry Bird in 1983, even though they never actually had to use the exception on Bird. Larry Coons, *Larry Coon's NBA Salary Cap FAQ*, CBA FAQ, http://www.cbafaq.com/salarycap.htm (last visited Feb. 21, 2017), *archived at* http://perma.cc/K9XV-FRTE.

Unlike the NFL, the NBA CBA includes limits on player salaries. A player who has completed fewer than seven Years of Service[p] has a maximum annual salary of 25% of the Salary Cap at the time of contract execution or 105% of the Salary for the final season of his prior contract, whichever is greater.[153] However, a player who has four Years of Service at the end of his Rookie Scale Contract, or a second-round pick or undrafted player who has four Years of Service following the end of the last season covered by his contract is eligible to receive, from his prior club only, 30% of the Salary Cap in effect at the time of contract execution, provided that the player has (i) been named twice to an All-NBA first, second, or third team or named Defensive Player of the Year, in the immediately preceding season or in two seasons during the immediately preceding three seasons, or (ii) been named as NBA MVP at least once during the preceding three seasons.[154]

A Player who has at least seven but less than ten Years of Service has a maximum annual salary of 30% of the Salary Cap in effect at the time of contract execution or 105% of the Salary Cap for the final season of his prior contract, whichever is greater.[155] A player with ten or more Years of Service has a maximum annual salary of 35% of the Salary Cap in effect at the time of contract execution or 105% of the Salary for the final season of his prior contract, whichever is greater.[156]

The 2017 CBA introduced an important exception to the rule limiting players with at least seven but less than ten Years of Service to 30% of the Salary Cap. Under the 2017 CBA,

> a player who has eight (8) or nine (9) Years of Service at the time the Contract is executed and rendered such Years of Service for the Team with which he first executed a Player Contract (or, if he was under a Player Contract for more than one Team during such period, changed Teams only by trade during the first four (4) Salary Cap Years in which he was under a Player Contract) shall be eligible to enter into a Designated Veteran Player Contract pursuant to which he receives from his Prior Team up to thirty-five percent (35%) of the Salary Cap in effect at the time the Contract is executed (the "Designated Veteran Player 35% Max Salary") if the player has met at least one of the following criteria at the time his Contract is executed: (i) the player was named to the All-NBA first, second, or third team, or was named

Defensive Player of the Year, in the immediately preceding Season or in two (2) Seasons during the immediately preceding three (3) Seasons; or (ii) the player was named NBA MVP during one of the immediately preceding three (3) Seasons (the "Designated Veteran Player 35% Max Criteria").[157]

The Designated Veteran Player rule was reportedly introduced in response to 2014 NBA MVP Kevin Durant leaving his original team, the Oklahoma City Thunder, for the Golden State Warriors prior to the 2016-17 season.[158] Had the rule existed at the time, the Thunder would have been able to offer Durant a contract with a higher annual salary than the Warriors which might have enticed him to stay with the club.

The mean annual salary in the NBA for the 2016–2017 NBA season is between $6.9 million and $8 million,[q] much more than the $2.7 mean salary for an NFL player. The median salary in the NBA for the 2016–2017 NBA season is between $4 million and $5 million. In 2016–17, the largest guaranteed contract in the NBA was Mike Conley's five-year deal worth $140,529,829 in gross value.[159] It is worth noting that NBA players generally have higher salaries than players in other professional sports leagues due, at least in part, to the fact that NBA rosters are much smaller. An NBA club's active roster is 12-13 players[160] while NFL active rosters are 46 players,[161] MLB active rosters are 25 players[162] and NHL active rosters are 23 players.[163]

Also unlike the NFL, the NBA CBA limits a veteran player's contract length. The default rule in the CBA is that a player contract may cover up to but no more than four seasons in length.[164] However, there are several instances where the CBA deviates from the default rule. For example, a player contract between a Qualifying Veteran Free Agent and his prior club may cover up to but not more than five seasons

---

p   A player is credited with a year of service for each year that he is on an NBA roster for at least one day during the regular season. 2017 NBA CBA, Art. I(iiii).

q   We rely on information from the NBA and spotrac.com in making this estimate. Spotrac.com, as of March 2017, maintained a database of 446 player contracts (including some partial-season contracts such as 10-day contracts) that demonstrated a mean salary of $6.9 million and a median salary of $4.0 million. See NBA Contracts, spotrac.com, http://www.spotrac.com/nba/contracts/ (last visited Mar. 13, 2017), archived at https://perma.cc/V7Y8-LA5M. In reviewing this Report, the NBA stated that the mean salary was approximately $8 million and the median salary was approximately $5 million. The NBA's determination of the mean salary is determined by dividing all player salaries by 396 players. 2017 NBA CBA, Art. 1, § 1(d). However, at any given time during the season, the number of players on NBA rosters is approximately 450. Thus, we believe the best statistics are likely somewhere between spotrac.com's and the NBA's. Basketball Reference, a well-regarded website, also provides data on this issue. Basketball Reference lists the mean NBA salary as $4.9 million and the median salary as $2.1 million. See 2016-2017 NBA Player Contracts, Basketball Reference, http://www.basketball-reference.com/contracts/players.html (last visited Mar. 13, 2017), archived at https://perma.cc/94UD-3RCG. However, Basketball Reference's salary database includes 607 contracts, far more than the approximately 450 NBA players on rosters at any given time, and also includes dozens of partial-season contracts for less than $100,000. Thus, we do not consider Basketball Reference's data sufficiently accurate to be used here.

and an extension of a Rookie Scale Contract may cover up to but no more than five seasons.[165] The mean contract length in the NBA during the 2016-17 season was 3.1 years.[166]

In sum, the contract rules provide significant advantages to a player's prior club. The prior club can offer a contract longer than other clubs and not have that contract count against the club's Salary Cap. In addition, players who have reached certain milestones, (such as All-NBA teams or MVP awards), are able to be paid a higher percentage of the Salary Cap by their prior club than by a new club. It is thus not surprising that the ten largest contracts in the NBA during the 2016–17 season were all contracts signed between a player and his existing club.[r]

---

5) GUARANTEED COMPENSATION

The NBA Uniform Player Contract ("UPC") permits NBA clubs to terminate a player's contract if the Player shall:

i   at any time, fail, refuse, or neglect to conform his personal conduct to standards of good citizenship, good moral character (defined here to mean not engaging in acts of moral turpitude, whether or not such acts would constitute a crime), and good sportsmanship, to keep himself in first class physical condition, or to obey the Team's training rules;

ii at any time commit a significant and inexcusable physical attack against any official or employee of the Team or the NBA (other than another player), or any person in attendance at any NBA game or event, considering the totality of the circumstances, including (but not limited to) the degree of provocation (if any) that may have led to the attack, the nature and scope of the attack, the Player's state of mind at the time of the attack, and the extent of any injury resulting from the attack;

iii at any time, fail, in the sole opinion of the Team's management, to exhibit sufficient skill or competitive ability to qualify to continue as a member of the Team . . . .; or

iv at any time, fail, refuse, or neglect to render his services hereunder or in any other manner materially breach this Contract.[167]

However, the CBA permits clubs and players to agree to "compensation protection," i.e., a guarantee of a player's contract in five circumstances, in the event of the player's: lack of skill; death; basketball-related injury; injury or illness; and, mental disability.[168] Compensation protections are negotiated terms in each player contract. However, the CBA requires that compensation protection be given in many circumstances. For sign-and-trade contracts,[s] the first season of the contract must be protected for lack of skill.[169] For Rookie Scale Contracts, all seasons must be protected for lack of skill and injury/illness for at least 80% of the player's Base Compensation.[170] Qualifying Offers made to a Restricted Free Agent must be protected for lack of skill and injury/illness.[171] Nevertheless, "[i]n practice, the majority of NBA contracts (especially for established veterans) are fully guaranteed. Non-guaranteed salary is most often used for fringe players (either at the beginning or end of their careers) or for the later years of long-term contracts (often in conjunction with benchmarks that allow the salary to become fully guaranteed over time)."[172] Data from spotrac.com gathered during January 2017 shows that 97.3% of NBA player compensation contracted for at that time was guaranteed,[173] as compared to about 44% of NFL player compensation.

While the NBA restricts clubs and players to compensation protection in just five scenarios, the NFL CBA does not limit the types of guarantees players and clubs can negotiate. Nevertheless, in practice, NFL contracts are generally only guaranteed against skill, injury, and Salary Cap. The fact that contracts in the NBA tend to be guaranteed more than those in the NFL is most likely a reflection of the leverage of the players in contract negotiations over time.

D) Compensation in the NHL

The most recent CBA agreed to by the NHL and National Hockey League Players Association ("NHLPA") was executed in 2013 and expires in 2022. In September 2019, both parties have the option of terminating the CBA, effective September 2020.[174]

---

r   The ten largest contracts in the 2016–17 season were: Mike Conley and the Memphis Grizzlies ($152.6m) Damian Lillard and the Portland Trailblazers ($139.9m); DeMar DeRozan and the Toronto Raptors ($139.0m); Bradley Beal and the Washington Wizards ($127.2m); Andre Drummond and the Detroit Piston ($127.2m); Anthony Davis and the New Orleans Pelicans ($127.2m); Carmelo Anthony and the New York Knicks ($124.0m); Nicolas Batum and the Charlotte Hornets ($120.0m); Chris Bosh and the Miami Heat ($118.7m); and, James Harden and the Houston Rockets ($118.0m). *NBA Contracts,* spotrac.com, http://www.spotrac.com/nba/contracts (last visited Jan. 30, 2017), *archived at* https://perma.cc/KR3K-M576.

s   A sign-and-trade contract is one in which a player signs with his prior club only to allow his prior club to then trade him to a new club. These transactions allow both clubs to take advantage of certain Salary Cap provisions, which ultimately benefits the player as well by enabling the desired transaction and contract.

1) THE NHL'S SALARY CAP

NHL players are collectively entitled to 50% of Hockey Related Revenues ("HRR").[175] Generally speaking, HRR "means the operating revenues . . . from all sources, whether known or unknown, whether now in existence or created in the future, . . . of each Club or the [NHL], . . . derived or earned from, relating to or arising directly or indirectly out of the playing of NHL hockey games or NHL-related events in which current NHL Players participate or in which current NHL Players' names and likenesses are used[.]"[176] The NHL's 2015–16 revenues were an estimated $4.1 billion.[177]

The NHL's Salary Cap structure includes both an Upper Limit and Lower Limit on club payrolls. To determine the Upper and Lower Limits, the parties multiply HRR by 50%, subtract player benefit costs, and then divide by the 30 NHL clubs to reach a midpoint.[178] The Lower Limit is reached by multiplying the midpoint by 85% and the Upper Limit is reached by multiplying the midpoint by 115%.

In the 2016–17 season, the Lower Limit is $54 million and the Upper Limit is $73 million.[179] Finally, the NHL's Salary Cap is considered "hard," because there are no exceptions permitting clubs to exceed the Salary Cap.

The NHL's Salary Cap is similar to the NFL's in that it has a hard upper limit (with a few exceptions) as well as setting some type of salary floor.

2) ROOKIE COMPENSATION

Almost all NHL rookies are "Group 1 Players"—players who signed their first contract between the ages of 18 and 24 and are still playing pursuant to the contract.[180] Group 1 Players are subject to the Entry Level System. The Entry Level System dictates the length of a player's rookie contract depending on the age at which the player first signed the contract:[181]

Table 5-F:

NHL Entry Level System

Age at First Contract Signing	Contract Length
18-21	3 years
22-23	2 years
24[t]	1 year

t   Players 25 and older are not subject to the Entry Level System and have no limits on their compensation. 2013 NHL CBA, § 9.1(b).

Group 1 Players' compensation may only take the form of NHL Paragraph 1 (base) salary,[182] signing bonuses, games-played bonuses, and performance bonuses.[183] The players' compensation in salary, signing bonuses and games-played bonuses cannot exceed $925,000 in any year of their first contract.[184] However, a player can negotiate with the club the opportunity to receive performance bonuses that can raise his compensation up to $3,775,000.[185] Moreover, the player is eligible for performance bonuses from the league that can raise his compensation several hundred thousand dollars.[186]

Once a player's rookie contract expires, he is no longer subject to the Entry Level System. At that point, the player is either subject to the club's exclusive rights or enters another Group depending on his age and experience level, as is explained next.

3) VETERAN COMPENSATION

Once a player is no longer subject to the Entry Level System, *i.e.*, his rookie contract has expired, he will typically transition from being a Group 1 Player into some other Group:

- **Group 2:** Players with expired contracts, who signed their first contract between the ages of 18 and 24 and have reached a certain level of experience: (1) for players who signed their first contract between the ages of 18 and 21, three years of minor league or NHL experience; (2) for players who signed their first contract between 22 and 23, two years of minor league or NHL experience; and, (3) for players who signed their first contract at 24 or older, one year of minor league or NHL experience.[187] Group 2 players are Restricted Free Agents, provided the club has made a Qualifying Offer.[188]

- **Group 3:** Players with expired contracts who have either played at least seven years in the NHL or are at least 27 years old.[189] Group 3 players are Unrestricted Free Agents.[190]

- **Group 4:** Players who, while still under contract, instead play in a league not affiliated with the NHL and then later try to return to the NHL.[191] Group 4 players are known as "Defected Players," and the NHL club from which the player defected retains the right to match any offer in the event the player returns to the NHL.

- **Group 5:** Players with expired contracts who have played at least ten years in the minor leagues or NHL and in the final year of their most recent contract did not earn more than the average salary.[192] Group 5 players are Unrestricted Free Agents,[193] but, in reality, any player who would meet the criteria for Group 5 status would already be a Group 3 player.[194]

The NHL and NHLPA nonetheless kept the Group 5 status in the CBA in the event it applied in future CBAs due to possible definitional or criteria changes.[195]

- **Group 6:** Players with expired contracts who are at least 25 years old, have played at least three seasons in the minor leagues, a European professional league while on loan from an NHL club, or the NHL and have played less than 80 NHL games (or 28 games if a goalie).[196] Group 6 players are Unrestricted Free Agents.[197]

In addition to the Groups listed above, clubs hold exclusive rights over their players who have an expired contract and less than three years of experience.[198] Provided the club offers the player a contract meeting certain criteria in the CBA, the player can only sign with his prior club.[199]

The NHL is the only Big Four league that takes age into consideration when determining free agent status.

In addition to the above-described scenarios, the NHL also has a salary arbitration mechanism for Restricted Free Agents. Players are eligible for salary arbitration depending upon the age at which they signed their first contract and their minor league, European league (while on loan from an NHL club) and NHL experience level:[200]

Table 5-G:
NHL Salary Arbitration Eligibility

Age at First Contract Signing	Minimum Years of Experience
18–20	4 years
21	3 years
22–23	2 years
24 and older	1 year

An eligible player is always entitled to elect salary arbitration,[201] while clubs can only elect salary arbitration in two situations. First, clubs can elect salary arbitration if the player's prior year salary exceeded $1,750,000,[202] a figure that is adjusted upward based on the mean salary in the league and equaled $1,953,297 in 2016. Second, the club can file for salary arbitration if an eligible player has not filed for salary arbitration by his July 5 deadline.[203] Once the salary arbitration process has commenced, the player and the club both then submit briefs on the player's value and can request either a one- or two-year contract, with some restrictions based on the player's experience level.[204] The arbitrator renders a decision within 48 hours and has

the discretion to choose the player's salary,[205] *i.e.*, unlike in MLB's salary arbitration process, the arbitrator is not bound to choose one side's position, but can determine the amount at his or her discretion.

4) MINIMUM, MAXIMUM, AND AVERAGE (MEAN) SALARIES

The minimum salary for an NHL player during the 2016–17 season is $575,000.[206]

As for maximum salaries, no player contract can provide for compensation in any year in excess of 20% of the Upper Limit.[207] In addition, NHL player contracts are restricted in terms of the variability of the salary over the term of the contract.[208] Generally speaking, these rules limit how much salaries can increase or decrease from year to year and prevent clubs from evading the Salary Cap. For purposes of counting a player's salary against the Salary Cap in any given year, the player's average salary over the term of the contract is used.[209] Thus, the variability rules prevent a club from adding years that the player is unlikely to play to the end of the contract for minimum compensation, which can have the effect of reducing the Salary Cap charge of the contract.

In 2010 (prior to the most recent CBA), the New Jersey Devils are alleged to have tried to do just that. The Devils and Ilya Kovalchuk agreed to a 17-year contract worth $102 million.[210] However, in the final five years of the contract, during which Kovalchuk would have been ages 39–44, Kovalchuk was due to earn only $550,000 per year, far short of the nearly $9 million per year that he was set to earn in the first 11 years of the contract.[211] The NHL invalidated the contract on the grounds that it was an illegal attempt to circumvent the Salary Cap, a decision that was upheld by an arbitrator.[212] The Kovalchuk case led to the creation of the variability rules in the 2013 CBA as well as a seven-year cap on player contract length (eight if the club is re-signing its own player).[213]

The NFL has some similar rules. Rookie contracts cannot increase more than 25% in the second year of the contract (to avoid possible circumvention of the Total Rookie Allocation),[214] and contracts extending beyond the life of the CBA cannot increase more than 30% (to avoid possible circumvention of the Salary Cap).[215]

The mean salary of an NHL player during the 2016–17 season was approximately $2,892,546,[216] slightly more than the estimated $2.7 million mean salary in the NFL. Additionally, the average contract was 3.5 years in length.[217]

5) GUARANTEED COMPENSATION

The NHL Standard Player Contract permits clubs to terminate player contracts at their discretion at certain times during the off-season.[218] This authority is broader than in the NFL CBA. However, in the NHL, if the club chooses to terminate the player's contract, it must "buy out" the player's contract. The portion of a player's salary that must be bought out is determined by his age. If the player is under 26 years of age at the time of termination, the club must pay the player, an amount equal to one-third of the player's base salary.[219] If the player is 26 years of age or older, the club must pay the player, an amount equal to two-thirds of the player's base salary.[220] Clubs must pay the buyout over twice as many years as are remaining on the term of the contract. Generally, clubs are still obligated to pay any amounts owed to the player in the form of a signing bonus even if they terminate the player's contract.[221]

In addition, unlike most NFL players' contracts, NHL players' contracts are guaranteed against injury. The Standard Player Contract provides that if a player is injured during the course of his employment as a hockey player and is subsequently unable to perform his duties as a hockey player, the club will continue to pay the player his base salary so long as the player is unable to play up until the expiration date of the contract.[222]

E) Compensation in the CFL

The most recent CBA agreed to by the CFL and the Canadian Football League Players Association ("CFLPA") was executed in 2014 and expires in 2019. The CFL CBA does not specify, but it stands to reason that all of the below amounts are in Canadian dollars.

1) THE CFL'S SALARY CAP

The CFL CBA sets both a maximum[223] and a minimum[224] amount each club can spend on player salaries:

Table 5-H:
CFL Salary Cap Ranges

Season	Range
2015	$4,450,000 – $5,050,000
2016	$4,500,000 – $5,100,000
2017	$4,550,000 – $5,150,000
2018	$4,600,000 – $5,200,00

By comparison, in 2016, the NFL's Salary Cap was $155.27 million,[225] more than 30 times than the that of the CFL (in Canadian dollars).

The 2006 CBA entitled players to 56% of league revenues.[226] However, this provision was eliminated in the 2010 CBA, which also included an increase in the Salary Cap.

The CFL's revenues in 2013 were estimated to be approximately $180 million, of which the players reportedly only received approximately 20%.[227] This number seems surprising considering the players' prior guarantee of 56% of revenues. Nevertheless, assuming the estimates of league revenue are accurate, the accuracy of the reported revenue split is borne out by simple calculations. There are nine teams in the CFL. Assuming all of them spent to the maximum of the Salary Cap in 2016, they would have spent $45,900,100 on player salaries collectively. That figure only represents only 25.5% of the CFL's estimated $180 million in revenue. The fact that three of the clubs make their financial statements public supports the estimate of the league's revenues.[228]

2) ROOKIE COMPENSATION

CFL rookies sign a one-year contract with a one-year club option.[229] If the club exercises the option, the contract must provide the player with at least the same level of salary and bonus payments (except signing bonus) that the player earned under the prior contract.[230] The club option can only be exercised once.[231]

3) VETERAN COMPENSATION

Upon expiration or termination of a player's rookie contract (including any option years), a player in the CFL becomes an Unrestricted Free Agent and can sign with any club without any compensation to the player's prior club.[232]

In contrast, NFL players are only Unrestricted Free Agents after the expiration of their rookie contract if they have obtained four Accrued Seasons—which would necessarily happen if the player plays until the expiration of his CBA-mandated four-year rookie contract.

4) MINIMUM, MAXIMUM, AND AVERAGE (MEAN) SALARIES

The minimum salary for an CFL player in the 2016 season was $52,000.[233] There are no maximum salaries in the CFL. Nevertheless, the Salary Cap imposes limitations on player salaries collectively.

The mean CFL player salary is approximately $80,000 per year.[234] This income is supplemented by signing bonuses and post-season playoff compensation.[235]

Many CFL players supplement their income with a secondary career, including the league's 2013 Most Outstanding Player, Calgary Stampeders running back Jon Cornish.[236] Although growth in league revenues suggests the number is decreasing, the Stampeders communications director estimated that 10% of the club's roster holds secondary jobs.[237] In 2014, the last year where such data was made public, the highest paid player in the CFL was reportedly B.C. Lions quarterback Travis Lulay, who earned a salary of approximately $450,000.[238]

5) GUARANTEED COMPENSATION

As a general matter, CFL contracts are not guaranteed.[239] The Standard Player Contract provides clubs the right to terminate the player's contract in five situations:

1 "in the opinion of the said Medical Committee, the Player is not completely fit to participate in football activities"[240];

2 "the Player fails at any time during the term of th[e] Contract to demonstrate sufficient skill and capacity to play football of the calibre required by the Club"[241];

3 "the Player's work or conduct in the performance of th[e] Contract is unsatisfactory"[242];

4 "where there exists a limit to the number permitted of a certain class of Player and the Player, being within that class, should not be included amongst the permitted number"[243]; and,

5 "termination of th[e] contract is in the best interest of the Club having regard for the competitiveness of the Club as a whole or the formation of a team with the greatest overall strength."[244]

These situations are very similar to the situations under which an NFL club can terminate a player's contract. Most importantly, both in the NFL and CFL, clubs can terminate contracts if the player is injured or no longer good enough.

Despite CFL clubs' termination rights, the CBA does provide certain veteran players with some level of protection. Players are entitled to 100% of their salary for the remainder of that season if their contract is terminated after a certain point in the season, depending on their level of experience:[245]

Table 5-I:
CFL Player Salary Protection Against Injury

Years of Experience	Required Games to Receive Salary
6 or more	9
5	10
4	11

The CFL's salary protection for certain veterans is similar to the NFL's Injury Protection[u] and Termination Pay[v] benefits.

Finally, CFL rookies receive signing bonuses which are typically considered guaranteed compensation. In 2015, the first overall pick of the CFL Draft, lineman Alex Mateas, received a signing bonus of $20,000.[246]

F) Compensation in MLS

MLS and the MLS Players Union ("MLSPU") agreed to the most recent CBA in 2015, which expires in 2020.

In analyzing the MLS compensation structure, it is important to understand how the labor relations dynamic between MLS and MLSPU is potentially different from that of the other sports leagues. MLS, formed in 1995, was structured in an effort to be considered a single-entity under the antitrust laws,[247] a distinction further explained below. In operational terms, rather than having each club owned and controlled by a different person or entity, as in the other sports leagues, all of the clubs in MLS are owned and controlled by Major League Soccer, LLC, a Delaware limited liability company.[248] Major League Soccer, LLC then has operator-investors, entities that have bought into MLS for the right to a certain amount of control over a single MLS club.[249] However, the amount of control is significantly less than in the other American sports leagues, as the clubs have to abide by strict MLS rules concerning

player compensation and transactions.[250] Generally, MLS negotiates the contracts with players and then allocates the players to the clubs,[251] or the clubs choose among the players hired by MLS.[252]

MLS' structure was designed to avoid the antitrust litigation and scrutiny common to the other professional sports leagues.[253] As we discussed in the beginning of this Chapter, Section 1 of the Sherman Antitrust Act prohibits contracts, combinations, or conspiracies that unreasonably restrain trade.[254] If an organization or joint venture is considered a single entity, there can be no multiplicity of parties agreeing to rules that might unreasonably restrain a market—such as the market for players' services through eligibility rules, a Salary Cap, or free agency rules as have often been the subjects of litigation in other leagues. In other words, without multiple parties there cannot be the contract, combination, or conspiracy necessary for antitrust scrutiny.[255]

Nevertheless, within a year of beginning play, in *Fraser v. Major League Soccer, L.L.C.,* several players sued MLS alleging that its rules on player compensation and mobility were violations of the antitrust laws. The United States District Court for the District of Massachusetts found that MLS was a single-entity and thus dismissed the plaintiffs' Section 1 antitrust claims.[256] The remainder of the plaintiffs' claims was dismissed after a jury found that the plaintiffs had failed to adequately allege a relevant market in which MLS had allegedly violated the antitrust laws.[257,w] On appeal, the United States Court of Appeals for the First Circuit was skeptical that MLS' structure constituted a single entity for purposes of antitrust law, but declared that the question "need not be answered definitively in this case."[258] The Court of Appeals nevertheless affirmed the dismissal of the plaintiffs' claims based on the jury's determination.[259] Thus, the effectiveness of MLS' efforts to be considered a single entity is questionable.

After the *Fraser* case, MLS players formed the MLSPU to negotiate terms and conditions of employment with MLS in a CBA.[260] However, without the clear threat of antitrust litigation (and the concomitant treble damages), the players and MLSPU potentially lack the authority and leverage of other professional sports unions.[261] But as MLS has grown both in revenues and clubs, control and financial investment by the operator-investors has increased, causing some to question whether MLS' operations are sufficiently

---

u   Where a player is injured in one season, fails the pre-season physical the next season because of that injury, and is terminated by the club as a result, the player is entitled to 50% of his salary for that season up to a maximum of $1.1 million in the 2015 season. If the player is still physically unable to play two seasons after the injury, he is entitled to 30% of his salary up to a maximum for $525,000 in 2015. A player is only entitled to Injury Protection once in his career. *See* 2011 NFL CBA, Art. 45.

v   A player with at least four years of experience who has his contract terminated after the first game of the season is entitled to the remainder of his salary for that season once in his career. 2011 NFL CBA, Art. 30.

w   The plaintiffs had also alleged that MLS had violated Section 2 of the Sherman Antitrust Act by monopolizing the market for the services of Division I professional soccer players in the United States, and Section 7 of the Clayton Act by combining in such a way as to substantially lessen competition. *See* Fraser v. Major League Soccer, L.L.C., 284 F.3d 47, 55 (1st Cir. 2002).

centralized to potentially be considered a single entity for purposes of antitrust law.[262]

In sum, because of MLS' structure, MLS—as compared to other professional sports leagues—is potentially less concerned that its rules concerning player compensation and employment are a violation of antitrust law, which would subject it to treble damages.[263] Consequently, MLS has more leverage in CBA negotiations with the MLSPU than other leagues do with their unions. This lack of union power is shown, in part, in MLS' compensation structures.

1) MLS' SALARY CAP

The Salary Cap for the 2017 season is $3,845,000,[264] and increases about 7% annually.[265] However, during the 2017 season, MLS clubs are permitted to acquire up to three players whose salaries exceed $480,625,[266] but whose salaries will only count against the Salary Cap in the amount of $457,500 (or less if they are under the age of 24).[267] These players, known as Designated Players, are considered important for MLS to attract and retain high-quality players who might otherwise play in Europe.[268] In the 2016 season, there were 49 designated players.[269] The 46 Designated Players for whom salary information is available earned an average of $1,766,329.[270] Of the 49 designated players, only 9 were American-born.[x]

MLS' revenues are approximately $600 million per year,[271] less than 5% of the NFL's approximately $14 billion in annual revenue.

2) ROOKIE COMPENSATION

Unlike the Big Four leagues, MLS does not have compensation rules specific to rookies.

3) VETERAN COMPENSATION

Prior to the 2015 CBA, veteran MLS players had no free agency. Under the old system, players with expired contracts could be redrafted by other MLS clubs without any say in where they were assigned.[272] The 2015 CBA initiated a limited form of free agency. Players with expired contracts who are 28 or older and have played at least eight years in MLS now have the ability to select their MLS club.[273] The players' salaries will be restricted based on their prior salaries: players who previously made more than $200,000

can receive a 15% increase; players who made between $100,000 and $200,000 can receive a 20% increase; and, players who made less than $100,000 can receive a 25% increase.[274]

4) MINIMUM, MAXIMUM, AND AVERAGE (MEAN) SALARIES

The minimum salary in MLS for the 2016 season was $62,500 per year.[275]

There is no maximum player salary in MLS.[276] However, the maximum amount a player's salary can count against the Salary Cap is $457,500 (unless they are a Designated Player).[277] There are also complicated accounting mechanisms by which clubs can "buy down" a player's Salary Cap charge.[278]

The mean salary of an MLS player in 2016 was $290,246, and the median salary was $108,900.[279] However, the average salary figure is skewed by the distribution of salaries. Out of 558 MLS players, 22 of them made $1 million per year or more, with four players (Michael Bradley, Gerrard Steven, Frank Lampard, and Kaka) making $6 million per year or more.[280] When these 22 players are removed from the calculation as outliers, the average salary of the remaining 536 players is only $169,886.[281] Similarly, when the salaries of the 46 Designated Players for whom salary information was available in 2016 are removed as outliers, the average salary drops to $156,847.[282] Due to these wide disparities in player income, the MLSPU made it a priority to try and establish a "middle class" in MLS, including by providing for some form of free agency and raising the minimum salary.[283]

5) GUARANTEED COMPENSATION

The contract of any player 24 years old or older who has at least one year of playing experience is automatically guaranteed,[284] meaning that it cannot be terminated "solely because of the quality of the Player's on-field performance or the fact that the Player may have sustained an injury during the performance of his duties as an MLS Player."[285] As a result, the majority of MLS player contracts are guaranteed.[286]

In 2016, the average MLS player contract had an average of $317,892 in guarantees.[287] However, if one removes the 46 Designated Players for whom there was salary information as outliers, MLS player contracts contain, on average, $168,821 in guaranteed compensation.[288]

---

x   The American-born players were Jozy Altidore, DaMarcus Beasley, Alejandro Bedoya, Matt Besler, Michael Bradley, Clint Dempsey, Maurice Edu, Tim Howard, and Graham Zusi.

G) Analysis

The below table summarizes some of the key provisions and figures concerning compensation structures in professional sports, subject to the various nuances and intricacies discussed above.

Table 5-J:

Comparisons of Leagues' Compensation Statistics and Policies

Benefit	NFL	MLB	NBA	NHL	CFL	MLS
Mean Annual Salary	$2.7 million	$4.25 million	$6.9-8 million	$2.89 million	$80,000	$290,246
Mean Career Length	5.0 years[289]	5.6 years[290]	4.8 years[291]	5.6 years[292]	3.2 years[293]	3.2 years[y]
Minimum Salary (2016)	$450,000	$507,500	$543,471	$575,000	$52,000	$62,500
Maximum Salary	No	No	Yes	Yes	No	No
Maximum Contract Length	No	No	Yes	Yes	No	No
Unrestricted Free Agency Rights	After four seasons	After six seasons	After five seasons for first round picks	Depends on age and experience	Upon expiration of rookie contract	28 years old and eight years of experience
Guaranteed Compensation	~ 44%	~ 100%	~ 90%	For injury and one-third or two-thirds of the player's salary	Almost none	For players 24 and older with 1+ years' experience
Salary Cap Type	Hard	Luxury Tax	Soft and Luxury Tax	Hard	Hard	Soft
Guaranteed Share of Revenue	Yes	No	Yes	Yes	No	No

At the beginning of this Chapter, we identified two key ways in which compensation and compensation structures affect player health: (1) influencing players' decisions about playing with injuries; and, (2) players' retirement planning and eventual retirement. We are most concerned with how compensation and compensation structures affect player behavior and decision-making concerning their health, *i.e.*, what are the consequences of the current compensation regimes on players' short- and long-term health. Unfortunately, these are questions that we cannot fully answer at the present.

To effectively and rigorously compare how the different leagues' compensation structures affect player health decisions would require the ability to control for the various levers, including free agency rules, salary and contract

y   Nick Schwartz, *The average career earnings of athletes across America's major sports will shock you*, For the Win Blog—USA Today (Oct. 24, 2013, 10:07 AM), http://ftw.usato-day.com/2013/10/average-career-earnings-nfl-nba-mlb-nhl-mls, *archived at* http://perma.cc/J8QL-Q3RG. Nevertheless, as pointed by the MLPSU in its review of this Report, the author of this article did not indicate how he arrived at the 3.2 years statistic. Moreover, MLSPU Executive Director Bob Foose stated that "this number is significantly misleading given the global nature of soccer (there are, I believe, professional leagues in over 80 countries around the world, typically with multiple such leagues in each country). We have not consistently tracked the total average career length of MLS players, but when we last did an exhaustive study, in 2013, the average MLS player (whose career was over) had played a total of just under 8.8 years of professional soccer over the course of that career. We haven't updated these numbers since then, but I don't have any reason to believe that these numbers have changed significantly." We believe this is a valid point and thus suggest caution in considering the mean career length of MLS players. Athletes in the other leagues rarely play in multiple professional leagues and thus the same concern is not present.

limitations, salary cap structure, and the level of guaranteed compensation. Additionally, one would likely also want to be able to control for other relevant factors, such as career length, career earnings and injury outcomes. The type and amount of health-related benefits, discussed at length in Chapter 3, also impact player compensation structures. Each of the leagues' compensation structures is an amalgam of these various levers and factors. This is a challenging analysis that requires more data than is currently available and thus we cannot fairly assess which leagues' overall compensation structures among the Big Four are best for players.[z]

There is, however, one compensation issue that is the subject of frequent discussion and thus merits further analysis: guaranteed compensation. As discussed above, many people believe that NFL player health could be improved through guaranteeing more of their compensation. The belief is that by guaranteeing a player's future compensation, he will not feel pressured to play through injuries to protect his status on the club. On this and related issues, many would argue that MLB's system is the most player-friendly, because compensation is almost entirely guaranteed, there is no

hard Salary Cap, there is no maximum salary, and, there is no maximum contract length.[294] It is thus not surprising that, as of February 2017, the 23 largest contracts among these sports leagues are all for MLB players.[aa] However, MLB players are not guaranteed a share of the revenue like in other leagues and must wait six years before becoming an Unrestricted Free Agent, the longest wait of the Big Four and thus it is not clear that their compensation arrangement is preferable.

The NFL and NFLPA are frequently criticized—by players,[295] the media[296] and academics, among others—for what is perceived as the lack of guaranteed contracts as compared to the other leagues.[297] However, the issue is complicated. As a preliminary matter, when discussing the compensation paid to players, one must also consider the benefits the players receive. As is discussed in Chapter 3 of this Report, the NFL generally provides a benefits package superior to those offered in all of the other leagues. The additional complications on this issue are discussed below in the Recommendation Section.

---

z   The CFL and MLS cannot realistically be compared to the Big Four due to their relatively small amounts of revenue and also the MLS' attempted single-entity structure.

aa Information about salaries and contracts was derived from data available on spotrac.com, the most reliable public source for information about professional sports contracts based on our analysis. Indeed, as of February 2017, there are 41 MLB contracts worth over $100 million while there are only 18 such contracts in the NBA, 12 in the NFL, and three in the NHL.

H) Recommendation

Recommendation 5-A: The NFL and NFLPA should research the consequences and feasibility of guaranteeing more of players' compensation as a way to protect player health.

As discussed above, guaranteed compensation in the NFL is a complicated issue. While many people—and players in particular—have expressed a desire for increased guaranteed compensation, it is not clear that fully guaranteed compensation would be beneficial to players *collectively* such that it ought to be preferred to the status quo.

As a preliminary matter, the NFLPA itself has expressed mixed views about the guaranteed contracts. In a 2002 editorial in *The Washington Post*, then-NFLPA Executive Director Gene Upshaw acknowledged that the possibility of guaranteed contracts "is severely undermined by the risk of a career-ending injury" and touted the benefits available to players as an alternative.[298] Then, in two reports issued by the NFLPA in or around 2002 and 2007 respectively, the NFLPA asserted that NFL player compensation is, in fact, largely guaranteed by explaining that more than half of all compensation *paid* to players is guaranteed.[299] However, importantly, this statistic does not mean that half of all compensation *contracted* was guaranteed—indeed, as discussed above, approximately 44% of all contracted compensation is guaranteed. Players are often paid guaranteed money (*e.g.*, a signing bonus or roster bonus) in the first or second year of the contract only to have the base salaries (the unguaranteed portions) in the later years of the contract go unpaid because the player's contract was terminated.

With this background in mind, there are several reasons why fully guaranteed compensation might not be beneficial to players *collectively*. First, while fully guaranteed contracts might be good for the players who receive them, it could result in many players not receiving any contract at all. If clubs were forced to retain a player of diminishing skill because his contract was guaranteed, a younger or less proven player might never get the opportunity to sign with the club.[300] Relatedly, clubs might continue to provide playing opportunities to the players with larger contracts in order to justify those contracts, preventing younger players from establishing themselves as starting or star players and earning higher salaries. It is also likely that under a system of guaranteed compensation, player salaries would decrease (at least in the short-term)—particularly the salaries of the highest paid players and players who are less certain to add value to a roster—as clubs would be more cautious about taking on the financial liabilities, especially given the Salary Cap in place in the NFL. Similarly, clubs also may seek to minimize their financial liabilities by reducing roster sizes, which might cost marginal players their jobs, while again reducing opportunities for young or unproven players to join a club.

There are also logistical challenges to implementing fully guaranteed contracts. The finances and operations of the NFL and its clubs are greatly intertwined with the fact that NFL contracts have never been fully guaranteed. Since 1993, NFL clubs have had to comply with a strict Salary Cap that necessarily influences the types of contracts clubs are willing to offer, including the possibility of guaranteed compensation. Fully guaranteed contracts would be a fundamental and monumental alteration to the current business of the NFL that, at a minimum, would require a gradual phasing in process.[ab]

It is possible that a rate of guaranteed contracts less than 100% but more than the current 44% is also optimal. Given the varying factors to be weighed and considered, it is not clear what percentage of guaranteed compensation would maximize player health for the most NFL players.

Clearly this is a complex issue, with the potential for substantial unintended consequences. Thus, we recognize the likely health value of guaranteed contracts, while simultaneously recognizing that it may not be the right solution for all players. Importantly, as discussed above, players who value a contractual guarantee over potentially higher but uncertain compensation may negotiate for that protection individually, as many currently do. Moreover, we expect that other

---

ab For example, one rule that would likely have to be removed is the NFL's requirement that clubs deposit into a separate account the present value, less $2 million, of guaranteed compensation to be paid in future years. 2011 CBA, Art. 26 § 9. Former NFL club executive Andrew Brandt believes clubs "hide behind" the funding rule to avoid guaranteeing player compensation, and have been largely successful in doing so. Andrew Brandt, Supplemental Peer Review Response (Nov. 6, 2015).

Recommendations Concerning Compensation – continued

recommendations made in this Report and, more importantly, our other Report, *Protecting and Promoting the Health of NFL Players: Legal and Ethical Analysis and Recommendations*, including key recommendations related to the medical professionals who care for players,[301] if adopted, would make great strides toward protecting and promoting player health such that guaranteed compensation would be less critical for that purpose.

Ultimately, we recommend further research into this question, including player and club perspectives, economic and actuarial analysis, and comprehensive consideration of the relevant trade-offs, ramifications, and potential externalities. In the meantime, we note that the trend toward greater use of contractual guarantees can help promote individual player health and allow individual negotiation by players based on their own goals and priorities.

Endnotes

1   *See, e.g.,* Josh Alper, *Sean Lee says it was his call to sit with $2 million on the line,* ProFootballTalk (Jan. 4, 2016, 10:46 AM), http://profootballtalk.nbcsports.com/2016/01/04/sean-lee-says-it-was -his-call-to-sit-with-2-million-on-the-line/, *archived at* https://perma.cc /69QS-FVPH.

2   *See* Thomas Richardson, Peter Elliotta, & Ronald Roberts, *The relation-ship between personal unsecured debt and mental and physical health: A systematic review and meta-analysis,* 33 Clinical Psychol. Rev. 8, 1148-62 (2013). Many experts have recognized that "financial insecurity can cause people to 'cut corners in ways that may affect their health and well-being,' like spending less on food, clothing, or prescrip-tions." Nadia N. Sawicki, *Modernizing Informed Consent: Expanding the Boundaries of Materiality,* Univ. Ill. L. Rev. (2016), *citing* Kevin R. Riggs, Peter A. Ubel, *Overcoming Barriers to Discussing Out-of-Pocket Costs With Patients,* 174 Jama Int. Med. 849 (2014); Peter A. Ubel, Amy P. Ab-ernethy, S. Yousuf Zafar, *Full Disclosure — Out-of-Pocket Costs as Side Effects,* 369 New Eng. J. Med. 1484 (2013). Indeed, to many, "financial well-being is certainly within the boundaries of most peoples' concept of health." *Id., quoting* Michael S. Wilkes & David L. Schriger, *Caution: The Meter is Running: Informing Patients About Health Care Costs,* 165 Western J. Med. 74, 78 (1996) (noting that "discussions about the cost of care are an important part of the physician-patient relationship").

3   *See, e.g.,* Melissa B. Jacoby, Teresa A. Sullivan, Elizabeth Warren, *Rethinking the Debates over Health Care Financing: Evidence from the Bankruptcy Courts,* 76 N.Y.U. L. Rev. 375 (2001) (empirical data demonstrating how many American families declare bankruptcy in the aftermath of illness or other healthcare crisis); Christopher Tarver Robertson, Richard Egelhof, Michael Hoke, *Get Sick, Get Out: The Medical Causes of Home Mortgage Foreclosures,* 18 Health Matrix 65 (2008) (empirically demonstrating and discussing the role that health crises have in home foreclosures).

4   *See, e.g.,* 2011 NFL CBA, Art. 1 ("'Salary Cap' means the absolute maxi-mum amount of Salary that each Club may pay or be obligated to pay or provide to players . . . at any time during a particular League Year"); 2017 NBA CBA, Art. 1, § 1(mmm) ("'Salary Cap' means the maximum allowable Team Salary for each Team for a Salary Cap Year, subject to the rules and exceptions set forth in [the CBA]").

5   The National League had begun play in 1876 and the American League in 1901. MLB was the result of a merger between the two leagues.

6   Joshua P. Jones, *A Congressional Swing and Miss: The Curt Flood Act, Player Control, and the National Pastime,* 33 Ga. L. Rev. 639, 642 (1999).

7   *Id.*

8   *See* American Needle, Inc. v. Nat'l Football League, 560 U.S. 183, 186 (2010), *citing* 15 U.S.C. § 1.

9   Fed. Baseball Club of Balt., Inc. v. Nat'l League of Prof'l Baseball Clubs, 259 U.S. 200 (1922).

10 *See* Nathaniel Grow, *Defining the "Business of Baseball": A Proposed Framework for Determining the Scope of Professional Baseball's Anti-trust Exemption,* 44 U.C. Davis L. Rev. 557, 566 (2010).

11 *See* Toolson v. N.Y. Yankees, 346 U.S. 356 (1953).

12 *See* Flood v. Kuhn, 407 U.S. 258 (1972).

13 *See id.* at 284.

14 In Radovich v. Nat'l Football League, 352 U.S. 445 (1957), the Supreme Court held that the NFL was not exempt from the antitrust laws. In Haywood v. Nat'l Basketball Ass'n, 401 U.S. 1204 (1971), the Supreme Court held that the NBA was not exempt from the antitrust laws. Lower courts have subsequently refused to extend baseball's antitrust exemption to professional hockey, Phila. World Hockey Club, Inc. v. Phila. Hockey Club, Inc., 351 F. Supp. 462, 466 n.3 (E.D. Pa. 1972); profes-sional golf, Blalock v. Ladies Prof'l Golf Ass'n, 359 F. Supp. 1260, 1263

(N.D. Ga. 1973); and professional tennis, Gunter Harz Sports, Inc. v. U.S. Tennis Ass'n, 665 F.2d 222, 223 (8th Cir. 1981).

15 *See* Chris Deubert & Glenn M. Wong, *Understanding the Evolution of Signing Bonuses and Guaranteed Money in the National Football League: Preparing for the 2011 Collective Bargaining Negotiations,* 16 UCLA Ent. L. Rev. 179, 187 (2009) (describing the various legal proceedings lead-ing to free agency in those sports).

16 *See* Glenn M. Wong, *Essentials of Sports Law,* Exs. 11.3–11.6 (4th ed. 2010) (providing CBA history for each of the Big Four leagues).

17 *See* Chris Deubert, Glenn M. Wong, John Howe, *All Four Quarters: A Ret-rospective and Analysis of the 2011 Collective Bargaining Process and Agreement in the National Football League,* 19 UCLA Ent. L. Rev. 1, 9–12 (2012) (discussing NFL-NFLPA labor relations between 1987 and 1993).

18 The NFL currently has television broadcasting agreements with ESPN, NBC, CBS, FOX, NFL Network and DirecTV. In addition, the NFL has a radio broadcasting agreement with Westwood One. In total, the broad-casting agreements bring in approximately $7 billion in annual revenue to the NFL. Kurt Badenhausen, *The NFL Signs TV Deals Worth $27 Billion,* Forbes (Feb. 14, 2011, 6:13PM), http://www.forbes.com/sites/ kurtbadenhausen/2011/12/14/the-nfl-signs-tv-deals-worth-26-billion/, *archived at* http://perma.cc/8PXK-2VNU.

19 NFL Ventures is responsible for negotiating all of the league's major sponsorship, marketing, and media rights deals. NFL Ventures, which Commissioner Goodell ran before becoming Commissioner, includes four wholly-owned subsidiaries: NFL Enterprises, NFL Properties, NFL Productions, and NFL International. *See* Tommy Craggs, *Exclusive: Leaked Documents Show Operating Profits for NFL Ventures Rose 29 Percent Last Year,* Deadspin (July 15, 2011, 1:10 PM), http://deadspin .com/5821386/audited-financials-operating-profit-for-nfl-ventures-lp -rose-from-999-million-to-13-billion-last-year, *archived at* http://perma .cc/3MNZ-XHLU.

20 NFL Network is the league-owned and operated television network de-voted full-time to the NFL, including broadcasting select Thursday night games. For more information, see www.nfl.com/nflnetwork.

21 NFL Properties is responsible for licensing, sponsorship, and market-ing. NFL Properties was the subject of Am. Needle, Inc. v. Nat'l Football League, 560 U.S. 183 (2010). NFL Properties was created by the 32 individual clubs to collectively market and license the clubs' individual intellectual property, such as names, colors, logos, and trademarks. In 2000, the clubs — through NFL Properties — granted Reebok an exclusive license to produce and sell trademarked headwear for the 32 clubs. American Needle — a former licensee and creator of NFL appar-eled headwear — could no longer create headwear with NFL logos and trademarks. American Needle challenged the exclusive license as an illegal restraint of trade by the 32 NFL clubs. The Northern District of Il-linois granted the NFL summary judgment after finding that NFL Proper-ties constituted a single entity for antitrust purposes, and therefore there was no contract, combination, or conspiracy to restrain trade. *See* Am. Needle, Inc. v. New Orleans La. Saints, 496 F. Supp. 2d 941, 943 (N.D. Ill. 2007). The Seventh Circuit affirmed. Am. Needle, Inc. v. Nat'l Football League, 538 F. 3d 736 (7th Cir. 2008). The Supreme Court reversed. Am. Needle, 560 U.S. 183. While the Court noted that NFL clubs "depend upon a degree of cooperation for economic survival," the necessity of cooperation does not transform concerted action into the independent action of a single entity. *Id.* at 198. Furthermore, that "even if league-wide agreements are necessary to produce football, it does not follow that concerted activity in marketing intellectual property is necessary to produce football." *Id.* at n.7.

22 NFL Enterprises is responsible for advertising, publicizing, promoting, marketing, and selling broadcasts of NFL games.

23 NFL Productions, also known as NFL Films, is the league-owned film

company that for over 50 years has produced award-winning films about the NFL. For more information see www.nflfilms.com.

24 NFL Digital is responsible for the league's technology and new media ventures, including www.nfl.com and NFL Mobile.

25 NFL CBA, Art. 12, § 6.

26 NFL CBA, Art. 12, §1, § 6.

27 Mike Florio, *NFL will reach $14 billion in 2017 revenue*, ProFootball-Talk (Mar. 6, 2017, 11:29 AM), http://profootballtalk.nbcsports.com /2017/03/06/nfl-will-reach-14-billion-in-2017-revenue/, *archived at* https://perma.cc/X57A-VRXU.

28 NFL CBA, art. 12, § 6(c)(ii).

29 NFL CBA, Art. 12, § 6(c)(i).

30 NFL CBA, Art. 1.

31 NFL CBA, Art. 12, § 2.

32 NFL CBA, Art. 12, § 6(c)(v).

33 *Adjusted Team Salary Caps*, NFLPA (Mar. 7, 2016), https://www.nflpa .com/news/all-news/2016-adjusted-team-salary-caps, *archived at* https://perma.cc/K9GZ-ZDGN.

34 Josh Alper, *Salary cap set at $167 million*, ProFootballTalk (Mar. 1, 2017, 11:12 AM), http://profootballtalk.nbcsports.com/2017/03/01/salary-cap -set-at-167-million/, *archived at* https://perma.cc/7W45-ERVP.

35 In reality, the NFL Salary Cap does permit for one exception for veteran players playing for the minimum salary. Players with at least four Credited Seasons who sign for the league minimum will only have their salary count against the Salary Cap as if the player only had two Credited Seasons. 2011 NFL CBA, Art. 27. This exception discourages clubs from hiring younger players over experienced veterans simply because they are younger. Also, each club's Salary Cap is uniquely based upon whether certain incentives were earned by the club's players in the previous season. 2011 NFL CBA, Art. 13, § 6(c)(ii–iii).

36 NFL CBA, Art. 12, § 9(a).

37 NFL CBA, Art. 12, § 8(b).

38 Chris Deubert & Glenn Wong, *All Four Quarters: A Retrospective And Analysis Of The 2011 Collective Bargaining Process And Agreement In The National Football League*, 19 UCLA Ent. L. Rev. 1, 52 (2012), *citing Rams Give Bradford 50M Guaranteed*, ESPN (July 31, 2010, 9:09 AM), http://sports.espn.go.com/nfl/news/story?id=5425041, *archived at* http://perma.cc/BZW8-GNTH.

39 Chris Deubert & Glenn Wong, *All Four Quarters: A Retrospective And Analysis Of The 2011 Collective Bargaining Process And Agreement In The National Football League*, 19 UCLA Ent. L. Rev. 1, 52 (2012), *citing Tom Brady Signs Extension*, ESPN (Sept. 11, 2010, 3:13 PM), http:// sports.espn.go.com/boston/nfl/news/story?id=5552561, *archived at* http://perma.cc/X69A-2G33.

40 *See* Chris Deubert & Glenn Wong, *All Four Quarters: A Retrospective And Analysis Of The 2011 Collective Bargaining Process And Agreement In The National Football League*, 19 UCLA Ent. L. Rev. 1, 52–60 (2012) (discussing changes to rookie compensation as part of 2011 CBA).

41 NFL CBA, Art. 7 § 3(a).

42 *Id.*

43 *Id.*

44 NFL CBA, Art. 7, § 1(e).

45 *See* Chris Deubert & Glenn Wong, *All Four Quarters: A Retrospective And Analysis Of The 2011 Collective Bargaining Process And Agreement In The National Football League*, 19 UCLA Ent. L. Rev. 1, 58–60 (2012). The formula for calculating the Total Rookie Allocation and each player's portion of the Total Rookie Allocation are intended to be secret to provide the clubs and players a range within which to negotiate a contract. However, prior to the 2011 League Year, an NFLPA employee inadvertently sent to all contract advisors the 2011 Total Rookie Allocations for each club, including for each drafted player. Consequently, all of the contract advisors and clubs knew the total amount of compensation each rookie was to receive. Additionally, the Salary Cap and Total Rookie Allocation

increase by the same percentage each year. Thus, contract advisors and clubs can easily determine a drafted player's share of the Total Rookie Allocation by examining the 2011 Total Rookie Allocations and increasing them the same percentage as the Salary Cap increased each year (a figure that is made public). *Id.*

46 *See* 2011 CBA, Art. 7 § 3(e) (prohibiting "option bonuses, option exercise fees, option nonexercise fees, Salary Advances . . . voidable year(s) provisions, buybacks of voidable year(s) provisions, and any 'contract within the contract' (i.e. terms and conditions of a contemplated superseding contract within the Rookie Contract)."); Chris Deubert & Glenn Wong, *All Four Quarters: A Retrospective And Analysis Of The 2011 Collective Bargaining Process And Agreement In The National Football League*, 19 UCLA Ent. L. Rev. 1, 52–60 (2012) (discussing changes to rookie compensation as part of 2011 CBA).

47 *See* Chris Deubert & Glenn Wong, *All Four Quarters: A Retrospective And Analysis Of The 2011 Collective Bargaining Process And Agreement In The National Football League*, 19 UCLA Ent. L. Rev. 1, 60–61 (2012).

48 *Id.* at 57–58. The Performance Incentive theoretically has the possibility of players risking injury to reach the playtime threshold necessary to earn the bonus. While this possibility exists, it is only one of many pressures that players feel to continue playing. Additionally, players are generally unlikely to know their cumulative playtime percentages during the season.

49 Michael David Smith, *Jared Goff expected to sign with Rams today*, ProFootballTalk (June 9, 2016, 10:00 AM), http://profootballtalk.nbcsports .com/2016/06/09/jared-goff-expected-to-sign-with-rams-today/, *archived at* https://perma.cc/3JBL-LSUY.

50 *Kalan Reed*, Spotrac, http://www.spotrac.com/nfl/tennessee-titans/kalan -reed/ (last visited June 23, 2016), *archived at* http://perma.cc/BY5K -PJ94.

51 *Id.*

52 NFL CBA, Art. 8, § 1.

53 *Id.*

54 NFL CBA, Art 1.

55 NFL CBA, Art. 8, § 2.

56 Weston Hodkiewicz, *Safety Banjo re-signs*, Green Bay Press-Gazette, Apr. 18, 2015, *available at* 2015 WLNR 11354235.

57 NFL CBA, Art. 9, § 2.

58 *See id.*

59 Curtis Crabtree, *Jermaine Kearse signs restricted free agent tender with Seahawks*, ProFootballTalk (May 5, 2015, 11:42 PM), http://profootballtalk.nbcsports.com/2015/05/05/jermaine-kearse-signs -restricted-free-agent-tender-with-seahawks/, *archived at* http://perma .cc/N78Z-ZJAM.

60 NFL CBA, Art. 1 ("'Unrestricted Free Agent' means a Veteran with four or more Accrued Seasons, who has completed performance of his Player Contract"); 2011 CBA, Art. 8, § 1 ("a player shall receive one Accrued Season for each season during which he was on, or should have been on, full pay status for a total of six or more regular season games").

61 NFL CBA, Art. 9, § 1(a).

62 *See* James Walker, *Breaking down Ndamukong Suh's record-setting contract*, ESPN, Mar. 12, 2015, http://espn.go.com/blog/nflnation/post/_ /id/163930/breaking-down-ndamukong-suhs-record-setting-contract, *archived at* http://perma.cc/GD65-SFMV.

63 NFL CBA, Art. 9 § 2(b).

64 For example, in 2015, former Detroit Lion Ndamukong Suh signed a six-year deal with the Miami Dolphins for $114 million, $60 million of which was guaranteed. Josh Alper, *Dolphins make it official with Ndamukong Suh*, ProFootballTalk (Mar. 11, 2015, 4:14 PM), http://profootballtalk .nbcsports.com/2015/03/11/dolphins-make-it-official-with-ndamukong -suh/, *archived at* http://perma.cc/2T5Z-367S.

65 *See* Chris Deubert & Glenn M. Wong, *Understanding the Evolution of Signing Bonuses and Guaranteed Money in the National Football League:*

Preparing for the 2011 Collective Bargaining Negotiations, 16 UCLA Ent. L. Rev. 179, 190–97 (2009) (discussing the different types of bonuses common in NFL player contracts).

66 *See* 2011 NFL CBA, Art. 13, § 6(c) (listing incentives permitted to be included in NFL players).

67 *See* Bert Bell/Pete Rozelle NFL Player Retirement Plan (Apr. 1, 2012) § 1.11 (defining "Credited Season"); 2011 NFL CBA, Art. 26, § 2 (same).

68 Gregg Rosenthal, *Winners, Losers from the NFL Lockout*, ProFootballTalk (July 25, 2011, 3:15 PM), http://profootballtalk.nbcsports.com/2011/07/25/winners-losers-from-the-nfl-lockout/, *archived at* http://perma.cc/FB28-XHSF.

69 NFL CBA, Art. 13, § 6(b)(i).

70 *Id.*

71 *See* James Walker, *Breaking down Ndamukong Suh's record-setting contract*, ESPN, Mar. 12, 2015, http://espn.go.com/blog/nflnation/post/_/id/163930/breaking-down-ndamukong-suhs-record-setting-contract, *archived at* http://perma.cc/GD65-SFMV.

72 *See* Sally Jenkins, *NFL's concussion priorities: Dodging blame, making players responsible*, Wash. Post, Dec. 3, 2015, https://www.washingtonpost.com/sports/redskins/nfls-concussion-priorities-dodging-blame-making-players-responsible/2015/12/03/1b8752f8-99d2-11e5-94f0-9eeaff906ef3_story.html, *archived at* https://perma.cc/JT6P-JX44 ("The heart of the NFL's concussion problem is not that players hide symptoms; it's a compensation structure that forces them to play hurt, or get cut.")

73 *See* 2011 NFL CBA, App. H. Notice of Termination; *see also id.*, at Art. 4 §5(d).

74 *See* Chris Deubert & Glenn M. Wong, *Understanding the Evolution of Signing Bonuses and Guaranteed Money in the National Football League: Preparing for the 2011 Collective Bargaining Negotiations*, 16 UCLA Ent. L. Rev. 179 (2009) (describing the various forms of guaranteed compensation in the NFL).

75 *See* Mike Florio, *The full Kaepernick contract details*, ProFootballTalk (Jun. 5, 2014, 12:46 AM), http://profootballtalk.nbcsports.com/2014/06/05/the-full-kaepernick-contract-details/, *archived at* http://perma.cc/B6W9-WVC7 (discussing details of Colin Kaepernick's 2014 contract with the San Francisco 49ers. Despite reports that Kaepernick had received $61 million guaranteed, only about $13 million was guaranteed against skill, injury, and Salary Cap).

76 *See* Chris Deubert, Glenn M. Wong, John Howe, *All Four Quarters: A Retrospective and Analysis of the 2011 Collective Bargaining Process and Agreement in the National Football League*, 19 UCLA Ent. L. Rev. 1, 61–63 (2012) (discussing the movement towards more guaranteed compensation). In 2012, Peyton Manning signed a five-year deal with the Denver Broncos for $96 million, $58 million of which was guaranteed. Mike Klis & Jeff Legwold, *Peyton Manning's $96 million deal with Broncos includes neck injury clause*, Denver Post, Mar. 20, 2012, http://www.denverpost.com/ci_20213659/peyton-mannings-deal-broncos-5-years-96-million, *archived at* http://perma.cc/4GMF-C92W. In 2014, J.J. Watt signed a six-year deal with the Houston Texans for $100 million, $51.8 million of which was guaranteed. *Texans give J.J. Watt $100M deal*, ESPN, Sept. 2, 2014, http://espn.go.com/nfl/story/_/id/11451373/jj-watt-houston-texans-reach-agreement-6-year-100-million-deal, *archived at* http://perma.cc/GUQ4-GP9J. And, in 2015, Ndamukong Suh signed a six-year deal with the Miami Dolphins for $114 million, $60 million of which was guaranteed. Josh Alper, *Dolphins make it official with Ndamukong Suh*, ProFootballTalk (Mar. 11, 2015, 4:14 PM), http://profootballtalk.nbcsports.com/2015/03/11/dolphins-make-it-official-with-ndamukong-suh/, *archived at* http://perma.cc/2T5Z-367S.

77 *See* Chris Deubert, Glenn M. Wong, John Howe, *All Four Quarters: A Retrospective and Analysis of the 2011 Collective Bargaining Process and Agreement in the National Football League*, 19 UCLA Ent. L. Rev. 1, 52–61 (2012) (discussing changes to rookie compensation scheme).

78 *Id.*

79 *See* 2011 NFL CBA, Art. 4, § 9. *See also* Chris Deubert, Glenn M. Wong, John Howe, *All Four Quarters: A Retrospective and Analysis of the 2011 Collective Bargaining Process and Agreement in the National Football League*, 19 UCLA Ent. L. Rev. 1, 48–51 (2012) discussing clubs' efforts to recoup portions of bonus money already paid to players); Chris Deubert & Glenn M. Wong, *Understanding the Evolution of Signing Bonuses and Guaranteed Money in the National Football League: Preparing for the 2011 Collective Bargaining Negotiations*, 16 UCLA Ent. L. Rev. 179, 202-26 (2009) (same).

80 *See* Chris Deubert & Glenn M. Wong, *Understanding the Evolution of Signing Bonuses and Guaranteed Money in the National Football League: Preparing for the 2011 Collective Bargaining Negotiations*, 16 UCLA Ent. L. Rev. 179, 194-95 (2009) (same).

81 *See* 2011 NFL CBA, At. 4, § 9(g) (discussing voiding of guarantees).

82 MLB CBA, Art. XXIII § B(2)

83 *MLBPA, MLB Announce Details of New Labor Agreement*, MLBPA (Dec. 2, 2016), http://www.mlbplayers.com/ViewArticle.dbml?DB_OEM_ID=34000&ATCLID=211336390, *archived at* https://perma.cc/4XUA-2DAW.

84 *MLBPA, MLB Announce Details of New Labor Agreement*, MLBPA (Dec. 2, 2016), http://www.mlbplayers.com/ViewArticle.dbml?DB_OEM_ID=34000&ATCLID=211336390, *archived at* https://perma.cc/4XUA-2DAW.

85 Maury Brown, *MLB Sees Record Revenues Approaching $10 Billion for 2016*, Forbes (Dec. 5, 2016, 3:22 PM), http://www.forbes.com/sites/maurybrown/2016/12/05/mlb-sees-record-revenues-approaching-10-billion-for-2016/#7704e2e21845, *archived at* https://perma.cc/775E-WE9A.

86 MLB CBA Art. XXI(A)(1).

87 UPC ¶¶ 10(a), (b).

88 Jeff Monhait, *Baseball Arbitration: An ADR Success*, 4 Harv. J. Sports & Ent. L. 105, 107 (2013). These players could be considered "Exclusive Rights Players" per the definition we provided in the Introduction to this Chapter.

89 Ed Edmonds, *A Most Interesting Part of Baseball's Monetary Structure—Salary Arbitration in Its Thirty-Fifth Year*, 20 Marq. Sports L. Rev. 1, 7 (2009).

90 *See* 2012 MLB CBA, Art. VI(E)(1)(a).

91 MLB CBA, Art. VI(E)(1)(b).

92 *Id.*

93 MLB CBA, Art. VI(E)(4).

94 MLB CBA, Art. VI(E)(5). The salary arbitration panel is distinct from the arbitration panel used to hear ordinary grievances under the CBA.

95 MLB CBA, Art. VI(E)(7).

96 *Id.* The criteria to be used in determining the player's salary include "the quality of the Player's contribution to his club during the past season (including but not limited to his overall performance, special qualities of leadership and public appeal), the length and consistency of his career contribution, the record of the Player's past compensation, comparative baseball salaries . . . , the existence of any physical or mental defects on the part of the Player, and the recent performance record of the Club including but not limited to its League standing and attendance as an indication of public acceptance." *Id.* at Art. VI, § E(10).

97 *Id.*, at Art. VI(E)(13).

98 *See* Eldon L. Ham & Jeffrey Malach, *Hardball Free Agency—The Unintended Demise of Salary Arbitration in Major League Baseball: How the Law of Unintended Consequences Crippled the Salary Arbitration Remedy—And How to Fix It*, 11 Harv. J. Sports & Ent. L. 63 (2010).

99 *MLBPA Info—Frequently Asked Questions*, MLB Players, http://mlb.mlb.com/pa/info/faq.jsp#minimum (last visited Aug. 27, 2015), *archived at* http://perma.cc/92LP-4YYP.

100 MLB CBA, Art. XX(B)(1). These players could be considered "Unrestricted Free Agents" per the definition we provided in the Introduction to this

Chapter. MLB does not have Restricted Free Agents.

101 Katie Stankiewicz, *Length of Contracts and the Effect on the Performance of MLB Players*, 17 Park Place Economist 76, 76–78 (2009), https://www.iwu.edu/economics/PPE17/stankiewicz.pdf, *archived at* http://perma.cc/M5CG-W6EY (surveying the related economics literature).

102 *Id.*

103 Jeff Todd, *Free Agent Contract Trends: 2007–08 To Present*, MLB Trade Rumors, Jan. 31, 2014, http://www.mlbtraderumors.com/2014/01/free-agent-contract-trends-2007-08-to-present.html, *archived at* http://perma.cc/4MWY-SU29.

104 *Id.*

105 Jayson Stark, *Stanton Wanted Flexibility for Marlins*, ESPN, Nov. 18, 2014, http://espn.go.com/mlb/story/_/id/11897600/giancarlo-stanton-325m-miami-marlins-heavily-backloaded, *archived at* http://perma.cc/VE7R-TWSS.

106 Jason Beck, *Tigers Announce Record Extension for Miggy*, Major League Baseball, Mar. 28, 2014, http://m.tigers.mlb.com/news/article/70257040/detroit-tigers-announce-eight-year-extension-for-miguel-cabrera, *archived at* http://perma.cc/MD5W-ANBB.

107 Cliff Corcoran, *Don't blame Cubs for taking advantage of rules with Kris Bryant*, Sports Illustrated, Mar. 18, 2015, http://www.si.com/mlb/2015/03/18/chicago-cubs-kris-bryant-scott-boras-theo-epstein-service-time, *archived at* http://perma.cc/KQ73-2BKX; C.J. Nitkowski, *Kris Bryant and the Service-Time Game,* Fox Sports, http://www.foxsports.com/mlb/just-a-bit-outside/story/chicago-cubs-kris-bryant-service-time-when-to-call-up-prospects-031115 (last visited Aug. 27, 2015), *archived at* http://perma.cc/P9ER-99TV.

108 Corcoran, *supra* n. 107; Nitkowski, *supra* n. 107. Jesse Rogers, *Kris Bryant, to hit cleanup in major league debut*, ESPN, Apr. 17, 2015, http://espn.go.com/chicago/mlb/story/_/id/12705857/chicago-cubs-call-kris-bryant, *archived at* http://perma.cc/WJ9M-2642.

109 Corcoran, *supra* n. 107; Nitkowski, *supra* n. 107; Rogers, *supra* n. 108.

110 *Id.*

111 *See* Ben Nicholson-Smith, *Recent Extensions For Pre-Arb Eligible Players*, MLB Trade Rumors, Apr. 10, 2012, http://www.mlbtraderumors.com/2012/04/recent-extensions-for-pre-arbitration-eligible-players.html, *archived at* http://perma.cc/5LVR-D26Y; Ken Rosenthal, *More extensions, less free agency,* Fox Sports (May 17, 2013, 4:01 PM), https://web.archive.org/web/20130921021255/http://msn.foxsports.com/mlb/story/more-contract-extensions-less-free-agency-robinson-cano-justin-verlander-joey-votto-felix-hernandez-kyle-lohse-051613, *archived at* https://perma.cc/88CH-HG57.

112 Bill Brink & Michael Sanserino, *Pirates, McCutchen agree on new contract,* Mar. 5, 2012, Pittsburgh Post-Gazette, http://www.post-gazette.com/sports/pirates/2012/03/05/Pirates-McCutchen-agree-on-new-contract/stories/201203050213, *archived at* http://perma.cc/7XYD-6UFE.

113 Bob Nightengale, *2016 MLB salaries: Royals way pays, while average salary hits $4.4 million*, USA Today, Apr. 4, 2016, http://www.usatoday.com/story/sports/mlb/2016/04/03/2016-mlb-salaries-payrolls/82592542/, *archived at* https://perma.cc/PK6Y-BP4B.

114 *See* 2012 MLB CBA, Art. VI(A)(1) (setting minimum salary at $500,000 plus cost of living adjustment); *MLB minimum salary remains at $507,500 for 2016*, ESPN.com (Nov. 18, 2015), http://espn.go.com/mlb/story/_/id/14161690/mlb-minimum-salary-remains-507500-2016, *archived at* https://perma.cc/A73N-E7U7.

115 Barry Krissoff, *Society and Baseball Facing Rising Income Inequality*, Soc'y for Am. Baseball Res. (Spring 2013), http://sabr.org/research/society-and-baseball-face-rising-income-inequality, *archived at* http://perma.cc/AHU7-KPX8.

116 *See* Jordan I. Kobritz, Jeffrey F. Levine, Steven C. Palmer, *Don Fehr Trades His Ball for a Puck: Will He Continue to Score?* 19 Vill. Sports & Ent. L.J. 521, 531 (2012) (describing contracts in MLB as "guaranteed"); Joseph P. Kahn, *Are long baseball contracts worth it?*, Bos. Globe, Apr. 5,

2015, *available at* 2015 WLNR 9933513 (same).

117 NBA CBA, Art. XXXIX, § 2.

118 NBA CBA, Art. VII, § 12(b)(3).

119 NBA CBA Art. VII, § 1(a).

120 NBA CBA, Art. VII, § 2(a).

121 *NBA salary cap for 2016-17 set at $94.143 million*, NBA (Jul. 2, 2016, 6:46 PM), http://www.nba.com/2016/news/07/02/nba-salary-cap-set/, archived at https://perma.cc/PA8P-6JTP.

122 Dan Feldman, *Report: NBA's 2017-18 Salary-Cap Projection Falls to $102 Million*, Pro Basketball Talk (Feb. 3, 2017, 10:00 PM), http://nba.nbcsports.com/2017/02/03/report-nbas-2017-18-salary-cap-projection-falls-to-102-million/, *archived at* https://perma.cc/U99B-MT4C.

123 Dan Feldman, *Report: NBA Projects Salary Cap to Reach $92 Million Next Season*, Pro Basketball Talk (Apr. 18, 2016, 12:12 PM), http://nba.nbcsports.com/2016/04/18/report-nba-projects-salary-cap-to-reach-92-million-next-season/, *archived at* https://perma.cc/D6T2-37UR.

124 NBA CBA Art. VII § 2(b).

125 Dan Feldman, *Report: NBA Revenue Projected to Reach $8 Billion Next Season*, Pro Basketball Talk (Sep. 16, 2016, 10:05 AM), http://nba.nbcsports.com/2016/09/16/report-nba-revenue-projected-to-reach-8-billion-next-season/, *archived at* https://perma.cc/73NP-QRJN.

126 *NBA salary cap for 2016-17 set at $94.143 million*, NBA (Jul. 2, 2016, 6:46 PM), http://www.nba.com/2016/news/07/02/nba-salary-cap-set/, archived at https://perma.cc/PA8P-6JTP.

127 *See* Feldman, *supra* n. 125.

128 NBA CBA, Art. VII, § 12(f)(1)(i).

129 *Id.*

130 NBA CBA, Art. VII, § 12(g).

131 Marc Stein, *Money well spent: Cavs owe $54M in luxury taxes, sources say,* ESPN (Jul. 3, 2016), http://www.espn.com/nba/story/_/id/16719485/cleveland-cavaliers-owe-54-million-luxury-taxes, *archived at* https://perma.cc/TVU2-TEDU.

132 NBA CBA Art. I § 1(jjj).

133 NBA CBA, Art. VIII § 1(a).

134 *Id.*

135 NBA CBA, Ex. B.

136 *See* Larry Coons, *Larry Coon's NBA Salary Cap FAQ*, CBA FAQ, http://www.cbafaq.com/salarycap.htm (last visited Feb. 2, 2017), *archived at* http://perma.cc/K9XV-FRTE.

137 *See id.*

138 *See NBA 2014 Draft Tracker,* Spotrac, http://www.spotrac.com/nba/draft/2016/ (last visited Feb. 2, 2017), *archived at* https://perma.cc/2KAS-MUKA (providing contract details for 2016 NBA Draft picks).

139 *See* 2017 NBA CBA, Art. XI, § 1(a).

140 *See id.; see also* Larry Coons, *Larry Coon's NBA Salary Cap FAQ*, CBA FAQ, http://www.cbafaq.com/salarycap.htm (last visited Feb. 2, 2017), *archived at* http://perma.cc/K9XV-FRTE.

141 *See* 2017 NBA CBA, Art. XI, § 1 (describing the circumstances under which a player become a Restricted Free Agent); 2017 NBA CBA, Art. 1, § 1(hhhh) ("'Veteran Free Agent' means a Veteran who completed his Player Contract (other than a 10-Day Contract) by rendering the playing services called for thereunder.")

142 NBA CBA, Art. XI, § 1.

143 *See* 2017 NBA CBA Art. XI, § 1(c).

144 NBA CBA, Art. XI § 1(a)(ii).

145 NBA CBA, Art. XI, § 5 (b).

146 NBA CBA, Art. XI, § 5(g).

147 *Id.*

148 *See* 2017 NBA CBA, Art. VII, § 6.

149 *CBA 101,* Nat'l Basketball Ass'n, http://www.nba.com/media/CBA101.pdf, *archived at* http://perma.cc/VH8S-9W55, at 5–8.

150 The NFL Salary Cap does permit for one exception for veteran players playing for the minimum salary. Players with at least four Credited Seasons who sign for the league minimum will only have their salary count against the Salary Cap as if the player only had two Credited Seasons. 2011 NFL CBA, Art. 27. This exception avoids clubs from hiring younger players over experienced veterans simply because they are younger.

151 *See* 2017 NBA CBA, Exhibit C.

152 *See id.*

153 NBA CBA, Art. II § 7(a)(i).

154 *Id.*

155 *See* 2017 NBA CBA, Art. II § 7(a)(ii).

156 *See* 2017 NBA CBA, Art. II § 7(a)(iii).

157 NBA CBA, Art. II, § 7(a)(ii).

158 Brian Windhorst & Marc Stein, *Sources: Warriors' Stephen Curry stands to benefit in new CBA*, ESPN (Dec. 15, 2016), http://www.espn.com /nba/story/_/id/18286141/under-new-cba-golden-state-warriors -guard-stephen-curry-get-deal-worth-more-200-million, *archived at* https://perma.cc/8X9D-2LBK.

159 *NBA Contracts*, spotrac.com, http://www.spotrac.com/nba/contracts/ (last visited Mar. 13, 2017), *archived at* https://perma.cc/V7Y8-LA5M.

160 NBA CBA, Art. XXIX, § 1.

161 NFL CBA, Art. 25, § 1.

162 Major League Rules, Rule 2(c)(2)(A).

163 NHL CBA, § 16.4(a).

164 *See* 2017 NBA CBA, Art. IX § 1.

165 *Id.*

166 *See NBA Contracts*, spotrac.com, http://www.spotrac.com/nba/ contracts/ (last visited Mar. 13, 2017), *archived at* https://perma.cc/V7Y8 -LA5M.

167 NBA CBA, Ex. A.

168 *See* 2017 NBA CBA, Art. II § 4. Negotiating over guarantees for mental disability is potentially troubling. A player and his agent may be unlikely to want to raise that issue as a point of negotiation for fear of causing the club to be concerned that the player suffers from a mental disability. Nevertheless, according to the NBA, many contracts in the NBA include guarantees for mental disability.

169 NBA CBA, Art. VII § 8(e)(1).

170 NBA CBA, Art. VIII § 1(c)(ii).

171 NBA CBA, Art. XI § 1(c)(i)(4).

172 Larry Coons, *Larry Coon's NBA Salary Cap FAQ #64*, CBA FAQ, http://www.cbafaq.com/salarycap.htm (last visited Aug. 27, 2015), *archived at* http://perma.cc/K9XV-FRTE; Tom Penn, *NBA Player Have Best Deal*, ESPN (Nov. 3, 2011 1:17 PM), http://espn.go.com/espn/ commentary/story/_/id/7181583/even-concessions-nba-players-best -deal-pro-athletes, *archived at* http://perma.cc/Z3SR-5JPK ("About 90 percent of all NBA contracts are fully guaranteed for payment on the day that they are signed by the player.")

173 *See NBA Contracts,* Spotrac.com, http://www.spotrac.com/nba/contracts (last visited Jan. 30, 2017), *archived at* https://perma.cc/KR3K-M576.

174 NHL CBA, § 3.1.

175 NHL CBA, § 50.4(b).

176 NHL CBA, § 50.1(a).

177 *See The Business of Hockey*, Forbes (Nov. 30, 2016), http://www.forbes .com/nhl-valuations/list/, *archived at* https://perma.cc/545K-NQBV (listing NHL clubs' estimated revenues).

178 NHL CBA, § 50.5(b).

179 James O'Brien, *The NHL's Salary Cap for 2016-17 is $73M*, Pro Hockey Talk (June 21, 2016, 8:54 PM), http://nhl.nbcsports.com/2016/06/21/ the-nhls-salary-cap-for-2016-17-is-73m/, *archived at* https://perma.cc /R4FW-WEWR.

180 NHL CBA, § 9.1(b).

181 NHL CBA, § 9.1(b).

182 A player's Paragraph 1 Salary is the player's salary as specified in Paragraph 1 of the SPC. *See* Ex. 1 to the 2013 NHL CBA ("The Club hereby employs the Player as a skilled hockey Player for the term of _____ League Year(s) commencing the later of July 1, 20 or upon execution of this SPC and agrees, subject to the terms and conditions hereof, to pay the Player a salary of _____ US Dollars ($_____).").

183 *See* 2013 NHL CBA, §9.3, §9.5.

184 NHL CBA, § 9.3.

185 The different performance bonuses available to players are described in Exhibit 5 of the 2013 NHL CBA.

186 *Id.*

187 NHL CBA, § 10.2(a)(i).

188 *Id.*

189 NHL CBA, § 10.1(a).

190 *Id.*

191 NHL CBA, § 10.2(b)(i).

192 NHL CBA, § 10.1(b).

193 *Id.*

194 NHL CBA at p. 502, letter from William L. Day, Deputy Commissioner, NHL, to Don Zavelo, General Counsel, NHLPA (Feb. 15, 2013).

195 *Id.*

196 NHL CBA, § 10.1(c).

197 *Id.*

198 *See* 2013 NHL CBA, § 10.2(c).

199 *Id.*

200 NHL CBA, § 12.1(a).

201 NHL CBA, § 12.2.

202 NHL CBA, § 12.3(a).

203 NHL CBA, § 12.3(b).

204 NHL CBA, § 12.9(b)-(c).

205 NHL CBA, § 12.9(n).

206 NHL CBA, § 11.12.

207 NHL CBA, § 50.6.

208 NHL CBA, § 50.7.

209 NHL CBA, § 50.5(d)(ii).

210 *NHL rejects Kovalchuk deal*, ESPN (Jul. 21, 2010), http://sports.espn.go .com/new-york/nhl/news/story?id=5397588, *archived at* https://perma .cc/88W2-CZY8.

211 *Id.*

212 Greg Wyshynski, *NHL lets NJ Devils off hook for Ilya Kovalchuk contract punishment*, Yahoo! Sports (Mar. 6, 2014, 1:18 PM), http://sports .yahoo.com/blogs/nhl-puck-daddy/nhl-lets-nj-devils-off-hook-for -ilya-kovalchuk-contract-punishment-181853523.html, *archived at* http://perma.cc/BM37-BDTJ.

213 *See* 2013 NHL CBA, § 50.8(b)(iv).

214 NFL CBA, Art. 7 3(e) ("No Rookie Contract may provide for an annual increase of more than 25% of the player's Year-One Rookie Salary unless such contract provides only for Paragraph 5 Salary equal to the then-applicable Minimum Active/Inactive Salary for each League Year of the Contract.")

215 NFL CBA, Art. 12, § 7.

216 *See NHL Contracts*, Spotrac.com, http://www.spotrac.com/nhl/contracts/ (last visited Jan. 30, 2017), *archived at* https://perma.cc/3FR9-GNRQ.

217 *Id.*

218 NHL Standard Player Contract, ¶ 13.

219 NHL Standard Player Contract, ¶ 13(d).

220 *Id.*

221 *See* James Mirtle, *David Clarkson and His Buyout-Proof Contract*, Globe & Mail, Apr. 2, 2014, http://www.theglobeandmail.com/sports/hockey

/leafs-beat/mirtle-david-clarkson-and-his-buyout-proof-contract/article17783243/?cmpid=rss1&click=dlvr.it, *archived at* http://perma.cc/L4GE-WF5Y (describing David Clarkson's signing-bonus-laden contract as "buyout-proof"); *Lightning to Buy Out Vincent Lecavalier*, Canoe, June 27, 2013, http://slam.canoe.com/Slam/Hockey/NHL/TampaBay/2013/06/27/20933546.html?cid=rsssportsslam!, *archived at* http://perma.cc/A7MA-3QE6 (reporting that the club would pay "the full amount of what's left on [Lecavalier's] signing bonus" as part of his buy-out).

222 NHL Standard Player Contract, ¶5(d).

223 *See 2014 CFL CBA*, § 30.01. The CFL's Salary Cap is formally known as the "Salary Expenditure CAP." *Id.*

224 CFL CBA, § 14.09.

225 *Adjusted Team Salary Caps*, Nat'l Football League Players Ass'n, Mar. 7, 2016, https://www.nflpa.com/news/all-news/2016-adjusted-team-salary-caps, *archived at* https://perma.cc/K9GZ-ZDGN.

226 CFL CBA, § 30.02 ("The parties agree that if during any one calendar year during the term of this Agreement the current economic conditions prevailing in the C.F.L. shall improve to the extent that the defined player's compensation is less than 56% of the defined gross revenue on a league wide basis, the C.F.L. and the Member Clubs in the C.F.L. shall pay to the C.F.L.P.A. the difference.")

227 Andrew Bucholtz, *What percentage of league-wide revenues did CFL players get in 2013 under the old CBA?*, Yahoo! Sports Can. (June 9, 2014, 6:49 PM), https://ca.sports.yahoo.com/blogs/cfl-55-yard-line/percentage-league-wide-revenues-did-cfl-players-2013-224954281.html, *archived at* http://perma.cc/F5NU-FWE3.

228 *Id.*

229 CFL Standard Player Contract, ¶ 15; *New five-year CBA ratified by CFL and CFLPA*, Can. Football League (June 13, 2014, 3:00 PM), http://www.cfl.ca/article/new-five-year-cba-ratified-by-cfl-and-cflpa, *archived at* http://perma.cc/EBL2-NRDA.

230 CFL Standard Player Contract, ¶ 15.

231 *Id.*

232 *See 2014 CFL CBA*, § 14.03 (discussing rights of free agents).

233 CFL CBA, § 9.

234 Emily Kaplan, *The CFL's Most Outstanding Player Moonlights as a Banker*, Monday Morning Quarterback with Peter King, Jun. 26, 2014, http://mmqb.si.com/2014/06/26/cfl-off-season-jobs-jon-cornish-calgary-stampeders/, *archived at* http://perma.cc/K6C7-2CM9.

235 Signing bonuses for non-veterans are rare, but signing bonuses of up to $75,000 for veterans have occurred. *See Frequently Asked Questions About Compensation*, Can. Football League Database, https://cfldb.ca/faq/compensation/ (last visited Aug. 28, 2015), *archived at* https://perma.cc/5VGW-3V9B; *see also* Victoria Revay, *Show me the money: CFL players' salaries*, Global News, Nov. 20, 2012, http://globalnews.ca/news/310679/show-me-the-money-cfl-players-salaries/, *archived at* http://perma.cc/Q373-RETY.

236 Emily Kaplan, *The CFL's Most Outstanding Player Moonlights as a Banker*, Monday Morning Quarterback with Peter King, Jun. 26, 2014, http://mmqb.si.com/2014/06/26/cfl-off-season-jobs-jon-cornish-calgary-stampeders/, *archived at* http://perma.cc/K6C7-2CM9.

237 *Id.*

238 *Roughriders sign quarterback Durant to contract extension*, Globe & Mail, Apr. 16, 2014, http://www.theglobeandmail.com/sports/football/roughriders-sign-quarterback-durant-to-contract-extension/article18042091/, *archived at* http://perma.cc/26WW-WDJU.

239 Aside from guarantees for veteran players, "CFL contracts are not guaranteed in the case of a player being released or beyond the current season in the case of a football-related injury." *See* Can. Football League Database *supra* note 235.

240 CFL Standard Player Contract, ¶ 6.

241 CFL Standard Player Contract, ¶10(a).

242 CFL Standard Player Contract, ¶10(b).

243 CFL Standard Player Contract, ¶10(c).

244 CFL Standard Player Contract, ¶10(d).

245 CFL CBA, Art. 15.

246 Justin Dunk, *Top CFL picks land rookie-record signing bonuses*, SportsNet (May 15, 2015, 11:19 AM), http://www.sportsnet.ca/football/cfl/top-cfl-picks-land-rookie-record-signing-bonuses/, *archived at* http://perma.cc/8NUF-A5J6.

247 *See* Fraser v. Major League Soccer, L.L.C., 97 F.Supp. 2d 130, 132-34 (D. Mass. 2000) (discussing MLS' structure, operations and origin, including meetings with NFL's antitrust counsel).

248 *See* Fraser v. Major League Soccer, L.L.C., 284 F.3d 47, 53–55 (1st Cir. 2002) (discussing MLS' structure and operations).

249 *Id.*

250 *Id.*

251 *Id.;* Kevin O'Riordan, *Dempsey Transfer Highlights Influence of MLS Single-Entity Economic Structure*, Bus. Of Soccer, Aug. 26, 2013, http://www.businessofsoccer.com/2013/08/26/dempsey-transfer-highlights-mls-single-entity-economic-structure/, *archived at* http://perma.cc/2TKQ-BQ4R.

252 *See* Order, Namoff v. D.C. Soccer LLC, No. 2012-CA-7050, at *2 (D.C.Sup.Ct. May 8, 2014) ("MLS has sole discretion to hire players and provides their salary and benefits[.]")

253 *See* Fraser v. Major League Soccer, L.L.C., 97 F.Supp. 2d 130, 132–34 (D. Mass. 2000) (discussing MLS' structure, operations and origin, including meetings with NFL's antitrust counsel); Michael McCann, *In pursuit of free agency, players could challenge MLS as single entity*, Sports Illustrated, Jan. 27, 2015, http://www.si.com/planet-futbol/2015/01/26/mls-cba-players-union-free-agency-single-entity-lawsuit, *archived at* http://perma.cc/JUV9-BGGP; Matthew J. Jakobsze, *Kicking "Single-Entity" to the Sidelines: Reevaluating the Competitive Reality of Major League Soccer After American Needle and the 2010 Collective Bargaining Agreement*, 31 N. Ill. U. L. Rev. 131, 132-33 (2010).

254 *See* American Needle, Inc. v. Nat'l Football League, 560 U.S. 183, 186 (2010), *citing* 15 U.S.C. § 1.

255 *See* Copperweld Corp. v. Independence Tube Corp., 467 U.S. 752 (1984) (parent corporation and wholly owned subsidiary were not legally capable of conspiring with each other under Section 1 of the Sherman Act).

256 *See* Fraser v. Major League Soccer, L.L.C., 97 F.Supp.2d 130, 135–36 (D.Mass. 2000).

257 *See* Fraser v. Major League Soccer, L.L.C., 284 F.3d 47, 55 (1st Cir. 2002).

258 *Id.* at 56–59.

259 *See id.*

260 *See About the MLS Players Union*, Major League Soccer Players Union, https://www.mlsplayers.org/about_mlspu.html (last visited Aug. 28, 2015), *archived at* http://perma.cc/P2XJ-MN4R.

261 *See* Michael McCann, *In pursuit of free agency, players could challenge MLS as single entity*, Sports Illustrated, Jan. 27, 2015, http://www.si.com/planet-futbol/2015/01/26/mls-cba-players-union-free-agency-single-entity-lawsuit, *archived at* http://perma.cc/JUV9-BGGP (discussing risks of MLSPU decertifying as players' labor representative and filing antitrust lawsuit); Matthew J. Jakobsze, *Kicking "Single-Entity" to the Sidelines: Reevaluating the Competitive Reality of Major League Soccer After American Needle and the 2010 Collective Bargaining Agreement*, 31 N. Ill. U. L. Rev. 131, 155 (2010) (same).

262 *See, e.g., id.;* Diana C. Taylor, *Aimed at the Goal?: The Sustainability of Major League Soccer's Structure*, 9 Willamette Sports L.J. 1 (2011); Order, Namoff v. D.C. Soccer LLC, No. 2012-CA-7050 (D.C.Sup.Ct. May 8, 2014) (finding MLS and D.C. United to be "concurrent employers" of players).

263 U.S.C. § 15 ("any person who shall be injured in his business or property by reason of anything forbidden in the antitrust laws may sue therefor in any district court of the United States in the district in which the

defendant resides or is found or has an agent, without respect to the amount in controversy, and shall recover threefold the damages by him sustained, and the cost of suit, including a reasonable attorney's fee").

264 *MLS Roster Rules and Regulations*, Major League Soccer, http://www .mlssoccer.com/league/official-rules/mls-roster-rules-and-regulations (last visited Mar. 8, 2017), *archived at* https://perma.cc/SC9V-2TW3.

265 Paul Tenorio, *Foose: New MLS CBA a 'watershed moment'*, Orlando Sentinel, Mar. 7, 2015, *available at* 2015 WLNR 7038891.

266 *MLS Roster Rules and Regulations*, Major League Soccer, http://www .mlssoccer.com/league/official-rules/mls-roster-rules-and-regulations (last visited Mar. 8, 2017), *archived at* https://perma.cc/SC9V-2TW3.

267 This information was provided by the MLSPU.

268 *See* Steven Goff, *D.C. United news and notes*, Wash. Post, Apr. 14, 2015, *available at* 2015 WLNR 10882564 (discussing D.C. United player Bill Hamid's weighing playing in Europe against earning a designated player salary); Daniel Boniface, *Kevin Doyle, Colorado Rapids agree to contract; June arrival expected*, Mar. 21, 2015, Denver Post, *available at* 2015 WLNR 8515066 (discussing Colorado Rapids' acquisition of English soccer player Kevin Doyle as a designated player); Steven Goff, *New CBA called 'win' for MLS players*, Wash. Post, Mar. 9, 2015, *available at* 2015 WLNR 7003801 (discussing designated player salaries and exception to Salary Cap); Gary Kingston, *As MLS evolves, so does the Beckham Rule; League's designated player clause is helping keep talented players in North America*, Vancouver Sun, Aug. 9, 2014, *available at* 2014 WLNR 21837206.

269 For the list of Designated Players, *see Designated Players, As of August 10, 2016*, Major League Soccer, http://pressbox.mlssoccer.com/ content/designated-players (last visited Sept. 14, 2016), *archived at* https://perma.cc/S5L7-ECRW..

270 These figures were calculated using data provided by the MLSPU at https://www.mlsplayers.org/salary_info.html, *archived at* https://perma .cc/54D9-22JG. The list of Designated Players is available at *Designated Players*, MLS (Aug. 3, 2016), http://pressbox.mlssoccer.com/content/ designated-players, *archived at* https://perma.cc/8HT2-E9DT.

271 *See* Chris Smith, *Major League Soccer's Most Valuable Teams 2016*, Forbes (Sep. 7, 2016, 10:32 AM), http://www.forbes.com/ sites/chrissmith/2016/09/07/major-league-soccers-most-valuable -teams-2016-new-york-orlando-thrive-in-first-seasons/, *archived at* https://perma.cc/K7B6-DJ86.

272 Richard Sandomir, *M.L.S. and Union Reach Deal Giving Free Agency to Veterans*, N.Y. Times, Mar. 4, 2015, http://www.nytimes.com/2015/03 /05/sports/soccer/mls-and-union-reach-deal-giving-free-agency-to -veterans.html?_r=0, *archived at* http://perma.cc/7KUK-FVWE.

273 *Roster Rules and Regulations*, Major League Soccer, http://pressbox .mlssoccer.com/content/roster-rules-and-regulations *(last visited Aug. 28, 2015), archived at* http://perma.cc/D885-JCL9, at § II(G)(2); 2015 MLS CBA, § 29.6(a)(i).

274 Jeff Carlisle, *The details on Major League Soccer's new collective bargaining agreement*, ESPN (Mar 4, 2015) http://www.espnfc.us/ major-league-soccer/19/blog/post/2332341/the-details-on-major -league-soccers-new-collective-bargaining-agreement, *archived at* http://perma.cc/QF79-8XLB; 2015 MLS CBA, § 29.6(b)(iii).

275 MLS CBA, § 10.1.

276 This information was provided by MLSPU.

277 *Roster Rules and Regulations*, Major League Soccer, http://pressbox .mlssoccer.com/content/roster-rules-and-regulations (last visited June 23, 2016), *archived at* https://perma.cc/2S5S-WHNQ.

278 *See id.*

279 These figures were calculated using data provided by the MLSPU. *See 2016 MLS Player Salaries: May 15, 2016: Alphabetical*, Major League Soccer Players Union, https://www.mlsplayers.org/images/May%2015 ,%202016%20Salary%20Information%20-%20Alphabetical.pdf (last visited Sept. 14, 2016), *archived at* https://perma.cc/PX9E-KMTX..

280 *See id.*

281 *See id.*

282 *See 2016 MLS Player Salaries: May, 2016: Alphabetical supra* n. 279.

283 *See* Steven Goff, *MLS union and management preparing for collective bargaining negotiations*, Wash. Post, Nov. 21, 2014, *available at* 2014 WLNR 32859557.

284 MLS CBA, § 18.6(b).

285 MLS CBA, § 2(x).

286 *MLS Announces CBA Changes*, U.S. Nat'l Soccer Players, Mar. 23, 2010, http://www.ussoccerplayers.com/2010/03/mls-announces-cba-changes .html, *archived at* http://perma.cc/HW5N-TSAV.

287 *See 2016 MLS Player Salaries: May, 2016: Alphabetical supra* n. 279.

288 *Id.*

289 *See What is average NFL player's career length? Longer than you might think, Commissioner Goodell says*, Nat'l Football League, Apr. 18, 2011, http://nflcommunications.com/2011/04/18/what-is-average -nfl-player%E2%80%99s-career-length-longer-than-you-might-think -commissioner-goodell-says/, *archived at* http://perma.cc/8UHQ-JMVX (discussing dispute between NFLPA's assertion that the average career is 3.5 years and the NFL's assertion that the average career is 6 years); *Average NFL Career Length*, Sharp Football Analysis, Apr. 30, 2014, http://www.sharpfootballanalysis.com/blog/?p=2133, *archived at* http://perma.cc/4EZY-E7ML (discussing disagreement between NFLPA and NFL and determining that the average drafted player plays about 5 years).

290 William D. Witnauer, Richard G. Rogers & Jarron M. Saint Onge, *Major league baseball career length in the 20th century*, 26 Population Res. & Pol'y Rev. 4, 371-386 (2007).

291 Susan Konig, *Financial Planning for the Pros*, 34 Registered Representative (Apr. 2010), *available at* 2010 WLNR 26366417.

292 *Average Length of an NHL Player Career*, QuantHockey.com, http://www .quanthockey.com/Distributions/CareerLengthGP.php (last visited Aug. 28, 2015), *archived at* http://perma.cc/95QB-X9P9.

293 Matthew Black, *Players rely on education, experience after CFL career*, Thunderbird, Mar. 31, 2011, http://thethunderbird.ca/2011/03/31/ players-bet-on-education-after-cfl-career/, *archived at* http://perma.cc /M92S-KNQ8.

294 *See, e.g.*, Matt Bowen, *Concussion in the NFL: The cost can be hard to calculate*, Chi. Trib., Sep. 16, 2010, *available at* 2010 WLNR 18355633 ("Without the guaranteed contracts we see in Major League Baseball or the NBA, NFL players will continue to sacrifice their health and their future by playing through concussions."); A. Jason Huebinger, *Beyond the Injured Reserve: The Struggle Facing Former NFL Players in Obtaining Much Needed Disability Assistance*, 16 Sport Law. J. 279, 283 (2009) ("The NFL is also fairly unique in its implementation of a hard salary cap, which also works to artificially reduce player salaries. Under a hard cap system, no team may exceed a given salary amount. Conversely, MLB and the NBA have much more relaxed caps, allowing for greater flexibility in negotiations between the team and a player. Arguably the greatest disadvantage facing current NFL players . . . is the lack of guaranteed contracts.").

295 *See, e.g.*, Mike Florio, *Adrian Peterson takes aim at the NFLPA*, Pro-FootballTalk (May 28, 2015, 9:18 PM), http://profootballtalk.nbcsports .com/2015/05/28/adrian-peterson-takes-aim-at-the-nflpa/, *archived at* http://perma.cc/GFQ6-QSCG (discussing Minnesota Vikings running back Adrian Peterson's complaints about guaranteed money in the NFL).

296 *See, e.g.*, Paul Needell, *Upshaw's legacy transcended the field*, Star-Ledger (Newark, NJ), Aug. 22, 2008, *available at* 2008 WLNR 15896505; Tim Tucker, *No guarantees in the NFL inside ball*, Atlanta J. & Const., Mar. 3, 2002, *available at* 2002 WLNR 4687719.

297 *See* A. Jason Huebinger, *Beyond the Injured Reserve: The Struggle Facing Former NFL Players in Obtaining Much Needed Disability Assistance*, 16 Sport Law. J. 279, 283 (2009); Matthew Levine, *Despite His Antics,*

T.O. Has a Valid Point: Why NFL Players Deserve a Bigger Piece of the Pie, 13 Vill. Sports & Ent. L.J. 425 (2006).

298 Gene Upshaw, *NFLPA's Upshaw Responds*, Wash. Post, Dec. 22, 2002, *available at* 2002 WLNR 15865309.

299 NFLPA, *A New Look at Guaranteed Contracts in the NFL* (circa 2002) (on file with authors) ("Over half of all salary earned by NFL players now is guaranteed"); Nat'l Football League Players Ass'n, *Guaranteed Contracts in Professional Team Sports: How Does the NFL Compare?* (circa 2007) (on file with authors) ("at least 52% of all compensation in the NFL is, in fact, 'guaranteed' to players.'")

300 Mike Florio, *Fully-guaranteed contracts could cause problems for teams, players,* ProFootballTalk (May 29, 2015, 9:55 AM), http://profootballtalk .nbcsports.com/2015/05/29/fully-guaranteed-contracts-could-cause -problems-for-teams-players/, *archived at* http://perma.cc/GE9E-YSME (discussing potential problems with guaranteed contracts in the NFL).

301 *See* Christopher R. Deubert, I. Glenn Cohen, Holly Fernandez Lynch, *Protecting and Promoting the Health of NFL Players: Legal and Ethical Analysis and Recommendations,* Recommendation 2:1-A (2016).

Eligibility Rules

Each of the leagues has rules governing when individuals become eligible to play in their leagues. While we fully acknowledge the unique nature and needs of the leagues and their athletes, we believe the leagues can learn from the other leagues' policies.

Leagues' eligibility rules affect player health in two somewhat opposite directions: (1) by potentially forcing some players who might be ready to begin a career playing for the leagues to instead continue playing in amateur or lesser professional leagues with less (or no) compensation and at the risk of being injured; and, (2) by protecting other players from entering the leagues before they might be physically, intellectually, or emotionally ready. As will be shown, the NCAA's Bylaws are an important factor in considering the eligibility rules and their effects on player health and thus must be included in this discussion. This issue too is discussed in our Recommendations.

In this Chapter we explain each of the leagues' eligibility rules as well as the rules' relationship to player health, if any. But first, we provide: (1) information on the eligibility rules' legal standing; (2) general information about the leagues' drafts that correspond to their eligibility rules; (3) an explanation of the NCAA and its relevance to the leagues' eligibility rules; and, (4) insurance options that might be available to players before joining one of the leagues.

So long as the leagues' eligibility rules are negotiated with the union, they will likely be exempt from the antitrust laws.

1) LEGAL STANDING OF THE ELIGIBILITY RULES

Each of the sports leagues we discuss in this Report, except MLS[a], consists of member clubs that are individually owned and operated, with the league serving as a centralized, governing body. The clubs compete both on and off the field, court, or ice.[1] Off the field, most notably, clubs compete in the labor market for players' services, bidding against one another on the terms of a contract in hopes of persuading a player to sign with their club. Eligibility rules put a limitation on this market by prohibiting certain potential players from participating in the market. The clubs—through the eligibility rules—have collectively agreed not to bid and contract for the services of particular classes of individuals.

The clubs' eligibility rules have the potential to violate the antitrust laws.[2] Section 1 of the Sherman Antitrust Act prohibits contracts, combinations or conspiracies that unreasonably restrain trade.[3] The eligibility rules restrain trade by prohibiting potential players from contracting with clubs. Whether this restraint is "unreasonable" requires a complicated antitrust analysis of a variety of legal and factual factors.[4]

Nevertheless, the leagues' eligibility rules have been generally treated as not subject to antitrust scrutiny. Certain collective actions by the clubs are exempt from antitrust laws under what is known as the non-statutory labor exemption. The non-statutory labor exemption exempts restrictions imposed by a multi-employer unit—such as sports clubs—where the restrictions were negotiated with a labor organization, i.e., a union, as part of the collective bargaining process.[5] For each of the professional sports leagues discussed in this Report, there is a corresponding union that represents the players and negotiates a collective bargaining agreement ("CBA") with the league. Consequently, based on at least the decision of the United States Court of Appeals for the Second Circuit in the Clarett case (explained below), it appears that so long as the eligibility rules are negotiated with the union, they will be exempt from the antitrust laws.[6,b]

The eligibility rules in the NFL, NBA, NHL, and CFL are all collectively bargained with those leagues' respective players associations and are thus exempt from antitrust law.[c] Below, we discuss each of these leagues' eligibility rules as well as the unique circumstances of MLB's and MLS' eligibility rules.

In most cases, the leagues' eligibility rules are designed, in part, to require players to enter the leagues through their respective drafts. As will be discussed below, the size of these drafts can have important impacts on player decisions concerning their eligibility. Table 6-A on the next page provides information about the drafts.

b   Some scholars have debated whether other Circuit Courts would find that eligibility rules are protected by the non-statutory labor exemption. See Marc Edelman and Joseph A. Wacker, Collectively Bargained Age/Education Requirements: A Source of Antitrust Risk for Sports Club-Owners or Labor Risk for Players Unions? 115 Penn St. L. Rev. 341 (2010); Michael A. McCann, Justice Sonia Sotomayor and the Relationship Between Leagues and Players: Insights and Implications, 42 Conn. L. Rev. 901 (2010). Also of note, in two cases involving now defunct professional sports league eligibility rules that were not negotiated with a union, the courts found that the rules did violate antitrust laws. See Linseman v. World Hockey Ass'n, 439 F. Supp. 1315 (D. Conn. 1977); Boris v. U.S. Football League, 83-cv-4980, 1984 WL 894 (C.D. Cal. Feb. 28, 1984).
c   Unions are empowered to negotiate terms and conditions that might affect future employees, even if those employees are not yet a part of the union's bargaining unit. See Clarett v. Nat'l Football League, 369 F.3d 124, 139 (2d Cir. 2004) (discussing union's rights to "preserve jobs for current players to the detriment of new employees and the exclusion of outsiders"); Wood v. Nat'l Basketball Assoc., 809 F.2d 954 (2d Cir. 1987) (denying prospective NBA player's antitrust challenge to CBA provisions negotiated between NBA and NBPA).

a   MLS' unique structure is discussed at length in Chapter 5: Compensation, Section F: Compensation in MLS.

Table 6-A:
Leagues' Drafts

	NFL	MLB	NBA	NHL	CFL	MLS
Month	April/May	June	June	June	May	January
Length	7 Rounds[7]	40 Rounds[8]	2 Rounds[9]	7 Rounds[10]	7 Rounds[11]	4 Rounds[12]
Approximate Number of Players	255	1,215	60	210	60	84

2) THE NCAA

The NCAA is a non-profit unincorporated association headquartered in Indianapolis through which the nation's colleges and universities govern their athletic programs. The NCAA consists of over 1,200 member institutions, all of which participate in the creation of NCAA rules and voluntarily submit to its authority.[13] The NCAA's member institutions hire a President to oversee its affairs, currently Mark Emmert, formerly the President of the University of Washington.

As will be demonstrated below, the majority of players in the leagues played college sports at NCAA member institutions and according to the NCAA's rules before joining their respective leagues. The NCAA's rules have a substantial impact on players and their decisions about when to join one of the professional leagues.

The NCAA Bylaws declare that "[o]nly an amateur student-athlete is eligible for intercollegiate athletics participation[.]"[14] Moreover, there must be "a clear line of demarcation between college athletics and professional sports."[15] Consequently, student-athletes are generally barred from receiving any compensation of any kind for their athletic ability other than a scholarship,[16] and stipends to cover the full cost of attendance.[17]

The NCAA Bylaws also limit a student-athlete's options concerning joining one of the leagues. The effect of certain NCAA Bylaws will be discussed in the course of this Chapter but here we highlight two specific Bylaws that affect player health and eligibility.

First, NCAA Bylaws generally prohibit players from hiring agents[18] or retaining a lawyer to represent them in contract negotiations.[19] Were they permitted in NCAA sports, agents and attorneys would have the ability to communicate with professional clubs about a player's prospects and also, if the player has been drafted but has collegiate eligibility remaining (as will be explained below), negotiate with the club so the player can make an informed decision about whether to return to college or turn professional. While some student-athletes may have the sophistication or support to do this by themselves, it stands to reason that they could benefit from the advice of experienced counsel. Nevertheless, NCAA Bylaws prohibit players from having lawyers who have any direct contact with professional clubs.[20]

There is, however, an important caveat to this discussion. In 2014, the NCAA approved allowing the five most competitive and highest revenue producing conferences (ACC, Big 12, Big Ten, Pac-12, and SEC) to write their own rules on certain matters.[21] As a result, in 2016, these conferences agreed to allow high school baseball players who are drafted to have an agent negotiate a potential contract with an MLB club.[22] The player must pay the agent a market rate and if the player chooses to enroll in college rather than sign with the MLB club, he must terminate the relationship with the agent.[23] This rule, which can be adopted by other conferences, will provide baseball players with a meaningful opportunity to consider whether to turn professional instead of enrolling in college.

Second, NCAA Bylaws effectively prohibit basketball and football student-athletes from returning to intercollegiate athletics if they are eligible for the draft but are undrafted.[d] College basketball student-athletes are, however, permitted

---

d   The NCAA's Bylaws suggest that these players can return but in reality they cannot. A basketball student-athlete can return to college if he declares his intention to do so "before the first day of the spring National Letter of Intent signing period for the applicable year." NCAA Division I Manual, Bylaw 12.2.4.2.1.1. The first day of the National Letter of Intent signing period for basketball is in April. *NLI Signing Dates for Prospective Student-Athletes Signing 2015–16 and Enrolling 2016–17*, Nat'l Letter of Intent, http://www.nationalletter.org/signingDates/ http://www.nationalletter. org/signingDates/ (last visited Sept. 23, 2015), *archived at* http://perma.cc/65MQ-DBAN. The NBA Draft is in June. Thus, the player cannot go through the Draft in June and still meet the April deadline to declare his intention to return in college. Similarly, a football student-athlete can return to college if he declares his intention to do so "within 72 hours following the National Football League draft declaration date." NCAA Division I Manual, Bylaw 12.2.4.2.3. The NFL requires student-athletes to declare for the NFL Draft by January 15. *See Unofficial underclassmen early entry list for 2015 NFL Draft*, Nat'l Foot League, Jan. 2, 2015, http://www.nfl.com/news/story/0ap3000000441827/article/unofficial-underclassmen-early-entry-list-for-2015-nfl-draft, *archived at* http://perma.cc/SD8M-PUXV. The NFL Draft is in April or May. Thus, the player cannot go through the Draft in April or May and still meet the January deadline to declare his intention to return to college.

to declare for the NBA Draft and attend pre-Draft work-outs and return to school provided they withdraw their name from the NBA Draft and had never hired an agent. Nevertheless, the players still are unable to actually weigh the results of having been drafted against the possibility of returning to school. Thus, players in both basketball and football must weigh whether they are physically, emotion-ally, and intellectually ready for the professional ranks, or to return to college and play for free while risking an injury that might jeopardize their ability to ever play professionally.

The NCAA and some of these Bylaws are currently the subject of lawsuits throughout the country. The lawsuits principally contend that the NCAA's prohibition against student-athletes earning pay while playing violates various legal doctrines and laws, notably the Sherman Antitrust Act's prohibition against agreements that unreasonably restrain trade.[24] Nevertheless, the NCAA Bylaws are still in existence as of today and thus play an important role in analyzing leagues' eligibility rules and their effect on player health.

To address the concerns of student-athletes who are weighing whether to turn professional, in 1990 the NCAA created the Exceptional Student-Athlete Disability Insur-ance ("ESDI") program.[25] We discuss the ESDI and other insurance options next.

3) PLAYERS' INSURANCE OPTIONS

In light of the NCAA's rules prohibiting players from being compensated while playing college sports (as many are effectively required to do for reasons explained below), some athletes might want insurance policies to protect against an injury preventing or reducing their future profes-sional earnings. Such athletes generally have two options: (a) the NCAA's ESDI program; and, (b) loss of value insur-ance policies through private insurers.

Student-athletes who demonstrate that they have the potential to be selected in the first three rounds of the NHL Draft, the first two rounds of the NFL Draft, or the first round of the NBA, MLB, or Women's National Basketball Association ("WNBA") Draft are eligible for the NCAA's Exceptional Student-Athlete Disability Insurance ("ESDI") program.[26] The program pays student-athletes a lump sum payment 12 months after determining that the player has suffered permanent total disability.[27]

The ESDI program, administered through HCC Specialty Underwriters Company, used to cap coverage at $5 mil-lion for projected first-round NFL Draft picks and men's basketball student-athletes,[28] while coverage for baseball, men's ice hockey and women's basketball was capped at $1.5 million, $1.2 million, and $250,000, respectively.[29] However, the amount of coverage is now determined by the insurer "based upon [the student-athlete's] prospec-tive status in the upcoming draft."[30] The premiums cost between $3,000 and $6,000 annually for each $1 million of coverage, depending on the sport and the player's position, which is considered a few thousand dollars less expensive than a private policy. Beginning in 2014, the NCAA has permitted colleges to pay the premiums on behalf of the player.[31] Alternatively, student-athletes may take out loans to pay for the insurance without losing their amateur status for the NCAA.[32] Approximately 40 to 50 athletes partici-pate in the ESDI program each year, and the majority of those athletes are college football players.[33]

In addition to the ESDI program, players might also con-sider obtaining a loss of value ("LOV") insurance policy through a private insurance company. LOV policies provide benefits to players whose draft stock, and thus the expected value of their contract, decreases due to injury.[34] For exam-ple, if a highly touted college player suffered an injury that prevented him from being the first overall pick in the draft, a LOV policy would have paid him the difference between the contract of the first overall pick and the player's actual, lesser contract.

In 2014, the NCAA approved permitting players to obtain loans based on the player's future earnings to pay for the premiums of LOV policies.[35] And because LOV policies are provided by private insurers rather than the NCAA, any player is able to obtain one if an insurance company is will-ing to provide coverage.

While LOV policies have reportedly become more common in recent years,[36] research has not revealed any publicly available data on how many players are obtaining the poli-cies or whether any have had difficult repaying the loans used to pay the premiums.

In 2015, for example, former Oregon and current NFL cornerback Ifo Ekpre-Olomu collected on a LOV policy.[37] Ekpre-Olomu was projected as a first round pick in the 2015 NFL Draft before tearing his ACL towards the end of the 2014 college season.[38] As a result of his injury, Ekpre-Olomu dropped to the seventh round of the NFL Draft.[39] Ekpre-Olomu's policy provided him with a $3 million pay-ment as a result.[40] In another instance, following the 2016 NFL Draft, former Notre Dame linebacker Jaylon Smith reportedly collected a $900,000 LOV policy after a knee injury dropped him from the first round into the second round of the Draft.[41]

With this background information covered, we are now ready to examine the NFL's player eligibility rules before comparing them to the other leagues.

A Player Eligibility Rules in the NFL

The 2011 NFL CBA provides that: "No player shall be . . . eligible for the [NFL] Draft, until three NFL regular reasons have begun and ended following either his graduation from high school or graduation of the class with which he entered high school, whichever is earlier."[42] Because there are no football leagues in the world comparable to the NFL in terms of skill and pay, the NFL's eligibility rule effectively requires almost all players to attend college for at least three seasons before they can enter the NFL Draft.[e]

The NFL's eligibility rule has faced legal challenges. In 2004, former Ohio State running back Maurice Clarett initiated an unsuccessful legal challenge to the NFL's eligibility rule. After a stellar freshman season in the fall of 2002 in which Clarett led Ohio State to the national championship, Clarett was suspended by the NCAA for the entire 2003 season due to a variety of NCAA rules infractions.[43] Rather than not play the 2003 season and then seek an uncertain reinstatement from the NCAA for the 2004 season, Clarett wished to enter the NFL Draft.[44] However, because he was not yet three years removed from his high school graduation, Clarett was ineligible for the Draft.

Clarett sued the NFL, arguing that the NFL's eligibility rule violated the antitrust laws. After initially winning in the United States District Court for the Southern District of New York, the United States Court of Appeals for the Second Circuit, in an opinion written by then-Judge Sonia Sotomayor, reversed. The Second Circuit held that the NFL's eligibility rule, even though it was not contained within the CBA, had been collectively bargained with the NFLPA and was thus immune from antitrust law pursuant to the non-statutory exemption.[45] In 2006, to help avoid future challenges, the NFL and NFLPA added the eligibility rule to the CBA.

The NFL's eligibility rule creates health-related pressures on two groups of potential players. We discuss each in turn.

First, the NFL's eligibility rule affects those college players who have already proven themselves as NFL prospects but are not yet eligible for the Draft. These players might be concerned about remaining healthy until they are eligible for the Draft (e.g., freshmen and sophomores). For example, in 2012, sophomore South Carolina defensive lineman Jadeveon Clowney established himself as the most dominant player in college football.[46] Many in the media argued that Clowney would have been the first overall pick in the 2013 Draft if not for the NFL's eligibility rule.[47] However, because of the eligibility rule, Clowney was forced to return to South Carolina for the 2013 season. Clowney had a less impressive 2013 season, including missing several games due to injuries. Clowney's diminished performance and missed game time caused some, including South Carolina's head coach Steve Spurrier, to speculate that Clowney was more concerned with protecting his NFL Draft status than playing college football.[48] Clowney was ultimately selected with the first overall pick in the 2014 NFL Draft.[49]

While Clowney's story still ended in him being highly drafted, there have been many players who suffered injuries in college and, as a result, saw their NFL Draft stock drop significantly. For example, Adewale Ogunleye, from the University of Indiana, was one of the country's best defensive players between 1996 and 1999 and considered leaving college early after his junior season in 1998. However, Ogunleye returned to college and suffered a knee injury during the 1999 season that caused him to go undrafted and left him unable to play in 2000.[50] Ogunleye ultimately went on to have a successful ten-year career in the NFL.

Clowney's former teammate at South Carolina, Marcus Lattimore, provides another interesting example. Lattimore, a running back who was First-Team All-SEC in his freshman year,[f] tore multiple ligaments in his knee in both his sophomore and junior seasons.[51] Lattimore was drafted by the San Francisco 49ers in the fourth round of the 2013 NFL Draft, but never played in an NFL game before

---

e   A notable exception was former University of Pittsburgh wide receiver Larry Fitzgerald. Fitzgerald had attended five years of high school and was thus eligible for the 2004 Draft after only two years of college football. Paul Zeise, *Fitzgerald Leaving Pitt Early for NFL*, Pittsburgh Post-Gazette, Feb. 10, 2004, *available at* 2004 WLNR 4854116. Fitzgerald was chosen with the third pick of the 2004 Draft and has had a stellar career with the Arizona Cardinals.

f   The SEC is widely regarded as the best college football conference. *After the SEC, which is the best conference in college football?* Nat'l Collegiate Athletics Ass'n, Sept. 2, 2014, http://www.ncaa.com/news/football/head-head/2014-08-22/after-sec-which-best-conference-college-football, *archived at* http://perma.cc/8JN2-AHAR; Clay Travis, *The SEC Is Dead, Long Live the SEC*, Fox Sports, Jan. 5, 2015, http://www.foxsports.com/college-football/outkick-the-coverage/the-sec-is-dead-long-live-the-sec-010515, *archived at* http://perma.cc/6C3W-LJVG.

retiring in 2014 due to ongoing knee problems.[52,g] Fortunately, Lattimore reportedly was eligible for a $1.7 million payment from a disability insurance policy.[53]

The Clowney, Ogunleye, and Lattimore stories all demonstrate the perils of being prevented from entering the NFL. A football player might suffer health problems at any time, but at least if the player is in the NFL, he will have earned (or be entitled to) some money before facing them.

The second group of potential players affected by the NFL's eligibility rule is comprised of those players who are eligible for the Draft and who also have college eligibility remaining (*e.g.*, juniors) but are considering entering the NFL Draft. These players (such as Ogunleye) often face a difficult choice between entering the Draft or playing another year of college football—during which time they may improve their skill and improve their Draft prospects, play for a championship at the collegiate level with their current teammates, and/or finish (or come closer to finishing) their educations, but also risk being injured.

The NFL's eligibility rule coupled with the short average duration of NFL careers, rookie contract structures, and free agency rules all place at least some pressure on players to leave college early for the NFL Draft. The mean career length of a drafted player is about five years.[54] NFL rookie contracts are limited to four years plus a club option for a fifth-year for first round picks and four years for all other Draft picks.[55] In addition, the form of rookie contracts is restrictive, limiting the amount players can potentially earn to amounts far below what Unrestricted Free Agents[h] might earn on the open market.[56] Finally, players cannot even become Unrestricted Free Agents until they have played at least four seasons.[57] Consequently, the typical player might only have one year left in his career when he is finally able to reach free agency and offer his services to the highest-bidding club.

All of this causes some players to believe they need to be in the NFL as soon as possible to capitalize on the limited timespan during which they can expect to be a healthy and productive NFL player. In particular, it is common to hear coaches or the media discuss the limited "lifespan" or "tread on the tires" for running backs.[58] If not for the NFL's eligibility rule, it is likely that some players would choose to enter the NFL Draft after their freshman or sophomore year of college, or maybe even high school, in order to maximize the perceived potential length of their NFL careers.

To assist these players, in 1994, the NFL created an Advisory Committee to help student-athletes determine their potential Draft round in the NFL Draft and assist them in making the decision of whether or not to leave school early.[59] The Advisory Committee is comprised of NFL club general managers, personnel directors, and scouts, and performs evaluations of student-athletes upon request from the student-athlete or his athletic department.[60] The Advisory Committee historically provided the student-athlete with an estimated range of rounds that the student-athlete should expect to be drafted (*e.g.*, rounds three through five).[61] In an effort to discourage players from entering the Draft early, the Advisory Committee's assessments are now separated into five categories: "As high as the first round; as high as the second round; as high as the third round; no potential to go in the first three rounds; and no potential to be drafted."[62] The Advisory Committee's assessments are confidential so it is thus impossible to judge their accuracy unless a player discloses them.

Despite the Advisory Committee's work, recent data suggests that many players declare for the NFL Draft before they are ready. In 2014, 45 of the 107 players (42%) who left college early were not drafted;[63] in 2015, 24 of the 84 early entrants (29%) went undrafted;[64] and, in 2016, 30 out of the 107 early entrants went undrafted (28%).[65i] Although those players had the opportunity to sign as undrafted free agents with any club, they were not guaranteed any compensation if they did so and their careers are likely to be shorter than those of drafted players.[66]

A player also cannot go through the Draft process and then, if not drafted, return to college football. Pursuant to NCAA Bylaws, a player who declares for the NFL Draft has only 72 hours to rescind his declaration or he cannot

---

g   Drawing on Lattimore's story, some recommended that Leonard Fournette, a star running back at LSU, not play his 2016 college season to avoid the risk of injury before becoming eligible for the 2017 NFL Draft. *See* Mike Florio, *Fournette definitely should take a year off in 2016*, ProFootballTalk (Sept. 30, 2015, 9:33 AM), http://profootballtalk.nbcsports.com/2015/09/30/fournette-definitely-should-take-a-year-off-in-2016/, *archived at* https://perma.cc/5XL4-6NJ4. Instead, Fournette obtained $20 million in insurance policies and played in the 2016 season. Mike Florio, *Leonard Fournette gets a pair of insurance policies*, ProFootballTalk (May 12, 2016, 10:05 PM), http://profootballtalk.nbcsports.com/2016/05/12/leonard-fourtnette-gets-a-pair-of-insurance-policies/, *archived at* https://perma.cc/2R2M-5DWK.

h   An Unrestricted Free Agent is a "player with four or more Accrued Seasons [who] . . . at the expiration of his Player Contract . . . shall be completely free to negotiate and sign a Player Contract with any Club, and any Club shall be completely free to negotiate and sign a Player Contract with such player without penalty or restriction[.]" 2011 NFL CBA, Art. 9, § 1(a).

i   It is important to know that while many (if not most) of the players who left college early did so because they thought they had the skill necessary to play in the NFL, at least some were likely forced to leave college for academic, personal, or institutional reasons.

return to play college football.[67] The NFL requires student-athletes to declare for the NFL Draft (which takes place in April or May) by January 15.[68] Thus, if a player has gone through the Draft in April or May, he is long past the January 18 (January 15 plus 72 hours) deadline to return to college football.

Even if the deadline for a player to rescind his declaration for the Draft were extended until after the Draft, NCAA Bylaws create an additional hurdle to players considering entering the Draft. A college football season ends in December or January but the NFL Draft is not until April or May. In that interim period, almost all prospective NFL players undergo extensive training to enable them to show off their skills at the NFL Combine and in other workouts in front of NFL clubs. The costs of that training and the player's living expenses during this time period—which are typically at least $30,000—are almost always paid for by agents. Consequently, to enter the NFL Draft, a player generally needs an agent—something forbidden by NCAA rules. Thus, a player who enters the NFL Draft and undertakes the requisite training to be drafted essentially gives up his NCAA eligibility, which prevents him from playing college football in the future.[69]

Despite the pressures the NFL's eligibility rule creates, the NFL's stated purposes for the rule are largely to protect player health. In the *Clarett* case, the NFL offered four reasons for its eligibility rule: "[1] protecting younger and/or less experienced players—that is, players who are less mature physically and psychologically—from heightened risks of injury in NFL games; [2] protecting the NFL's entertainment product from the adverse consequences associated with such injuries; [3] protecting the NFL clubs from the costs and potential liability entailed by such injuries; and [4] protecting from injury and self-abuse other adolescents who would over-train—and use steroids—in the misguided hope of developing prematurely the strength and speed required to play in the NFL."[70]

The NFL's eligibility rule imposes a strict delay on when players can enter the league. Given the injury concerns about playing football, players are often anxious to get to the NFL as soon as possible to maximize their potential earnings. Nevertheless, players must weigh their desire to enter the league with an understanding of whether or not they are physically prepared for the NFL.

Now that we have an understanding of the NFL player eligibility rules we are ready to compare them to the other major leagues.

B) Player Eligibility Rules in MLB

As a preliminary note, comparing player eligibility rules between the NFL and MLB from a health perspective is likely of diminished significance due to the different injury rates in the sports, discussed at length in Chapter 2. With that note in mind, we detail the player eligibility rules in MLB and their substantial difference from those of the NFL.

Players' eligibility to play in MLB depends on where the player is a resident. The eligibility rules differentiate players who are residents from the United States[j] or Canada from those who are not.

American and Canadian players who have never previously contracted with a major or minor league baseball club[k] are subject to MLB's First-Year Player Draft, known as the "Rule 4 Draft," because the Draft is set out in Rule 4 of MLB's Major League Rules[l] ("MLR")—but not the CBA.[m] Additionally, when players are eligible for the Rule 4 Draft depends on their education status.

The principal result of the Rule 4 Draft is that, generally, once a player enters college, he cannot enter the Draft again until after his junior year of college (unless he is 21). If the player plays beyond his junior year, he cannot enter the Draft until his collegiate eligibility has expired, which is typically after his senior year. Next, we provide a more detailed description of the Rule 4 Draft's nuances.

---

j   The "United States" includes "the 50 States of the United States of America, the District of Columbia, Puerto Rico, and any other Commonwealth, Territory or Possession of the United States." Major League Rule 3(a)(1). Additionally, a "resident of the United States" includes anyone who "enrolls in a United States high school or college or establishes a legal residence in the United States on the date of the player's contract or within one year prior to that date." Major League Rule 3(a)(1)(A).

k   Minor league baseball generally refers to lower levels of baseball in which players almost always play before reaching MLB. Minor League Baseball ("MiLB") is an organization of 15 different minor leagues with 176 teams, almost all of which are affiliated with an MLB club. *See General History,* Minor League Baseball, http://www.milb.com/milb/history/general_history.jsp (last visited June 23, 2016), *archived at* http://perma.cc/2WHA-44D2. In addition to MiLB, there are independent minor leagues that are not affiliated with MLB or MLB clubs in any way.

l   In addition to the CBA, many of MLB's rules are set out in a document entitled Major League Rules. Many of the Major League Rules have not been collectively bargained with the MLBPA, but the CBA does mention and amend some of the Rules. To the extent the Major League Rules and CBA conflict, the CBA controls.

m   The Major League Rules are not the CBA and are not necessarily collectively bargained with the MLBPA. While the CBA mentions multiple Major League Rules, and news reports indicate that changes to the Rule 4 Draft resulted from negotiations of the 2011 CBA, *see MLB, MLBPA reach new five-year labor agreement,* Major League Baseball, Nov. 22, 2011, http://m.mlb.com/news/article/26025138/, *archived at* http://perma.cc/48JZ-CUHX. MLB's eligibility rules are not an explicit part of the CBA and thus might be slightly more prone to an antitrust attack as compared to the eligibility rules of the NFL, NBA, NHL, and CFL for the reasons discussed in the Introduction of this Chapter.

High school players are not eligible for the Draft—and thus not eligible for MLB—while "the student is eligible for participation in high school athletics."[71] High school athletic eligibility typically terminates at the earlier of eight semesters of enrollment or graduation.[72] A high school player may become eligible for the Draft prior to graduation if he has become ineligible for high school competition due to his age, because he has completed the maximum number of allowable semesters of attendance without graduation, or if "the maximum number of seasons in which the player was eligible to participate in any major sport has passed," though in no case may a high school player be obligated "to report for service prior to the normal graduation of the class with which [he] originally entered high school."[73] Additionally, a high school player who drops out of high school prior to the expiration of his athletic eligibility must remain out of school for "365 days including the date of withdrawal" before he is eligible for the Rule 4 Draft.[74]

Of the 1,216 players drafted in 2016's Rule 4 Draft, only 300 (24.7%) were drafted directly out of high school.[75] The remaining players all played at least some college or junior college baseball. However, once a player decides to enter college, his eligibility for the Rule 4 Draft becomes restricted.

Subject to a number of exceptions discussed below, a college[76] player is ineligible for the Rule 4 Draft from the "date [he] attends the first class in [his] freshman year" until "the graduation of the class with which [he] originally entered college," or the graduation of a subsequent undergraduate class "if [he] retains eligibility to play baseball at [his] college in [that] year."[77]

The general rule that a college player is not eligible until the graduation of the class with which he entered college does not apply to a college player:

1 who is at least 21 years old and is currently between school years;

2 who has completed [his] junior year and is currently between school years;

3 who has completed the full period of [his] eligibility for intercollegiate baseball;

4 whose association with [his] college has been terminated by reason of scholastic deficiency[78]; or,

5 who withdraws from college and remains out [of college] for at least 120 days (including the date of withdrawal).[79]

Some high school players may also enter junior colleges. Junior college players are eligible for the Draft after either their first or second year at the school.[80]

MLB's different rules result in the possibility that a player can be drafted multiple times. A player drafted after high school may choose to enter college instead of signing. Players might believe they will have more opportunity to play and develop in college than in the minor leagues. Then, if the player enters a four-year college, he cannot be drafted again until he is 21 years of age or after his junior year. If he is still not ready to sign, he can return for his senior season. In each case, the player does not choose to enter the Draft—he is automatically subject to the Draft. Therefore, a player could be drafted after high school, after his junior year of college, and then a third time after his senior year of college.[n]

While MLB's Draft rules provide considerable flexibility, there have been occasions where players thought they were sufficiently prepared for MLB before they could be drafted. After completing his sophomore year of high school in 2009, during which he batted .626, Bryce Harper earned his General Educational Development ("GED") and enrolled in a junior college to face better competition.[81] After one year in junior college, Harper was selected as the first overall pick in the 2010 Rule 4 Draft at the age of 17. Nevertheless, Harper's situation (and talent) is considered anomalous.

We now discuss the eligibility rules for foreign (i.e., non-U.S./non-Canadian) players, assuming they have not entered an American or Canadian college or otherwise become a resident of the United States. These foreign players are never subject to the Rule 4 Draft.[82] Instead, an international player is eligible to sign a professional contract if he is "17 years old at the time of signing, or . . . will attain age 17 prior to either the end of the effective season for which the player has signed or September 1 of such effective season, whichever is later."[83]

In lieu of a draft, MLB clubs engage in a competitive scouting and bidding process for international talent, particularly as the rate of foreign-born players has increased. In 2016, 27.5% of players on clubs' opening day rosters were foreign-born.[84] Moreover, 22.3% of all MLB players were from South or Central American countries.[85]

---

n   It is even possible to be drafted four times. Some players go from high school to junior college, where you can be drafted after your second year. Hypothetically, a player could be drafted after high school, enter a junior college and be drafted after junior college, then enroll in a four-year college, be drafted after his junior year, and be drafted a fourth time after graduating from, or completing his eligibility at, the four-year college.

Unfortunately, the scouting and bidding process has been fraught with problems. In Latin American countries, young baseball players—some not even in their teens—are often found and then controlled by "buscones," or street agents.[86] The buscones control MLB clubs' access to the players and can effectively sell the players to the clubs, taking a portion of the players' signing bonus for themselves.[87] MLB club personnel have also been caught defrauding their clubs by taking a portion of the signing bonus allocated for the player (and often splitting it with the buscone).[88] In addition, there are widespread problems with identity fraud. Players desperate to reach MLB claim to be younger than they are or might even pretend to be someone else entirely.[89] While MLB and MLB clubs have taken steps to prevent identity fraud and to eliminate the influence of buscones (by having their own academies), many have also argued that the best way to resolve the issues is through an international Draft.[90]

The 2011 CBA created an International Talent Committee charged with "discuss[ing] the development and acquisition of international players, including the potential inclusion of international amateur players in a draft, and to examine the rules and procedures pursuant to which international professional players sign contracts with clubs."[91] As part of its mandate, the International Talent Committee was to provide the MLBPA and MLB with advice on "[t]he appropriate age at which international amateur players should be signed to professional contracts."[92] Other than its first meeting in 2012,[93] our research has not revealed any output from the International Talent Committee. At the time of this writing there was still no draft for international players.

During the 2016 CBA negotiations, it was reported that MLB and the MLBPA seriously discussed the possibility of a draft for international players.[94] However, the sides were not able to reach an agreement. Instead, the parties agreed that Clubs would be subject to a "Signing Bonus Pool" that limited the amount of compensation Clubs could provide to international players.[95] The Signing Bonus Pool is a maximum of $5.75 million, growing annually with league revenues.[96]

Importantly, regardless of how a player ends up with an MLB club—whether through the Draft or as an international signee—almost all players will play several seasons with the minor league clubs affiliated with the MLB club that drafted them before signing an MLB contract[97] or playing in an MLB game, if they ever even do. Indeed, only about 17% of drafted players ever reach the major leagues.[98] Players signed to minor league contracts are not members of the MLBPA and are not entitled to the same rights and benefits as major league players.[99] Whereas the minimum salary for a major league player was $507,500 in 2016,[100] minor league players often earn between $10,000 and $20,000 per season.[101]

Additionally, for either domestic or international players, health generally would not be a factor in considering how to proceed with their professional eligibility.

International players generally want to get into international camps or onto minor league clubs affiliated with MLB clubs as soon as possible, i.e., as soon as they are eligible. MLB's eligibility rule permits international players to sign at age 17 (or slightly earlier) and thus is a minimal (if any) barrier to entry for international players. These camps and clubs generally provide international players with the best resources—including coaching, housing, and healthcare—that they have ever experienced, while also increasing their chances of one day making the Major Leagues. In doing so, these players forfeit the right to ever play college baseball—an unlikely career trajectory for international players anyway. Thus, international players generally gain little by not entering into a professional contract as soon as they are able.

MLB's eligibility rules also do not create health-related concerns for American and Canadian players. MLB's eligibility rules do not prevent American and Canadian players, apart from very rare circumstances (e.g. Bryce Harper), from entering MLB as soon they believe it is in their best interests. They have the opportunity to become a major leaguer at various times and as early as age 17. By the time a player reached the skill level necessary to be drafted by an MLB club, he almost certainly would have reached the age of 17. Thus, the eligibility rule generally does not force players to make difficult decisions concerning their health.

NCAA eligibility rules, however, can affect an American or Canadian player's choices. American or Canadian players who have been drafted by MLB clubs often have to consider whether to forego a signing bonus worth tens or hundreds of thousands of dollars from an MLB club to play or continue playing in college. Choosing to remain in college subjects the player to the risk of career-ending or threatening injury without compensation. As discussed above, the NCAA's ESDI program attempts to alleviate some of these concerns.

The NFL and MLB eligibility rules are very different. The NFL eligibility rules effectively require a player to play three years in college and permit the player one chance to determine when is best for him to enter the NFL. In contrast, MLB eligibility rules allow a player to be drafted multiple times, including right out of high school.

The differences in the rules are perpetuated by the NCAA's rules and also the role of agents. A player becomes ineligible for NCAA competition once he signs with an agent.[102] However, to be drafted in MLB, a player does not need an agent. MLB's Draft is held in June—shortly after a high school or college player would have finished his season and thus their prior results will largely determine their Draft performance. As discussed above, college football players almost always need the help of an agent to prepare for the NFL Draft—help that is forbidden by NCAA rules. As a result, even if the NFL adopted a system whereby players have the ability to be drafted multiple times like that of MLB, it would be useless due to the NCAA's rules.

The number of rounds in each league's draft also plays an important role. The MLB Draft has 40 rounds. Additionally, MLB clubs generally do not even sign many of the players they draft and, of the athletes they do sign, all of them will have to prove themselves in the minor leagues before reaching the MLB club. Consequently, MLB clubs have much more flexibility in drafting players who might not yet be ready for MLB. In contrast, the NFL Draft is only seven rounds and every player will immediately join the NFL club, creating considerably more pressure on NFL clubs to use each and every Draft pick wisely. NFL clubs do not have the luxury of drafting players who might instead prefer to return to college.

 ## C) Player Eligibility Rules in the NBA

The NBA's eligibility rules differentiate between American players and international—including Canadian—players.[103]

American players must meet three criteria to be eligible for the NBA Draft, summarized as follows:

1. The player is or will be at least 19 years old during the calendar year in which the Draft is held;[104]

2. At least one NBA season must have elapsed since the player's graduation from high school (or the graduation of the class with which the player would have graduated high school);[105] and,

3. The player must meet one of the following seven conditions:

   a. The player has graduated from a four-year college or university in the United States (or is to graduate in the calendar year in which the Draft is held) and has no remaining intercollegiate basketball eligibility; or,

   b. The player is attending or previously attended a four-year college or university in the United States, his original class in such college or university has graduated (or is to graduate in the calendar year in which the Draft is held), and he has no remaining intercollegiate basketball eligibility; or,

   c. The player has graduated from high school in the United States, did not enroll in a four-year college or university in the United States, and four calendar years have elapsed since such player's high school graduation; or,

   d. The player did not graduate from high school in the United States, and four calendar years have elapsed since the graduation of the class with which the player would have graduated had he graduated from high school;[o] or,

   e. The player has signed a player contract with a 'professional basketball team not in the NBA' . . . and has rendered services under such contract prior to the January 1, immediately preceding such Draft; or,

   f. The player has expressed his desire to be selected in the Draft in a writing received by the NBA at least sixty days prior to such Draft (an "Early Entry" player)[.][106]

International players must meet two criteria to be eligible for NBA Draft:

1. The player must be at least 19 years old during the calendar year in which the Draft is held;[107] and,

2. The player must meet one of the following three conditions:

   a. The player is or will be twenty-two years of age during the calendar year of the Draft; or,

   b. The player has signed a player contract with a "professional basketball team not in the NBA" . . . that is located in the United States, and has rendered services under such contract prior to the Draft; or,

---

o   As a result of this specific rule, some players can be eligible for the NBA Draft by intentionally not graduating from high school. For example, prior to the 2016 NBA Draft, it was reported that Jonathan Isaac, a high school player, was considering going straight from high school to the NBA. Isaac was in his 5th year of high school and thus the class with which Isaac entered high school had already graduated. Provided Isaac did not complete high school, he would have been eligible for the 2016 NBA Draft. Nevertheless, Isaac ultimately chose to attend college instead. *See* Dan Feldman, *Will Jonathan Isaac Jump from High School to NBA Draft?*, Pro Basketball Talk (Feb. 11, 2016, 10:40 PM), http://nba.nbcsports.com/2016/02/11/will-jonathan-isaac-jump-from-high-school-to-nba-draft/, *archived at* https://perma.cc/XPB4-NYYB. Had Isaac graduated from high school but did not enroll in college, he would have had to wait four calendar years until he would be eligible for the Draft. 2017 NBA CBA, Art. X, § 1(b)(ii)(C).

c. The player has expressed his desire to be selected in the Draft in a writing received by the NBA at least sixty days prior to such Draft (an '"Early Entry" player).[108]

The NBA's eligibility rules and their evolution have been controversial. Prior to 1971, the NBA required players to be four years removed from high school graduation in order to be eligible for the Draft.[109] In 1970, Spencer Haywood, a former Olympic basketball player who chose to play in the professional American Basketball Association ("ABA")[110] rather than finish college, sued the NBA, alleging that the NBA's eligibility rule violated the antitrust laws.[111] The United States District Court for the District of California agreed and enjoined the NBA from enforcing its eligibility rule.[112] Two weeks after the District Court's decision, the United States Court of Appeals for the Ninth Circuit stayed the injunction pending the NBA's appeal.[113] However, two weeks later, the Supreme Court of the United States reinstated the injunction.[114] Haywood and the NBA then settled the case, with the NBA agreeing to allow players who were less than four years removed from high school graduation to enter the NBA if they if they could demonstrate "financial hardship."[115] In 1976, the eligibility rule was removed in its entirety.[116]

Despite the NBA's removal of the eligibility rule, almost all players continued to spend at least some time in college before entering the NBA.[117] Between 1976 and 1995, no players entered the NBA without first attending college.[118] In 1995, Chicago high school star Kevin Garnett was chosen with the fifth overall pick in the Draft, beginning a wave of high school players trying to make the leap straight to the NBA. Between 1995 and 2005, 39 high schoolers were selected in the NBA Draft.[119]

However, some high schoolers went undrafted[p] or otherwise had unsuccessful NBA careers, causing many to believe that they had tried to make the NBA too soon.[120] As a result, the NBA sought and obtained the current eligibility rule as part of the 2005 CBA.[121] Nevertheless, many have also criticized the current eligibility rule for the creation of so-called "one-and-done" players, that is, players who play one season of college basketball (as required by the eligibility rule), before entering the NBA Draft.[122] These players are able to enroll in college, take the minimum number of classes in their first semester, go to some of their classes as the college basketball season winds down in their second

semester, declare for the Draft, and drop out of school having completed only four or five general education classes.[123] Since the initiation of the current eligibility rule, 95 players have left college after only one season and were drafted by an NBA club (a mean of 8.6 per Draft), with mixed success in the NBA.[124]

There are also college players who are eligible for the Draft but, if they have collegiate eligibility remaining, debate whether to return to college. For these players, the NBA's eligibility rule is not a concern but only their readiness for the NBA and the potential for injury at the collegiate level. The NCAA's ESDI program, discussed above, is an attempt to alleviate some of the concerns about possible injury. In addition, beginning in 2016, the NCAA amended its rules to permit underclassmen players to participate in the NBA's pre-Draft Combine to allow players to better gauge their Draft potential.[125] Following the Combine, a player now has ten days to withdraw from the Draft and return to college (provided he never signed with an agent).[126]

Instead of playing NCAA basketball, some American players have chosen instead to go play professionally in foreign countries before entering the NBA Draft,[127] with mixed success. In 2008, Brandon Jennings, a highly acclaimed high school basketball player from California, decided to play professional basketball in Italy instead of playing college basketball. After one season in Italy, Jennings was selected 10th overall in the 2009 NBA Draft and has had, as of the publication of this Report, a successful NBA career.[128] Jeremy Tyler, another California basketball player who, in 2009, opted to play professionally overseas rather than play college basketball in the United States, had less success.[129,q]

In addition to playing NCAA basketball or overseas, players have one other option before they are eligible for the NBA. Players can play in the NBA Development League ("D-League").[r] The D-League, started in 2001, is the NBA's official minor league, consisting of 22 clubs with players hoping to reach the NBA.[130] Indeed, more than 30% of current NBA players have played in the D-League at some

---

p   The players would have been unable to pursue college basketball if they had signed an agreement with an agent, *see* NCAA Division I Manual, § 12.1.2 ("An individual loses amateur status and thus shall not be eligible for intercollegiate competition in a particular sport if the individual . . . [e]nters into an agreement with an agent."). Most, if not all, of the players signed with agents in hopes of increasing their chances of being drafted.

q   Tyler decided to leave high school after his junior year and play professional basketball in Israel and Japan until he was NBA eligible. While Tyler eventually made it to the NBA as a second round NBA Draft pick in 2011, he was not a successful NBA player and currently plays in China. As another example, in 2014, Emmanuel Mudiay from Texas went to play in China rather than for an American college. Mudiay, who escaped from war in the Congo as a child, chose playing overseas due to potential problems concerning the NCAA's academic eligibility and amateurism requirements. In the 2015 NBA Draft, Mudiay was selected with the seventh overall pick by the Denver Nuggets.

r   Beginning with the 2017-18 season, the D-League will officially be known as the "G-League" as part of a sponsorship agreement with Gatorade. Dan Feldman, *D-League? It's Now the G-League*, Pro Basketball Talk (Feb. 14, 2016, 9:50 AM), http://nba.nbcsports.com/2017/02/14/d-league-its-now-the-g-league/, *archived at* https://perma.cc/8KN3-GL8J.

point.[131] Of most relevance, the minimum age to play in the D-League is 18 years old, one year younger than the NBA's requirement.[132] However, no high school player has ever foregone the NCAA for the D-League[s] and most D-League players are undrafted former college players or NBA veterans trying to make a comeback.[133] The low salaries (reportedly between $19,500 and $26,000[134]) likely deter players from considering the D-League as their best option.[t]

The NBA's eligibility rule is generally considered the most controversial in sports. To its critics, the rule prevents young men capable of playing in the NBA from pursuing their chosen career (or at least choosing to try to play in the NBA) and instead forces them to enroll in college for a brief period of time even if they have no interest in academics.[135] Others believe requiring players to mature more before entering the NBA is essential for their development as both players and people.[136] Additionally, some have suggested that by having rookies play at least one year of college basketball, they will be more familiar to fans and thus be more interesting and marketable to NBA fans.[137] For these reasons, leading up to the 2017 CBA negotiations, the NBA suggested requiring players to be at least two years removed from high school before entering the NBA Draft.[138] Nevertheless, the NBPA resisted those suggestions and no changes were made to the eligibility rule in the 2017 CBA.[139]

The NBA and NFL eligibility rules are similar in that they both effectively require players to play at least some time in college. While the NBA requires one year and the NFL requires three years, both leagues' rules are generally designed to keep players out of the professional leagues until they are sufficiently physically and mentally mature, thus arguably protecting both the players and the clubs' investments in those players.

D) Player Eligibility Rules in the NHL

To be eligible to play in the NHL, a player must be at least 18 years old and have sufficient vision in both eyes (a requirement discussed further below).[140,u] To reach the NHL, players are subject to the NHL Draft unless the player is at least 22 years old or is at least 21 years old and played hockey for at least one season in North America when he was 18, 19, or 20.[141]

The NHL's Draft and eligibility rules are complicated by the heavily international nature of the NHL. In the 2016–17 season, 48% of the players were born in Canada, 24.8% were born in America, and the remaining 27.2% of players were from 13 different European nations.[142] All players are subject to the NHL Draft, regardless of their nationality.

The five principal sources of NHL Draft picks are: (1) the Canadian Hockey League, an organization of three hockey leagues (Quebec Major Junior Hockey League, Ontario Hockey League, and the Western Hockey League) ("Canadian Juniors"); (2) the United States Hockey League ("USHL"), an American junior hockey league; (3) American colleges; (4) players playing in European

---

s   In 2009, Latavious Williams did go directly from high school to the D-League. However, Williams had little choice—after committing to play at the University of Memphis, Williams could not meet NCAA academic requirements to play.
t   Players that entered the D-League would be ineligible to play NCAA basketball.

u   News reports have indicated that the NHL is considering trying to raise the minimum age to 19. *See* Allan Muir, *Notebook: Draft age change in store?* Sports Illustrated (Mar. 8, 2016), http://www.si.com/nhl/2016/03/07/nhl-draft-age-change-world-cup-over-35-team-players, *archived at* https://perma.cc/9L6C-8CL4.

professional leagues; and, (5) American high schools.[143] The Canadian Juniors are for players between the ages of 16–20 and operate like a semi-professional league: the players generally continue to be in school of some kind and receive a few hundred dollars a month as a stipend.[144] The NCAA considers Canadian Juniors to be professional leagues due to the compensation and benefits the players receive.[145] Consequently, many young players face a difficult choice between playing hockey for American colleges or playing in Canadian Juniors.[146] About 50% of NHL players played in Canadian Juniors,[147] while about 30% of NHL players went to an American college.[148] While the USHL is also for players between the ages of 16–20, it does not provide players a stipend and thus they retain their NCAA eligibility.

The NHL's eligibility rules provide flexibility for players. High school and college players can be drafted and choose to instead play college hockey. The drafting NHL club generally holds the player's rights until he graduates college, meaning no other club can draft or sign the player.[149] In the case of non-North American players, the drafting NHL club holds the player's rights for four years if the player is 18 or 19, or two years if he is 20.[150] After each collegiate season, the player can decide whether to return to college or to begin his NHL career with the club that drafted him.

The purpose of the NHL's age requirement is unclear. However, in deciding to return to college as opposed to enter the NHL, several players have cited the need to continue to grow physically and to gain weight to be prepared for the NHL.[151] Thus, assuming age is a proxy for physical size, the NHL's eligibility rule prevents players who might not be physically ready for the NHL from entering prematurely.

Concerning the vision requirement mentioned above, the NHL By-Laws declare ineligible "[a] player with only one eye, or one of whose eyes has a vision of only three-sixtieths (3/60ths) or under."[152] In the 1970s, NHL draftee Greg Neeld, who had lost his left eye in a Juniors game, sued the NHL, alleging that the rule violated the antitrust laws. The NHL's rule was ultimately determined to be reasonable and not in violation of the antitrust laws.[153] The United States Court of Appeals for the Ninth Circuit determined that "the primary purpose and direct effect of the League's by-law was not anticompetitive but rather safety," as there was "bound to be danger to players who happen[ed] to be on Neeld's blind side."[154]

The NHL's eligibility rules are generally flexible and do not force players to either abstain from entering the NHL or to enter the NHL. Players have a variety of options and generally enter the Draft when their skills and size have sufficiently developed to play in the NHL.

The NHL's eligibility rule is similar to MLB's in that it provides players multiple opportunities to determine when to enter the NHL. The NHL's eligibility rule thus differs from the NFL's in many of the same ways that MLB's rule does. Prospective NHL players—like prospective MLB players—can easily be drafted without the assistance of an agent, and thus do not need to risk their NCAA eligibility to consider whether to turn professional like prospective NFL players do. Additionally, prospective NHL players—also like prospective MLB players—will have to prove themselves in the minor leagues before reaching the NHL. The minor league system provides NHL—and MLB—clubs several years to develop their draft picks into productive professionals. In contrast, the NFL does not have a minor league and thus NFL clubs are under pressure to draft players who are going to have an impact in a relatively short period of time.

E) Player Eligibility Rules in the CFL

The CFL's eligibility rules depend on whether the player is a National Player or an International Player. National Players are those who are Canadian citizens at the time of signing the player's first CFL contract, or a player who was physically resident in Canada for an aggregate period of five years prior to turning 18 years old.[155] International Players are players who do not meet the criteria to be a National Player.[156]

National Player eligibility is further differentiated based on whether the player plays in the Canadian Interuniversity Sport ("CIS") League, Canada's equivalent of the NCAA, or in the NCAA or National Association of Intercollegiate Athletics ("NAIA," the NCAA's much smaller American competitor).

National Players who play in the CIS are eligible for the CFL Draft three years after completing their first year of CIS eligibility.[157] Under the CIS By-laws, a football player is "charged with a year of eligibility for each year of competition where the athlete participated in" more than one regular-season game.[158] Thus, under normal circumstances, a National Player is not eligible for the CFL Draft until he has played four years of college football. This rule was created in 2013 to eliminate the ability of "redshirt" juniors to enter the CFL Draft. In college athletics, when a player is "redshirted," it means he will not compete in athletics that season,[v] and that

---

v   Student-athletes red-shirt for several reasons: (1) as freshman, to allow for a transition to the athletic and academic rigors of college; (2) due to an injury; and, (3) to improve their academic standing.

season will not count against the number of seasons that the player is permitted to play. Therefore, a redshirted player would not be charged with a year of eligibility under CIS By-laws. A redshirted junior would be a fourth-year player academically but who has only played three seasons of college football (having sat out the redshirt season). The CFL's current eligibility rules no longer permit redshirt juniors to enter the CFL Draft.[159]

National Players who play NCAA or NAIA football are only eligible for the CFL Draft after they have completed their senior year of eligibility.[160] Thus, redshirt juniors playing college football in the United States are also barred from the CFL Draft. Before the rule changes in 2013, juniors who were National Players playing college football in the United States could be drafted by CFL clubs but still return for their senior season.[161] The CFL club would retain rights to the player upon their graduation.[162] The prior regime required CFL clubs to speculate on which National Players would choose to leave college after their junior season for the CFL or choose to instead return to college and play a senior season with the hopes of maybe making the NFL.[163] The change was made to improve predictability in the Draft as to which National Players would actually play in the CFL.[164]

In stark contrast to the rules for National Players and the rules of the NFL, the CFL imposes no age or education requirements for International Players.[165] Thus, American high school players could choose to play in the CFL as opposed to playing college football in the United States. Although our research has not revealed a case where that actually occurred, we have found at least one case where it was considered. In 2009, star high school running back Bryce Brown was reportedly considering foregoing college for the CFL.[166] Brown ultimately chose to attend the University of Tennessee and later Kansas State University before being selected in the 2012 NFL Draft.

While the CFL eligibility rules permit American players to enter at any time, they are very restrictive of National Players. Effectively, a National Player cannot join the CFL until he has played four years of college football. While the rule might assist National Players in obtaining their college degree, it also subjects them to the wear and tear of four years of college football before they can consider becoming professional. It is likely that some National Players believe they are physically prepared for the CFL prior to graduation and would prefer to enter the CFL earlier so as to avoid the risk of injury or diminished skill. However, the CFL rules do not permit a National Player to make that choice.

The CFL's eligibility rule is more restrictive than that of the NFL's. Whereas the NFL's rule only requires players to play

three years of college football, the CFL requires four years of college for National players (the only players relevant for this discussion). Additionally, the CFL's eligibility rule does not appear to be concerned with player health — but is instead principally concerned with CFL clubs' ability to know which players are likely to play in the CFL.

F) Player Eligibility Rules in MLS

In contrast to all of the other leagues, MLS does not have an eligibility rule. Players need not be of a certain age or have reached a certain level of education to play in MLS. Indeed, in the 2016 season, there were 18 teenagers on MLS rosters, with the youngest player being 16.[167] Notably, Freddy Adu began playing with MLS' D.C. United club in 2004 at the age of 14.[168]

Although there is no eligibility rule, players arrive at MLS via a wide variety of paths. The path by which a player arrives at MLS determines the process by which the player reaches his club:

1. Allocation Process: U.S. Men's National Team players, elite youth U.S. National Team players, and former MLS players returning to MLS after playing with a non-MLS club for a transfer fee of greater than $500,000 are allocated to clubs pursuant to MLS' Allocation Ranking List (which is in the reverse order of the prior season's standings).[169]

2. SuperDraft: Clubs can nominate players to be in the MLS SuperDraft and only nominated players can be drafted.[w] College players, non-collegiate international players, and players from Generation adidas are eligible for the Super Draft.[x]

---

w   Although it is called the "SuperDraft," the SuperDraft is simply MLS' draft.

x   "Generation adidas is a joint program between MLS and adidas that is dedicated to developing exceptional domestic talent in a professional environment. Each year, a handful of top domestic collegiate underclassmen and youth national team players are signed by the league and placed in the SuperDraft through this program." Generation adidas players may also receive an education stipend. Importantly, Generation adidas players are on a club's Supplemental Roster and are not charged against the team's salary budget. *Roster Rules and Regulations*, § II(C), MLS.com, http://pressbox.mlssoccer.com/content/roster-rules-and-regulations (last visited May 18, 2015), *archived at* http://perma.cc/48QQ-VC4S. Generation adidas is designed to prevent the best underclassmen from going to play in Europe. Brooke Tunstall, *Does MLS Block College Underclassmen from Draft?*, Am. Soccer Now (Jan 17, 2014, 6:39 PM), http://americansoccernow.com/articles/does-mls-block-college-underclassmen-from-draft, *archived at* http://perma.cc/3862-WDCR. As a result of the Generation adidas program, generally only players who have exhausted their collegiate eligibility are nominated to be in the SuperDraft. *Roster Rules and Regulations, supra*. The impact of the Generation adidas program is also discussed in Chapter 3: Health-Related Benefits.

3. Discovery Process: Clubs can scout and sign players who are not under contract to MLS and who are not subject to the Allocation Process or SuperDraft.[170] The Discovery Process is typically used to sign foreign players who were not nominated for the SuperDraft.[171]

4. Homegrown Players: Clubs may sign a player to his first professional contract without subjecting him to the SuperDraft if the player has been a member of the club's youth academy for at least one year.[172]

Normally, MLS' different drafting and signing processes do not place pressure on players. There are a wide variety of soccer leagues around the world and generally, if a player is good enough, he will have opportunities. MLS' rules are generally designed to assist MLS in competing against more talented and better paying European leagues for players' services. For example, players signed to Generation adidas contracts are given incentive-laden contracts that provide the opportunity for greater compensation than if the player had completed his college degree while also placing money in escrow for them to complete their college education.[173]

The Generation adidas education payments are similar to the NFL's Tuition Assistance Plan, which reimburses players for tuition, fees, and books from attending an eligible education institution. However, while the Generation adidas program is limited to only some elite players, all current NFL players with at least one Credited Season are eligible for the Tuition Assistance Plan. Former players with at least five Credited Seasons are also eligible provided that the costs are incurred within four years of the player's last season.

Now that we have reviewed the policies of the major leagues we are ready to analyze the NFL's policies by comparing them to these leagues' policies.

G) Analysis

The leagues' eligibility policies vary. MLS has the most liberal eligibility policy, with no minimum age requirement, while, by requiring several years of college, the NFL and CFL are the most restrictive.

All of the eligibility rules seemingly are at least partially concerned with when a player is "ready" to enter a professional league. Readiness is an important concept, but difficult to define. In our view, a player is ready when he is able

to enter the league safely, in terms of protecting his health,[y] and maximize his success across various domains, including physically, mentally, and emotionally. Each of the leagues, often through negotiations with the unions, has made a judgment as to when they think the typical player is ready, or at least ready enough. In so doing, the leagues have helped protect clubs from drafting and investing in players who are not ready, and also potentially helped to protect players who need more time to prepare for a successful and healthy career.[z] However, without more empirical analysis, we cannot say for certain when players—individually or collectively—are ready and thus whether the eligibility rule is fair or successful. No such data currently exists and would be challenging to gather. We discuss this issue further in the Recommendations.

The NBA is the one league that potentially has the data to inform its eligibility rule. Between 1995 and 2005, 35 high schoolers were selected in the NBA Draft.[174] Concerned that many of these players were not ready for the NBA, the NBA instituted its current eligibility rule in the 2005 CBA. Since the initiation of the current eligibility rule, 95 players have left college after only one season and were drafted by an NBA club.[175] One could, in theory, compare the career and health outcomes of the high schoolers that entered the NBA with those of the one-and-done players and with upperclassmen to potentially evaluate whether the NBA's eligibility rule has been effective at preventing players from entering the NBA before they are ready.[aa] Such a comparison would be helpful, if not conclusive (in part because of selection effects and other research design problems), in understanding the value of delaying eligibility. Indeed, in 2017, NBA Commissioner Adam Silver discussed the need for the eligibility rule to be "studied" more closely,

---

y   As a reminder and as discussed in the Introduction, Section F: Scope, we define health for purposes of this Report as "a state of overall wellbeing in fundamental aspects of a person's life, including physical, mental, emotional, social, familial, and financial components."

z   On this point, it is interesting to note that in Europe, soccer and basketball players often begin playing professionally in their mid-to-late teens. *See, e.g., Next Generation 2015: 50 of the best young talents in world football,* The Guardian, Oct. 7, 2015, http://www.theguardian.com/football/ng-interactive/2015/oct/07/next-generation-2015-50-of-the-best-young-talents-in-world-football, *archived at* https://perma.cc/PTR6-T8SJ; Lang Whitaker, *Here's Footage of 14-Year-Old Ricky Rubio,* NBA.com (Nov. 7, 2014, 10:22 AM), http://allball.blogs.nba.com/2014/11/07/heres-footage-of-14-year-old-ricky-rubio/, *archived at* https://perma.cc/WK5W-R777.

aa   Indeed, there has been some research on this issue. An analysis of first-round draft picks from 1989–2000 by Ryan Rodenberg and Jun Woo Kim concluded that "players who are drafted at a younger age relative to other draftees have, on average, more successful NBA careers." Moreover, the authors concluded that "there is no evidence that players who played one year of college basketball, while controlling for other factors, perform better than individuals who moved into the NBA straight from high school." Ryan Rodenberg and Jun Woo Kim, *Testing the On-Court Efficacy of the NBA's Age Eligibility Rule,* 8 J. Quantitative Analysis in Sports 1 (2012). While this analysis is interesting, some might argue that it does not address one of the core purposes of the eligibility rule: preventing young men who give up their eligibility to play at the college level by entering the Draft early from having their careers derailed by being drafted in the second round or not drafted at all.

including better understanding various factors that affect or are affected by the rule.[176] While the NBA's consideration of this issue is laudable, the data from any such study would have limited generalizability to the other leagues due to the different demands of each sport.

The Women's Tennis Association ("WTA") provides a useful example. WTA's eligibility rule, probably more than any other sports organization, is the result of considerable analysis and study. In the early 1990s, there was concern about the well-being and career longevity of teenage players competing on the WTA Tour.[177] At the time, fourteen- and fifteen-year-old players were permitted extensive play on the WTA Tour.[178] As a result, in 1994, the WTA Tour formed an Age Eligibility Commission to study the Tour's eligibility rule.[179] The Age Eligibility Commission, consisting of sports medicine and sports science professionals, gathered and analyzed extensive anecdotal, statistical, medical, and scientific evidence. Among the data gathered was evidence that an early start to a player's career correlated to an earlier departure from the Tour.[180] Based on such evidence, the Commission recommended a revised eligibility rule,[181] adopted in 1995, that instituted a graduated maximum number of tournaments for players beginning at age 14 and with no limits after players reach age 18.[182] In 2004, the Age Eligibility Commission's successor, the Age Eligibility Advisory Panel, conducted an extensive re-examination of the rule, again gathering a variety of anecdotal, statistical, medical, and scientific evidence.[183] The Age Eligibility Advisory Panel concluded that the 1995 rule change had been helpful to young players and enhanced their career longevity, while recommending some minor tweaks.[184]

> The NCAA's rules create a problem for players who have the potential to reach the NFL but who are required — or might prefer — to continue playing college football.

The comparison of the leagues' policies highlights two clear issues with the NFL's eligibility rule, but, generally, neither is of the NFL's making.

First, the NFL's requirement that players effectively play at least three years of college football might ensure that only sufficiently physically mature players enter professional football, but it also requires players to risk their physical health longer without getting paid—and in a sport with higher injuries rates than that of the other leagues, as discussed in Chapter 2: Injury Rates and Policies. While the NCAA's ESDI program tries to alleviate some of these issues, players have legitimate concerns that they will suffer a career-altering or ending injury before they are able to reach the professional level and earn any money from their athletic skills. This is at least in part a problem resulting from the NCAA's prohibition on student-athletes being compensated. Whether the NCAA's rules are fair is beyond the scope of this Report, but it is clear that the rules create a problem for players who have the potential to reach the NFL but who are required—or might prefer—to continue playing college football.

Second, in light of the fact that players are not paid for playing in college, it is understandable that many want to enter the NFL as soon as possible. Specifically, players will want to enter the NFL after their junior year of college, the first time they are permitted under the NFL's eligibility rule. However, whether the player is ready for the NFL is a difficult question to answer and may not be resolved until many years later—if ever. If the player is undrafted, NCAA rules effectively prohibit the player from returning to college football, and the player's football future is in serious doubt. Once again, although this problem intersects with the NFL's eligibility rule, it is the primary result of the NCAA's rules, not the NFL's.

Ultimately, without more data, it is unclear what the optimal eligibility rule is in any of the leagues. Thus, it is also unclear whether any of the leagues can learn from each other on this issue. As a result, we cannot assess the reasonableness of the NFL's current eligibility rule. The rule seemingly prevents players from joining the NFL before they are ready, which both protects those players from injury in the NFL and protects the clubs from investing in players who are not yet ready to play at a professional level. While there are likely to occasionally be players who are ready to join the NFL before the end of their junior season,[ab] there are going to be outliers to any rule and, without data suggesting otherwise, we cannot say the NFL's eligibility rule is not reasonable or sufficiently considerate of player health. For this reason our main recommendation is for the NFL to continue to gather data to permit a better evidence-based evaluation of its current policy, as well to consider the interplay of its rules with the NCAA's.

---

ab For example, in 2007, the Houston Texans drafted Amobi Okoye with the tenth overall pick at the age of 19. Okoye, originally from Nigeria, began college at the age of 15 in light of his academic performance. See Steve E. Cavezza, "Can I See Some ID?": An Antitrust Analysis of NBA and NFL Draft Eligibility Rules, 2010 Den. U. Sports & Ent. L.J. 22, 50–51 (2010).

H) Recommendations

Recommendation 6-A: The NFL should consider performing or funding research analyzing when a player might be "ready" for the NFL.

Currently, the NFL's eligibility rule appears to be the NFL's best guess as to when players, as a general rule, are ready to play in the NFL. However, we are unaware of any rigorous body of data to support the NFL's eligibility rule as it is currently written. While the NFL's eligibility rule seems reasonably protective of player health based on what is currently known, data could substantially buttress the rule—or prompt changes to it as necessary. For the sake of player health, the NFL should make efforts to gather this data.

Among the data that might be valuable in this context are: players' ages when they enter the league; players' height and weight; players' position; players' professional results; players' injury histories; players' financial health; players' education; players' psychological health; and, players' post-career activities. This and other data may need to be gathered before, during, and after the player's career, as relevant; there may also be questions related to the precise definition of player success for purposes of this analysis, although certain thresholds on either end of the spectrum will be evident. While some of this data does currently exist, the ideal comparison would be between players who entered the league under the current rule and those who entered earlier (or later) on an alternative rule. Because the current eligibility rule has been in place for decades, direct comparison is difficult. However, it is possible that the NFL—potentially with the help of others—could learn something from the data that is already available, for example, comparing the outcomes of players who enter the league at different ages beyond the eligibility threshold. Of course, this will not answer the question of how *individual* players might fare if they could enter the league even earlier than the current rule permits,[ac] but it may nonetheless provide some helpful information for comparison between players who are younger or older at entry.

Recommendation 6-B: The NFL should reconsider the interplay of its eligibility rules with the NCAA's rules as they concern player health and take appropriate action if necessary.

The NFL's eligibility rule coupled with the realities of the NCAA's rules cause tremendous pressure on prospective and future NFL players. While these NCAA rules are not the NFL's creation, the NFL should nevertheless acknowledge that the football careers of prospective or future NFL players are substantially affected by the NCAA's rules and take steps within its power to address those problems. The combination of the two organizations' rules creates situations that many find inequitable and it is thus appropriate for the NFL to reconsider its eligibility rules' applicability in those situations and whether anything can be done to change them.[ad]

---

ac Given more advances in health technology, it is theoretically possible that leagues could adopt an individualized approach, using specific metrics to determine whether a particular player was "ready." However, such an approach also raises concerns with the Americans with Disabilities Act and the Genetic Information Nondiscrimination Act, as discussed in our article, *Evaluating NFL Player Health and Performance: Legal and Ethical Issues*, 165 U. Penn. L. Rev. 227 (2017).

ad Despite criticism on this issue, the NFL reportedly is not considering any changes to its eligibility rules. *See* Mike Florio, *NFL not considering a change to the three-year rule*, ProFootballTalk (Oct. 31, 2015, 10:38 PM), http://profootballtalk.nbcsports.com/2015/10/31/nfl-not-considering-a-change-to-the-three-year-rule/, *archived at* https://perma.cc/34JC-M66Y.

Endnotes

1   *See* American Needle, Inc. v. Nat'l Football League, 560 U.S. 183, 196-97 (2010) ("The teams compete with one another, not only on the playing field, but to attract fans, for gate receipts, and for contracts with managerial and playing personnel.")

2   *See* Clarett v. Nat'l Football League, 369 F.3d 124, 137 (2d Cir. 2004) (discussing application of antitrust law to NFL's eligibility rule).

3   *See* Am. Needle, Inc. v. Nat'l Football League, 560 U.S. 183, 186 (2010), *citing* 15 U.S.C. § 1.

4   *See id.* at 203, n.10, *quoting* Board of Trade of Chicago v. United States, 246 U.S. 231, 238 (1918) ("The true test of legality is whether the restraint imposed is such as merely regulates and perhaps thereby promotes competition or whether it is such as may suppress or even destroy competition. To determine that question the court must ordinarily consider the facts peculiar to the business to which the restraint is applied; its condition before and after the restraint is imposed; the nature of the restraint and its effect, actual or probable. The history of the restraint, the evil believed to exist, the reason for adopting the particular remedy, the purpose or end sought to be attained, are all relevant facts. This is not because a good intention will save an otherwise objectionable regulation or the reverse; but because knowledge of intent may help the court to interpret facts and to predict consequences.")

5   *See* Brown v. Pro Football, Inc., 518 U.S. 231 (1996).

6   *See* Clarett v. Nat'l Football League, 369 F.3d 124 (2d Cir. 2004) (NFL's eligibility rule immune from antitrust scrutiny as a result of non-statutory labor exemption).

7   NFL CBA, Art. 6, § 2(a).

8   *Draft FAQ*, Major League Baseball, http://mlb.mlb.com/mlb/draftday/faq.jsp (last visited May 13, 2015), *archived at* http://perma.cc/4HA7-4D8L.

9   NBA CBA, Art. X, § 3.

10 NHL CBA, Art. 8, § 8.2.

11 *CFL Draft Expanded to seven rounds*, Can. Football League, May 1, 2013, http://cfl.ca/article/cfl-draft-expanded-to-seven-rounds, *available at* http://perma.cc/SB4N-ZJYQ.

12 *Roster Rules and Regulations*, Major League Soccer, http://pressbox.mlssoccer.com/content/roster-rules-and-regulations (last visited Sept. 22, 2015), *archived at* http://perma.cc/9BLN-R7QD.

13 *See Who We Are*, Nat'l Collegiate Athletics Ass'n, http://www.ncaa.org/about/who-we-are (last visited Sept. 23, 2015), *archived at* http://perma.cc/RXA5-4FLL; *Membership*, Nat'l Collegiate Athletics Ass'n, http://www.ncaa.org/about/who-we-are/membership (last visited Sept. 23, 2015), *archived at* http://perma.cc/6BTQ-G7QS (describing membership as more than 1,200 schools).

14 NCAA Division I Manual, Bylaw 12.01.1.

15 NCAA Division I Manual, Bylaw 12.01.2.

16 *See* NCAA Division I Manual, Bylaw 12.02.9 ("Pay is the receipt of funds, awards or benefits not permitted by the governing legislation of the Association for participation in athletics."); *id.* at Bylaw 12.02.10 ("A professional athlete is one who receives any kind of payment, directly or indirectly, for athletics participation except as permitted by the governing legislation of the [National Collegiate Athletic] Association."); *id.* at Bylaw 12.1.2.1 (discussing "Prohibited Forms of Pay"); *id.* at 12.2 (regulating "Involvement With Professional Teams"); *id.* at 12.4 (regulating employment of student-athletes and requiring that student-athlete compensation be "[a]t a rate commensurate with the going rate in that locality for similar services"); *id.* at 12.5 (regulating "Promotional Activities"); *id.* at Bylaw 12.01.4 ("A grant-in-aid [a scholarship] administered by an educational institution is not considered to be pay or the promise of pay for athletics skill, provided it does not exceed the financial aid limitations set by the [National Collegiate Athletic] Association's membership.")

17 *See* O'Bannon v. Nat'l Collegiate Athletic Ass'n, 802 F.3d 1049, 1054-55 (9th Cir. 2015) ("In August 2014, the NCAA announced it would allow athletic conferences to authorize their member schools to increase scholarships up to the full cost of attendance. The 80 member schools of the five largest athletic conferences in the country voted in January 2015 to take that step, and the scholarship cap at those schools is now at the full cost of attendance.")

18 NCAA Division I Manual, Bylaw 12.1.2 ("An individual loses amateur status and thus shall not be eligible for intercollegiate competition in a particular sport if the individual . . . [e]nters into an agreement with an agent.")

19 NCAA Division I Manual, Bylaw 12.3.2.

20 NCAA Division I Manual, Bylaw 12.3.2.1 ("A lawyer may not be present during discussions of a contract offer with a professional organization or have any direct contact (in person, by telephone or by mail) with a professional sports organization on behalf of the individual. A lawyer's presence during such discussions is considered representation by an agent.") In Oliver v. Natl. Collegiate Athletic Assn., 920 N.E.2d 203 (Ohio Com.Pl. 2009), a college baseball player obtained a permanent injunction against the enforcement of this Bylaw. However, to avoid that result, the NCAA appealed the decision, and settled with the player for $750,000 in exchange for the vacatur of the court's decision. Thus, the rule stands. *See* Glenn M. Wong, Warren Zola, Chris Deubert, *Going Pro in Sports: Providing Guidance to Student-Athletes in a Complicated Legal & Regulatory Environment*, 28 Cardozo Arts & Ent. L.J. 553, 583-85 (2011) (discussing the *Oliver* case).

21 Brian Bennett, *NCAA board votes to allow autonomy*, ESPN (Aug. 8, 2014), http://espn.go.com/college-sports/story/_/id/11321551/ncaa-board-votes-allow-autonomy-five-power-conferences, *archived at* https://perma.cc/Y6B9-5FP8.

22 Teddy Cahill, *High School Draftees Permitted to Have Agent*, Baseball America, Jan. 15, 2016, http://www.baseballamerica.com/draft/high-school-draftees-permitted-agent/#gFU7SYlRjVxSdxzY.97, *archived at* https://perma.cc/YS4K-4ZHX.

23 *Id.*

24 *See, e.g.,* O'Bannon v. Nat'l Collegiate Athletic Ass'n, 802 F.3d 1049, 1054-55 (9th Cir. 2015); *In re Nat'l Collegiate Athletic Ass'n Grant-in-Aid Cap Antitrust Litigation*, 14-md-2541, 2016 WL 4154855 (N.D. Cal. Aug. 5, 2016).

25 *See Student-Athlete Insurance Programs*, Nat'l Collegiate Athletics Ass'n, http://www.ncaa.org/about/resources/insurance/student-athlete-insurance-programs (last visited Sept. 23, 2015), *archived at* http://perma.cc/MHL6-7T3A [hereinafter NCAA ESDI Program]. See also Glenn M. Wong & Chris Deubert, *The Legal and Business Aspects of Disability Insurance Policies in Professional and College Sports*, 17 Vill. Sports & Ent. L.J. 473, 506 (2010).

26 *See* Wong & Deubert, *supra* n 25.

27 *Id.* at 507–08.

28 *Id.*

29 *Id.*

30 *Student-Athlete Insurance Programs*, Nat'l Collegiate Athletics Ass'n, http://www.ncaa.org/about/resources/insurance/student-athlete-insurance-programs (last visited Sept. 23, 2015), *archived at* http://perma.cc/MHL6-7T3A.

31 *See* Michael David Smith, *Clemson buys $5m insurance policies for Deshaun Watson*, ProFootballTalk (Aug. 17, 2016, 4:18 PM), http://nhl.nbcsports.com/2016/10/11/nhl-plans-on-fining-teams-who-violate-new-concussion-protocol/, *archived at* https://perma.cc/M5PM-LS96; Barry Petchesky, *FSU Paid For Jameis Winston's Insurance Policy On His Draft Stock*, Deadspin (Aug. 5, 2014), http://deadspin.com/fsu-paid-for-jameis-winstons-insurance-policy-on-his-dr-1616301588, *archived at* http://perma.cc/DVB5-YGN7.

32 *See* Wong & Deubert, *supra* n 25.

33 *See* Wong & Deubert, *supra* n 25 at 507; *see also* Petchesky, *supra* n. 31.

34 Wong & Deubert, *supra* n. 25 at 495–96.

35 Bryan Fischer, *NCAA issues waiver allowing greater access to insurance,* Nat'l Football League, Oct. 15, 2014, http://www.nfl.com/news/story/0ap3000000411358/article/ncaa-issues-waiver-allowing-greater-access-to-insurance, *archived at* http://perma.cc/E85A-ZZPM.

36 Zac Jackson, *Report: Browns CB becoming first to collect loss of draft value insurance,* ProFootballTalk (Oct. 2, 2015, 11:48 AM), http://profootballtalk.nbcsports.com/2015/10/02/report-browns-cb-becoming-first-to-collect-loss-of-draft-value-insurance/, *archived at* https://perma.cc/KUG6-5CER (reporting that "many top college players are taking out such policies").

37 Dennis Dodd, *Ekpre-Olomu expected to be first to collect on loss of draft value insurance,* CBS Sports (Oct. 2, 2015, 1:37 AM), http://www.cbssports.com/collegefootball/writer/dennis-dodd/25324664/ekpre-olomu-expected-to-be-first-to-collect-on-loss-of-draft-value-insurance, *archived at* https://perma.cc/QT3Q-S4WE.

38 *Id.*

39 *Id.*

40 *Id.*

41 Michael David Smith, *Jaylon Smith will receive insurance payment, Myles Jack won't,* ProFootballTalk (Apr. 29, 2016, 10:33 PM), http://profootballtalk.nbcsports.com/2016/04/29/jaylon-smith-will-receive-insurance-payment-myles-jack-wont/, *archived at* https://perma.cc/7Q4P-3HAV.

42 NFL CBA, Art. 6 § 2(b).

43 *See* Clarett v. Nat'l Football League, 306 F.Supp.2d 379, 387 (S.D.N.Y. 2004), *rev'd* 369 F.3d 124 (2d Cir. 2004).

44 *See id.*

45 Clarett v. Nat'l Football League, 369 F.3d 124 (2d Cir. 2004).

46 *See South Carolina's Jadeveon Clowney is Heisman frontrunner,* Augusta Chronicle (GA), Aug. 11, 2013, *available at* 2013 WLNR 19791739.

47 Michael David Smith, *Clowney sees himself as the No. 1 overall pick,* ProFootballTalk (Feb. 6, 2014, 3:17 PM), http://profootballtalk.nbcsports.com/2014/02/06/clowney-sees-himself-as-the-no-1-overall-pick/, *archived at* http://perma.cc/T8FW-T28R ("Clowney almost certainly would have been the No. 1 overall pick in the 2013 NFL draft if not for the NFL's rule requiring players to be at least three years out of high school before they enter the draft.")

48 Mike Florio, *Clowney passes on one game, Spurrier goes passive aggressive,* ProFootballTalk (Oct. 6, 2013, 10:16 AM), http://profootballtalk.nbcsports.com/2013/10/06/clowney-passes-on-one-game-spurrier-goes-passive-aggressive/, *archived at* http://perma.cc/2LJ4-WVND; Michael David Smith, *Clowney: I'm fully committed, not thinking about the NFL draft,* ProFootballTalk (Oct. 6, 2013, 6:36 PM), http://profootballtalk.nbcsports.com/2013/10/08/clowney-im-fully-committed-to-my-team-not-thinking-about-the-nfl/, *archived at* http://perma.cc/9F2K-QUES.

49 *See* Curtis Crabtree, *Warren Sapp jumps on bandwagon of Jadeveon Clowney criticism,* ProFootballTalk (Apr. 22, 2014, 1:33 AM), http://profootballtalk.nbcsports.com/2014/04/22/warren-sapp-jumps-on-bandwagon-of-jadeveon-clowney-criticism/, *archived at* https://perma.cc/J4UR-ERK6; Michael David Smith, *Mayock: Clowney can be the best player in the NFL, if he wants it,* ProFootballTalk (Apr. 23, 2014, 1:25 PM), http://profootballtalk.nbcsports.com/2014/04/23/mayock-clowney-can-be-the-best-player-in-the-nfl-if-he-wants-it/, *archived at* http://perma.cc/T5N6-696B.

50 Rich Gosselin, *Injured college stars have NFL value,* Dallas Morning News, Sept. 20, 2002, *available at* 2002 WLNR 13720468.

51 Cindy Boren, *49ers' Marcus Lattimore considering retirement,* Wash. Post, Nov. 3, 2014, *available at* 2014 WLNR 30777868.

52 Cindy Boren, *49ers' Marcus Lattimore retires, ends longshot NFL career before it even began,* Wash. Post, Nov. 5, 2014, *available at* 2014 WLNR 31019273.

53 *Id.*

54 *See What is average NFL player's career length? Longer than you might think, Commissioner Goodell says,* Nat'l Football League, Apr. 18, 2011, http://nflcommunications.com/2011/04/18/what-is-average-nfl-player%E2%80%99s-career-length-longer-than-you-might-think-commissioner-goodell-says/, *archived at* http://perma.cc/8UHQ-JMVX (discussing dispute between NFLPA's assertion that the average career is 3.5 years and the NFL's assertion that the average career is 6 years); *Average NFL Career Length,* Sharp Football Analysis, Apr. 30, 2014, http://www.sharpfootballanalysis.com/blog/?p=2133, *archived at* http://perma.cc/4EZY-E7ML (discussing disagreement between NFLPA and NFL and determining that the average drafted player plays about 5 years).

55 NFL CBA, Art. 7, § 3.

56 Chris Deubert, Glenn M. Wong, John Howe, *All Four Quarters: A Retrospective and Analysis of the 2011 Collective Bargaining Process and Agreement in the National Football League,* 19 UCLA Ent. L. Rev. 1, 52-61 (2012).

57 *Id.*

58 *See* Willie T. Smith III, *For the love of Mike,* Greenville News (Greenville, SC), Aug. 24, 2014, *available at* 2014 WLNR 23306853 (South Carolina head coach Steve Spurrier saying he would recommend running back Mike Davis enter the NFL because "The lifespan of a running back is only a certain number of years."); Paolo Bovin, *Cardinals, RB Gordon appear to be perfect fit,* Ariz. Republic, Apr. 26, 2015, *available at* 2015 WLNR 12199272 (discussing the short "lifespan" on NFL running backs); Evan Woodbery, *Hightower still pursuing a dream, Hopes for comeback rest with the Saints,* New Orleans Times Picayune, Feb. 15, 2015, *available at* 2015 WLNR 4668527 (same); Greg Logan, *Johnson a good fit in Jets' Attack,* Newsday, Sept. 20, 2014, *available at* 2014 WLNR 26127868 (discussing the "tread" on veteran running back Chris Johnson's "tires").

59 *See* Mike Chappell, *Chancy Proposition: Underclassmen who Enter Draft Weigh the Risks; Colts' Bashir Doesn't Regret Leaving School,* Indianapolis Star, Apr. 14, 2002, at C1; John McClain, *'Bama's Palmer to Enter Draft Now/All-America Receiver Alters Decision,* Hous. Chron., Jan. 11, 1994, *available at* 1994 WLNR 4953475.

60 *See* Brent Schrotenboer, *Dad: Brown Will Be Back in Scarlet and Black in 2010,* San Diego Union-Trib., Jan. 16, 2010, http://www.sandiegouniontribune.com/news/2010/jan/16/dad-brown-will-be-back-scarlet-and-black-10/, *archived at* https://perma.cc/GU6Z-WFP6 (discussing decision of San Diego State wide receiver Vincent Brown to return for his senior season after receiving a projection that he would not be taken in the first three rounds).

61 *See* Scott Hotard, *LSU's Black a Forgotten Man by NFL,* Baton Rouge Advoc., May 3, 2010, *available at* 2010 WLNR 9154729; Manish Mehta, *Warren Steps Up for Jets,* Star-Ledger (Newark, N.J.), May 1, 2010, *available at* 2010 WLNR 9064474.

62 Albert Breer, *NFL implementing changes to address underclassmen issue,* Nat'l Football League, Jul. 18, 2014, http://www.nfl.com/news/story/0ap2000000365987/article/nfl-implementing-changes-to-address-underclassmen-issue, *archived at* https://perma.cc/M7BM-DYL7.

63 *Id.*

64 Michael David Smith, *24 early entries went undrafted,* ProFootballTalk (May 3, 2015, 4:49 PM), http://profootballtalk.nbcsports.com/2015/05/03/24-early-entries-went-undrafted/, *archived at* https://perma.cc/XKE3-42AS.

65 Zac Jackson, *30 early entrants go undrafted,* ProFootballTalk (Apr. 30, 2016, 7:21 PM), http://profootballtalk.nbcsports.com/2016/04/30/30-early-entries-go-undrafted/, *archived at* https://perma.cc/8UVC-4PQH.

66 *See Average NFL Career Length,* Sharp Football Analysis, Apr. 30, 2014, http://www.sharpfootballanalysis.com/blog/?p=2133, *archived at* http://perma.cc/4EZY-E7ML (showing that drafted players tend to have longer careers).

67 NCAA Division I Manual, Bylaw 12.2.4.2.3 (providing that a football

68 *See Unofficial underclassmen early entry list for 2015 NFL Draft*, Nat'l Football League, Jan. 2, 2015, http://www.nfl.com/news/story/0ap3000000441827/article/unofficial-underclassmen-early-entry-list-for-2015-nfl-draft, *archived at* http://perma.cc/SD8M-PUXV.

69 Some college coaches have expressed their disappointment in not permitting undrafted underclassmen the opportunity to return to college football. *See* Mike Florio, *Should undrafted underclassmen be allowed to return to college?* ProFootballTalk (May 11, 2016, 11:50 AM), http://profootballtalk.nbcsports.com/2016/05/11/should-undrafted-underclassmen-be-allowed-to-return-to-college/, *archived at* https://perma.cc/J9RY-ZJH5.

70 *See* Clarett v. Nat'l Football League, 306 F.Supp.2d 379, 408 (S.D.N.Y. 2004), *rev'd* 369 F.3d 124 (2004).

71 Major League Rule 3(a)(2)(A).

72 *See, e.g., Eligibility Guide for Participation in High School Athletics*, Ohio High School Athletic Ass'n, June 8, 2014, http://www.ohsaa.org/eligibility/EligibilityGuideHS.pdf, *archived at* http://perma.cc/5MAB-Q64V.

73 Major League Rule 3(a)(2)(A)(i)–(iii).

74 Major League Rule 3(a)(2)(A).

75 *Draft 2016 — Draft Tracker*, Major League Baseball, http://m.mlb.com/draft/tracker/#!ft=round&fv=1 (last visited Feb. 7, 2017), *archived at* https://perma.cc/2YGN-JDAK.

76 For purposes of the Major League Rules, a "college" is an institution that confers four-year degrees and is "represented by a baseball team which participates in inter-collegiate competition," a definition that "includes but is not limited to all members of the NCAA and the National Association of Intercollegiate Athletics ("NAIA")." Major League Rule 3(a)(3)(A).

77 Major League Rule 3(a)(3)(B).

78 A college player seeking eligibility because he was terminated due to scholastic deficiency must apply to the Commissioner for eligibility. Major League Rule 3(a)(3)(F)(i).

79 Major League Rule 3(a)(3)(E)(i)–(v).

80 *First-Year Player Draft*, Major League Baseball, http://mlb.mlb.com/mlb/draftday/rules.jsp (last visited Oct. 24, 2016), *archived at* https://perma.cc/RA2T-A8YN.

81 Matt Youmans, *Harper ready to give college try*, Las Vegas Rev.-J., Jun. 14, 2009, http://www.reviewjournal.com/sports/harper-ready-give-college-try, *archived at* http://perma.cc/452J-6DPK.

82 *See* Major League Rule 4(a) (restricting Rule 4 Draft eligibility).

83 Major League Rule 3(a)(1)(B)(i)–(ii).

84 Craig Calcaterra, *Opening Day Rosters Have 238 Players Born Outside of the United States*, Hardball Talk (Apr. 4, 2016, 4:44 PM), http://mlb.nbc-sports.com/2016/04/04/opening-day-rosters-have-238-players-born-outside-of-the-united-states/, *archived at* https://perma.cc/AP4J-4PLY.

85 *Id.*

86 Matt Kalthoff, *Out of Sight, Out of Mind: Confronting the Legal, Economic and Social Issues Raised by Major League Baseball's Peculiar Treatment of Foreign Talent*, 29 Conn. J. Int'l L. 353, 360-65 (2014) (describing the buscon industry).

87 *Id.*

88 *Id.*

89 *Id.*

90 *See id.*; Dustin Williamson, *Part of the Team: Building Closer Relationships Between MLB Teams and Independent Agents in the Dominican Republic Through an MLB Code of Conduct*, 2 NYU J. Intell. Prop. & Ent. L. 369 (2013); Rick J. Lopez, *Signing Bonus Skimming and a Premature Call for a Global Draft in Major League Baseball*, 41 Ariz. St. L.J. 349 (2009).

91 MLB CBA Attachment 46 § I(A).

92 *Id.* § I(D)(2).

93 *International Talent Committee to seek input from foreign baseball experts*, Major League Baseball, Jan. 18, 2012, http://m.mlb.com/news/article/26379998/international-talent-committee-to-seek-input-from-foreign-baseball-experts, *archived at* http://perma.cc/82KF-4ZNY.

94 Craig Calcaterra, *Report: MLB, Union Negotiating the Implementation of An International Draft*, Hardball Talk (Oct. 17, 2016, 4:23 PM), http://mlb.nbcsports.com/2016/10/17/report-mlb-union-negotiating-the-implementation-of-an-international-draft/, *archived at* https://perma.cc/4GGM-DGNV.

95 *MLBPA, MLB Announce Details of New Labor Agreement*, MLBPA (Dec. 2, 2016), http://www.mlbplayers.com/ViewArticle.dbml?DB_OEM_ID=34000&ATCLID=211336390, *archived at* https://perma.cc/4XUA-2DAW

96 *Id.*

97 Players drafted in the Rule 4 Draft must sign minor league contracts. *See MLB, MLBPA reach new five-year labor agreement*, Major League Baseball, Nov. 22, 2011, http://m.mlb.com/news/article/26025138/, *archived at* http://perma.cc/48JZ-CUHX.

98 Matt Eddy, *One In Six Picks Will Click On Trek From Draft To Majors*, Baseball Am., Jul. 22, 2013, http://www.baseballamerica.com/draft/one-in-six-draft-picks-will-click/, *archived at* http://perma.cc/X89T-7K2M.

99 *See* Michael McCann, *In lawsuit minor leaguers charge they are members of 'working poor'*, Sports Illustrated, Feb. 12, 2012, http://www.si.com/mlb/2014/02/12/minor-league-baseball-players-lawsuit, *archived at* http://perma.cc/A89J-YTHJ (discussing lawsuit brought by minor league players against MLB concerning their wages).

100 MLB CBA, Art. VI, § A(1).

101 Michael McCann, *In lawsuit minor leaguers charge they are members of 'working poor'*, Sports Illustrated, Feb. 12, 2012, http://www.si.com/mlb/2014/02/12/minor-league-baseball-players-lawsuit, *archived at* http://perma.cc/A89J-YTHJ.

102 NCAA Division I Manual, § 12.1.2 ("An individual loses amateur status and thus shall not be eligible for intercollegiate competition in a particular sport if the individual . . . [e]nters into an agreement with an agent.").

103 An "'international player' is a player: (i) who has maintained permanent residence outside of the United States for at least the three (3) years prior to the Draft while participating in the game of basketball as an amateur or as a professional outside of the United States; (ii) who has never previously enrolled in a college or university in the United States; and, (iii) who did not complete high school in the United States." 2017 NBA CBA Art. X § 1(c).

104 *See* 2017 NBA CBA, Art. X § 1(b)(i).

105 *Id.*

106 *See* 2017 NBA CBA, Art. X § 1(b)(ii)(A)-(G).

107 *See* 2017 NBA CBA, Art. X § 1(b)(i).

108 NBA CBA, Art. X, § (1)(b)(ii)(G).

109 Denver Rockets v. All-Pro Management, Inc., 325 F.Supp. 1049, 1055 (C.D.Ca. 1971).

110 The ABA was a professional basketball league that attempted to compete against the NBA from 1967–1976. *See Remember the ABA — Home*, Remember the ABA, http://www.remembertheaba.com/ (last visited Sept. 24, 2015), *archived at* http://perma.cc/WR9N-DME8. When the ABA folded, four of its clubs (New York Nets, Denver Nuggets, Indiana Pacers, and San Antonio Spurs) merged into the NBA. *Id.*

111 Denver Rockets, *supra* n. 109 at 1060.

112 *See id.* at 1067.

113 Denver Rockets v. All-Pro Management, Inc., 71-cv-1089, 1971 WL 3015 (9th Cir. Feb. 16, 1971).

114 Haywood v. Nat'l Basketball Ass'n, 401 U.S. 1204 (1971).

115 *How NBA Policy Changed*, Seattle Times, Oct. 29, 1997, available at 1997 WLNR 1485502.

116 *Id.*

117 Moses Malone (1974), Darryl Dawkins (1975), and Bill Willoughby (1975) were the only players to join the NBA straight from high school in the

years immediately following the *Haywood* case. *High School Star Seeks Jump to NBA,* Orlando Sentinel, May 12, 1995, *available at* 1995 WLNR 4649503.

118 *See id.*

119 This information was provided by the NBA.

120 *See* Roscoe Nance, *Teen draftees grounded until 19 under new deal,* USA Today, Jun. 22, 2005, *available at* 2005 WLNR 9883069.

121 *Id.*

122 *See* Tim Sullivan, *You can blame NCAA for a lot, but not for the one-and-done rule,* Courier-J. (Louisville, KY), Mar. 6, 2014, *available at* 2014 WLNR 6290752; Bill Dwyre, *One-and-done shouldn't be satisfying to anyone,* L.A. Times, Apr. 11, 2009, *available at* 2009 WLNR 6798286.

123 Glenn M. Wong, Warren Zola, Chris Deubert, *Going Pro in Sports: Providing Guidance to Student-Athletes in a Complicated Legal & Regulatory Environment,* 28 Cardozo Arts & Ent. L.J. 553, 578 (2011).

124 Neil Greenberg, *A look at how one-and-done players perform in the NBA,* Wash. Post, Apr. 8, 2015, http://www.washingtonpost.com/news/fancy-stats/wp/2015/04/08/a-look-at-how-one-and-done-players-perform-in-the-nba/, *archived at* http://perma.cc/U5N4-ZJ9H (describing 68 players as having left college after only one season beginning with the 2006 NBA Draft through the 2014 NBA Draft); There were 13 one-and-done players in the 2015 NBA Draft and 14 in the 2016 NBA Draft.

125 Jim Vertuno, *NCAA rule change to allow NBA evaluation flexibility,* NBA (Jan. 13, 2016, 7:06 PM), http://www.nba.com/2016/news/01/13/ncaa-convention-draft-status-flexibility/, *archived at* https://perma.cc/BR97-U23T.

126 *Id.*

127 *See* Scott Cacciola, *Australia Emerges as the New Front in the College Recruiting Wars,* N.Y. Times, Nov. 12, 2016, https://www.nytimes.com/2016/11/13/sports/basketball/australia-college-basketball-recruiting.html, *archived at* https://perma.cc/KC49-6WQ4.

128 Dave Telep, *NBA Star Jennings' Advice to Aquille Carr,* ESPN, Mar. 13, 2013, http://insider.espn.go.com/blog/dave-telep/post/_/id/3311/nba-star-jennings-advice-to-aquille-carr, *archived at* https://perma.cc/V8R6-B63E.

129 Ethan Sherwood Strauss, *A Moment of Clarity for Jeremy Tyler,* ESPN, July 13, 2013, http://espn.go.com/blog/truehoop/post/_/id/61544/a-moment-of-clarity-for-jeremy-tyler, *archived at* http://perma.cc/V27B-N3WB.

130 *Frequently Asked Questions: NBA Development League,* NBA Development League, http://dleague.nba.com/faq/ (last visited Feb. 3, 2017), *archived at* https://perma.cc/8QKN-VKYC.

131 *Id.*

132 *NBA D-League FAQ,* Nat'l Basketball League, http://www.nba.com/dleague/santacruz/dleague_faqs.html (last visited Sept. 24, 2015), *archived at* http://perma.cc/34EW-7QVY.

133 *Id.* Some NBA owners and analysts argue that the D-League should replace collegiate sports as the traditional path for NBA players, but believe that the D-League must improve its incentives and competitiveness before this can happen. *See* Time MacMahon, *Cuban: D-League better for prospects,* ESPN, Mar. 6, 2014, http://espn.go.com/dallas/nba/story/_/id/10538276/mark-cuban-says-nba-d-league-better-option-ncaa, *archived at* https://perma.cc/6FNR-Q3WC.

134 Chris Reichert, *Source: NBA D-League to change salary structure in 2016/17,* Upside & Motor (2016), http://upsidemotor.com/2016/07/15/nba-d-league-salary-money/, *archived at* https://perma.cc/C7H2-N2UQ.

135 Art Tellem, *Turn One-and-Done Into None-and-Done,* N.Y. Times, Jun. 28, 2014, http://www.nytimes.com/2014/06/29/sports/basketball/turn-one-and-done-into-none-and-done.html, *archived at* http://perma.cc/KQ4Z-36R4.

136 Kiki VanDeweghe, *N.B.A. Eligibility Rule Is Good for the Game,* N.Y. Times, Jul. 12, 2014, http://www.nytimes.com/2014/07/13/sports/basketball/nba-eligibility-rule-is-good-for-the-game.html, *archived at* http://perma.cc/WJ3U-CC2T.

137 *See* Zach Harper, *Commissioner Adam Silver still wants age limit of 20 for draft eligibility,* CBS Sports (Nov. 24, 2014, 7:38 PM), http://www.cbssports.com/nba/eye-on-basketball/24838071/commissioner-adam-silver-still-wants-age-limit-of-20-for-draft-eligibility, *archived at* https://perma.cc/TX6U-QH6M; Steve Kerr, *The Case for the 20-Year-Old Age Limit in the NBA,* Grantland, May 8, 2012, http://grantland.com/features/steve-kerr-problems-age-limit-nba/, *archived at* https://perma.cc/BU6U-8T8R.

138 *NBPA leader Michele Roberts: 'Be happy with one-and-done,'* Sports Illustrated, Feb. 15, 2015, http://www.si.com/nba/2015/02/15/nba-age-limit-michele-roberts-adam-silver-one-and-done, *archived at* http://perma.cc/38K7-QGUN.

139 *See* David Aldridge, *NBA, NBPA reach tentative seven-year CBA agreement,* NBA.com (Dec. 14, 2016, 8:18 PM), http://www.nba.com/article/2016/12/14/nba-and-nbpa-reach-tentative-labor-deal, *archived at* https://perma.cc/X5U4-YA73.

140 NHL CBA, Art. 8, § 8.4(a); NHL By-Law § 12.7.

141 NHL CBA, Art. 8, § 8.4(a).

142 *See Active NHL Players Totals by Nationality—Career Stats,* QuantHockey.com, http://www.quanthockey.com/nhl/nationality-totals/active-nhl-players-career-stats.html (last visited Nov. 30, 2016), *archived at* https://perma.cc/8682-9DBY.

143 Generally only about 20 players are drafted out of high schools each year, or about 10% of drafted players. S*ee* Mike Morreale, *NHL teams grab 20 high-schoolers in draft,* Nat'l Hockey League (Jun. 23, 2010, 4:31 PM), http://www.nhl.com/ice/news.htm?id=635956, *archived at* http://perma.cc/Q4ZR-VHC3; Mike Morreale, *NHL teams draft record 22 high school players,* Nat'l Hockey League, Jun. 26, 2010, http://www.nhl.com/ice/news.htm?id=533004, *archived at* http://perma.cc/PFZ4-GCW8.

144 *See* Katie Strang, *Lawsuit seeks to have junior players paid minimum wage,* ESPN, Jan. 29, 2015, http://espn.go.com/blog/nhl/post/_/id/34346/lawsuit-seeks-to-have-junior-players-paid-minimum-wage, *archived at https://perma.cc/5DAL-NPGU.*

145 NCAA Division I Manual Bylaw 12.2.3.2.4 ("Ice hockey teams in the United States and Canada, classified by the Canadian Hockey Association as major junior teams, are considered professional teams under NCAA legislation.")

146 Andrew Podnieks, *A Battle Across the Border in Recruiting,* Feb. 9, 2011, N.Y. Times http://www.nytimes.com/2011/02/10/sports/hockey/10hockey.html, *archived at* http://perma.cc/E9TP-UW5N.; Marc Bianchi, *Guardian of Amateurism or Legal Defiant? The Dichotomous Nature of NCAA Men's Ice Hockey Regulation,* 20 Seton Hall J. Sports & Ent. L. 165 (2010).

147 Marc Bianchi, *Guardian of Amateurism or Legal Defiant? The Dichotomous Nature of NCAA Men's Ice Hockey Regulation,* 20 Seton Hall J. Sports & Ent. L. 165, 175 (2010).

148 Andrew Podnieks, *A Battle Across the Border in Recruiting,* Feb. 9, 2011, N.Y. Times http://www.nytimes.com/2011/02/10/sports/hockey/10hockey.html, *archived at* http://perma.cc/E9TP-UW5N.

149 NHL CBA, Art. 8, § 8.6(c).

150 NHL CBA, Art. 8, § 8.6(d).

151 *See, e.g.,* Aaron Portzline, *Blue Jackets: Defenseman Mike Reilly to Return to College, Add to Game and Frame,* Columbus Dispatch, July 11, 2014, http://bluejacketsxtra.dispatch.com/content/stories/2014/07/11/still-room-for-growth.html, *archived at* http://perma.cc/L3XW-HBT7 (explaining University of Minnesota's Mike Reilly's decision to return to college to put on muscle after adding 36 pounds already in two years of college); Colin Dambrauskas, *Johnny Gaudreau Playing Big—Wants to Join Flames,* HockeyBuzz (July 16, 2013, 12:35 p.m.), http://www.hockeybuzz.com/blog/Colin-Dambrauskas/Johnny-Gaudreau-Playing-Big---Wants-to-Join-Flames/171/52843, *archived at* http://perma.cc/9MZN-NSWC (quoting Calgary Flames' prospect Johnny Gaudreau as saying, "Hopefully they want me next year at the end of the year and hopefully I can come in and make an impact for them. If I play well this

year *and put on the right weight*, I think I might be able to do it.") (emphasis added); *Lightning's Jonathan Drouin Selected Top Prospect by NHL.com*, Tampa Bay Lightning, Sept. 9, 2014, http://lightning.nhl.com/club/news.htm?id=729872, *archived at* http://perma.cc/4R9A-X6DG (noting that David Pastrnak will "need at least one more season in Sweden to get bigger and stronger" and that "[a]t 5-10 and 180 pounds . . . 18-year-old [Kevin Fiala] will need at least one more season with HV 71 in Sweden to get bigger and stronger).

152 NHL By-Law § 12.7.

153 Neeld v. Nat'l Hockey League, 594 F.2d 1297, 1300 (9th Cir. 1979) ("the record amply supports the reasonableness of the by-law"). Under the rule of reason, "the factfinder weighs all of the circumstances of a case in deciding whether a restrictive practice should be prohibited as imposing an unreasonable restraint on competition," including "'specific information about the relevant business' and 'the restraint's history, nature, and effect.'" Leegin Creative Leather Products, Inc. v. PSKS, Inc., 551 U.S. 877, 885 (2007) (citations omitted).

154 Neeld, 594 F.2d at 1300. In addition to the *Neeld* case, there was a legal challenge to the age eligibility requirements of professional hockey — albeit a challenge to the World Hockey Association ("WHA"), a 1970s competitor of the NHL. In *Linseman v. World Hockey Ass'n*, 439 F. Supp. 1315 (D.Conn. 1977), 19-year-old Ken Linseman challenged the WHA's requirement that players be at least 20 years old. The United States District Court for the District of Connecticut granted Linseman a preliminary injunction against the application of the rule, finding that it was not "directed to any valid purpose." Linseman played one year in the WHA before it folded in 1979.

155 CFL CBA, § 14.02.

156 *Id.*

157 *CFL adjusts eligibility rules for Draft*, Can. Football League, Sept. 6, 2013, http://cfl.ca/article/cfl-adjusts-eligibility-rules-for-draft, *archived at* http://perma.cc/YWE9-J535.

158 CIS By-laws, Policies and Procedures, § 40.10.4.1.3(c), available at http://en.cis-sic.ca/information/members_info/bylaws_policies_procedures.

159 *CFL adjusts eligibility rules for Draft*, *supra* n. 157.

160 *Id.*

161 Murray McCormick, *Forde heats up CFL draft talk*, Postmedia News (Can.), May 9, 2014.

162 *See* Greg Mancina, *CFL drafts Saginaw Valley back*, Saginaw News (Mich.), Oct. 3, 2008, *available at* 2008 WLNR 19073005.

163 *See* Lowell Ullrich, *Ullrich: CFL draft as mysterious as ever*, Postmedia News (Can.), May 12, 2014 (discussing changes to CFL Draft structure); Murray McCormick, *Forde heats up CFL draft talk*, Postmedia News (Can.), May 9, 2014.

164 *See id.*

165 *See* Pete Thamel, *Bryce Brown to the C.F.L.?*, N.Y. Times, Feb. 4, 2009, *available at* http://thequad.blogs.nytimes.com/2009/02/04/bryce-brown-to-the-cfl/?_r=0, *archived at* http://perma.cc/3DPM-XSY5.

166 *Id.*

167 *See Players*, Major League Soccer, http://www.mlssoccer.com/players?sort=age&order=ASC (last visited June 23, 2016), *archived at* https://perma.cc/8Y7N-FQEW; *see also* Paul Tenorio *Young stars increasingly on fast track*, Wash. Post, Apr. 14, 2010, *available at* 2010 WLNR 26726087 (discussing lack of age requirement in MLS and the number of teenage players).

168 *See* Jenna Merten, *Raising a Red Card: Why Freddy Adu Should Not Be Allowed to Play Professional Soccer*, 15 Marq. Sports L. Rev. 205 (2004).

169 *Roster Rules and Regulations*, Major League Soccer, http://pressbox.mlssoccer.com/content/roster-rules-and-regulations (last visited May 18, 2015), *archived at* http://perma.cc/48QQ-VC4S.

170 *Id.*

171 Avi Creditor, *A look inside the MLS discovery process*, Goal (Feb 26, 2013 1:00 AM), http://www.goal.com/en-us/news/1110/major-league-soccer/2013/02/26/3780299/avi-creditor-a-look-inside-the-mls-discovery-process, *archived at* https://perma.cc/8VQP-9A8C.

172 *Roster Rules and Regulations*, MLS.com, http://pressbox.mlssoccer.com/content/roster-rules-and-regulations (last visited May 18, 2015), *archived at* http://perma.cc/48QQ-VC4S.

173 L. E. Eisenmenger, *McCabe Explains Generation adidas*, U.S. Soccer Players, Jan. 8, 2010, http://www.ussoccerplayers.com/2010/01/mccabe-explains-generation-adidas.html, *archived at* http://perma.cc/CS4G-2QY5 (quoting an MLS player agent as saying: "The challenge is how to keep players here in the MLS. The only way is to overpay a little bit to keep them.") The education related benefits of the Generation adidas program are also discussed in Chapter 3: Health-Related Benefits.

174 Glenn M. Wong, Warren Zola, Chris Deubert, *Going Pro in Sports: Providing Guidance to Student-Athletes in a Complicated Legal & Regulatory Environment*, 28 Cardozo Arts & Ent. L.J. 553, 577 (2011).

175 Neil Greenberg, *A look at how one-and-done players perform in the NBA*, Wash. Post, Apr. 8, 2015, http://www.washingtonpost.com/news/fancy-stats/wp/2015/04/08/a-look-at-how-one-and-done-players-perform-in-the-nba/, *archived at* http://perma.cc/U5N4-ZJ9H (describing 68 players as having left college after only one season beginning with the 2006 NBA Draft through the 2014 NBA Draft); There were 13 one-and-done players in the 2015 NBA Draft and 14 in the 2016 NBA Draft.

176 Ohm Youngmisuk, *Adam Silver: Age issue 'needs to be studied' outside CBA negotiations*, ESPN (Feb. 19, 2017, 12:10 PM), http://www.espn.com/nba/story/_/id/18715853/nba-commissioner-adam-silver-says-age-issue-worth-looking-deeper-cba, *archived at* https://perma.cc/SB5P-H549.

177 *See* Bartlett H. McGuire, *Age Restrictions in Women's Professional Tennis: A Case Study of Procompetitive Restraints of Trade*, 1 J. Int'l Media & Ent. L. 199 (2007).

178 *Id.* at 207.

179 *Id.* at 207–08.

180 Bartlett, *supra* n. 177, at 209.

181 *Id.*

182 WTA 2016 Official Rulebook, § XV.

183 Bartlett, *supra* n. 177, at 211–12.

184 *Id.* at 217–18.

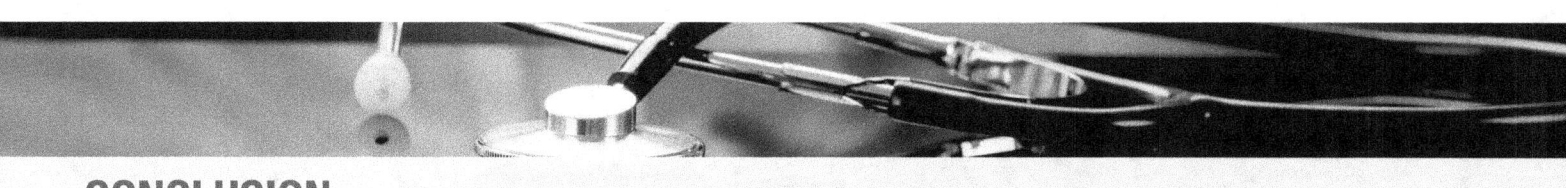

CONCLUSION

We began this Report by explaining the pressing need for research into the overall health[a] of NFL players; the need to address player health from all angles, both clinical and structural; and the challenges presented in conducting such research and analysis. The issues and parties involved are numerous, complex, and interconnected. To address these issues — and ultimately, to protect and improve the health of NFL players — requires a diligent and comprehensive approach to create well-informed and meaningful recommendations for change.

We believe part of that comprehensive approach is for the NFL and NFLPA to learn from other professional sports leagues when possible. In many respects, the leagues and their games are very different and thus it can be challenging to draw comparisons. Nevertheless, the leagues face a series of common issues, such as labor negotiations, stadiums and arenas, fan interest, multimedia platforms, and many others. But perhaps the most important issue is player health. In recent years, each of the leagues has had to make a fresh and comprehensive examination of its player health policies and practices. We anticipate the leagues will continue to engage in this examination for many years to come.

The leagues have the opportunity to learn a great deal from one another in light of their shared interest in player health. In this Report we have identified many areas in which the policies and practices of the NFL concerning player health appear superior to those of the other leagues. Indeed, the NFL's player health provisions are generally the most protective of player health among the relevant comparators. Nevertheless, we also identified several areas in which the policies and practices of the NFL concerning player health could potentially be improved by comparison to the other leagues:

1. The CFL CBA, unlike the NFL CBA, requires that pre-season physicals "to determine the status of any pre-existing condition" be performed by a neutral physician.

2. The standard of care articulated in the NHL and MLS CBAs, unlike the NFL CBA, seemingly requires club doctors to subjugate their duties to the club to their duties to the player *at all times*.

3. MLB, unlike the NFL, has a concussion-specific short-term injury list.

4. The MLB, NHL, and CFL injury reporting policies, unlike the NFL, do not require the disclosure of the location on the body of a player's injury.

5. MLB, the NBA, and the NHL, unlike the NFL, generally offer health insurance to players for life.

6. Among the Big Four leagues, the retirement plan payments offered by the NFL are the lowest.

7. MLB and NHL players, unlike in those in the NFL, are vested in their pension plans on the first day they play in the league.

8. The NBA and CFL, unlike the NFL, offer treatment to players who have violated their performance-enhancing substance policies.

---

a   As explained in the Introduction, Section F: Scope, we define health for purposes of this Report as "a state of overall wellbeing in fundamental aspects of a person's life, including physical, mental, emotional, social, familial, and financial components."

9. The amount of player compensation that is guaranteed in the NFL is substantially lower than in the other Big Four leagues.

10. The NFL has the most prohibitive eligibility rule of the leagues (except the CFL).

It is important to note that where we have identified these differences, we have also explained the different nuances and contexts. In many cases, the NFL's policies might be justifiably different than the other leagues and perhaps even superior, despite their apparent deficiency. Thus, it is essential that all of these differences be examined in a full and fair context.

There is still, however, room for improvement, as each Chapter's Recommendations show. Additionally, our Recommendations are only as useful as their implementation. For these reasons, we make the following final Recommendations.

Final Recommendation 1: The leagues and unions should continue to coordinate on player health issues and to consider each other's policies and practices.

Indications are that the leagues do communicate with each other concerning common issues on a regular basis. Similarly, the unions communicate on common issues. This coordination is assisted by the fact that many doctors, lawyers, and other professionals are advisors to multiple leagues or unions. It is important that the leagues and unions continue—and perhaps increase—their level of coordination on player health issues. As many of the leagues have increased their interest in and funding of research—particularly medical research—concerning player health issues, valuable data is being created that can help inform other leagues' policies and practices. We urge the leagues to share this data—not just with each other but with all researchers. Moreover, by combining resources the leagues might be able to take on broader and better projects than they can alone. Finally, as leagues continue to make advancements in player health policies and practices, it is important that the other leagues and unions take note of those advancements, consider their possible application to their respective organizations, and make the necessary changes to protect and promote player health. The leagues are tremendously powerful and influential institutions—by working together, they can maximize their ability to be positive change agents in player health.

Final Recommendation 2: The media, academics, the leagues, and the unions should continue to police the advancement of player health.

Following this Report, we do not intend to be a passive voice in the process of improving player health. It is our hope to be able to periodically review progress on the issues discussed in this Report and provide additional reports. However, in addition to any progress reports from the authors of this Report or the Football Players Health Study at Harvard University, we urge and trust that others—in particular the leagues and unions—will heed the message of this Report and hold other stakeholders accountable.

* * *

NFL football has a storied history and holds an important place in this country. The men who play it deserve to be protected and have their health needs met and it is our fervent hope that they will be met. We hope this Report furthers that cause.

Learning from Other Leagues

Major League Baseball
- Concussion-specific injury list
- No disclosure of player injury location
- Length and amount of health insurance for former players
- Earlier pension accrual date
- More guaranteed compensation
- Eligibility age and education

National Hockey League
- No disclosure of player injury location
- Length and amount of health insurance for former players
- Earlier pension accrual date
- More guaranteed compensation
- Eligibility age and education

National Basketball Association
- Length and amount of health insurance for former players
- Treatment for performance-enhancing substance usage
- More guaranteed compensation
- Eligibility age and education

Canadian Football League
- Neutral doctor pre-season physical
- No disclosure of player injury location
- Treatment for performance-enhancing substance usage

Major League Soccer
- More guaranteed compensation
- Eligibility age and education

Appendices

APPENDIX A \ COMPILATION OF RECOMMENDATIONS

Below, for ease of reference, is a compilation of all of the Recommendations made in this Report.

1) Club Medical Personnel

Recommendation 1-A:
Pre-season physicals for the purpose of evaluating a player's prior injuries should be performed by neutral doctors.

The CFL requires pre-season physicals for the purpose of evaluating a player's prior injuries to be performed by a neutral doctor. The NFL should adopt the same rule. The use of neutral doctors ensures that players' medical history is being recorded in an accurate manner, *i.e.*, in a manner that correctly details a player's injury history and the ways in which those prior injuries are manifesting themselves today. Clubs—and thus club doctors—have an incentive to minimize players' injuries and declare them fit to play in order to avoid further financial liability. For example, if an NFL player is injured during one season, and fails the pre-season physical the next season, the player is entitled to an Injury Protection benefit, an amount equal to 50% of his Paragraph 5 Salary (*i.e.*, base) for the season following the season of injury, up to a maximum payment of $1,150,000 (in 2016).[1] If the player is still injured during the next pre-season, he can obtain Extended Injury Protection, a benefit that permits a player to earn 50% of his salary up to $500,000 for the *second* season after suffering an injury that prevented the player from continuing to play. Additionally, similar to the CFL, if the club doctor finds that a player is healthy enough to play, a player's potential Injury Grievance[a] is undermined. In these situations, the club doctor, acting in the interests of the club, might be motivated to find that the player is healthy enough to play during the pre-season physical, preventing the player from receiving

benefits and compensation to which he is entitled. While we do not know if such practices are common or widespread, in our Report *Protecting and Promoting the Health of NFL Players: Legal and Ethical Analysis and Recommendations*, we provided examples from players attesting that such situations do occur.[2] Whatever the frequency, a structural conflict still exists and needs to be addressed. A neutral doctor avoids the potential for bias, and ensures players are receiving their just compensation and care.

As discussed in the Introduction, the NFL declined to review this Report. However, MLB did provide comments on the Report which may provide insight into the viewpoints of the other professional leagues. In reviewing a draft of this Report, MLB expressed its disagreement with this recommendation, stating:

The recommendation (1-A) that preseason physical examinations be performed by a neutral doctor misses the point of the PPE [preparticipation physical evaluation]. Continuity of care is an important aspect of player health care and it is the view of our medical experts that having a separate physician for the preseason exam would result in worse care during the season. The recent Consensus Monograph on PPE, which was prepared by several national physician groups and is viewed as the governing document on these types of exams, does **not** include a recommendation for independent physicians.

While we generally agree with MLB that continuity of care is important, we disagree with MLB's comment for several reasons.

First, it is important to understand we believe there is a structural conflict of interest whereby NFL club doctors provide care to players while also providing services for the club.[b] As a result, players have business reasons to be concerned about the outcome of the pre-season physical. As explained above, club doctors may not accurately record a

---

a   An Injury Grievance is "a claim or complaint that, at the time a player's NFL Player Contract or Practice Squad Player Contract was terminated by a Club, the player was physically unable to perform the services required of him by that contract because of an injury incurred in the performance of his services under that contract." 2011 NFL CBA, Art. 45, § 1.

b   In our Report *Protecting and Promoting the Health of NFL Players: Legal and Ethical Analysis and Recommendations* we set forth a comprehensive recommendation to address this issue. We propose restructuring NFL club medical staff in such a way that the doctor treating the players has as his or her only concern the well-being of the player-patient and has no advisory role to the club.

player's condition, which can negatively affect his contract status and benefits to which he is entitled.

Second, our recommendation would not affect continuity of care as MLB's comment seems to suggest. Assuming doctors working for the club continue to treat players (which is not what we recommend as explained in footnote b), the club doctor would have full access to the results of the pre-season physical and is also permitted to re-examine the player at any time, including during the pre-season. However, a physical performed by a neutral doctor should be used to establish the player's pre-existing conditions in order to better protect the player's business interests.

Third, MLB's reference to the consensus monograph[c] is misplaced. The monograph specifically states that it "is intended to provide a state-of-the-art, practical, and effective screening tool for physicians who perform PPEs for athletes in *middle school, high school, and college.*"[3] Thus, the monograph does not apply to *professional sports*, and does not speak to the issues raised above.

2) Injury Rates and Policies

Recommendation 2-A: The NFL, and to the extent possible, the NFLPA, should: (a) continue to improve its robust collection of aggregate injury data; (b) continue to have the injury data analyzed by qualified professionals; and, (c) make the data publicly available for re-analysis.

As explained above, each of the Big Four leagues and MLS seems to have a quality injury tracking system, allowing for the accumulation of current information about the nature, duration, and cause of player injuries. As stated above, we rely on this data in this Report because it provides the best available data concerning player injuries, although we cannot independently verify the data's accuracy. Nevertheless, if accurately collected, this data has the potential to improve player health through analysis by qualified experts so long as it is made available to them. In particular, analysis potentially could be performed to determine, among other things, the effects of rule changes, practice

habits, scheduling, new equipment, and certain treatments, while also identifying promising or discouraging trends and injury types in need of additional focus.[4] Notably, the NFL already conducts this type of analysis through Quintiles.

However, the NFL does not publicly release its aggregate injury data (nor does any other league).[5] The NFL does release some data at its annual Health & Safety Press Conference at the Super Bowl. However, the data released at the Press Conference is minimal compared to the data available and the analyses performed by Quintiles. For the data to have the potential meaningful applications mentioned above, it must be made available in a form as close to its entirety as possible. Such disclosure would permit academics, journalists, fans, and others to analyze the data in any number of ways, likely elucidating statistical events, trends, and statistics that have the opportunity to improve player health. To be clear we are recommending the release of more *aggregate* data, not data that could lead to identification of the injuries of any particular player or cause problems concerning gambling.

Publicly releasing injury data, nevertheless, comes with complications that we must acknowledge. While more transparency in injury reporting is necessary, the nuances of such data can easily be lost on those without proper training. Sports injury prevention priorities in public health can be swayed by public opinion and heavily influenced by those with the most media coverage. Making injury data publicly available may allow those with the media access to dictate the agenda regardless of the actual implications of the data. As a result, it may be harder for injury trends that may be more hazardous, but less visible in the media, to get the attention they need, even when the data clearly shows the importance of these issues. Thoughtful, balanced, peer-reviewed results may have difficulty competing against those statistics which garner the most media attention. For this and other reasons, in our report *Protecting and Promoting the Health of NFL Players: Legal and Ethical Analysis and Recommendations*, we recommended that "[t]he media . . . engage appropriate experts, including doctors, scientists, and lawyers, to ensure that its reporting on player health matters is accurate, balanced, and comprehensive."[6] The medical, scientific, and legal issues concerning player health are extremely complicated, which demands that the media take care to avoid making assertions that are not supported or that do not account for the intricacies and nuance of medicine, science, and the law.

---

c   *See* Am. Acad. Pediatrics, Preparticipation Physical Evaluation (4th ed. 2010). This monograph was created through the coordination of the American Academy of Family Physicians, American Academy of Pediatrics, American College of Sports Medicine, American Medical Society for Sports Medicine, American Orthopaedic Society for Sports Medicine, and the American Osteopathic Academy of Sports Medicine.

In light of these concerns, one possible intermediate solution is to create a committee of experts that can review requests for data and determine whether or not the usage of the data is appropriate and will advance player health. Indeed, the Datalys Center for Sports Injury Research and Prevention performs this role concerning access to NCAA student-athlete injury data.[7] Moreover, such committees have also been formed in the clinical research setting.[8]

Recommendation 2-B: Players diagnosed with a concussion should be placed on a short-term injured reserve list whereby the player does not count against the Active/Inactive 53 man roster until he is cleared to play by the NFL's Protocols Regarding Diagnosis and Management of Concussions.[d]

According to the leading experts, 80–90% of concussions are resolved within seven to ten days.[9] Thus, concussion symptoms persist for longer than ten days for approximately 10–20% of athletes. In addition, there are a variety of factors that can modify the concussion recovery period, such as the loss of consciousness, past concussion history, medications, and the player's style of play.[10] Consequently, a player's recovery time from a concussion can easily range from no games to several games. The uncertain recovery times create pressure on the player, club, and club doctor. Each roster spot is valuable and clubs constantly add and drop players to ensure they have the roster that gives them the greatest chance to win each game day. As a result of the uncertain recovery times for a concussion, clubs might debate whether they need to replace the player for that week or longer. The club doctor and player might also then feel pressure for the player to return to play as soon as possible. By exempting a concussed player from the 53 man roster, the club has the opportunity to sign a short-term replacement player in the event the concussed player is unable to play. At the same time, the player and club doctor would have some of the return-to-play pressure removed.

In fact, MLB already has such a policy. MLB has a seven-day Disabled List (as compared to its normal 10- and 60-day Disabled Lists) "solely for the placement of players who suffer a concussion."[11]

Why treat concussions differently than other injuries in this respect? This is a fair question to which there are a few plausible responses. First, in terms of the perception of the game by fans, concussions have clearly received more attention than any of the other injuries NFL players might experience and thus the future of the game depends more critically on adequately protecting players who suffer from them. Second, concussions are much harder to diagnose than other injuries, such that there may be a period of uncertainty in which it would be appropriate to err on the side of caution.[12] Third, both players and medical professionals have more difficulty anticipating the long-term effects of concussions as compared to other injuries, given current scientific uncertainties concerning brain injury.[13] Fourth, and perhaps most importantly, it is much harder to determine the appropriate recovery times for concussions as compared to other injuries.[14] These reasons all support a recommendation to exclude concussed players from a club's Active/Inactive roster, but we recognize that the key feature of players potentially feeling or facing pressure to return before full recovery may be shared across any injury a player may experience. Thus, it may also be reasonable to consider extending this recommendation to injuries beyond concussions.[e]

In reviewing a draft of our Report, *Protecting and Promoting the Health of NFL Players: Legal and Ethical Analysis and Recommendations,* the NFL argued that "[t]he current NFL roster rules actually provide greater flexibility" than is recommended here.[15] The NFL explained that because "[t]here is no limitation on how long a player may be carried on the 53-man roster throughout the season without being 'activated,' . . . a player who is concussed routinely is carried on his club's 53-man roster without being activated until he is cleared."[16] However, for the reasons explained above, we believe concussions should be treated differently. All 53 spots on the roster are precious to both the club and the players. The uncertainty surrounding recovery from a concussion presents unique pressures that can be lessened with the approach recommended here.

Indeed, the NFL's practice has been to treat concussions differently from other injuries. As part of its Concussion Protocol, players suspected of having suffered a concussion

---

d   This recommendation also appears as Recommendation 7:1-E in our Report *Protecting and Promoting the Health of NFL Players: Legal and Ethical Analysis and Recommendations.* Due to the fact that the recommendation was inspired by MLB's concussion-specific DL list, we include it here as well.

e   We recognize that this new injured reserve list is subject to gaming by clubs, whereby a club might designate a player as concussed in order to add another player and effectively expand the roster. We do not view this this concern to be sufficient to outweigh the health benefits of the proposal. Moreover, all injury lists are subject to some risk of being gamed in this manner, and thus the issue is not unique to what we propose.

during a game are examined by doctors unaffiliated with the club, and to be cleared to play in the next game they must be cleared by doctors unaffiliated with the club. For all other injuries, club doctors are the only ones to examine and clear players to play. Additionally, in 2016, the NFL sent a memo to all clubs directing them not to comment on a player's progress in returning from a concussion.[17] Instead, the NFL directed clubs to state only "that the player is in the concussion protocol under the supervision of the medical team, and the club will monitor his status."[18] This is in contrast to the clubs' open discussion of players' other injuries.

The Washington football club essentially proposed our recommendation at the 2016 owners' meetings. Washington proposed amending the NFL bylaws to provide that a player who has suffered a concussion, and who has not been cleared to play, be placed on the club's Exempt List, and be replaced by a player on the club's Practice Squad on a game-by-game basis until the player is cleared to play. Unfortunately, the proposal was not adopted.

Recommendation 2-C: The NFL should consider removing the requirement that clubs disclose the location on the body of a player's injury from the Injury Reporting Policy.

In our Report *Protecting and Promoting the Health of NFL Players: Legal and Ethical Analysis and Recommendations*, we recommend the NFL consider fining and/or suspending players if they discuss or encourage targeting another player's injury.[19] However, the need for this Recommendation would be reduced if the NFL's Injury Reporting Policy did not openly disclose the location on the body of players' injuries, a requirement imposed only by the NFL, NBA and MLS.

The gambling-related interests of full disclosure likely do not outweigh the risks of targeting by other players created by the Injury Reporting Policy.[20] While additional data—including from federal law enforcement authorities—could inform this analysis—it seems unlikely that the risks of injury information being sold on a black market are so high to justify a known risk of players intentionally aiming to hit a player in an area known to be injured because of the Injury Reporting Policy. Similarly, we see no inequity in clubs not knowing the full extent of an opposing club's player injuries. Consequently, we recommend that the NFL consider removing the requirement that clubs disclose the location of a player's injury from the Injury Reporting Policy.

3) Health-Related Benefits

Recommendation 3-A: The NFL and NFLPA should consider whether change is necessary concerning player benefit plans.

As discussed above, we identified three potential areas of concern regarding the benefit plans offered by the NFL. Also as discussed above, the benefits available to NFL players must be viewed in the context of one another: increasing one benefit might mean a decrease in another benefit. Below, we identify and discuss possible changes to the benefit plans, the implementation of which must be weighed collectively.

- The NFL and NFLPA should consider providing former players with health insurance options that meet the needs of the former player population for life: While the NFL provides significant benefits to former players, players likely do not take full advantage of those benefits due to the associated administrative burdens.[21] Additionally, a consistent and reliable health insurance plan seems preferable to ad hoc and uncertain benefits. The NFL and NFLPA should consider whether it would be more appropriate to shift some of the value of benefits away from the unplanned benefits (*e.g.*, disability benefits and the health reimbursement account) to more stable health insurance options.[f] Where players have only played one or two seasons (and perhaps games), there might be questions as to whether it is appropriate to provide lifetime health insurance to someone who was employed for such a short period of time. On the other hand, only a few games or seasons can have life-lasting effects on a player. One option worth considering is tiering health insurance benefits and allowing those with less Credited Seasons to qualify for some but not full benefits.

- The NFL and NFLPA should consider increasing the amounts available to former players under the Retirement Plan: The monthly retirement benefits represent a more stable benefit than the other valuable but still uncertain benefits. Consequently, the NFL and NFLPA should consider whether it would be more beneficial to shift some of the value of benefits away from the unplanned benefits to the more stable Retirement Plan monthly payments.

---

f   According to columnist Mike Freeman, the NFLPA did analyze the potential costs of providing NFL players with health insurance for life and found the cost to be approximately $2 billion. Mike Freeman, *Two Minute Warning: How Concussions, Crime, and Controversy Could Kill the NFL (and What the League Can Do to Survive)*, xxv (2015).

- The NFL and NFLPA should consider reducing the vesting requirement for the Retirement Plan: The purpose of the NFL's three-year vesting requirement is unclear. The vesting requirement results in a considerable portion of former players being unable to collect any retirement benefits. We acknowledge that there may be appropriate policy reasons for such a limitation, such as a determination as to when a player has sufficiently contributed to the NFL. Indeed, many employers require a certain number of years of service before accruing certain benefits.[g] If the vesting requirement is instead principally motivated by cost, then the distribution of benefits among former players should be reconsidered to determine what is maximally beneficial for player health. In other words, is the current distribution of benefits among former players, which largely excludes players with less than three years of experience, preferred by the NFL, NFLPA, and players, or would it be preferable to reduce the benefits to players with more than three years of experience to provide some benefits to those with less than three years of experience? While these considerations are not easy and require a delicate balance, the exclusion of a significant portion of former players from the Retirement Plan requires an examination of the vesting requirement. As with health insurance benefits, one option worth considering is tiering Retirement Plan benefits and allowing those who have played less than three Credited Seasons to qualify for some if not full benefits.

4) Drug and Performance-Enhancing Drug Policies

Recommendation 4-A: The NFL should consider amending the PES Policy to provide treatment to any NFL player found to have violated the PES Policy.

The NFL and the other leagues recognize that substance abuse is a serious medical issue and, as a result, provide players with robust counseling and treatment. As discussed above, PES usage has been shown to be associated with a variety of serious physical and mental ailments. However, only the NBA and CFL offer treatment for players who have used PES. In light of the potential negative health consequences associated with PES usage and the treatment provided by the NBA and CFL for PES usage, it seems prudent for the NFL to consider providing treatment to PES

users similar to that provided for by the Substance Abuse Policy's Intervention Program.

There is an important clarification to this Recommendation. As stated earlier in this Chapter, we are not focused on the competitive advantage concerns associated with PES use or the discipline imposed by the leagues for drug or PES usage. We are focused on the health implications of drug and PES policies. Thus, our Recommendation should not be read to suggest that because players might need treatment for PES usage that they should not be disciplined—as is the case for first time offenders of the Substance Abuse Policy.

As discussed in the Introduction, the NFL declined to review this Report. However, MLB did provide comments on the Report which may provide insight into the viewpoints of the other professional leagues. MLB did not agree with this Recommendation, stating:

> There are no established treatment programs for PEDs, and since the recidivism rate for PEDs is fairly low, there is no support for the position that this class of prohibited substances warrants a response based on treatment. It is also an established practice of not just MLB, but all other professional leagues and international anti-doping organizations that the use of PEDs affects the integrity of play and should be responded with a disciplinary perspective as opposed to a clinical one. Our experts advise not including "PED treatment programs" as a recommendation in the report.

As a preliminary matter, we note that the NBA and CFL do provide treatment to PES users. Thus, there is a disagreement among the leagues (and potentially also the unions) on this issue, suggesting further research is needed.

We further reply to MLB with a clarification and with a disagreement. We understand sports organizations' need to discipline players who have violated PES policies. Our recommendation does not seek the elimination or reduction of discipline for PES violations in any way. Instead, we believe it is appropriate to consider providing players who have violated the PES Policy with counseling, regardless of any discipline imposed. This is where we and MLB disagree.

MLB rejects counseling for PES use on the grounds that "[t]here are no established treatment programs for PEDs." As discussed above, experts in the field recommend and do provide treatment for PES usage and its associated problems. Whether these programs are sufficiently "established," is beyond our expertise, but it nonetheless is an issue worth further consideration.

---

g   The principal distinction would be that employers require a certain number of years of service to, in part, encourage employees to continue working for them rather than obtaining employment elsewhere. This incentive structure is not needed in the NFL—where the vast majority of players play in the NFL for as long as they are able.

5) Compensation

Recommendation 5-A: The NFL and NFLPA should research the consequences and feasibility of guaranteeing more of players' compensation as a way to protect player health.

As discussed above, guaranteed compensation in the NFL is a complicated issue. While many people—and players in particular—have expressed a desire for increased guaranteed compensation, it is not clear that fully guaranteed compensation would be beneficial to players *collectively* such that it ought to be preferred to the status quo.

As a preliminary matter, the NFLPA itself has expressed mixed views about the guaranteed contracts. In a 2002 editorial in *The Washington Post*, then-NFLPA Executive Director Gene Upshaw acknowledged that the possibility of guaranteed contracts "is severely undermined by the risk of a career-ending injury" and touted the benefits available to players as an alternative.[22] Then, in two reports issued by the NFLPA in or around 2002 and 2007 respectively, the NFLPA asserted that NFL player compensation is, in fact, largely guaranteed by explaining that more than half of all compensation *paid* to players is guaranteed.[23] However, importantly, this statistic does not mean that half of all compensation *contracted* was guaranteed—indeed, as discussed above, approximately 44% of all contracted compensation is guaranteed. Players are often paid guaranteed money (*e.g.*, a signing bonus or roster bonus) in the first or second year of the contract only to have the base salaries (the unguaranteed portions) in the later years of the contract go unpaid because the player's contract was terminated.

With this background in mind, there are several reasons why fully guaranteed compensation might not be beneficial to players *collectively*. First, while fully guaranteed contracts might be good for the players who receive them, it could result in many players not receiving any contract at all. If clubs were forced to retain a player of diminishing skill because his contract was guaranteed, a younger or less proven player might never get the opportunity to sign with the club.[24] Relatedly, clubs might continue to provide playing opportunities to the players with larger contracts in order to justify those contracts, preventing younger players from establishing themselves as starting or star players and earning higher salaries. It is also likely that under a system

of guaranteed compensation, player salaries would decrease (at least in the short-term)—particularly the salaries of the highest paid players and players who are less certain to add value to a roster—as clubs would be more cautious about taking on the financial liabilities, especially given the Salary Cap in place in the NFL. Similarly, clubs also may seek to minimize their financial liabilities by reducing roster sizes, which might cost marginal players their jobs, while again reducing opportunities for young or unproven players to join a club.

There are also logistical challenges to implementing fully guaranteed contracts. The finances and operations of the NFL and its clubs are greatly intertwined with the fact that NFL contracts have never been fully guaranteed. Since 1993, NFL clubs have had to comply with a strict Salary Cap that necessarily influences the types of contracts clubs are willing to offer, including the possibility of guaranteed compensation. Fully guaranteed contracts would be a fundamental and monumental alteration to the current business of the NFL that, at a minimum, would require a gradual phasing in process.[h]

It is possible that a rate of guaranteed contracts less than 100% but more than the current 44% is also optimal. Given the varying factors to be weighed and considered, it is not clear what percentage of guaranteed compensation would maximize player health for the most NFL players.

Clearly this is a complex issue, with the potential for substantial unintended consequences. Thus, we recognize the likely health value of guaranteed contracts, while simultaneously recognizing that it may not be the right solution for all players. Importantly, as discussed above, players who value a contractual guarantee over potentially higher but uncertain compensation may negotiate for that protection individually, as many currently do. Moreover, we expect that other recommendations made in this Report and, more importantly, our other Report, *Protecting and Promoting the Health of NFL Players: Legal and Ethical Analysis and Recommendations*, including key recommendations related to the medical professionals who care for players,[25] if adopted, would make great strides toward protecting and promoting player health such that guaranteed compensation would be less critical for that purpose.

---

h   For example, one rule that would likely have to be removed is the NFL's requirement that clubs deposit into a separate account the present value, less $2 million, of guaranteed compensation to be paid in future years. 2011 CBA, Art. 26 § 9. Former NFL club executive Andrew Brandt believes clubs "hide behind" the funding rule to avoid guaranteeing player compensation, and have been largely successful in doing so. Andrew Brandt, Supplemental Peer Review Response (Nov. 6, 2015).

Ultimately, we recommend further research into this question, including player and club perspectives, economic and actuarial analysis, and comprehensive consideration of the relevant trade-offs, ramifications, and potential externalities. In the meantime, we note that the trend toward greater use of contractual guarantees can help promote individual player health and allow individual negotiation by players based on their own goals and priorities.

6) Eligibility Rules

Recommendation 6-A: The NFL should consider performing or funding research analyzing when a player might be "ready" for the NFL.

Currently, the NFL's eligibility rule appears to be the NFL's best guess as to when players, as a general rule, are ready to play in the NFL. However, we are unaware of any rigorous body of data to support the NFL's eligibility rule as it is currently written. While the NFL's eligibility rule seems reasonably protective of player health based on what is currently known, data could substantially buttress the rule—or prompt changes to it as necessary. For the sake of player health, the NFL should make efforts to gather this data.

Among the data that might be valuable in this context are: players' ages when they enter the league; players' height and weight; players' position; players' professional results; players' injury histories; players' financial health; players' education; players' psychological health; and, players' post-career activities. This and other data may need to be gathered before, during, and after the player's career, as relevant; there may also be questions related to the precise definition of player success for purposes of this analysis, although certain thresholds on either end of the spectrum will be evident. While some of this data does currently exist, the ideal comparison would be between players who entered the league under the current rule and those who entered earlier (or later) on an alternative rule. Because the current eligibility rule has been in place for decades, direct comparison is difficult. However, it is possible that the NFL—potentially with the help of others—could learn something from the data that is already available, for example, comparing the outcomes of players who enter the league at different ages beyond the eligibility threshold. Of course, this will not answer the question of how *individual* players might fare if they could enter the league even earlier

than the current rule permits,[i] but it may nonetheless provide some helpful information for comparison between players who are younger or older at entry.

Recommendation 6-B: The NFL should reconsider the interplay of its eligibility rules with the NCAA's rules as they concern player health and take appropriate action if necessary.

The NFL's eligibility rule coupled with the realities of the NCAA's rules cause tremendous pressure on prospective and future NFL players. While these NCAA rules are not the NFL's creation, the NFL should nevertheless acknowledge that the football careers of prospective or future NFL players are substantially affected by the NCAA's rules and take steps within its power to address those problems. The combination of the two organizations' rules creates situations that many find inequitable and it is thus appropriate for the NFL to reconsider its eligibility rules' applicability in those situations and whether anything can be done to change them.[j]

7) Conclusion

Final Recommendation 1: The leagues and unions should continue to coordinate on player health issues and to consider each other's policies and practices.

Indications are that the leagues do communicate with each other concerning common issues on a regular basis. Similarly, the unions communicate on common issues. This coordination is assisted by the fact that many doctors, lawyers, and other professionals are advisors to multiple leagues or unions. It is important that the leagues and unions continue—and perhaps increase—their level of coordination on player health issues. As many of the leagues have increased

---

i   Given more advances in health technology, it is theoretically possible that leagues could adopt an individualized approach, using specific metrics to determine whether a particular player was "ready." However, such an approach also raises concerns with the Americans with Disabilities Act and the Genetic Information Nondiscrimination Act, as discussed in our article, *Evaluating NFL Player Health and Performance: Legal and Ethical Issues*, 165 U. Penn. L. Rev. 227 (2017).

j   Despite criticism on this issue, the NFL reportedly is not considering any changes to its eligibility rules. *See* Mike Florio, *NFL not considering a change to the three-year rule*, ProFootballTalk (Oct. 31, 2015, 10:38 PM), http://profootballtalk.nbcsports.com/2015/10/31/nfl-not-considering-a-change-to-the-three-year-rule/, *archived at* https://perma.cc/34JC-M66Y.

their interest in and funding of research—particularly medical research—concerning player health issues, valuable data is being created that can help inform other leagues' policies and practices. We urge the leagues to share this data—not just with each other but with all researchers. Moreover, by combining resources the leagues might be able to take on broader and better projects than they can alone. Finally, as leagues continue to make advancements in player health policies and practices, it is important that the other leagues and unions take note of those advancements, consider their possible application to their respective organizations, and make the necessary changes to protect and promote player health. The leagues are tremendously powerful and influential institutions—by working together, they can maximize their ability to be positive change agents in player health.

Final Recommendation 2: The media, academics, the leagues, and the unions should continue to police the advancement of player health.

Following this Report, we do not intend to be a passive voice in the process of improving player health. It is our hope to be able to periodically review progress on the issues discussed in this Report and provide additional reports. However, in addition to any progress reports from the authors of this Report or the Football Players Health Study at Harvard University, we urge and trust that others—in particular the leagues and unions—will heed the message of this Report and hold other stakeholders accountable.

Endnotes

1   NFL CBA, Art. 45, § 2.

2   See Christopher R. Deubert, I. Glenn Cohen, Holly Fernandez Lynch, *Protecting and Promoting the Health of NFL Players: Legal and Ethical Analysis and Recommendations,* Recommendation 1:1-F (2016).

3   Am. Acad. Pediatrics, Preparticipation Physical Evaluation 3 (4th ed. 2010).

4   For examples of such studies in high school and college sports, *see* Barry P. Boden et al., *Catastrophic Injuries in Pole Vaulters, A Prospective 9-Year Follow-up Study,* 40 Am. J. Sports Med. 1488 (2012); Frederick O. Mueller and Robert C. Cantu, *Catastrophic injuries and fatalities in high school and college sports, fall 1982–spring 1988,* 22 Med. & Sci. in Sports & Exercise 737 (1990).

5   Some of the studies discussed in this Report were the result of the leagues' willingness to provide some injury data upon request. While it is commendable that the leagues occasionally provide the data when requested, this does not entirely address the concerns outlined in Recommendation 1.

6   Christopher R. Deubert, I. Glenn Cohen, Holly Fernandez Lynch, *Protecting and Promoting the Health of NFL Players: Legal and Ethical Analysis and Recommendations,* Recommendation 17:1-B (2016).

7   *See The Datalys Center for Sports Injury Research and Prevention,* NCAA, http://www.ncaa.org/health-and-safety/medical-conditions/datalys-center-sports-injury-research-and-prevention (last visited Aug. 3, 2016), *archived at* https://perma.cc/2M75-B24L.

8   *See, e.g., Data transparency,* GlaxoSmithKline, http://www.gsk.com/en-gb/behind-the-science/innovation/data-transparency (last visited June 20, 2016), *archived at* https://perma.cc/M5HN-NLHN; *Frequently Asked Questions,* the YODA Project, http://yoda.yale.edu/frequently-asked-questions-faqs#Data (last visited June 20, 2016), *archived at* https://perma.cc/2Z98-R7HC.

9   *See* Paul McCrory et al., *Consensus statement on concussion in sport: the 4th Int'l Conference on Concussion in Sport held in Zurich, November 2012,* 47 Br. J. Sports Med. 250, 251 (2013).

10 *Id.* at 253.

11 MLB CBA, Att. 36, ¶ 2.

12 *See* Paul McCrory et al., *Consensus statement on concussion in sport: the 4th Int'l Conference on Concussion in Sport held in Zurich, November 2012,* 47 Br. J. Sports Med. 250, 250–58 (2013) (discussing the challenges of and best practices for diagnosing concussions).

13 *See id.*

14 *See id.* at 252-58 (discussing generally the challenges of determining when an athlete has recovered from a concussion).

15 Letter from Larry Ferazani, NFL, to authors (July 18, 2016).

16 *Id.*

17 Mike Florio, *NFL tells teams to stop commenting about concussed players,* ProFootballTalk (Nov. 11, 2016, 7:50 PM), http://profootballtalk.nbcsports.com/2016/11/11/nfl-tells-teams-to-stop-commenting-about-concussed-players/, *archived at* https://perma.cc/Z7ML-ZP7W.

18 *Id.*

19 Christopher R. Deubert, I. Glenn Cohen, Holly Fernandez Lynch, *Protecting and Promoting the Health of NFL Players: Legal and Ethical Analysis and Recommendations* Recommendation 7:4-B (2016).

20 Mike Florio, *Disclosure of injury information continues to put NFL players in a delicate spot,* ProFootballTalk (July 10, 2015, 12:34 PM), http://profootballtalk.nbcsports.com/2015/07/10/disclosure-of-injury-information-continues-to-put-nfl-players-in-a-delicate-spot/, *archived at* http://perma.cc/PYL4-KMRY ("many players would like to keep [injury information] secret, in order to keep an opponent from hitting, poking, and/or kicking the injured region.")

21 For more on this issue, *see* Christopher R. Deubert, I. Glenn Cohen, Holly Fernandez Lynch, *Protecting and Promoting the Health of NFL Players: Legal and Ethical Analysis and Recommendations,* Recommendation 7:3-B (2016).

22 Gene Upshaw, *NFLPA's Upshaw Responds,* Wash. Post, Dec. 22, 2002, *available at* 2002 WLNR 15865309.

23 NFLPA, *A New Look at Guaranteed Contracts in the NFL* (circa 2002) (on file with authors) ("Over half of all salary earned by NFL players now is guaranteed"); Nat'l Football League Players Ass'n, *Guaranteed Contracts in Professional Team Sports: How Does the NFL Compare?* (circa 2007) (on file with authors) ("at least 52% of all compensation in the NFL is, in fact, 'guaranteed' to players.'")

24 Mike Florio, *Fully-guaranteed contracts could cause problems for teams, players,* ProFootballTalk (May 29, 2015, 9:55 AM), http://profootballtalk.nbcsports.com/2015/05/29/fully-guaranteed-contracts-could-cause-problems-for-teams-players/, *archived at* http://perma.cc/GE9E-YSME (discussing potential problems with guaranteed contracts in the NFL).

25 *See* Christopher R. Deubert, I. Glenn Cohen, Holly Fernandez Lynch, *Protecting and Promoting the Health of NFL Players: Legal and Ethical Analysis and Recommendations,* Recommendation 2:1-A (2016).

APPENDIX B \ COMPILATION OF SUMMARY TABLES

Below, for ease of reference, is a compilation of all of the tables summarizing the leagues' various policies and practices at the end of each Chapter of this Report. Explanatory footnotes and citations are included in the full Chapters. Note that Chapter 6: Eligibility Rules does not include a summary table.

Table 1-C:
Summary of Club Medical Personnel Policies and Practices

Do the Leagues' policies:	NFL	MLB	NBA	NHL	CFL	MLS
QUALITY OF MEDICAL CARE						
Require retention of doctors?	Yes	Yes	Yes	Yes	No	No
Require retention of athletic trainers?	Yes	Yes	Yes	Yes	Yes	No
Require sports-specific certification for doctors?	Yes	No	Yes	Yes	No	No
Set forth a standard of care?	Yes	No	No	Yes	No	Yes
DISCLOSURE AND PLAYER AUTONOMY						
Require medical staff to disclose communications with club to player?	Yes	No	No	No	No	No
Require club to pay for second opinion?	Yes	Yes	Yes	Yes	No	Yes
Provide club doctor right to determine a player's course of treatment?	No	No	Yes	Yes	No	Yes
Entitle players to surgeon of their choice?	Yes	No	No	Yes	No	No
Entitle players to medical records?	Yes	Yes	Yes	Yes	Yes	Yes
Require players to submit to physicals upon request?	Yes	Yes	Yes	No	Yes	Yes
CONFIDENTIALITY						
Permit non-medical club personnel to obtain and disclose player health information?	No	Yes	Yes	Yes	No	Yes
Require players to inform club of care by other medical professionals, regardless of payment source?	No	If baseball-related	Yes	No	No	No
CONFLICTS OF INTEREST						
Insulate club medical staff from influence by coaches and other club personnel?	No	No	No	No	No	No
Prohibit healthcare providers from paying for right to provide care?	Yes	Yes	Partially	Unknown	No	No

Table 2-L:

Comparison of Leagues' Regular Season Injury Statistics[a]

	NFL	MLB	NBA	NHL	CFL	UEFA	MLS
Electronic Tracking System	Yes	Yes	Yes	Yes	No	N/A	Yes
Mean Injuries Per Season	1,511.0	1,516.6	369.8	728.0	N/A	N/A	N/A
Rate of Injuries Per Player-Season	0.69	0.93	0.88	0.85	N/A	N/A	N/A
Mean Concussions Per Season	160.0	18.0	9.0	93.0	57.0	N/A	N/A
Rate of Concussions Per Player-Season	0.073	0.016	0.019	0.108	N/A	N/A	N/A
Concussions As Percentage of Injuries	10.5%	1.8%	2.4%	12.8%	N/A	1.9%	N/A
Mean Injuries Per Game	5.90	0.45	0.16	0.59	N/A	0.53	N/A
Rate of Injury Per Player-Game	0.064	0.016	0.016	0.016	N/A	0.038	N/A
Regular Season Games Per Player-Injury	15.60	62.50	62.50	62.50	N/A	N/A	N/A
Most Common Injury/ Injured Body Part	Concus-sion	Upper leg (thigh)	Ankle Sprain	Head	N/A	Thigh	N/A
Concussions Per Game	0.625	0.007	0.007	0.067	0.704	0.010	N/A
Rate of Concussion Per Player-Game	0.00679	0.00026	0.00035	0.00180	0.00800	0.00072	N/A
Games Per Concussion Per Player	147.10	3,846.15	2,857.14	555.56	125.00	1,388.89	N/A

Table 2-M:

Comparison of Leagues' Injury Policies

	NFL	MLB	NBA	NHL	CFL	UEFA	MLS
Authorized to Disclose Injuries (Existence and Nature)	By waiver	Yes	Yes	Yes	No	N/A	Yes
Required to Disclose Existence of Injuries	Yes	No	Yes	Yes	No	N/A	Yes
Required to Disclose Nature of Injuries	Yes	No	Yes	No	No	N/A	Yes

a   We remind the reader that we use the data that we consider the most reliable—and generally the most recent—in order to provide the most accurate assessment of injury rates in sports today. We also remind the reader that our data is limited to regular season data.

Table 3-I:
Comparison of Leagues' Benefits

Benefit	NFL	MLB	NBA	NHL	CFL	MLS
Pension Plan	Yes	Yes	Yes	Yes	Yes	No
Pension Plan Vesting Requirement	3 years (post 1992)	1 day	3 years	1 day	9 games	N/A
Severance Plan	Yes	No	No	No	No	No
401k Plan	Yes	Yes	Yes	Yes	No	Yes
Other Deferred Compensation Plan	Yes	No	Yes	No	No	No
Health Insurance (Current Players)	Yes	Yes	Yes	Yes	Yes	Yes
Health Insurance (Former Players, other than COBRA)	5 years	For life potentially	For life potentially	For life potentially	No	No
Life Insurance	Yes	Yes	Yes	Yes	Yes	Yes
Dental Insurance	Yes	Yes	Yes	Yes	Maybe	Yes
Health Reimbursement Account	Yes	No	Yes	No	No	No
Long Term Care Insurance	Yes	No	Potentially	No	No	No
Wellness Benefits	Many	Some	Some	None	None	None
Disability Benefits (Current Players)	Yes	Yes	Yes	Yes	Maybe	Yes
Disability Benefits (Former Players)	Yes	Yes	No	No	No	No
Neurocognitive Disability Benefits	Yes	No	No	Only for current players	No	No
Workers' Compensation	Yes	Partial	Yes	Yes	Prohibited by law	Yes
Education-Related Benefits	Yes	No	Yes	Yes	No	For some players
Joint Health-Specific Committee(s)	Yes	Yes	Yes	Yes	Yes	Yes

Table 4-I:
Comparison of Leagues' PES Policies[b]

Feature	NFL	MLB	NBA	NHL	CFL	MLS
Independent administration	Yes	Yes	Yes	Yes	Yes	Yes
Urine tests permitted	Yes	Yes	Yes	Yes	Yes	Yes
Blood tests permitted	Yes	Yes	Yes	No	Yes	No
Maximum number of annual tests for player without prior violation	24	No maximum	Nine	No maximum	No maximum	No maximum
Therapeutic Use Exemptions available	Yes	Yes	Yes	Yes	Yes	No
Treatment available	No	No	Yes	No	Yes	Yes
Safe harbor for self-referrals	No	No	No	No	Yes	No
Discipline for first violation	Two–Six games	80 games	25 games	20 games	Two games	League discretion
Discipline for second violation	Ten games	162 games	55 games	60 games	Nine games	League discretion
Discipline for third violation	Two years	Life	Two years (subject to reinstatement)	Two years	One year	League discretion
Discipline for fourth violation	NA	NA	NA	NA	Life	League discretion
Confidential violations	Until discipline	Until discipline	Until discipline	Until discipline	Until discipline	Until discipline
Neutral appeal rights	In part	Yes	Yes	Yes	Yes	No

b For context, the NFL regular season is 16 games, the MLB regular season is 162 games, the NBA and NHL regular seasons are 82 games, the CFL regular season is 18 games, and the MLS regular season is 34 games.

Table 4-J:

Comparison of Leagues' Drugs of Abuse Policies

Feature	NFL	MLB	NBA	NHL	CFL	MLS
Independent administration	Yes	Yes	Yes	Yes	No Policy	Yes
Urine tests permitted	Yes	Yes	Yes	Yes	No Policy	Yes
Blood tests permitted	No	No	No	No	No Policy	No
Maximum number of annual tests for player without prior violation	One	No tests	Six	No tests	No Policy	No maximum
Therapeutic Use Exemptions available	Yes	Yes	Yes	No	No Policy	No
Treatment available	Yes	Yes	Yes	Yes	No Policy	Yes
Safe harbor for self-referrals	Yes	Maybe	Yes	Yes	No Policy	Yes
Discipline for first violation	None	None	No (Marijuana); One year for rookies only or two years (other drugs)	None	No Policy	Determined by Program Professionals evaluation
Discipline for second violation	Fine (Marijuana); Four games (other drugs)	15–25 games	$25,000 fine (Marijuana); 2 years for rookies or self-referrals (other drugs)	Suspended during treatment	No Policy	League discretion
Discipline for third violation	4–6 games	50–75 games	Five games (Marijuana)	Minimum of six months	No Policy	League discretion
Discipline for fourth violation	10 games (Marijuana); One year (other drugs)	At least One year	Ten games (Marijuana)	Minimum of one year	No Policy	League discretion
Confidential violations	Yes	Yes	Yes	Yes	No Policy	Until discipline
Neutral appeal rights	Yes	Yes	Yes	Yes	No Policy	No

Table 5-J:
Comparisons of Leagues' Compensation Statistics and Policies

Benefit	NFL	MLB	NBA	NHL	CFL	MLS
Mean Annual Salary	$2.7 million	$4.25 million	$6.9-8 million	$2.89 million	$80,000	$290,246
Mean Career Length	5.0 years	5.6 years	4.8 years	5.6 years	3.2 years	3.2 years
Minimum Salary (2016)	$450,000	$507,500	$543,471	$575,000	$52,000	$62,500
Maximum Salary	No	No	Yes	Yes	No	No
Maximum Contract Length	No	No	Yes	Yes	No	No
Unrestricted Free Agency Rights	After four seasons	After six seasons	After five seasons for first round picks	Depends on age and experience	Upon expiration of rookie contract	28 years old and eight years of experience
Guaranteed Compensation	~ 44%	~ 100%	~ 90%	For injury and one-third or two-thirds of the player's salary	Almost none	For players 24 and older with 1+ years' experience
Salary Cap Type	Hard	Luxury Tax	Soft and Luxury Tax	Hard	Hard	Soft
Guaranteed Share of Revenue	Yes	No	Yes	Yes	No	No

APPENDIX C \ GLOSSARY OF TERMS & RELEVANT PERSONS & INSTITUTIONS

88 Plan: A program that provides benefits for former NFL players suffering from dementia, ALS, or Parkinson's disease.

401(k) Savings Plan: A retirement plan available to NBA players who can contribute a portion of their salary, subject to the maximum amounts permitted by the Internal Revenue Code.[1] NBA clubs match up to 140% of players' allowed contributions.[2]

ACC: *See* Accountability and Care Committee.

Accountability and Care Committee ("ACC"): A committee consisting of the NFL Commissioner or his designee; the NFLPA Executive Director or his designee; and six additional members "experienced in fields relevant to health care for professional athletes," three appointed by the Commissioner and three by the NFLPA Executive Director. The ACC is to "provide advice and guidance regarding the provision of preventive, medical, surgical, and rehabilitative care for players by all clubs."[3]

Accrued Season: Generally speaking, a season in which an NFL player is on a club's roster for at least six games.

AHMS: *See* Athlete Health Management System.

AMA: *See* American Medical Association.

American Medical Association ("AMA"): a voluntary professional association for physicians and the source of the predominant code defining ethical medical practice.

Anti-Drug Program: The NBA-NBPA policy prohibiting players from using PES and drugs of abuse.

Athlete Health Management System ("AHMS"): The NHL's electronic medical records system.

Big Four: A label sometimes used to collectively describe the NFL, MLB, NBA, and NHL, due to similarities in their structures and positions in the American sports landscape.

Board of Certification for the Athletic Trainer: The accredited certification program for entry-level athletic trainers, which sets the standards and codes of conduct for the practice of athletic training.

BOC: *See* Board of Certification for the Athletic Trainer.

Canadian Athletic Therapists Association ("CATA"): A voluntary professional membership association for certified athletic trainers across all levels of competition in Canada. CATA's American counterpart is NATA.

Canadian Football League ("CFL"): A professional football league consisting of nine member clubs, all of which are located in Canada. The CFL began play in 1958, has its headquarters in Toronto, and is currently looking for a new Commissioner. The CFL's 2015 revenues were an estimated $200 million.

Canadian Football League Players Association ("CFLPA"): A labor organization representing CFL players. The CFLPA was formed in 1965,[4] has its headquarters in Stoney Creek, Ontario; and is led by President Scott Flory, a 15-year CFL veteran.

Canadian Interuniversity Sport: The organization that governs intercollegiate athletics in Canada. CIS' American counterpart is the NCAA.

CATA: *See* Canadian Athletic Therapists Association.

CBA: *See* Collective Bargaining Agreement.

CFL: *See* Canadian Football League.

CFLPA: *See* Canadian Football League Players Association.

CIS: *See* Canadian Interuniversity Sport.

Club: A professional sports franchise.

COBRA: *See* Consolidated Omnibus Budget Reconciliation Act.

Collective Bargaining Agreement ("CBA"): "A contract between an employer and a labor union regulating employment conditions, wages, benefits, and grievances."[5] Each of the sports leagues is governed by a CBA.

Commissioner: The Chief Executive Officer of a league.

Consolidated Omnibus Budget Reconciliation Act ("COBRA"): A federal law that requires continuation coverage to be offered to covered employees, their spouses, former spouses, and dependent children when group health coverage would otherwise be lost due to certain specific events, including, as would be relevant in the NFL, "the termination (other than by reason of such employee's gross misconduct), or reduction of hours, of the covered employee's employment."[6]

Credited Season: Generally speaking, a season in which an NFL player is on a club's roster for at least three games.

Disability & Neurocognitive Benefit Plan: Provides eligible NFL players with disability benefits, including benefits based on neurocognitive disability.

Disabled List ("DL") (MLB): A roster designation for MLB players who are injured and are unable to play. The MLB has a 60-day, 10-day, and 7-day DL. Players on the Disabled List do not count towards the club's 25-man roster.

Disabled List ("DL") (MLS): A roster designation for MLS players who are injured and are unable to play. The player must remain on the DL for a minimum of six matches.

DL: *See* Disabled List.

Draft: A process by which a league's clubs (or, in the case of MLS, the league itself) select players to join the league. Players selected are typically college or high school student-athletes, but, in some sports, can also include international players.

eBIS: *See* Electronic Baseball Information System.

Electronic Baseball Information System ("eBIS"): An electronic system that MLB clubs use to complete the Standard Form of Diagnosis for Disabled List applications and which links with players' electronic medical records.

ESDI: *See* Exceptional Student-Athlete Disability Insurance Program.

Exceptional Student-Athlete Disability Insurance Program ("ESDI"): An NCAA insurance program available to collegiate student-athletes who demonstrate that they have the potential to be selected in the first three rounds of the NHL Draft, the first two rounds of the NFL Draft, or the first round of the NBA, MLB, or Women's National Basketball Association Draft, and which pays the student-athletes a lump sum payment 12 months after determining that the player has suffered permanent total disability.

Exclusive Rights Player: A player whose contract has expired but, because he only has a minimal amount of experience—which varies among the leagues—can only sign a contract with his prior club provided that club offers him a contract that meets the minimum requirements outlined in the CBA. Exclusive Rights Players have no leverage and thus generally must accept the contract offered by the club, which is typically for or near the league minimum.

Extended Injury Protection: An Injury Protection benefit that permits an NFL player to earn 50% of his salary up to $500,000 for the *second* season after suffering an injury that prevented the player from continuing to play. *See also* Injury Protection.

Fédération Internationale de Médecine du Sport ("FIMS"): The world's leading sports medicine organization, comprised of national sports medicine associations across five continents which seeks to maximize athlete health and performance.

FIMS: *See* Fédération Internationale de Médecine du Sport.

Former Player Life Improvement Plan: A medical plan that permits qualifying former NFL players (and in some cases their dependents) not otherwise covered by health insurance to receive reimbursement for medical costs for "joint replacements, prescription drugs, assisted living, Medicare supplemental insurance, spinal treatment, and neurological treatment."

Free Agency: A system by which players are able to sign contracts with new clubs after a certain number of seasons played, provided their prior contract is expired. *See* Unrestricted Free Agent and Restricted Free Agent.

Health and Injury Tracking System ("HITS"): An electronic system linked to MLB players' electronic medical records that allows MLB to monitor, study, and analyze injuries in baseball.

HealtheAthlete: An electronic medical record system used by NBA and MLS clubs.

Health Reimbursement Account (NBA): A program that helps to pay out-of-pocket healthcare expenses after players are no longer employed by an NBA club.

Health Reimbursement Account (NFL): A program that helps to pay out-of-pocket healthcare expenses after players are no longer employed by an NFL club and after the period of extended medical coverage under the NFL Player Insurance Plan that is paid by the NFL has ended.

HITS: *See* Health and Injury Tracking System.

Injured List: A roster designation for CFL players who are injured and are unable to play. The CFL has either a six-game or one-game Injured List. Players on either Injured List do not count towards the club's 44-man roster.

Injured Non-Roster List: A roster designation for NHL players who fail the pre-season physical. Players on the Injured Non-Roster List do not count towards the club's 23-man roster.

Injured Reserve ("IR") (NFL): A roster designation for players who are injured and are unable to return that season, with the exception of one player per season per club who can be placed on the IR but designated to be able to return. Players on IR do not count towards the club's 53-man Active/Inactive List.

Injured Reserve ("IR") (NHL): A roster designation for players who are injured and are unable to return for a minimum of seven days. Players on IR do not count towards the club's 23-man roster.

Injury Protection: A benefit available to NFL players where the player has met the following criteria: (1) "[t]he player must have been physically unable, because of a severe football injury in an NFL game or practice, to participate in all or part of his club's last game of the season, as certified by the club physician following a physical examination after the last game; or the player must have undergone club-authorized surgery in the off-season following the season of injury; and (2) [t]he player must have undergone whatever reasonable and customary rehabilitation treatment his club required of him during the off-season following the season of injury; and (3) [t]he player must have failed the pre-season physical examination given by the club physician for the season following the season of injury because of such injury and as a result his club must have terminated his contract for the season following the season of injury." In 2016, an NFL player could receive Injury Protection in "an amount equal to 50% of his Paragraph 5 Salary for the season following the season of injury, up to a maximum payment of" $1,150,000. A player is only entitled to Injury Protection once in his career.[7] *See also* Extended Injury Protection.

Injury Report: Generally, a list of injured players, each injured player's type or location of injury, and the injured player's status for the upcoming game. The detail provided by each league's Injury Report varies.

Intervention Program: A program for testing, evaluating, and treating NFL players pursuant to the Substance Abuse Policy.

IR: *See* Injured Reserve.

Joint Committee on Player Safety and Welfare ("Joint Committee"): An NFL-NFLPA committee consisting of three club representatives and three NFLPA representatives which discusses "player safety and welfare aspects of playing equipment, playing surfaces, stadium facilities, playing rules, player-coach relationships, and any other relevant subjects."[8] The Joint Committee is merely advisory and has no binding decision-making authority.

Joint Committee on Players' Safety and Welfare: A CFL-CFLPA committee which discusses player safety and welfare aspects of playing equipment, playing surfaces, stadium facilities, playing rules, player-coach relationships, drug abuse prevention programs, and any other relevant subjects.

Joint Drug Prevention and Treatment Program ("Joint Program"): The MLB-MLBPA policy prohibiting players from using PES and drugs of abuse.

Joint Health and Safety Committee: An NHL-NHLPA committee consisting of five members from each party, and which is responsible for "mak[ing] recommendations to the NHL and the NHLPA for consideration and approval regarding all issues related to Player health and regarding the safety of the playing environment."[9]

Joint Program: *See* Joint Drug Prevention and Treatment Program.

Joint Safety Committee: An MLS-MLSPU committee that is responsible for making "recommendations to the Commissioner concerning safety procedures."[10]

Legacy Benefit: As part of the 2011 CBA, the NFL contributed $620 million in benefits to players who played prior to 1993 through credits as part of the Retirement Plan. Players who played before 1975 received a $124-per-month credit and those who played between 1975 and 1992 received a $108-per-month credit.

Long Term Care Insurance Plan: Provides medical insurance to cover the costs of long-term care for NFL players (but not their family members).

Major League Baseball ("MLB"): The world's premier professional baseball organization, consisting of 30 member clubs. MLB began play in 1903, has its headquarters in New York City, and is led by Commissioner Rob Manfred. MLB's 2015 revenues were an estimated $10 billion.

Major League Baseball Players Association ("MLBPA"): A labor organization representing MLB players. The MLBPA was formed in 1953,[11] has its headquarters in New York City and is led by Executive Director Tony Clark, a 15-year MLB veteran.

Major League Baseball Players Benefit Plan: A comprehensive plan to MLB players and former MLB players that includes pension, investment, disability, and insurance components.

Major League Soccer ("MLS"): A professional soccer league consisting of 20 clubs. MLS began play in 1996, has its headquarters in New York City, and is led by Commissioner Don Garber. MLS' 2016 revenues were an estimated $600 million.

Major League Soccer Players Union ("MLSPU"): A labor organization representing MLS players. The MLSPU was formed in 2003,[12] has its headquarters in Bethesda, Maryland, and is led by Executive Director Bob Foose.

MLB: *See* Major League Baseball.

MLB Team Physicians Association ("MLBTPA"): A voluntary professional membership association for MLB club doctors. MLBTPA's "mission is to maintain the earned trust of the athletes and teams of Major and Minor League Baseball, as well as the public, by providing the highest quality medical care and services aimed at securing and enhancing their safety, health and well-being."[13]

MLBTPA: *See* MLB Team Physicians Association.

MLS Team Physicians Society ("MLSTPS"): A voluntary professional membership association for MLS club doctors. MLSTPS' stated mission is "[t]o be a global leader and collaborator in the science of soccer medicine focused on research, education and athlete care."[14]

MLS: *See* Major League Soccer.

MLSTPS: *See* MLS Team Physicians Society.

NATA: *See* National Athletic Trainers Association.

National Athletic Trainers Association ("NATA"): A voluntary professional membership association for certified athletic trainers across all levels of competition. NATA's stated mission "is to enhance the quality of health care provided by certified athletic trainers and to advance the athletic training profession." NATA's Canadian counterpart is CATA.

National Basketball Association ("NBA"): The world's premier professional basketball league, consisting of 30 member clubs. The NBA began play in 1946, has its headquarters in New York City, and is led by Commissioner Adam Silver. The NBA's 2016–17 revenues are projected to be $5.2 billion.

National Basketball Athletic Trainers Association ("NBATA"): A voluntary professional membership association for NBA club athletic trainers.

National Basketball Players Association ("NBPA"): A labor organization representing NBA players. The NBPA was formed in 1954,[15] has its headquarters in New York City, and is led by Executive Director Michelle Roberts.

National Collegiate Athletic Association ("NCAA"): A nonprofit unincorporated association headquartered in Indianapolis through which America's colleges and universities govern their athletic programs. The NCAA consists of over 1,200 member institutions, all of which participate in the creation of NCAA rules and voluntarily submit to its authority.

National Hockey League ("NHL"): The world's premier professional hockey league, consisting of 30 members clubs. The NHL began play in 1917, has its headquarters in New York City, and is led by Commissioner Gary Bettman. The NHL's 2015–16 revenues were an estimated $4.1 billion.

National Hockey League Players Association ("NHLPA"): A labor organization representing NHL players. The NHLPA was formed in 1957, has its headquarters in Toronto, and is led by Executive Director Don Fehr, who served as Executive Director of the MLBPA from 1985–2009.

National Football League ("NFL"): The world's premier professional football league, consisting of 32 member clubs. The NFL began play in 1920, has its headquarters in New York City, and is led by Commissioner Roger Goodell. The NFL's 2017 revenues are estimated to reach $14 billion.

National Football League Players Association ("NFLPA"): A labor organization representing NFL players. The NFLPA was formed in 1956,[16] has its headquarters in Washington, DC, and is led by Executive Director DeMaurice Smith.

National Labor Relations Act ("NLRA"): A federal labor law statute which governs labor relations between employees and employers in the private sector and obligates both sides to negotiate in good faith concerning the wages, hours, and other terms and conditions of employment.

National Labor Relations Board ("NLRB"): An independent agency of the United States government responsible for administering and enforcing the provisions of the NLRA, including investigating and remedying unfair labor practices.

NBA: *See* National Basketball Association.

NBATA: *See* National Basketball Athletic Trainers Association.

NBA Team Physicians Society ("NBATPS"): A voluntary professional membership association for NBA club doctors.

NBATPS: *See* NBA Team Physicians Society.

NCAA: *See* National Collegiate Athletic Association.

NFL: *See* National Football League.

NFL Injury Surveillance System ("NFLISS"): The standardized system, created in 1980, used by the NFL and NFL clubs to track and analyze NFL injuries and to provide data for medical research. Injury information is entered by club athletic trainers. Since 2011, the NFLISS is managed by the international biopharmaceutical services firm Quintiles.

NFLISS: *See* NFL Injury Surveillance System.

NFLPA: *See* National Football League Players Association.

NFL Physicians Society ("NFLPS"): A voluntary professional membership association for NFL club doctors. NFLPS' mission is "to provide excellence in the medical and surgical care of the athletes in the National Football League and to provide direction and support for the athletic trainers in charge of the care for these athletes."

NFLPS: *See* NFL Physicians Society.

NHL: *See* National Hockey League.

NHL Team Physicians Society ("NHLTPS"): A voluntary professional membership association for NHL club doctors.

NHLTPS: *See* NHL Team Physicians Society.

NLRA: *See* National Labor Relations Act.

NLRB: *See* National Labor Relations Board.

Paragraph 5 Salary: An NFL player's base salary. Paragraph 5 salaries are typically non-guaranteed, except for better players and even then only for some seasons of the player's contract.

PBATS: *See* Professional Baseball Athletic Trainers Society.

PED: *See* Performance-Enhancing Substance(s).

PES: *See* Performance-Enhancing Substance(s).

PES Policy: *See* Policy on Performance-Enhancing Substances.

Performance-Enhancing Substance(s) ("PES"): Substances that have the potential to enhance a player's performance in ways that the league, sports, and/or medical community has determined to be unfair, unnatural, and/or unsafe. Also sometimes referred to as "Performance-Enhancing Drugs."

PFATS: *See* Professional Football Athletic Trainers Society.

PHATS: *See* Professional Hockey Athletic Trainers Society.

Physically Unable to Perform ("PUP") List: A roster designation for NFL players who have failed the pre-season physical and are unable to participate in training camp but are expected to be able to play later in the season. A player on the PUP List cannot practice or play until after the sixth game of the regular season and does not count towards the club's 53-man Active/Inactive List during that time.

Player Annuity Program: An NFL plan that provides deferred compensation to players.

Player Insurance Plan: An NFL player insurance plan that provides players and their family with life insurance, accidental death and dismemberment insurance, medical coverage, dental coverage, and wellness benefits. The wellness benefits include access to clinicians for mental health, alcoholism, and substance abuse; child and parenting support services; elder care support services; pet care services; legal services; and, identity theft services.

Players' Pension Plan: A plan that provides pension benefits to NBA players who have at least three years of service in the league.

Policy and Program on Substances of Abuse ("Substance Abuse Policy"): The NFL-NFLPA policy prohibiting players from using common street drugs, such as cocaine, marijuana, amphetamines, opiates, opioids, PCP, and MDMA (ecstasy). The Substance Policy includes treatment and disciplinary provisions.

Policy on Performance-Enhancing Substances ("PES Policy"): The NFL-NFLPA policy prohibiting players from using PES. The PES Policy includes disciplinary *but not* treatment provisions.

Post-Career Income Plan: A retirement plan that purchases annuities for NBA players to provide a source of post-employment income.

Professional Baseball Athletic Trainers Society ("PBATS"): A voluntary professional membership association for MLB club athletic trainers. "PBATS mission is to serve as an educational resource for the Major League and Minor League Baseball athletic trainers. PBATS serves its members by providing for the continued education of the athletic trainer as it relates to the profession, helping to improve his understanding of sports medicine so as to better promote the health of his constituency—professional baseball players."[17]

Professional Football Athletic Trainers Society ("PFATS"): A voluntary professional membership association for NFL club athletic trainers.

Professional Hockey Athletic Trainers Society ("PHATS"): A voluntary professional membership association for NHL club athletic trainers.

Professional Soccer Athletic Trainers Society ("PSATS"): A voluntary professional membership association for MLS club athletic trainers.

Prohibited Substances Committee: A committee consisting of one NBA representative, one NBPA representative, and three jointly selected representatives who advise the NBA and NBPA on its anti-drug policy.

PSATS: *See* Professional Soccer Athletic Trainers Society.

Restricted Free Agent: A player whose contract has expired and who can sign a contract with any club. However, because the player has only a certain (but more than minimal) amount of experience (which varies among the leagues), the player's prior club is entitled to a right of first refusal on a contract offered by another club. But, the prior club only retains the right of first refusal if it had already made an offer meeting certain minimal criteria outlined in the CBA ("Qualifying Offer"). Additionally, if the player signs with a new club, his prior club will be entitled to some form of compensation, typically draft picks. Restricted Free Agents have minimal leverage as clubs generally prefer not to pay the required compensation to the prior club. *See also* Unrestricted Free Agent.

Retiree Medical Plan: An NBA plan that provides health insurance to former NBA players.

Retirement Plan (NFL): An NFL retirement plan that provides eligible players with retirement benefits, and offers survivor benefits for players' wives and family.

Retirement Plan (NHL): An NHL retirement plan that provides eligible players with retirement and disability benefits.

Safety and Health Advisory Committee ("SHAC"): A committee comprised of representatives of MLB clubs and the MLBPA, formed to "deal with emergency safety and health problems" and to review player working conditions.[18]

Salary Cap: Generally, the maximum amount of money that a club can spend on its players' salaries collectively in a season. In MLB, the "salary cap" is called the Tax Threshold.

Second Career Savings Plan: A 401(k) plan that helps NFL players save for retirement in a tax-favored manner. All NFL players are eligible for the Plan, regardless of the number of Credited Seasons.

Severance Pay: A benefit available to NFL players as severance for each Credited Season.

Substance Abuse Policy: *See* Policy and Program on Substances of Abuse.

Termination Pay: An NFL player benefit whereby a player who has at least four years of credited service under the Retirement Plan is eligible to receive the unpaid balance of his Paragraph 5 Salary for a season after having had his contract terminated during that season, provided he was on the club's Active/Inactive List for at least one game that season. A player is entitled to Termination Pay only once during his career.

Therapeutic Use Exemption ("TUE"): A policy that permits an athlete to use a banned substance without violating a drug policy for the treatment of a diagnosed medical condition.

TUE: *See* Therapeutic Use Exemption.

Tuition Assistance Plan: A benefit that entitles qualifying current and former NFL players to reimbursement for tuition, fees, and books from attending an eligible education institution.

UEFA: *See* Union of European Football Associations.

Union of European Football Associations ("UEFA"): A European soccer organization whose members generally include the best soccer clubs in the world and who play in some of the best soccer leagues in the world (such as the English Premier League and Spain's La Liga).

Unrestricted Free Agent: A player whose contract has expired and, because he has a higher level of experience (defined variously across the leagues), can sign a contract with any club without his prior club retaining any rights concerning the player. Unrestricted Free Agents have far more leverage and options as compared to Exclusive Rights Players or Restricted Free Agents. Becoming an Unrestricted Free Agent is an important opportunity that allows players to offer their services to any and all clubs at the highest price the market will bear (within the confines of the CBA). *See also* Free Agency and Restricted Free Agent.

VEBA: *See* Voluntary Employees' Beneficiary Association.

Voluntary Employees' Beneficiary Association ("VEBA"): Provides employees with benefits as permitted under Section 501(c)(9) of the Internal Revenue Code, such as "life, sick, accident, or similar benefits [for] members or their dependents, or designated beneficiaries."[19]

WADA: *See* World Anti-Doping Agency.

World Anti-Doping Agency: An international agency funded by sports organizations and governments with its principal focus on eliminating the use of PES in sports. WADA publishes annually a "Prohibited List" that lists prohibited substances. The WADA Code and the Prohibited List are the governing anti-doping documents of all Olympic sports organizations and most sports organizations worldwide.

Workers' Compensation: A state-based system which provides workers injured during the course of their employment with wages and medical benefits and which, as a tradeoff, generally bars employees from suing their employers and co-employees for negligence.

Endnotes

1   NBA, CBA, Art. IV, § 2(a).

2   *See* Jay MacDonald, *Professional Athletes' Big-League Tax Bills*, Fox Bus., Mar. 15, 2012, http://www.foxbusiness.com/personal-finance/2012/03/15/professional-athletes-big-league-tax-bills/; Sean Hanley, *Estate Planning Attorney Guide for Retirement*, Hanley Law (Aug. 21, 2013), http://hanleylaw.com/estate-planning-attorney-retirement; Mark Riddix, *Top Pro Athlete Pension Plans*, Investopedia, July 16, 2010, http://www.investopedia.com/financial-edge/0710/top-pro-athlete-pension-plans.aspx. *See also Top 15 Sports Organizations with the Best 401k Plans*, BrightScope, June 25, 2013, http://blog.brightscope.com/2013/06/25/top-15-sports-organizations-with-the-best-401k-plans/ (rating the plan as the best in professional sports, in part because of generous contributions of NBA clubs).

3   CBA, Art. 39, § 3.

4   *Id.*

5   Black's Law Dictionary (9th ed. 2009).

6   U.S.C. § 1163(2).

7   CBA, Art. 45, § 1.

8   CBA, Art. 50, § 1.

9   NHL CBA, § 34.9.

10 MLS CBA, § 24.1.

11 *See* Glenn M. Wong, *Essentials of Sports Law*, § 11.3 (4th ed. 2010) (providing history of the unions in the Big Four sports leagues).

12 *Id.*

13 *Home,* Major League Baseball Team Physicians Association, http://mlbtpa.org/ (last visited Aug. 25, 2015), *archived at* http://perma.cc/2JTM-XMJ5.

14 *Home,* MLS Team Physician Society, http://www.mlsteamdocs.com/ (last visited Aug. 26, 2015), *archived at* http://perma.cc/QJ7E-82SN.

15 *Id.*

16 *History,* Nat'l Football League Players Ass'n, https://www.nflpa.com/about/history (last visited Aug. 7, 2015), *archived at* https://perma.cc/3D2R-8EQG?type=pdf [hereinafter "NFLPA History"].

17 *About,* Professional Baseball Athletic Trainers Society, http://pbats.com/about/ (last visited Aug. 25, 2015), *archived at* http://perma.cc/G9FP-42CS.

18 MLB CBA, Art. XIII, § A(1).

19 *Voluntary Employee Beneficiary Association — 501(c)(9),* IRS (Jan. 13, 2015), http://www.irs.gov/Charities-&-Non-Profits/Other-Non-Profits/Voluntary-Employee-Beneficiary-Association-501%28c%29%289%29. The VEBA is funded through 1% of Basketball Related Income. 2011 NBA CBA Art. IV § 4(c).

INDEX